GLOBAL PROJECT FINANCE, HUMAN RIGHTS AND SUSTAINABLE DEVELOPMENT

Many infrastructure projects around the world are funded through the project finance method, which often combines private financing with public sector backing from multilateral finance institutions such as the World Bank/IFC. This examination of the theoretical and practical implications of such funding begins with a discussion of the relationship between the structuring of these projects and finance, policy and legal disciplines, especially in the form of investment law, human rights and environmental law. A number of case studies are then examined to provide practical insights into the application (or otherwise) of human rights and sustainable development objectives within such projects. While these perspectives do not conclude that the project finance method necessarily detracts from the application or implementation of human rights and sustainable development objectives, they do highlight the potential damage that can result from the prioritization of investment returns at the expense of human rights and environmental protection standards.

SHELDON LEADER is a graduate of Yale and Oxford Universities. He is a professor of law, and the Director of the Essex Business and Human Rights Project. He works in the area of economic relations and human rights, as well as in legal theory. He has provided analyses of the human rights impacts of investment agreements for civil society organizations and for governments, most recently in Kosovo for the Organization for Security and Cooperation in Europe (OSCE). Among his publications are *Human Rights on the Line* (2003) (with Andrea Shemberg); and 'The Place of Labor Rights in Foreign Direct Investment', in A. Morris and S. Estreicher (eds.), *Global Labor and Employment Law* (2010). He formulated the basic principles for the Human Rights Undertaking governing the BTC pipeline, the first legally binding human rights commitment incorporated into an international investment contract.

DAVID ONG is a reader at the School of Law, University of Essex, where he teaches and researches in the fields of public international law and environmental law. He has served as a technical expert and resource person for United Nations Development Programme (UNDP) activities on oil- and gas-producing developing countries, as well as for the OSCE Mission in Kosovo, alongside Professor Leader.

GLOBAL PROJECT FINANCE, HUMAN RIGHTS AND SUSTAINABLE DEVELOPMENT

Edited by

SHELDON LEADER

and

DAVID ONG

CAMBRIDGE UNIVERSITY PRESS
Cambridge, New York, Melbourne, Madrid, Cape Town,
Singapore, São Paulo, Delhi, Tokyo, Mexico City

Cambridge University Press
The Edinburgh Building, Cambridge CB2 8RU, UK

Published in the United States of America by Cambridge University Press, New York

www.cambridge.org
Information on this title: www.cambridge.org/9780521762601

© Cambridge University Press 2011

First published 2011

Printed in the United Kingdom at the University Press, Cambridge

A catalogue record for this publication is available from the British Library

Library of Congress Cataloguing in Publication data
Global project finance, human rights and sustainable development / edited by
Sheldon Leader, David Ong.
p.   cm.
ISBN 978-0-521-76260-1 (hardback)
1. Infrastructure (Economics) – Finance.   2. Human rights.   3. Sustainable
development.   I. Leader, Sheldon   II. Ong, David
HC79.C3G56   2011
338.9′27–dc22
2010030732

ISBN 978-0-521-76260-1 Hardback

CONTENTS

CONTRIBUTORS

DR ÖZGÜR CAN KAHALE is an academic and a legal practitioner specializing in project finance transactions particularly in emerging markets. She has worked on major power and infrastructure project financings in Europe and the Middle East which involved private international banks, export credit agencies and multilateral financings. She taught law at postgraduate level in Middlesex and Essex Universities, UK, and worked as a senior research officer for the University of Essex. She has an LLM in international human rights law from the University of Essex and a Ph.D. from Lancaster University. Her Ph.D. thesis, entitled 'Private investment and protection of human rights', focuses on the national and international legal actions that states should take in order to protect human rights while developing infrastructure projects, providing public services and exploiting natural resources; and emphasizes the importance of building human rights protection mechanisms into national and international investment laws.

LORENZO COTULA is a senior researcher in law and sustainable development at the International Institute for Environment and Development (IIED), based in the UK. His work focuses on the role of law in sustainable development, particularly in the areas of land/natural resource rights, foreign investment, governance and human rights. Before joining IIED in 2002, Lorenzo worked on several assignments with the Food and Agriculture Organization of the UN and with two Italian NGOs. He holds a law degree *cum laude* from the University La Sapienza of Rome, an M.Sc. (Distinction) in development studies from the London School of Economics, and a Ph.D. in law from the University of Edinburgh.

ANNIE DUFEY is Director of Energy, Sustainability and Climate Change at the Environment and Energy Area of Fundación Chile in Santiago, Chile. Between 2004 and 2008 she was a senior researcher in the

Environmental Economics Programme at the International Institute for Environment and Development in London on the linkages between trade, investment and sustainable development in several economic sectors and on biofuels, examining the impacts on developing countries. Annie also worked in Santiago, Chile, with Recursos e Investigación para el Desarrollo Sustentable and Centro de Investigación y Planificación del Medio Ambiente on trade and sustainable development issues and for Gemines Consultores. Annie holds a degree in economics from the University of Chile, and a Master's in environment, development and policy from the University of Sussex, UK.

CLAUDIA GIRARDONE is a senior lecturer in finance at the Essex Business School, University of Essex, UK. Her research focus is on financial management and strategies of financial services firms and modelling bank efficiency and productivity. Her most recent work includes a textbook entitled *Introduction to Banking* (2006) and articles on efficiency, integration and competition in banking markets. She has published widely in specialist finance and economics journals.

MARYANNE GRIEG-GRAN is a principal researcher in environmental economics at the International Institute for Environment and Development (IIED) with over twenty-five years' experience of working on sustainable development. Maryanne works on the economic aspects of natural resource management in developing countries, including valuation of forest resources, impact assessment of market-based instruments for conservation and sustainable resource management, and the links between investment and sustainable development. Experience prior to joining IIED in 1994 includes four years as an environmental economist for Environmental Resources Management, four years in Papua New Guinea on investment promotion and industrial development and four years in the Ministry of Agriculture and Water Resources in Mexico. Maryanne has a Master's degree in economics from Warwick University and a Bachelor's degree in economics and sociology from Keele University, UK.

RASMIYA KAZIMOVA, Ph.D. candidate, School of Law, University of Essex, UK, is a lawyer with a background in international law, international environmental law and international human rights law. She has worked with the State Oil Company, State Petrochemical Company, as well as the Ministry of Fuel and Energy of Azerbaijan. Prior to this, she practised as a legal expert with the Omni Consultants commercial law firm on compatibility of Azerbaijani law with the *acquis* of the EU. She also worked as a researcher in an EU-funded project on social regulation of TNCs, and the ESRC-funded research project on which this book is based. Since 2005, she has been teaching constitutional and administrative law, as well as business and human rights law at the University of Essex, UK.

NII ASHIE KOTEY is the Dean of the Faculty of Law, University of Ghana. Professor Kotey has been deeply involved in development, higher education and civic issues for over twenty years. He has practised law, consulted, advocated democratic governance and human rights, and organized civic groups. As a specialist in natural resources, environmental and human rights law, he has undertaken research work, participated in national and international conferences, and prepared advisory papers for many national and foreign clients. He has published widely both nationally and internationally. He has been a visiting lecturer in Nigeria and a visiting scholar in the USA, the Netherlands and the UK.

DIANA MORALES is the Programme Manager at the Essex Transitional Justice Network (ETJN) in the UK. Her work focuses on the different mechanisms used to address human rights abuses in countries emerging from conflict, with a particular interest in the economic dimensions of transitional justice and state responsibility. Before joining the ETJN team, she has worked for the International Bar Association and as an independent consultant on a variety of human rights issues mainly focusing on transitional justice, rule of law, administration of justice and human rights for projects in countries such as Colombia, Ecuador, Bolivia and Zimbabwe.

JUDITH SCHÖNSTEINER, LLM, is Assistant Professor for International Law at the Diego Portales University in Chile, and conducting her doctoral studies at the School of Law, University of Essex, UK. She specializes in international human rights law, with a focus on business and human rights in Latin America, and has worked as a researcher on an EU-funded project on social regulation of the overseas activities of European TNCs, as well as the ESRC-funded project on which this book is based.

STUART SNAITH is lecturer in finance at the Essex Business School, University of Essex, UK. His research is in international finance, with recent work focusing on the purchasing-power parity and forward premium puzzles. Recent publications appear in specialist economic journals.

TAMARA WIHER FERNANDEZ is currently working for the Office of the UN High Commissioner for Human Rights in Colombia, in particular on indigenous and Afro-Colombian issues and related right to free prior and informed consultation. This includes the impact of large-scale infrastructure projects on economic, social and cultural rights. She has experience working for the UN Development Programme, NGOs and the Swiss Foreign Department on various issues related to international human rights and humanitarian law. Tamara holds an LLM in international human rights law from the University of Essex, UK, where her research focused on human rights risk management in investment. She also participated in the ESRC-funded project on which this book is based.

ABBREVIATIONS

ACHR	American Convention on Human Rights
ASEAN	Association of South East Asian Nations
BIT	bilateral investment treaty
CAO	Compliance Advisor/Ombudsman
CDAP	Caspian Development Advisory Panel
CEDAW	Convention on the Elimination of all Forms of Discrimination Against Women
CERD	[UN] Committee on the Elimination of Racial Discrimination
CESCR	[UN] Committee on Economic, Social and Cultural Rights
CITES	Convention on International Trade in Endangered Species
CSR	corporate social responsibility
DFID	UK Department for International Development
EBRD	European Bank for Reconstruction and Development
ECA	export credit agency
ECE	Economic Commission for Europe
ECHR	European Convention on Human Rights and Fundamental Freedoms
ECtHR	European Court of Human Rights
EHS	[WB Group] Environmental Health and Safety
EMMP	environmental management and monitoring plan
EP	Equator Principle/Equator Principles
EPA	Environmental Protection Agency
EPFI	Equator Principles Financial Institution
ESCR	[UN Committee on] Economic, Social and Cultural Rights; economic, social and cultural rights
ESIA	environmental and social impact assessment
ESRC	Economic and Social Research Council
EU	European Union
FDI	foreign direct investment
GATT	General Agreement on Tariffs and Trade
GDP	gross domestic product
GESY	governance and efficiency of economic systems
GIIP	good international industry practice
HGA	host government agreement
HRIA	human rights impact assessment
HRMP	human rights management plan

HSE	health, safety and environment
IACtHR	Inter-American Court of Human Rights
IBLF	International Business Leaders Forum
IBRD	International Bank for Reconstruction and Development
ICCPR	International Covenant on Civil and Political Rights
ICESCR	International Covenant on Economic, Social and Cultural Rights
ICJ	International Court of Justice
ICRG	International Country Risk Guide
IEC	independent environmental consultant
IFC	International Finance Corporation
IFI	international financial institution
ILO	International Labour Organization
IMO	International Maritime Organization
ISO	International Standards Organization
ISRP	Independent Scientific Review Panel
ITLOS	International Tribunal for the Law of the Sea
IUCN	International Union for the Conservation of Nature
LIBOR	London Interbank Offered Rate
MEA	multilateral environmental agreement
MIGA	Multilateral Investment Guarantee Agency
MNC	multinational corporation
MNE	multinational enterprise
MOU	memorandum of understanding
NGO	non-governmental organization
OECD	Organization for Economic Cooperation and Development
OPIC	[US] Overseas Private Investment Corporation
OSPAR	Paris Convention on the Protection of the Marine Environment of the North East Atlantic
PF	project finance
PIFI	public international financial institution
plc	public limited company
PRI	political risk insurance
PS	[IFC] Performance Standards
PSA	production-sharing agreement
R&D	research and development
SEA	strategic environmental assessment; social and environmental assessment
SEMS	social and environmental management system
SIA	social impact assessment
SPV	special purpose vehicle
TIA	transnational investment agreement
TNC	transnational corporation

TRIMs	Trade-Related Investment Measures [Agreement]
UDHR	Universal Declaration of Human Rights
UN	United Nations
UNCTAD	UN Conference on Trade and Development
UNDP	United Nations Development Programme
UNEP	United Nations Environment Programme
VCLT	Vienna Convention on the Law of Treaties
WB	World Bank
WTO	World Trade Organization

PART I

The framework

1

An introduction to the issues

SHELDON LEADER[1]

To someone interested in the social and environmental impact of foreign direct investment (FDI), a focus on project finance (PF) might seem to be a small corner of concern, not worth straying into for too long. That would be a mistake. The closer one looks at the relationships between corporate decision making, lenders' disciplines and the social and environmental impacts of projects, the more the techniques of PF emerge as important forces at work when human rights and environmental values are at stake.

PF provides a set of refined tools for the spreading and mitigating of risks between corporations, host states, lenders and those contractors involved in building and operating a project. At the same time, civil society is producing its own increasingly refined tools for measuring the potential gains and losses to the populations affected by this investment strategy. PF has arguably become one of the most closely watched modes of international finance, as various bodies assess the risk to social and environmental standards by projects to which this form of lending is extended. There are positive and negative elements in the picture. Positively, the finance provided in this way has sometimes provided a bridge to very large social gains, generating revenues that give host governments the space to fund major work in housing, health care and education. Negatively, praise is sometimes brought up short by those whose lives are overturned by a project because of its pollution; accidents during its construction or operation; seizure of lands; and many other impacts. In short, PF provides a prism through which pass many of the fundamental tensions

This book is the result of a project entitled 'Global Project Finance, Rights, and Sustainable Development', which formed part of the World Economy and Research Programme funded by the Economic and Social Research Council (ESRC). The authors wish to thank the ESRC for its generous support.
[1] With the help of Rasmiya Kazimova and Judith Schönsteiner.

characterizing the relation between basic rights, sustainable development and foreign direct investment.

As civil society, both national and international, raises the pressure for meaningful social accountability of business, PF is often in its sights – either intentionally or without realizing it. Demands made for protection of local populations sometimes place particular requirements on this financing technique that it may not be well equipped to handle. Because of certain structural features of PF, a company borrowing under a PF scheme may not easily cede to civil society's demands because of its perception that there is little room for manoeuvre left by the conditions set by lenders. Of concern here are some of the largest projects in the world, many playing a central part in the politics and societies of those countries receiving the investment. A measure of this concern is to be seen in a special meeting which focused on the impact of PF called by the UN's Special Representative on Human Rights and Transnational Corporations, Prof. John Ruggie.[2] It has also been the subject of a report by International Alert, an organization interested in the links between PF and social conflict.[3] The investment community has been taking its own initiatives towards meeting the demand for accountability. Lenders have been developing social and environmental standards that are the most elaborate criteria yet to have been deployed by the international financial community aimed at controlling the impact of what they do. Two leading examples of these standards are, in the public sector, the International Finance Corporation's (IFC) performance standards, meant to control eight different types of potential damage.[4] In the private sector, major lending banks concerted with PF have banded together to formulate the Equator Principles (EP).[5]

---

[2] See report of the United Nations High Commissioner on Human Rights on the sectoral consultation entitled 'Human rights and the financial sector', 16 February 2007 A/HRC/4/99, 6 March 2007, available at: http://198.170.85.29/UNHCHR-finance-sector-consultation-report-6-Mar-2007.pdf.

[3] The report focused on the relationship between PF and social conflict. See International Alert, 'Conflict and project finance: exploring options for better management of conflict risk' by Corene Crossin and Jessie Banfield, January 2006.

[4] Latest version, April 2011, with draft amendments at www.ifc.org/policyreview. Note that human rights are not specifically included. For critique, see 'Joint Civil Society Statement' (at http://accountabilityproject.org).

[5] At: www.equator-principles.com. These, sometimes referred to collectively as IFC/EP standards, themselves draw both on international norms, such as International Labour Organization (ILO) conventions, as well as domestically formulated criteria, and will be considered in later chapters.

Can the norms for a better environment, human rights and related concerns be adequately satisfied by an investment community aiming to hold onto the full commercial benefits offered by PF? The jury is still out. The aim of this book is to look at the different dimensions of the issue, setting a framework for tackling that question. It draws on, but looks beyond, the views of academics, basing itself on interviews with a variety of actors involved practically in the process.

It is important, first of all, to describe briefly the elements of project finance and to sketch, in an introductory way, the main points of contact with social and environmental issues with which we will be concerned.

The elements

Project finance

Project financing is a method of funding in which the lenders 'base credit appraisals on the projected revenues from the operation of the facility, rather than the general assets or the credit of the sponsor of the facility, and rely on the assets of the facility . . . as collateral for the debt'.[6] It is to be distinguished from those modes of finance in which the general assets of a sponsoring company, often owning several projects, are wholly or in part the subject of claims by the lender in the event of a failure to repay the loan.[7]

This relatively sparse definition needs to be placed within the corporate structure tailored for it. We can use here a classic model: a parent company or a group of companies in a consortium (project sponsors) are typically set up as a project company, or special purpose vehicle (SPV), the latter usually owning the land, machinery, operating funds and other assets directly connected to its owning and operating the pipeline, dam, hydroelectric plant, etc. which is the target of the investment. The controlling equity in the SPV will be held by the project sponsor(s), sometimes accompanied by equity participation from the host state. A loan is then made to the SPV by private banks or public lenders, without – or with limited – recourse to the parent in the event of default on the loan. Instead,

---

[6] S. L. Hoffman, *The Law and Business of International Project Finance* (2nd edn, Boston: Kluwer, 2001), pp. 4–5.

[7] *Ibid.*, pp. 6–7.

as the definition indicates, the lender's recourse will be to the assets of the SPV.[8]

This arrangement has several noteworthy characteristics:

- The project sponsor is protected from threats to its assets that would otherwise be posed by a venture's failure. The sponsor stands to lose the money it has already invested in the SPV, but its explicit understanding with the lender is that the latter will not have recourse against its other assets. This autonomy is buttressed by the fact that the SPV is a separate legal entity and its sponsors, as shareholders, enjoy limited liability.
- Emphasis is placed by the lender on predictable revenue flow. This concern, while also present in lending against general assets of a sponsor, is here heightened. Were the loan to have been made to the project sponsor, the latter would normally be obligated to pay the loan back from its general revenues, coming from all of the projects in which it is involved. In PF, however, the loan is repaid from one source only: a single project. This typically leads to a heightened emphasis on meeting target dates for construction accompanied by penalties for failure to do so, paving the way for the start of operation and generation of revenue. This is accompanied by a focus on the need to keep project costs as closely as possible to their initial predicted amounts.

These two factors lead to certain intensified concerns on the part of both lenders and borrowers that can have social and environmental impacts. These concerns are also present in other modes of financing, but can be stronger here:

- *Regulatory stability*: Lenders as well as other parties to the project have a strong interest in discouraging the host state from introducing changes in law or regulation that will have a negative impact on project costs, and hence can put pressure on the ability of the project to meet its loan repayment targets.
- *Allocation of risk*: While such allocations are a concern in all projects, those financed by PF place particular emphasis on a spread of risks that will induce the relevant parties to help meet project deadlines and keep expenses within the expected limits.

---

[8] This non-recourse element functions primarily during the operational phase of the project. The earlier construction phase is often accompanied by some form of recourse the lender will have to the sponsor directly. There are many variants and qualifications to this picture, but it is a good starting point.

- *Presumption in favour of meeting of costs from within project revenues*: Given the insulation of the project from its sponsor's own liabilities, there is a concern to avoid calling on further funds from sponsors to meet unexpected problems with the project.

These concerns can generate both positive and negative effects on societies hosting a project:

- *Positive*: The needs for predictability of return on project investment may encourage a particularly careful calculation of environmental/social risks, given the impact these can have on steady cash flow. As will be seen in later chapters, where the lender has recourse against the project sponsor's assets, there can be less inducement to pay close attention to such factors. The assessment of these risks is called for by the performance standards set by several major public and private lenders, most notably by the IFC and Equator banks.
- *Negative*: On the other side, there is the possibility that risks of certain types of damage to local populations might be heightened by some of the pressures on project timing and performance, as well as techniques of risk management, in PF. Our investigations indicate that this may be so, for example, when unrealistic completion deadlines for construction are set; stringent stabilization requirements freezing regulatory change are placed on host governments; or the possibility exists for project sponsors to abandon a project that is underperforming, with potential loss to third parties. The concern for stability might sometimes be intense enough to pull against an investor's endorsement of democracy in the host country, in favour of the more predictable environment that a strong non-democratic form of government can provide.[9]
- *Issues shared with other modes of finance*: Finally, there is a set of concerns that involve problems of projects financed by PF which would also be shared to the same extent by other modes of finance: e.g. complicity with human rights violations; shortcomings in the due diligence processes conducted by the financial institutions – as will be discussed in several of the chapters in Parts II and III.

---

[9] This is one possible explanation for the correlations between forms of government and the price of loans discussed in Chapter 8.

The standards for evaluating social impacts of PF

'Basic' and 'human' rights and duties

The fundamental rights of concern throughout this work fall into two overlapping categories, as will be seen in more detail in Chapter 3. First, there are internationally recognized human rights that come from recognized sources. For these purposes such sources include the International Covenant on Civil and Political Rights (ICCPR) and the International Covenant on Economic, Social and Cultural Rights (ICESCR) as well as more narrowly focused human rights conventions. Second, at some points a wider category, 'basic' rights, is used. They are the fundamental entitlements that are formulated in instruments such as the 1972 Stockholm Declaration of the United Nations Conference on the Human Environment, and the 1992 Rio Declaration on Environment and Development. Finally, within the class of basic rights and duties will be those entitlements and obligations imposed on borrowers by the requirements of the IFC as well as Equator Principles banks (hereafter IFC/EP standards), several of which coincide with the international norms mentioned.

How should one deploy basic rights as a critical tool for evaluating the impacts of private investment? How, in turn, should these critical standards be used in evaluating PF projects? There are several elements in an answer, each of which will be more fully developed in Parts I and II.

Comparing rights-based development and rights-based investment

Host states have obligations to respect, protect and fulfil certain basic rights of their populations, and these in turn have been woven into the guidelines for rights-based development: guidelines developed by the UN High Commissioner for Human Rights.[10] Investors can come under an overlapping, but also diverging, set of obligations

---

[10] For the UN's approach to rights-based development, see UN High Commissioner on Human Rights, 'Rights-based Approaches', available at www.unhchr.ch/development/approaches-04.html, last reviewed on 5 January 2008. For a discussion of the conceptual framework of a rights-based approach to development, see Jakob Kirkemann Hansen and Hans-Otto Sano, 'The Implications and Value-added of a Rights-based Approach', in B. A. Andreassen and S. P. Marks (eds.), *Development as a Human Right: Legal, Political, and Economic Dimensions* (Cambridge, MA: Harvard School of Public Health, 2007), at 42. See also L. VeneKlasen *et al.*, 'Rights-based Approaches and Beyond: Challenges of Linking Rights and Participation', Institute of Development Studies, Working Paper 235, Brighton, 2004.

corresponding to the same rights. The difference between the two sets of duties is one of scope. This can be seen if we consider the example of the right of access to water – an example to be treated in more detail in Chapter 3.[11] Consider an investment in a pipeline project that uses water to such an extent that the supply to the local population falls below minimal standards set by international instruments. The host state could legitimately impose, in fulfilment of its obligation to protect this basic right, regulations requiring the pipeline not to block this access. At that point the obligations of the investor and those of the host state converge: both aim at a portion of the guarantees involved in rights-based development. Not only that, but were the host state to fail to enforce protection of this right in its own domestic rules, there would nevertheless be independent grounds on which the investor could be held responsible for the damage done to the water supply. It could, for example, be held to have broken a basic condition of its loan from an Equator Principles bank. The same would be true were the project company to violate fundamental labour rights as defined in certain ILO conventions. These are conventions which bind the host states, but also form part of the lending conditions set by the Equator banks and the IFC.[12]

An investor's human rights obligations do not completely mirror the host state's responsibilities for rights-based development. Yet over a significant terrain those responsibilities coincide. It is in this domain and others like it that tensions can appear which are of central concern to this book. Even though the private investor might acknowledge, at a general level, that it has to respect these rights, it may aim to determine their content and weight in a way that weakens their protective potential. This can happen as the web of contracts framing an investment are drawn up and given effect. One of the tasks of these chapters is to see how the disciplines of PF might stand behind these problematic features of the legal framework, and then to see what changes to PF arrangements might be made in order to avoid the problem.

---

[11] See 'What Price for the Priceless? Implementing the Justiciability of the Right to Water', 120 (2007) *Harv. L. Rev.*, 1067.

[12] For example, ILO Conventions No. 182 on Worst Forms of Child Labour, No. 176 on Health and Safety in Mines, No. 167 on Health and Safety in Construction or No. 154 on Collective Bargaining, available at: www.ilo.org/ilolex/english/convdisp1.htm, last reviewed 3 March 2008.

Rights on both sides of the fence

It is tempting to place the concern for basic rights on the side of a population that can be damaged by a project, and the concern for other goals, such as commercial objectives, on the side of the investor. Such a division does not work. There are situations in which the choice of PF as a technique can clearly help a host state discharge its own human rights responsibilities. Water supplied by private sources might reach the neediest parts of the population; and schools or hospitals financed from tax revenues generated by a petroleum pipeline might do the same. Yet, at the same time, as pipelines or water facilities are built, they may themselves do damage: to people, to environments and to property. The real issue at that point might be better cast as a matter of choosing between two courses of action, each with its own distinct impact on human rights. Is it, for example, better to take a step towards fulfilling a basic right to adequate medical care on a national level via tax revenues from a project, but at the expense of allowing construction to move at a pace that destroys the health of some of a local population, or should the adjustment between the two sets of rights move in the opposite direction? Where does the drive for commercial profit legitimately fit into this picture? This clash of fundamental entitlements stands in the background, and sometimes in the foreground, of the enquiries in the following chapters.

Property rights of the investor

In this book it will be important to include in the mix of relevant basic rights those of the investor. We shall work with a model in which the investor enjoys a right to protection of its property via internationally recognized human rights norms. It is tempting, as some do, to construct policy around the denial of this fundamental status to property rights, and in particular to the rights of the investor. Our approach will be to admit the right to property fully into the picture, but will then turn to the question of the appropriate adjustment between this entitlement and competing fundamental rights of those who are affected by any given investment project. It is here that the appropriate constraints on the operation of PF can be constructed. They will not be built on the assumption that the property rights of the investor must automatically take second place, but also that those property rights are not automatically dominant. They must enter into a balance. Understanding the terms of this balance will be a major underlying theme in the analyses at various points in the book. They provide a dynamic way of assessing the qualities of project financing in various settings.

The chapters to come

In Part I of the book we set out the relevant fundamentals of PF, as well as of those elements of human rights, environmental and rights-based development standards that are engaged by FDI. The book then moves in Part II to a consideration of certain special topics where one can observe the positive and negative features of project finance at work. This is in turn followed by case studies in Part III. The book ends with a chapter in which proposals for reform of the international management of project finance are set out.

2

The linkages between project finance and sustainable development

ANNIE DUFEY AND MARYANNE GRIEG-GRAN

Introduction

Since the beginning of this decade there has been a marked increase in flows of private capital to developing countries from just under US$200 billion in 2001 to over US$1 trillion in 2007 before the global financial crisis in 2008 curtailed these increases in flows.[1] These flows consist of foreign direct investment (FDI), portfolio investment, private bank lending and remittances. Much of this was FDI, which by the mid-1990s had become the most important source of external finance for developing countries and reached over US$500 billion in 2007.[2] A large share also corresponded to private debt (just under US$500 billion in 2007) of which the major part corresponded to debt contracted by enterprises in developing countries.[3] During the same period, net official development assistance was small by comparison reaching a little over US$100 billion from 2005 onwards.[4] Private capital flows, and FDI in particular, far outweigh development assistance and therefore constitute a significant leverage point for sustainable development. But there are major debates

[1] World Bank, *Global Development Finance: Charting a Global Recovery* (Washington, DC: IBRD/World Bank, 2009), table 2.1.
[2] E. Arnal and A. Hijzen, *The Impact of Foreign Direct Investment on Wages and Working Conditions* (OECD Social Employment and Migration Working Papers No. 68, OECD, 2009), available from the OECD's website.
[3] 'Between 2003 and 2007, firms based in emerging markets raised $1.2 trillion in external debt via syndicated bank deals and bond issues, while only $237.2 billion went to the sovereign sector' (World Bank, *Global Development Finance*).
[4] World Investment Report *Transnational Corporations, Agricultural Production and Development* (New York and Geneva: UNCTAD/UN, 2009), figure 1.4 Net capital flows to developing countries, 2000–2009.

about the impact of FDI on host countries, and about whether its economic benefits are achieved at the expense of environmental damage and social inequity, and indeed whether the economic benefits are all that they are claimed to be.

The rise of project finance[5] as a way of financing large foreign invest-ment projects in strategic sectors such as oil and gas and mining adds another dimension to this debate. This is because it brings another group of actors, the project finance banks, into the decision making and negotiation on FDI projects. Project finance lending world-wide grew from US$14 billion in 1994 and US$62 billion in 2002 to US$180 billion in 2006.[6] During the period 2002 to 2006, just under 30 per cent of this lending was in Asia, Africa and Central and South America.[7] This chapter examines how the use of project finance to support FDI in large resource-based and infrastructure projects in developing countries affects the likelihood of negative or positive impacts on the sustainable development potential of host countries. It reviews first the concept of sustainable development, emphasizing its multidimensional nature and its evolution over time into a broad framework for national and international development objectives and strategy. This is followed by a discussion of FDI and project finance and how they are related. The chapter then reviews the debates on the impacts of FDI on sustainable development and explores how the use of project finance affects these impacts. A final section offers conclusions on the links between project finance and sustainable development.

---

[5] Project finance is a method of funding in which the lender looks primarily to the revenues generated by a single project, both as the source of repayment and as security for the exposure. Project finance may take the form of financing of the construction of a new capital installation, or refinancing of an existing installation, with or without improve-ments. In such transactions, the lender is usually paid solely or almost exclusively out of the money generated by the contracts for the facility's output, such as the electricity sold by a power plant. The borrower is usually an SPV that is not permitted to perform any function other than developing, owning and operating the installation (source: 'Equator Principles and Basle Committee on Banking Supervision, International Convergence of Capital Measurement and Capital Standards ("Basel II")', November 2005, available at: www.bis.org/publ/bcbs118.pdf).

[6] B. Esty and A. Sesia 'An Overview of Project Finance and Infrastructure Finance' (2007), 2006 Update, Harvard Business School.

[7] *Ibid.*

The concept of sustainable development

Sustainable development, while much used in both government policy and in the academic literature has been subject to a number of inter-pretations and has evolved since its first appearance in the 1980s.[8]

An early and much-cited definition of sustainable development came from the World Commission on Environment and Development in 1987, the so-called Brundtland Commission: 'development that meets the needs of the present without compromising the ability of future generations to meet their own needs'.[9] This has often been perceived as being primarily about inter-generational equity and ensuring that over-reaching of ecological limits does not reduce the opportunities open to future generations. In fact, further explanation of the definition specified that it contained two key elements: both the idea of environmental limits and the concept of needs, in particular the essential needs of the world's poor, to which overriding priority should be given.

In 1992 the concept of sustainable development was given further elaboration in the Rio Declaration on Environment and Development which was adopted by more than 178 governments at the United Nations Conference on Environment and Development (UNCED) held in Rio de Janeiro, Brazil, 3 to 14 June 1992. Also for the first time a Commission on Sustainable Development within the United Nations (UN) was created in December 1992 to ensure effective follow-up of UNCED, to monitor and report on implementation of the agreements at the local, national, regional and international levels.

The Rio Declaration in its Principle 1 affirmed that human beings are at the centre of concerns for sustainable development and are entitled to a healthy and productive life in harmony with nature. While the Declaration emphasized the integration of environment and develop-ment it made explicit reference to the need for poverty eradication: 'All States and all people shall cooperate in the essential task of eradicating poverty as an indispensable requirement for sustainable development, in order to decrease the disparities in standards of living and better meet

---

[8] For a detailed discussion of the evolution of the sustainable development concept, and its application in a major primary resource sector see 'The Minerals Sector and Sustainable Development', ch. 1 in MMSD, *Breaking New Ground. The Report of the Mining, Minerals and Sustainable Development Project* (London: Earthscan, 2002).

[9] *Our Common Future: Report of the World Commission on Environment and Development*, Annex to UN Doc. A/42/427, 4 August 1987, ch. 2 'Towards Sustainable Development'.

the needs of the majority of the people of the world' (Principle 5). It also highlighted the particular needs of developing countries: 'The special situation and needs of developing countries, particularly the least developed and those most environmentally vulnerable, shall be given special priority' (Principle 6). While it did not mention human rights specifically, it affirmed the right to development (Principle 3) and urged participation of all concerned citizens and access to information in addressing environmental issues (Principle 10).

Agenda 21, the implementation plan that accompanied the Rio Declaration made the multidimensional nature of sustainable development clear, calling for improvement or restructuring of policy decision making so that consideration of socio-economic and environmental issues is fully integrated and a broader range of public participation assured (Chapter 8). Of its four sections, one was on social and economic issues and another on natural resource management. This led to the common articulation of sustainable development as involving three dimensions or pillars, social, economic and environmental, often within an institutional or governance framework.[10]

The Johannesburg Declaration in 2002[11] went further in spelling out and broadening the concept of sustainable development, making reference to the 'interdependent and mutually reinforcing pillars of sustainable development – economic development, social development and environmental protection – at the local, national, regional and global levels'. Like the Rio Declaration, it affirmed the need for poverty eradication but went further in pointing explicitly to the threat posed to global prosperity by the 'deep fault line' between rich and poor and the ever increasing gap between the developed and developing worlds. It also recognized as threats to sustainable development a wide range of conditions: 'chronic hunger; malnutrition; foreign occupation; armed conflict; illicit drug problems; organized crime; corruption; natural disasters; illicit arms trafficking; trafficking in persons; terrorism; intolerance and incitement to racial, ethnic, religious and other hatreds; xenophobia; and endemic, communicable and chronic diseases, in particular HIV/AIDS, malaria and tuberculosis'. In this way it broadened still further the scope of actions to promote sustainable development.

---

[10] See for example, *Towards a Sustainable Paper Cycle*. A report prepared by IIED for the World Business Council on Sustainable Development (London: IIED, 1996).
[11] World Summit on Sustainable Development, Johannesburg, South Africa.

It also explicitly mentioned the need to strengthen governance at all levels for the effective implementation of Agenda 21 and other plans for making sustainable development happen. Another area in which it went further than the Rio Declaration was in reference to the private sector which in pursuit of its legitimate activities was considered to have a duty to contribute to the evolution of equitable and sustainable communities and societies. Private sector corporations were urged to enforce corporate accountability within a transparent and stable regulatory environment.

The UN's Division for Sustainable Development sums up the concept in the following way: 'Sustainable development requires looking at the totality of social, economic and environmental concerns. It also needs the involvement not only of Governments but also of civil society and the private sector.'[12] Sustainable development is therefore a broad concept which has evolved since its first articulation over twenty years ago but which provides a useful frame of reference for examining the impacts of investment projects. Nevertheless, it is also challenging because of the large number of aspects to cover. The UN Commission on Sustainable Development (CSD) has a core set of no fewer than fifty indicators to track progress in the achievement of sustainable development.[13]

FDI and the role of project finance

The essential characteristics of FDI are that it is investment made to establish a lasting interest in enterprises operating outside of the economy of the investor, implying a long-term relationship between the direct investor and the direct investment enterprise, and that it is undertaken with the intention of exercising a significant degree of influence on the management of the enterprise.[14] The Organization for Economic Cooperation and Development (OECD) recommends the use of the criterion of ownership by the investor of 10 per cent or more of the voting power of the enterprise as a threshold for FDI.[15] Thus a spectrum

---

[12] United Nations Department of Economic and Social Affairs (DESA), Division for Sustainable Development in Brief, Selected key issues, 'National Sustainable Development Strategies', available at: www.un.org/esa/desa/aboutus/keyissues.html.

[13] UN DESA, *Indicators of Sustainable Development: Guidelines and Methodologies* (3rd edn, New York: United Nations).

[14] *OECD Benchmark Definition of Foreign Direct Investment* (4th edn, Paris: OECD).

[15] *Ibid.* See also World Investment Report, *Transnational Corporations*, which in its Definitions and Sources notes that 'An equity capital stake of 10% or more of the ordinary shares or voting power for an incorporated enterprise or its equivalent for an

of companies, from minority-owned foreign affiliates, to equity joint ventures through to 100 per cent foreign-owned subsidiaries, can be considered as involving FDI. The investment made by the foreign investor takes the form of equity, but can also include reinvested earnings and shareholder loans.

Project finance, being bank lending rather than equity, is not included in the statistics on FDI volume but it is often a crucial part of the financing package for foreign investment projects. As has been indicated in Chapter 1, project finance typically involves the creation of a special purpose company (or what will be hereafter referred to as a special purpose vehicle, or SPV), in which the sponsoring companies take an equity stake, while the remaining finance is secured as loans from project finance banks. The lenders look to the revenues from the project for the repayment of the debt and to the assets of the project as the security.[16] Usually a number of banks are involved in providing the finance and in developing countries there is often participation from an official multilateral, regional or bilateral financing institution such as the International Finance Corporation (IFC) or European Bank for Reconstruction and Development (EBRD).

Project finance has been important in increasing the financing options open to large capital-intensive projects in developing countries with high political risk. For example mining projects in such countries used to be financed mainly through equity but in the 1990s increasingly project finance was used in conjunction with finance from official sources such as IFC.[17] According to Esty and Sesia,[18] three trends in the 1990s, privatization, deregulation and globalization, led to increasing use of project finance in a wider range of sectors in both developed and developing countries. This is not to say that project finance is always associated with FDI. In some cases it involves only domestic companies or just the public sector or a consortium of state-owned and domestic companies. Similarly, not all FDI involves the use of project finance. But it is the use of project finance investment to enable FDI that is the

---

unincorporated enterprise, is normally considered as the threshold for the control of assets'.

[16] Esty and Sesia, 'An Overview of Project Finance'.

[17] Alyson Warhurst and Nia Hughes, *Financing the Global Mining Industry: Project Finance*. Mining and Environment Research Network, Working Paper 150, University of Warwick.

[18] Esty and Sesia, 'An Overview of Project Finance'.

focus of this chapter. The key issue here is whether the mode of financing through project finance affects the impact of foreign investment projects.

The impacts of FDI on sustainable development

This section examines the debates and evidence on the impacts of FDI on the three main pillars, economic, environmental and social, of sustainable development.

FDI is commonly characterized[19] as:

- efficiency-seeking where the aim is to take advantage of low costs of production usually labour related, to produce for export;
- market-seeking where the objective is to produce for a large domestic market; and
- resource-seeking where the host country has natural resources available for exploitation.

A further distinction is often made between greenfield FDI, where a new facility is established, and mergers and acquisitions (M&A), where an existing enterprise is taken over. The latter is often associated with privatization of state-owned enterprises. Worldwide most FDI is M&A but for developing countries, greenfield investment has typically been important.[20] This reflects the opportunities for resource-seeking FDI in oil and gas, hydropower and minerals in developing countries where large injections of capital are needed to enable exploitation of these resources. A marked increase in M&A investment was observed in developing countries between 2001 and 2008.[21] Nevertheless, M&A investment was estimated by the World Bank to represent about 30 per cent of FDI to developing countries in 2007 and 2008, suggesting that greenfield FDI was still the main type of inward investment for these countries.[22]

These distinctions are important because the nature and extent of the impacts of FDI on sustainable development depend to some degree on the type of FDI involved.

[19] See for example J. Dunning, 'Re-evaluating the Benefits of Foreign Direct Investment', *Transnational Corporations* 3(1) (1994).
[20] World Investment Report, *Cross-border Mergers and Acquisitions and Development* (New York and Geneva: UN/UNCTAD, 2000).
[21] World Investment Report, *Transnational Corporations*.
[22] World Bank, *Global Development Finance*, p. 54 and figure 2.18.

FDI and the economic dimension of sustainable development

The main positive economic impact claimed for FDI is that it increases economic growth through a number of different pathways. This is first through its effect on investment. For developing countries as a whole, there is a positive but weak relationship between FDI as a share of gross domestic product (GDP) and gross fixed capital formation,[23] providing some support for a view that FDI may increase investment in host countries.

When FDI is export oriented, it can lead to creation of new markets for the country's output, boosting export revenues and foreign exchange, which in turn can lead to economic growth. This effect is more pronounced when greenfield investment is involved. More generally economic growth can be generated through the multiplier effects of local purchases of inputs and labour.[24]

Another way in which FDI can contribute to economic growth is through transferring advanced technology from industrialized to developing economies – the so-called spillover or contagion effect. Spillover effects can occur in several ways as normally companies engaged in FDI invest in the infrastructure, human resources, research and development (R&D), and other factors that will ensure the profitability of their investments. These actions may in turn benefit the surrounding community or the economy at large. According to the OECD (2002) technology transfer and diffusion work take place through four interrelated channels:

- vertical linkages with suppliers or purchasers in the host countries;
- horizontal linkages with competing or complementary companies in the same industry;
- migration of skilled labour; and
- the internationalization of R&D.

The evidence of positive spillovers is strongest and most consistent in the case of vertical linkages, in particular, the backward linkages with local suppliers in developing countries.[25]

---

[23] UNCTAD, *World Investment Report, 2003* (UNCTAD/WIR/2003, Geneva: UNCTAD), p. 77.

[24] M. Grieg-Gran, 'Towards Sustainable FDI in Asia Report', prepared for the Proposed SIGN3 Asia Initiative Sustainable Investment Global Network for Asia, IIED, April 2002.

[25] OECD, *Foreign Direct Investment for Development: Maximising Benefits, Minimising Costs* (Paris: OECD, 2002).

However, the enclave nature of many foreign enterprises raises concerns about their minimal linkages to the rest of the economy. Foreign enterprises may seek to protect technology rents rather than transfer technology, reducing or eliminating hoped-for spillovers and externalities.[26] Criticisms are also often made of the heavy reliance on imports of raw materials and capital equipment and use of expatriate staff in management positions, all of which serve to reduce the contribution to the national economy. For example it has been argued that the export-oriented strategy based on FDI, adopted by Singapore, Malaysia and Thailand in the 1980s to 1990s, did not result in the same sorts of linkages and technology spillovers compared to Taiwan and South Korea.[27] The enclave risks are especially associated with resource-based industries and foreign firms that split production processes among different countries/regions.

Not only may FDI have minimal linkages with the rest of the host economy, it may crowd out local firms that are competing in the same domestic or export markets. The empirical evidence, however, is mixed and location specific. While some studies have found that FDI has stimulated national investment – a crowding-in impact – especially in Asia, crowding out was frequent in Latin America.[28]

A cross-country empirical analysis of 1981 to 1999 found that the effect of FDI on growth is ambiguous depending very much on the sector to which it is channelled. FDI to the primary sector is associated with a negative impact on growth, while FDI to manufacturing is found to have a positive impact.[29]

FDI may increase host government revenues enabling public expenditure on growth-enabling activities. These revenue effects are both direct (through corporate taxes paid by the enterprises themselves) and indirect (when FDI raises economic growth and therefore the economy's total tax base).[30] But the use of generous tax concessions or direct financial incentives by host governments to attract FDI can offset the

---

[26] L. Zarsky and K. P. Gallagher, 'Searching for the Holy Grail? Making FDI Work for Sustainable Development'. Analytical Paper (Switzerland: WWF, 2003).

[27] G. Felker and K. S. Jomo, 'New Approaches to Investment Policy in the ASEAN', 4 (2000) Asian Development Bank Policy Institute.

[28] UNCTAD, *World Investment Report, 2003*.

[29] L. Alfaro, 'Foreign Direct Investment and Growth. Does the Sector Matter?' Harvard Business School. Available at: www.people.hbs.edu/lalfaro/fdisectorial.pdf.

[30] T. Addison and G. Mavrotas, 'Foreign Direct Investment, Innovative Sources of Development Finance and Domestic Resource Mobilization' (Helsinki, Finland: UNU-WIDER, 2004). Revised paper for Track II, Global Economic Agenda, Helsinki Process on

potential FDI benefits through increase of government revenues – in particular when these incentives surpass the level of the FDI spillover benefits. Much depends also on the use made of additional government revenues. A major concern is that FDI revenues and the granting of incentives can be fertile ground for rent-seeking and corruption, dissipating any increases in government revenue and undermining systems of corporate and political governance in the host country.[31] In such circumstances FDI can support or create anticompetitive industries (i.e. monopolies), distort local politics and thwart regulation.[32]

Another type of argument relates to FDI benefits as a stable source of capital. Compared to other types of capital flows, FDI is claimed to be relatively stable – by definition foreign investors make a long-term commitment and are less likely than portfolio investors to pull out suddenly in response to financial crises. Authors such as Lipsey[33] and Nunnenkamp provide examples for the case of East Asian countries, where FDI declined considerably less than portfolio investment during the Asian crisis in 1997 to 1998.[34] More recently, the global financial crisis appears to have affected FDI flows to developing countries less than other types of capital. Portfolio equity flows to developing countries declined by 90 per cent between 2007 and 2008, private debt flows declined by nearly 80 per cent but FDI actually increased slightly, although its rate of growth was greatly reduced.[35] In this context, FDI might be of particular relevance for countries with less-developed financial systems and regulation, given its ability to withstand financial shocks. However, it has also been claimed that FDI can create instability through increasing financial volatility.[36]

Globalization and Democracy. Available at: www.helsinkiprocess.fi/netcomm/ImgLib/24/89/hp_track2_addison_mavrotas.pdf, p. 5.

[31] M. Blomstrom, 'The economics of international investment incentives', Stockholm School of Economics, presented at the ECLAC/World Bank Seminar on Globalization, Santiago de Chile, 6–8 March 2002, available at: www.eclac.org/prensa/noticias/noticias/2/9272/blomstrom.pdf; C. Oman, *Policy Competition and Foreign Direct Investment* (Paris: OECD Development Centre, 2001).

[32] Blomstrom, 'Economics'; Zarsky and Gallagher, 'Searching for the Holy Grail?', 3.

[33] R. Lipsey, *Foreign Direct Investors in Three Financial Crises*, Working Paper 8084 (Cambridge, MA: National Bureau of Economic Research, 2001).

[34] P. Nunnenkamp, *To What Extent Can Foreign Direct Investment Help Achieve International Development Goals?*, Kiel Working Paper No. 1128 (Kiel: Kiel Institute for World Economics, October 2002).

[35] World Bank, *Global Development Finance.*

[36] Zarsky and Gallagher, 'Searching for the Holy Grail?'

FDI and the environmental dimension

FDI can affect the environment through three main routes: FDI environmental performance; FDI impacts on the production scale or on economic growth; and FDI structural impact or influence on the pattern of resource use.

FDI environmental performance

One of the main expected FDI environmental benefits is that foreign firms will help to drive up standards in developing countries by transferring both cleaner technology and better management expertise in controlling environmental impacts. The technology that foreign investors bring with them is likely to be relatively advanced, newer and less environmentally damaging than the ones available in the host countries.[37] Given that financial constraints are among the most important barriers to investment in environmentally preferable technology in developing countries,[38] access to capital implied by FDI may relieve one of the key constraints on investment in cleaner technology.

However, the evidence is rather mixed. While in some countries FDI performs better than domestic investment (e.g. Chile),[39] in other countries (e.g. Ghana and Zambia)[40] it has exerted downward pressure on environmental requirements. In others (e.g. Mexico) FDI has brought cleaner technologies only in industries where new core technologies are required.[41] This leads to a conclusion that FDI performs no better than national investment and that the environmental performance of a particular foreign firm depends on the strength of local regulation, the industry sector it is in and the particular company culture in relation to environmental commitment and corporate social responsibility.[42]

[37] OECD, *Foreign Direct Investment and the Environment: An Overview of the Literature* (Paris: OECD, 1997).
[38] *Ibid.*
[39] See N. Borregaard and A. Dufey, 'Environmental effects of foreign direct investment versus domestic investment in the mining sector in Latin America'. Paper prepared for OECD conference 'FDI and Environment – Lessons from Mining', 7–8 February 2002, Paris.
[40] See C. N. Boocock, 'Environmental impacts of foreign direct investment in the mining sector in sub-Saharan Africa'. Background document, for OECD conference on FDI (as n. 39).
[41] Working Group on Development and Environment in the Americas, *Globalization and Environment: Lessons from the Americas* (Washington, DC: Heinrich Böll Foundation, 2004), 51.
[42] Zarsky and Gallagher, 'Searching for the Holy Grail?'

A major debate in the literature on FDI is whether environmental regulation influences firm location decisions. The argument is that dirty and poorly performing firms from industrialized countries will be attracted to or tend to agglomerate in low-standard developing countries – creating the so-called 'pollution havens'[43] – due to the lower costs of complying with environmental regulations. However, Zarsky in her 1999 empirical review of FDI performance observes that the bulk of studies have found no evidence to support this hypothesis. While there are cases of foreign firms that clearly perform like 'environmental renegades' in host countries, there are also cases where foreign firms have brought with them higher standards and better management practices.[44]

UNCTAD's World Investment Report therefore suggests that most investment location decisions are not made on the basis of environmental criteria and that environmental costs are typically a small element in these decisions. As a result the imposition of higher environmental standards seems more likely to generate a technological response, rather than leading to capital flights.[45]

In a context of intense competition for attracting FDI, and given the absence of global overarching environmental standards, there is the concern that those host governments seeking to attract FDI are reluctant to make higher-than-average environmental demands on foreign firms. In a so-called 'race to the bottom' they may even be tempted to offer lower-than-average environmental demands to enhance the attractiveness of an overall package. Alternatively, it is thought that foreign investors may persuade governments to relax environmental standards as a condition for investment. However, as suggested before, evidence on this point tends to be ambiguous. Zarsky's 1999 review argued that policy makers are sensitive to potential effects of higher environmental standards on foreign investors. While they may not weaken standards in order to attract investors there will be a 'regulatory chill' effect on further environmental and social improvements for fear of losing competitive advantage in relation to other locations.

---

[43] Zarsky, 'Havens, halos and spaghetti: untangling the evidence about foreign direct investment and the environment'. Background document, for OECD conference on FDI and the Environment (The Hague, 28–9 January 1999) (Paris: OECD, 1999).

[44] *Ibid.*

[45] UNCTAD, *Making FDI Work for Sustainable Development* (UNCTAD/DITC/TED/9, Geneva: UNCTAD, 2004).

FDI environmental impact associated with economic growth

Maybe the most significant FDI environmental concern relates to the scale effect of FDI operations. As long as investment and hence output expand – given a fixed pollution intensity[46] and composition of production – scale effects on the environment are expected to be negative accelerating environmental degradation.[47] Although some observe that the scale effect occurs under domestic or foreign investment alike, the point is that foreign firms are usually larger than domestic ones and, in some cases, only foreign firms have the capabilities to invest in a particular sector.[48]

The counter-argument to the scale effect is that as long as FDI has a positive impact on economic growth, over time this can generate environmental improvements. This is because as incomes increase with economic growth, environmental quality is more likely to become a political priority for citizens and because governments have more possibilities to invest additional wealth in sound environmental policy.[49] This is the traditional Environmental Kuznets Curve (EKC) hypothesis, which posits that environmental quality first worsens and then improves as per capita income rises. However, the validity of the EKC hypothesis – especially in the context of developing countries – is questioned by an increasing number of studies.[50] The implication is that it would be incorrect to assume that environmental impacts of FDI-led growth will automatically be offset as income increases.[51]

FDI impacts on the pattern of resource use (structural effect)

A different FDI environmental impact concerns the shift in the pattern of resource use, or the so-called structural effect. To the extent that trade and investment liberalization promote a more efficient resource allocation among economies, structural effects are expected to be positive, as

---

[46] Pollution intensity refers to volume of emissions per unit of output.

[47] See M. Araya, 'FDI and the Environment: What Empirical Evidence Does – and Does not – Tell Us', ch. 2 in L. Zarsky (ed.), *International Investment for Sustainable Development: Balancing Rights and Rewards* (London: Earthscan, 2005).

[48] Zarsky, 'Havens, halos'; Oman, *Policy Competition*.

[49] Araya, 'FDI and the Environment'.

[50] H. Nordstrom and S. Vaughan 'Trade and Environment', Special Studies 4 (Geneva: WTO, 1999); Zarsky and Gallagher, 'Searching for the Holy Grail?'; Araya, 'FDI and the Environment'.

[51] Araya, 'FDI and the Environment'.

goods will be produced with lower input and capital per unit of output worldwide.[52]

In addition, a structural shift seems to be taking place in inward FDI to developing countries, as FDI investors are increasingly targeting the service (tertiary) sector and giving less emphasis to the manufacturing sector.[53] Although such a shift would be, in principle, environmentally good,[54] it should be acknowledged that each type of service – finance, transport, utilities, tourism – generates a different environmental impact, and more research is needed to understand the nature of the environmental impact associated with each of them. Moreover, FDI in primary sectors has remained stable or has slightly increased.[55] In regions such as Latin America, FDI is primarily targeting the primary sectors such as mining.

FDI and the social dimension of sustainable development

There are a number of arguments that FDI can lead to poverty reduction, directly and indirectly. But for most of these there are counter-arguments and the magnitude of the impact is case specific.

FDI has been highlighted as a key element for economic growth, and in turn growth has been pointed out as the single most important factor affecting poverty reduction.[56] But the first of these linkages is contested as discussed earlier under the economic dimension of sustainable development and the second has also been the subject of much debate. Dollar and Kraay's much-cited cross-country analysis found that poverty reduction was highest in countries with high average income growth.[57] But another cross-country study found that the magnitude of the poverty reduction effect observed depends critically on how economic growth is defined.[58] Single country studies of the growth and poverty relationship

---

[52] Araya, 'FDI and the Environment'.
[53] According to Arnal and Hijzen, *Impact of Foreign Direct Investment*, manufacturing's share of FDI stock in developing countries over the period 1990 to 2005 decreased from 44 per cent to 32 per cent, while the share of service sectors increased from 47 per cent to 58 per cent.
[54] B. S. Gentry, *Private Capital Flows and the Environment: Lessons from Latin America* (Cheltenham, UK: Edward Elgar, 1998).
[55] Arnal and Hijzen, *Impact of Foreign Direct Investment*.
[56] M. Klein, C. Aaron and B. Hadjimichael, Foreign Direct Investment and Poverty. World Bank Policy Research Working Papers No. 2613, June 2001.
[57] D. Dollar and A. Kraay, 'Growth is Good for the Poor', *Journal of Economic Growth*, 7(3) (2002), 195–225.
[58] R. H. Adams, 'Economic Growth, Inequality and Poverty: Estimating the Growth Elasticity of Poverty', *World Development*, 32(12) (2004), 1989–2014.

in Indonesia[59] and the Philippines[60] show some linkage but not as strong as that suggested by the Dollar and Kraay study.

In more general terms, jobs generated by FDI projects are expected to yield benefits in terms of poverty reduction. Indeed, it is estimated that employment in foreign affiliates of multinational companies reached 53 million workers in 2002, two and a half times the number in 1982.[61] By 2006, this had increased to 73 million, equivalent to 3 per cent of the global workforce.[62] FDI can lead to poverty reduction if employment is generated for unskilled labour or if capacity building and training is built into the activity.[63] But job creation may also be jeopardized when foreign companies are capital intensive and employ few local staff – though this often reflects the nature of the sector – i.e. mining. Indirect job generation can also be minimal where FDI companies have few linkages with local companies, relying instead on imports. Moreover, this may lead to the crowding out of more labour-intensive domestic activities. The type of investment is also important. FDI in greenfield projects is more likely to generate employment than M&A.[64]

FDI can generate much-needed revenues for underfunded governments to spend on social infrastructure such as health and education. Many foreign investors also invest substantially in supporting the development of a safety net for the poor in the community where they operate. On the other hand, FDI has also been linked to social disruptions as a consequence of accelerated commercialization in less developed countries.[65]

FDI and labour standards: the 'race to the bottom' hypothesis also applies to labour standards. Critics of FDI allege that foreign firms tend to locate in countries with lower wages, lower taxes and weaker social standards. They thus contribute to a 'race to the bottom' where countries are forced to lower their standards to attract FDI and so not lose investments and jobs.

[59] A. Balisacan, E. M. Pernia and A. Asra, *Revisiting Growth and Poverty Reduction in Indonesia: What Do Subnational Data Show?* ERD Working Paper Series No. 25, Economics and Research Department, Asian Development Bank.
[60] A. M. Balisacan and E. M. Pernia, *Probing Beneath Cross-National Averages: Poverty, Inequality and Growth in the Philippines.* ERD Working Paper Series No. 7 Economics and Research Department, Asian Development Bank.
[61] UNCTAD, *World Investment Report.*
[62] Arnal and Hijzen, *Impact of Foreign Direct Investment.*   [63] Grieg-Gran (2002).
[64] Arnal and Hijzen, *Impact of Foreign Direct Investment.*
[65] OECD, *Foreign Direct Investment for Development.*

Evidence supporting a race to the bottom on labour standards is rather ambiguous. On the one hand, FDI may help to improve labour standards, for instance, because foreign investors tend to be concerned about their reputation in developed country markets.[66] This would apply more to efficiency-seeking FDI than market-seeking FDI. But there is little cross-country empirical evidence to provide support for this positive effect.[67] On the other hand, there are cases where FDI and their suppliers have been criticized for poor labour standards including worker abuse, inadequate protection of worker health and safety, use of child labour and complicity in the violation of human rights.[68] Studies of export processing zones have shown how in some cases – e.g. the Philippines – workers in these zones do not enjoy the same labour rights in terms of unionization as workers outside the zones.[69]

FDI and inequality: FDI may accentuate inequality particularly where certain areas are targeted for inward investment – e.g. export processing zones – or between individuals as those working in foreign-owned companies may enjoy better working conditions and remuneration. Research from Mexico, Venezuela, several countries in sub-Saharan Africa and Indonesia provides some evidence to support this.[70] Moreover, most FDI may increase urban–rural inequality as it tends to concentrate in urban areas where there is economic development.

In addition, skilled workers may benefit significantly more from FDI than unskilled workers.[71] As FDI tends to apply more advanced technologies than local firms, it is frequently concentrated in relatively skill-intensive sectors (such as resource extraction and sophisticated

---

[66] Arnal and Hijzen, *Impact of Foreign Direct Investment.*   [67] *Ibid.*
[68] Zarsky and Gallagher, 'Searching for the Holy Grail?'
[69] S. Kuruvilla, C. Erickson, M. Anner, M. V. Amante and I. Ortiz, *Globalisation and Industrial Relations in the Philippines* (Bangkok: ILO, Regional Office for Asia and the Pacific, 2000).
[70] B. Aitken, A. E. Harrison and R. Lipsey, 'Wages and Foreign Ownership: A Comparative Study of Mexico, Venezuela and the United States', *Journal of International Economics*, 40(314) (1996), 345–71; R. E. Lipsey and F. Sjöholm, 'Foreign Firms and Indonesian Manufacturing Wages: An Analysis with Panel Data', *Economic Development and Cultural Change*, 55(1) (2006), 201–21; O. Morrisey and D. W. Te Velde, 'Do Workers in Africa get a Wage Premium if Employed in Firms Owned by Foreigners?', *Journal of African Economies*, 12(1) (2003), 41–73 – all reviewed by Arnal and Hijzen, *Impact of Foreign Investment.*
[71] Nunnenkamp, *To What Extent?*

manufacturing). A study carried out by Te Velde in 2003[72] seems to support this finding as it shows that income differentials in Latin America have become more accentuated during periods of high FDI inflows, demonstrating that FDI has potentially led to increases in wages for skilled labour, while wages for unskilled labour have been more stable.

Summary of the evidence

Overall, the effects of FDI on sustainable development – whether positive or negative – are context dependent. There have been some very positive experiences and also some very negative ones. It is also the case that FDI can be positive on one dimension of sustainable development, and negative on the others. Moreover, it is not always the economic dimension that is positive at the expense of the others. Some foreign companies have been found to have better environmental and social performance than locally owned ones, but their economic spillover effects may be minimal. There is also little evidence that one type of FDI, whether export oriented or market seeking or resource seeking, is better for sustainable development than another. Export-oriented FDI may be influenced by the demands of the buyers and may have better environmental and social performance than FDI focused on the domestic market. But market-seeking investment may contribute more to the economic dimension of sustainable development through its linkages with the local economy. However, resource-seeking FDI is widely considered to pose the most risks because of the nature of the sectors involved.

The following factors may be considered to affect the impact of FDI:

- the host country's policies – the extent to which it adjusts policies in positive or negative ways to attract investment;
- the nature of the company – interest in corporate social responsibility (CSR) and concern about reputation;[73]
- the market that the company is targeting – final consumers or business to business in developed or developing countries, as this

---

[72] D. W. Te Velde, 'Foreign Direct Investment and Income Inequality in Latin America' Overseas Development Institute, 2003 available at: www.odi.org.uk/resources/download/1298.pdf.

[73] For example in the mining sector, companies that are members of ICMM (International Council on Mining and Metals) agree to adhere to codes of practice.

affects how sensitive the market is to sustainable development concerns;

- scrutiny and pressure brought to bear by civil society; and
- the policies of the financial institutions backing the project.

Does financing through PF have an influence?

The rise in project finance as a mode of financing of FDI raises the issue of whether it can accentuate these positive and negative impacts or whether it is neutral.

To establish why project finance might affect the impacts of FDI it is necessary to examine its essential characteristics which distinguish it from other types of finance for investment projects. And in turn to consider whether these distinguishing characteristics have any link with the factors identified above that influence the impact of FDI. It is first necessary to take into account the types of project and sector that are most likely to involve this type of financing. Statistics on foreign debt contracted by developing country corporations (which is the category within which project finance will be classified) show that while financial institutions in developing countries receive a large amount,[74] a large share corresponds to resource-based industries such as oil and gas (24 per cent in 2007) and mining (6 per cent in 2007) as well as infrastructure, for example telecommunications (11 per cent in 2007) and utility and energy (6 per cent in 2007).[75] These sectors are typically not closely linked to consumers in developed countries, and it is therefore unlikely that the markets targeted by the companies concerned are environmentally or socially sensitive. There is also very little to suggest that project sponsor companies seeking project finance are any different in terms of their practices and concerns about reputation than those seeking other types of finance.

The use of project finance is however very relevant to the other three factors listed above, the policies of the host country, the extent of civil society scrutiny and the policies of the institutions giving financial backing to the project. These factors are discussed below.

---

[74] The finance sector received the highest amount among sectors in 1998 to 2000, and 2004 to 2006. In 2001–3 and 2007–8, the highest amount was contracted by the oil and gas sector. in World Bank, *Global Development Finance*, table 3.1, p. 75. The financial institutions contracted this debt presumably to finance their lending within the country.

[75] Calculated from *ibid.*

Impact on host country policies and ability to pursue sustainable development

The complex contractual arrangements involved in project finance to allocate risk, and in particular the need for an agreement with the host country government, have implications for host country policies.[76] There is a concern that the agreements entered into to meet the requirements of the lenders may interfere with the host government's ability to pursue sustainable development goals. This would exacerbate any negative impacts of FDI. Particular concerns have been expressed about the stabilization clauses which are often a feature of host government agreements (HGAs). These clauses aim to 'freeze in place each of the significant investment assumptions made by the project company over which the government has control'.[77] This is necessary from the lender's perspective because changes in government policies could affect the project cash flow and ability to repay the loan.

The case of the Baku–Tbilisi–Ceyhan (BTC) pipeline project[78] shows the controversies associated with HGAs and their stabilization clauses. The agreements signed between the project sponsor, and the governments of the three countries, Turkey, Georgia and Azerbaijan, through which the pipeline passes, raised concerns with civil society groups because of their economic equilibrium clause. This clause states that the host government has to pay the project consortium substantial compensation for any changes in law or other actions that will disturb the economic equilibrium of the project.[79] A further concern was that each HGA had a privileged legal status overriding all conflicting domestic law, present and future. They thus appeared to take precedence over existing environmental and social laws. In Georgia, this enabled the overriding of the national Water Act in order to develop the pipeline right of way.[80]

[76] See Chapter 5, in this book.
[77] S. L. Hoffman, *The Law and Business of International Project Finance* (2nd edn, Boston, MA: Kluwer Law International), 2001 p. 228. See also A. Shemberg, 'Stabilization Clauses and Human Rights' (IFCUN, 2008), S. Leader, 'Human Rights, Risks, and New Strategies for Global Investment', *Journal of International Economic Law*, 9 (2006), 657–705, and Amnesty International, *Human Rights on the Line* (London: Amnesty International, 2003).
[78] See Chapter 12 in this book.
[79] Chapter 12 in this book, citing Amnesty International, *Human Rights on the Line*.
[80] Chapter 12 in this book, citing USAID, 'Multilateral Development Bank Assistance Proposals', at n. 59.

This was not just a 'regulatory chill' but a potential regulatory down-grading. However, subsequently a number of clarifying legal documents were produced which addressed many of the concerns raised by civil society organizations.[81]

It is not clear, however, that such arrangements are peculiar to project finance. Analysis of mining sector regulation in Africa suggests that they are part of a broader process of liberalizing investment and developing investor-friendly mining codes.[82] In Tanzania, the Mining Act 1998 was the result of a World Bank-financed Mineral Sector Technical Assistance Project which aimed to introduce a legal, regulatory and fiscal frame-work conducive to private investment in mining.[83] This act provided for development agreements (s. 10) which would enable companies to negotiate fixed tax rates throughout the life of the project, as well as other incentives and special guarantees and waivers of company liability for environmental problems.

As with any project, the outcome depends on how the risks are allocated and mitigated and how well the host country negotiates its position.[84] Governments may, for example, undertake responsibility for the wrong risks such as construction cost overruns which are usually better managed by the project company.[85] Another scenario is that a government takes on too much risk, leaving the project company with insufficient financial responsibility to deter it from excessive risk tak-ing.[86] It is argued though[87] that one-sided political risk mitigation may not be in the long-term interests of investors. By creating the perception of governments being bullied to accept unfavourable risk mitigation alternatives, it generates a new risk that may threaten the project in the long term. Once significant amounts of foreign capital have been com-mitted to the project, the relative bargaining positions of investor and host government change. The host government gains in power and can force renegotiation.

---

[81] Chapter 12 in this book, citing Carpenter and Labadi, 'Striking a Balance', at n. 58; Zarsky and Gallagher, 'Searching for the Holy Grail?'.

[82] B. Campbell (ed.), *Regulating Mining in Africa: For Whose Benefit?* Discussion Paper 26 (Uppsala: Nordiska Afrikainstitutet, 2004).

[83] P. Butler, 'Tanzania: Liberalisation of Investment and the Mining Sector. Analysis of the Content and Certain Implications of the Tanzania 1998 Mining Act', in Campbell (ed.), *Regulating Mining in Africa*.

[84] On risk allocation in this context, see Chapter 5, in this book.

[85] Hoffman, *Law and Business*.   [86] *Ibid.*   [87] *Ibid.*

However, it has also been suggested[88] that project finance could be less vulnerable to renegotiation than other types of financing. For example, where a company finances a project with corporate finance it would respond to high political or sovereign risk by increasing the rate of return required from the project. The argument is that this high required return is itself a risk factor as it might create the perception of excessive return earned at the expense of the host government. This could increase the risk of expropriation. Reducing sovereign risk through 'careful structuring' in a project finance approach to financing means that a lower rate of return can be sought by the sponsors and the project is therefore less vulnerable to *ex post* renegotiation.[89]

Ultimately, it comes down to how the risks are allocated and mitigated and the effects on the host government as well as the external effects on other stakeholders. The latter type of effect though may not be given high priority by the host government. Moreover, there may well be different views within the country or between local, national and international stakeholders as to what is an acceptable risk and return trade-off. These negotiating issues are not exclusive to projects financed through project finance, and apply to any project involving an agreement between investors and a host government. The World Investment Report, which in 2007 looked at extractive industries, summed up the issue as follows:

> Unequal bargaining power between large TNCs and governments may lead to less than optimal outcomes of negotiations for a host country, especially since the short-term profit maximization motives of the TNCs do not necessarily coincide with the longer term development objectives of a host country.[90]

It goes on to suggest that some of the mining codes adopted and mining agreements negotiated in the 1980s and 1990s in developing countries in a context of historically low mineral prices may have been overgenerous to foreign investors.

---

[88] Benjamin C. Esty, 'The economic motivations for using project finance', current draft February 2003, working paper, Harvard Business School (available at HBS's website).
[89] *Ibid.*
[90] World Investment Report, *Transnational Corporations, Extractive Industries and Development* (New York and Geneva: UNCTAD/UN, 2007), ch. V, 'Development Implications for Host Countries', p. 129.

At most the use of project finance can be considered as an additional pressure point for decisions potentially detrimental to sustainable development in situations where bargaining power is unequal or host governments are poorly informed or lack negotiating capacity.

Civil society scrutiny and policies of financial institutions

The use of project finance may open up investments to greater civil society scrutiny directly and indirectly through the involvement of high-profile financial institutions.

Companies receiving project finance as SPVs are typically highly leveraged and owned by one to three sponsors whose equity in the project company is almost always privately held.[91] As the requirements for public information provision are not as onerous for privately held companies as for listed companies, this appears to close off an avenue for civil society scrutiny. What makes the difference though in this case is the involvement of particular types of financial institutions, official development financing institutions with a development mandate and the so-called Equator Banks.

The development finance institutions because of their official nature have a greater requirement for information disclosure. Because of their development mandate, they are under greater pressure than private banks to apply strict environmental and social standards. But through the Equator Principles (EP) this environmental and social responsibility has been extended to private banks.

The majority of private project finance banks have now signed up to the EP which commit them to apply World Bank/IFC social and environmental risk management procedures in assessing the projects they finance. As will be seen more fully in Chapters 3 and 4, the EP are an industry standard adopted in June 2003 which provide a framework for commercial banks to review, evaluate and mitigate/avoid environmental and social impacts and risks associated with project finance activities. These were introduced and signed up to by ten banks in 2003 and updated in 2006. In 2007, three-quarters of all international financing transactions for major projects in developing and emerging states complied with the standards.[92]

---

[91] Esty, 'Economic motivations'.
[92] S. Bergius, 'Environmental standards loom ever larger in banks' ENDS Agenda! Environmental Data Services. Available at the EP website: www.equator-principles.com.

The case study of the BTC pipeline shows how it was the involvement of the IFC that led to the disclosure of the HGAs signed between each of the host governments, Azerbaijan, Georgia and Turkey and project sponsors. This enabled civil society groups to comment on the contracts and to highlight areas that conflicted with sustainable development and human rights goals.

The same point emerges from the comparison of two mining concessions in Ghana involving FDI (Chapter 14, in this book). One, Newmont Ghana Gold Ltd (NGGL) financed through project finance and with IFC participation, and the other, AngloGold Ashanti, a South African multinational company financed through equity and corporate finance.[93] The authors of the case study note that AngloGold has been reluctant to disclose most independent assessment reports on its operations, while documents related to NGGL are available on the IFC website. Moreover they suggest that NGGL's operations are subject to higher standards of compliance than AngloGold Ashanti and that therefore a project finance mechanism may be preferable to conventional forms of financing.

As well as increasing disclosure and hence public scrutiny, another likely effect of the project finance contractual arrangements is to broaden the range of risks addressed. In theory, the non-recourse nature of the loans means that there is greater attention to risks and more extensive due diligence[94] undertaken by the lenders than for other types of finance. But the inclusion of social and environmental factors in the risk assessment has not been automatic. It has taken some bad experiences with controversial projects for financial institutions to recognize that certain factors, such as impacts on environment and societies in which the projects are located, could represent serious risks to their financial exposure and therefore should be an integral part of due diligence. In the case of WestLB, a decisive turning point was its experience with the controversial OCP pipeline in Ecuador for which it was one of the largest

---

[93] Until 2004, the mining operations were owned by Ghana-based Ashanti Goldfields and became part of AngloGold Ashanti in April 2004 when the business combination of Ashanti and South African-based AngloGold came into effect. Obuasi Country Report, available at: www.anglo gold.com/NR/rdonlyres/EC62C8CA-4F9A-4D74-B33F-322DF7137EF4/0/obuasi_report.pdf.

[94] Due diligence is an important process for risk identification in project financing. It is an interdisciplinary process involving legal, technical, environmental, social and financial specialists, designed to detect events that might result in total or partial project failure (Hoffman, *Law and Business*).

financiers. The OCP pipeline project was widely criticized for the conflicts it caused with indigenous populations and the scant regard given to
the interests of local indigenous people. The resulting criticism of
WestLB prompted it to take part in the initiative that was to become
the EP.[95]

The EP now provide a common framework for the project finance
banks to assess and address a wide range of social and environmental
factors.

Conclusions

The impacts of FDI on sustainable development are case specific, and
generalizations cannot be made. Similarly the implications of using
project finance in FDI projects depend very much on the context.
While the contractual arrangements with host country governments
that are a feature of project finance represent risks for sustainable
development, the outcome depends on how the negotiations are conducted, what is taken into account and the range of short, medium and
long-term risks that are taken into consideration. For this reason, it is
difficult to show firm evidence that the use of project finance is magnify-
ing the negative impacts of FDI on sustainable development as compared
with other types of financing. Nevertheless, it is important to identify
opportunities to introduce legal remedies to address the risks posed
by project finance to sustainable development (see Part II and Chapter
15 of this book).

The case for project finance having a positive effect on the FDI and
sustainable development relationship seems stronger. Mechanisms such
as the EP which provide signatory banks with a common approach for
assessment of economic, environmental and social risks associated with
their lending, are broadening the scope of due diligence procedures and
opening up projects to greater scrutiny from civil society. But again it is
how the EP are applied that matters.

Moreover the approaches adopted for project finance are being transferred to other types of finance. For example HSBC applies the EP to
export finance loans where the use of proceeds is known to be directly
related to projects.[96] WestLB rejected two corporate loans and an export

---

[95] Bergius, 'Environmental Standards'.
[96] HSBC Holdings plc Sustainability Report 2008.

finance transaction on the basis of the EP.[97] This is important for sectors such as pulp and paper where the use of project finance has been extremely limited.[98]

Project finance is playing an increasingly important role in developing-country economies. Continued action to introduce legal remedies for some of the risks project finance represents to sustainable development, as well as improvement in the application of existing mechanisms such as the EP, is crucial.

---

[97] Bergius, 'Environmental Standards'.
[98] M. Spek, *Financing Pulp Mills: An Appraisal of Risk Assessment and Safeguard Procedures* (Bogor, Indonesia, Centre for International Forestry Research, 2006; available at: www.cifor.cgiar.org/publications/pdf_files/Books/Bspek0601.pdf).

3

Project finance and the relevant human rights

ÖZGÜR CAN KAHALE

Introduction

This chapter aims to set out the human rights standards that project finance (PF), as a species of foreign direct investment (FDI), must meet. The benchmarks set by such standards are largely the same as they are for FDI in general even though, as will be seen, there are particular pressures on such rights that PF can sometimes bring to bear. This chapter therefore fits PF into a wider context, looking at a range of sectors and examples of projects, some making use of this financing technique and some not. Later in the book, particular PF mechanisms and projects will be the focus.

Developed-country multinational enterprises (MNEs) are the leading sources of FDI, accounting for 84 per cent of global outflows.[1] Hence, MNEs have become increasingly important, particularly in developing countries, and, in some cases, assume functions performed previously by the public sector.[2] Furthermore, with economic globalization the developing world has assumed the role of manufacturer, while the developed world has moved into the production of services, whereby investors compensate the scarcity of capital in developing economies by borrowing money from lenders to realize projects, thereby frequently utilizing PF.

There is considerable evidence to suggest that when FDI projects are insufficiently monitored or regulated, human rights suffer, especially in developing host states. There have been reports about the way in which MNEs have benefited from the lower production costs available

---

[1] Ochoa, C., 2003, p. 5; UNCTAD, *World Investment Report*, 2007, p. 1.
[2] Sanchez-Moreno, M. and Higgins, T., 2004, p. 5.

through systemic violations of core labour and anti-discrimination standards in Asia and Latin America.[3] Similar claims have been made regarding the extraction of natural resources. Many developing countries have opened up their borders to welcome foreign firms in the extractive industries such as mining, oil extraction and logging in isolated parts of their territories, which are often the last refuge of indigenous peoples.[4] While these opportunities for business generate growth, they also present a risk to human rights.[5]

The human rights considered here are those found in UN instruments. In 1966, the General Assembly of the United Nations adopted the two Covenants on human rights, which, together with the 1948 Universal Declaration of Human Rights, are referred to as 'the International Bill of Human Rights'. These instruments provide the backbone of modern human rights protection mechanisms.[6] As of 3 July 2009, the International Covenant on Civil and Political Rights (ICCPR) has 160 parties, and the International Covenant on Economic, Social and Cultural Rights (ICESCR) has 166 parties.[7] These documents, which reflect a strong consensus, largely set the meaning of human rights in contemporary international society, and are regarded as authoritative statements of international norms.[8] Therefore, the human rights discussed below are all linked to the International Bill of Rights and other relevant UN treaties.

Rather than simply list these rights, it is more informative to consider some of the sectors in which serious issues about them have arisen.

[3] Weiler, T., 2004, p. 4.   [4] Daes, E. A., 2001, p. 1.
[5] International Committee of the Red Cross, 2006, p. 7.
[6] Adopted during the 1495th and 1496th plenary meetings of 16 December 1966.
[7] Information obtained from the United Nations Treaty Collection Database website on 3 July 2009.
[8] Donnelly says that the Universal Declaration of Human Rights and the International Human Rights Covenants – often referred to collectively as the International Bill of Human Rights – provide a widely accepted list of internationally recognized human rights. They encompass a wide range of personal, legal, civil, political, economic, social and cultural rights, and further elaboration of this list has been in a variety of single-issue treaties and declarations on such topics as discrimination, women's rights and genocide, that it is generally agreed that these rights form an interdependent and interactive system of guarantees. Donnelly, J., 2003, pp. 228–9 and p. 23. There are also a number of regional conventions and additional treaties covering particular groups or subjects (such as women's and children's rights or the prohibition against torture). Furthermore the United Nations Charter imposes on its member states the obligation to promote 'universal respect for and observance of human rights and fundamental freedoms'.

Extractive industries

The extractive industries sector includes mining and metals and oil and gas. The deals which use PF methods in extractive industries totalled US$13.7 billion in the first half of 2009.[9] This sector usually requires a large amount of capital and it has been the most common source of allegations of human rights abuses. The claims usually advanced are that a range of civil, political, economic, social and cultural rights are, as a direct consequence of the exploitation of natural resources, adversely affected.[10] Violations of civil and political rights have been caused by land disputes and forcible relocations, denials of freedom of speech, torture, disappearances, extra-judicial killings and arrests. The use of bonded and child labour and infringements of the right to association and assembly, have caused labour rights violations. One also finds allegations of denials of women's rights, violations of indigenous peoples' rights, denials of the right to health, housing and water, and economic, social and cultural rights violations.[11]

For example, in the *Ogoni* case involving oil extraction by Shell and the Nigerian state company, the African Commission on Human and Peoples' Rights found Nigeria in violation of the right to food, housing and protection against forced eviction, among others.[12] Another example is the Mining Act in the Philippines. In order to lure foreign investors, the Act provides assurance to mining companies that they will be the priority when apportioning access to water in their areas, among other privileges.[13] The majority of Filipinos depend on land and water resources for their livelihood.[14] Nettleton argues that the Philippines concern themselves mainly with promotion of mining to international investors and that they neglect the need to regulate the mining industry to protect human rights. He further emphasizes that, in addition to the unwillingness to regulate, the Department of Environment and Natural Resources is not capable of effectively regulating the mining industry

---

[9] *Infrastructure Journal*, Global Infrastructure Finance Review, 2009.
[10] Forest Peoples' Programme and Tebtebba Foundation, 2006, p. 64.
[11] Woicke, P., 2005, p. 338.
[12] African Commission on Human and Peoples' Rights, 2001–2002, p. 43.
[13] Such as: 100 per cent foreign ownership of mining firms guarantees the direct flow of capital, profits, equipment and loan services out of the country; reduction in the royalty on gold to 2 per cent; assured non-expropriation; reduction in excise taxation from 5 to 2 per cent; and tax holidays (Balane, W. I., 2006).
[14] Balane, W. I., 2006.

to ensure the protection of the people and the environment from mining hazards, and that in the past it has often failed in its duty to manage, monitor and regulate.[15]

Land acquisitions for mining operations have often been one of the most problematic sources of conflict.[16] While land acquisitions by a government for a company, or by the company directly, may comply with national law, this is no guarantee that the acquisition process will not violate international human rights law or that it follows basic notions of fair and equitable process and compensation.[17] The Centre on Housing Rights and Evictions reported that on 8 January 2007, private police forces and the armed forces evicted 80 Mayan-Q'eq'chi families from the community of La Pista and 228 families from La Union, in the region of El Estor, Izabal, Guatemala. The Canadian Mining Company, Skye Resources, holds an exploratory mining licence for 300 sq. km of land in the municipality of El Estor, and the evictions took place to clear the area for mining facilities.[18] However, in 2001 the Inter-American Court held that the state must adopt legislative, administrative and any other measures to delimit, demarcate and title lands and territories belonging to indigenous peoples.[19]

Extractive industries frequently operate in hitherto isolated areas of developing countries, which are often the last refuge of indigenous peoples and their cultural diversity.[20] The majority of complaints submitted by indigenous peoples to intergovernmental human rights bodies involve alleged rights violations in connection with resource extraction.[21] The Committee on the Elimination of Racial Discrimination found 28 instances; the Human Rights Committee found 13; and the Committee on Economic, Social and Cultural Rights found 15 instances

[15] Balane, W. I., holds that mining law was devised at the request of mining companies, and on the recommendation of international financing agencies such as the World Bank, the Asian Development Bank and the United Nations Development Programme. See Balane, W. I., 2006.
[16] Woicke, P., 2005, p. 343.   [17] Woicke, P., 2005, p. 344.
[18] Centre on Housing Rights and Evictions, 17 January 2007.
[19] Mayagna (Sumo) Awas Tingni Community Case, Judgment of August 31, 2001. Series C No. 79, para 164; Forest Peoples' Programme and Tebtebba Foundation, 2006.
[20] Working paper on combating racism against indigenous peoples submitted by Mrs E. I. A. Daes, a member of the Working Group on Indigenous Populations of the Sub-Commission on the Promotion and Protection of Human Rights. UN Doc. A/CONF.189/PC.3/4, 20 July 2001, para. 4.
[21] For a list of these cases, see Box 2, p. 21, Forest Peoples' Programme and Tebtebba Foundation, 2006.

of violation of indigenous peoples' rights in connection with extractive industries in different countries between 1996 and 2006.[22] The UN Committee on the Elimination of Racial Discrimination said that one of the reasons it adopted a General Recommendation on indigenous peoples in 1997 is because in many regions of the world indigenous peoples' rights have been seriously jeopardized since they have lost their land and resources to commercial companies and state enterprises.[23]

The UN Special Rapporteur on the situation of human rights and fundamental freedoms of indigenous people observes:

> [r]esources are being extracted and/or developed by other interests (oil, mining, logging and fisheries) with little or no benefits for the indigenous communities that occupy the land . . . [i]n numerous instances the rights and needs of indigenous peoples are disregarded, making this one of the major human rights problems faced by them in recent decades.[24]

The Committee on the Elimination of Racial Discrimination in its concluding observations regarding Ecuador stated that in the exploitation of the subsoil resources located subjacent to the traditional lands of indigenous communities, mere consultation of these communities prior to exploitation fell short of meeting the requirements set out in the Committee's General Recommendation 23 on the rights of indigenous peoples. The Committee recommended that the prior informed consent of these communities should be sought, and that the equitable sharing of benefits to be derived from such exploitation be ensured.[25] In 2006, the Inter-American Commission recommended that the indigenous peoples' consent to the exploitation of natural resources on their traditional territories should always be required by law.[26]

---

[22] Forest Peoples' Programme and Tebtebba Foundation, 2006, p. 12.

[23] General Recommendation XXIII (51) concerning Indigenous Peoples. Adopted at the Committee's 1235th meeting of 18 August 1997. UN Doc. CERD/C/51/Misc.13/Rev.4, para. 3.

[24] Report of the Special Rapporteur on the situation of human rights and fundamental freedoms of indigenous peoples, Mr Rodolfo Stavenhagen, submitted pursuant to Commission Resolution 2001/57. UN Doc. E/CN.4/2002/97, para. 56.

[25] CERD, 2003, para. 16.

[26] See Inter-American Commission on Human Rights, Report on Admissibility and Merits No. 09/06, 12 Saramaka Clans, Case 12.338 (Suriname), 2 March 2006, para. 230, cited in Forest Peoples' Programme and Tebtebba Foundation, 2006. Suriname's Mining Bill of 2004 was also deemed racially discriminatory by the UN Committee on the Elimination of Racial Discrimination on the grounds that it denies indigenous peoples access to judicial remedies and fails to require their agreement to mining.

The extraction of natural resources without regard to human rights might deprive people of their means of subsistence and impinge on their right to determine their development. As exemplified above, forced evictions to carry out mining activities left many indigenous peoples without land. This infringes Article 47 of the ICCPR and Article 25 of the ICESCR, which says:

> Nothing in the present Covenant shall be interpreted as impairing the inherent right of all peoples to enjoy and utilise fully and freely their natural wealth and resources.

The United Nations Declaration on the Rights of Indigenous Peoples also confirms this, stating in Article 20 that:

> Indigenous peoples have the right to maintain and develop their political, economic and social systems or institutions, to be secure in the enjoyment of their own means of subsistence and development, and to engage freely in all their traditional and other economic activities.[27]

The extraction of natural resources in developing countries can also cause violations of the right to freedom of expression and freedom of association and assembly. For example, Amnesty International reported that protests against the gold mine run by the Australia-based Normandy Mining Company (widely known by its former name, Eurogold) in Bergama, Turkey, have led to violations of the right to freedom of expression in Turkey.[28] The people of Bergama have been protesting against the mine for about twelve years, asserting that it is doing damage to the environment and jeopardizing human health because of the cyanide-leaching method used at the mine. The *Turkish Daily News* reported on 16 September 2000 that the gendarmerie had taken some protesters into custody, and that gendarmerie command asked the Public Prosecutor's Office to charge them with being members of an illegal Marxist organization. The gendarmerie is quoted as saying:

> The members of the Environmental Activity Committee and the heads of public committees and their members were organised against the integrity of the state. In order to prevent demonstrations that could cause more problems in the future, those people who are members of illegal organisations should be charged.

[27] Report of the Human Rights Council, 61st session, Agenda item 68, 7 September 2007, A/61/L.67.
[28] Amnesty International, 2003, p. 24.

Over the years, there have been other attempts to imprison protesters for non-violent opposition to the mine in Bergama.[29]

The extractive industry is the sector with the most operations in the least-developed countries. Of the thirty-two countries in the low human development section of the United Nations Development Programme Human Development Index, twenty-two have experienced conflict at some point since 1990.[30] In some of these countries conflict was caused or exacerbated by a phenomenon known as the 'resource curse', where extraction of natural resources revenue fuels tensions.

Extractive industries and conflict

Natural resources such as oil, diamonds, gold or timber, in theory, should favour a country's rapid economic and social development but millions of people in resource-rich countries have seen their lives devastated by the misuse of FDI revenues.[31] In an expert meeting on FDI and natural resources organized by UNCTAD it was stated that many mineral-rich countries have failed to realize the potential of economic development in the exploitation of their endowments, since the social and economic outcome of involving MNEs in the extractive industries is dependent on good governance.[32]

Developed-country MNEs are still the main players in terms of investment in oil and gas, with some developing country state-owned companies emerging as important outward investors.[33] The extractive industries sector is inherently limited in its choice of investment sites because it must invest in countries that possess the natural resources whether there are human rights abuses or not.[34] While most investors prefer to engage in democratic states that are economically and politically stable, those involved in the extractive industry are more constrained by the location of resources.[35]

---

[29] Amnesty International, 2003, p. 24.

[30] *International Alert*, 2006, p. 5.

[31] Le Billon, P., 2005, p. 7 and p. 11. Le Billon says that compared to less-well-endowed countries, resource-rich countries have been on average poorer and less competently governed and observed a lower economic growth rate over the past thirty years.

[32] UNCTAD, 2007, para. 12.   [33] UNCTAD, 2007, para. 5.

[34] Other industries, however, have far greater flexibility in selecting locations for investment. For example, efficiency-seeking FDI may (or may not) choose countries in which there is a greater respect for human rights. Blanton, S. and Blanton, R., 2005, p. 6.

[35] International Law Commission, 2001, p. 11.

The unequal sharing out of the benefits of natural resources extraction is associated with creating or perpetuating conflict and the onset of civil war.[36] If a government is party to a conflict, sometimes revenues collected from natural resources such as taxes, royalties or profits go towards boosting the conflict.[37] Therefore, in a country with a repressive regime that abuses human rights, investors are capable of bolstering the corrupt regime and increasing its staying power. This was the case of the financial and technical support provided by international business in South Africa during apartheid.[38] Governments in resource-dependent countries tend to be more corrupt as they have discretionary control over large resource rents, used often to strengthen their power and resist international pressure.[39] For example, the Chadian government used part of the US$25 million sign-on bonus from the World Bank for the Chad–Cameroon pipeline to buy arms, presumably to keep the opposition at bay.[40]

Another example is in Sudan. Sudan's 1,600 km-long oil pipeline has been operating since 1999, guarded by 4,000 Chinese troops in a country torn apart by civil war – mainly between the oil-rich South and the governing North – a conflict which has caused 4 million deaths since it began in 1956.[41] In 1999, a link was observed between oil revenues received by the government and increases in military expenditure;

[36] Rosser, in a literature survey he ran, says that the literature contains numerous studies that suggest that natural resource abundance and conflict are related. However, while there is strong evidence to support the notion of a resource curse, it is by no means conclusive. A study run by Collier and Hoeffler found that natural resources increased the risk of civil wars. Reynal-Querol conducted a similar study, focused on examining the association between natural resources and the onset of ethnic and non-ethnic civil wars. Using data from a sample of 138 countries between 1960 and 1995, she found that natural resource abundance was an important variable in explaining the incidence of non-ethnic civil wars and other forms of political violence. See Rosser, A., 2006, p. 9; Dine, J., 2005, p. 183.

[37] International Alert, 2006, p. 3.

[38] Forcese, C., 2001, p. 72.   [39] Le Billon, P., 2005, p. 20.

[40] The World Bank had the Chadian government adopt Revenue Management Law to ensure the channelling of oil revenues into efforts at poverty alleviation, with an emphasis on the local population in the oil-producing region. While there were a number of questions raised about the effectiveness of the revenue management provisions and safeguards, generally, the public scrutiny and various monitoring mechanisms may have helped to reduce potential human rights violations. The abolition of the Revenue Management Law and associated mechanisms in 2005 caused embarrassment to the World Bank, forcing a major rift between the Chadian government and the Bank. Brodnig, G., 2006, p. 9.

[41] Goodland, R. J. A., 2005, p. 10.

there was no evidence that significant economic or other benefits (increased expenditure on social services) from oil development were accruing to indigenous communities in the Western Upper Nile.[42] Commenting on the involvement of a consortium headed by Talisman Oil Companies Gagnon *et al.* assert:

> [n]umerous credible reports have found that oil development in Upper Nile has exacerbated civil conflict and assisted the war aims of the Government of Sudan, facilitating violations of human rights by government forces, government-backed forces and rebel groups. The human rights situation in the oil region steadily deteriorated during Talisman's presence. Forced displacement of indigenous populations and attacks on civilian settlements by government and pro-government forces increased. The company benefited from human rights violations committed by the government as systematic displacement carried out by government and pro-government forces enhanced security for its oil operations. Talisman Energy was unable to influence the government to allocate oil revenues for social development. Government and pro-government forces continued to use oil facilities and infrastructure for military and human rights abusing purposes.[43]

Chad and Sudan are not isolated instances. Shell in Nigeria, British Petroleum in Colombia and Unocal, Total and Premier Oil in Burma (Myanmar) are other cases where the implication is that investors are involved in a conflict through the formation of business relationships with the governments of host states.[44] Academics and non-governmental organisations (NGOs) argue that MNEs commit human rights violations through complicity when they provide assistance to the state in circumstances when the MNE knew or ought to have known that its acts or omissions would encourage the perpetrator.[45] John Ruggie, the Special Representative of the United Nations Secretary-General on the issue of human rights and transnational corporations and other business

---

[42] Several government of Sudan officials also acknowledge that oil revenues contribute to arms manufacturing capability. Gagnon *et al.*, 2003, p. 43; Zarsky, L., 2005, p. 92.

[43] Gagnon *et al.*, 2003, p. 3.

[44] International Law Commission, 2001, p. 11.

[45] According to International Alert even if the company has not committed an illegal act directly and even if it did not intend for such an act to be committed if it can be established that the company has aided, abetted, assisted, facilitated, contributed to, encouraged, or provided support to such acts, then the company's officials run the risk of prosecution under international criminal law, and the company may be accused of being complicit in human rights abuses if such abuses follow. See International Alert, 2006, p. 11; Gagnon *et al.*, 2003, pp. 7–8.

enterprises, in his report in April 2008 refers to complicity as indirect involvement by companies in human rights abuses causing actual harm, committed by another party including governments and non-state actors.[46]

The mere presence of a business opportunity may induce a regime to increase its repressive activities and engage in the abuse of human rights. A regime may use repressive means to supply resources to a company by, for example, clearing people off oil-rich lands.[47] Fig reports that

> [d]iamonds [were] discovered in the Central Kalahari Game Reserve in Botswana, and the San people for whom the reserve was created, were ordered to leave by the government. This measure was seen as providing great assistance to the mining company Debswana, a co-ownership of De Beers Corporation (South Africa) and the government of Botswana. The community engaged in a campaign to have their rights restored, and gained huge international support. In litigation, the courts of Botswana pronounced that they could return to their land. Some have, but they still face water cut-offs, destruction of their housing, closure of key services and infrastructure. This makes their return so much more difficult. The community's human rights continue to be ignored by the state. There are a number of cases in Africa where resource extraction occurs at the expense of communities, who are forced off their ancestral lands and expected to survive under adverse conditions.[48]

Repressive regimes often impose projects on local people without providing substantial benefits to them. In the process, frequently environmental degradation occurs destroying the health, livelihoods and even the lives of the people.[49] Among the human rights violations in conflict zones where the extraction of natural resources is active are abduction, detention, exploitation, indiscriminate attacks and intentional targeting of people that violate the right to liberty and security of the person.[50] Conscription of children into the armed forces and militia violates the rights of the child.[51] Bombing, burning of shelters, pillage and the destruction of objects necessary for survival violates the right to housing and an adequate standard of living.[52] Rape and other sexual brutality

---

[46] Ruggie, J. G., 2008, para. 73.   [47] Forcese, C., 2001, p. 78.   [48] Fig, P., 2007, para. 2.
[49] The litigation against Unocal, Chevron, Shell, Freeport, Texaco and Rio Tinto in the US under ATCA are examples of resource extraction on lands inhabited by ethnic minorities. See Herz, R., 2001, p. 265.
[50] ICCPR, Article 9.
[51] Convention on the Rights of the Child, Articles 38–39.
[52] ICESCR, Article 11.

violates the rights of women, rights enshrined in the ICCPR, as well as the Convention on the Elimination of All Forms of Discrimination against Women (CEDAW). Attacks targeting members of ethnic, racial or religious groups violate the rights enshrined in the International Convention on the Elimination of All Forms of Racial Discrimination (ICERD). Dispersal of families, forced abandonment of the means of a livelihood, denial of access to humanitarian and/or medical assistance, denial of access to food, water, clothing and education, violate all the rights protected in the ICESCR.[53]

Building infrastructure

The roles of the public and the private sectors in the development of infrastructure have evolved considerably throughout history. While in the nineteenth century privately financed infrastructure projects were commonplace, the international trend during most of the twentieth century has been towards the public provision of infrastructure.[54] Many developed and most developing countries' governments regarded the services that infrastructure projects provide – water and sewer systems, telecommunications services, and electricity – as public goods and, therefore, public monies funded such services.[55]

The current reverse trend began in the 1980s with the expansion of international and local markets and the opening of borders to foreign investment. Private companies seeking funds for infrastructure projects through international capital markets sought contracts for build-and-operate projects to recoup costs and to garner a profit.[56] As developing countries have struggled to modernize and industrialize, their demand for infrastructure development has grown at a staggering rate.[57] Nowadays, most countries' privately financed infrastructure projects through PF are an important tool in meeting national needs.[58]

Growing infrastructure demand and supply in developing countries has caused intense discussion about its impact on human rights.[59] Dams are an example of these big projects. Built to generate electricity, control floods and

---

[53] Gagnon *et al.*, 2003, pp. 148–63.
[54] United Nations Commission on International Trade Law, 2001, p. 1.
[55] Banani, D., 2003, p. 2; McCutcheon, E. D., 1998, p. 8.
[56] Likosky, M., 2003, p. 66.   [57] Banani, D., 2003, p. 2.
[58] United Nations Commission on International Trade Law, 2001, p. 6.
[59] Likosky, M., 2003, p. 65.

provide water for drinking and irrigation,[60] while they bring substantial benefits, the social costs of their construction have also been considerable. Some large-scale dams have displaced people, disrupted the lives of the communities into which the displaced people have moved, and deprived riverine communities, particularly those downstream of the dams, of their livelihoods.[61] In some cases, the reservoirs or rivers transformed by dams have deprived whole societies of their access to natural resources and their cultural heritage. Experts have estimated that the construction of large dams has displaced between 40 and 80 million people worldwide.[62] The *Report of the World Commission on Dams* found that indigenous peoples suffer a great deal of human rights abuses during the construction of dams. For example, displacement of the people from their native land, environmental change and social disruption threatened peoples' right to a decent living, culture, health and livelihood. It also widened gender gaps since women bore an unequal share of the social cost and they were often discriminated against in the sharing of benefits.[63] Host states and investors have been the target of strong criticism. In some cases, activists and NGOs have even targeted, leading banks to call on them to withdraw from financing such projects. The Narmada dams in India, the Ilisu dam in Turkey and the Three Gorges dam in China were all subject to such demands.[64]

Dam construction is a small proportion of FDI in infrastructure projects. Other examples include building pipelines, ports, toll roads, factories, airports and similar infrastructural projects. Different projects come with various threats to human rights. During the operation of a privatized oil transportation company in Bolivia, an oil spill in the Desaguadero River caused numerous human rights violations, including the right to water, the right to health, and other rights pertaining to indigenous peoples.[65] With

---

[60] Bradlow holds that between 160 and 320 new dams become operational each year. See Bradlow, D. D., 2001, p. 15.

[61] See Report of the World Commission on Dams, 2000, p. 16.

[62] Bradlow says that commonly the definition of 'affected persons' governments have used in determining who to compensate excludes downstream communities and landless and indigenous people. The result is that often only those with legal title to land receive compensation. Consequently, many adversely affected people receive inadequate compensation for their loss. See Bradlow, D. D., 2001, p. 15.

[63] Report of the World Commission on Dams, 2000, p. 17.

[64] International Alert, 2006, p. 7. Public outcry ensued as the result of a well-orchestrated non-governmental campaign, which led the World Bank to withdraw support for a series of state-sponsored dam projects along the Narmada River in India. See Likosky, M., 2003, p. 65.

[65] The company was owned 50/50 by Shell and Enron. See Sanchez-Moreno, M. and Higgins, T., 2004, p. 36.

the spill, the communities in the vicinity could not collect their water from the contaminated river (they had long suffered neglect in the provision of water services as they were not connected and could not afford to purchase water from other sources). The Bolivian government failed to ensure that the company maintained its pipes in good condition, had an emergency spillage and an emergency mitigation plan. This entailed a breach by Bolivia of its human rights obligation to protect the right to water, health and a healthy environment.[66]

Poor public consultation and participation during the design phase of projects has been a major issue in infrastructure building.[67] In some cases, NGOs alert the rest of the world to peoples' opinions about the activities of investors. In other cases, due to lack of ability or capability, vulnerable peoples' opinions do not attract the attention of the outside world.[68] A result of this is that communities around the project zone feel isolated and ignored and this can give rise to social unrest. The lives of people around infrastructure projects can alter substantially. Often the assumption is that people will automatically benefit from new infrastructure projects without acknowledging that it may also have a significant negative impact on them. For example, a transport project will usually mean improved access to the marketplace and encourage changes to agricultural production, such as promoting mass crop production. This in turn may cause the land around the project to gain in value, prompting landowners to evict the squatters from their land so they can sell it to industrial farmers.

Water and sewage

Today a mere 5 per cent of the world's population receive their water from private companies, leaving the door open for tremendous growth in the worldwide water industry.[69] There is a large and growing industry of private-service providers who compete for the opportunity to finance, build, and operate water facilities worldwide.[70] An organized commercial water business has evolved, considered as 'the infrastructure sector

---

[66] Sanchez-Moreno, M. and Higgins, T., 2004, p. 36.
[67] For further issues relating to consultation on design see Chapter 5, text accompanying n. 45.
[68] Baxi has proposed a call for an international moratorium on the construction of large dams until there is an installation of participatory policy-making processes. Baxi, U., 2001, p. 10.
[69] Tisdale, M., 2004, pp. 1–6.   [70] Seidenstat et al., 2002, p. 3.

with the greatest promise'.[71] The two largest water corporations in the
world are French Suez operating in seventy countries and German RWE,
where together they capture nearly 40 per cent of the existing private-
water market share.[72] According to observers, private-sector participation in water services seems to be an irreversible trend in developing
countries. In some countries, such as Ecuador and Chile, moreover,
some water-concession awards are for seventy-year periods or are even
indefinite.[73] PF in the water and sewage sector totalled US$797 million in
the first half of 2009.[74] After the economic crisis in 2009, it was the only
sector that grew both in the deal size and the number of transactions
after being the smallest sector by volume in the second half of 2008.[75]

Although there is much debate around the need for private-sector
participation in the water sector, so far, scant attention has been paid to
how it is 'governed'[76] in order that peoples' right to water is respected.
General Comment 15 of the UN Committee on Economic, Social and
Cultural Rights holds that people are entitled to sufficient, safe, acceptable, physically accessible and affordable water for personal and domestic uses.[77] The Committee recognized there and in General Comment 6
that the right to water is essential to the realization of Article 11 of the
ICESCR, the right to an adequate standard of living, as well as Article 12,
the right to enjoyment of the highest attainable standard of health.[78]
Measured against these benchmarks, the privatization programmes in
Asia, Africa and Latin America are documented failures for not providing the poor with water of acceptable quality for reasonable prices.[79]

Investors can influence the regulatory framework for water and this
can lead to the neglect of certain objectives related to human rights. For
example, in Argentina Aguas Argentinas, the private water-service provider that took over water distribution services after privatization did not
serve the slum communities because the latter did not have a title to the
land on which they lived.[80] This restriction goes against the principle laid

[71] Haarmeyer in Seidenstat et al., 2002, pp. 8–9.
[72] Information obtained from the following websites: Suez, Human Rights and the
Business Resource Centre, and Public Citizen.
[73] United Nations Conference on Trade and Development, October 2003, p. 10.
[74] Infrastructure Journal, Global Infrastructure Finance Review, 2009, p. 18.
[75] Infrastructure Journal, Global Infrastructure Finance Review, 2009, p. 18.
[76] Haarmeyer in Seidenstat et al., 2002, p. 207.
[77] UN Committee on Economic, Social and Cultural Rights, 2003, para 2.
[78] Bachand, R. and Rousseau, S., 2003, p. 32.
[79] United Nations Conference on Trade and Development, October 2003, p. 10.
[80] Gutierrez et al., 2003, p. 7.

down by the Committee on Economic, Social and Cultural Rights, which does not tie the right to any particular title to land but rather to the persons in need. Framing private-investor involvement in a way that explicitly recognizes the importance of reaching the poor is therefore essential. The most common way of doing this is to define universal access to the service as one of the major performance goals. In the absence of this specification, there is a risk that the poor may be excluded from privately provided services, especially if the revenue yield is higher for serving wealthy and middle-class consumers.[81] There are a variety of ways to meet universal-service objectives, one way being to incorporate in the contract obligations for the investor to provide the water-supply service to an increasing proportion of residents, regardless of the title or the right to live in their residences, with increasing targets set for access each year.[82]

Physical and economic accessibility should accompany one another, in the absence of which the increase in the price of services causes violation of the right to water. For example, Zmag reported in 2001 in South Africa that a massive cholera outbreak had spread from rural areas in Kwa-Zulu Natal Province to the outskirts of Johannesburg. It made hundreds of thousands sick and killed at least 300 people who had to turn to polluted and cholera-infected water systems after they could no longer afford the water prices (increased by 300 per cent) of the new privately owned water companies.[83] However, recently in South Africa, in a decision involving the right to water for the poor of Phiri Township, the High Court held that the forced installation of a pre-payment water-meter system without the option of an 'all available' water supply option was unconstitutional and unlawful.[84] The Court ordered the City of Johannesburg to provide each applicant and other similarly situated residents of Phiri, with a free basic water supply of 50 litres per person, per day.

---

[81] Panggabean, A., 2005, p. 12.   [82] Panggabean, A., 2005, p. 12.

[83] In 2003, village, town and city councils throughout South Africa were trying to cancel their contracts with water multinationals. The urban councils were contractually obliged to pay the debts to the water companies, which the poor and unemployed could not afford. Nevertheless, the government continued to restrict access to water. Nowicki, A., 2003.

[84] Section 27(1) of the South African Constitution guarantees everyone the right to access to 'sufficient water'. Section 39(1) (b) of the Constitution requires courts to consider international law when applying the South African Bill of Rights and states a preference for interpreting legislation consistently with international law. Case No: 06/138665 – see *Residents of Phiri*, in the bibliography at the end of this chapter.

Health care

Health services have emerged as a dynamic investment area with a ninefold increase between 1990 and 2001.[85] Similar to the water industry, the FDI stock in the health services industry is still relatively small, leaving huge potential for the future growth of the health industry. For example between 1974 and 1989, total private health-care expenditures in Chile rose substantially, while public health-care expenditures declined, and although public health expenditures since the return to a democratic regime in 1990 have been increasing, growth in private health-care expenditure in Chile still outstrips that of public health care.[86]

International finance institutions have taken a free-market approach to financing health care, saying that even strong economies can no longer afford to pay for public services, and that weak economies in the third world must strip themselves of their large bureaucracies if they are to remain eligible for loans.[87] There is some concern that privatization in some transitional economies is leaving serious gaps in the health-care system.[88] There are claims that rural health in China has suffered from the privatization of health care, leaving it without a social safety net.[89] Until recently, in Turkish private hospital emergency rooms, it was common practice to hold a patient hostage until their relatives could pay for the treatment received.[90] This is despite a communiqué sent by the Turkish Ministry of Health in 2003 preventing this practice.[91]

Article 12 of the ICESCR recognizes the rights of everyone to enjoy the highest attainable standard of physical and mental health. General Comment 14, of the Committee on Economic, Social and Cultural Rights, the authoritative interpretation of Article 12, says that in order

[85] United Nations Conference on Trade and Development, October 2003, p. 6.
[86] Labonte et al., 2004.   [87] Turshen, M., 1999, p. 1.
[88] United Nations Division for Public Economics and Public Administration, 1999, p. 4.
[89] United Nations Division for Public Economics and Public Administration, 1999, p. 4.
[90] Information gathered from reputable Turkish newspapers including Milliyet, 6 September 2007, Hurriyet, 30 July 2006, Haber7, 24 October 2005, among others.
[91] Communiqué regarding release of patients from hospitals, 30 March 2004, No. 5089, from the Minister of Health, Recep Akdag. Following media and public outrage over the situation, reports suggest that now, instead of holding people hostage, private hospital emergency rooms in Turkey turn away patients unless they are able to prove that they can pay for the treatment. Evrensel, 14 May 2008, Zaman, 18 December 2008, Sabah, 10 April 2006, among others.

to protect the right to health, states are required to do a variety of things: assure medical services in the event of sickness;[92] adopt legislation to ensure equal access to health care and health-related services provided by third parties;[93] and ensure privatization of the health sector does not constitute a threat to the availability, accessibility, acceptability and quality of health facilities.[94]

Economic accessibility – in other words affordability – of health facilities, goods and services, especially for the vulnerable in society, is one of the most important issues. Privatization of health-care systems without appropriate guarantees of universal access to affordable health care reduces availability and can lead to the violation of the right to health.[95] Costs associated with health services discourage people from seeking medical help. For example, in the World Bank report compiled by Deepa Narayan, *Can Anyone Hear Us?*, Moldavian families said they were afraid to go to the doctor due to anticipated expense.[96] The introduction of fees or cost-recovery policies, when applied to basic health services for the poor can easily result in significantly reduced access to services, which are so essential for the enjoyment of the right to health recognized in the ICESCR.[97] By causing exclusion of certain people from access to health care because of their inability to pay, states are not only violating their obligation to protect the right to health but this also constitutes discrimination on the grounds of property, which the Covenant also prohibits.[98]

Proponents of privatization claim that charging for health care can have substantial positive impacts on the efficiency of health-care financing.[99] However, the World Health Organization (WHO) holds that there is insufficient evidence that competition and private initiative leads to

---

[92] United Nations Committee on Economic Social and Cultural Rights, General Comment No. 14, the Right to the Highest Attainable Standard of Health, 2000, para. 12.
[93] General Comment No. 14, para. 1.
[94] General Comment No. 14, paras. 1, 8 and 12.
[95] Fourth World Conference on Women, 1995, para. 93.
[96] Narayan, 1999, p. 218.
[97] United Nations Committee on Economic Social and Cultural Rights, Globalisation and Economic, Social and Cultural Rights, 1998, para. 3.
[98] Among the extremely poor in Zambia, six out of ten people, despite being sick, did not go for a consultation at a health facility. In a recent survey in Lusaka, almost half of those who considered themselves ill did not seek health care because of lack of money. Afronet and Raid and Citizens for a Better Environment, 2000, p. 55. Article 2.2 of the ICESCR specifically precludes discrimination on grounds of property.
[99] Turshen, M., 1999, p. 42.

better-quality health services.[100] In the private provision of such services, quality of care is often a delicate balance of competing objectives between efficiency and resource generation. It is conceivable, therefore, that cost containment strategies and/or profitability objectives could compromise efforts to improve service quality.[101] The US Physicians for a National Health Program say that competition in health care creates wastefulness and increased prices. For example, when hospitals compete they often duplicate expensive equipment in order to corner more of the market for lucrative procedure-oriented care. This drives up overall medical costs to pay for the equipment and encourages over-treatment. Furthermore, competition among insurers results in avoiding the sick, cherry-picking and denial of payment for expensive procedures.[102] Borgenhammar supports this by saying patient risk might be calculated in a different way, to the detriment of the patient, if there is a profit incentive.[103]

Additionally, the involvement of private providers in health services may divert attention from preventing illness at the community level and focus on individual health and payment for treatment.[104] Prevention may be low priority, as the effect of such neglect may only be obvious after some years.[105] The public sector is the critical element in community health; the private sector is no more efficient and does not provide higher quality in the critical areas of preventive and curative services for the rural poor.[106] The private sector will not adequately provide some services, unless regulated by the state. These include vaccination services and the treatment of contagious diseases.[107] A health-care system concerned with communities tries to cope with outbreaks of new infectious diseases. However, in Africa, cutbacks in state spending on health services, coupled with the shift to private provision, have caused a shrinking number of national laboratories able to investigate new and emerging infectious diseases and outbreaks.[108]

Tursen points out that the private health-care system may also absorb scarce health personnel trained mainly at the expense of the state.[109] For

[100] Cited in Turshen, M., 1999, p. 42.
[101] Muschell, J., 1999, p. 114.
[102] Physicians for a National Health Care Program, 2009.
[103] Borgenhammar, E., 1999, p. 111.   [104] Turshen, M., 1999, p. 3.
[105] Borgenhammar, E., 1999, p. 111.   [106] Turshen, M., 1999, p. 58.
[107] United Nations Division for Public Economics and Public Administration, 1999, p. 4.
[108] Turshen, M., 1999, p. 7.   [109] Turshen, M., 1999, p. 57.

example, in Turkey, 30 per cent of doctors work for private hospitals where only 14 per cent of the national health-care service provision is by private hospitals, and, furthermore, private hospitals spend 30 per cent of the budget designated for health care by the state.[110] Similarly, in Brazil, private health care provides 120,000 physicians and 370,000 hospital beds to the richest 25 per cent of the population, while the public system has just 70,000 physicians and 565,000 hospital beds for the remaining 75 per cent.[111] With the efficiency and benefits derived from competition, FDI can help individuals to receive better treatment once they get ill. However, the right to health means more than just treatment. It should have a strong focus on community health via disease prevention, as well as individual health via cure.

Initiatives for control: the EP and the IFC's project standards

The purpose of this exercise has been to emphasize the importance to investors of studying human rights impacts of projects in advance. In the sectors mentioned, PF is an important mode of finance. The Equator Principles (EP), formulated by the major commercial banks providing project finance are a good example of specific and uniform standards which can help integrate evaluation of human rights impact of projects into PF.[112] Under the EP, financial institutions working in the project finance sector undertake not to provide loans or advisory services unless investors can demonstrate that the project will be constructed and operated in accordance with specific social and environmental standards.[113] The World Bank's International Finance Corporation (IFC) parallels this with their own standards that have to be met by borrowers.

This general framework of the ten broad EP requires banks to do a baseline review of proposed projects that have capital costs of US$10 million or more, and to categorize them A, B or C, depending on their perceived social and environmental impacts. Category A[114] indicates

---

[110] Demirduzen, H., 2008.   [111] Labonte *et al.*, 2004.

[112] Equator Principles, www.equator-principles.com.

[113] Conceived with the help of the IFC in 2002, the first set of EP launched in 2003. A subsequent updating process took place in 2006, leading to a newly revised set of EP released in July 2006. See Watchman *et al.*, 2007, p. 6.

[114] Based on available data from banks that subscribed to the EP, about one in six projects in 2005 were categorized as 'A'. See Aizawa, M., 2007, p. 10.

high risk, B indicates medium risk, and C indicates low risk.[115] For all
Category-A projects – and, if considered appropriate, Category-B projects – the EP require the preparation of an Environmental and Social
Management Plan which addresses mitigation, action plans, monitoring
and management of risks. The World Bank Group expect the project to
comply with its standards as well as relevant national standards. For
example, during the construction of a thermal power plant, the World
Bank Group's Thermal Power Guidelines for New Plants[116] (or the
Thermal Power Rehabilitation of Existing Plants as the case may be)
and the World Bank Group Environmental, Health and Safety
Guidelines[117] are applied, as well as the national laws. Companies are
required to develop an action and management plan for all impacts
identified. This includes a monitoring component to consult with communities and disclose outcomes (although there is no requirement to
establish that broad community support was obtained for the project);[118]
establish grievance mechanisms to ensure community engagement
throughout the project and resolve concerns about environmental and
social impacts; and obtain an independent review by an environmental
and social impact expert for all Category-A and some qualifying
Category-B projects.[119] The introduction of grievance procedures and
the requirement for an independent expert appraisal and community
consultation are steps towards effectively monitoring compliance with
the EP.[120]

The strength of the EP/IFC guidelines over other initiatives, such as
OECD Guidelines or the Draft UN Norms, is that the EP is very precise

---

[115] www.equator-principles.com/index.html. These criteria include the type, location,
sensitivity and scale of the project and the nature and magnitude of its potential
environmental and social impact. The line between Category-A and Category-B projects is blurred but the impacts of the latter tend to be reversible or capable of mitigation
in general. The assessment is to be done individually by the banks (with assistance from
their environmental consultant if necessary) in accordance with internal guidelines and
based on the IFC environmental and social screening criteria.

[116] For the full text, see the IFC website: www.ifc.org/ifcext/enviro.nsf/AttachmentsByTitle/
gui_thermnew_WB/$FILE/thermnew_PPAH.pdf.

[117] For the full text, see the IFC website: www.ifc.org/ifcext/enviro.nsf/Content/
EnvironmentalGuidelines.

[118] The objectives of the consultation are to ensure communities that could experience
disruption from projects have the opportunity to express their views beforehand on the
risks, impacts and mitigation measures, and that the sponsor may consider the comments and respond to them. See Watchman et al., 2007, p. 7.

[119] Major, E., 2006, pp. 10–11.   [120] Watchman et al., 2007, p. 9.

about what it is that banks need to do. This precision is what gives the EP initiative unique strength over others. For example, the Draft UN Norms say in Article 14 with regard to Environmental Protection:

> The transnational corporations and other business enterprises shall carry out their activities in accordance with national laws, regulations, administrative practices, and policies relating to the preservation of the environment of the countries in which they operate as well as in accordance with relevant international agreements, principles, objectives, responsibilities, and standards with regard to the environment as well as human rights, public health and safety, bioethics, and the precautionary principle; and shall generally conduct their activities in a manner contributing to the wider goal of sustainable development.[121]

As opposed to a general obligation of this sort, the EP refers to the World Bank/IFC guidelines and explicitly specifies, for example, how much pollutant a thermal power plant may release.[122] The specificity of this obligation makes it easy for the investors to measure, and banks to monitor.

Many foreign investors working in developing countries are familiar with the environmental standards of the World Bank Group. However, the EP takes in more than these standards by requiring consideration of social issues and stating that projects to which the EP applies develop in a socially responsible manner.[123] With the EP, the World Bank Group's standards in project implementation extend to projects where the World Bank is not involved. Furthermore, the introduction of a 'uniform' approach to the environmental and social impacts of investment projects has meant that financial institutions can measure the environmental and social compliance of investors.[124] It has been claimed that the EP exercise a growing influence on emerging-market projects since they require

---

[121] United Nations Sub-Commission on the Promotion and Protection of Human Rights, 2003.

[122] See *IFC Guidelines on Thermal Power: Guidelines for New Plants* in the *Pollution Prevention and Abatement Handbook* at www.ifc.org/ifcext/enviro.nsf/AttachmentsByTitle/gui_thermnew_WB/$FILE/thermnew_PPAH.pdf.

[123] A more pragmatic driving force behind the EP is an attempt to level the playing field for all private financial institutions involved in PF. This is as a result of private financial institutions working together with international financial institutions (such as the IFC), who are required to apply social and environmental standards, thereby increasing operating costs for the project and reducing the revenue available to the private banks. If all major lenders involved in project financing apply similar standards, all lenders should face the same costs.

[124] Watchman *et al.*, 2007, p. 7.

investors to pay greater attention to the environmental and social impacts of their projects. In June 2003, ten banks had adopted the EP. As at February 2009, that number had risen to sixty-five financial institutions.[125] Research reveals that 88 per cent of the US$31 billion debt underwritten in emerging markets was pledged to deals compliant with the EP.[126]

However, in order for the EP to become an effective instrument in the protection of human rights, they need to refer to human rights explicitly instead of referring to social impact assessment (SIA). SIA refers to socio-economic impacts, land acquisition and land use, involuntary settlement and impact on indigenous peoples and communities.[127] These do not cover all the human rights PF projects can violate. The use of human rights impact assessment (HRIA) is essential and an SIA cannot take its place. Once the HRIA becomes an integral part of the EP, and the content and the process of the assessment unified to the satisfaction of all parties concerned, the EP could be an effective tool to protect human rights in PF. An additional advantage of embedding HRIA in the EP is the guidance it offers to EP-users on how to classify projects. Furthermore, addressing environmental impact assessment (EIA), SIA and HRIA under one umbrella might prevent the overlaps that could occur, particularly between SIA and HRIA. These points will be developed further in the book.

Conclusion

PF projects are an important tool in meeting national infrastructure needs or extracting resources. At the same time, lenders of PF can find themselves caught up in accusations of complicity or other forms of involvement in abuses committed by those projects. The EP mark an

---

[125] Information obtained from www.equator-principles.com.
[126] Please note that the EP criteria are divided into high-income countries, non-OECD and non-high-income OECD countries, as defined by the World Bank's development indicators. The high-income category comprises high-income OECD countries and high-income non-OECD countries. The EP were conceived to deal almost exclusively with environmental and social issues in emerging markets and not in high-income economies. It is assumed that current environmental laws in high-income countries, such as those in Western Europe, North America and parts of the Asia Pacific and Middle East, already address the environmental and social impacts of a project. In fact, it is understood that the environmental and social standards are higher than those in emerging markets. Ellis, S. and Caceres, V., 2007, p. 2–6.
[127] Watchman, P., 2006, p. 15.

important step forward. Instead of using their own judgement to classify investment projects and setting their own standards, banks can now consult the EP for the accepted norm. This prevents certain lenders from doing the minimum just to keep up appearances or undermining others' efforts to gain the competitive edge. The EP standards take a step closer to meeting the Ruggie Report's demand that companies' specific responsibilities be made explicit instead of allowing a retreat into a language of general obligations where gaps appear through which responsibilities may slip.[128] The examples given above demonstrate how human rights are threatened if they are not taken into account in the first stages of design, construction and operation of projects. As some impacts occur at the beginning and others in the operation phase, different rules and regulations should govern both, which are incorporated during the design phase of projects. These, and other features of PF, will be considered in the chapters to come.

Bibliography

African Commission on Human and Peoples' Rights (2001–2002) *15th Annual Activity Report of the African Commission on Human and Peoples' Rights* (Nigeria: Social and Economic Rights Action Centre and the Centre for Economic and Social Rights), Annex V.

Afronet and Raid and Citizens for a Better Environment (2000) 'Zambia: Deregulation and the Denial of Human Rights'. Retrieved 8 February 2006 from www.rsc.ox.ac.uk/PDFs/rrzambia00.pdf.

Aizawa, M. (2007) 'The Equator Principles in Action: Creating a Community of Learning', *Infrastructure Journal*, 42.

Amnesty International (2003) 'Human Rights on the Line – The Baku–Tbilisi–Ceyhan Pipeline Project'.

Bachand, R. and Rousseau, S. (2003) 'International Investment and Human Rights: Political and Legal Issues', in Rights and Democracy, *Investment in Developing Countries: Meeting the Human Rights Challenge* (Ottawa, Canada).

Balane, W. I. (2006) 'Stay as Regulator, Stop Being Promoter of Mining'. MindaNews, Davao City. Retrieved 1 September 2008 from www.minesandcommunities.org/article.php?a=4194.

Banani, D. (2003) 'International Arbitration and Project Finance in Developing Countries: Blurring the Public/Private Distinction', *Boston College International and Comparative Law Review*, 26, 355.

---

[128] Ruggie, J. G., 2008, para. 6.

Bangladesh Water Development Board (2001) *Environment and Social Impact Assessment of Gorai River Restoration Project*, Dhaka, Ministry of Water Resources, Government of Bangladesh.

Baxi, U. (2001) 'What Happens Next Is up to You: Human Rights at Risk in Dams and Development', *American University International Law Review*, 16, 1507.

Becker, H. A. (1997) *Social Impact Assessment: Method and Experience in Europe, North America and the Developing World* (London and Bristol, PA: UCL Press).

Blanton, S. and Blanton, R. (2005), *What Attracts Foreign Investors?* Annual Meeting of the Mid-west Political Science Association, Chicago, IL.

Borgenhammar, E. (1999) 'Privatization of the Health Sector: An Overview', in United Nations Division for Public Economics and Public Administration, *Privatization of Public Sector Activities* (New York: United Nations).

Bradlow, D. D. (2001) 'The World Commission on Dams' Contribution to the Broader Debate on Development Decision-Making', *American University International Law Review*, 16, 1531.

Brodnig, G. (2006) 'This is the President of the World Bank Calling' in Amnesty International, *Human Rights, Trade and Investment Matters*.

Burdge, R. J. (2004) *Concepts, Process, and Methods of Social Impact Assessment* (Middleton, WI: Social Ecology Press).

Carley, M. and Bustelo, E. (1984), *Social Impact Assessment and Monitoring: A Guide to the Literature* (Boulder, CO: Westview Press).

Center on Housing Rights and Evictions (17 January 2007) 'Canadian Mining Company Forcibly Evicts Impoverished Mayan-Q'eqchi' Communities'. Retrieved 4 July 2008 from www.cohre.org/view_page.php?page_id=251.

Chapman, A. (2002) 'Core Obligations Related to the Right to Health', in Chapman, A. and Russell, S., *Core Obligations: Building a Framework for Economic, Social and Cultural Rights* (Antwerp and New York, Intersentia, Transnational Publications).

Committee on World Food Security (2004) 'Report of the Intergovernmental Working Group for the Elaboration of a Set of Voluntary Guidelines to Support the Progressive Realization of the Right to Adequate Food in the Context of National Food Security', General Affairs and Information Department, 127th Session – Report of the 30th Session.

Communiqué regarding release of patients from hospitals, 30 March 2004, No. 5089, from the Minister of Health, Turkey, Recep Akdag.

Daes, E. A. (2001) *Working Paper on Combating Racism Against Indigenous Peoples*, UN Doc. A/CONF.189/PC.3/4, Working Group on Indigenous Populations of the Sub-Commission on the Promotion and Protection of Human Rights.

De Feyter, K. (2005) *Human Rights: Social Justice in the Age of the Market* (New York: Zed Books).

Demirduzen, H., Istanbul Doctors' Association General Secretary (8 July 2008) 'Health Services in the World'. Reported by Akyol, K. BBC Turkish Radio. Retrieved 19 July 2008 from www.bbc.co.uk/turkish/indepth/story/2008/07/080707_nhs_files.shtml.

Dine, J. (2005) *Companies, International Trade and Human Rights*, (Cambridge and New York, Cambridge University Press).

Donnelly, J. (2003) *Universal Human Rights in Theory and Practice* (Ithaca, NY: Cornell University Press).

Ellis, S. and Caceres, V. (2007) 'Equator Principles Review H2 2006: The Reformed Standards Maintain their Momentum', *Infrastructure Journal*, 42.

Engström, V. (2002) 'Who Is Responsible for Corporate Human Rights Violations?' Institute for Human Rights. Retrieved 18 May 2006 from http://web.abo.fi/instut/imr/norfa/ville.pdf.

Escher, A. and Bradlow, D. (1999) *Legal Aspects of Foreign Direct Investment* (The Hague and London: Kluwer Law International).

FIAN International (2006) 'Voluntary Guidelines on the Right to Adequate Food: From Negotiation to Implementation'. Retrieved 5 September 2007 from www.fian.org.

Fig, D. (June 2007) 'Natural Resource Extraction and Human Rights-Based Abuses in Africa: Opinions, Problems, and Perspectives', *Southern Africa Resource Watch*, 4.

Forcese, C. (2001) "Human Rights Mean Business: Broadening the Canadian Approach to Business and Human Rights", in Isfahan, M. and Oosterveld, V., *Giving Meaning to Economic, Social, and Cultural Rights* (Philadelphia, PA: University of Pennsylvania Press).

Forest Peoples' Programme and Tebtebba Foundation (2006) 'Indigenous Peoples' Rights, Extractive Industries and Transnational and Other Business Enterprises'. Retrieved 14 June 2007 from www.business-humanrights.org/Documents/Forest-Peoples-Tebtebba-submission-to-SRSG-re-indigenous-rights-29-Dec-2006.pdf.

Fourth World Conference on Women (1995) 'Beijing Declaration and Platform for Action', A/CONF.177/20 (1995) and A/CONF.177/20/Add.1 (1995).

Gagnon, G., Macklin, A. and Simons, P. (2003) 'Deconstructing Engagement: Corporate Self-Regulation in Conflict Zones – Implications for Human Rights and Canadian Public Policy', in Social Sciences and Humanities Research Council and the Law Commission of Canada, *Relationships in Transition* (Toronto).

Goodland, R. J. A. (2005) *Oil and Gas Pipelines: Social and Environmental Impact Assessment* (Fargo, ND: International Association of Impact Assessment).

Gutierrez, E., Calagus, B., Green, J. and Roaf, V. (2003) 'Synthesis Report: New Rules, New Roles: Does PSP Benefit the Poor?' Retrieved 20 October 2004 from

www.wateraid.org.uk/in_depth/policy_and_research/private_sector_participation/
    default.asp?PrefType=UK.
Haarmeyer, D. and Coy, D. (2002) 'Overview of Private Sector Participation in the
    Global and US Water and Wastewater Sector', in Seidenstat, P.,
    Haarmeyer, D. and Hakim, S., *Reinventing Water and Wastewater
    Systems – Global Lessons for Improving Water Management* (New York,
    John Wiley & Sons, Inc.).
Herz, R. (2001) 'Holding Multinational Corporations Accountable', in
    Barnhizer, D., *Effective Strategies for Protecting Human Rights: Prevention
    and Intervention* (Aldershot, Hampshire and Burlington, VT: Ashgate).
IFC Performance Standard 1, Social and Environmental Assessment and
    Management Systems, issued on 6 April 2006.
Infrastructure Journal, Global Infrastructure Finance Review, 2009.
Inter-American Commission on Human Rights (1997) 'Report on the Situation of
    Human Rights in Ecuador', OEA/Ser.L/V/II.96.
International Alert (2006), *Conflict-Sensitive Project Finance: Better Lending
    Practice in Conflict-Prone States* (London).
International Business Leaders Forum and International Finance Corporation
    (2007) *Guide to Human Rights Impact Assessment and Management*.
International Committee of the Red Cross (2006) 'Business and International
    Humanitarian Law: An Introduction to the Rights and Obligations of
    Business Enterprises under International Humanitarian Law'. Retrieved
    23 April 2007 from www.icrc.org/Web/eng/siteeng0.nsf/html/p0882.
International Law Commission (2001) Report of the International Law
    Commission, 53rd Session (New York).
Labonte, R., Schrecker, T., Sanders, D. and Meeus, W. (2004) *Fatal Indifference:
    the G8, Africa and Global Health* (Lansdowne, South Africa: University of
    Cape Town Press; Ottawa, Canada: International Research Development
    Centre).
Le Billon, P. (2005) *Fuelling War: Natural Resources and Armed Conflict*,
    (Abingdon, Oxon and New York: Routledge).
Likosky, M. (2003) 'Mitigating Human Rights Risks under State-Financed and
    Privatized Infrastructure Projects', *Indiana Journal of Global Legal Studies*,
    10, 65.
Likosky, M. (2006) *Law, Infrastructure and Human Rights* (Cambridge and New
    York: Cambridge University Press).
Major, E. (2006) 'The Equator Principles, project finance and stabilization
    clauses', LL.M. coursework for the University of Essex.
Mander, H., Asif, M. and Sasi, K. P. (2004) *Good Governance: Resource Book*
    (Bangalore, Books for Change).
Marcks, E. (2001) 'Avoiding Liability for Human Rights Violations in Project
    Finance', *Energy Law Journal*, 22, 301.

McCutcheon, E. D. (1998) 'Think Globally, (En) Act Locally: Promoting Effective National Environmental Regulatory Infrastructures in Developing Nations', *Cornell International Law Journal*, 31, 395.

Muchlinski, P. (1995) *Multinational Enterprises and the Law* (Oxford, UK and Cambridge, MA: Blackwell).

Muschell, J. (ed.) (1999) 'A View from the World Health Organisation', in United Nations Division for Public Economies and Public Administration, *Privatization of Public Sector Activities* (New York: United Nations).

Narayan, D. (1999) *Can Anyone Hear Us? Voices from 47 Countries* (New York: World Bank, 1999).

Nowicki, A. (22 October 2003) 'What went wrong in the "New South Africa"?', *Znet*. Retrieved 13 August 2006 from www.zmag.org/znet/viewArticle/9667.

Ochoa, C. (2003) 'Advancing the Language of Human Rights in a Global Economic Order: An Analysis of a Discourse', *Boston College Third World Law Journal*, 23(1).

Organization of African Unity (entered into force 20 November 1999). 'African Charter on the Rights and Welfare of the Child'. OAU Doc. CAB/LEG/24.9/49 (1990).

Ott, D. H. (1987) *Public International Law in the Modern World* (London: Pitman).

Panggabean, A. (2005) *Using Market Mechanisms to Expand Access to Basic Services in Asia Pacific: Public–Private Partnerships for Poverty Reduction* (Manila: Asian Development Bank).

Penfold, B. (2004) *Labour and Employment Issues in Foreign Direct Investment: Public Support Conditionalities*, Working Paper No. 95 (Geneva: International Labour Organization).

Physicians for a National Health Care Program (2009) Retrieved 13 May 2009 from www.pnhp.org.

Residents of Phiri, Lindiwe Mazibko, Grace Munyai, Jennifer Makoatsane, Sophia Malekutu, and Vusimuzi Paki (the Applicants) v. *City of Johannesburg, Johannesburg Water, South African Minister of Water Affairs and Forestry, and Centre on Housing Rights and Evictions* (the Respondents), (case no. 06/138665), summarized in *International Judicial Monitor*, published by the American Society of International Law and the International Judicial Academy, September 2008 issue, High Court of South Africa.

Rosser, A. (2006) *The Political Economy of the Resource Curse: A Literature Survey*, Institute of Development Studies, Working Paper 268.

Ruggie, J. G. (July 2006) *Human Rights Impact Assessments: Discussion Paper*, Business and Human Rights website. Retrieved on 25 January 2007 from www.business-rights.org.

Ruggie, J. G. (2008) *Protect, Respect and Remedy: A Framework for Business and Human Rights*, Report of the Special Representative of the Secretary-

General on the issue of human rights and transnational corporations and other business enterprises, A/HRC/8/5, United Nations.

Salomon, M. (2005) 'Towards a Just Institutional Order: A Commentary on the First Session of the UN Task Force on the Right to Development', *Netherlands Quarterly of Human Rights*, 23(3), 409–38.

Sanchez-Moreno, M. and Higgins, T. (2004) 'No Recourse: Transnational Corporations and the Protection of Economic, Social, and Cultural Rights in Bolivia', *Fordham International Law Journal*, 27, 1663.

Seidenstat, P., Haarmeyer, D. and Hakim, S. (2002) *Reinventing Water and Wastewater Systems: Global Lessons for Improving Water Management* (New York: Wiley).

Smith, J., Bolyard, M. and Ippolito, A. (1999) 'Human Rights and the Global Economy: A Response to Meyer', *Human Rights Quarterly*, 21.

Sociological Association of Turkey (1994) *Survey on the Problems of Employment and Resettlement in areas which will be affected by Dammed Lakes in the Gap Region*, p. 30, South-eastern Anatolia Project Regional Development Administration, GAP, 1994.

Tisdale, M. (2004) 'The Price of Thirst: The Trend towards the Privatization of Water and its Effect on Private Water Rights', *Suffolk University Law Review*, 37, 535.

Turkish Environmental Impact Assessment Decree dated 16 December 2003, no. 25318.

Turshen, M. (1999) *Privatizing Health Services in Africa* (New Brunswick, NJ: Rutgers University Press).

UK's Official Export Credit Agency: Ilisu Hydroelectric Power Dam in Turkey, Government-commissioned reports examining the issues surrounding the Ilisu Hydroelectric Dam, 2000.

United Nations (1945) Charter of the United Nations, signed on 26 June 1945, in San Francisco, at the conclusion of the United Nations Conference on International Organization, came into force on 24 October 1945.

United Nations (1966) International Covenant on Civil and Political Rights. Adopted and opened for signature, ratification and accession by General Assembly Resolution 2200A (XXI) of 16 December 1966. Entry into force 23 March 1976, in accordance with Article 49.

United Nations (1966) International Covenant on Economic, Social and Cultural Rights. Adopted and opened for signature, ratification and accession by General Assembly Resolution 2200A (XXI) of 16 December 1966. Entry into force 3 January 1976, in accordance with Article 27.

United Nations (1981) Convention on the Elimination of All Forms of Discrimination against Women, entered into force 3 September 1981 by a General Assembly Resolution 34/180, 34 UN.

United Nations (1990) 'International Convention on the Rights of the Child', entered into force 2 September 1990 by General Assembly Resolution 44/25, Annex, 44 UN.

United Nations (2007) Report of the Human Rights Council, 61st session. Agenda item 68, 7 September 2007, A/61/L.67.

United Nations Commission on International Trade Law (2001) 'UNCITRAL: Legislative Guide on Privately Financed Infrastructure Projects' (New York: United Nations).

United Nations Committee on Economic Social and Cultural Rights (1998) 'Statement on Globalization and Economic, Social and Cultural Rights'. Office of the United Nations High Commissioner for Human Rights, Geneva, Switzerland.

United Nations Committee on Economic, Social and Cultural Rights (2000) General Comment 14 'The Right to the Highest Attainable Standard of Health'. Reprinted in Compilation of General Comments and General Recommendations adopted by Human Rights Treaty Bodies, UN Doc. HRI/GEN/1/Rev.6 at 85 (2003). UN Doc. E/C.12/2000/4 (2000).

United Nations Committee on Economic Social and Cultural Rights (2003) General Comment 12 'Right to Adequate Food'. Reprinted in *Compilation of General Comments and General Recommendations adopted by Human Rights Treaty Bodies*, UN Doc. HRI/GEN/1/Rev.6 at 62 (2003). UN Doc. E/C.12/1999/5 (1999).

United Nations Committee on Economic Social and Cultural Rights (2003) General Comment 15 'The Right to Water'. Reprinted in *Compilation of General Comments and General Recommendations adopted by Human Rights Treaty Bodies*, UN Doc. HRI/GEN/1/Rev.6 at 105 (2003). UN Doc. E/C.12/2002/11 (2002).

United Nations Committee on the Elimination of Racial Discrimination (1997) 'General Recommendation on indigenous peoples'. 1235th meeting of 18 August 1997. UN Doc. CERD/C/51/Misc.13/Rev.4.

United Nations Committee on the Elimination of Racial Discrimination (2003) Concluding Observations: Ecuador. UN Doc. CERD/C/62/CO/2.

United Nations Conference on Trade and Development (2003) 'Foreign Direct Investment and Performance Requirements: New Evidence from Selected Countries'.

United Nations Conference on Trade and Development (2007) 'Expert Meeting on FDI in Natural Resources'.

United Nations Conference on Trade and Development (2007) *World Investment Report*.

United Nations Division for Public Economics and Public Administration (1999) 'Privatization of Public Sector Activities: With a Special Focus on

Telecommunications, Energy, Health and Community Services'. New York, United Nations.

United Nations High Commissioner for Human Rights (2006) 'Frequently Asked Questions on a Human Rights-based Approach to Development Cooperation'. UN Doc. HR/PUB/06/8. New York and Geneva.

United Nations Sub-Commission on the Promotion and Protection of Human Rights (2003) 'Draft Norms on the Responsibilities of Transnational Corporations and Other Business Enterprises with Regard to Human Rights'. UN Doc. E/CN.4/Sub.2/2003/12.

Vanclay, F. and Burdge, R. (1995) 'Social Impact Assessment', in Vanclay, F. and Bronstein, D., *Environmental and Social Impact Assessment* (Chichester and New York: Wiley).

Watchman, P. (2006) 'The Equator Principles: Raising the Bar on Social Impact Assessments?', in Amnesty International, *Human Rights, Trade and Investment Matters.*

Watchman, P., Johnston, B. and Baines, T. (2007) 'Equator Principles: Consultation, Assessment and Accountability', *Infrastructure Journal*, 42.

Weiler, T. (2004) 'Balancing Human Rights and Investor Protection: A New Approach for a Different Legal Order', *Boston College International and Comparative Law Review*, 27, 429.

Woicke, P. (2005) 'Putting Human Rights Principles into Development Practice through Finance: The Experience of the International Finance Corporation', in Alston, P. and Robinson, M., *Human Rights and Development: Towards Mutual Reinforcement* (Oxford University Press).

World Commission on Dams (2000) *Dams and Development: A New Framework for Decision-Making.*

Zarsky, L. (ed.) (2005) *International Investment for Sustainable Development: Balancing Rights and Rewards* (London and Sterling, VA: Earthscan).

4

Applying international environmental principles to project-financed transnational investment agreements

DAVID ONG

Introduction

How does environmental law provide a regulatory framework for the operation of project finance? In answering this question, this chapter will first introduce the basic precepts of the international law for environmental protection, before highlighting certain difficulties arising from efforts so far, and then outlining how some of these difficulties are being surmounted. In particular, this chapter will suggest that the discipline of project finance is not only subject to international environmental law, but is a contributor to carving out special characteristics of that body of norms. The international law for environmental protection is now evolving into its own sub-discipline that both draws from traditional international law for environmental protection, as well as establishing its own set of applicable environmental principles and other specific aspects such as international compliance mechanisms.

Unlike international human rights law or world trade law, international environmental law does not have an all-encompassing global treaty regime that provides general rules for global environmental protection. Both the above sub-disciplines of public international law are governed by rules articulated within globally applicable multilateral treaties. For example, the 1966 International Covenant on Civil and Political Rights (ICCPR) in respect of the international protection of human rights, and the 1994 World Trade Organization (WTO) Agreement and 1947/1994 General Agreement on Tariffs and Trade (GATT) in respect of world trade law. However, there is no equivalent, globally applicable, multilateral instrument codifying the general international legal principles for environmental protection, save perhaps for the 1992 Rio Declaration on Environment and Development,[1] which is strictly speaking, a non-binding international instrument. Thus, the general environmental principles articulated within the Rio Declaration, which states reaffirmed their commitment to in the 2002 World Summit on Sustainable Development (WSSD, 2002),[2] nevertheless have to be independently shown as binding upon states under customary international law. Such a requirement almost inevitably leaves the international environmental lawyer attempting to rely on these principles as authoritative under international law on the back foot, in the sense that they are then charged with the burden of proof to show that the specific environmental principle they are relying upon is both globally applicable and legally binding on the opposing state in the instant case before the international tribunal concerned.

This exercise in determining the actual *substantive* 'rules', as opposed to 'principles' of international environmental law is almost always a difficult task to perform in the absence of a globally accepted treaty providing for their universal application; or consistent state practice, based on a common understanding of these 'principles', as being both applicable and binding 'rules' on the individual state(s) concerned. This is due to the paramount difficulty of discerning a cumulative and collective state of mind on the part of states for the fulfilment of the psychological aspect of customary international law, normally expressed as *opinio juris sive necessitatis*. This in turn highlights the *systemic* problem inherent in public international law, namely that it is ultimately reliant upon a bilaterally oriented judicial dispute settlement system for the resolution of differences between its principal actors – the states, whereas international environmental law has as its principal aim nothing less than the protection of the global environment in its entirety.

Thus, a further argument put forward in this chapter is that transnational non-state actors now play a significant role that in turn obliges them to be independently observant of, and accountable to, international law. Indeed, they have already begun the process of accepting and

---

[1] Declaration of the UN Conference on Environment and Development (UNCED), UN Doc.A/COF.151/26/Rev.1. Adopted on 5 June 1992.

[2] See para. 8 of the Johannesburg Declaration on Sustainable Development, adopted as an Annex to Resolution 1 (Political Declaration) at the 17th plenary meeting of the WSSD on 4 September 2002. For access to all documentation arising from this summit, also known as Rio+10, or the Johannesburg Summit, see *Report of the World Summit on Sustainable Development*, Johannesburg, South Africa, 26 August–4 September 2002. Doc.A/CONF.199/20 (re-issued) at: www.wssd.org.

internalizing the applicable international norms within their respective fields. While the nature of these internalization efforts has so far been self-regulatory in character, it is important to note that this consensual approach in fact replicates the process by which states themselves enter into international legal obligations, whether in treaty or customary form. Other similarities between transnational, and international, law-making will also be highlighted to confirm this social internalization process whereby international norms are increasingly being accepted and applied by transnational actors both between and within themselves. The time has therefore come to recognize these transnationally oriented normative efforts for what they truly represent: law-making endeavours that are often coupled with sanctioning mechanisms to both forestall and respond to non-compliant behaviour on the part of the transnational organization/club/network/community member.

International law for global environmental protection?

The international law for environmental protection has developed through the adoption of a multitude of multilateral treaty regimes addressing specific environmental threats. In the main, these treaties can be categorized in the following manner: first, there are globally applicable treaties but issue-specific treaties. Examples of such treaties include the 1987 Montreal Protocol to the 1985 Vienna Convention on Substances that Deplete the Ozone Layer, and the 1973 Convention on International Trade in Endangered Species (CITES). Second, there are treaties that are expressly confined to a clearly defined regional space, most usually in the form of a semi-enclosed sea, for example, but encompass within their overall regulatory framework several pollution sources into that well-defined region. Examples of these types of treaties include a whole slew of regionally focused marine environmental protection conventions. Several of these are managed by the United Nations Environment Programme (UNEP) Regional Seas Programme, such as the Barcelona Convention for the Mediterranean Sea (1976), the Cartagena Convention for the Wider Caribbean Region (1983), and the Nairobi Convention for Eastern African Region (1985), respectively, to name but a few of these regional seas conventions. Many others also form part of the global network of regional seas programmes even if they are not actually managed by the UNEP itself, such as the Bucharest Convention for the Black Sea (1992), the Lima Convention for the Protection of the Marine Environment and Coastal Areas of the

South-East Pacific (1981), as well as the regionally oriented (but not exclusively so) Economic Commission for Europe (ECE) treaties such as the 1979 Geneva Convention on Long Range Transboundary Air Pollution, and its related Protocols.

When coupled with the continuing evolution of general environmental principles, it is possible to envisage a relatively seamless international legal sub-system, consisting of overarching general principles to guide state behaviour, together with individual treaty rules establishing specific legal obligations and standards, all of these acting to constrain the environmentally damaging effects of state activities. The combination of these globally applicable environmental treaties that cover certain specific environmental issues and regional treaties which in turn cover several different but related environmental threats gives much succour to international environmental lawyers. Indeed, it is possible to suggest that a gradual knitting process is under way here, with the global and regional regulatory threads becoming entwined over time to form a warming blanket of universal regulation (whether global and/or regional in form) covering all manner of general and specific environmental threats. Against this apparently serendipitous outcome, however, it is certainly possible to ask whether this veritable Topsy of multilateral environmental agreements (MEAs) is either necessary, or effective.

Moreover, from the vantage point of general, public international law, certain *systemic* problems persist. These are at least twofold in nature. First, gaps remain in both the coverage and participation of global and regional environmental treaties. As to the latter issue, it is noticeable that certain regions in the world are much better regulated than others. In particular, the western and northern European regions, incorporating Scandinavia and also including their marine regions, namely, the northeastern Atlantic ocean, *inter alia*, encompassing the Bering, North and Baltic Seas, as well as the Mediterranean Sea, are the subject of a range of regional environmental treaties. Examples are as follows in chronological order: the 1976 Barcelona Convention on the Mediterranean Sea, 1979 Geneva Convention on Long Range Transboundary Air Pollution, the 1991 Espoo Convention, 1992 Paris Convention, the 1994 Baltic Convention, the 1998 Aarhus Convention. This is notwithstanding all of the environmental protection regulations and directives promulgated by the relevant European Union (EU) institutions, to be implemented and enforced within each of the (currently) twenty-seven Member States of the EU. Given the geopolitical, economic and other circumstances of other, relatively underdeveloped regions, there is little prospect in the short- to medium-term time-frame for this regulatory gap to be bridged, at least in terms of the range of environmental threats covered by individual regional instruments. In respect of the former issue, as noted above, the third-party (*pacta tertis*) rule of international treaty law prevents the imputation of arguably any treaty obligation on a non-party state, no matter how well supported the treaty is, short of its universal acceptance by all states. Neither can this *systemic* difficulty be easily bridged by reference to soft-law instruments, as this function of soft law as a supplement to hard-law instruments is by definition limited in its application to the parties to the hard-law, treaty instrument in the first place. Second, even the present international regulatory framework of global and regional treaties covering a whole range of environmental threats – general and specific – cannot be easily expanded to cover newly perceived environmental threats. Indeed, the growth in environmental treaty specialization sometimes occurs in the full knowledge of existing environmental treaty regimes related to, and even overlapping, the subject matter of the new instruments. This legal reality serves yet again to highlight the disparity inherent in international environmental law between the multitude of global and regional environmental treaties and the relative paucity in the development of accepted general customary rules to address new environmental threats.

Thus, the steady accretion of international environmental treaties that include provisions purporting to apply these environmental principles does not necessarily lead us to the assumption that these principles can or will be invoked, and perhaps more importantly, applied within international dispute settlement proceedings as rules of customary or general international law. This much can be discerned from the jurisprudence of the International Tribunal for the Law of the Sea (ITLOS) and associated arbitral tribunals, as in the 2001 *MOX Plant (Ireland* v. *United Kingdom)* case, for example. In this case, ITLOS refused to grant the provisional measures requested by Ireland in this case relying on the application of the precautionary principle, even though it was expressly provided for in at least one of the treaties invoked by Ireland, namely, the 1992 Paris Convention on the Protection of the Marine Environment of the North East Atlantic (OSPAR). Notions of applying 'best treaty practice', in this context, where several different treaty instruments are arguably equally applicable to the matters at hand, appear to have fallen on stony ground, at least at the provisional measures stage of such proceedings. Neither have arguments based on Article 31.3(c) of the 1969 Vienna Convention on the Law of Treaties (VCLT) regarding the application of other 'relevant international rules' to the interpretation of a treaty,[3] proved successful at ensuring the cross-fertilization and thus possible application of principles and rules from one treaty to another.[4] At least not within the WTO context and not in respect of the precautionary principle, for example: the WTO Panel in the recent *EC-Biotech Products* case held that this provision was limited in its application strictly to treaty instruments that *all* WTO Members to the dispute were party to.[5] This meant that neither the 1992 Biodiversity Convention, nor its 1999 Cartagena Protocol on Biosafety, could be regarded as falling within the scope of Article 31.3(c) and thus deemed to be applicable to the United States in this context.

Thus, there is a continuing sense of uncertainty among international legal academics, practitioners, governments and even judicial bodies, both international and domestic, as to the legal status and application of the main principles of 'international environmental law', defined here as the specific sub-discipline of public international law devoted to global environmental protection. This consideration of the underlying uncertainties afflicting international environmental law begins by observing that this field of public international law has developed on two main fronts. On the one hand, through the articulation of a set of general principles aimed at guiding states towards ensuring environmental protection; and on the other hand, through the adoption of specific treaty regimes addressing particular environmental problems, often through the establishment of detailed and technical international regulatory regimes aimed at controlling specific environmental threats. Both these trends are now well established and can be argued to support each other within the development of an overall international legal framework providing for both specific treaty rules to address particular environmental problems and general environmental principles that serve as authoritative interpretive guidelines to fill the gaps and resolve any uncertainties that remain both between and within these specific environmental treaty regimes. These environmental principles are also meant to govern state behaviour in their daily interaction with other

[3] Article 31.3(c) of the 1969 VCLT provides that: 'There shall be taken into account, together with the context: ... (c) any relevant rules of international law applicable in the relations between the parties.'
[4] As mooted by Philippe Sands, 'Treaty, Custom and the Cross-fertilization of International Law', *Yale Human Rights and Development Law Journal*, 1 (1998), 58–106.
[5] Full title: *EC-Biotech Products* (US, Canada, Argentina, v. EC), WT/DS291R, WT/DS292R, WT/DS293R, 29 September 2006.

states in the international arena, where these interactions can result in adverse environmental change.

Sustainable development and other applicable international environmental principles

The overall goal or objective of this general and specific interaction between environmental principles and specific environmental treaty rules and standards within the legal sub-discipline of international environmental law is the achievement of 'sustainable development'.[6] What, then, are the applicable international environmental principles accepted by states to achieve the sustainable development goal? Among the most significant and well accepted (by states, if not necessarily well implemented) of these environmental principles are as follows: (a) the environmental integration principle, entailing the inclusion of environmental considerations within socio-economic development activities; (b) the preventive and precautionary principles, providing that such activities do not cause environmental harm or damage; (c) the polluter-pays principle, requiring that polluters should pay for the environmentally damaging causes of their activities; (d) the environmental impact assessment (EIA) principle, providing that the environmental impact of proposed socio-economic activities is fully accounted for; and (e) the principle of public participation on environmental issues in decision-making processes relating to such socio-economic development activities.

The integration principle

This principle provides for the integration of environmental considerations into socio-economic policies and is defined in Principle 4 of the 1992 Rio Inter-Governmental Declaration on Environment and Development, as follows: 'In order to achieve sustainable development, environmental protection shall constitute an integral part of the development process and cannot be considered in isolation from it.' There is

---

[6] 'Sustainable development' was first authoritatively defined as: 'development that satisfies the needs of present generations without compromising the ability of future generations to meet their own needs', by the World Commission on Environment and Development (WCED) led by Gro Harlem Brundtland, the former Norwegian Prime Minister. See WCED, *Our Common Future* (Oxford University Press, 1987), p. 43.

continuing uncertainty over the extent to which the integration principle applies beyond the realm of the state or government policy making, and especially whether it extends to cover non-governmental entities generally and companies, in particular.[7] For example, should the integration principle be included and applied to contractual arrangements between host states and investing companies for major infrastructure projects within so-called transnational investment agreements (TIAs) or host government agreements (HGAs) that are clearly part of the 'development process' for the countries involved in these state-investor agreements? An affirmative answer to this question would mean that at least in respect of TIAs/HGAs, *all* the parties to these networks of contractual-type arrangements included within these agreements undertake that considerations of the highest standards of environmental protection form at least an implied term in the implementation of these agreements. It can then be presumed that any activity pursued by the contracting parties, in particular the investing companies concerned is governed by these highest applicable environmental standards.

The preventive and precautionary principles

These two principles are increasingly taken together and constitute the single most important principle for environmental protection as they embody the imperative requirement of environmental law for *a priori* measures to prevent harm to the environment, rather than *ex post facto*, reactive responses providing for responsibility and liability to compensate for remedial measures to be taken for damaged environments. Principle 15 of the Rio Declaration provides that, '[I]n order to protect the environment, the precautionary approach shall be widely applied by States according to their capabilities. Where there are threats of serious and irreversible damage, lack of full scientific certainty shall not be used as a reason for postponing cost-effective measures to prevent environmental degradation.' In spite of the compromised language, ambiguous phrases and qualifying clauses contained within this statement of the principle, it nevertheless highlights the main thrust of current environmental law-making processes.

---

[7] David Ong, 'The Impact of Environmental Law on Corporate Governance: International and Comparative Approaches', *European Journal of International Law*, 12(4) (September 2001), 685–726.

The polluter-pays principle

There are different conceptions of this principle, ranging from a simple, but arguably simplistic, interpretation requiring actual polluters to be liable for the environmental consequences of their activities, to the more sophisticated interpretation that envisages this principle as the application of a well-known concept within economics of requiring the internalization of environmental costs incurred from polluting activities that are usually left to society as a whole to absorb. Principle 16 of the 1992 Rio Declaration favours the latter approach: 'National authorities should endeavour to promote the internalisation of environmental costs and the use of economic instruments, taking into account the approach that the polluter should, in principle, bear the cost of pollution.'

Increasingly, however, the emphasis of the polluter-pays principle in legal terms is focusing also on liability for what is known as 'pure' environmental damage, or ecological damage, i.e., damage to natural elements of the environment, especially wildlife species and their habitats. Principle 13 of the Rio Declaration, for example, provides that 'States shall develop national law regarding liability and compensation for victims of pollution and *other environmental damage*' (emphasis added). This trend is also in line with a wider conception of what the phrase 'environmental protection' should entail. Multilateral treaties providing for civil liability on behalf of so-called ultra-hazardous industrial activities such as oil tanker shipping and nuclear power generation now expressly include the possibility of including as a separate liability heading, claims for clean-up measures aimed at restoring damaged aspects of the natural environment, in addition to the traditional tort liability headings of personal injury, property damage and economic loss.[8] A good example of the recent emphasis on compensating for the rejuvenation of wildlife damage is the inclusion of such claims under a separate liability heading under the European Community's Environmental Liability Directive. It is now also a well-known concept in US federal environmental legislation, such as the 1980 Comprehensive Environmental Response, Compensation and Liability Act (CERCLA) and related case law.

---

[8] For a discussion of this trend, see David Ong, 'The Relationship between Environmental Damage and Pollution: Marine Oil Pollution Laws in Malaysia and Singapore', in Michael Bowman and Alan Boyle (eds.), *Environmental Damage in International and Comparative Law* (Oxford University Press, 2002), pp. 191–212.

The principle of environmental impact assessment (EIA)

This principle is now provided for in numerous multilateral, bilateral and domestic environmental instruments. In the 1992 Rio Declaration, Principle 17 provides that: 'Environmental impact assessment, as a national instrument, shall be undertaken for proposed activities that are likely to have a significant adverse impact on the environment'. The almost universal application of this principle within developed, transitional and even developing-country economies, is a typical example of the progressive changes wrought by environmental regulations and their impact on general trade and investment relationships. While it cannot be emphasized too strongly that an EIA exercise merely requires the assessment of environmental impacts and thus does not of itself oblige the entity whose activities are negatively impacting on the environment necessarily to mitigate such impacts, it is nevertheless the case that the publication of information relating to these impacts clearly fulfils the transparency requirement implicit in both the principles of access to environmental information and public participation in environmental decision-making discussed below.

The importance of greater transparency for ensuring better accountability is especially pertinent in situations where these infrastructure projects have negative impacts on wildlife habitats. While local communities can reasonably be expected to make use of public consultation mechanisms provided for them under the EIA process, such mechanisms will clearly not be useful to the wildlife itself, without a well-organized, grassroots support network among the local community to raise the issue of potential destruction of such wildlife habitat by the planned infrastructure projects. Building such local support for wildlife habitat preservation among impoverished communities who are being offered relatively large sums of local currency as compensation for the sale or use of their land is not an ideal situation for ensuring the prioritization of such wildlife habitat. A further development and link between the EIA principle discussed here and the integration principle discussed above is the concept of a strategic environmental assessment (SEA). SEA represents a progressive evolution in the standard EIA exercise and is now required on a regional basis by the Member States of the European Union, especially in the context of marine environmental protection within their offshore jurisdictions. While the EIA process now embodies a proactive approach, the SEA simply operates on a much larger scale than the individual projects that are subject to EIAs. Moreover, each SEA exercise is both comprehensive in its coverage of nearly all aspects of development projects with environmental implications, as well as subject to review by stakeholder groups, to ensure the final version of the SEA is as up to date and as accurate as possible.

The principles of access to environmental information, public participation in the environmental decision-making process, and access to environmental justice

Principle 10 of the Rio Declaration provides that: 'Environmental issues are best handled with the participation of all concerned citizens, at the relevant level.' It then goes on to highlight three aspects of such citizen participation, beginning with the need to have access to environmental information, especially in respect of hazardous activities; moving on to providing opportunities for public participation, and finally, allowing effective access to judicial proceedings to seek redress for any failings in respect of the first two aspects.

All these elements are present in a range of regional environmental treaties. For example, the 1991 Espoo Convention on Transboundary Environmental Impact Assessment, provides that each State Party must establish an EIA procedure that permits public participation in respect of the proposed activities listed under Appendix I that are likely to cause a significant adverse transboundary impact. Such public participation includes notification and consultation. Building on the successful entry into force of the Espoo Convention, the ECE adopted the 1998 Aarhus Convention on Access to Information, Public Participation in Decision-Making and Access to Justice in Environmental Matters is regarded as being the most advanced international treaty on public participation in environmental issues so far. Article 4 of this Convention provides for access to 'environmental information', with a broad definition of what this constitutes under Article 2(3). It then follows this up with a fairly comprehensive right to public participation in various environmental decision-making processes described under Articles 6, 7 and 8, and particularly in relation to certain activities specified in Annex I to the Convention, as well as activities that 'may have a significant effect on the environment'. Especially significant in this context is the fact that for the purposes of the definition of 'the public concerned' as the public affected or likely to be affected by such environmental decision-making pro-cesses, non-governmental organizations (NGOs) shall be also deemed to have an interest. However, both of these regional treaties are ECE

conventions and thus geographically limited in their application only to
certain European and North American states. Thus, their progressive
application of the principles of access to environmental information,
public participation and even judicial review of environmental decision-
making processes must be replicated within other regional or bilateral
agreements across the world before it can be argued that their present
formulations transcend their individual instruments to inform the development of, and moreover, contribute to the customary sources of international environmental law.

At a practical level, the implementation of these principles is therefore
of the utmost importance to ensure local communities not only have a
voice but are confident that their voice will be heard. However, it should
be noted that all three aspects of this right, namely, to environmental
information, public participation and access to justice, merely constitute
the provision of procedural, rather than substantive, rights. A substantive right to a healthy or clean environment is not as well established
under international law as the procedural rights enumerated above. Such
a right to a healthy environment would arguably establish a clear presumption against which any environmental interferences would have to
be justified in explicit terms.

On the other hand, the provision of access to information, public
participation rights and access to justice remedies does suffer from a
major defect when it attempts to ensure 'pure' environmental or ecological protection, especially in respect of wildlife and their habitats, in
that such provision must be further coupled with a *locus standi* provision
allowing suitably committed and competent environmental NGOs to
utilize these procedural rights and remedies on behalf of elements of the
natural environment that would otherwise not be represented in this
respect. Just as when we noted that liability for 'pure' environmental
damage must be claimed and utilized for the restoration of damaged
natural ecosystems on their behalf by appropriately committed, competent, knowledgeable and well-established environmental NGOs, so must
procedural rights to access information, participate and challenge any
threats to wildlife and their habitats be allowed to be taken up on their
behalf by these same NGOs before the national courts of the host states
concerned. However, it is still very much the case that the explicit legal
recognition of such a role for environmental NGOs has so far been
mainly confined to the legal systems of a handful of developed or
industrialized countries. Conversely, such provisions for allowing claims
for compensation of environmental damage and legal representation of

wildlife interests by NGOs within the formal procedures providing for the exercise of environmental rights are not always forthcoming within the legal systems of developing countries and/or transitional economies. Waelde for example has bemoaned the fact that the negotiations for the 1994 Energy Charter Treaty missed an opportunity to at least partly fill the international legal lacuna over transboundary harm caused by corporate activities by giving 'teeth' to environmental obligations in the form of citizen and NGO litigation rights against energy industry polluters or their governments and treating environmental misconduct as an international delict giving rise to civil and even criminal liability.[9]

These principles are now well accepted by states both in terms of their legal status as applicable environmental 'principles' and their commonly accepted meanings. However, their specific implementation, both between and within states, as required of customary international environmental 'rules' remains in doubt. The continuing legal difficulties raised by these principles for the progressive development of international environmental 'rules' (as opposed to 'principles') of law are twofold in nature: first, they are usually articulated in non-legally binding international instruments such as Declarations, Resolutions and Programmes of Action. Second, the question arises as to whether these environmental 'principles', currently articulated in 'general' terms within these international instruments, have developed into much more normatively significant 'rules' of customary international law, containing specific rights and duties for individual states in the environmental protection field.

Within this context, several eminent commentators have examined the still arguably 'soft' law status of these environmental principles with a view to determining their precise legal nature under international law. Boyle, for example, observes that '[t]hey may lack the supposedly harder edge of a "rule" or an "obligation", but they are certainly not legally irrelevant. As such they constitute a very important form of law, which may be "soft", but which should not be confused with "non-binding" law.'[10] In a more recent study on normative hierarchy in international law, focusing *inter alia* on soft law, Shelton too notes the inherent

[9] T. W. Waelde, 'Sustainable Development and the 1994 Energy Charter Treaty: Between Pseudo-Action and the Management of Environmental Investment Risk', in F. Weiss, E. Denters and P. de Waart (eds.), *International Economic Law with a Human Face* (The Hague: Kluwer Law International, 1998), pp. 223–70, at p. 235.
[10] Alan Boyle, 'Some Reflections on the Relationship of Treaties and Soft Law', *International and Comparative Law Quarterly*, 48(4) (October 1999), 901–13, at 907.

paradox of such allegedly non-legally binding instruments in that they nevertheless allow conforming states to put political pressure on dissenting states into conforming to the soft-law norms contained within these instruments. However, she cautions that 'generally ... States cannot demand that others conform to legal norms the latter have not accepted'.[11] Shelton therefore concludes that 'nonbinding norms and informal social norms can be effective and offer a flexible and efficient way to order responses to common problems. They are not law and they do not need to be in order to influence conduct in the desired manner.'[12] The flexibility of such environmental principles, due to the non-legally binding nature of their sources and their hortatory rather than imperative language, does however come at a price. This price is their uncertain legal status under international law: are they general 'principles' or specific customary 'rules' of international environmental law?

Several of these environmental principles have now also been invoked by states in the context of legal claims against other states adjudicated before international tribunals. As Boyle observes in this respect, '[t]hey may lay down parameters which affect the way courts decide cases or the way an international institution exercises its discretionary powers. They can set limits, or provide guidance, or determine how conflicts between other rules or principles will be resolved.'[13] The continuing difficulty identified here is to translate these environmental principles in such a way as to be able to provide a clear delineation of their implications upon traditional international law concepts such as state sovereignty. In this respect, judicial pronouncements from international tribunals seized of these issues arguably leave much to be desired in terms of confirming the global application of these principles as rules of customary international law above and beyond the environmental treaty regimes where these principles are reiterated as specific rules. Indeed, the analysis of a number of significant cases before different international tribunals, namely, the International Court of Justice (ICJ), the WTO Panels and Appellate Body and the International Tribunal for the Law of the Sea (ITLOS), suggests that there is a lack of confirming jurisprudence in favour of the application of significant environmental principles, such that there is arguably a lack of a certain 'animating spirit' within international

---

[11] Dinah Shelton, 'Normative Hierarchy in International Law', *American Journal of International Law*, 100(2) (April 2006), 291–323, at 319.

[12] Shelton, 'Normative Hierarchy', at 322.

[13] Boyle, 'Some Reflections', at 907, and also his references in fn. 1, at 901.

environmental law. This lack of an 'animating spirit' does not allow these undoubtedly well-accepted, but generally worded and in themselves non-binding, environmental principles to be applied in such a way that they can transcend their specific articulation within individual environmental treaties, and facilitate their transition to rules of customary international law providing for environmental protection. Such customary rules of international environmental law can then be employed or utilized by international tribunals to better decide so-called 'hard cases', entailing consideration of specific international legal limitations on state sovereignty and consequentially also over the autonomy and discretion usually afforded to states over potentially environmentally damaging activities within their territories, or subject to their jurisdiction or control.

Unfortunately, this is simply not the case at the present time. More worryingly, it is suggested here that the reason why international tribunals are apparently reluctant to confirm the place of such well-known environmental 'principles' as applicable 'rules' within the customary international law between states is due to the reality of a situation that there is arguably precious little evidence from domestic state practice alone that states abide by, and perhaps more importantly, actually implement these general environmental principles fully, both as between themselves, and within their domestic legal regimes. This is so even where these principles are now articulated more specifically in individual treaty regimes, addressing particular environmental problems identified for concerted action by these very same states. Constant and uniform, if not universal, implementation of these environmental principles is still found to be wanting. This suggests that states have actually accepted these principles merely as guidance for their domestic environmental policies, rather than implementation within their environmental laws.

Thus, the really critical questions regarding the legal status and application of these general environmental principles remain unanswered. Have they transcended their status as environmental 'principles' to become 'rules', such that they should now be directly applicable to states as part of customary international law? Perhaps more importantly, where these environmental principles have been invoked in disputes between states, have they been confirmed as the applicable customary international rules by the international tribunals tasked with adjudicating between such disputing states? Or, do they remain only general environmental principles, and thereby act as mere guidelines for state behaviour in the environmental policy-making field, without the obligatory character inherent to rules of customary international law? To paraphrase de Sadeleer, have these general environmental principles made the successful transition from 'political slogans to legal rules'? Moreover, if they have successfully become legal rules – what kind of international obligations do they entail? Do they convey the traditional, bilateral type of international obligation, owed only as between individual states? Or, as advocated by certain international environmental lawyers, do they form overarching multilateral rules entailing *erga omnes* obligations owed by each state to every other state, on the basis that *all* states have an interest in global environmental protection. The conception of this latter type of obligation is arguably still nascent in its development, even within general international law. As Fitzmaurice notes, 'many aspects of the legal character of *erga omnes* obligations are still arguable', and furthermore, it is 'unclear the extent to which States are responsible in relation to the environment towards the community of States generally'.[14] The precise legal implications of such *erga omnes* obligations have arguably yet to be spelled out by any international tribunal. Since the development of international environmental principles, apart from the 'golden' or primary rule against transboundary environmental damage, are almost by definition meant to be *erga omnes* in their application, it is interesting to note that the ICJ declined an opportunity to enunciate on this very issue in respect of the Australian application to intervene in the 1995 *Nuclear Tests* case, brought by New Zealand against France.[15] Moreover, the further question as to whether *erga omnes* obligations (even where they can be proved to apply to a particular situation) in turn give rise to the exercise of an *actio popularis* right by any state to enforce such obligations was also not addressed by the ICJ in the initial, 1974 *Nuclear Tests* cases.[16]

The dilemma that international environmental law now finds itself in as a result of the lack of authoritative judicial decisions and confirming

---

[14] Malgosia Fitzmaurice, 'International Responsibility and Liability', in Daniel Bodansky, Jutta Brunnée and Ellen Hey (eds.), *The Oxford Handbook of International Environmental Law* (Oxford University Press, 2007), pp. 1010–35, at p. 1011 and pp. 1020–2.

[15] See Request for an Examination of the Situation in Accordance with Paragraph 63 of the Court's Judgment of 20 December 1974 in the Nuclear Tests (*New Zealand* v. *France*) case, *ICJ Reports* (1995) 288. The Australian application to intervene was on the basis that the obligations allegedly owed by France to New Zealand were of an *erga omnes* character.

[16] *Nuclear Tests Cases* (*Australia* v. *France, New Zealand* v. *France*), *ICJ Reports* (1974) 253, at 387.

state practice as to the binding legal status of important environmental principles is at least in part due to these *substantive* and *systemic* problems inherent to the discipline of public international law itself, which raise particular problems for the field of international environmental law. Chief among these is the *substantive* legal issue that the generally applicable environmental principles are contained within non-binding international instruments and therefore can only act as a guide and not an imperative of inter-state behaviour, whereas the specific rules and obligations are contained within treaty regimes and therefore struggle to transcend the bounds of the individual treaties and their parties to inform and bind all states as a matter of general or customary international law, alongside the general principles and specific treaty rules. As Sands notes: '[t]he international community has not adopted a binding international instrument of global application which purports to set out the general rights and obligations of the international community on environmental matters.'[17]

A taxonomic representation of international and transnational, non-state actor agreements

Moving on from our examination of the legal status and content of the individual environmental principles that have evolved within what is now clearly a distinct field or sub-discipline of international law, namely, 'international environmental law', we should note the different types of international and transnational actors and agreements within this new field. In fact, however, the fields of international law and international relations have witnessed a general increase in the numbers and types of transnational actors and agreements, involving different permutations of both states and non-state actors purporting to refine, elaborate and/or apply well-known and well-accepted principles and rules of behaviour. This phenomenon is now well documented and in itself can arguably be seen as a concrete indication of the increasing influence of transnational non-state actors within international society. Two relationships in particular are of special interest in this regard: first, the relationship between these non-state actor agreements and the sources of international legal authority, which technically apply only between states. Second, the relationship between the transnational, non-state actors and states

---

[17] Philippe Sands, *Principles of International Environmental Law* (2nd edn, Cambridge University Press, 2003), p. 234.

themselves, within the traditional framework for international law-making. Before we examine these relationships in detail below, we should first attempt a taxonomic representation of the various categories of international (state–state) and transnational (state–non-state and non-state–non-state) agreements. This can best be seen as a spectrum stretching from classical state-to-state agreements at one end to exclusively private, non-state actor agreements, such as the Equator Principles (EP), which will be considered in more detail below.

Within this spectrum, there are also TIAs between states and non-state actors in the form of business entities such as multinational or transnational corporations (MNCs/TNCs). These arguably 'mixed', public–private, state–non-state actor agreements are regulated by a rapidly developing international legal framework governing the protection of foreign investment within individual host states by non-state actors such as MNCs/TNCs. This legal framework is now established through multilateral treaties such as the International Convention for the Settlement of Investment Disputes (ICSID), the Trade-Related Investment Measures (TRIMs) Agreement within the WTO, and other relevant treaties such as the Energy Charter Treaty, as well as accumulated state practice in the form of literally hundreds of bilateral investment treaties (BITs) agreed between states across the whole world. However, these treaties do not expressly regulate the substantive legal relationship between the state and non-state actors (usually MNCs/TNCs) concerned. Thus, the international rules governing foreign investment by such business entities within host states are to be found in the accumulated state–non-state actor TIAs or HGAs themselves and the outcomes of transnational litigation between their state–non-state parties in the event of disputes arising. Through such transnational litigation, this type of 'mixed', state–non-state TIA provides a means by which international law applies to disputes beyond the traditional relationship between states only, reaching into the legal relationship between states and non-state actors. Such litigation has thereby also elevated the legal status of the non-state actors (MNCs/TNCs) involved to the same (international) level as that of states.

The subset of transnational agreements that arguably contains the most innovative type of such agreements, namely, those involving *only* non-state actors. Of these, one mixed, quasi-public–private transnational actor is the International Standards Organization (ISO), which establishes international standards for a variety of industries. The second, arguably truly transnational, non-state actor agreement is the EP, which were adopted by transnationally active, private commercial banks. Of the two non-state actors highlighted here, the EP can be regarded as the prime example of a 'transnational', rather than 'international', agreement. The ISO and the Equator Principles are both transnational agreements providing for principles and standards adopted by mixed, quasi-public– private, or even entirely *private*, non-state actors, rather than the *public* institutions of states. Thus, the term transnational agreements can be utilized to denote the TIAs between states and MNC/TNCs, and the ISO (involving state and non-state actors), as well as those transnational agreements (adopted by non-state actors only), such as the EP.

Case study of a transnational, non-state actor agreement: the EP

Turning now to the EP as an example of a transnational agreement adopted by non-state actors, we shall try to draw out the international norm-internalization process that is arguably taking place here. Such an assessment must first consider both the provenance (private sector commercial lending banks) and the normative 'density' (in terms of their potentially binding legal authority) of these EP.

The EP have also been considered in Chapter 2. The aim here is to link these principles to the concerns of environmental protection. As has been seen in Chapter 2, these Principles were drafted by a group of commercial lending banks which, along with the World Bank Group's International Finance Corporation (IFC), were intent on establishing a banking industry framework for addressing environmental and social risks in the 'project finance' sector.[18] 'Project finance' (PF)-type projects, as indicated in Chapter 1 and as will be treated again in Chapter 5, entail a high exposure to risk on the part of the lending bank and are more likely to be located in higher-risk countries. Such commercial lending practices to firms that are often located in foreign jurisdictions have given the banks concerned a more significant stake in the borrowers' financial performance. This relationship in turn provides the banks with

---

[18] As indicated in Chapter 2, 'project finance' is generally described as a bank-lending method whereby the lender relies primarily on the revenues generated by a specific project run by a so-called special purpose entity (SPE) – a specific project company, as the source of repayment for the original loan, as well as the security for the exposure of the lending bank itself. It can thus be distinguished from *corporate finance*-type projects, whereby the lending bank's capital exposure is secured *both* on the corporate assets of the investing company (usually a foreign multinational or transnational company (MNC/TNC)) as well as the project company (or SPE)'s assets and revenues.

not only a financial, but perhaps more importantly, a corporate 'reputational', incentive to consider the environmental, social (and other) risks entailed by these projects. This is especially the case where these PF-type projects involve large-scale extractive and/or infrastructure-type development activities, such as oil and gas exploration, mining, dam-building and the laying down of highways/motorways, etc. Both the scale and impacts of these projects also brought the companies and banks involved to the attention of campaigning environmental and human rights NGOs. Hence, the perceived need for the adoption of the 'Equator Principles' in June 2003.[19] These Principles represent a common and coherent set of environmental and social policies and guidelines that are applicable globally and across all industry sectors. Each participating financial institution has adopted the Principles individually and declared that it will put into place internal policies, procedures and processes that are consistent with these Principles. Notwithstanding the explicitly 'soft' or non-binding nature of these Principles, they have arguably become the standard for assessing and managing environmental and social risk within project financings. Furthermore, a significant aspect of the process through which these Principles arose exposes the close links between these Principles and the environmental, social and health and safety guidelines and conditionalities utilized by the state-funded multilateral/global financing institutions such as the World Bank to assess their (public) funding and/or technical support for socio-economic development projects located mainly within developing countries. This is because many of these projects ultimately rely on a mixture of public and private sources for funding and credit provision, especially when they concern the building and operation of large infrastructure projects. In this respect, it is important to note that as of 30 April 2007, new versions of the World Bank Group's Environmental, Health and Safety Guidelines (also known as the EHS Guidelines) are now in use. The new EHS Guidelines were developed as part of a two and a half year review process. They are technical reference documents with general and industry-specific examples of Good International Industry Practice

---

[19] See the 'Equator Principles': an industry approach for financial institutions in determining, assessing and managing social and environmental risks in project financing. Accessible at: www.equator-principles.com. Hereinafter, the 'Equator Principles' will be called the 'Principles' and the commercial lending banks that have adopted them will be called the 'Equator Banks'. As of mid-2007, the 'Equator Principles' had received fifty-one Equator Bank signatories that accounted for nearly 90 per cent of emerging market project finance – about US$28 billion in 2006.

(GIIP). They contain the performance levels and measures that are normally acceptable to the IFC and are generally considered to be achievable in new facilities at reasonable costs by existing technology. Significantly, when host country regulations differ from the levels and measures presented in the EHS Guidelines, projects are expected to achieve whichever is *more* stringent.[20] Thus, the 'Equator Principles' represent the establishment of a common framework for the *private* PF industry based on external and respected benchmarks established by *public* sector international financial institutions, namely, the World Bank and IFC Guidelines. Thus, *international* norms are being refined and implemented by *transnational* entities because, rather than in spite, of the fact that these entities usually operate beyond the control of any single state.

It is also possible to discern that the substantive aspects of the principles and standards within these EHS Guidelines in themselves ultimately derive from a variety of international human rights, labour, as well as both general and specific environmental, instruments. The human rights and labour standards arise, for example, from the 1966 ICCPR and the International Covenant on Economic, Social and Cultural Rights (ICESCR) respectively, as well as many ILO Conventions, whereas the environmental instruments concerned range from the 1992 Rio Declaration to environmental treaties such as the 1998 Aarhus Convention. This last environmental treaty, along with Principles 10 and 17 of the Rio Declaration alluded to above, are clearly the original sources of international legal authority for Principle 5 of the EP requiring 'consultation and disclosure' of the social and environmental impacts of the proposed infrastructure and other socio-economic development projects applying for Equator Bank loans. Moreover, under Principle 6 and subject to certain qualifications, the borrower is enjoined to establish a grievance mechanism, the existence of which the borrower has to inform any communities affected by the project. Other principles such as the need for a social and environmental assessment (SEA) of the project and the integration of environmental considerations within the Action Plan and Social and Environmental Management System of the project are also included in Principles 2 and 4, respectively.

The EP were revised in July 2006, allowing us to assess their progressive development in the internalization of principles and standards of international environmental law within transnational actors like the

---

[20] These EHS Guidelines and related information are accessible at: www.ifc.org/.

Equator Banks. This assessment is timely, considering that the implementation by the Equator Banks of the initial version of these Principles
did not receive overwhelming approval from the environmental and
human rights protection NGOs shadowing these banks' activities in
this field. See, for example, a report on the performance of the 2003
version that came to the following conclusion: 'In sum, preliminary
analysis suggests that one year after the launch of the Equator
Principles, levels of implementation at endorsing banks varies greatly.'[21]
In the revision process that followed, leading to the second, 2006 version
of these Principles, twenty-five NGOs and other stakeholders were
explicitly consulted as to how the Principles could be improved,
although concerns remain as to the efficacy of their implementation.

One positive effect of such stakeholder consultation prior to the
adoption of the revised 2006 version of the EP is the creation of a
reasonably level 'playing field' for the majority of potentially competitive
private loan providers that have agreed to be guided by these Principles
in their lending practices. As noted above, this level 'playing field' is also
broadly in line with the environmental and social guidelines and standards adopted for public sector institutional funding of the same types of
projects. The scope for 'free rider'-type actions by rival Equator Banks
competing against each other to undercut the loan rates offered is
reduced by their collective acceptance of the EP, although not entirely
eliminated given the consensual nature of these Principles. On the other
hand, non-Equator banks are of course free to act in this way and this
represents an obvious lacuna in the present regime. In this connection,
Prakash and Potoski's 'green club' theory is a powerful conceptual tool to
explain the Equator Banks' 'membership' of these Principles, despite the
threat posed to their business by non-Equator banks. This theory posits
that the reputational and other benefits of club membership, coupled
with the threat of exclusion as an informal but effective sanction, can be
utilized to exert a strong pull towards membership of such clubs.[22]
Moreover, the participating banks concerned are acutely aware of their
exposure to NGOs, media and general public scrutiny over their lending

[21] See BankTrack, *Principles, Profit or Just PR? Triple P Investments under the Equator Principles: An Anniversary Assessment* (June 2004), at 38. A second anniversary report, entitled: *Unproven Principles*, was published in 2005. Both these reports are accessible at: www.banktrack.org.
[22] Aseem Prakash and Matthew Potoski, *The Voluntary Environmentalists: Green Clubs, ISO 14001, and Voluntary Environmental Regulations* (Cambridge University Press, 2006), pp. 17–27 and 34–80.

activities. Thus, despite their consensual, rather than compulsory, character, most if not all these banks are now able to show a significant level of internalization of these Principles within their lending criteria and practice. A newly incorporated Principle 10 also requires the banks to commit to publicly available reports, on at least an annual basis, about their EP implementation processes and experience. While this informational requirement will assist others (especially NGOs) to monitor the Equator Banks' implementation records in this regard, the voluntary nature of this requirement will not prevent 'shirking' of responsibilities from occurring.

The application of international environmental principles to the EP

In the revised, 2006 Statement of these Principles, the so-called Equator Principles Financial Institutions (EPFIs) undertake that they 'will only provide loans to projects that conform with the following ten Principles', each of which is now considered in turn.

Principle 1: Review and categorization

This provides that when a project is proposed for financing, the EPFI will, as part of its internal social and environmental review and due diligence, categorize such project based on the magnitude of the potential impacts and risks in accordance with the environmental and/or social screening criteria of the IFC. Exhibit I, which is annexed to the EP describes three categories, ranging in level of seriousness or concern from Category A – projects with potentially significant adverse social or environmental impacts that are diverse, irreversible or unprecedented; to Category B – projects with limited adverse social or environmental impacts that are few in number, generally site specific, largely irreversible and readily addressed through mitigation measures; and Category C – projects with minimal or no social or environmental impacts. Such categorizations certainly allow for the proper prioritization of efforts to ensure that the projects with the highest social and environmental impacts are subject to the greatest scrutiny by the banks concerned. In fact, as we will see below, only projects designated as either Category A or Category B will require an SEA by the borrowing company.

Principle 2: Social and environmental assessment (SEA)

This is a key requirement that the EP Banks are required to place upon the would-be borrowing companies. The borrower has to conduct an SEA process to the EPFI's satisfaction. An illustrative list of the potential social and environmental issues to be addressed in the SEA documentation is provided in Exhibit II, also annexed to the Equator Principles themselves. This list is fairly comprehensive in scope but there is no suggestion that it is exhaustive in any way. It can presumably therefore be seen as the minimum requirements for the participating EPFIs and they would be free either to add more issues to this list, or strengthen the language describing these social and environmental issues, thereby making these requirements more stringent for the borrowing company to fulfil in order to get the EPFI's approval. On the other hand, there is a risk here that the lending banks concerned will regard the Exhibit II list of social and environmental issues as the only issues that they need to check against in order to accept the borrowing company's SEA. In which case, simply being seen to address these social and environmental issues will be the maximum requirement for the borrowing company. Nevertheless, the SEA: 'should also propose mitigation and management measures relevant and appropriate to the nature and scale of the proposed project'.

Principle 3: Applicable social and environmental standards

Once the SEA has raised the social and environmental issues that need to be addressed, the next question that arises is the standard of protection that needs to be applied to these issues. Here, a distinction is made on the one hand between projects located in non-OECD and non-High Income OECD countries,[23] and on the other hand, projects within the High-Income OECD countries. In the former group of countries, the SEA will reference standards laid down in the applicable IFC Performance Standards (attached in Exhibit III to the present Principles) as well as the applicable Industry Specific Environmental, Health and Safety (EHS) Guidelines (attached to Exhibit IV). The SEA for projects within these countries 'will establish to a participating EPFI's satisfaction the project's overall compliance with, or justified deviation from, the respective (IFC) Performance Standards and EHS Guidelines. Again, the danger here will be that these standards are not taken as the minimum requirements but as the maximum level of performance expected of the borrowing

[23] As defined by the World Bank Development Indicators database. These categories will presumably include all developing and less-developed countries (LDCs).

company, which it would be unreasonable to expect them to exceed. In the two TIAs (BTC and Chad–Cameroon) noted above, certain clauses could conceivably allow such a company to bring a claim before an international arbitral tribunal alleging illegal regulatory taking amounting to expropriation, when subjected to new EHS standards that are higher than those that prevailed at the time of signing the Agreement. The regulatory, permitting and public comment process requirements for High-Income OECD countries are generally seen as meeting or exceeding the above IFC Performance Standards and EHS Guidelines. Thus, if the required SEA successfully complied with the national law requirements for such projects, this would be considered 'an acceptable substitute' for these Standards and Guidelines and any further requirements in Principles 4, 5 and 6, below. The EPFI however must still categorize and review the project in accordance with Principles 1 and 2 above.

This presumption that developed country legal systems are more likely to apply the appropriate social and environmental standards that in turn need to be addressed in the SEA for the EPFI concerned is at least arguably an example of the application of common but differentiated responsibilities principle between industrialized and developing countries. This principle purports to require states' historically different contributions to global environmental degradation to be taken into account when formulating their respective obligations in addressing this major issue. Thus, Principle 7 of the 1992 Rio Declaration provides, *inter alia*, that: 'In view of the different contributions to global environmental degradation, states have common but differentiated responsibilities.'

Principle 4: Action Plan and Management System

Again for the non-OECD countries and non-High Income OECD countries, the borrower has to prepare an Action Plan (AP) which addresses the relevant findings of the SEA exercise and draws on the conclusions of the assessment. The AP will describe and prioritize between the mitigation measures, corrective actions, and monitoring measures necessary to manage the impacts and risks identified in the SEA. The AP may therefore range from a brief description of routine mitigation measures to a series of documents (e.g., resettlement action plan, indigenous peoples plan, emergency preparedness and response plan, decommissioning plan, etc.). The level of detail and complexity of the AP and the priority of the identified measures and actions will be commensurate

with the project's potential impacts and risks.[24] While there is certainly a
need for flexibility of response in such matters, it is notable that the AP is
not necessarily subject to approval by the EPFI – it merely needs to be
prepared by the borrower, who presumably decides on the appropriate
level of detail that should be included within it.

Moreover, the borrowers will build on, maintain or establish a Social
and Environmental Management System addressing the management of
these impacts and risks, and the corrective actions required to comply
with the host country laws, IFC Performance Standards and EHS
Guidelines. This Social and Environmental Management System will
incorporate the following elements: (a) Social and Environmental
Management System; (b) a management programme; (c) organizational
capacity; (d) training; (e) community engagement; (f) monitoring; and
(g) reporting.[25] For projects in High-Income OECD countries, the EPFIs
may also require an AP but this need only be based on host country laws,
which are again deemed to be 'an acceptable substitute' for the IFC
standards.

Principle 5: Consultation and disclosure

For Category A and B projects located in non-OECD or non-High
Income OECD countries, the host government, borrowing company or
third party expert must consult with so-called project 'affected communities' in a structured and culturally appropriate manner.[26] Moreover, for
projects with significant adverse impacts on affected communities, the
process will ensure their free, prior and informed 'consultation' and
facilitate their informed participation as a means to establish, to the
satisfaction of the EPFI, whether a project has adequately incorporated
affected communities' concerns. 'Consultation' in this context should be
'free' (free of external manipulation, interference or coercion, and intim-
idation), 'prior' (timely disclosure of information) and 'informed' (relevant, understandable and accessible information), and apply to the
entire project process and not to the early stages of the project alone.
Additionally, the borrower will tailor its consultation process to the
language preferences of the affected communities, their decision-making

[24] See fn. 3 to Principle 4, 'Equator Principles', as n. 19 above.
[25] See fn. 3 to Principle 4, 'Equator Principles', as n. 19 above.
[26] 'Affected communities' in this context are defined as 'communities of local population
within the project's area of influence who are likely to be adversely affected by the
project. See fn. 4 to Principle 5, 'Equator Principles', as n. 19 above.

processes, and the needs of disadvantaged or vulnerable groups. Last but not least, consultation with indigenous peoples must conform to the specific and detailed requirements laid down in IFC Performance Standard 7. In order to accomplish these consultation and disclosure requirements, the borrower is placed under the further duties of ensuring that the SEA and AP documentation, or summaries thereof, are made available to the public for a reasonable minimum time period in the relevant local language and in a culturally appropriate manner. The borrower must also document the consultation process and its results. Finally, for projects with adverse social and environmental impacts, disclosure should occur early in the assessment process and in any event before the project construction commences, and on a continuing basis.

This is indeed a far-reaching set of requirements, which if implemented fully by the borrower, appears to more than implement the three elements of the principle of citizen participation provided in Principle 10 of the Rio Declaration, and discussed above, on the applicable environmental principles to states in such contexts. The question is how far the EPFI concerned can actually both require and ensure the full implementation of all three components of this principle, as well as the further aspects of language and indigenous peoples' needs, in respect of the borrower. This raises a more general issue, namely, apart from refusing to provide the PF loan in the first place, once the project is under way how can the EPFI/Equator Bank concerned exert any kind of pressure or sanction against the borrower for non-performance of any of these specific requirements?

Principle 6: Grievance mechanism

For all Category A projects and Category B projects 'as appropriate' that are located in non-OECD or non-High Income countries, the borrower is enjoined to establish a grievance mechanism, the existence of which the borrower has to inform the affected communities. However, the grievance mechanism to be established is subject to the following qualifiers: (a) this mechanism is scaled to the level of risk and adverse impacts of the project; and (b) it is part of the management system. The former qualifier is understandable, albeit affording the borrower much discretion to decide on the scope and method of the grievance mechanism employed. This is especially pertinent when it is considered that Category B projects will be subject to a grievance mechanism only 'as appropriate', presumably from the borrower's perspective? The second qualifier is subject to more serious concerns, as follows. First, it is clear that this mechanism does not have to amount to an independent and objective dispute settlement mechanism for addressing community grievances. Its explicit attachment to the project management system undermines any notion of such objectivity or independence in its procedures. Second, there is nothing in this requirement under Principle 6, or indeed in the consultation and disclosure requirements under Principle 5 above, that deals with the issue of standing for NGOs concerned with nature conservation and wildlife protection issues to participate in such grievance mechanisms, where these issues are not raised by the 'affected communities' concerned. Such NGOs will not necessarily be encompassed within the definition of 'affected communities', except perhaps if they have among their membership, individuals from these 'affected communities'. Moreover, Richardson observes that the Equator Banks themselves do not see the Principle 6 'Grievance Mechanism' as 'a formal dispute resolution system that can confer obligations or liabilities against them'.[27]

Principle 7: Independent review

For all Category A projects, and again Category B projects 'as appropriate', an independent social 'or' environmental expert 'not directly associated' with the borrower will review the SEA required under Principle 2, the AP required under Principle 4, and consultation process document required under Principle 5, to assess the borrower's compliance with the EP, and thereby assist with the fulfilment of the EPFI's due diligence requirements.

Responses to this requirement would focus on the fact that the 'independent' expert may not in fact be completely independent from the borrower, and may not necessarily be an expert in both social and environmental issues, as expertise in one of these two subject areas appears to be a sufficient qualification for this position. Apart from these specific issues, it is again important to make the general observation that while the participating Equator Banks or EPFIs adopted the EP, it is in fact the borrower that is expected to fulfil the requirements laid down by these Principles. A possible disjuncture therefore exists within this relationship between the participating parties, whereby those that

---

[27] Benjamin J. Richardson, 'Financing Sustainability: The New Transnational Governance of Socially Responsible Investment', 17 *Yearbook of International Environmental Law*, 2006 (2008), 73–110, at 92.

have accepted these Principles (the Equator Banks) may not actually have either the willpower or priority to exert pressure, or the capacity to place sanctions, against the parties (the borrowing companies) that are actually enjoined to apply the EP themselves.

Principle 8: Covenants

This preceding point has particular resonance in respect of the detailed covenants that the borrowers are required to enter into within their financing documentation for the project concerned. These covenants extend to the following areas:

(1) Compliance with all relevant host country social and environmental laws, regulations and permits in all material respects.
(2) Compliance with the AP during the construction and operation of project in all material respects.
(3) Provision of periodic reports in a format agreed with the EPFIs, although the frequency of these reports is proportionate to the severity of impacts, or as required by law, as long as these are at least on an annual basis. Moreover, these reports need to fulfil any formal documentation requirements of the AP and show compliance with the relevant social and environmental laws, regulations and permits.
(4) Decommissioning of the facilities, where applicable and appropriate, in accordance with an agreed decommissioning plan.

A number of observations can be made here. First, as Richardson notes, 'while the borrowers must adhere to environmental covenants included in the loan agreement, the [Equator Bank] lenders themselves are not contractually bound to comply with the EP or to enforce them against their borrowers'.[28] On the other hand, the significant question here relates to how the above covenants can be enforced on the borrower, in the event of a dispute arising over its compliance with them. Principle 8 provides that: '[w]here a borrower is not in compliance with its social and environmental covenants, EPFIs will *work with* the borrower to bring it back into compliance to the extent feasible, and if the borrower fails to re-establish compliance within an agreed grace period, EPFIs *reserve the right to exercise remedies*, as they consider appropriate' (emphasis added). Quite apart from the fact that the 'remedies' alluded to here are not specified, there is an altogether more significant

---

[28] Richardson, 'Financing Sustainability', at 92.

observation to make at this juncture. As noted previously, given the
'non-recourse' element of the type of financing utilized for PF projects, it is difficult to see what type of remedy the EPFIs can utilize
that does not simultaneously also increase their own exposure to the
risk that the project might fail. The consequences of such failure
would be the loss of the Equator Bank's loan to the borrowing special
purpose entity (SPE), without any recourse to the parent corporation
of the SPE concerned. This realization of the limited scope for
manoeuvre by the EPFIs/Equator Banks significantly reduces the
deterrent effect of the above statement.

Principle 9: Independent monitoring and reporting

To ensure continuous monitoring and reporting throughout the life of
the loan, the EPFIs will require the appointment of an independent
environmental and/or social expert for all Category A projects, and
also for Category B projects but only 'as appropriate', or require the
borrower to retain qualified and experienced external experts to verify its
monitoring information which should be shared with EPFIs. While the
thrust of this Principle is clear, the alternative and arguably much weaker
option given to the borrower to fulfil its requirements in the second part
of Principle 9 is clearly open to abuse.

Principle 10: EPFI reporting

Finally, each EPFI commits to publicly available reports, on at least an
annual basis, about its EP implementation processes and experience,
subject to confidentiality considerations. This last phrase arguably provides much scope for hindering transparency, in that it is not limited
only to matters of commercial confidentiality and therefore may be
relied upon by the Equator Banks to include all manner of sensitive
information.

   So, how successful have the EP been in securing the application of
the relevant social and environmental principles by Equator Banks
and their borrowing companies? This question can be approached
from both the institutional and empirical perspectives. At the former,
institutional level, a study by an international law firm conducted in
2005, prior to revision of the EP in 2006, reported that several
Equator Banks have entered into structured dialogues with stakeholders and NGOs about the social and environmental aspects of their
lending. This study concludes positively on the way the EP have
influenced financial markets generally and redefined bank lending

considerations.[29] At the latter, empirical level, however, other reports have still found instances of Equator Bank funding of unsustainable projects.[30] As Richardson concludes, the overall evidence so far is patchy, and points to the need for more comprehensive solutions for promoting socially and environmentally responsible financing generally, beyond the private finance sector.[31]

The internalization of international environmental principles within transnational non-state actors?

The fields of international law and international relations have witnessed increasing numbers and types of transnational actors and agreements, involving different permutations of both states and non-state actors purporting to refine, elaborate and/or apply well-known and well-accepted principles and rules of behaviour. This phenomenon is now well documented and in itself can arguably be seen as a concrete indication of the increasing influence of transnational non-state actors within international society. When considering the relationship between these transnational, non-state actors and the states themselves, it should first be noted that these transnational actors display a number of similar characteristics to states themselves. Through various globalizing trends and processes, they too now exhibit international, or at least transnational, characteristics in their relationships. Moreover, they too are increasingly autonomous in their relationships with other similar transnational entities. Within the context of transnational or multinational corporations for example, it is becoming increasingly difficult to categorize such business entities, so multifaceted and multilayered have their existence and activities within the international and domestic scenes become. Indeed, it has been proposed that such entities should now be seen as 'global', rather than 'multinational', actors on the world stage. Moreover, these 'globally integrated enterprises' are ready to partner governments in contributing 'new forms of commerce, learning and good governance' in fields as diverse as health care, education, securing

---

[29] Freshfields Bruckhaus Deringer, *Banking on Responsibility* (July 2005), cited in Richardson, 'Financing Sustainability', at 89–92.

[30] See J. Monahan, 'Principles in Question', *The Banker* (March 2005); and R. Bulleid, 'Putting Principles into Practice', *Environmental Finance* (June 2004), both cited in Richardson, 'Financing Sustainability', at 92.

[31] Richardson, 'Financing Sustainability', at 94.

shipping lanes and electronic commerce, as well as addressing the myriad social and environmental challenges posed by globalization.[32]

When this phenomenon of the rising numbers and involvement of transnational non-state actors in significant areas of international relations is viewed through the prism of reduced and withdrawing state involvement in important areas of governance and its replacement by these quasi-autonomous, or mixed public–private-type, or even wholly private, non-state actors, it becomes imperative that the level of accountability hitherto obtaining against states in the performance of their international legal obligations is not similarly withdrawn. This is notwithstanding the many difficulties encountered by states in ensuring compliance to applicable rules of international law, whether in treaty or customary form, as well as their enforcement in cases of a clear breach of these rules. International lawyers are engaged in continuous efforts to address these issues of non-compliance and enforcement.[33] There is arguably a need to ensure that if and when the state retreats, a regulatory and hence accountability vacuum does not result at the global governance level. Special-interest NGOs, especially in the environmental, human rights and labour standards fields, have campaigned against the perceived takeover, especially by private entities, of what had previously been conceived as state-controlled fields, or areas, of regulation. Significantly, the need to provide a normative framework has increasingly become recognized and accepted even by the transnational or multinational business entities that now conduct much of the international business transacted around the world. The policy and academic focus on this shift from public to 'private' or self-regulation has arguably been most pronounced in the field of international labour standards, particularly when such standards are perceived to be under threat from globalizing forces. However, it is also evident within many other fields including human rights and environmental protection. On the other hand, caution has been expressed about the assumption that self-regulation has simply come about due to the withdrawal of the state from its hitherto omniscient regulatory function. Nor can the alternative perspective of a perceived threat of new and more stringent regulation by the state and/or its associated bodies also adequately explain the

---

[32] Samuel J. Palmisano, 'The Globally Integrated Enterprise', *Foreign Affairs* 85(3) (May/June 2006) 127–36.
[33] See, for example, Geir Ulfstein (ed.), with Thilo Marauhn and Andreas Zimmermann, *Making Treaties Work* (Cambridge University Press, 2006).

self-regulatory impulse or drive. For business entities, as well as for states before them, the level of certainty that such an international or transnational normative framework provides, however prone individual norms may be to non-compliance, or even abuse, is infinitely preferable to the chaotic, 'free for all' situation that might otherwise ensue in an anarchic world society. Thus, it should not necessarily be assumed that in adopting transnational agreements between themselves providing normative frameworks and guidelines on a consensual and technically non-binding basis, the entities involved are merely responding to either the regulatory concerns of states, or the human rights and environmental issues raised by special interest groups.

Within this context, Haufler has enumerated at least three reasons why the private sector places limits on its own behaviour, even if these limits are not very constraining and perhaps more significantly are weakly enforced. These are: (a) risk reduction; (b) reputation enhancement; and (c) learning.[34] From the last of these reasons, namely, corporate 'learning', we can discern a shift in attitude and strategy from 'defensive reaction' to 'opportunity grasping'. Indeed, many private actors have departed from the reactive or responsive attitudes of their peers and clearly hope to achieve a number of implicit or even explicit goals in their private or self-regulatory efforts. In this respect, a further perspective contributed by Prakash and Potoski, describes the positive effects of 'clubbing together' by business corporations within particular fields.[35] According to them, 'club' theory provides at least 'two salient institutional dimensions – club standards, which specify the systems and programs firms need to put in place to join a club and retain its membership, and monitoring rules which specify monitoring and enforcement mechanisms established by program sponsors to ensure that members adhere to club rules'.[36] As they note: '[e]ffective green clubs induce participating firms to incur the private costs of undertaking progressive environmental action beyond what they would take unilaterally.'[37] Whether or not these explicit and/or implicit goals are ultimately achieved, it is suggested here that the behavioural patterns shown by

---

[34] Virginia Haufler, *A Public Role for the Private Sector* (Washington, DC: Carnegie Endowment for International Peace, 2001), pp. 20–51.

[35] Prakash and Potoski, *Voluntary Environmentalists*, pp. 46–7.

[36] Prakash and Potoski, *Voluntary Environmentalists*, p. 31.

[37] Prakash and Potoski, *Voluntary Environmentalists*, p. 31. In this context, 'green clubs' are defined as 'codified programs and practices that firms pledge to adopt and follow' (p. 17).

these non-state actor entities in adopting the normative frameworks described below and their implementation strategies for these norms display many of the characteristics of states themselves in their negotiation and implementation of international norms through international 'soft law' instruments. For example, the formal nature of these transnational agreements underscores their acceptance of the overarching normative framework applying equally to states, despite the fact that they are usually described as 'voluntary' or 'self-regulatory'.

Similarly, transnational law, like international law, envisages compliance with its self-regulatory efforts predominantly through internalization or socialization processes, rather than in response to the threat of sanctions per se. Indeed, legal writers have predicted that such 'transnational legal processes' would facilitate the 'norm-internalization' taking place within the state and non-state actors involved.[38] According to Koh, the study of 'transnational legal process' involves 'the theory and practice of how public and private actors – nation-States, international organizations, multinational enterprises, non-governmental organizations, and private individuals – interact in a variety of public and private, domestic and international fora to make, interpret, enforce and ultimately, internalise rules of transnational law'.[39] This description of the evolution of 'transnational law' as the outcome of an iterative process leading to the embedding of agreed substantive norms is readily identifiable as being similar to the role of state practice in the formation of international law. The only difference being that the practice of states in this connection was at least traditionally limited to 'practice' attributable to clearly identifiable state, governmental, or at least public sector-related, organs or actors. As noted previously, this public–private distinction is becoming more difficult to distinguish.

For example, the EP are clearly now the pre-eminent self-regulation instrument in their respective fields, and their principles and standards are both accepted and applied by a significant number of the private project finance lending banks around the world. This phenomenon in and of itself arguably demands attention from international lawyers in terms of the possible status of the EP as evidence of the further crystallization of these social rights and environmental protection principles into rules of customary international law. The continuing institutional

---

[38] Harold Hongju Koh, 'Transnational Legal Process', *Nebraska Law Review*, 75 (1996), 181.
[39] Koh, 'Transnational Legal Process', at 183–4.

development of environmental principles and standard-setting through well-known international organizations such as the UN (IMO), WTO (Codex) and ISO has now progressed to less well-known but arguably equally significant 'transnational' rather than international, non-state actor agreements, such as the EP. This new phenomenon of transnational, non-state actor agreements presents a further challenge to the solely inter-state law-making function of international law generally, and international environmental law, in particular.

On the other hand, questions persist, principally over the uncertain legal status of the non-state actors involved in these transnational agreements such as the EP, and the difficulty of relying on these Principles, whether as new, complementary or alternative sources of international law. Moreover, as noted above, the apparent inability of the Equator Banks to regulate or otherwise constrain the behaviour of the borrowing company after a loan is approved and funds have been transferred is exacerbated by the 'non-recourse' nature of the PF-type loan vehicle. In effect, this means that despite lack of direct control over the operations and assets of the loan, the Equator Bank is nevertheless dependent for the repayment of its loan on the stream of revenue flowing from the project and is therefore going to be wary of any constraints it places on the borrowing company's actions or omissions on the environmental and social aspects of the project, for fear that this will interfere with its vital source of revenue constituting its repayment. All these questions and issues combine to create a continuing atmosphere of uncertainty surrounding the enforcement of these Principles.

A further, more generic question that can be noted here is whether there can in fact be truly 'international' or 'global' standards on all contentious issues, in the sense that a vast majority of the different types of states and non-state actors in a diverse world would all accept and apply the same standards. This point is pertinent when we deal with essentially non-binding standards established by a transnational network of non-state actors, such as the ISO. Problems have arisen for example in similar types of exercises conducted in respect of international labour standards, under the auspices of the ILO. The controversies surrounding the extent to which ostensibly well-accepted international labour standards have in fact not been implemented within ILO Member states have even resulted in calls for a reiteration and arguably the 're-entrenchment' of 'core labour standards' previously thought to be entrenched but which have turned out not to be so after all.[40] However,

---

[40] Philip Alston, '"Core Labour Standards" and the Transformation of the International Labour Rights Regime', *European Journal of International Law*, 15(3) (2004), 457–521.

this issue may not necessarily be resolved by the apparently simple expedient
of reverting to traditional treaty law-making by states.

Finally, another difficulty posed by the increasing scope for norm-
iteration, refinement and application by transnational, non-state actor
networks is their perceived lack of accountability. Within the Equator
Principles context, the need for transparency and accountability in the
EPFI decision-making processes was highlighted as a major deficiency in
the previous (2003) version of the Principles. The BankTrack Equator
Principles Anniversary Report noted that a lack of information undermined the ability of the public and of the endorsing (Equator) Banks to
assess the implementation, effectiveness and, ultimately, integrity of the
Principles.[41]

Conclusions

Even though the international law for environmental protection is grad-
ually becoming a specific field or sub-discipline in itself, namely, of
'international environmental law', this still fledgling field of public international law suffers from both *substantive* and *systemic* difficulties.
International environmental law has thus fallen *between* the development of general environmental principles, mainly enunciated in non-
binding international instruments (such as the 1992 Rio Declaration on
Environment and Development) and binding international environmental treaties which are nevertheless sector specific in their orientation,
or even when comprehensive in their approach to (several) environmental threats, are *regional* rather than *global*, in their geographical
scope of application. This developmental 'gap' between general environmental principles and specific treaty rules points towards a *substantive*
failing within international environmental law as a viable sub-discipline
of public international law generally.[42]

International environmental law also suffers from the following *systemic* difficulties inherent to public international law. First, it is difficult
to impute generally applicable customary rules of international environmental law from globally applicable but sector-specific treaties, or even

---

[41] BankTrack, *Principles*, at 38.
[42] For a detailed analysis of the issues raised by this critical assessment of the progress of
international environmental law, see David Ong, 'International Environmental Law's
"Customary" Dilemma: Betwixt General Principles and Treaty Rules', *Irish Yearbook of
International Law*, Vol. 1 (inaugural vol.), 2006 (Oxford: Hart, 2008), pp. 3–60.

comprehensive regional treaty networks addressing several common environmental threats. This situation is both highlighted and exacerbated by the lack of an equally comprehensive, globally applicable treaty covering all major environmental threats. The *pacta tertis* rule regarding the applicability of treaties to non-parties is a further obstacle in this respect, as is the lack of authoritative jurisprudence in the decisions of international courts and tribunals seized of environmental issues to date. Second, environmental treaty compliance procedures, while performing a valuable role in ascertaining compliance to the specific treaty regime concerned, do not yield authoritative judgments contributing to an understanding of the application of the accepted environmental principles for the wider international community as decisions of international courts and tribunals would do.

Thus, international environmental law is evolving along a different trajectory than other, also comparatively recently established sub-disciplines of international law, such as international human rights and WTO law. Its effective implementation by states is often the outcome of a focused and detailed iterative multilateral regulatory *process*, rather than the result of an established set of rules enunciated in a globally applicable treaty and confirmed in a series of definitive judgments by international tribunals resolving mainly bilateral dispute situations. Thus, it is the increasing numbers and strength of patterns and networks of international environmental *governance*, rather than the development of coherent international environmental law *jurisprudence*, arising from mounting instances of international environmental litigation, which defines the progress of international environmental law as a viable sub-discipline of public international law.

In any case, the relative unsuitability of international litigation for ensuring global environmental protection is well documented. Given the reactive nature of such international litigation, which generally arises only when a breach of an international obligation is deemed to have occurred, often already resulting in environmental damage, it may be seen that an institutionalizing, process-based approach would better fulfil a preventive role than relying on litigation. Such an approach will arguably be more successful in attempting to *internalize* these well-known and well-accepted environmental principles, which have nevertheless until now still not been fully implemented within domestic legal regimes. This approach also accords with what is surely the ultimate priority of both international and domestic environmental law worldwide; namely, the prevention of environmental harm, rather than the allocation of fault, blame and liability for its remediation. Indeed, the prevention of environmental damage can arguably only be fully achieved as a result of the *internalization* of these environmental principles within both international and domestic societies. Should such an *internalization* process be ultimately successful, then the need for traditional international legal remedies, which are still largely predicated upon the notion of bilateral (state vs. state) disputes, would arguably be obviated.

In this context, an *internalizing* approach can also be discerned within continuing efforts to strengthen the global governance of, and remedies against, private non-state actors in respect of the environmental impact of their activities. Therefore, this essay also suggests that it is the increasing numbers and strength of patterns and networks of international and transnational *governance*, resulting in the social internalization and thus effective implementation of norms by states *and* non-state actors, which ultimately defines the progress of any field of international law, and especially, international environmental law. Such progress is often the outcome of a focused and detailed iterative multilateral/transnational regulatory *process*. This alternative regulatory approach will arguably be more successful in attempting to *internalize* international environmental principles and standards within non-state actors, such as the Equator Banks in the form of the EP, especially when these environmental principles have not been fully implemented within domestic legal regimes.

PART II

Special topics

5

Risk management, project finance and rights-based development

SHELDON LEADER

Analyses of project finance (PF) are usually concerned with the distribution of risks between the participants in designing, building and operating an undertaking, each party looking to find the right balance between its exposure and its returns. This chapter has a different focus: it looks at the potential impact that such calculations by the parties can have on the society in which the project is located. The analysis will first identify the relevant components of risk management; it then considers the objectives of each of the project participants as they negotiate with one another over appropriate risk allocations; and it then considers how different allocations can affect the risks that the surrounding society incurs from the building and operation of a mine, oil pipeline or projects with similar potential impacts.

The question

What is the appropriate relationship between the management of two types of risk arising in project finance: risks to returns for the project participants – from lenders through to subcontractors; and risks of damage to the basic rights of third parties – individuals or groups located in areas in which the project functions; as well as in the wider society? By 'basic' rights I will for these purposes understand the entitlements indicated in the norms of the International Finance Corporation (IFC) as well as Equator Banks (hereafter IFC/EP standards). These overlap with, while not covering the same terrain as, elements of international human rights law, but they are a useful benchmark for these purposes, not least because they have grown out of concerns of the finance industry itself.

The author wishes to thank Rasmiya Kazimova and Judith Schönsteiner for their assistance.

The relevant elements in PF

We can use here a classic model of PF. The project sponsor(s), made up of a parent company, or set of companies in a consortium, set up a project company, or special purpose vehicle (SPV), which owns the assets of the project: e.g. a pipeline. The controlling equity in the SPV will be held by the sponsor, and a loan is made to the SPV covering the rest of the investment, without recourse to the sponsor's assets. This non-recourse element functions primarily during the operational phase of the project. The earlier construction phase is often accompanied by some form of recourse the lender will have to the sponsor directly. There are many variants and qualifications to this picture, but it is a good starting point.

This arrangement has several characteristics. Emphasis is placed on the benefit of protecting the project sponsor from financial liability apart from its equity investment – the 'off balance sheet' factor – which is provided via the non-recourse element in the loan. Emphasis is also placed on predictable revenue flow: this concern, also present in lending against general assets of a sponsor, is here heightened,[1] as there is no payment of the loan from general corporate funds, backed by general corporate asset guarantees in case of default. Instead, there is exclusive reliance on the revenue stream from the project, backed only by the assets of the project itself (owned by the SPV) as collateral in the event of default.

These two features strongly affect the approach to risk management in PF and generate a particular set of potential social impacts of those risk management policies. The impacts are both positive and negative. On the positive side, current practices of PF have ushered in a greater awareness by the investment community of those social impacts, having induced the establishment of the Equator Principles among major private lending banks, paralleling the IFC's performance standards. But at the same time PF carries within itself certain systematic features that can make it difficult to satisfy those very standards, as well as the wider requirements of international human rights and environmental law. PF, in other words, is a potential source of both

---

[1] On this point, see e.g. S. L. Hoffman, *The Law and Business of International Project Finance: A Resource for Governments, Sponsors, Lenders, Lawyers and Project Participants* (2nd edn, The Hague: Kluwer Law International, 2001), pp. 6–7, 10–11.

progress and of obstruction in fulfilling the objectives of rights-based development.[2]

Risk management strategies in PF and their potential impacts

The categories of risk arising in PF fall into two broad groups: there is the set of risks that mark possible types of significant damage to the project's progress, which if they materialize will make it more difficult for the investors and contractors to realize their projected returns; and there are risks marking possible damage to third parties: employees, local communities and the wider society. The latter risk may in turn either be seen as a problem on its own, or it may be seen as a problem because of the way in which it can have an impact on the first set of interests: those of one or more of the parties participating in the project. In this latter case, the protection of third-party interests is perceived as instrumental to project performance.

Where the two risk management agendas line up in a complementary fashion, we have the positive effects of PF, manifested in the aspirations of the Equator Principles and IFC Performance Standards. The case usually made for the Principles and Standards is that even if they are costly to implement, they are good for business via the investor's ability to anticipate and avoid various claims for social and environmental damage that would upset plans.[3] The standards would, for example, induce companies to tolerate a reduction in project revenue coming from a decision by the host state to stop the construction or operation of a project because of its impact on local populations, knowing that a consultation process with the communities can in the long term benefit the project. Where the two risk management agendas are competitors, because one or more of the parties has managed to transfer away the cost of meeting a risk, we have the potentially negative effects of PF. For our

---

[2] United Nations High Commissioner for Human Rights: 'Essentially, a rights-based approach integrates the norms, standards and principles of the international human rights system into the plans, policies and processes of development.' www.unhchr.ch/development/approaches-04.html. See also S. P. Marks, 'The Human Rights Framework for Development: Seven Approaches', Working Paper No. 18, François-Xavier Bagnoud Centre for Health and Human Rights, Harvard University (2003), available at: www.hsph.harvard.edu/fxbcenter/FXBC_WP18–Marks.pdf.

[3] See generally on the business case, D. Vogel, *The Market for Virtue: The Potential and Limits of Corporate Social Responsibility* (Washington, DC: Brookings Institution Press, 2005), and M. Conroy, *Branded! How the Certification Revolution is Transforming Global Corporations* (Gabriola Island, BC, Canada: New Society Publishers, 2007).

purposes we can take the Equator Principles and IFC standards as a benchmark for measuring those effects.[4]

Three components of risk management

There are three distinct parts of a risk management policy that are important: avoidance, allocation and mitigation.

Risk avoidance

The policy of avoidance calls for measures to prevent or reduce the chance of damage happening. This may include technologies for better protecting, for example, health and safety or the environment, standards on which the IFC or EP banks will insist for higher-risk projects.[5] It also includes protocols for the construction or operation of a project, such as indications of the appropriate speed at which it should function if health and safety are not to be jeopardized, or the way in which its sites or access routes are to be established.[6] This second set of avoidance protocols is important for our purposes, and one principle that is central can be called the 'avoidance over compensation' priority. The IFC, for example, in its formulation of project standards, says that:

> The measures and actions to address identified impacts and risks will favor the avoidance and prevention of impacts over minimization, mitigation, or compensation, wherever technically and financially feasible. Where risks and impacts cannot be avoided or prevented, mitigation measures and actions will be identified so that the project operates in compliance with applicable laws and regulations, and meets the requirements of Performance Standards 1 through 8.[7]

---

[4] The degree of integration of these project standards is uneven. A representative of an industry association who was interviewed on 3 July 2007 indicated that she had not come across a contract in which Equator Principle requirements formed part of the undertakings between the parties. Interviews with lenders, however, indicated key projects in which the standards did form part of the loan agreements (public and private lenders, interviewed on 22 June 2006 and 27 February 2006 respectively). Thanks to Judith Schönsteiner for the former point. All interviewees will be referred to with the pronouns she/her.

[5] See for example the IFC's classification of projects, including Category C projects which 'need not [comply with] any specific requirements' (IFC Policy on Social and Environmental Sustainability, paras. 18 and 28, available at the IFC's website).

[6] This was an issue, e.g., in the Chad–Cameroon pipeline project. See discussion below.

[7] International Finance Corporation, Performance Standard 1: Social and Environmental Assessment and Management Systems, April 2006, para. 14, available at the IFC's website.

Risk allocation

Risk allocation is largely accomplished via negotiated agreements among project participants. The resulting rise or fall in risk to third parties, which we will consider in a moment, is not here termed a risk 'allocation'. This is a piece of terminological legislation in order to allow us to distinguish the spread of risks among parties who negotiate over the distribution of responsibility for avoiding certain problems, who have to consent before the allocation can be binding, as opposed to local populations which incur risks of damage to health, land or their environment as a result of the negotiation process but cannot, because they are not parties to the negotiations, be said to assume responsibility for them.

Insofar as principles play a role in negotiation over risk allocation, there are several that are candidates, embraced with different degrees of enthusiasm by the various parties. The principles are: (a) allocate the risk to the party best able to control it (the dominant guideline); (b) allocate the risk to the party with resources adequate to address it (e.g. strong contractors sometimes assume liability for damage even though a weaker subcontractor is better placed to prevent the damage); (c) allocate the risk to the party which stands to profit most from the project (e.g. the reason host governments sometimes give for transferring risk for changes in law to project companies and accordingly to project sponsors by potentially decreasing the return on their equity in those companies).[8] Negotiation among project parties may refer to these principles, but is itself a process, not a principle. As such, parties in it may try to deploy one or more of the three principles mentioned, or none at all. In the latter case, they may be content to prevail or lose simply because the balance of bargaining power allows this to happen.

Examples of resulting allocations are:

- classic stabilization clauses – the host state bears the risk of regulatory change;

---

[8] An example of the last principle would be a negotiating position according to which in case of rise in market prices of oil, and as a result of a consequent increase in the share of profits of project sponsors from the project, the risk of change in environmental, social and even tax legislation could be shifted from a state (as a party best able to control that risk) to the parties that would be benefiting most from the project. The party advancing this argument should be ready to face counter-claims that increased profits of project sponsors would lead to increase in amount received as taxes on the realized profit, etc. This point is owed to Rasmiya Kazimova.

- fixed date and budget contract provisions – contractor bearing risk for failures to meet completion deadlines and doing so at predicted cost; and
- risk of default in servicing the project loan – borne by the SPV.

Risk mitigation

These are measures that do not distribute responsibility for risk, but instead reduce the overall risk for one or more of the project participants. Any given mitigating measure may or may not heighten risk to third parties in turn. The central form of mitigating device is project insurance, which will be treated in a later chapter.[9] A further important form of mitigation is the reduction of certain types of legal liability. This can take the form of immunity from certain taxes and other regulations.[10] For example, a representative clause in a contract governing the provision of a public utility stipulates that the project 'is not subject to any laws or regulations respecting . . . e.g. rates for public utilities or financial or organizational activities of public utilities'.[11]

Other clauses have been known to restrict liability for the building or operation of the project to intentional damage, thus removing responsibility based on negligence and areas of strict liability otherwise introduced by standards for health and safety and environmental protection.[12] Finally, there is the example of removal of certain financial risks that come from the creation of tax-free zones. Uruguay, for example, has done this for the two pulp mills considered in one of the case studies discussed in Part III. Both pulp mills were granted Free Zone status. According to Article 19, Law NR 15.921: 'Users of the Free Zones shall be exempted from all national tax, created or to be created, including those requiring by law a specific exemption, as regards any activity carried out therein.'[13] By this provision, the project is insulated from tax changes which are understood as a regulatory risk.

---

[9] Chapter 9 by Rasmiya Kazimova.

[10] Examples from interviews held in Azerbaijan by Rasmiya Kazimova in the period 1 to 23 May 2007.

[11] Hoffman, *Law and Business*, p. 201.

[12] See, for example, Article 20.2 of the Azeri–Chirag–Guneshli Production Sharing Agreement of 20 September 1994, available at: subsites.bp.com/caspian/ACG/Eng/agmt1/agmt1.pdf.

[13] Republic of Uruguay, Ley de zonas francas n°. 15921 del 17 de diciembre de 1987 available at: www.zonafrancacolonia.com/ley.htm.

The objectives of each of the project participants in risk management

It is tempting to try to understand and evaluate the social impacts of foreign direct investment (FDI) in two-party terms: as a conflict between investors, along with those aligned with their interests, opposed to those in the wider society who are affected by what the investors do. In fact, the impact of PF, as that of other species of foreign direct investment, is often the outcome of confrontations from within the camp of those normally taken to be on the side of the investor. They make up the full list of project participants: lender, project sponsor, SPV, as well as various project contractors. These parties have partly different and partly overlapping aims and approaches to these three areas of risk management: avoidance, allocation and mitigation. We can see this by first understanding the objectives of these participants separately; and then by considering how they compete or align with one another as the parties negotiate. It is the outcome of these negotiations that is important for third parties. The latter sometimes stand on the sidelines, with little participation in shaping of policy, and at other times their interests are taken up by the state as their representative, as will be seen.

We are not concerned here with the full range of aims and risks for the parties, but only with those which can have an impact on society via potential damage to environment, health and safety, and analogous concerns.

The lender

These are commercial banks or public bodies, often providing the finance for a project in a combination of inputs from the private and public sectors. The main objective of the private lenders is to realize a return on their loans, while the objective of the public sector lenders is, depending on the entity, to combine that incentive with their mandate to further development in the host country and/or if they are an organ of a particular state, as are export credit agencies, to respect the legal obligations that their home government must respect in its investing activity. Provided it enters the planning phase early enough (an issue considered in Chapter 15), the lender is in a position to influence the construction and operation of a project via the conditions attached to the loan, embodied for example in the Equator Principles and IFC project standards, as described in Chapter 3.[14] Failure to respect these conditions can lead either to an outright refusal to finance the project, or to a cancellation and recall of the loan in circumstances of serious breach. The associated risk that the lenders run is that there will be events that interfere with the predicted timing and volume of revenue flow to the project so as to service the loan. These interferences can come from a range of directions. They include changes of policies and laws by the host government, negative reactions by local populations to the project or alterations in the international demand for a product, such as petroleum or iron ore. The lender will seek an allocation and mitigation of risks that will minimize the impact on it of these events perturbing the servicing of the loan.

The sponsor

This is the party with often the greatest direct influence over the day-to-day business of projects. The influence is exercised via the sponsor's position as owner of the equity in the SPV, and this is often complemented by its role as the project operator and provider of inputs into the phase of construction. British Petroleum, Mittal Steel and Firestone Rubber Co. are prominent examples, but for the purposes of understanding the impacts of risk management policies, it is also important to understand the place of less-well-known companies, which are often less sensitive to their reputations among the general public. The main objective of the sponsor is to meet or surpass its anticipated return on equity. A secondary aim is to satisfy the lender's requirement. While the SPV's obligation to repay the loan takes precedence over any obligations it has to allocate revenue to equity, the sponsor has no such obligation to the lender.[15] This separation between the two can be socially significant. If the sponsor judges the continuation of the operation of a project to be too costly in terms of further equity contributions or other funds it is asked to contribute, then it is in a position to allow the company to go into liquidation. The sponsor is, in short, in a position to 'walk away' if it

---

[14] Lenders are not always deterred from investing despite being brought in after the bulk of the technical and operational features of the project have been established. However, they will then seek to offset any risks they perceive as a result of shortcomings in design by looking for further guarantees of repayment. On this point, see *Standard & Poor's Global Project Finance Yearbook*, for the year 2007, p. 92, available at www2.standardsandpoors.com.

[15] This is so when the construction phase of the project, itself accompanied by limited recourse to sponsor assets, has finished.

deems this appropriate to its overall corporate strategy.[16] Barring its having behaved in a way that would merit piercing the corporate veil between itself and its SPV, or holding it liable under other principles, the sponsor will have no responsibility under general principles of corporate law in most jurisdictions. This complements its immunity under the terms of the non-recourse bank loan. If it is to avoid undue risk to its existing equity investment, withdrawal from the project may be the sponsor's most rational course of action.

The SPV

The SPV's primary objective is to maximize project income levels. Its associated risk is that of failing adequately to service the demands of the lender and of equity. If there is a mixed set of equity holders, forming a consortium, then it is also the obligation of the SPV's board of directors to provide fair balance among shareholders. The company's status as SPV does not detract from this fundamental feature: it is like other subsidiaries in that respect, and this feature is potentially important when considering the competing interests among sponsors, as when a minority share is held by either a host state or a state company with different outlooks than the other commercial equity holders might have. This means that the objectives of an SPV, as defined in law, will not always be completely aligned with the objectives of any given sponsor. At the same time it will, as theories of finance suggest, be under the effective control of one or more of the sponsors.[17] This potential tension between the legal status of an SPV and the pattern of its corporate governance can have impacts on risk management, with attendant social consequences on, for example, environment or health of local communities.

---

[16] 'The legal ability to "walk away" from a project that is significantly underperforming gives substantial leverage in renegotiating/restructuring funding arrangements' (International Power plc, presentation on Capital Structure and Project Finance by Mark Williamson and Tony Moore, available at: www.ipplc.com). While lenders' agreements often contain provisions aimed at preventing voluntary liquidation of a project company, this usually does not amount to a requirement that the sponsor continue to contribute equity when it feels that doing so is not worthwhile. At that point, unless there are contributions from another source, the project company would quickly go into involuntary liquidation.

[17] For an account of the way in which the SPV is more tightly controlled than is the typical subsidiary, see Benjamin Esty, 'The Economic Motivations for Using Project Finance' (on file at Harvard Business School, 2003).

The project contractor

Much of the project's activity is in the hands of its contractors. They range from companies, often multinationals, engaged in construction of the project through to small suppliers of local labour and goods. The main objective of contractors is to earn their bargained-for return from either the SPV, with whom they have contracted, or, in their capacity as subcontractors, from other contractors. The associated risk is that of interferences with that expected return due to external factors or to their own failures of execution of their undertaking. Many contractors in the chain of agreements making up the project risk losses as a result of a fixed-date and budget feature of the construction contract which makes it difficult to foresee events that might result in an increased price of the contract, late delivery or failure to perform at agreed levels. The contractor will typically want to limit risks of any change in the cost of the project, to provide excuses for late delivery, and to provide sufficient time to satisfy performance guarantees. The lender will want to have limited recourse to sponsors to pay the contractor for the work performed if the financing documents require the lender to make payments directly to the contractor.[18]

The place of corporate social responsibility

For each of these participants in PF, it is important to locate the impact of principles of corporate social responsibility (CSR) in thinking about risk management. While the detail of such an impact obviously varies, depending on features of the roles of lender, sponsor, SPV or contractor, there are some shared aspects of responsibility that are important to identify. These concern the appropriate balance between two elements: on the one hand, the basic rights of those affected by a project; and on the other, the fact that the parties to the project have as their core objective the earning of adequate return on their investment. Principles of CSR can then take two forms: first, they might require the body to enlarge on its objectives so that it positively assists the host country to build capacity in various domains so as to render development sustainable.[19] On the

---

[18] Hoffman, *Law and Business*, p. 49.
[19] This accords with the IFC's definition of sustainable development and its view that the corporate role in such development calls for such positive contributions. See *Banking on Sustainability* (Washington, DC: IFC, 2007), p. 13 ('Defining sustainability'), available at riskybusiness.wordpress.com/2007/03/30/new-ifc-report-banking-on-sustainability-march-2007.

other hand, CSR principles also demand that the company avoid certain types of damage to society, and it is here that risk management enters into the picture: CSR provides a set of tools for filtering out some methods of dealing with project risk that are dangerous to society and so needing careful control.

It seems at first glance to add nothing here to invoke the *social* responsibility of enterprises engaged in risk management of this sort. If we know that a company should avoid certain levels of environmental damage or damage to health and safety, then this looks no different from what has happened for generations as companies are prevented from committing frauds, providing cover for enemy aliens, etc. However, that ignores an important point. In the area of risk management there are issues of adjustment between competing interests to focus on, and principles of social responsibility can strongly affect the way in which this adjustment is carried out. For example, when an SPV is under an obligation via the EP/IFC standards to avoid certain types of damage to the environment, this requirement is to be placed alongside the need to respect the EP/IFC principle that avoidance of damage is to be favoured over compensation for it. Taken together, these two parts of the stand-ards identify the types of damage of concern – be it to social or environ-mental interests – and then they permit the company to cause that damage when this 'cannot be avoided ... (in the light of what is) ... financially feasible'.[20]

Much turns on the way in which these terms are to be understood, and it is here that the impact of CSR principles can be felt. Once the damage that a project risks causing is identified, a spectrum of solutions is opened up – with avoidance at one end and compensation for the damage caused at the other. There is a point on that spectrum at which a company decides that it should stop trying to achieve the former and instead opt for the latter. In deciding where that point is located, management knows from the EP/IFC principles that it cannot select the commercially most *convenient* stage at which to move to the compensation solution, but that it may move to it only when avoidance of the damage is not technically or financially feasible: this is a point beyond the *capacity* of the available technology or of the financial structure to accommodate extra costs.

This is where principles of CSR can make a difference. They call for an altered approach to identifying where the limits of that capacity lie. The

---

[20] IFC Performance Standard 1.

change involves a different direction of adjustment between commercial and non-commercial concerns. [21] That is, it makes a difference to know whether one is searching for a version of the protection of basic environmental or social rights that, from among alternatives, does least damage to established commercial arrangements in project finance; or whether one is searching from among alternative means of carrying forward those commercial arrangements the method that does least damage to the basic rights.[22] The demand for CSR can be understood as inviting the banks and companies to switch from the former form of adjustment to the latter at certain key points. Unless such an alteration happens, the promise behind the IFC's call to treat certain social damage as a priority, via its demand that avoidance of harm takes priority over its compensation, can turn out to be empty. The danger in turn is that the project can begin to make trade-offs that the wider society will find fundamentally unacceptable. The project company and contractors may, for example, knowingly run a higher level of risk to the environment by refusing the implementation of expensive measures that would call for stopping or slowing the project, since their calculations may show that it is better to run the risk of damage happening and then to compensate.[23] Every measure that stops or slows down a project delays the flow of revenue. If the lender's and project sponsor's common priority is to start that flow as soon as possible, and then to stabilize it, it can make more sense to pay for damage out of a reserve fund held by the SPV, and then to replenish

---

[21] This resembles what some human rights analysts call 'reverse flow'. Rather than taking account of human rights risks because of their impact on the viability of an investment, the aim is to reverse the order of concerns: assessing the impact of an investment on prospects for protecting human rights. The seminal writing on this topic is by Ashley Campbell, *The Private Sector and Conflict Prevention Mainstreaming* (Carleton, Canada: Country Indicators for Foreign Policy, 2002), available at: www.carleton.ca/cifp/. This section has benefited from analysis contributed by Tamara Wiher.

[22] On directions of adjustment, see S. Leader, 'Collateralism', in R. Brownsword (ed.), *Global Governance and the Search for Justice* (Oxford: Hart Publishing, 2005) pp. 53–67; and S. Leader, 'Two Ways of Linking Economic Activity to Human Rights', *International Social Science Journal*, 185 (2005), 541ff.

[23] One consequence of following this logic too far is to be seen in a scandal that involved the Ford Motor Company. In producing the Ford Pinto it was discovered that the car had design faults that could aggravate fatalities in accidents. Ford was aware of this design flaw but allegedly decided it would be cheaper to pay off possible lawsuits for resulting deaths rather than engage in a costly recall of all Pintos. This decision led to substantial lawsuits and badly damaged the reputation of the company. For the decision, see *Grimshaw* v. *Ford Motor Co.*, 174 Cal. Rptr. 348 (Ct. App. 1981). Research on this point has been carried out by Rajat Khosla.

the fund out of fresh project revenues, rather than stop the project in order to rectify the risk, and thereby temporarily cut off the revenue stream.[24] The alternative facing the project sponsor is to feed the reserve fund out of its own fresh equity contributions or operating funds, which it will be typically less happy about doing than it is to rely on project revenue. The boundary between the interruptions to project plans that are and are not 'financially feasible' is thus strongly affected by the disciplines of PF.

For example, the building of the Chad–Cameroon oil pipeline raised problems of dust control, as heavy vehicles passed through populated areas, posing a health hazard for those in surrounding villages.[25] This was a difficulty aggravated by the high speed with which operations have been carried out: the pipeline having been terminated a year before the deadline.[26] Equivalent problems, arising from the speed at which the completion of work has happened, have confronted other pipeline projects.[27] The drive for such speed makes sense in terms of the ground rules for PF. Analysts often point to the fact that the lender wants to reach as quickly as possible the point at which the reimbursement of its loan begins, given that there is no revenue stream to service the loan coming from a company's several projects, but only this one.[28] As a prop to this objective, the project will often offer bonuses to contractors for work that comes in ahead of schedule. Interviews among contractors have established that these bonuses can often make the difference between some profit or none for their work, given the highly competitive bidding

---

[24] 'A reserve fund is an account mandated by the debt documentation for the purpose of setting aside funds designed for use to ameliorate the effects of a project risk. The account can be funded from the construction budget, equity contributions, a draw on a letter of credit, a call on a guarantee, from project cash flow, or any combination of these sources' (Hoffman, *Law and Business*, p. 664).

[25] The legal power to use the roads is granted by the Consortium–Chad Convention for the Development of Oil Fields, Article 8.2. On the dust problem, see Report by the Bank Information Center 2003, p. 2, available at: www.siteresources.worldbank.org.

[26] 'The speed of construction work stands in marked contrast to the substantial delays of measures intended to ensure the welfare of local people and protection of the environment, some of which may never see the light of day' (Report by the World Rainforest Movement January 2003, available at: www.wrm.org.uy/countries/Cameroon/Horta. html). Compare similar issues for the BTC pipeline, Baku–Ceyhan Campaign, BP's pipeline record, available at: www.bakuceyhan.org.uk/more_info/bp_ pipeline.htm.

[27] The effects of the emphasis on speed in completing pipeline projects, are detailed above, n. 26.

[28] Jeffrey Delmon, *Project Finance, BOT Projects and Risk* (The Hague: Kluwer Law International, 2005), p. 292.

environment that often accompanies projects. Pressure is thereby created that pushes the company more easily towards the compensation
solution, so as to keep work going, and away from the avoidance solution, which would slow the pace of work down.[29] Were the consortium
owning the project companies in Chad and Cameroon to have looked for
a way of adjusting its commercial objectives so as to do less damage to
health concerns, it could have held to the original schedule for project
completion, thereby giving more time to make the changes to the access
roads that would have reduced considerably the impact of the dust
generated. The company and the lenders would have stayed within
their initial commercial plans: they would have delayed reimbursement
of the loan, but at a lesser social cost.

This is not to say that such pressures of timing arise solely from the
constraints of project finance. In any given situation, the pressures may
well arise for other reasons. A pipeline may rush to completion in order
to fit in with wells beginning to produce; or in order to meet market
demand that will soon peak. The pressures arising from the terms of loan
reimbursement are therefore only one factor among several potential
ones. What can be aimed at, however, is the tempering of one of the
pressure points in this combined picture: that contributed from this
mode of finance.

What if it becomes clear that serious social and environmental
damage is threatened even if a project remains within its planned
constraints of price and timing for completion? Initial calculations of
costs involved in avoiding that damage may have been inaccurate, and
now turn out to be too high for the project to be viable. The project can
survive only by using the less expensive compensation alternative. In
the circumstances of PF, this point can be reached more quickly than it
is when lending is made against the full balance sheet of the project
sponsor. As seen in Chapter 1, an SPV usually operates with a large
proportion of its income already spoken for by the lender. In addition,
it services that loan via a single income stream coming from a single
project, not the multiple streams from several projects that feed into
the servicing of a typical corporate loan. This will mean that the ability
of an SPV to take the measures necessary to avoid damage by slowing
or stopping a project will depend on how it can manage to do so while

---

[29] The risks posed by attempts to speed the construction of the project, often prompted by
the offer of bonuses for early completion, have been emphasized in interviews with
transnational engineering firms, granted on condition of preserving anonymity.

still giving the lender the comfort that its expectations about reimbursement will be met. That will depend on the reserves held by the SPV: reserves available both to make the changes necessary to the project in order to avoid the damage, and to meet the ongoing financial obligations.

This pushes calculations in a direction that PF planners do not find congenial. As several authors in the theory of finance argue, the SPV is intended to be an entity with relatively low reserves: both as a means to keep it under the tight control of the project sponsor and in order to make it less attractive for host governments as an object of expropriation.[30] If the SPV opts for compensation to third parties as and when damage happens, this will also make demands on its reserve funds, but it is likely to be a lesser demand than that involved in stopping the flow of revenue: spending money on structural changes to the project while reimbursing the loan at the same time. As a result, the project can slip more easily into trading off health, safety and environmental concerns against commercial demands. Projects may do more social damage when financed this way.

It is in these scenarios drawn from the example of the Chad–Cameroon project that a tension emerges between the social and environmental standards that certain lenders try to bring to bear on investment, and the constraints imposed by the need to show returns on the investment that they are in fact providing. If lenders and borrowers are to create projects able to give adequate place to the avoidance of damage, then it may be necessary at certain points to carve out exceptions to the classic non-recourse model. That is, if lenders and borrowers are to take seriously the priority accorded to the avoidance of damage by slowing or stopping projects, this might only be a realistic prospect if either the sponsor is required to help meet the project company's shortfall in funds, or the lender relaxes its reimbursement schedule to make room for such delays. Negotiation among the parties, reflecting the impact of CSR, would add this necessary element of flexibility to the positions, with important potential effects on the surrounding society.

---

[30] C. Hainz, and K. Stefanie, 'Project Finance: Managing Risk in International Syndicated Lending', Limburg Institute of Financial Economics, 2006, available at: www.fdewb. unimaas.nl/finance/workingpapers.

The host state

We have kept a separate place for the host state, since it occupies an ambiguous role in project-financed undertakings: it can be a project participant and a representative of its subjects. It is often said that the state faces a clash between these two: between its commercial and public interest roles. This, it is submitted, is a mistake. We should instead assume that the state has as a constraint on all that it does the requirement that it comply with basic rights of its subjects. This covers its commercial as well as its non-commercial activity.[31] The rights it must respect range from the property rights of investors through to the rights of its subjects to protection of their health, safety and environment. Whether or not the state manages to satisfy the demands of those rights is, of course, the central question. However, in asking that question, it is wrong to place the commercial concerns of the state on one side of the scale, and its human rights responsibilities on the other. Instead, these responsibilities for basic rights can appear in both places.

As a participant in the project, the state can be found as one of its owners: as a holder of equity in the SPV. This entitles it to earn a share of project profit in addition to what it receives under the heads of corporate tax, royalties on goods or services sold by a project, and related sources of revenue. In turn, this project revenue should, in principle, be allocated according to priorities that basic rights would stipulate: public health, education, etc., before servicing other state activities. Alongside this, the state has a role that stands away from any ownership of the project, and instead regulates it as an outsider. Here it must in principle provide sufficiently robust remedies for subjects suffering from various types of particular damage that a project might do,[32] as well as place requirements on projects promoting capacity building, contribution to local health improvement schemes, etc. This second role may incline the state to bring requirements to bear on the project that the first role would reject: by stopping a project in order to protect land or environmental or health and safety rights; allowing it to be stopped by workers'

---

[31] For this point, see S. Leader 'Human Rights, Risks and New Strategies for Global Investment', *Journal of International Economic Law*, 9 (2006), 657–705, at 662.

[32] The obligation of a state to provide an adequate and effective remedy in the case of alleged human rights violations is enshrined in most human rights treaties, e.g. ICESRC Art. XX, ECHR Art. 13, ACHR Arts. 8 and 25.

exercise of their right to strike; or more positively, by requiring the project to make use of local employees as part of its mandate to build the capabilities of its subjects.[33]

This does not mean that each time the state makes demands for a share of project revenue, or each time it stops a project in order to avoid certain damage, it is servicing a basic right of its citizens. However, in both situations it is possible that those basic rights are at stake: when a portion of revenue is routed to fundamental medical or educational needs; or when the project is forced to operate at a speed that avoids, for example, jeopardizing the right to life.

It follows that the state faces two distinct types of risk of failing to satisfy the basic rights of its subjects as it regulates a project:

- Project *revenue* risk to basic rights: the risk of failing to meet its obligations to satisfy its subjects' basic rights via the project's financial returns failing to meet targets.
- Project *activity* risk to basic rights: the risk of failing to meet its obligations to satisfy its subjects' basic rights via failing to orient adequately project activity in directions that avoid damaging them, or failing to provide them with local employment opportunities, medical facilities in remote areas, etc.

The difficult problem, in trying to regulate this part of the state's function with the tools of basic rights, is one of fixing priorities among these competing concerns: when should the revenue risk take priority over the activity risk, and when should the priority be reversed? We will return to this question below as we consider the state's role as a party to negotiations over the shape of a project.

Alliances and conflicts among the project participants

Each of the parties sometimes occupies several roles simultaneously on any given project. Contractors, for example, are sometimes equity holders and project sponsors may also contract with the project as operators. For the purposes of understanding the issues involved,

---

[33] This could be along lines indicated by Amartya Sen *Development as Freedom* (Oxford University Press, 2001), p. 14. For the role of Sen's approach in PF, see Carl Bjerre, 'Project Finance, Securitization and Consensuality', Part II, *Duke J. of Comp. & Int'l L.*, 12 (2002), 411.

however, it is best to set out the roles separately and then to see how they relate to one another in negotiation over risk allocation and mitigation.

Lenders vs. project sponsors/SPV

The international lender will rarely have direct liability to third parties in a host country for damage done.[34] However, it can find its returns at risk when the project fails to operate smoothly. Among the important perturbing events are claims for damages by third parties in the host country, or injunctions granted for the protection of individuals' rights. The lender will ideally look for a solution whereby its debtor – the SPV – keeps its loan repayment in focus. A lender will therefore welcome the possibility that an SPV claims an indemnity for lost income due to damage caused by those it had contracted to build and operate the project. As one author puts it, the lender's objective is that the risk for such an impediment is 'completely transferred away from the project company'.[35] This leaves the SPV free to concentrate on its task of assuring repayment of the loan as scheduled in timing and in amount. The risks of mistakes that may prevent this happening, such as negligent construction or operation, are passed onto those participants best placed to try to avoid the risk, and which must indemnify the project company for lost revenue arising from their failures. In an ideal world, this aligns the interests of the lender with those of the project company when negotiations about allocations of risk take place. However, in the real world, tensions arise in this couple, since the project company might not have been able to transfer away all such risk in particular cases. It will then need to be in a position to meet claims with its reserve funds either while the project carries on, or in the worst case, if the project is stopped. This in turn creates a potential competition between the interests of project sponsor and lender. The latter typically wants to see the former

---

[34] However, it can in principle incur such liability. There is literature that suggests that this might be possible as a result of a high degree of control by the lender of the borrower, see: K. T. Lundgren, 'Liability of a Creditor in a Control Relationship with its Debtor', *Marquette L. Rev.* 67 (1984), 523; and Jeffrey John Hass, 'Insights into Lender Liability: An Argument for Treating Controlling Creditors as Controlling Shareholders', *University of Pennsylvania Law Review*, 135(5) (1987), 1321–63. M. Likosky mentions an example where Indonesian individuals sued Japanese lenders in Japan, in *Law, Infrastructure and Human Rights* (Cambridge University Press, 2006), p. 43.

[35] J. Delmon, *Project Finance*, p. 115.

required to contribute more resources necessary to keep up those reserves as a cushion preventing upsets to the loan payments, while the former typically wants to resist such calls. Our interviews have shown that this tension is a persistent feature in negotiation.[36]

The potential impacts of the different negotiated solutions on third parties in these circumstances are important. To the degree that a sponsor is required to inject further operating funds into the SPV, the space increases for the SPV to allow projects to alter their planned course in order to avoid damage; and to the degree that the sponsor is insulated from any further calls, the SPV's room for manoeuvre shrinks. This conflict can carry over into considerations of corporate survival. Recall that SPVs are usually more highly leveraged than are typical subsidiaries. The room to meet unexpected expense arising from failures in project design or realization is correspondingly narrow. A sizeable demand can cause the SPV to tip over into bankruptcy more quickly than it would for normal companies with a wider range of mutually supporting income streams coming from several projects. Here, the lender may well want the SPV to survive in more circumstances than might the project sponsor. The latter, as mentioned earlier, may have no reputational worries. Indeed, Prof. Esty has observed that most project sponsors are not concerned about their reputations, unlike the headline multinationals such as BP which clearly do have such concerns. The sponsor may therefore be willing to take risks with a project, including the risk of causing damage to the host society, where the lender will want to avoid those same risks.[37]

These factors make it understandable that the IFC/EP standards are taken as seriously as they are in non-recourse PF and less so where the lender has full recourse to the assets of the project sponsor.[38] Interviews with banks indicate that they are less concerned with the precise qualities of a project that is part of a portfolio of various projects undertaken by a company to which they have lent.[39] When the income stream is narrowed to a single, more fragile, source the IFC/EP standards can be seen as a useful way of avoiding bad surprises. Requiring the borrower to respect the standards is a way of stabilizing the future for the investor. The positive effect can

---

[36] Interviews with public lenders and academics, June 2006. See also Delmon, *Project Finance*, p. 72.

[37] Delmon, *Project Finance*, pp. 85ff.; with regard to reverse flow analysis, see pp. 98–9.

[38] See also Chapter 14 by Nii Ashie Kotey and Poku Adusei, case study on Newmont and AngloGold Mining projects in Ghana.

[39] Interview with representative of private bank, 24 June 2006.

widen out to political considerations: a lender will take a view of the qualities of a social and political system that will be more or less secure for its loan, and this can and does include a consideration of the human rights record of the host country. On this point, Chapter 8, correlating loan pricing and indicators that can be understood as proxies for human rights performance is informative.[40] The case studies in Part III also indicate the convergence of lender and CSR interests.

Lenders vs. unsecured creditors

There is a further potential point of tension between lenders and other project participants: this concerns unsecured creditors – individuals or companies with claims under contract, or accident victims who have obtained judgment in their favour. The bank or IFC's loan is typically secured by a charge against project assets, while the position of contractors and victims of damage is often – with some exceptions – unsecured. The latter will therefore come behind secured interests in the event of an SPV going into liquidation. The only exceptions arise where domestic law of the host country has carved out special protection for certain interests, such as that of wages owed to employees and tax owed to the state. However, the position of others is usually not secured with a charge over project assets. Given the relatively thin reserves in many SPVs, these individuals and groups can be at greater risk of receiving nothing from a liquidated company than they would be were there recourse to the sponsor, while the lenders may have emerged fully reimbursed by the assets of the SPV. This is a domain in which negotiation between the interested parties does not go on. The lender's priority over other creditors is put in place at the time the loan is initially worked out. By the time the position of others falls for consideration, the bulk of the project assets may have been spoken for. In the developing world, this exposure can have serious social consequences.

Sponsors vs. the SPV

It might seem surprising to oppose these two bodies. The classic picture of PF seems to line up the interests of sponsor and SPV as fully complementary. The international companies making their investments are often said to create what is essentially a passive company in the host

---

[40] See Chapter 8 in this book.

country: an entity charged with taking orders from the sponsor while insulating the sponsor from responsibility towards the lender and third parties. However, the picture is more complex, and the complexity can affect the societies in which the companies operate. There are two related features of the sponsor–SPV relationship which can push the latter to greater independence from the interests of a sponsor than might be expected.

The first is that for reasons of liability arising under corporate law, the SPV may wish to display greater independence than is conveyed by the view that it is the sponsor's puppet. On classic principles of corporate law, to be found in most jurisdictions, when the directors of a subsidiary follow the day-to-day orders of the dominant shareholders, they may be deemed no longer to be managing an independent company. The corporate veil, normally fixed between the two companies as separate entities, and shielding the sponsor from liability, could be pierced. It is therefore important that the SPV display a degree of real and not sham independence from close management by the parent, as leading authors on PF recommend.[41] Failing this, third parties might be able to make their claims directly against the sponsor.

A second element, fuelling this potential need for an SPV's management to function independently, is that the company often has a mixed shareholding, made up of several sponsors in a consortium, to which the host state or a state company may be added as an equity holder. The members of this consortium might disagree among themselves about best policy for the project: some might want it to pay closer attention to the demands of social responsibility by, for example, altering the pace of work as in our earlier example, while others might want to proceed with full speed despite the greater risks of damage to people or the environment that might ensue. In classic corporate law these conflicts of perspective among equity holders are common, and the law's response is to insulate the company's directors from the need to obey the day-to-day orders of the shareholders on matters of management. If that fails, then the veil risks being pierced.[42] A company's constitution can carve out particular areas of policy that require shareholder consent, such as decisions about transactions above a certain value, but that constitution

---

[41] Hoffman, *Law and Business*, pp. 126–7.

[42] The reasons for piercing the corporate veil are usually restricted to such cases as outlined by Esty, 'Economic Motivations'. There might be arguments in favour of piercing the veil for other reasons. For such arguments see below, regarding recommendations.

cannot cede close managerial power across a wide spectrum of company policy.

This principle has the potential to limit the ability of the majority shareholder in the SPV to dictate policy to the minority, as well as to management. This could in turn mean that management can have a role in balancing competing perspectives among project sponsors about the appropriate response to the demands of the society in which they operate: management is charged with the fiduciary duty to act in the best interests of the SPV, as is true of management of any wholly owned subsidiary in a corporate group, or in any company with multiple share-holdings. If the corporate veil is not to be vulnerable to piercing, there must be a margin of freedom in the management of the local company owning a pipeline, dam or water system to adopt policies of greater social responsibility – mirroring that management's closeness to the social conditions in the host country. Some sponsors might be interested in minimizing their contribution of further resources to an SPV, being ready to 'walk away' from an investment by liquidating the company (assuming there is no market for their shares), while other sponsors might want to carry on, out of closer identification with the host country. Depending on how tightly the sponsors tie themselves to one another via a shareholders' agreement, and tie the hands of management in the company's constitution, the management of the SPV will have legal room for manoeuvre on the point. The interests of the host society can be affected by the configuration of control that emerges, and the remedies available under each scenario.

To illustrate the possibilities here, consider the earlier example of dust control. Recall that the choice in front of the project company on the Chad–Cameroon pipeline was to reduce dust emission by slowing down the pace of the pipeline's construction while staying within the deadline for completion, or carrying on with the existing speed and paying compensation as and when damage, provoked by the higher level of dust, produced claims by victims. If management is not tied to needing consent from the sponsors before slowing down the pace of construction, then there is room for that management to take an approach that gives greater place to the right to a safe environment.

Tight sponsor control over management decisions such as this, coupled with shareholder agreements imposing unanimity on the relevant matter, can result in SPV policy representing the lowest common denominator of views among, for example, sponsors linked in a consortium. However strongly one set of sponsor–shareholders might believe that the SPV should give greater room to local health and safety interests, if another group opposes it, the shareholders are not able to speak with one voice. A looser structure of control allows these different perspectives to make themselves felt in SPV policy: this will be particularly relevant when a dominant international sponsor confronts or is confronted by other international companies that are weaker, as well as by local private and public body equity holders.

Project contractors vs. lenders, sponsors and SPVs

Project contractors want to protect the returns which they have been granted via contract in two ways: one is to insulate the project as a whole from threats to its survival, which if it fails may make them vulnerable as unsecured creditors; and the second is to protect their undertakings to one another and to the project company to meet the deadlines and deliver the quality of result that they have promised. Taking the latter first, the undertakings about completion are a matter of negotiation, in which the lenders, sponsor and SPV have a shared interest in allocating all risk of failure to meet the target to the contractor. Typically this is achieved by a turnkey undertaking, where the contractor promises to deliver the result on a certain date, at a certain quality and at a certain price. This best serves the lenders, sponsors and SPVs' interest in a predictable balance between cost and revenue, as well as the ability to rely on the revenue stream beginning as soon as possible. As one author puts it, 'the project company will want to commence operation of the project as soon as possible in order to earn maximum revenue and improve return on investment'.[43] This is complemented by the desire of the project sponsor to complete the construction phase of the project as soon as possible so as to move away from the lender's limited recourse against its assets and into the more protected terrain of non-recourse finance.

The contractor, on the other hand, often wishes to avoid tight and inflexible deadlines, and other features of fixed-date and budget contracts. Interviews with contractors have shown this to be a major cause of concern, the complaint often being that the deadlines are worked out at the stage of project design, with little or no consultation with the contractors themselves.[44] This mirrors a similar complaint from lenders

---

[43] Delmon, *Project Finance*, p. 131.

[44] Interview, on condition of anonymity, with transnational engineering company. A similar concern has been voiced by a representative of the insurance industry, anonymous.

about designing the post-construction phase of the project without early consultation.[45] In turn, these fixed-date and budget features are said by some contractors to create a risk to social concerns. Companies pressed to meet tight schedules may take short cuts that could harm the environment or individuals.[46] This brings the interests of contractors and lenders as well as those of sponsors into conflict with one another, and interests of third parties can be affected by the outcome of the negotiation.

Contractors vs. subcontractors

A further problem for the host society can arise from the way in which contractors allocate risk among themselves. This will typically happen in subcontracting. The head contractor will typically agree with the project company (SPV) to assume the risk of failing to meet certain deadlines as well as fixed-price and quality requirements. The head contractor may in turn allocate to the subcontractor the risk of failure to meet its own undertakings. This may itself involve a simple risk of having to absorb any extra cost of failing to meet the contractual target, such as reduction of profits, or it may mean the more extreme solution of requiring the defaulting contractor to meet all extra costs of the parties arisen due to his failure, in the form of liquidated damages for breach of the contract.[47] In some circumstances there may be, for good reasons of social policy, priority given to local enterprises in providing some or all of the relevant subcontracting. Some of these may be relatively weak in resources. If these are allocated the risk of failing to perform, they may not be able to absorb the extra cost and become insolvent. In turn, this may render them unable to meet their obligations to third parties, including potential victims of negligently caused accidents. Some engineering companies have consequently worked with models in which the risk of the subcontractor failing to perform is borne by the head contractor.[48]

---

[45] Interview with two major private banks, 27 February 2006 and 13 March 2006 respectively.

[46] Hoffman, *Law and Business*, pp. 126–7, and an interviewee working in the insurance industry who requested anonymity, on 8 March 2007. The point has been confirmed in an interview with representatives of an engineering firm on 19 March 2007.

[47] Delmon, *Project Finance*, p. 210.

[48] Interview with representatives of the engineering industry on 23 July 2007. See also Delmon, *Project Finance*, pp. 73ff.

Finally, the contractor's interest in project survival may add to its incentives to assume more risk than it normally would: in particular to assume the risk of failure by some of its subcontractors. While this might raise its costs, it in turn will demand a greater contract return in compensation.

Host states vs. other participants

Political risk

In negotiating over project *revenue* risk, the state in its capacity as equity holder will find itself aligned with the policies of the project sponsors: it will be concerned to see a stable return on its own equity share as well as its revenue from tax. This could lead it to accept responsibility for all political risk, including the risk of changes in law and regulation affecting the economic equilibrium of the project, in order to secure the investment deal in the first place.[49] However, it is also possible – and increasingly common – that the host state will want to place some of the risk for these changes on the project company. In this case an upper limit is often placed on the degree of loss to be borne.[50] This is true, for example, in the Nam–Theun II hydroelectric project, in which the project company must accept the first $500,000 of loss in such circumstances for any one year and up to $5,000,000 aggregate loss for all changes up to the concession period of twenty-five years.[51] The lender will often want the

---

[49] Economic equilibrium being a phrase often used in stabilization to indicate the overall balance between costs and revenue. See, for example, the Azeri–Chirag–Guneshli PSA, of 20 September 1994, Art. XXIII, cl. 23.2, available at: subsites.bp.com/caspian/ACG/Eng/agmt1/agmt1.pdf. While its equity share might incline the state to accept wide-ranging restrictions on its regulatory role in a project, this may be less convincing as a reason for accepting restrictions on its ability to alter the tax charged or tariff prescribed for products of the project. Here, the state has an interest in striking a balance between providing enough assurance of stability so as to attract suitable investors, while not providing so much assurance that its scope for domestic policy making is hampered because it is not able to finance those priorities. Delmon observes in this context: 'the legal principle of fettering discretion may mean that the regulator cannot be bound by contract to set tariffs [in water or sanitation projects] in a particular manner. The project company may need some other contractual or financial remedy to address regulatory risk' (*Project Finance*, p. 109).

[50] See Delmon, *Project Finance*, pp. 107–8 for situations in which the state wants to place this risk on the project company – 'up to a specified monetary limit, or subject to limitations'.

[51] Concession Agreement between the Government of the Lao People's Democratic Republic and Nam Theun 2 Power Company Limited, 2 October 2002, paras. 5.2 (ii) for the concession period, and para. 6.3 (a)(i) A–C for the amounts. See Memorandum on Legal Issues by O. Can and S. Leader, for International Rivers Network, 30 May 2005, available at: www.international.rivers.org.

project company to maintain an amount in its reserve account to meet such costs.[52]

Equally, in its concern to control revenue risk to the project, the host state may be willing to offer risk-mitigating provisions to the project, such as wholesale exemptions from certain laws. It may, for example, agree with the project company and its contractors to exempt them from certain claims in tort damages, limiting liability to damage intentionally rather than accidentally caused as indicated earlier.

If, however, the host state's focus is on protection against project *activity* risk, it will be less willing to entertain a wide stabilization clause when it comes to promises concerning changes in project regulation, and less committed to the mitigation device of carving out certain legal immunities from those regulations. It will be more concerned to see the project submitted to the same requirements as are other projects in the country.

The host state's enthusiasm for its role in sharing project revenue and for its role as regulator of project activity often varies with the relative strength of one branch of government over the other: the executive branch may be more enthusiastic about giving dominance to the state's revenue share in the project, while parliament and the judiciary – including constitutional courts – may place greater emphasis on reducing the risk of damage from project activity. The solution will depend on the configuration of power within the state, as well as between the state and civil society. Local groups who feel they are suffering more from the activity of the project than they are gaining from the revenue generated by the project are likely to resist the project, and to have more or less well-organized means of doing so, depending on the circumstances in the host society.[53]

Commercial risk

The state sometimes accepts commercial risk, such as construction cost overruns or the risk of declining demand for or lack of availability of a project product. An extreme example of this is the 'hell or high water contract'. This type of contract provides that the state as buyer of goods commits itself to purchasing the relevant output whether or not there is a demand for it, and whether or not it is in fact available; the availability of

---

[52] Delmon, *Project Finance*, p. 108.

[53] See D. Szablowski, *Transnational Law and Local Struggles: Mining, Communities and the World Bank* (Oxford: Hart, 2007), pp. 2–4ff.

the good, e.g. electricity or water, is subject to the possibility that *force majeure* events or technical failures might interfere with supply.[54]

Potential impacts of host-state choices in risk management

On the positive side, in both its role as sharer of revenue and as controller of project activity, the host state has an interest in seeing the IFC and EP standards succeed, and wherever possible be reflected in its domestic law and policy. The legitimacy of any given project can be measured by: the state's ability to meet basic requirements standards in the allocation of the project's revenue; the prevention of project damage; and in some cases, obliging project activity to extend itself to improving the provision of basic services to its subjects which the state may not be in a position to provide itself.

At the same time, there are certain potential negatives. To the degree that the host state assumes commercial risks, it may, in the words of one author, 'remove important incentives from the private sector for selecting sound projects for development and managing costs'.[55] Furthermore, if the revenue share of the state is allowed to dominate the host-state's relationship with investors, then this can place constraints on its ability to protect project activity-based rights such as those in the workplace. At the same time, revenues may help the state fulfil basic rights which are unrelated to the project, e.g. improve the education or health systems. These competing factors can be seen in the potential effects of widely drawn stabilization clauses, requiring the state to compensate the project for any legal or regulatory change, even if these changes are made for the protection of basic rights or of the environment. For example, stabilization clauses have been considered to be one of the major concerns about the oil and gas agreements of Azerbaijan. Interviews with representatives of civil society have established that in 1994, just after the signing of the Azeri–Chirag–Guneshli (ACG) production-sharing agreement (PSA), the PSA Specialist, Mr Peter Wells warned that environmental standards had developed further. As a result, the standards exploited in the development of ACG were not keeping pace with the general standards as early as 1994 and the stabilization clause has prevented the application of newer standards to the PSA.[56]

---

[54] Hoffman, *Law and Business*, p. 175.   [55] *Ibid.* p. 111.
[56] This point stems from interviews held in Azerbaijan by Rasmiya Kazimova (1–23 May 2007).

The UN echoes this concern. In its report, *Human Rights, Trade and Investment*,[57] the UN Commission on Human Rights argued that there is a danger of tying the hands of host states too tightly if broad interpretations of limitations on regulatory change are given effect. The UN is here pointing to interpretations of the 'indirect expropriation' principle, whereby the state is obliged to compensate the investor for legal changes which are deemed to have a severe impact on any given project.[58] As will be seen in Chapter 6, its warnings apply with equal or greater force to stabilization clauses. The latter often call for compensation for *any* legal change that upsets the economic equilibrium of the project: they are not confined to changes with a particularly severe impact on that equilibrium that would for example lead to the insolvency of the SPV.

One can also expect a host state, as revenue earner from a project financed by PF, to exhibit relative caution in imposing the IFC's priority of avoidance over compensation. This would align it with the interests of most of the other parties to the project, as they work out the optimal strategy for risk management. However, in so aligning itself, the state may become party to heightening the risk of project damage to local communities. It might thereby face the warning of experts that, as one puts it, 'the risk structure of a project can allocate too much risk to that host country, leaving the project company with insufficient financial responsibility for taking excessive risks'.[59] The problem is aggravated by the fact that it is often not the country as a whole which is at risk, but a specific region that may be already disadvantaged or neglected. The spread of gains and losses arising from foreign direct investment in developing countries is often uneven, with rural areas taking much more of the costs and risks of development, and less of its benefits than do urban areas. The Niger Delta region in Nigeria,[60] or the Amazon region in Northern Ecuador,[61] both

---

[57] 'High Commissioner for Human Rights, Human Rights, Trade and Investment', 2/7/2003, E/CN.4/Sub.2/2003/9, available at: www.unhchr.ch/Huridocda/Huridoca.nsf/(Symbol)/E.CN.4.Sub.2.2003.9.En?Opendocument.

[58] See also L. Cotula, Sustainable Markets Investment Briefing 3, The regulatory taking doctrine, IIED 2007, available at: www.iied.org/pubs/pdf/full/17014IIED.pdf.

[59] Hoffman, *Law and Business*, pp. 110ff.

[60] UNDP, Niger Delta Human Development Report, Abuja 2006, at 23, available at: web.ng.undp.org/documents/nigeria-delta-hdr.pdf.

[61] See for example Inter-American Commission on Human Rights, Country Report on Ecuador 1997, esp. Chapter VIII, available at: www.cidh.org/countryrep/ecuador-eng/index%20-%20ecuador.htm. See also: UN System in Ecuador, Ecuador's Northern

experiencing substantive investment by foreign extractive industry companies but suffering from historic neglect, may serve as examples, though this is an issue for further research.[62] What is clear is that regional inequalities are significant, and can be aggravated by a host state that pays less attention to preventing the local damage done by a project in order to favour the flow of its overall project income, much of which will go to funding its objectives elsewhere in the country.[63]

Proposals for reform

Drawing the appropriate line between the avoidance of and compensation for damage

The arrival of the IFC/EP standards marks an important step in social risk management for foreign direct investment. It adds a series of internationally recognized rights and interests to those which project participants are accustomed to considering. As these rights and interests are brought onto the agenda, however, they risk being effectively removed again if a project company or contractor is allowed to reach too easily for the option of paying compensation to the victim for violating a project standard. It is one thing for a project company to cause damage for which it is not held responsible since the impact is not deemed serious enough, as would be true if water quality affected by a project were, while reduced, not considered a health risk. It is quite another for a project to be entitled to go ahead and create a health risk that is damagingly high and to plan to pay compensation to the victims as and when the risk matures. The fundamental message sent by the IFC/

Border: Assessment and Recommendations of the Inter-Agency Mission of the United Nations System in Ecuador, 2004; and, recently, UN Special Rapporteur on the Right to the Highest Attainable Standard of Health, Closing Remarks to the Press, 18 May 2007, Quito, Ecuador. The government of Ecuador designed a policy programme to address issues of education, health care, etc. in 2007, called Plan Ecuador, see: www.mmrree.gov. ec/mre/documentos/pol_internacional/plan_ecuador/indice.htm.

[62] Some economists point to the relative dependence by host states on foreign investment as being a generator of inequality, and link this to the power that the firms exercise over host-state policy. One symptom of that influence would be found in the willingness of the state to give priority to its stake in lowering a project's revenue risk at the expense of supervising the control of the project's activity risk. See A. Alderson and F. Nielsen, 'Income Inequality, Development and Dependence: A Reconsideration', *American Sociological Review*, 64(4) (1999), 606, at 627.

[63] S. M. Ravi Kanbur, *Spatial Disparities in Human Development: Perspectives from Asia* (Tokyo: United Nations University Press, 2005), at pp. 2 and 103. A point owed to Judith Schönsteiner.

EP standards is that this second option should only be a last resort. In doing this, the standards come closer to expressing a core principle of prevention in international human rights law.[64] Such strategies, says the High Commissioner for Human Rights, 'permit no "trade-offs" between development and rights'.[65] In the context of risk management, this means that host societies should not be faced with the prospect that investors are too easily trading off interests in preserving the environment, health or safety against commercial advantage, even though there comes a point at which an enterprise's own basic property rights might be at stake in a concern that their project cannot survive a particular demand.

Societies do engage in legitimate trade-offs between viable projects and the basic rights of the potential victims of those projects. When accepting the design of motorways or nuclear reactors, often built and operated by the private sector with PF, host states knowingly increase risks to the lives of their citizens. Society at that point shifts away from the belief that such damage cannot be traded against economic interests, and accepts instead the need to do so. However, it is dangerous to shift from the level of risk that *society* finds acceptable as the motorway or reactor is built, and which it establishes via dialogue with enterprises in the relevant industries to see what is technically and financially feasible, through to a different level of risk that a *particular company* imposes because it finds some of the costs of avoidance of damage unacceptable. If standards of adequate protection of health, as set by the host society, call for accepting extra project costs in order to achieve adequate dust control on the Chad–Cameroon pipeline, then the project company should not be entitled to refuse to implement that control on the ground that it slows the project down too much, even if prepared to compensate victims of its decision to carry on. There should be no gap, that is, between host state and company in drawing the IFC/EP line between avoidance and compensation.

At the international level, what is 'technically and financially feasible' as a cost to be borne in avoiding certain risks should be set by the IFC and the Equator Banks for a sector of economic activity as a whole, such as the extractive industries, via consultation with relevant stakeholders. Such an industry standard would both level the playing field among

---

[64] See also Chapter 3.
[65] UN High Commissioner of Human Rights, Rights-based approaches, available at: www.unhchr.ch/development/approaches-04.html.

competitors, and assure minimum protection of third parties and the environment. This should in turn provide a benchmark which project participants would need to respect in any given undertaking. If a particular level of technology is established as necessary for the avoidance of certain damage across an industry, then no single company should be in a position to invoke the IFC proviso, claiming that it was not financially feasible for it to keep to that standard.[66] It should either keep to the standard or not undertake the project. It is only this approach that would avoid project sponsors keeping their SPVs thinly resourced in order to be able to claim that a particular level of protection was not, in the vocabulary of the IFC/EP standard, 'financially feasible'. If a company does want to move ahead with a given project in such circumstances, a mechanism would need to be built into project-financing arrangements requiring further contributions of operating funds from the project sponsor. Another solution might be to make delay in loan servicing legitimate when this frees the funds necessary to cover the costs in meeting an IFC/EP standard.

Integrating the chain of project participants

A persistent complaint among the parties involved in a project-financed undertaking is that the whole process is too fragmented. Contractors, as has been seen, complain of being presented with completion deadlines that have been worked out by project sponsors with little prior consultation with those who may be asked to meet such deadlines.[67] Lenders seeking to impose IFC/EP requirements complain about being brought into a project at too late a stage, when its primary characteristics are fixed.[68] Project insurers say, to quote one, that 'the earlier a project is fully risked, from both a financial and insurance prospective, the better it

---

[66] This argument does not accept that 'industry standards' as they presently function provide a benchmark for adequate environmental or health and safety standards. They appear in many investment agreements, but are often unilaterally worked out by the companies themselves, with little or no involvement of other stakeholders. See, for example, the critique of industry standards in the host-government agreements for the BTC pipeline in *Human Rights on the Line* (London: Amnesty International UK, 2003). See also A. Wawryk, 'International Environmental Standards in the Oil Industry: Improving the Operations of Transnational Oil Companies in Emerging Economies', *Oil, Gas and Energy Law Intelligence*, 1 (2003), 1. Available at: www.gasandoil.com/ogel/samples/freearticles/roundup_09.htm.

[67] Interview with a representative from a construction company, 19 March 2007.

[68] Interview with a representative from a major private bank, 13 March 2006.

is for all involved in the project'.[69] The advantage of integrating a wide range of parties into the project's basic features at an early stage is that this can affect the terms of negotiation over risk allocation. If, for example, project sponsors have been led to see the need for a more realistic deadline for completion of the construction phase in the first place, then when it comes to negotiation over who is to bear the risk of failing to meet that deadline, the contractor will not be caught between the pressure to meet an unrealistic set of timing requirements, tempting the contractor to take short cuts with safety in order to do so, and the prospect of indemnifying the parties concerned if that deadline is not met.

Corporate governance and the sponsor–SPV relationship

If project companies are to be sufficiently flexible in producing the responses that principles of CSR require, as explored above, then it is necessary to enlarge the classic picture of the closely controlled relationship between project sponsor and SPV advanced by theories of corporate finance. There needs, in the structure of corporate governance, to be greater accommodation of the principles that lead courts to respect an SPV's distinct corporate personality only on condition that it display sufficient freedom from comprehensive control by shareholders over company decision making. Management must be allowed to function more as does a classic subsidiary in a corporate group or single company with multiple shareholders. It must have sufficient freedom to find balances between its commercial goals and social interests – balances which may be called for if a company is to be as socially responsible as the IFC/EP standards require.

At the same time that the SPV should have greater autonomy in decision making, the project sponsor should incur greater accountability for the actions of the SPV than it presently does. In terms of risk allocation, the sponsor can effectively transfer all risk for project failure to the SPV, while the SPV in turn tries to transfer as much of such risk as it can to the other project participants. The project sponsor is doubly insulated: by its preservation as shareholder in a limited liability company, protected from claimants against the company who are owed money by it; and by the preservation of its assets from claims by the project lender. If the

---

[69] Communication from an interviewee working in the insurance industry, 20 July 2007.

sponsor has kept the resource base of the SPV deliberately low – as certain theorists and practitioners of PF advocate – then it may well force the SPV into liquidation, with strong social costs, by refusing to put more operating funds in so as to meet future obligations. If the result of such an allocation of resources is to expose third parties to important levels of risk that will in effect be uncompensated; or if it is clear that an injection of more funds would avoid that risk altogether in a particular situation, then as argued earlier, third parties should have recourse for their claims against the sponsor, or the sponsor should be required, in order to avoid their corporate veil being pierced, to inject more funds into the SPV.[70] This can be complemented by willingness of lenders, themselves wanting to see full respect accorded to their social and environmental standards under IFC/EP principles, to be more flexible about the schedule of reimbursements of the loan.

Negotiation of security for judgment creditors in event of liquidation

Courts in some major commercial jurisdictions have invalidated the priority that certain creditors have been given as a result of their privileged position of influence over the debtor company.[71] The principle here is that such insider positions should not be allowed to force others, no less deserving of having their obligations satisfied, to go empty handed. That is a principle which PF could incorporate into its functions. If lenders wish to promote the social standards that the IFC/EP standards promise, then there should be negotiation in any given country with the host government over fair principles of allocation of funds when an SPV goes into liquidation. This would not leave the lender unprotected, but it would involve dialogue and negotiation between international lenders and other stakeholders over this important element of risk allocation.

---

[70] The basis here for piercing the veil would be on the ground of deliberate undercapitalization. This is recognized in some systems of corporate law, but not all. For a treatment of the issue, see W. P. Hackney and T. G. Benson, 'Shareholder Liability for Inadequate Capital', *U. Pitt. L. Rev*, 43 (1982), 837.

[71] See e.g. *Re Southard* [1979] 3 All England Reports 556 (UK).

The position of the host government

The host government is in a central position to influence the risks that a project poses to the society it governs. As has been seen, the state can here affect the basic rights of its subjects in two ways: via a fair allocation of the overall revenue the project generates according to priorities set by rights of the general population to adequate housing, education or health care; and by the advantages and disadvantages a project produces by its operation in the locality in which it is situated. When there is a clash between the demands of basic rights that are serviced by project revenues, and the basic rights serviced by local project activity, which should take precedence? As has been seen, this question arises in concrete form when the host state has to balance its interests as equity holder, wanting a steady and timely stream of project income, against its obligations as project regulator, required at certain points to interrupt the flow of that income. It is submitted that the latter must take precedence over the former. The reason is that the state is predominantly concerned with limiting the damage that a project may do when it regulates project activity, while the revenue it collects from the project is properly trained not on avoiding damage but on improving the prospects of its population. The latter is, of course, crucially important, and gives priority in calls on project revenue to those groups that can claim their entitlement to the fulfilment of their internationally recognized social and economic rights. However, the progressive improvement in the provision of resources servicing a basic right should not, it is submitted, take precedence over the need to prevent individuals or groups from being pulled below their current levels of enjoyment of non-derogable basic rights[72] – the lower level arising from pollution or health and safety damage.[73]

---

[72] Non-derogable rights are those treaty rights enjoyment of which cannot be suspended during public emergencies, and which usually cannot be restricted for reasons of public interest, etc.

[73] The ICESCR establishes that states have to 'achieve progressively the full realization of the rights recognized' in the Covenant (Art. 2). The text of the treaty is available at: www2.ohchr. org/english/law/cescr.htm. The Covenant has been ratified by 157 states (as of 8 December 2007). The Committee on Economic, Social and Cultural Rights has interpreted this obligation as meaning that 'any deliberately retrogressive measures in that regard would require the most careful consideration and would need to be fully justified by reference to the totality of the rights provided for in the Covenant and in the context of the full use of the maximum available resources'. See General Comment No. 3, The Nature of State parties obligations (Art. 2.1), para. 9, available at: www.unhchr.ch/tbs/doc.nsf/(Symbol)/94bdbaf59-b43a424c12563ed0052b664?Opendocument. This point is owed to Judith Schönsteiner.

It follows that the host state must aim at allocations of project risk that reflect these priorities. It should not accept responsibility for political risk, for example, that would make it responsible for all legal changes that incur extra project costs. Some of those legal changes are necessary in order to prevent damage to local populations according to internationally recognized standards. Equally, it should not permit mitigations of risk that would also allow damage to be done that would normally be preventable. Special investment zones should not permit the lifting of such obligations, nor should projects be insulated from the full range of laws controlling negligence, as was seen earlier.

Conclusion

An adequate policy of risk management in PF must be embedded in a wide set of concerns, ranging from principles of corporate governance through to an appreciation of the particular weight that basic rights, such as those focused on environmental and health and safety concerns, carry when adjusted against the demands of commercial viability for a project. The arguments advanced here are designed to relieve a major point of conflict in risk management: between the aspirations behind the important social standards promulgated by certain public and private lenders, and the threat to those aspirations arising from the structure of the finance that the lenders are themselves providing. It is a conflict that can be resolved, but only by careful consideration of the legal and financial frameworks that the other chapters in this book take as their focus.

6

Freezing the balancing act? Project finance, legal tools to manage regulatory risk, and sustainable development

LORENZO COTULA

Framing the issue

In project financing, debt repayment is primarily ensured through the revenues generated by the project. Effective mitigation and allocation of the risks that may affect these revenues are therefore paramount for the 'bankability' of proposed investments. These risks include commercial aspects, for example linked to currency or interest rate fluctuations, or to changing demand for project output. But they also include risks of a non-commercial nature, namely political, fiscal and regulatory risks. Indeed, regulatory changes may significantly affect project revenues, through increasing costs or delaying implementation. Changes in tax regimes may have similar effects. Once the bulk of a long-term, capital-intensive investment is made, the balance of negotiating power tends to shift away from the project sponsor in favour of the host state; the project thus becomes vulnerable to host government action that may undermine project revenues or even the project's financial viability.[1]

This situation has led to the development of legal tools to manage regulatory risk. Such tools may be based on international investment treaties, as in the case of the regulatory taking doctrine; and on contractual commitments entered into by the host state, such as stabilization clauses. Under the regulatory taking doctrine, regulation that undermines the investment's commercial viability may be deemed as a taking of property, and require the host state to compensate the project sponsor.[2] Under commonly used stabilization clauses, the host government

---

[1] Thomas Wälde and Abba Kolo, 'Environmental Regulation, Investment Protection and "Regulatory Taking" in International Law', *Int'l & Comp. LQ* 50 (2001), 811, at 819.

[2] Other treaty-based tools, such as the free and equitable treatment standard, are also relevant but are only cursorily mentioned here.

commits itself not to change the regulatory framework in a way that affects the economic equilibrium of the project, and to compensate the sponsor if it does so.

These legal devices can help shelter investment from arbitrary host-state interference. Stabilization clauses are a direct corollary of a fundamental risk allocation principle in project finance: that risk be allocated to the party that is best able to control it (the host government, in the case of regulatory risk). This chapter explores whether these devices may also distort the pursuit of sustainable development – broadly defined here as the policy imperative to balance economic, environmental and social considerations so as to meet 'the needs of the present without compromising the ability of future generations to meet their own needs'.[3] Indeed, sustainable development goals such as environmental protection or promotion of local livelihoods may require host-state action over the duration of an investment project; such action may affect project revenues, and therefore fall within the scope of a stabilization clause – or, in the most extreme cases, can be deemed as a regulatory taking. The chapter builds on earlier debates about the implications of the regulatory taking doctrine for environmental regulation; and on more recent discussions about the potential 'chilling effect' created by stabilization clauses on efforts to advance human rights or promote sustainable development.[4]

---

[3] *Our Common Future: Report of the World Commission on Environment and Development* ('Brundtland Report'), Annex to UN doc. A/42/427, 4 August 1987, available at: www.un-documents.net/wced-ocf.htm (last accessed on 9 September 2009), para. 27.

[4] As for the academic literature, see: Sheldon Leader, 'Human Rights, Risks, and New Strategies for Global Investment', *J. Int'l Econ. L.* 9 (2006) 657; Olivier de Schutter, 'Transnational Corporations as Instruments of Human Development', in P. Alston and M. Robinson (eds.), *Human Rights and Development: Towards Mutual Reinforcement* (Oxford University Press, 2005), 403. As for the work of human rights organizations, see the reports by Amnesty International UK (London: Amnesty International UK), 'Human Rights on the Line: The Baku–Tbilisi–Ceyhan Pipeline Project' (2003) and 'Contracting out of Human Rights: The Chad–Cameroon Pipeline Project' (2005); and Global Witness, 'Heavy Mittal? A State within a State: The Inequitable Mineral Development Agreement between the Government of Liberia and Mittal Steel Holdings NV' (2006). Most recently, Andrea Shemberg has undertaken a study for the IFC and the UN Special Rapporteur on Human Rights and Transnational Corporations and Other Business Enterprises ('Stabilization Clauses and Human Rights'); the study was released on 11 March 2008, and is available at: www.ifc.org/ifcext/enviro.nsf/AttachmentsByTitle/p_StabilizationClausesandHumanRights/$FILE/Stabilization+Paper.pdf. For a sustainable development perspective, see International Institute for Environment and Development: (IIED) and partners, 'Lifting the Lid on Foreign Investment Contracts: The Real Deal for Sustainable Development' (IIED, 2005); Lorenzo Cotula, 'Strengthening Citizens' Oversight of Foreign Investment: Investment Law and Sustainable Development', 4. Investment Contracts (IIED, 2007).

First, the chapter recalls the key elements of the international law on regulatory takings, and compares them to the legal standards applicable under a selection of stabilization clauses. This analysis reveals that increasingly broad stabilization clauses tend to ensure a level of regulatory stability that far exceeds that accorded by international law under the regulatory taking doctrine. Second, the chapter analyses options to reconcile managing regulatory risk with ensuring continued host-state capacity to pursue sustainable development goals. This part focuses on stabilization clauses, as they potentially create much more far-reaching constraints on state action. The conclusion summarizes key findings and discusses possible ways forward.

The regulatory taking doctrine

Under international law, host states have the sovereign right to expropriate assets and regulate activities within their jurisdiction, based on the principle of permanent sovereignty of states over natural resources. This principle was affirmed in UN General Assembly Resolution 1803 of 1962, and is generally recognized as being a principle of customary law.[5]

However, international law sets conditions with which host states expropriating foreign investors' assets must comply. Namely, takings must be for a public purpose, in a non-discriminatory way, on the basis of due process, and against the payment of compensation. These requirements are spelled out in a large number of international instruments,[6] bilateral investment treaties[7] and arbitral awards.[8] They are widely regarded as being part of customary international law, although controversy still exists on the international standard of compensation.

---

[5] Articles 1 and 4 of UN General Assembly Resolution on the Permanent Sovereignty over Natural Resources (Resolution 1803 (XVII) of 1962). See also: *Texaco Overseas Petroleum Company and California Asiatic Oil Company* v. *Government of the Libyan Arab Republic*, [1977] 53 ILR 389 [*Texaco*]; *Amoco International Finance Corp.* v. *Iran, Iran–US Claims Tribunal* [1987] 15 Iran–US CTR 189 [*Amoco*]; *Government of Kuwait* v. *American Independent Oil Co.* (*Aminoil*), Arbitration Award, [1982] 21 ILM 976 [*Aminoil*].

[6] For instance, UN General Assembly Resolution 1803, above n. 5, at para. 4.

[7] See, for example: NAFTA article 1110(1); ASEAN Investment Agreement, article VI(1); Energy Charter Treaty, article 13.1.

[8] For example, *Case Concerning Factory at Chorzów* (*Claim for Indemnity*), 1928 PCIJ (ser. A) No. 17; *British Petroleum Exploration Company (Libya) Ltd* v. *Government of the Libyan Arab Republic*, [1973] 53 ILR 329 [*British Petroleum*]; *American International Group* v. *Iran, Iran–US Claims Tribunal*, [1983] 4 Iran–US CTR 96; and see also the *Texaco, Amoco* and *Aminoil* cases, above n. 5.

International law defines in very broad terms the 'taking of property' to which these four conditions for lawful expropriation apply. In establishing whether a taking has occurred, the government's *intention* to expropriate and the form of government interference are 'less important' than the *impact* of government action on the investor's assets.[9] Such an impact may include regulatory measures that substantially affect the *value* of the investor's property rights, in particular, regulatory measures that interfere with property rights 'to such an extent that these rights are rendered so useless that they must be deemed to have been expropriated'.[10] As a result, a taking may occur even where no formal transfer of ownership takes place, for instance, where the investor is 'deprived of fundamental rights of ownership' through taxation or regulation, provided that this deprivation is 'not merely ephemeral' ('regulatory taking' or 'indirect expropriation').[11]

This broad definition of taking is explicitly affirmed in most recent investment treaties. For example, article 1110(1) of the North American Free Trade Agreement (NAFTA) requires compensation for both 'direct' and 'indirect' expropriation; the latter includes 'measures tantamount to expropriation'. In *Metalclad* v. *Mexico* (a NAFTA case), the arbitral tribunal held: 'Expropriation under NAFTA includes not only open, deliberate and acknowledged transfer of title in favour of the host State, but also covert or incidental interference with the use of property which has the effect of depriving the owner, in whole or in significant part, of the use of reasonably-to-be-expected economic benefit of property even if not necessarily to the obvious benefit of the host State.'[12]

In this specific case, the tribunal found that the arbitrary denial of a construction permit and the adoption of an 'ecological decree' establishing a protected area in the project site amounted to indirect expropriation, as they prevented the operation of the investor's waste management facility. The facility had obtained all of the necessary federal permits but was opposed by the municipality (which denied the construction permit) and by the state government (which issued the ecological decree).

A broad definition of expropriation to include regulatory takings provides a tool to deal with regulatory risk. But it has also raised

[9] *Tippetts, Abbett, McCarthy, Stratter* v. *TAMS–AFFA Consulting Engineers of Iran, Iran–US Claims Tribunal* [1984] 6 Iran–US CTR 219, at 225–6 [*Tippetts*].
[10] *Starrett Housing Corp.* v. *Iran, Iran–US Claims Tribunal* [1983] 4 Iran–US CTR 122, at 154 [*Starrett*].
[11] *Tippetts*, above n. 9, at 225.
[12] *Metalclad Corporation* v. *United Mexican States, ICSID*, Arbitration Award, 30 August 2000, 40 (2001) ILM 36, para. 103 [*Metalclad*].

concerns over a possible 'regulatory chill' – the idea that the obligation to pay compensation for regulatory change may make it more difficult for host states to regulate in 'socially desirable' areas such as human rights or environment protection – including to comply with their evolving international obligations.

International awards suggest that the threshold beyond which the obligation to pay compensation is triggered is quite demanding, however. In *Pope & Talbot* v. *Canada* (another NAFTA case), the arbitral tribunal argued that, for a regulatory taking to occur, a 'substantial deprivation' of property rights must be shown, whereby the investor 'will not be able to use, enjoy, or dispose of the property'. Criteria to assess the extent of the deprivation include whether the investor is in control of the investment, whether the government manages the day-to-day operations of the company, whether the government interfered with payment of the project dividends, and whether the investor retains full ownership and control of the investment.[13] In other words, the regulatory taking doctrine can only be relied on where government interference results in very major economic impacts on the investment project.

The 'substantial deprivation' test developed in *Pope & Talbot* reflects the dominant orientation of international arbitrators. It seems equivalent to the test of 'radical deprivation' used in *Tecmed* v. *Mexico*.[14] It has been explicitly followed in several recent arbitral awards, including *CMS Gas Transmission Company* v. *Argentina*, which found that no expropriation had occurred;[15] *LG&E Energy* v. *Argentina*, which also found no expropriation;[16] *Siemens* v. *Argentina*, which found that host-state measures did amount to expropriation;[17] *Enron* v. *Argentina*, which found no expropriation;[18] *Vivendi* v. *Argentina*, which found that

---

[13] *Pope & Talbot Inc.* v. *Government of Canada*, Award on the Merits of Phase 2, 10 April 2001, para. 100.

[14] *Técnicas Medioambientales Tecmed, SA* v. *United Mexican States*, ARB(AF)/00/2, 23 May 2003, 43 ILM (2004) 133, para. 115.

[15] *CMS Gas Transmission Company* v. *Argentine Republic*, Case No. ARB/01/8 (12 May 2005), 44 ILM 1205 (2005), paras. 262–4.

[16] *LG&E Energy Corp., LG&E Capital Corp. and LG&E International Inc.* v. *Argentine Republic*, 3 October 2006, ICSID Case No. ARB/02/1, 46 ILM 36 (2007). This tribunal held that the substantial deprivation test is 'not satisfied where the investment continues to operate, even if profits are diminished' (para. 191).

[17] *Siemens AG* v. *Argentina*, ICSID Case No. ARB/02/08, Award, 6 February 2007, available at: http://ita.law.uvic.ca/documents/Siemens-Argentina-Award.pdf, para. 271.

[18] *Enron Corporation and Ponderosa Assets, LP* v. *Argentine Republic*, ICSID Case No. ARB/01/3, Award, 22 May 2007, available at: http://ita.law.uvic.ca/documents/Enron-Award.pdf, para. 245.

expropriation had occurred;[19] *Sempra* v. *Argentina*, which found no expropriation.[20]

Stabilization clauses

Concept, content and rationale

The level of stability required in project finance goes well beyond that accorded by general international law through the regulatory taking doctrine. Regulation that does not affect the very viability of an investment project, and that therefore is unlikely to attract compensation under the regulatory taking doctrine, may nevertheless have profound implications for the cash flow generated by the investment project. As project finance heavily relies on projected cash flows, sponsors and lenders typically seek higher levels of stability than those provided by general international law.

Stabilization clauses are a legal device for doing this. They involve a contractual (or legislative) commitment by the host government not to alter the regulatory framework governing an investment project outside specified circumstances – such as investor consent, automatic or negotiated restoration of the economic equilibrium (e.g. through longer contract durations, higher tariffs or lower taxes), and/or payment of compensation. Stabilization commitments respond to investors' need for protection from regulatory change that may adversely affect the investment, particularly as the balance of negotiating power shifts in favour of the host state during project implementation.[21]

---

[19] *Compañia de Aguas del Aconquija SA and Vivendi Universal* v. *Argentine Republic*, ICSID Case No. ARB/97/3, Award, 20 August 2007, available at: http://ita.law.uvic.ca/ documents/Vivendi AwardEnglish.pdf, paras. 7.5.11 and 7.5.34.

[20] *Sempra Energy International* v. *Argentine Republic*, ICSID Case No. ARB/02/16, Award, 28 September 2007, available at: www.ita.law.uvic.ca/documents/SempraAward.pdf, para. 284.

[21] On stabilization clauses, see Nagla Nassar, *Sanctity of Contracts Revisited: A Study in the Theory and Practice of Long-Term International Commercial Transactions* (Dordrecht and Boston: M. Nijhoff, 1995); Thomas Wälde and George N'Di, 'Stabilising International Investment Commitments', *Texas Int'l. LJ*, 31 (1996), 215; Piero Bernardini, 'The Renegotiation of the Investment Contract', *ICSID Rev. – FILJ* 13(1) (1998) 411–25; Peter Muchlinski, *Multinational Enterprises and the Law* (Oxford: Blackwell, 1999); Klaus Peter Berger, 'Renegotiation and Adaptation of International Investment Contracts: The Role of Contract Drafters and Arbitrators', *Vanderbilt Journal of Transnational Law*, 36(3) 2003, 1347–80; Peter D. Cameron, *International Energy Investment Law – The Pursuit of Stability* (Oxford University Press, 2010). For

Discussions about stabilization devices were popular in the 1970s and early 1980s, when the outcome of several high-profile arbitrations depended on the legal effects attributed to stabilization clauses embodied in oil concession contracts.[22] In the early 1990s, interest in these clauses seemed to have subsided, with international attention shifting to the booming number of investment treaties.

However, recent years have witnessed renewed interest in stabilization devices, particularly with regard to investment projects in developing and transition economies. Evolution in contractual practice points to a shift away from 'freezing clauses' (whereby the applicable domestic law is the one in force at the time the contract is concluded, to the exclusion of subsequent legislation)[23] toward greater use of 'economic equilibrium clauses' (which link regulatory change to restoration of the economic equilibrium of the project, including through payment of compensation[24]), mainly because of the greater flexibility and versatility associated with the latter clauses. In some cases, freezing and economic equilibrium clauses are combined in the same contract – for instance, in the Chad–TOTCO Convention of Establishment for the Chad–Cameroon oil pipeline,[25] and in the host government agreements (HGAs) for the Baku–Tbilisi–Ceyhan (BTC) oil pipeline.[26]

the author's own work on this, see: L. Cotula, 'Reconciling Regulatory Stability and Evolution of Environmental Standards in Investment Contracts: Towards a Rethink of Stabilization Clauses', *Journal of World Energy Law & Business*, 1(2) (2008), 158–79 and 'Pushing the Boundaries vs Striking a Balance: Some Reflections on Stabilization Issues in Light of *Duke Energy International Investments* v. *Republic of Peru*', *Transnational Dispute Management*, 7(1) (2009).

[22] See e.g. Christopher Greenwood, 'State Contracts in International Law: The Libyan Oil Arbitrations', *BYBIL*, 53 (1982), 27.

[23] Charles Leben, La Théorie du Contrat d'Etat et l'Evolution du Droit International des Investissements 302 R.D.C. Collected Courses 201 (2003); Wälde and N'Di, 'Stabilising International Investment Commitments'. Freezing clauses feature for instance in the contractual arrangements for the Chad–Cameroon oil development and pipeline project, a project-financed pipeline: see articles 24 and 30 of the 'Convention of Establishment' between the Republic of Cameroon and the Cameroon Oil Transportation Company (COTCO), approved with Law 97-16 of 7 August 1997 and signed in 1998 [Cameroon–COTCO Convention].

[24] Economic equilibrium clauses feature for instance in the contractual arrangements for the West African Gas Pipeline (WAGP): West African Gas Pipeline International Project Agreement (IPA) between Benin, Ghana, Nigeria and Togo, on the one hand, and the West African Gas Pipeline Company Ltd, on the other, signed on 22 May 2003 [WAGP IPA], article 36.

[25] Convention d'Etablissement between the Republic of Chad and the Tchad Oil Transportation Company (TOTCO), signed on 10 July 1998 and approved with Law 015/PR/98 of 1998, article 21.3.

[26] Host Government Agreement between the Government of Turkey and the MEP Participants, 19 October 2000, articles 7.2, 10.1(iii) and 21.1.

Stabilization clauses are seen as important by lenders, particularly in project finance.[27] Lenders are interested in a secure stream of revenue to ensure timely debt repayment. Regulatory change that undermines projected cash flows may affect the debt repayment schedule. Because of this, lenders may require tight stabilization clauses as a condition for the 'bankability' of the project – which in turn increases pressure on the investor to extract such a clause from the host state.[28]

Legal value and effect

International awards suggest that arbitrators tend to consider stabilization clauses as valid and with legal effect under international law. Even if ultimately stabilization commitments cannot prevent government interference, they have significant implications for the obligation to pay compensation and for its amount. In *Texaco v. Libya*, the arbitrator held that stabilization commitments are a manifestation and exercise of state sovereignty – not its alienation – and are therefore valid and with legal effect.[29] This view was followed, with some variants, in *Kuwait v. Aminoil*,[30] *AGIP v. Congo*[31] and *Revere Copper v. OPIC*.[32]

Overall, this case law points to payment of compensation as the main legal effect of a breach of a stabilization commitment. Thus, in *AGIP Company v. People's Republic of the Congo*, the arbitrators found that nationalization in breach of a stabilization clause was 'irregular' and required the host government to pay compensation.[33] In *Liamco*, the arbitrator held that nationalization in breach of a stabilization clause is a source of liability to pay compensation.[34] In *Texaco*, the arbitrator ordered *restitutio in integrum* – that is, restoration of the conditions existing before the illegal government interference. But even here, the *restitutio* ruling proved impossible to enforce in the face of host government opposition, and the parties eventually settled with compensation. In a sense, the above-mentioned shift in contractual practice from

---

[27] Wälde and N'Di, 'Stabilising International Investment Commitments', at 228–9.
[28] Shemberg, 'Stabilization Clauses and Human Rights'.
[29] *Texaco*, above n. 5, paras. 66–8.   [30] *Aminoil*, above n. 5.
[31] *AGIP Company v. People's Republic of the Congo*, 30 November 1979, 21 ILM 726 (1982) [*AGIP*].
[32] *Revere Copper & Brass, Inc. v. Overseas Private Investment Corporation (OPIC)*, 24 August 1978, 56 ILR 257 [*Revere Copper*].
[33] AGIP, above n. 31, at para. 88.
[34] *Libyan American Oil Company (Liamco) v. Government of the Libyan Arab Republic*, 12 April 1977, 62 ILR 140.

freezing to economic equilibrium clauses mirrors the dominant orientation of the arbitral case law – whereby stabilization commitments cannot ultimately prevent regulatory change but do require payment of compensation to restore the economic equilibrium.

The amount of compensation depends on a range of factors – the costs incurred by the investor because of the violation (e.g. higher costs caused by regulatory change in breach of a freezing clause); the investor's legitimate expectations generated by the presence of a stabilization clause (as held by arbitrators in *Liamco* and *Aminoil*);[35] the restoration of the economic equilibrium, in the case of economic equilibrium clauses.

Additional insights about the legal value and effect of stabilization clauses were provided by more recent cases not primarily concerned with such clauses. In *Methanex* v. *US*, the arbitral tribunal held that non-discriminatory, public-purpose and due-process regulation 'is not deemed expropriatory and compensable *unless specific commitments had been given* by the regulating government to the then putative foreign investor contemplating investment that the government would refrain from such regulation'.[36] The 'unless' provision of this statement implies that regulation in breach of stabilization commitments would require payment of compensation.

Tensions between investor protection and the sovereign right to regulate were also addressed in *Parkerings* v. *Lithuania*, with regard to the concepts of 'fair and equitable treatment' and 'legitimate expectations'. In this context, the arbitral tribunal reiterated the legal value of stabilization commitments. It may be worth quoting in full a paragraph from this award (emphasis added):[37]

> It is each State's undeniable right and privilege to exercise its sovereign legislative power. A State has the right to enact, modify or cancel a law at its own discretion. *Save for the existence of an agreement, in the form of a stabilisation clause or otherwise, there is nothing objectionable about the amendment brought to the regulatory framework existing at the time an investor made its investment.* As a matter of fact, any businessman or investor knows that laws will evolve over time. What is prohibited however is for a State to act unfairly, unreasonably or inequitably in the exercise of its legislative power.

---

[35] *Aminoil*, above n. 5, paras. 148–9 and 158–9.
[36] *Methanex Corp.* v. *United States of America*, 3 August 2005, available at: www.state.gov/documents/organization/51052.pdf, para. IV.D.7 (emphasis added).
[37] *Parkerings-Compagniet AS* v. *Lithuania*, Award, 11 September 2007, ICSID Case No. ARB/05/8, available at: http://ita.law.uvic.ca/documents/Pakerings.pdf, para. 332.

Most recently, the arbitral tribunal in *Duke* v. *Peru* held that changes in administrative and interpretive practice breached a tax-burden stabilization commitment made by the government of Peru to a foreign investor through a set of 'Legal Stability Agreements', and awarded compensation.[38]

The legal value of stabilization clauses may be reinforced by provisions in investment treaties, whereby a state commits itself to honour contractual undertakings vis-à-vis nationals of another state party ('umbrella clause').[39] In *CMS Gas Transmissions* v. *Argentina*, international arbitrators held that umbrella clauses make *iure imperii* violations of contractual stabilization commitments (to the exclusion of purely commercial disputes arising out of a contract) a breach of the investment treaty.[40] In addition, the *Parkerings dictum* suggests that the existence of a stabilization commitment may be a source of 'legitimate expectations' for the investor, which may trigger the application of 'fair and equitable treatment' provisions included in applicable investment treaties.

Two qualifications need to be made, however. First, the *Texaco, Aminoil, AGIP* and *Revere Copper* awards all involved expropriation claims rather than lesser forms of regulatory change. Economic equilibrium clauses like the tax-burden provision involved in *Duke* v. *Peru* do not prevent host-state regulation so long as the economic equilibrium is restored. But freezing clauses establish a more fundamental limitation of state sovereignty, compared to commitments not to expropriate and to economic equilibrium clauses. Therefore, it remains doubtful that such a fundamental limitation of sovereignty would be enforceable if a host state were to impose unilaterally new regulation on an investment project. Indeed, doubts on the ability of freezing clauses to prevent host-state regulation have been expressed by several commentators.[41]

Second, legal validity under international law does not evade issues concerning the legality of stabilization clauses under the domestic law of the host state, including constitutional principles on the separation of

---

[38] *Duke Energy International Peru Investments No. 1 Ltd* v. *Republic of Peru*, Award on the Merits, 18 August 2008, ICSID Case No. ARB/03/28 [*Duke*]. Tax-burden commitments are effectively a type of economic equilibrium clause, as they commit the host government to maintain the overall tax burden while enabling changes to tax rules.

[39] See, for example, Article 10(1) of the Energy Charter Treaty.

[40] *CMS Gas Transmission Company* v. *Argentine Republic*, Award, ICSID ARB/01/8, 12 May 2005, 44 ILM 1205, paras. 296–303.

[41] Berger, 'Renegotiation and Adaptation', refers to the legal validity of freezing clauses as 'questionable' (at 1360); in the same sense, see also Bernardini, 'Renegotiation of the Investment Contract', at 415.

powers and on the competence of the executive to enter into commitments that purport to prevail over legislation adopted by parliament
(freezing and consistency clauses). Issues concerning legality under
domestic law are likely to vary across national legal systems. Where stabilization commitments are indeed unconstitutional, the implications of this may
be complicated by the longstanding principle of international law whereby
states cannot plead the provisions of their domestic legal system to justify
non-compliance with, or legal challenges to their international obligations.
In *Revere Copper* v. *OPIC*, the arbitral tribunal held that 'under international
law the commitments made in favor of foreign nationals are binding notwithstanding the power of Parliament and other governmental organs under
the domestic Constitution to override or nullify such commitments'.[42]

Yet, if an analogy is made between treaties and contracts, insights may
come from article 46 of the Vienna Convention on the Law of Treaties.
While confirming the general principle that states cannot invoke domestic law rules, this provision also contains an exception for 'rules of . . .
internal law of fundamental importance'. Arguably, constitutional provisions such as the principle of separation of powers do constitute
internal rules of fundamental importance, which the host state cannot
violate through entering into investment contracts and which a diligent
investor should be aware of before concluding such contracts with the
host state.[43]

Threshold

The obligation to pay compensation for violations of a stabilization
clause creates the need to determine the threshold beyond which this
obligation is triggered. Given the great diversity of stabilization clauses,
trigger events vary considerably depending on the specific contractual
formulation. Under freezing clauses, the host state must usually pay
compensation if it applies regulatory changes to the investment project.
On the other hand, economic equilibrium clauses are only triggered
where the economic equilibrium of the contract is affected; at this
point, parties to the contract come under an obligation to restore the
economic equilibrium; failure to do so triggers a violation of the clause.

Some economic equilibrium clauses provide guidance for determining
at what point the economic equilibrium can be deemed to have been

[42] *Revere Copper*, above n. 32, at 1321.
[43] I am indebted to Professor Sheldon Leader on this point.

affected. For instance, the clauses included in the contract for the West African Gas Pipeline (WAGP) refer to a standard of 'material' impact ('material adverse affect' or 'material decrease in project benefits or company value').[44] The economic equilibrium clause used in the BTC contracts, on the other hand, merely refers to regulatory change impairing implementation or adversely affecting value – without requiring these effects to be 'material'.

Compared to the regulatory taking doctrine and despite significant variation across contracts, stabilization clauses tend to lower significantly the threshold beyond which host states must pay compensation. Freezing clauses require payment of compensation for regulatory change regardless of its impact. Economic equilibrium clauses entail a shift from 'substantial deprivation' of property rights to lesser impacts on the economic equilibrium of the project. Even the standard of 'material impact' used in some economic equilibrium clauses appears to be significantly lower than 'substantial deprivation'. What is required for this threshold to be met is not government interference that affects the very viability of an investment project but, rather, less intrusive forms of government action that affect the cost–benefit equilibrium of the investment.

On the other hand, the amount of compensation payable for breach of a stabilization clause is not necessarily comparable to that payable under the regulatory taking doctrine. By definition, a regulatory taking entails a substantial deprivation of property rights. The amount of compensation reflects therefore the fact that an expropriation has taken place. But stabilization clauses may trigger payment of compensation for lesser interferences in the economic equilibrium of the contract. Apart from extreme cases where breach of a stabilization clause amounts to expropriation, the aim is to compensate the investor not for a full expropriation, but for the actual damage suffered.[45] Compensation for lesser breaches of stabilization clauses is therefore likely to be lower than compensation for takings. However, in cases involving a regulatory taking, the existence of a stabilization clause may increase the amount of compensation for the taking beyond what would be payable under general international law, due to the legitimate expectations that such a clause generates.[46]

[44] IPA for the WAGP, above n. 24, article 36.
[45] In *Duke*, above n. 38, the arbitral tribunal held that an investor suffering damage for breach of a tax-stabilization commitment is 'entitled to be made whole for the damages suffered' (para. 458; on the ensuing calculation of the quantum, see paras. 460–88).
[46] See e.g. *Liamco*, above n. 34, at 196–202; and *Aminoil*, above n. 6, paras. 148–9 and 158–9.

Implications for host-state regulation in pursuit of sustainable development

The first three sections of this chapter showed that, while the regulatory-taking doctrine protects investments from the 'substantial deprivation' of property, broadly formulated stabilization clauses may cover a much wider range of host-state action. Effective legal tools to manage regulatory risk are seen as a key ingredient for structuring investment projects – even more so in project financing, where the need to manage risk is heightened by the role that projected cash flows play in credit appraisal and debt repayment. This section discusses the implications of these legal tools for government action in pursuit of sustainable development.

On the one hand, risk-management devices can protect investment projects that may themselves be beneficial to sustainable development. For instance, stabilization clauses can protect renewable energy projects that may be undermined by the arbitrary removal of public subsidies or tax breaks. This protection can help promote 'socially desirable' investments. But, on the other hand, too sweeping stabilization commitments may unduly constrain state action in pursuit of sustainable development. This issue would be at stake where state action aiming to raise social and environmental standards is capable of affecting the economic equilibrium of an ongoing investment project, and it would seem particularly pressing in countries where the health of public finances is a major concern.

Examples of such action may include measures to minimize local environmental impacts, such as introducing strict liability in particular industries, or tightening compensation or local consultation requirements.[47] It may also include regulation adopted in the wake of new technological advances or of the discovery of new hazards; and regulation to tackle climate change (through introducing or tightening carbon taxation or emission trading schemes, for instance).

By its very nature, sustainable development entails an evolving – rather than one-off – balancing act between social, economic and environmental considerations. Changing circumstances (e.g. new technologies, newly discovered hazards) may call for a change in the balancing act embodied by the

---

[47] For a US domestic case where tighter consultation requirements resulted in the regulatory taking of a mining concern, see *United Nuclear Corp. v. US*, 912 F.2d 1432 (Fed. Cir. 1990), United States Court of Appeals, Federal Circuit, 24 August 1990.

existing regulatory framework. In the words of the Brundtland Report, 'sustainable development is not a fixed state of harmony, but rather a process of change in which the exploitation of resources, the direction of investments, the orientation of technological development, and institutional change are made consistent with future as well as present needs'.[48]

In addition, the host state may be required to take measures in order to comply with evolving international law. Over the past few decades, the international law on sustainable development has undergone remarkable change. A growing body of international law on environmental protection has emerged through an increasing number of international environmental treaties, reflecting, in part, the momentum generated by international conferences such as the 1972 UN Conference on the Human Environment in Stockholm and the 1992 UN Conference on Environment and Development in Rio, as well as through the increasing integration of environmental aspects in treaties with a broader remit.[49] The International Court of Justice (ICJ)[50] and other international dispute settlement bodies[51] have also begun to pay more attention to environmental issues. Activities that only a few decades ago were subject to very limited environmental regulation are now subject to stricter standards. In addition, international environmental law increasingly emphasizes prevention and minimization of environmental damage, rather than compensation for damage incurred – as evidenced, for example, by the growing number of international provisions concerning environmental impact assessment.[52]

---

[48] Brundtland Report, para 30.

[49] See, for instance, Article 32 of the 2000 ACP–EU Cotonou Agreement, and Article 19 of the 1994 Energy Charter Treaty.

[50] See, for instance, the Case Concerning the Gabčíkovo–Nagymaros Project (Hungary v. Slovakia), [1997] ICJ Rep. 92 (25 September), 37 ILM 162 (1998) [Gabčíkovo–Nagymaros].

[51] See, for instance, the WTO case United States – Import Prohibition of Certain Shrimp and Shrimp Products, Report of the Appellate Body, Doc. AB-1998-4, WT/DS58/AB/R (12 October 1998), 38 ILM 121 (1998).

[52] See principle 17 of the 1992 Rio Declaration on Environment and Development, 13 June 1992, 31 ILM 874 (1992); the 1991 Convention on Environmental Impact Assessment in a Transboundary Context, 30 ILM 800 (1991); Article 19 of the 1994 Energy Charter Treaty; Article 206 of the 1982 UN Convention on the Law of the Sea, 21 ILM 1261 (1982); and Article 14 of the 1992 Convention on Biological Diversity, 31 ILM 818 (1992). More generally, as the ICJ stated in Gabčíkovo–Nagymaros, '[i]n the field of environmental protection, vigilance and prevention are required on account of the often irreversible character of damage to the environment and of the limitations inherent in the very mechanism of reparation of this type of damage' (above n. 50, para. 140).

Similarly, international social standards have been raised considerably as a result of developments in international human rights and labour law. In the human rights field, international law has undergone major development since 1948, when the Universal Declaration of Human Rights (UDHR) was adopted. This has happened, among other things, through the adoption of new treaties, both at global level (particularly the 1966 UN Covenants) and at the regional level (e.g., in Africa, the 1981 African Charter on Human and Peoples' Rights and subsequent Protocols); through case law applying international treaties;[53] and through 'General Comments' issued by UN bodies responsible for overseeing implementation of international treaties, which clarify the meaning of treaty provisions. The past few decades have also witnessed a clarification of international human rights standards, the strengthening of international institutions responsible for overseeing them, and growing numbers of states becoming parties to international human rights treaties. Evolutions in international law may create state obligations to take action under national law.

The issue is whether host-state action in pursuit of sustainable development may well fall within the scope of a stabilization clause if, for instance, it raises the costs of an ongoing investment project. The extent of this depends on the wording of the clause and on the nature of the regulatory measures. Tax stabilization clauses are less likely to affect social and environmental regulation. But even a purely tax stabilization commitment may raise sustainable development issues. Taxation is not just a source of government revenues – it is also a tool for public policy, including in social and environment matters. With regard to environmental regulation, this is highlighted by the growing shift away from 'command-and-control' approaches towards more incentives-based forms of regulation – whereby behaviour is promoted or discouraged through tax incentives rather than prohibitions and sanctions.

Stabilization clauses with a broader scope than tax liability are more likely to affect action in pursuit of sustainable development, particularly if they are not limited to arbitrary or discriminatory measures. Some

---

[53] For instance, in the often-quoted 'Ogoniland' case, the African Commission on Human and Peoples' Rights found that human rights such as the right to food and water were implicitly recognized in the African Charter on Human and Peoples' Rights; it clarified the content of explicitly recognized rights, such as peoples' right to dispose freely of their natural resources; and clarified the nature of state obligations with regard to economic, social and cultural rights; SERAC (*Social and Economic Rights Action Centre*) and CESR (*Center for Economic and Social Rights*) v. Nigeria, Communication No. 155/96, 27 October 2001, (2001) AHRLR 60 (ACHPR 2001).

clauses are framed in very broad terms to encompass *any* regulation that may affect the project, and may even explicitly include social and environmental regulation. Clauses along these lines are included, for instance, in the above-mentioned HGAs for the BTC oil pipeline. Article 7(2) of the BTC–Turkey HGA requires the government of Turkey to restore the economic equilibrium if this is affected:

> directly or indirectly, as a result of any change (whether the change is specific to the Project or of general application) in Turkish Law (*includ-ing* any Turkish Laws regarding Taxes, *health, safety and the environment*) ... including changes resulting from the amendment, repeal, withdrawal, termination or expiration of Turkish Law, the enact-ment, promulgation or issuance of Turkish Law, the interpretation or application of Turkish Law (whether by the courts, the executive or legislative authorities, or administrative or regulatory bodies). (Article 7(2)(xi), emphasis added)

This provision is very broad in that: (a) it defines regulatory change in very broad terms, to encompass not only legislation but also judicial or administrative interpretation of existing legislation (and article 7(2)(vi) explicitly includes ratification of international treaties); (b) it covers both general legislation and discriminatory measures that target the invest-ment project; and (c) it explicitly includes regulation in health, safety and environmental matters.

Arguably, the use of project finance creates incentives for such broader stabilization clauses. Indeed, as debt repayment and credit appraisals crucially depend on projected cash flow, managing risk becomes partic-ularly important – as reflected in the typically very complex 'webs of contracts' that mitigate risk and distribute it among the many entities involved in the project (e.g. sponsor, host government, lenders, suppli-ers, service providers, off-takers). Sponsors may come under pressure to extract sweeping stabilization commitments to increase the 'bankability' of the project. However, empirical evidence on a possible correlation between project finance, on the one hand, and use and breadth of stabilization clauses, on the other, is still limited. As with all contract negotiations, a wide range of factors will affect the drafting to stabiliza-tion clauses – from negotiating power and skills through to the estab-lished contractual practice of the law firms or in-house counsels involved. The BTC project, which features the particularly broad stabi-lization clauses cited above, was funded through project finance. But other projects, not involving project finance, present similarly broad stabilization clauses.

The broadening of stabilization commitments is compounded by recent arbitral awards that have adopted a rather broad approach to interpreting these commitments. In *Duke* v. *Peru*, the tribunal found that the tax-burden stabilization commitment at stake covered not only amendments to applicable tax law, but also changes in its interpretation and application by administrative or judicial bodies.[54] The tribunal also found that a breach may occur even in absence of interpretive/administrative change, if interpretation or application is 'patently unreasonable' or 'arbitrary'.[55] This goes beyond the already broad formulation of the BTC clauses, and signals a shift away from the more restrictive interpretation of stabilization commitments on state sovereignty grounds, followed in *Aminoil* (where the tribunal held that supposition commitments had to be expressly stipulated for, and restrictively interpreted).[56]

Broadly formulated and interpreted stabilization commitments may create disincentives for host states to enact regulation or ratify treaties raising social and environmental standards, and to apply such standards to ongoing investment projects. Doing so would require the state to restore the economic equilibrium of the contract, or to compensate the investor. For poorer states where public finances are not in a healthy shape due to resource constraints and/or debt burdens, this legal liability may make it more difficult to raise social and environmental standards. In this sense, commitments on regulatory stability may shelter the economic equilibrium of an investment project from changes in environmental and social standards, and may as a result 'freeze' a non-optimal balance between social, environmental and economic considerations.

Alternatively, host states may exclude ongoing investment projects from the application of the regulatory change. In other words, they may still adopt new regulation but insulate from it investment projects covered by stabilization clauses. This method raises issues for the coherence of the overall legal framework, as similar investment projects may be governed by different rules. It raises problems in light of two factors:

- the often considerable size of investment projects where wide-ranging stabilization clauses are used, both in economic terms

---

[54] *Duke*, above n. 38, paras. 216 and 219.   [55] *Ibid.* paras. 222–3 and 227.
[56] *Aminoil*, above n. 5, para. 95.

relative to the host state's national economy, particularly in poorer developing countries, and in terms of possible social and environmental impacts;[57] and

- the usually long duration of investment contracts, possibly spanning several decades.

As a result of these two factors, applying new social and environmental standards only to future investment projects may delay the application of new regulation to a major share of economic activity for several decades.

Whether the outcome is 'regulatory chill' or 'selective regulation' that excludes ongoing investment projects, the operation of stabilization clauses may entail the continued application of social and environmental regulation below international standards for decades to come. This is particularly problematic in poorer developing countries where the national legal framework setting social and environmental standards at project inception may not be well developed.

In addition, this situation shifts to the host state the risk of currently unknown social and environmental hazards which may be discovered in future and which may be prevented or minimized through new regulation. For instance, should new research show that technology or materials used for an investment project are harmful for human health or the environment, host-state regulation that bans or restricts such technology or materials may attract the obligation to compensate the investor – thereby creating disincentives for host states to regulate and/or to apply new regulation to ongoing projects.

Stabilization clauses may also create distortions in legal policy, with host states favouring ways to pursue sustainable development goals that are less costly for ongoing investment projects – even if they are less

---

[57] See, for instance, the considerable importance of the Chad–Cameroon pipeline project for the national economy of Chad and the important concerns raised by civil society on the project's social and environmental standards in both Chad and Cameroon. For example, see: Centre pour l'Environnement et le Développement, *Broken Promises: The Chad–Cameroon Oil and Pipeline Project: Profit at any Cost* (2001), at: www.foe. org./camps/intl/worldbank/brokenpromises.pdf; and Centre pour l'Environnement et le Développement, 'The Chad–Cameroon Oil and Pipeline Project: A Call for Accountability' (2002), at: www.edf.org/documents/2134Chad-Cameroon.pdf. These concerns led to the establishment of two World Bank Inspection Panels; see http:// web.worldbank.org/external/projects/main?pagePK=64283627&piPK=73230&theSiteP K=40941& menuPK=228424 &Projectid=P044305.

effective in pursuing their goal. This may entail, for instance, favouring compensation for environmental damage over injunctions to prevent damage from occurring in the first place. This situation can occur because injunctions may negatively affect the speed of project implementation (and therefore the economic equilibrium of the project) – for instance, by requiring that construction works be halted until compliance with new regulation is assured.[58] Issues of pace in implementation are particularly acute in project financing, as delays may have knock-on effects on projected cash flows.

In making it more costly for host states to take measures in social and environmental matters, and in favouring measures that are less costly to the project even if they are less effective, broad stabilization clauses may trigger tensions between different host government obligations – namely between the obligation to honour contractual commitments (*pacta sunt servanda*), possibly backed by umbrella clauses embodied in investment treaties, on the one hand, and the obligation to comply with evolving international (human rights, environmental) law, on the other. Their focus on safeguarding the economic equilibrium may also foster tensions between the three pillars of sustainable development – economic, social and environmental: it may shelter the economic pillar from possible negative impacts flowing from social and environmental measures, and it may 'freeze' suboptimal balances between the three pillars.

In practice, legal claims are only part of the story in the long-term contractual relationships that typically characterize investment projects. Much depends on the balance of negotiating power between the different stakeholders involved in the project – foreign investors and host states, but also lenders, non-governmental organizations (NGOs), local groups affected by the project, and others. Recent experience with renegotiation of investment contracts, particularly in the oil and gas sector, illustrates that even tight stabilization clauses may not prevent host-state action backed by political determination and changes in the balance of negotiating power. Such balance of power tends to evolve as a result of changing circumstances, of the unfolding of the different stages of project implementation (from negotiation to construction through to operation and decommissioning),[59] and of the economic and political cycles

---

[58] As argued by Leader, 'Human Rights, Risks'.

[59] For instance, the investor's negotiating power tends to decrease after the construction phase, when the investor depends on the host state honouring its commitments in order to be able to recover costs and make profits.

characterizing the relevant industry (e.g., as for the petroleum sector, changes in oil prices and in availability of capital and technology).[60]

However, these considerations do not affect the relevance of the above discussion. Legal claims based on stabilization clauses provide 'markers', 'magnetic points' that may be relied on by the investor or the host state, thereby influencing their negotiating power and possibly affecting negotiation outcomes.[61] Using concepts developed by Tai-Heng Cheng, I would argue that broad stabilization commitments tend to shift negotiating power from the host state to the investor through four types of processes: 'trigger', whereby investors are vested with enforceable entitlements; 'drain', whereby the exercise of state sovereignty is constrained as a result of those entitlements; 'transfer', whereby the power lost by host states does not 'vanish' but is devolved to other actors such as foreign investors or arbitral tribunals; and 'restore', whereby the host state can ultimately restore its power (for instance through payment of compensation), but at a price that can be quite steep.[62]

Besides relations between investor and the host state, stabilization clauses may affect other aspects of the balance of negotiating power, in a way that may make new regulation more unlikely. First, governments are not monolithic entities – different agencies and even different officials may have different priorities and agendas. For example, the ministry responsible for environmental protection and that in charge of petroleum operations, or even the national oil company, may have very different interests with regard to new regulation. The obligation to pay compensation under broad stabilization commitments may provide ammunition to those resisting regulatory change, and undermine the negotiating power of those agencies that are pushing for change.

The obligation to pay compensation may also affect negotiations between the host state and NGOs calling for tighter social and environmental standards to be applied to the investment project. The host state may resist NGO demands by claiming that it has 'tied hands' as a result of its contractual obligations. This is particularly an issue where, lacking genuine commitment to pursue sustainable development goals, the host state is ready to use the social or environmental concerns as a lever for

---

[60] T. Wälde, 'Rule of Law and the Resource Industries Cycles: Acquired Rights vs the Pressures Inherent in the Political Economy of the International Energy and Resource industries', *Journal of World Energy Law & Business*, 1(1) (2008).

[61] Wälde, 'Rule of Law'.

[62] T. Cheng, 'Power, Authority and International Investment Law', *Am. U. Int'l L. Rev.* (2005), 465, at 470–99.

renegotiating the distribution of control and economic benefits;[63] but also to drop pursuit of those concerns once its higher-priority economic objectives are achieved.

This analysis suggests that, from a legal point of view, stabilization clauses may create a 'regulatory chill' on measures in pursuit of sustainable development goals – and they may do so to a more significant degree than the regulatory taking doctrine. This conclusion does not change when the analysis of legal claims is brought together with an analysis of evolving power relations among stakeholders involved in an investment project – as stabilization clauses may affect the balance of negotiating power between those stakeholders in a way that makes it more difficult to improve applicable standards.

Reconciling regulatory stability with continued host-state ability to regulate in pursuit of sustainable development

Investment contracts are carefully negotiated deals. Their provisions define a delicate economic equilibrium shaped by the allocation of rights, obligations and risks. The contract would be undermined if one of the parties could rely on a different body of law (including international law) to alter that equilibrium in an arbitrary way.

At the same time, freezing the regulatory framework, or requiring the host state to bear the costs of any regulatory change, would lead to unsatisfactory situations where regulation is required by changing circumstances or evolving international law. This situation requires exploring options to reconcile the regulatory stability provided by stabilization clauses, itself a legitimate need for investors, with continued host-state ability to reassess the balancing act at the heart of sustainable development, and take measures to correct that balance if needed.

This section explores two such options: (a) carefully limiting the scope of stabilization clauses; and (b) adopting an evolutionary approach to their application. These two options are complementary and mutually reinforcing. Their adoption would redefine the legal claims of the investor and the host state; but also, indirectly, shift the balance of negotiating power between these stakeholders. As a result, these options may ease some of the constraints on host-state action discussed in the previous section.

---

[63] See for instance the recent renegotiations in the Sakhalin and Kashagan petroleum projects in Russia and Kazakhstan, respectively.

Limiting the scope of the stabilization clause

Contractual practice with stabilization clauses developed as an attempt to shelter investors from arbitrary host-state interference at a time when the bulk of the investment has been made and the balance of negotiating power shifts in favour of the host state. Yet, over the past few decades, the gradual broadening of the scope of stabilization clauses has brought within their remit much more than just arbitrary treatment. The stabilization clauses used in some contracts are not limited to arbitrary (e.g. discriminatory) regulatory change. The clauses used in the BTC HGAs explicitly include both discriminatory treatment and regulation of general application.

A first way of reconciling regulatory stability with host-state ability to regulate in pursuit of sustainable development entails rolling back the scope of stabilization clauses to their original focus on arbitrary treatment. At the very minimum, this involves excluding social and environmental regulation that genuinely pursues a public purpose from the remit of these clauses – even more so where such regulation is required by evolving international law.

With regard to human rights, the merits of this approach have been discussed by Sheldon Leader.[64] According to this author, state sovereignty is limited by the international obligation to realize fundamental human rights. In providing commitments to the investor, the host state cannot impair the human rights held by individuals and groups that may be affected by the investment project. Therefore, stabilization clauses are valid and legally binding, but their scope is restricted in that they cannot impair the human rights held by third parties; and they cannot prevent genuine host-state action to realize human rights progressively. In other words, this approach entails building a human rights exception into stabilization clauses, whether explicitly or implicitly; host-state regulation to promote the full realization of human rights is outside the scope of the stabilization clause.[65]

This approach may be broadened beyond the human rights field to encompass the broader range of international law obligations relating to sustainable development. It is accepted that host states may commit themselves not to exercise their sovereign *rights*, such as the right to nationalize. As discussed above, this argument was central in the reasoning developed by the *Texaco* arbitrator to reconcile stabilization

---

[64] 'Human Rights, Risks'.   [65] *Ibid.*

clauses with state sovereignty.[66] It must also be accepted, however, that states may not contract out of compliance with their *obligations* under international law. Indeed, it is well established in international law that state sovereignty is not unlimited, but qualified, among other things, by international obligations concerning the realization of human rights and the protection of the environment.[67] Therefore, states cannot commit themselves not to exercise rights they do not have – such as a right to exercise sovereignty in a way that does not take account of international obligations. In other words, states cannot commit themselves not to take measures that they are required to take under international law. On the basis of this reasoning, the scope of stabilization clauses is limited by a 'compliance with international law' exception, whether explicitly or implicitly.

An example of *explicit* exception, concerning human rights rather than sustainable development, is provided by the 2003 BTC Human Rights Undertaking. The undertaking is a unilateral commitment of the BTC consortium not to interpret the very broad stabilization clause that is included in the BTC contracts (cited earlier) in a way that prevents host-state regulation from pursuing human rights goals, provided that such regulation meets specified requirements aimed at preventing host-state abuse. While the undertaking is a unilateral commitment on the part of the consortium, it 'constitutes a legal, valid and binding obligation' and cannot be revoked without the consent of the host states.[68]

Under the undertaking, the BTC consortium commits itself not to assert claims that are inconsistent with host-state regulation, provided that this is:

> reasonably required by international labour and human rights treaties to which the relevant Host Government is a party from time to time [or] otherwise . . . required in the public interest in accordance with domestic law in the relevant Project State from time to time, provided that such domestic law is no more stringent than the highest of European Union standards as referred to in the Project Agreements, including relevant EU directives . . . those World Bank standards referred to in the Project

---

[66] *Texaco*, above n. 5.

[67] In environmental matters, this is explicitly stated in Principle 2 of the Rio Declaration on Environment and Development, above n. 52.

[68] The Baku–Tbilisi–Ceyhan Pipeline Company, 'BTC Human Rights Undertaking', 22 September 2003, sections 3(e) and 6. The undertaking was published by the BTC as a response to pressure from human rights and environmental groups (including Amnesty International UK's, 'Human Rights on the Line'). On 'BTC Human Rights Undertaking', see de Schutter, 'Transnational Corporations'; and Leader, 'Human Rights, Risks'.

Agreements, and standards under applicable international labour and human rights treaties.[69]

The undertaking also commits BTC not to seek compensation under the economic equilibrium clause 'in connection with ... any action or inaction by the relevant Host Government that is reasonably required to fulfil the obligation of the Host Government under any international treaty on human rights (including the European Convention on Human Rights), labour or HSE in force in the relevant Project State from time to time to which such Project State is then a party'.[70]

The BTC Human Rights Undertaking is an innovative tool seeking to strike a balance between ensuring the stability of the investment climate and enabling the host state to adopt legislation in pursuit of human rights or environmental goals. It does not repeal the broad stabilization clauses embodied in the BTC HGAs. However, it commits the BTC consortium not to invoke these clauses against any regulatory measures that are genuinely pursuing human rights or environmental goals.

It is interesting to note that the BTC Undertaking itself makes no explicit reference to limiting the scope of the stabilization clause to arbitrary treatment alone. In practice, its provisions can still be used to distinguish arbitrary action from interventions that genuinely pursue a public purpose. First, the undertaking requires that regulation be 'reasonably required' to comply with international obligations or to meet a public need. While this expression is admittedly vague, it can provide a first legal hook for discerning the public purpose or arbitrariness of state action.

Second, the undertaking refers to international treaties as a benchmark to define whether government action falls within the 'exception' established by the undertaking. In other words, new human rights or environmental regulation is within the scope of the exception only if it is in line with international standards. This is important to the investor since introducing exceptions to the stabilization clause creates the risk that such exceptions are used by the host state as a 'Trojan horse' to introduce measures harming the investment project with only minimal links to (real or spurious) human rights or environmental concerns.

At the same time, the formulation of the undertaking effectively sets a cap on host-state action: the host state is exempted from the obligation to compensate only if the regulatory change does not go beyond

---

[69] The Baku–Tbilisi–Ceyhan Pipeline Company, 'BTC Human Rights Undertaking', at section 2(a).
[70] *Ibid.* at section 2(d).

internationally recognized standards. This may not be an issue in countries where domestic legislation is significantly below international
standards. But it may cause problems in areas where international standards themselves are not well developed, and in cases where host states
need to respond quickly to new (or newly discovered) social or environmental hazards which are not yet tackled by international standards.

In addition, the undertaking is an *ex-post* tool, which was negotiated
only *after* a very broad stabilization clause had been signed and as a
result of civil society mobilization against that clause. While the undertaking does emphasize its binding nature, questions remain as to the
value that international arbitrators would attach to it should a dispute
arise. This is particularly so given that, far from being a mutually agreed
amendment to the investment contract, the undertaking is a unilateral
commitment entered into by the investor alone. Arguably, integrating an
exception into the contract itself and during the negotiation phase is a
preferable solution.

An interesting example of this solution is provided by the economic
equilibrium clause included in Mozambique's Model Exploration and
Production Concession Contract 2008. This specifically excludes non-
discriminatory legislation concerning the protection of health, safety,
labour or the environment, or the regulation of any category of property
or activity – provided that social and environmental standards embodied
in such legislation are 'reasonable and generally accepted in the international petroleum industry'.[71]

Mozambique's Model Concession Contract explicitly refers to discrimination as a ground for discerning what is within or without the
scope of the stabilization clause (differently to the BTC contracts, which
explicitly include non-discriminatory regulation). In Mozambique's
Model Concession Contract, the key factors to consider when determining whether a new regulatory measure falls within the exception are:
(a) whether it is discriminatory; (b) whether it relates to specified issues,
namely the protection of health, safety, labour or the environment, or the
regulation of property (which would seem to include measures to
strengthen the protection of affected local property rights); (c) whether
the measure is 'reasonable' and its standards are generally accepted in the
international petroleum industry.

The BTC undertaking and Mozambique's Model Exploration and
Production Concession Contract illustrate ways of building explicit

---

[71] Article 27(13).

exceptions into stabilization clauses, whether *ex post* or *ab initio*. However, even in very broad stabilization clauses, a 'compliance with international law' exception must be deemed to be implicitly included. This follows from the recognition that while host states can use stabilization clauses to commit themselves not to exercise their sovereign rights, they cannot use them to avoid compliance with their international obligations – as discussed above. In other words, what host states can commit themselves to with stabilization clauses is limited by their obligations under international law – including international human rights and environmental law.

At the very minimum, this implicit exception must be deemed to include changes in applicable standards flowing from the crystallization of new norms of customary international law, and from the clarification or progressive development of the host state's existing treaty obligations (e.g. through case law or through the work of treaty bodies such as conferences of the parties or committees monitoring the implementation of human rights treaties). It should also include changes stemming from the ratification of treaties produced by international organizations of which the host state is a member – such as the UN or regional organizations. Indeed, although the host state is strictly speaking not under an international obligation to ratify the treaty, doing so may be part of its responsibilities as member of the relevant organization – membership that was (or should have been) well known to the investor when negotiating the investment contract.

While a 'compliance with international law' exception limits the scope of stabilization clauses even where it is not explicitly stated, express formulation is likely to improve clarity and certainty in contractual relations – not only with regard to the existence of such exception but also to its scope and conditions. The project sponsor, the lenders and the host state all stand to gain from greater clarity and certainty.

In addition, greater care in defining the explicit scope of stabilization clauses can make a difference for host-state regulation that, though in line with evolving international law, is not actually required by it – and cannot therefore be considered as part of a 'compliance with international law' exception, whether implicit or explicit. In many key areas of sustainable development, international rules remain unclear. In addition, the urgency of circumstances – for instance, upon discovery of a new major health or environmental hazard – may require swift action that cannot be postponed until international agreement is found.

Stabilization clauses may well be framed so as to enable host-state action in social and environmental matters, so long as such action is reasonable and non-discriminatory. It is worth noting that the exceptions to the stabilization clause in Mozambique's Model Exploration and Production Concession Contract do not refer to exempted host-state action as having to be 'required' by international law.

More generally, the remark made by the arbitral tribunal in *Aminoil* – that stabilization commitments are a 'particularly serious' limitation of state sovereignty[72] – would seem to require tying the scope of stabilization commitments to the regulatory stability genuinely needed by the project. If tax, exchange rate, tariff structures or other similarly specific issues are the real concern for sponsors or lenders, any stabilization commitments can be tailored to these needs, rather than being uncritically lifted from pre-existing contract models. Stabilization commitments may also be explicitly limited to changes having material impact on the project, to the exclusion of lesser impacts. Finally, a stabilization commitment may have shorter duration than the full contract term when justified by economic and financial considerations.[73]

In these important respects, a change in contractual practice is desirable, and the BTC and Mozambique Model Concession Contract examples may provide a starting point to develop new contractual formulations.

Evolutionary approach

The second approach to enabling evolution of applicable social and environmental standards relates to the content and interpretation of stabilization clauses, rather than to their scope. It entails privileging those types of clauses that can more easily adjust to changes in applicable standards; and interpreting these clauses in an evolutionary way. This 'evolutionary' approach complements the first approach centred on scope – namely, by dealing with changes in applicable standards that are *within* the scope of the stabilization clause.

---

[72] *Aminoil*, above n. 5, at para. 95.
[73] See for example section 2.06 of the 2003 Stability Agreement between AngloGold Ltd and the government of Ghana: the contract has a duration of fifty years, but its freezing clause applies for fifteen years only.

In *Gabčíkovo–Nagymaros*, the ICJ held that, while new legal developments such as the emergence of new norms of international environmental law do not undermine existing treaty obligations, new
developments must be taken into account in the implementation of
those obligations. On this basis, the ICJ called on the parties to enter
into negotiations to redefine the infrastructure project, particularly in
relation to its environmental dimensions.[74]

The evolutionary approach applied to treaty obligations in *Gabčíkovo–
Nagymaros* may also be applied to contractual obligations.[75] Thus, following *Gabčíkovo–Nagymaros*, developments in international law are to be
taken into account in the implementation of *existing* contractual obligations, particularly through the renegotiation of the terms of the contract.[76]
In *Aminoil*, a majority of the arbitral tribunal held that the concession
contract at stake 'ha[d] undergone great changes since 1948' when it was
first signed. In particular, the host state had introduced new elements in the
contractual relationship, and the investor had tacitly acquiesced to these
changes. The result was not 'a departure from [the] contract' but, rather, 'a
change in the nature of the contract itself, brought about by time, and the
acquiescence or conduct of the Parties'.[77] The stabilization clause, argued
the majority, was not isolated from the contract but was part of it.
Therefore, the clause lost its 'former absolute character'.[78]

Contractual provisions on applicable 'industry standards' in social and
environmental matters may facilitate some degree of evolution in the
interpretation of the contract. For instance, Article 13 of the Cameroon–
COTCO Establishment Convention concerning the Chad–Cameroon
pipeline[79] requires COTCO to conduct construction, operation and maintenance works in accordance not only with domestic legislation as specified
in the contract but also with 'the international technical and safety standards prevailing in the petroleum industry relating on the one hand to the
management and the protection of the environment and on the other hand
to the protection of the population'. Formulae of this type are commonly
used in foreign investment contracts.[80]

[74] *Gabčíkovo–Nagymaros*, above n. 50.
[75] As argued by Abba Kolo and Thomas Wälde, 'Renegotiation and Contract Adaptation in
the International Investment Projects: Applicable Legal Principles and Industry
Practices', *Transnat'l Dispute Mgmt*, 1 (2004), 1.
[76] *Ibid.*   [77] *Aminoil*, above n. 5, at para. 101.
[78] *Ibid.*, at para. 100.   [79] WAGP IPA, above n. 24.
[80] For instance, see also Article 19.8 of the WAGP IPA, above n. 24.

The weakness of these provisions is their vagueness – the wording is usually elusive and no international standards applicable in the petroleum industry have been clearly defined as yet. As a result, they offer limited or no possibility for enforcement by the host state. Yet the elusive wording may also be a strength, as reference to standards external to the contractual relationship introduces an element of flexibility. This flexibility can enable evolution in applicable social and environmental standards despite broad stabilization clauses. It may be argued that the content of the industry standards referred to in the contract must be defined in light of evolving international law.

Although this solution in itself does not enable the host state to regulate in breach of a stabilization clause, it may allow for international standards to apply to the project. It also sets a reference that has to be taken into account in any contract renegotiation process, and it may strengthen the type of 'evolutionary' arguments applied in *Aminoil*, where substantial evolution in the overall contractual relationship within the context of a very long-term contract was held to have affected the strength of the stabilization clause itself.

Compared to freezing clauses, economic equilibrium clauses coupled with flexible clauses on social and environmental standards appear to lend themselves more easily to adjustments in applicable standards aimed at bringing these in line with evolving international law. While freezing clauses aim to 'freeze' the regulatory framework applicable to the project, economic equilibrium clauses aim to preserve the economic equilibrium of the contract. Regulatory changes which would violate freezing clauses may still be consistent with economic equilibrium clauses if they do not alter the economic equilibrium of the contract, or if the parties restore that equilibrium once it has been affected. In this sense, economic equilibrium clauses are more conducive to adopting an evolutionary approach than freezing clauses.

Through its integration in the more flexible economic equilibrium clauses, the evolutionary approach proposed here makes business sense and is in line with established contractual practice. It does not undermine the sponsor's (and lenders') need to manage risk. Indeed, sponsors and lenders are primarily interested in projected cash flows. Unlike freezing clauses, economic equilibrium clauses do not prevent host-state action – but they do shelter project revenues from negative impacts flowing from it. They therefore strike a better balance between protecting the cash flows, on which debt repayment depends, and enabling evolution in applicable rules. Requirements to compensate the sponsor for adverse impacts may still create disincentives for host-state action falling within the scope of the clause (and as discussed this should exclude measures that directly pursue sustainable development). But economic equilibrium clauses may also provide ways to restore the equilibrium other than lump-sum compensation – for instance, where relevant, by automatically extending the term of the contract. Project financing may restrict options in this respect, as extending the contract duration is likely to affect the debt repayment schedule.

Conclusion

Regulatory stability is a key concern in project finance. Legal devices to manage regulatory risk respond to the sponsors' and lenders' need for stability of the regulatory framework, on which commercial viability and debt repayment depend. But, if inappropriately structured, these devices may also make it more difficult for host states – particularly poorer ones – to take action in pursuit of sustainable development goals, if this affects the economic equilibrium of the investment project or undermines its commercial viability. In other words, commitments on regulatory stability shelter the economic equilibrium of an investment project from changes in environmental and social standards, and may as a result 'freeze' a non-optimal balance between social, environmental and economic considerations. These issues are particularly pressing in the case of stabilization clauses.

Indeed, under international law, host-state action raising social and environmental standards may constitute a regulatory taking if it affects the viability of an investment project to such an extent that the investment must be deemed to have been expropriated. Stabilization commitments, possibly backed up by 'umbrella clauses' in investment treaties, may take regulatory stability a step further. Changes in social and environmental standards may require the host state to compensate the investor for losses incurred. The threshold triggering payment of compensation tends to be considerably lower than that which is applicable to regulatory takings (changes to the 'economic equilibrium' of the project rather than 'substantial deprivation' of property rights).

These tensions between investment protection and sustainable development goals are all the more important given that waves of privatization in low and middle-income countries over the past two decades have resulted in private investment being increasingly relied on in the provision of public services. For instance, private investment in water supply in countries such as Argentina and Tanzania has resulted in international arbitration proceedings between investors and host states. Water provision is a business opportunity and involves economic/commercial considerations; but it also raises important social and environmental issues – for instance, with regard to the realization of the internationally recognized right to water.

Practical measures may be taken to avoid these negative consequences, and to reconcile the investor's legitimate need for regulatory stability with maintaining the capacity of the host state to regulate in pursuit of sustainable development goals. While recognizing that any provisions would need to be tailored to the specific contractual relationship, the scope of stabilization clauses should be restricted to the regulatory stability genuinely needed by the project. As discussed, if tax, exchange rate, tariff structures or other similarly specific issues are the real investor's (or lender's) concern, any stabilization commitments should be tailored to these needs. Stabilization commitments should be limited to changes having material impact on the project – to the exclusion of lesser impacts. A stabilization clause may also have shorter duration than the full contract term when justified by economic and financial considerations.

If protection against arbitrary treatment is what stabilization clauses are for, this should be made clear in the text of the provision and public interest regulatory changes should be excluded from these commitments. At the very minimum, it is possible to exclude from the scope of stabilization social or environmental regulations in line with evolving international law. Limitations may be explicit, as in the BTC Human Rights Undertaking and in Mozambique's Model Exploration and Production Concession Contract. But while express formulation improves clarity and certainty, a 'compliance with international law' exception must be deemed to exist even in absence of express formulation. Indeed, international treaties (on human rights, for example) cannot be derogated from by contracts, and exceptions to the scope of stabilization commitments exist implicitly even where not explicitly provided for in the contract – and it makes business sense to clarify the scope of this protection through explicit exceptions so as to reduce uncertainty.[81]

---

[81] A. Sheppard, and A. Crockett, 'Stabilisation Clauses: A Threat to Sustainable Development?', forthcoming in M. C. Cordonier-Segger, M. Gehring and A. Newcombe (eds.), *Sustainable Development in World Investment Law* (The Hague: Kluwer Law International), also conclude that it is advisable to make explicit provision subjecting the stabilization clause to the host-state's obligations under international treaties on human rights, health, safety and environmental standards.

An evolutionary approach to formulating and interpreting stabilization clauses may also enable a degree of evolution in social and environmental standards. This evolutionary approach entails preferring economic equilibrium clauses over freezing clauses; featuring flexible social and environmental standards clauses in the contract; and building *de minimis* exceptions (e.g. 'material' impact) into the threshold triggering the application of economic equilibrium clauses.

These methods of reconciling regulatory stability with evolution in social and environmental standards make 'business sense'. Integrating an explicit 'compliance with international law' exception is good for business because that requirement can be deemed to exist in any event even where not explicitly stated in the contract. An explicit exception would increase certainty by clarifying what is within and what is outside the scope of the stabilization clause. It may also provide the opportunity for international benchmarking along the lines of the BTC Human Rights Undertaking. Similarly, providing for evolution in contract interpretation makes business sense given that in the real world circumstances change, and attempts to freeze the contract are unlikely to go far.

7

Human rights impact assessments and project finance

TAMARA WIHER FERNANDEZ

The added value of human rights impact assessments

The importance of human rights and environmental impact assessments in project finance

Effective risk management is particularly important in project finance investments; first, because this financing technique is often used for investments in politically unstable developing countries and for socially and environmentally sensitive infrastructure or natural resource extraction projects. Project participants aim at reducing the risk by spreading it between the participants. Such a project finance structure can increase the availability of loans for a project.[1] Second, project finance is risky business due to its limited or non-recourse nature. Lenders can only look to the revenues generated by the borrowing project company for repayment of their loans. They do not have recourse to the project sponsor if the project company has difficulty repaying the debt.[2] The decisive criterion for granting a loan to a project is therefore its future success. However, there are a variety of factors influencing the cash flows of a project that are difficult to anticipate.[3] Moreover, project companies have often low

---

[1] C. Crossin and J. Banfield, 'Conflict risk in project finance: exploring options for better management of conflict risk: a background paper' (London: International Alert, 2006), available at: www.eca-watch.org (accessed: 5 November 2009).

[2] *Ibid.* p. 6. G. D. Vinter, *Project Finance – A Legal Guide* (3rd edn, London: Sweet & Maxwell, 2006), p. 180.

[3] K. Backhaus and H. Werthschulte, 'Identification of Key Risk Factors in Project Finance – A "Project-Type" Based Simulation Approach', *Journal of Structured Finance*, 11(4) (2006), 71, citing Benjamin C. Esty, 'Why Study Large Projects? An Introduction to Research on Project Finance', *European Financial Management*, 10(2) (2004), 213–24.

reserves and their capacity to cover unanticipated costs can easily be exhausted.[4]

A deteriorating human rights situation in the host country or allegations of environmental spills, for example, could affect the revenue flow of a project negatively. The relationship between an investment project and the human rights and the environment of its host community is a 'two-way street':[5] The project can, on the one hand, have important impacts on the economic and social development of the area and thereby influence directly and indirectly the human rights situation of its society. On the other hand, a project operating in a developing country can itself be threatened by risks arising from human rights problems in that country.[6] These could include clients defaulting on loans due to social and environmental problems or costly litigation for complicity with the host government's human rights violations or because of abuses committed by other project participants. A client's failure or lapse in addressing environmental and social issues can hurt the business, which in turn can hurt the bank that has supported it. Such risks may indirectly lead to a loss of customers, investors or revenue. An institution's poor social and environmental practices – including its association with socially and environmentally problematic investments, projects or clients – can lead to negative publicity that damages the brand value.[7]

This calls for proactive strategies, a need highlighted by John Ruggie, Special Representative of the UN Secretary-General on human rights

---

[4] C. Hainz and S. Kleimeier, 'Project finance as a risk-management tool in international syndicated lending', Discussion Paper No. 183 (Governance and the Efficiency of Economic Systems (GESY), December 2006). Available at: www.gesy.uni-mannheim.de/dipa/183.pdf (accessed: 5 November 2009).

[5] Crossin and Banfield, 'Conflict risk', p. 9. International Alert uses this term to describe the relation between project finance and conflict.

[6] IFC/IBLF, *Guide to Human Rights Impact Assessment and Management (HRIA) Road-Testing Draft* (June 2007), p. 2. In June 2007 the IBLF, IFC and the Global Compact jointly produced this draft Guide to be tested by businesses. After a road-testing phase, the revised online version of the Guide was launched on 25 June 2010, during the Global Compact Leaders Summit, in New York (available at: www.guidetohriam.org/ welcome).

[7] IFC, *Banking on Sustainability, Financing Environmental and Social Opportunities in Emerging Markets* (Washington, DC, 2007), pp. 40f. E. Marcks, 'Avoiding Liability for Human Rights Violations in Project Finance', *Energy Law Journal*, 22 (2001), 301, at 313–14. Recently, Canadian mining company Goldcorp has commissioned an external HRIA after pension funds and ethical investors threatened to sell their shares in Goldcorp due to allegations of human rights abuses and environmental damages in one of Goldcorp's mines in Guatemala. See BBC News, 21 August 2008, 'Unease over Guatemalan Gold Rush', at: news.bbc.co.uk/1/hi/programmes/crossing_continents/7569810.stm (accessed: 5 November 2009); and www.hria-guatemala.com (accessed: 5 November 2009).

and transnational corporations. In his April 2008 Report, Professor Ruggie has called for the implementation of a due diligence process through which the company will become aware of and address adverse human rights impacts.[8] Risks are to be managed by all parties to a project: not only by the company that is at the 'front line', operating a project, but also by financiers and insurers which provide the means for project companies to operate and can be a source of leverage.[9] By integrating possible human rights threats effectively into their risk management processes, all project participants can take preventive action against potential human rights challenges that may lie in evolving or future projects rather than reacting to challenges as they arise.[10]

The assessment of potential risks and impacts is at the basis of every risk management process in investment. In order to avoid, allocate or mitigate risk, parties to a project first need to identify the risk to be managed. The human rights or environmental risks posed by or affecting a project, its employees and the surrounding community have so far, if at all, been assessed mainly by environmental and social impact assessments (ESIAs).

In this chapter the insufficiencies of currently performed impact assessments will be highlighted and the case will be made for HRIA in project finance. The next section will then present the current discussion on HRIA in business and some of the HRIA tools that have recently been developed, for example by the International Finance Corporation (IFC) and several non-governmental organizations (NGOs), and that may be used in the future by project finance participants.[11] These tools will be analysed and compared to each other according to their compatibility with the logic of project finance mechanisms as well as their compliance

---

[8] Human Rights Council (HRC) A/HRC/8/5, 7 April 2008, *Protect, Respect and Remedy: A Framework for Business and Human Rights*, paras. 54 and 56f.

[9] UNHCHR, *Human rights and the financial sector*, report of the sectoral consultation, A/HRC/4/99 (6.3.2007), para. 6.

[10] IFC/IBLF *Guide*, p. 2.

[11] In very few cases have companies operating projects in developing countries commissioned an HRIA from external consultants. See for example Gare A. Smith and Bennett Freeman, 'Human rights assessment of the proposed Tangguh LNG project', presented to BP Indonesia (19 April 2002), or Goldcorp Inc. who have recently commissioned a consultancy firm to elaborate an HRIA that will be peer reviewed by the NGO International Alert, see www.hria-guatemala.com. This chapter, however, analyses not individual initiatives but proposed tools for HRIA that could be used by a wider range of companies or affected communities or are specifically geared to project finance operations.

with international human rights standards. It will be asked whether they address particular human rights concerns resulting from project finance-specific features such as the non-recourse nature that creates a heightened concern of project participants for a predictable revenue flow.

Traditional impact assessment by project finance investors

Currently, investors have access to a variety of techniques and standards to assess the non-commercial risks associated with investing in projects in developing countries. These include country- and project-level risk indicators, political risk analysis (PRA) and ESIA.[12] While country-level risk ratings are a useful tool to measure levels of market risk, the indicators they use are too broad to take into account specific human rights risks.[13] PRA measures several indicators related to the human rights situation in a country, such as the level of democracy, internal divisions along ethnic or economic lines, or public security that might be affected by violent conflict.[14] However, these indicators do not cover the human rights issues in a country comprehensively. Also, such an assessment only allows the project participants to protect themselves against some human rights risks but does not provide the same level of protection to the involuntary risk bearers, the communities affected by a project.[15] Furthermore, the risk perception of affected communities might differ significantly from that collected from official sources for PRA. Another limitation of PRA is that often it is conducted at a certain moment of the project history but not continuously monitored and adapted to the often ephemeral political landscape of developing countries. In particular in project finance transactions PRA tends to be treated as a separate activity disconnected from project cash flows rather than integrated into the wider risk assessment process. Frequently, the results of the analysis are only used to determine levels of risk but not as a management tool to actively avoid or reduce a risk.[16]

---

[12] Crossin and Banfield, 'Conflict risk', p. 11.

[13] *Ibid.*, p. 13.

[14] Standard & Poor's, *Sovereign Credit Ratings: A Primer* (2006), p. 7, available at: www.bus.ucf.edu/borde/download/KR_sovereign_APrimer_Eng.pdf (accessed: 9 November 2009).

[15] The NGO Working Group on EDC (Halifax Initiative Coalition (HIC)), 'Risk, responsibility and human rights. Taking a rights-based approach to trade and project finance' (discussion paper, final revised version, July 2004) p. 12.

[16] Crossin and Banfield, 'Conflict risk', pp. 13–14.

ESIAs are intended to predict specifically negative environmental and social impacts arising from a project and to identify ways to either avoid or mitigate these impacts. Environmental impact assessment frameworks have been developing since the 1970s and are now required for most large projects. Normally, host-state legislation requires a comprehensive written technical evaluation of likely environmental impacts conducted in advance before concessions are given or projects are allowed to proceed.[17] ESIAs additionally consider social impacts and can thereby help to prevent or reduce a significantly broader spectrum of project-related 'side effects'. They also contain mechanisms to ensure stakeholder participation in the decision-making process.[18]

Similar to host governments of corporate projects, lenders such as the IFC or private banks also require impact assessments as a precondition for financing a project; for example in the IFC Performance Standard 1 on social and environmental assessment and management systems or the Equator Principles (EP).[19] Both sets of standards establish criteria for the appraisal of a proposed project, involving the assessment of its social and environmental aspects, and of its monitoring and supervision.[20] To recall the points in Chapter 3, the IFC evaluates and categorizes projects into three categories (A, B or C) depending on the potential degree of impact and the resulting level of scrutiny to which the projects will be subject:[21] while category A projects potentially have the most significant adverse social and environmental impacts and require a full environmental impact assessment, category B project impacts are not irreversible and can be addressed by mitigation measures, and category C projects' negative effects are negligible.[22]

[17] Engineers Against Poverty (EaP), 'A systematic approach to project social risk and opportunity management' (briefing note for project managers of large infrastructure and extractive industry projects), p. 3, available at the EaP's website www.engineersagainstpoverty.org/_db/_documents/social_risk_management_briefing_note.pdf (accessed: 6 November 2009).
[18] D. Szablowski, *Transnational Law and Local Struggles: Mining, Communities and the World Bank* (Oxford and Portland, OR: Hart Publishing, 2007), pp. 49–50.
[19] See Chapter 3. IFC Performance Standards on Social and Environmental Sustainability, PS 1 on Social and Environmental Assessment and Management Systems, para. 4; available at the IFC's website (accessed: 9 November 2009); 'The Equator Principles, A financial industry benchmark for determining, assessing and managing social and environmental risk in project financing' (July 2006), Principle 2: Social and Environmental Assessment (see: www.equator-principles.com).
[20] Szablowski, *Transnational Law*, pp. 102–3.   [21] IFC PS 1.
[22] IFC Policy on Social and Environmental Sustainability (April 2006); available at the IFC's website (accessed: 9 November 2009); IFC PS 1, paras. 8–11. See also Szablowski, *Transnational Law*, p. 103.

Commensurate with the level of risks and impacts a project presents, the borrower will establish a social and environmental management system (SEMS) including an ESIA, a management programme, organizational capacity, training for employees and contractors, community engagement, monitoring of the management programme and reporting.[23] Equator Banks require an Action Plan for category A and B projects, defining actions needed to implement mitigation and monitoring measures necessary to manage the risks identified in the impact assessment.[24]

Shortcomings of traditional impact assessments

In general, the ESIAs and management systems prescribed by some governments,[25] the IFC and the Equator Banks can potentially satisfy some concerns over the protection of the environment and human rights of affected communities. However, these traditional risk assessment and management strategies aim at mitigating social and environmental risks rather than promoting and protecting human rights. They address only a limited number of directly impacted human rights such as the right to property where a project is using land previously inhabited by local residents or is operating near indigenous territory. Thereby they can miss important human rights conditions embedded in a particular society, such as restrictions on freedom of expression or collective bargaining.[26] The IFC PS and EP have been criticized for not demanding an explicit assessment of potential impacts on internationally protected human rights. Without an adequate procedural framework for conducting human rights due diligence, project sponsors will not be alerted to the full range of human rights risks their project could be facing.[27]

---

[23] IFC PS 1; EP 4.   [24] EP 4.

[25] In Australia, for example, several laws require the assessment of social and environmental impacts of projects in the field of mining and infrastructure, and India in 2008 made it mandatory for companies to conduct a social impact assessment in the case of the displacement of over 200 people. See O. Lenzen and M. d'Engelbronner, *Guide to Corporate Human Rights Impact Assessment Tools* (Utrecht 2009), p. 13.

[26] UNHCHR, Human Rights Impact Assessments Discussion Paper, prepared for UN Special Representative to the Secretary-General on business and human rights, Professor John Ruggie, Draft for Discussion 18 July 2006, paras. 5 and 6.

[27] S. Herz, K. Genovese, K. Herbertson and A. Perrault, The International Finance Corporation's Performance Standards and the Equator Principles: Respecting Human Rights and Remedying Violations?, Submission to UN Special Representative to the Secretary General on Human Rights and Transnational Corporations and other

Although current ESIAs and management systems promote engagement with interested parties to a certain extent, the implementation of
meaningful community participation in the whole process of project
management has proved to be difficult. The IFC promotes early engagement with local communities in the pre-feasibility phase of a project, in
order to cultivate proactively 'relationships that can serve as "capital"
during challenging times'.[28] It describes community engagement as
involving the company's timely disclosure of information and the 'free,
prior and informed consultation' of local communities, meaning that the
disclosed information must be relevant, understandable and accessible
for these communities.[29]

Indeed, ESIA processes in developing countries have created
opportunities for public participation in decision making and in
negotiation of conflicts regarding large private sector development
projects. However, without technical support, adequate time and
resources it is impossible for affected communities in developing
countries to engage meaningfully with the often very complex
ESIAs. It seems that in practice, the foreign companies' community
relations programmes are on the one hand often used as a tool to
gain access to a community employing sometimes culturally inadequate methods or exercising pressure. This is particularly problematic in the case of indigenous communities on their ancestral
lands being approached by companies in a culturally insensitive
way, not respecting their traditional authorities or even using
bribery.[30] On the other hand, these engagement programmes are

Business Enterprises (August 2008), pp. 11–12. HRC, *Protect, Respect and Remedy: A
Framework for Business and Human Rights*, Report of the Special Representative of the
Secretary-General on the issue of human rights and transnational corporations and
other business enterprises, John Ruggie, A/HRC/8/5 (7.4.2008), para. 61.

[28] IFC, 'Stakeholder Engagement: A Good Practice Handbook for Companies Doing
Business in Emerging Markets' (May 2007), pp. 2–6, available at the IFC's website
(accessed: 9 November 2009).

[29] IFC PS 1, paras. 19–22. EP 5.

[30] See the example of Muriel Mining Corp. explorations in Colombia on holy territory of
Embera indigenous peoples and Afro-Colombian ancestral lands with a flawed process
of consultation using signatures of leaders from communities outside the project area
and signatures obtained under pressure as well as bribing of local community for agreement
to project operations and defamation of leaders and NGOs that oppose the mining
project. See: http://justiciaypazcolombia.com/Rio-Tinto-in-Colombia-joint and the
Justicia y Paz Communiqué regarding Accusations by the Muriel Mining Corporation
Against Indigenous Peoples and Human Rights Defenders, at: http://justiciaypazcolom-
bia.com/Acusaciones-de-la-Muriel-Mining (accessed: 14 November 2009).

often defensive tactics of companies responding to human rights campaigns by NGOs and community groups in order to avoid project disruption, whether by NGO or community activities.[31]

Ineffective stakeholder relations can lead to distrust between the project company and the local population which in turn can impact negatively on the project itself. In the case of the two gold mines in Ghana[32] the destruction of local farmers' livelihoods could have been avoided if the company's resettlement and compensation plan had been elaborated in closer consultation with the affected farmers and if the company's grievance mechanism had been adequate and effective. Instead the expropriated farmers criticize the compensation as too meagre and distrust the NGO hired by the company for community relations.[33]

The corporate responsibility to respect human rights requires companies to offer an effective grievance mechanism for people whose rights were adversely affected by a project. Such grievance mechanisms may be specific to a given project or company or they may be linked to multi-stakeholder or industry initiatives.[34] The IFC has created a compliance adviser/ombudsman who can mediate in case of grievances and disputes and considers claims based upon violations of international law.[35] However, the financial institutions subscribing to the EP have not yet as a group adopted an initiative-wide grievance process.[36] The Equator Banks only require project sponsors to establish a

---

[31] M. B. Likosky, *Law, Infrastructure and Human Rights* (New York: Cambridge University Press, 2006), pp. 47f.

[32] See Part III, Chapter 14 on the Newmont and AngloGold Mining Projects in Ghana.

[33] See Chapter 14, pp. 00–0.

[34] HRC, *Protect, Respect and Remedy*, paras. 93 and 100.

[35] IFC Compliance Advisor/Ombudsman (CAO), *Operational Guidelines* (April 2007), p. 21. See for example the CAO's audit report of the IFC's investments in palm-oil production in Indonesia where the CAO found that the World Bank ignored its own environmental and social protection standards when it approved loan guarantees despite its awareness of significant environmental and social issues and risks inherent in the oil-palm sector in Indonesia. CAO, Audit Report C-I-R6-Y08-F096 (19 June 2009).

[36] HRC, *Protect, Respect and Remedy*, para. 100. Herz *et al.*, *IFC's Performance Standards*, p. 13. This has been criticized by the NGO network BankTrack in its recent submission to the OHCHR consultation on operationalizing the framework for business and human rights presented by the SRSG Prof. John Ruggie, 5–6 October: A. Missbach, Banking it Right: The 'Protect, Respect and Remedy' Framework Applied to Bank Operations, available at: www.banktrack.org/download/banktrack_submission_to_the_ohchr_consultation (accessed: 9 November 2009).

project-level grievance mechanism 'to receive and facilitate resolution of the affected communities' concerns and grievances about the
client's environmental and social performance'.[37] But they do not
require all the minimum due process standards recommended by
Prof. Ruggie, UN Special Representative on Human Rights and
Transnational Corporations. Grievance mechanisms should, for
example, be independent from project sponsors to ensure legitimacy, and not integrated into the sponsor's organizational structure.[38] It has been suggested that Equator Banks should, in addition
to requiring project-level grievance mechanisms, establish their own
system for ensuring compliance with the EP on the ground by
receiving complaints directly from affected communities. This
would enable the Equator Banks to guarantee that important environmental and social lending conditions are being met and that
activities financed by them are not causing significant adverse
impacts.[39]

Furthermore, the effectiveness of impact assessments can be threatened by a conflict between the host government's interests in economic
growth and its obligations to protect the environment and human rights.
The risks identified in an impact assessment may not be addressed
properly because the interest in obtaining an important investment
outweighs the concerns over potential social or environmental problems.
In practice, it seems that the social component of impact assessments,
including questions relating to human rights, is given a secondary role
and that its findings are often neglected;[40] the consequence of this
practice is that a category of 'slow burn' risks remains unaddressed,
meaning that they will escalate years later when it is too late for mitigation.[41] Project proponents tend to consider the impact assessment
process rather as a bureaucratic requirement to be fulfilled in order to
obtain project approval and not as an important component of the

---

[37] PS 1, para. 23 and EP 6.
[38] HRC, *Protect, Respect and Remedy*, para. 92. Herz *et al.*, *IFC's Performance Standards*,
    p. 13.
[39] Missbach, Banking it Right.   [40] Szablowski, *Transnational Law*, p. 51.
[41] T. F. Maassarani, D. Tatgenhorst and J. P. Margo, 'Extracting Corporate Responsibility:
    Towards a Human Rights Impact Assessment', *Cornell International Law Journal*,
    40 (2007), 136–69, 148, citing Donal O'Neill, 'Impact Assessments: Preventing
    Slow-Burn Issues from Bursting into Flames', *Compact Quarterly*, 2 (2005) at:
    www.enewsbuilder.net/globalcompact/e_article000375801.cfm?x=b11,0,w   (accessed:
    9 November 2009).

project planning and implementation cycle. After approval of a project, the protection and mitigation measures established through the impact assessment as conditions or recommendations for the success of the project, risk not being implemented.[42]

Moreover, ESIAs originate from the regulatory systems of the developed world and are therefore of limited applicability in developing countries. While the deficiency of not addressing the totality of impacts a project can have is compensated in developed countries by state regulatory mechanisms, the operations of project companies in the developing world are under-regulated or existing regulation is not consequently implemented. This lack of regulation could be balanced by incorporating an HRIA into the risk management process of projects operating in the developing world.[43] Using an HRIA could help a company determine the extent to which the lack of sufficient legislation or good practice in the host country might undermine or put at risk the company's international commitment to respect and protect human rights.[44]

Deficient enforcement of client compliance with ESIAs by the lenders

It seems that in practice financial institutions are under such competitive and time constraints that implementation of a thorough risk appraisal is often discouraged. This has in the past been partly due to the large amounts of liquidity in the financial system which allow lenders to keep risk assessments superficial.[45] It has been alleged that lenders have tried to circumvent the exigency of an ESIA by categorizing a project as category B or C despite the anticipated impacts justifying a higher categorization or they have overlooked a borrower's unsatisfactory impact assessments instead of insisting on an assessment that conforms to EP or IFC Performance Standards (PS).[46] In the case of the

---

[42] I. Verocai, 'Environmental and Social Impact Assessment for Large Dams: Thematic Review from the Point of View of Developing Countries' (Contributing Paper) (2000), pp. 3, 8 and 9.

[43] Maassarani et al., 'Extracting Corporate Responsibility', 149.

[44] IFC/IBLF HRIA Guide, p. 19.

[45] M. Spek, Financing Pulp Mills: An Appraisal of Risk Assessment and Safeguard Procedures (Bogor, Indonesia: CIFOR, 2006), p. 68.

[46] In November 2004, the Executive Vice President of IFC requested that CAO audit IFC's environmental categorization of the Amaggi Expansion Project in Brazil. The CAO

World Bank's financing of the palm oil industry in Indonesia, for example, an internal audit found that the IFC failed to examine the subsidiaries that source the raw materials and ignored issues such as the absence of publicly available EIAs for the subsidiary companies. Instead, the IFC let commercial pressures prevail and overly influence the categorization of the projects and the scope and scale of environmental and social due diligence.[47]

Under the current economic crisis companies and lenders are under an even stronger pressure to cut costs, promote efficiency, increase productivity and maintain strong profit returns and competitiveness. Nowadays, it may seem contrary to their mindset to dedicate time and money towards assessing social and environmental risks thoroughly. However, it is exactly the laxness in the risk assessment and the gaps in the regulation of the financial sector that have contributed to the financial crisis – the same failures that also constitute what the Special Representative John Ruggie has called the 'permissive environment for corporate wrongdoing in relation to human rights'.[48]

The IFC, the Equator Banks and export credit agencies (ECAs) still seem to lack adequate in-house capacity to effectively assess and integrate social, environmental and in particular human rights issues into their risk management processes.[49] NGOs have criticized the IFC for allegedly permitting its clients a significant degree of leeway in the application of the PS, and tolerating non-compliance as long as clients continue to improve their performance, thereby encouraging

deemed the categorization of the project to be unjustifiable in light of the failure of IFC to assure itself adequately as to the quality of the design and implementation of the project's Environmental and Social Management System (ESMS); see CAO's website (accessed: 22 October 2009). Sakhalin II project, see BankTrack, Unproven Equator Principles; a BankTrack statement, Utrecht, June 2005, p. 8; available at BankTrack's website (accessed: 22 October 2009).

[47] See the audit report of the IFC CAO, above n. 35, pp. 21f. and 30: The auditor concluded that the IFC incorrectly labelled a loan as 'Category C', because the IFC based its decision on the argument that, as a trade facility, the project would have limited or no environmental or social impacts, and thereby excluded the supply chain from its investment decision-making process.

[48] HRC, *Business and Human Rights: Towards Operationalizing the 'Protect, Respect and Remedy' Framework, Report of the Special Representative of the Secretary-General on the issue of human rights and transnational corporations and other business enterprises*, A/HRC/11/13 (22 April 2009), para. 119.

[49] Spek, *Financing Pulp Mills*, p. 55; interview with David Hunter, Asst. Professor of Law, American University Washington College of Law, Washington, DC, and Chair of the Board of Directors of the Bank Information Center (accessed: 19/20 June 2007).

unsustainable practices.[50] Although the IFC and Equator Banks have the right to take remedies such as recalling a loan in case of borrower non-compliance with standards,[51] it is questionable whether they would actually employ such a sanction as it could harm them as well.[52]

Furthermore, within public international financial institutions (PIFIs) there seem to exist perverse incentives that are an obstacle to taking a human rights-based approach to project financing. There are pressures within the World Bank to lend despite negative outcomes and built-in incentives among ECAs, the IFC and MIGA to support riskier projects because of higher insurance premiums and bonuses for employees based on the volume of transactions they make.[53] This stands in contrast with the interest PIFIs should have in mitigating their own reputational risk: as the loans or guarantees are provided specifically for a particular project, the banks or the insurers are often criticized by NGOs or activists for supporting a project that has become controversial or has led to violent conflict or human rights abuses.[54]

Added value of HRIA to project finance

An HRIA distinguishes itself from a traditional ESIA by broadening its scope of analysis, going further than the existing narrow economic criteria on which projects are assessed and rooting the assessment process in international human rights standards such as the Universal Declaration of Human Rights (UDHR), the International Covenants on Civil and Political Rights (ICCPR) and on Economic, Social and Cultural Rights (ICESCR). Taking a human rights-based approach, HRIAs identify rights-holders and duty-bearers[55] and have the added value of not only assessing facts but also perceptions of being wronged that are generated by the concept of rights

---

[50] Halifax Initiative Coalition [HIC] (ed.), *One Step Forward, One Step Back: An Analysis of the International Finance Corporation's Sustainability Policy, Performance Standards and Disclosure Policy* (May 2006), pp. 1 and 7.

[51] EP 8; IFC Policy on Social Environmental Sustainability, para. 26.

[52] Spek, *Financing Pulp Mills*, p. 68.

[53] HIC, 'Risk, responsibility and human rights', p. 13.

[54] International Alert, *Conflict-Sensitive Project Finance: Better Lending Practice in Conflict-Prone States* (September 2006), pp. 4–9.

[55] O. Lenzen and M. d'Engelbronner, *Guide to Corporate Human Rights Impact Assessment Tools* (Utrecht: Drukkerij Libertas, 2009), p. 9.

itself.[56] An HRIA provides an integrated assessment identifying the impact on and measuring the fulfilment of the whole range of interdependent and interrelated human rights rather than only some specific rights that at first sight may be directly affected by the proposed project activity.[57] This should include the human right to a healthy environment as well as accounting for the impacts of project activities on corruption as this often falls within the corporate sphere of influence.[58] An HRIA and management plan leads to the integration into company management plans of measures to respect, protect and fulfil the human rights guaranteed to all rights-holders.[59]

According to the human rights-based approach there should be no trade-off between human rights and investors' needs or development goals of a host country. The fact that the benefits and the negative impacts of a project or investment are often not distributed equally among the different interested parties can be balanced out by conducting an effective HRIA and addressing its findings in a spirit of non-discrimination.[60] Project development should focus on equity, participation of affected communities, and the sharing of costs and benefits.[61] This is particularly true for project finance schemes, because project sponsors, as opposed to some other multinationals, act as 'agents of development' in developing countries; they typically create infrastructure and industrial units on which other businesses depend, the tenders they bid for name development goals, and the IFIs they deal with are development banks.[62]

---

[56] Nomogaia Foundation, A Methodology for Human Rights Impact Assessment, Draft Version, Phase 2, Step 7: Rightsholder Engagement, p. 23. See: www.nomogaia.org/HRIA/Entries/2010/9/23_A_Methodology_for__Human_Rights_Impact_Assessment_2.html (accessed: 9 November 2009).

[57] UNHCHR HRIA, Human Rights Impact Assessments, para. 8; HIC, 'Risk, responsibility and human rights', p. 16f.

[58] Maassarani, Extracting Corporate Responsibility, p. 152.

[59] UNHCHR HRIA, Human Rights Impact Assessments, para. 8; HIC, 'Risk, responsibility and human rights', pp. 16f.

[60] Lenzen and d'Engelbronner, Guide, p. 17.

[61] HIC, 'Risk, responsibility and human rights', p. 17.

[62] T. Sorell, 'Project Financing in Developing Countries, New Corporate Social Responsibility, Human Rights, and Multinationals', Essex Human Rights Review, 51 (2008), 7.

The traditional ESIA's shortcomings with regard to the consultation of affected communities, as discussed above (pp. 179–83), are exacerbated in project finance by the risk allocation process between the different project participants. In principle, risk should be allocated to the party that wants to or can best control the occurrence of the risk.[63] In practice, however, risk tends to be allocated on the basis of the commercial and negotiating strength of project participants. Delmon suggests that 'the stronger party will allocate risk that it does not want to bear to the weaker party'.[64] As argued by Sheldon Leader in Chapter 5, it is the outcome of these negotiations, influenced by competing risk management objectives and unequal bargaining powers, which leads to the rise or fall of risks borne by third parties such as the local population. However, as affected communities are not party to these negotiations, their voice is not heard enough in the process of risk allocation.[65]

The influence that third parties can take over the risks they have to bear is further restrained by the international investment protection framework consisting of host government agreements, bilateral investment treaties, etc. The internationalization of contracts between a project company and the host government removes the foreign investment transaction from the sphere of the host country's law.[66] Stabilization clauses contained in these contracts, predominantly in those between investors and non-OECD countries, can either insulate investors from having to implement new environmental and social laws or provide investors with an opportunity to be compensated for compliance with such laws.[67] As a consequence, host states are deterred from implementing new and more progressive human rights or environmental legislation in fulfilment of their international obligations.[68] Thereby

[63] Scott L. Hoffman, *The Law and Business of International Project Finance* (2nd edn, The Hague: Kluwer Law International, 2001), p. 45.
[64] J. Delmon, *Project Finance, BOT Projects and Risk* (The Hague: Kluwer Law International, 2005), p. 125. Hoffman, *Law and Business*, p. 37.
[65] Chapter 5, pp. 115ff.
[66] M. Sornarajah, *The International Law on Foreign Investment* (2nd edn, Cambridge University Press, 2004), pp. 407–17.
[67] UN Special Representative of the Secretary-General on Business and Human Rights, *Stabilization Clauses and Human Rights*, a joint research project conducted with IFC, May 2009; available at the IFC's website (accessed: 1 November 2009).
[68] Amnesty International, *Contracting Out of Human Rights: The Chad–Cameroon Pipeline Project* (London, 2005), available at AI's website (accessed: 24 October 2008), pp. 21–2.

these agreements stabilize the investment climate but at the same time curtail the power of the domestic judiciary to enforce human rights,[69] and frustrate the right of victims of corporate abuses to an effective judicial remedy.[70]

This imbalance between the protection of private investors' interests and those of affected individuals and communities could be mitigated by the implementation of an HRIA. An HRIA would promote a consequent consultation and participation of all stakeholders from the pre-feasibility stage on and the inclusion of their concerns into project agreements and management plans.[71] An HRIA aims at ensuring a transparent decision-making process inclusive of affected communities and civil society, through participatory risk analysis that draws on the perspectives and needs of those living in areas affected by a project. Such an assessment takes a more people-centred perspective than the purely technical and financial cost–benefit analysis. Furthermore, it can contribute to risk mitigation, in particular in conflict settings, as shared decision-making furthers trust, relieves tensions and creates a sense of ownership in the project for all stakeholders, including local communities. It also enables a company to address the risk of potential allegations of human rights violations.[72]

Implementing an HRIA could prevent project participants from considering effects of their projects on local communities merely as 'negative externalities', thereby marginalizing third-party interests and painting

[69] R. Bachand and S. Rousseau, *International Investment and Human Rights: Political and Legal Issues, A Background Paper* (Montreal: Rights and Democracy, 2003), pp. 29f.

[70] UDHR Article 8: Right to an effective remedy. AI, *Contracting Out of Human Rights*, pp. 24 and 34f.

[71] According to Prof. Ruggie's report, HRIAs could also examine whether human rights protection clauses have been adequately built into HGAs and other investment contracts. Human Rights Council, *Report of the Special Representative of the Secretary-General on the issue of human rights and transnational corporations and other business enterprises, Human rights impact assessments – resolving key methodological questions*, A/HRC/4/74 (5 February 2007), para. 24. HIC, 'Risk, responsibility and human rights', pp. 19f.

[72] Crossin and Banfield, 'Conflict Risk', pp. 18–19. HIC, 'Risk, responsibility and human rights', p. 19. IFC/IBLF *Guide*, pp. viii and 6. M. Drakos, T. Maassarani and R. J. Tarek, Evidentiary submission re: Human Rights Impact Assessment to the Joint Committee on Human Rights of the House of Commons of the UK (1 May 2009), Principle 5. See: http://198.170.85.29/Drakos-Maassarani-Radon-submission-to-UK-Joint-Committee-1-May-2009.pdf (accessed: 10 November 2009).

them as being of secondary importance.[73] Greater knowledge of the risks a project might face can present a possibility for project lenders and insurers to lower the risk–reward trade-offs they have to make when deciding whether to support a project.[74] Also, to conduct this forecast of potential problems surrounding a project's impact prior to production can serve as a kind of insurance system and prevent higher costs and inefficiency of problem-solving once production is under way.[75] An HRIA can lead to improved decision making by projects, consistent with international standards and based on informed participation and empowerment of the affected communities. What is more, HRIA could even promote the beneficial impacts of a project on the fulfilment of human rights in the host country. It would contribute to the raising of human rights awareness, the identification of good business practices and policies in furtherance of human rights and sustainable economic development.[76]

In light of these realizations and because of the growing awareness of business and human rights issues in general, the call for HRIAs for companies and projects has become louder. The implementing provisions of the UN Norms on the Responsibilities of Transnational Corporations and Other Business Enterprises with Regard to Human Rights state that companies should conduct periodic evaluations of their impact on human rights.[77] Subsequently, the OHCHR recommended that tools should be developed to 'assist businesses in implementing their responsibilities, in particular through the development of … methodologies for undertaking human rights impact assessments'.[78] Until today, several organizations have developed frameworks for HRIAs for private sector projects.[79] These new HRIA tools are still in a road-testing

---

[73] Carl S. Bjerre, 'Project Finance and Consent', in Michael B. Likosky (ed.), *Privatising Development: Transnational Law, Infrastructure and Human Rights* (Leiden: Martinus Nijhoff Publishers, 2005), p. 436.

[74] Crossin and Banfield, 'Conflict risk', pp. 18–19. HIC, 'Risk, responsibility and human rights', p. 19. IFC/IBLF, *Guide*, pp. viii and 6.

[75] Drakos *et al.*, Principle 3.   [76] Maassarani, *Extracting Corporate Responsibility*, p. 152.

[77] Commission on Human Rights, *Norms on the responsibilities of transnational corporations and other business enterprises with regard to human rights*, UN Doc. E/CN/Sub.2/ 2003/12/Rev.2 (26 August 2003).

[78] Commission on Human Rights, *Report of the United Nations High Commissioner on Human Rights on the responsibilities of transnational corporations and related business enterprises with regard to human rights*, E/CN.4/2005/91 (15 February 2005).

[79] UNHCHR, HRIA Discussion Paper, paras. 6 and 7. For a list of recent initiatives, see paras. 20–2 of this discussion paper or IFC/IBLF, *Guide* p. 7.

phase and the assessment of their practical implementations for companies and financial institutions is still ongoing.[80] As the development of international legislation in the field of human rights and business is still lagging behind, HRIAs have the potential to become the leading tool for companies to assume their responsibility in human rights issues. Furthermore, the recent financial and credit crisis may have the positive effect that public and private financial institutions will hold their clients more accountable not only in the economic areas but also in regard to their human rights performance. Requiring borrowers to perform an HRIA could be the perfect tool for this purpose.[81]

New developments in HRIA and how they relate to project finance

In the following, the question will be asked how far the recently developed HRIA tools that may be used in the future by project finance participants have integrated human rights concerns resulting from project finance practices and to what extent these proposed HRIAs are compatible with project finance strategies. After a short general presentation of these new tools and the current debate around HRIAs, the analysis will focus on project finance-specific features such as their non-recourse nature and the resulting heightened concern of project participants for a predictable revenue flow. As a consequence of this concern for a steady cash flow, project participants aim at stabilizing the legal and political environment of the project and push for an early start of project operations and revenue generation. This in turn can lead to time and financial pressures on constructors, insufficient stakeholder consultation and a general preference to postpone the solution of social or environmental problems until revenue has started to flow. At this stage, however, human rights issues or environmental damage cannot be prevented or mitigated anymore and the only remaining option is compensation. The following analysis will show how the new HRIA tools take into account these project finance-specific characteristics and respond to the potential threat they pose to human rights.

---

[80] UNHCHR, *Human rights and the financial sector*, para. 63.
[81] Lenzen and d'Engelbronner, *Guide*, pp. 12 and 40.

Proposals for HRIA and their communalities

Current HRIA tools and reports have emerged from the established practice of ESIA and pull together the best practices from these areas. As will be shown, HRIAs risk facing similar deficiencies and problems of implementation in project finance transactions as ESIA. However, they also present an opportunity to take an approach to project finance that is more focused on the particularities of human rights demands.

Various HRIA tools that are complementary in that they focus on different needs and audiences have been developed by international organizations, NGOs, think-tanks or industry groups. A small number of individual companies have privately commissioned an HRIA for specific projects.[82] Although the following analysis is based on a broad spectrum of recent developments in the HRIA sector, it focuses on a few particular tools and reports that are designed to be used by a group of companies or stakeholders and have either a particular focus on project finance investments or take a unique perspective (Rights & Democracy). The most important tool currently available for project financing is the IFC and International Business Leaders Forum (IBLF) joint HRIA and Management Guide, which was sent on a road-testing phase in 2007 and which is currently coming to an end.[83] Other HRIA tools that are geared towards project finance investments include the HRIA model developed by the Halifax Initiative Coalition's Working Group on EDC (the Canadian export credit agency) in 2004 based on the 'best practices' existing at that time;[84] in the subcategory of conflict-risk assessment International Alert and IISD lead the conflict-sensitive business practice process.[85] Rights & Democracy has developed an HRIA tool which, although designed for the use of affected communities, contains an assessment questionnaire that points to some human rights issues relevant to the project finance context.[86] At the beginning of 2009,

---

[82] See above n. 11.

[83] IFC/IBLF, *Guide*, For the details of the the the revised version of the *Guide*, see above n. 6.

[84] HIC, 'Risk, responsibility and human rights'.

[85] International Alert, see: www.international-alert.org/peace_and_economy/index.php?t=1 (accessed: 10 November 2009); International Institute for Sustainable Development: www.iisd.org/security/business/conflict.asp. (accessed: 10 November 2009).

[86] Rights & Democracy, Investing in Human Rights: A Three Volume Initiative. Volume I: *Human Rights Impact Assessments for Foreign Investment Projects: Learning from community experiences in the Philippines, Tibet, the Democratic Republic of Congo, Argentina, and Peru* (2007); Volume II: *Getting it Right: A step-by-step guide to assess the impact of foreign investment on human rights* (2008); and Volume III: *Human Rights and Bilateral Investment Treaties: Mapping the role of human rights law within*

Aim for Human Rights published a Guide to Corporate Human Rights
Impact Assessment Tools in which it summarizes most of the currently
available options.[87]

These HRIA tools have various common features. The methodology
they propose for the assessment and management of human rights issues
surrounding a project is divided into several steps.[88] In most HRIA
proposals these steps are similar while the order of the steps might
vary slightly. First, the need for an assessment and its scope should be
determined. Business sector-specific standards or categorizations such as
those used by the IFC may serve as criteria.[89] The context of the host
country, the project and the relevant stakeholders must be identified.[90]
Before assessing human rights impacts, a baseline report should set the
current human rights situation against which the impacts of the project
can be measured.[91] At this stage at the latest, consultation with potentially affected communities will become crucial; several HRIA proposals
recommend including risk-bearers from the very outset of the assessment process.[92]

Having set the baseline, the expected human rights impacts of the
project can now be assessed. For some proposed HRIA tools this represents a more participatory process inclusive of interested parties than for
others. The HRIA should analyse comprehensively the possible options
for a project and propose the most 'human rights friendly' alternative to
the project management. The Halifax Initiative suggests doing an
options assessment *before* the impact assessment and in collaboration
with the affected communities.[93] A recent article in *International Affairs
Review*[94] proposes that HRIA should assess the equity of a project's

---

investor-state Arbitration (2009). See: www.dd-rd.ca/site/publications/index.php?
   id=2094&subsection=eatalogue (accessed: 10 November 2009).
[87] Lenzen and d'Engelbronner, *Guide*.
[88] *Ibid.*, p. 36.   [89] IFC/IBLF HRIA, *Guide*.
[90] Nomogaia Foundation, pp. 16f. *Methodology*, HRC, *Protect, Respect and Remedy*, para. 61.
[91] Business Leaders Initiative on Human Rights Ltd (BLIHRL), *Guide for Integrating
    Human Rights into Business Management*, 2nd edn, Processes and Procedures Step 1,
    at: http://blihr.zingstudios.com/home (accessed: 25 October 2009). Aim for Human
    Rights' Human Rights Impact Resource Centre (HRIRC), Eight Step Approach to
    HRIA, Step 1, at: www.humanrightsimpact.org/hria-guide/steps/step/resources/view/
    8/user_hria_homapproachstep/ (accessed: 1 November 2009).
[92] IFC/IBLF, *Guide*. Drakos *et al.*, Principle 2.
[93] HIC, 'Risk, responsibility and human rights: taking a rights-based approach to trade and
    project finance', discussion paper prepared by the NGO Working Group on EDC
    (Ottawa, 2004), p. 21.
[94] M. Tatgenhorst Drakos, 'The Corporate Human Rights Impact Assessment: Top-Down
    and Bottom-Up', *International Affairs Review*, 18(1) (2009).

impacts, determine its positive and negative impacts and any potential unbalanced distributions between communities to avoid retaliations by disenfranchised groups. All findings of the HRIA should be made available to stakeholders and integrated into corporate decision making and the company's due diligence process; they should be institutionalized throughout the corporate management structure, for example integrating them into a human rights management plan (HRMP) that defines the mitigation measures to address the identified risks and impacts.[95] Closing the project cycle, the implementation of this HRMP has to be monitored and evaluated to ensure that lessons learned can be used in the formulation of future policies and projects.[96] Regular updating of HRIA with follow-up compliance assessments is necessary as the human rights situation around a project evolves and to ensure continuous improvement of a project's human rights performance.[97]

Assessment of the impact of investment protection agreements

Due to the non-recourse nature of project finance where the repayment of a loan is not backed by a strong asset base but relies exclusively on the revenue stream from the project, investors are more concerned about the predictability and stability of this revenue flow than in corporate finance. As was mentioned above, this concern for stability is the driver behind project finance strategies to secure regulatory stability in investment agreements with host governments via stabilization and arbitration clauses. These provisions can have a chilling effect on good faith government changes in policy to fulfil human rights obligations and result in a lack of protection of people affected by a project. Host government agreements are taken out of the state's jurisdiction and disputes are subject to private arbitration only. Project sponsors can thereby increase their leverage over host governments and obtain favourable conditions for their investments such as tax cuts or lower workers protection standards in the project area.[98] This stands in contrast with the corporate

[95] *Ibid.* The article enumerates seven cross-cutting basic principles that should guide the corporate HRIA; this section corresponds to principles 4, 5 and 6. The arguments exposed in this article have been submitted to the UK House of Commons in Drakos *et al.*, Evidentiary submission, above n. 72.
[96] BLIHRL, Eight Step Approach to HRIA, Steps 7 and 8.
[97] IFC/IBLF, *Guide*, p. 12. Drakos *et al.*, Principles 7. Nomogaia Foundation, *Methodology*, p. 30. HRC, *Protect, Respect and Remedy*, paras. 62 and 63.
[98] AI, *Contracting Out of Human Rights*, pp. 28–31 and 34–5.

responsibility to respect human rights 'as companies should ensure the agreements they negotiate will not interfere with the enjoyment of rights and the state's ability to protect against abuse'.[99]

Nevertheless, most HRIA tools do not address human rights issues resulting from these investment protection agreements. Rights & Democracy, however, has taken up this issue indirectly in isolated points of its questionnaire for community HRIAs. It asks for example whether national laws on occupational health and safety have been recently changed to the benefit of the project.[100] In order to analyse the impact of a project in more detail, the question could be amended to ask whether a special regime for the project was established and whether it weakened or strengthened health and safety laws. The questionnaire also asks about the legal remedies for victims of industrial accidents. This points to the important issue of legal standing of victims of human rights abuses by the project. In that regard, the IFC/IBLF HRIA Guide recommends that companies should not interfere with potential victims' access to local judicial mechanisms.[101] However, if this recommendation is taken seriously, then one could argue that obstructing access to the judiciary and to the protection from new human rights legislation for local residents should be avoided from the outset by not integrating over-restrictive stabilization clauses in the investment contracts.

After piloting its questionnaire in several countries, Rights & Democracy found in its report that the HRIA methodology should include an analysis of the role played by the company's home state in promoting the investment through trade and investment facilitation services and negotiation of bilateral and other investment treaties.[102] Certainly, this would be helpful in order to gain clarity over the effect the contractual framework of a project finance has or will have on the human rights situation in a host country before even the impacts of the project's operations are assessed. Thus, an HRIA could reveal the tension points between the project finance stabilizing requirement and a state's obligation to implement international human rights treaties and its citizens' right to a remedy for human rights violations; it could furthermore

---

[99] UN Special Representative of the Secretary-General on Business and Human Rights, *Stabilization Clauses*, Annex 1, p. 3.

[100] Rights & Democracy, Draft Research Guide, pp. 28f.

[101] IFC/IBLF, *Guide*, p. 55.

[102] International Centre for Human Rights and Democratic Development, *Human Rights Impact Assessments for Foreign Investment Projects* (Quebec, Legal Deposit, 2007), p. 25.

recommend to the project management investment contract clauses that balance out the requirements of stabilization and international human rights obligations. The UN High Commissioner for Human Rights stated that when balancing investors' rights with individual rights, state human rights obligations or the protection of the environment, the conditional nature of investors' rights which are defined in order to meet some wider goal, such as sustainable human development, has to be taken into account.[103] By including an analysis on the impact of investment protection agreements, the HRIA would contribute to a human rights-based approach to development in host countries ensuring that the realization of one right is not favoured over another.

At what commercial price avoidance of human rights violations?

The traditional approach of the investment community to managing threats to third parties' human rights is risk based;[104] from that perspective the materialization of a risk represents a cost that is weighed against the benefits of the project: only if the cost of post-violation compensation outweighs the cost of prevention might the latter be an option.[105] This is contrary to the rights-based approach[106] adopted by the human rights community. From a human rights point of view the priority is to *avoid* any human rights violation or environmental degradation from the outset of a project.[107] If damage is not avoidable, then measures to minimize damages should be taken and compensation must be provided for the victims.[108]

The IFC PS and its HRIA Guide clearly take such a preventive approach to risk management, favouring measures that avoid and

---

[103] Commission on Human Rights, *Human Rights, Trade and Investment*, E/CN.4/Sub.2/2003/9 (2 July 2003), para. 37.

[104] Compare with the discussion in UNHCHR, *Human rights and the financial sector*, para. 22.

[105] Compare with issues of compensation over avoidance in Leader, Chapter 5.

[106] A Human Rights Based Approach (HRBA) is used for example by development agencies such as the United Nations Development Programme and it stresses the primacy of international human rights instruments. According to Professor Ruggie two elements of the HRBA could prove useful in HRIA for business: (a) using international human rights law as a guiding principle; and (b) a discussion of rights-holders and duty-bearers. HRC, A/HRC/4/74 (5.2.2007), para. 27.

[107] UNHCHR, HRIAs Discussion Paper, para. 3. HRC, *Protect, Respect and Remedy*, para. 23f.

[108] The IFC PS adopt the same list of priorities in the Objectives of PS 1.

prevent negative impacts over measures for compensation of damage.[109] However, the IFC PS also limit the requirement to avoid risk to situations where it is 'technically and financially feasible'.[110] By conditioning risk management measures on these criteria, the IFC recognizes the legitimacy of commercial boundaries to the fulfilment of human rights. Thereby it shows flexibility to adapt its standards to the requirements of project finance. As was highlighted in Chapter 5, this leeway given to project managements by the IFC could be misused to interpret the provisions of the Guide as allowing them to prioritize in some cases their interest in the profitability of the project over avoidance of human rights violations. This could be a particular risk with project companies which are often thinly resourced in terms of reserve funds for unforeseen events. Having to invest large sums in environmental and human rights risk avoidance before the project company has even started to generate revenue flow can easily be considered financially 'non-viable' by the borrower.[111]

Similarly, the IFC/IBLF HRIA Guide only urges a company to 'choose the most effective option to address human rights issues over which it has *direct control*' (emphasis added); where the company has only indirect control the IFC allows the choice of options to be limited by lack of resources and expertise, a negative response of business partners, and the lack of supportive international or local conditions.[112] The IFC does not seem to count the host government as under the direct control of a foreign project. Although the Guide suggests that 'in those areas where it does not have direct control, a company will need to assess the level of influence that it can exercise on the behaviour of others',[113] the project might escape assessment regarding a large part of its influence over decisions that have consequences for human rights, such as contracts with the host government, joint projects in stakeholder engagement, or changes in national law and exemptions for the project. According to Professor Ruggie's 2009 report, thus, any risk, whether it is controllable or not, merits a similar level of due diligence, because all human rights challenges and impacts of a project can pose material risks to the company and its stakeholders.[114]

---

[109] IFC PS 1, Objectives, above n. 19. IFC/IBLF, *Guide to HRIA*, above n. 6, p. 2.
[110] IFC PS 1, para. 14. See analysis by Leader in Chapter 5.
[111] Leader, Chapter 5, pp. 110ff.   [112] IFC/IBLF, *Guide*, p. 48.
[113] *Ibid.*, p. 3.   [114] HRC, *Business and Human Rights*, para. 51.

As opposed to the IFC standards, other HRIA tools leave less room for compromise and take more clearly a human rights-based approach. The Halifax proposal, for example, requires a preliminary 'Comprehensive Options Assessment' for every project, placing equal weight on social, environmental, technical and economic factors. This process should review alternatives to the proposed project site, technology, design and operation that might improve the respect, protection and fulfilment of the rights of the affected community.[115] The IFC/IBLF HRIA Guide also suggests that during the actual impact assessment stage operative alternatives to eliminate or otherwise address each identified human rights challenge should be assessed. In order to identify the most effective and acceptable alternative, consultation with affected stakeholders is advisable. The IFC/IBLF Guide states that a company's existing human rights policies and commitments will determine what non-negotiable issues are and guide the choice of alternatives. There is, however, no reference to international human rights law here and a minimum standard for such company human rights policies is not specified. The Guide suggests that a company 'may well find that the preferred human rights approach is also the best financial, environmental or social approach'.[116] However, here again, in order to avoid human rights violations, more resources would have to be invested in the HRIA process allowing for a meaningful choice between different project options and the participation of affected communities in the decision-making process.

According to Professor Ruggie's report on HRIA 'a medium-sized enterprise should not be expected to allocate the same amount of funding and staff time to an HRIA as a multinational'.[117] It is arguable that the criterion should be the human rights footprint of a project rather than the size of the project company. Otherwise special purpose vehicles (SPVs) will escape strict requirements due to their low reserves, although their sponsors may be large multinational companies (MNCs) that could well afford an extensive and costly HRIA and management programme. Several HRIA tools and business and human rights guides thus recommend that the level of detail and complexity of a management programme, the priority of the identified measures and actions and the resources allocated for it should be 'commensurate with the project's risks and impacts'.[118]

---

[115] 'Risk, responsibility and human rights', p. 21.
[116] IFC/IBLF, *Guide*, p. 46.   [117] HRC, *HRIAs*, para. 38.
[118] 'Risk, responsibility and human rights', p. 20. IFC PS 1, para. 14. BLIHRL, *Guide*, Processes and Procedures Step 3.

Financial and time constraints during project construction vs.
contractor compliance with human rights standards

Contractors of projects can bring with them a range of particular human
rights challenges such as poor health and safety standards for workers,
disruption of the local community and its infrastructure and services,
and the use of substandard materials in construction. On the other hand,
hiring local labour and local subcontractors can cement relationships
with important local stakeholders.[119] The heightened concern in project
finance for predictable revenue flow puts contractors under pressure to
finish the construction of a project early because the other parties want to
begin project operation as soon as possible to maximize revenue and
improve return on investment. The construction contractor bears the
risk of timely completion; sanctions will be imposed for failure reflecting
the losses the project company will incur.[120] This pressure on the constructor, pushed by bonuses offered for early completion, can lead a
constructor to neglect for example standards for environmental protection resulting in health hazards for the local residents. During the
construction of several oil pipelines in Chad and Cameroon, respiratory
diseases were caused by dust pollution from heavy vehicles passing
through populated areas.[121] Furthermore, victims claiming compensation for environmental damage or human rights violations committed by
the project, risk not receiving anything due to the non-recourse nature of
project finance and the back-to-back risk allocation away from the SPV
towards subcontractors which may have even less resources to cover
extra costs than the SPV.[122]

An HRIA will therefore need to consider the particular practices and
challenges of contractors engaged in the project, since any of their
human rights issues will reflect on the project's outcome. It is recommended that contractors follow qualification process and include guidelines for suppliers and contractual agreements with customers and
suppliers to ensure that risks are minimized, managed or eliminated,
and opportunities are maximized.[123] The IFC advises companies to
extend the wordings of their bidding documents for contractors involved

[119] IFC/IBLF, *Guide*, pp. 28f.   [120] Delmon, *Project Finance*, p. 131.
[121] Leader, Chapter 5, p. 128. K. Horta and Environmental Defense, *The Chad/Cameroon
Oil and Pipeline Project – Reaching a Critical Milestone* (January 2003). See: www.wrm.
org.uy/countries/Cameroon/Horta.html (accessed: 11 November 2009).
[122] Leader, Chapter 5, pp. 130–1, 135.
[123] BLIHRL, *Guide*, Processes and Procedures Step 4.

in construction, operation and decommissioning to 'reflect the companies' full human rights requirements'.[124] It is argued here that such a provision should be based on applicable international human rights law rather than on companies' norms that might be too varied and might not reflect the newest standards. The IFC/IBLF Guide continues that 'where necessary, sharing information, guidance, training and technology, as well as including incentives, will contribute to managing the project risks'.[125] Contrary to current project finance practices, the time pressure on construction contractors should thus rather be diminished and not increased by bonuses offered for early completion. An HRIA tool should therefore include specific questions assessing the contractual conditions beneficial or detrimental to the respect of human rights and the environment by contractors. This would further reveal the pressure points between project finance time and financial constraints on contractors and their margin to respect and protect human rights and the environment. The HRIA team could thereby give more detailed and informed recommendations to the project management regarding the integration of environmental and human rights concerns in construction contracts.

The IFC/IBLF Guide acknowledges that despite continuing debate about how far a company's responsibility should reach down the supply chain it is generally accepted that a high degree of responsibility lies with the principal company. It recommends that the project management should control compliance of contractors and suppliers with its human rights policies. Where direct control is not possible it should provide training to contractors and monitor their performance in order to manage the project risks better.[126] Thereby it seems to suggest that an SPV or even the sponsors could be held accountable for a contractor's human rights performance and that, as a minimum, the perception of the project will be directly affected by the contractors' activities. Apart from constituting a risk of liability, human rights violations by contractors could be considered as a product flaw and a quality control issue. Human rights management plans should therefore require that compliance with human rights be mandatory in all contracts and provide for penalties against abusive contractors.[127]

---

[124] IFC/IBLF, *Guide*, pp. 28f.   [125] *Ibid.*

[126] Evidentiary submission, above n. 72, Drakos *et al.* recommend that staff should be trained and management protocols designed to allow for supervision of contractors in order to avoid or mitigate risks identified in the HRIA, Principle 5.

[127] Interview with Peter Frankental, Economic Relations and Human Rights, Amnesty International, 3 March 2008.

Improved stakeholder consultation and participation

Recently developed HRIAs highlight the need to strengthen the involvement of rights-holders and risk-bearers into assessment and decision-making processes of a project. The IFC/IBLF HRIA Guide emphasizes stakeholder consultation, for example with local community leaders, and the use of local sources such as other organizations operating in the area in order to accumulate the information necessary for the baseline survey and the HRIA.[128] It gives detailed recommendations on how to engage with interested parties explaining requirements for effective consultation with different groups such as employees, vulnerable members of the local community, NGOs and other knowledgeable parties. If in-house knowledge on human rights issues is not available, in particular in case of sensitive issues, the IFC recommends resorting to external expertise.[129]

The Halifax Initiative Coalition takes consultation standards even further and would like to see the affected communities involved in the pre-feasibility stage and to design a decision-making process that is more participatory. Before carrying out the actual HRIA they recommend conducting a preliminary and comprehensive assessment of alternatives for a project with the participation of affected communities. Agreements on alternatives negotiated between the project sponsor and the people would become part of the project framework.[130] However, the fact that companies often try to secure the rights to an area before engaging with communities currently contradicts early participation of rights-holders.[131]

With regard to indigenous and tribal peoples directly affected by a project, the ILO Convention 169 on Indigenous and Tribal Peoples requires from signatory states that they lead good faith consultations 'with the peoples concerned, through appropriate procedures and in particular through their representative institutions',[132] and 'with the *objective of achieving agreement or consent* to the proposed measures'

---

[128] IFC/IBLF, *Guide*, p. 33.
[129] *Ibid.*, pp. 41–4. In addition, the IFC Stakeholder Engagement Handbook gives further guidance on this.
[130] HIC, 'Risk, responsibility and human rights', p. 21.
[131] HIC, *Risk, Responsibility and Human Rights: Assessing the Human Rights Impacts of Trade and Project Finance*, Final Report (2004), p. 25.
[132] Convention (No. 169) concerning Indigenous and Tribal Peoples in Independent Countries, adopted on 27 June 1989 by the General Conference of the International Labour Organization (ILO) at its 26th session, Article 6(1a).

(emphasis added).[133] Environmental, social, spiritual or cultural impact assessments of planned development projects should be 'carried out, in co-operation with the peoples concerned'.[134] The language used in the UN Declaration on the Rights of Indigenous Peoples – free prior and informed *consent* – suggests that consultations with indigenous communities should have the nature of negotiations towards mutually acceptable arrangements prior to decisions over proposed measures.[135] In their General Comments the CERD and CESCR Committees have also repeatedly recommended that governments seek the 'informed consent' of indigenous peoples on resource exploitation projects affecting them.[136]

While these legal instruments establish responsibilities of states, it is increasingly expected that private sector companies follow these norms within their respective spheres of influence and do not interfere with states' obligations under international law.[137] The IFC PS 7 requires that IFC clients will conduct free, prior and informed *consultation* with indigenous peoples and seek their *informed participation*,[138] in a process that leads 'to broad community support for the project'.[139] The IFC/IBLF HRIA Guide, on the other hand, seems to interpret the ILO Convention 169 as saying that 'the convention ... requires consultation with representatives of indigenous peoples in a way that *gives them a voice* in the design, implementation and evaluation of ... the project' (emphasis

[133] ILO Convention 169, Article 6(2).   [134] *Ibid.* Article 7(3).
[135] Declaration on the Rights of Indigenous Peoples, Articles 19 and 32 Paragraph 2, A/61/L.67 (7 September 2007). The HIC supports the concept of free prior and informed consent and suggests consent be sought at the preparatory stage of a project via a consultation and participation plan for the feasibility study. See HIC, 'Risk, responsibility and human rights', pp. 19f.
[136] Concluding Observations of the Committee on the Elimination of Racial Discrimination: Ecuador, CERD/C/62/CO/2, 21/03/2003, para. 16. Concluding Observations of the Committee on the Elimination of Racial Discrimination: Guatemala, CERD/C/GTM/CO/11, 15/05/2006, para. 19. Concluding Observations of the Committee on the Elimination of Racial Discrimination: Guyana, CERD/C/GUY/CO/14, 04/04/2006, paras. 14 and 19. Concluding Observations of the Committee on Economic, Social and Cultural Rights: Colombia, E/C.12/Add.1/74, 30/11/2001, paras. 12 and 33. Concluding Observations of the Committee on Economic, Social and Cultural Rights: Ecuador, E/C.12/1/Add.100, 07/06/2004, para. 35.
[137] HRC, *Report of the Special Rapporteur on the situation of human rights and fundamental freedoms of indigenous people*, James Anaya, A/HRC/12/34 (15.7.2009), para. 56.
[138] IFC PS 7, para. 9.
[139] IFC PS 7, Guidance Note 7 Indigenous Peoples (31 July 2007), G19, available at the IFC's website (accessed: 11 November 2009).

added).[140] This would suggest that the IFC's standard of consultation is watered down compared to the one prescribed by international human rights law. However, for high-risk projects such as extractive and agro-industrial projects and probably most projects likely to affect indigenous peoples on their traditional lands, the IFC requires good faith negotiations with a 'successful outcome' including a memorandum of understanding or joint statement which cannot mean anything else than some form of agreement.[141]

The Special Rapporteur on the situation of human rights and fundamental freedoms of indigenous peoples, James Anaya, states that the right to free, prior and informed consent should not be interpreted as giving indigenous peoples a veto power over decisions that may affect them, but rather as 'establishing consent as the objective of consultations with indigenous peoples'.[142] The importance of achieving consent necessarily depends on the circumstances and the indigenous interests involved. Private companies should endeavour to always make their activities conform to international law on the rights of indigenous peoples. However, the state responsibility to consult with indigenous peoples concerned cannot be avoided by delegating it to a private company. Consultations on development activities affecting indigenous peoples should take place as early as possible and before concessions to private companies are granted.[143] The main goal of consultations between governments, companies and affected communities should be to avoid the imposition of the will of one party over another and instead work towards reaching a consensus through negotiations in which imbalances of power are overcome.[144]

Taking measures to promote the effective participation of project-affected people in the decision-making process involves the provision of human, financial, technical and legal resources in all phases of the project cycle.[145] This may include the hiring of experts with the knowledge and language skills needed to engage effectively with indigenous

[140] IFC/IBLF, *Guide*, p. 77.
[141] Forest Peoples Programme and Tebtebba Foundation, *Indigenous Peoples' Rights, Extractive Industries and Transnational and Other Business Enterprises*, a Submission to the Special Representative of the Secretary-General on human rights and transnational corporations and other business enterprises, 29 December 2006, p. 51.
[142] HRC, *Human rights and fundamental freedoms of indigenous peoples*, para. 46.
[143] *Ibid.* paras. 47, 54 and 56.   [144] *Ibid.* paras. 49 and 55.
[145] HIC, 'Risk, responsibility and human rights', Annex V – Illustrative screening mechanism for reviewing HRIAs by PIFIs, pp. 43f.

or rural communities. Such an undertaking can be costly and demands the allocation of funds by the project from the beginning. This, however, is not easily reconciled with the need in project finance to keep expenditures as low as possible before the project starts to generate revenue. By including these expenditures already in the project planning costs covered by the sponsors, the problem that SPVs do not have enough resources to take such costly measures, could be avoided. Early and effective stakeholder engagement is a definite advantage for project finance investments because it can contribute to avoiding conflict and thereby prevent costly interruptions of construction or production. As was discussed above (p. 188), including affected communities in the decision-making processes can serve as a conflict-risk mitigation strategy, fostering trust and legitimacy and relieving tensions.[146] However, it has to be kept in mind that an engagement process will not always go smoothly, and, while large-scale participation is to be encouraged, it should be clearly regulated, in order for the HRIA process not to be weakened through delays and an overstretched budget.[147]

While a comprehensive ESIA can serve to reduce future grievances from project-affected communities, the need for an effective mechanism to address such complaints will always exist and forms a vital part of the corporate responsibility to respect human rights.[148] Mechanisms at the company level contribute greatly to early warning and risk management to identify, mitigate and resolve grievances before they escalate and result in abuses and lawsuits.[149] Thus, all new HRIA proposals provide for some form of complaints or mediation procedure for people whose rights are adversely affected by a project, at least during project construction and operation. Many of them go further and promote community consultation from the very outset of a project, suggesting that an independent grievance mechanism be established from the pre-feasibility stage on and with the participation and agreement of interested parties.[150] This would promote the legitimacy, transparency and predictability of non-judicial grievance mechanisms; principles that

---

[146] See also International Alert, *Conflict-Sensitive Project Finance*, p. 10.
[147] Lenzen and Engelbronner, *Guide*, p. 10.
[148] IFC, Good Practice Note, *Addressing Grievances from Project-Affected Communities*, Guidance for Projects and Companies for Designing Grievance Mechanisms (Washington, DC, September 2009), p. ii. HRC, *Protect, Respect and Remedy*, para. 93.
[149] HRC, *Business and Human Rights*, para. 91.
[150] IFC/IBLF, *Guide*, p. 54. HIC, 'Risk, responsibility and human rights', p. 21.

according to Professor Ruggie should underpin these tools.[151] The IFC Good Practice Note on grievance mechanisms recommends scaling the mechanism to the project's risk and adverse impact on affected communities anticipated by the ESIA. It recognizes that if a project affects rights-holders with significant cultural differences, such as indigenous peoples or societies with segregation of roles and responsibilities, a tailored approach may be needed to ensure that every group is able to raise concerns.[152] Furthermore, to be effective, such a procedure should be confidential, accessible and free of charge. The project company should react speedily to allegations of human rights violations, investigate them, and remedy any violation that is confirmed.[153]

The IFC/IBLF Guide does not literally mention the principle of avoidance, but it states that a company should 'amend its management processes to avoid recurrence of the violations' and review its business relationships in case violations are committed by third parties (e.g. contractors).[154] In the example of pipeline constructions in Chad and Cameroon creating dust pollution the constructors would thus have had to adapt the pace of the construction and improve the quality of access roads in order to stop the health hazard resulting from the dust. Furthermore, as issues should be resolved speedily and fairly, the project cannot wait until the beginning of its operation and the start of revenue flows to pay out compensations to the victims of this dust problem, but should try to find a solution immediately.

This requirement is incompatible with the common project finance feature of preferring to compensate damages out of the project revenue flow.[155] However, postponing the solution of human rights complaints or not providing for a grievance mechanism at all appears as a short-sighted management decision also in project finance. Unaddressed grievances such as health problems caused by excessive dust could cost the company more in the long run; increased tensions could result in higher risk management, security and personnel costs, expensive lawsuits and reputational costs.[156] Slowing down the construction of the

---

[151] HRC, *Protect, Respect and Remedy*, para. 92. See also IFC, *Addressing Grievances*, above n. 148, principle 4, p. 13.

[152] IFC, *Addressing Grievances*, principles 1 and 2, pp. 7ff.

[153] IFC/IBLF, *Guide*, pp. 54, 55. HIC, 'Risk, responsibility and human rights', p. 34. IFC, *Addressing Grievances*, principle 3, p. 11.

[154] IFC/IBLF, *Guide*, p. 54.   [155] Leader, Chapter 5.

[156] HIC, 'Risk, responsibility and human rights', p. 13. Crossin and Banfield, 'Conflict risk', pp. 9f.

pipeline may be a better option than risking the total disruption of it or a stop of operations.

In addition to requiring project-level grievance mechanisms, financial institutions seeking to improve compliance with human rights standards in the conduct of the projects they support, should look more towards collaborative models for complaint mechanisms. There exist already a number of voluntary codes, multi-stakeholder initiatives and investor-led standards,[157] but many initiatives, such as the EP, still lack grievance procedures and Professor Ruggie found evidence showing that this erodes their perceived legitimacy.[158] For the Equator Banks to be able to ensure that the projects they finance are not causing significant adverse impacts, a process for hearing concerns from affected communities unfiltered through their clients is needed.[159] Collaborative grievance procedures could facilitate access for complainants providing a single avenue for recourse to multiple organizations or companies. This would, furthermore, reduce the costs for the individual entities involved which could be particularly attractive for thinly resourced SPVs and the people affected by their operations.[160]

Ensuring compliance with standards through HRMPs

According to the IFC/IBLF HRIA Guide the management of a project will have to decide, based on the HRIA, which proposed alternatives or mitigation measures for identified human rights challenges it will adopt. These decisions will then be integrated in the overall project

[157] See for example the IFC's CAO. It is independent of IFC management and reports directly to the President of the World Bank Group. The CAO responds to complaints from those affected by IFC-financed projects and oversees audits of IFC's social and environmental performance, particularly in relation to sensitive projects. Source: IFC's Policy on Social and Environmental Sustainability, Section 4. www.ifc.org/sustainability.

[158] HRC, *Business and Human Rights*, para. 106.

[159] BankTrack, *Banking it Right*, Submission to OHCHR consultation on operationalizing the SRSG's framework for business and human rights, October 2009, p. 8. See: www.reports-and-materials.org/BankTrack-submission-to-Ruggie-1-Oct-2009.pdf (accessed: 11 November 2009).

[160] HRC, *Protect, Respect and Remedy*, para. 101. The SRSG has launched a global wiki called Business and Society Exploring Solutions – A Dispute Resolution Community (www.baseswiki.org) for sharing, accessing and discussing information about non-judicial mechanisms that address disputes between companies and their external stakeholders. See also HRC, *Business and Human Rights*, para. 108.

management plan and disclosed to affected stakeholders.[161] Similarly, and in more detail, the Halifax Initiative proposes a 'Human Rights Protection Plan' describing measures to respect, protect and fulfil human rights and mitigate adverse effects, as well as to develop negotiated and binding agreements between project sponsors and the affected communities for compensation.[162] Such compensation measures could include not only the direct provision of goods and resources but also the provision of means by which goods and resources can be generated, such as agricultural land or training for self-employment.[163] Agreeing on compensation and mitigation measures beforehand can help a project sponsor to calculate the costs of human rights management more realistically and can build trust with communities and prevent future conflict. However, it also means that project sponsors will have to allocate enough funds to the HRIA and management process before the project even begins to generate revenues. Again, this poses the same problem as the financing of consultations with stakeholders at an early stage.

Step 8 of the IFC/IBLF Guide suggests that companies continuously monitor and evaluate the human rights management process and adopt corrective action in case of failure to implement human rights management measures.[164] As opposed to the IFC PS or the EP, this HRIA is designed as an internal process of a company's due diligence and therefore its implementation depends on the goodwill and the good governance of the company.

The Halifax Initiative, on the other hand, proposes that project sponsors be held accountable by their PIFIs for appropriate financial and human resources set aside throughout the project cycle to monitor and enforce the 'Human Rights Protection Plan'. Indeed, for the effective functioning of such management plans, the commitment of insurers, lenders and governments to ensure compliance will be crucial. Project sponsors will approach financial institutions or ECAs with the final HRIA trying to secure additional funding or insurance for the project. These institutions have the responsibility to insist on the sponsor's implementation of the mitigation measures and negotiated resettlement, compensation and benefit sharing plans, identified in the HRIA.[165] In their submission to the UK House of Commons, Drakos, Maassarani and

[161] IFC/IBLF, *Guide*, pp. 50 and 54.
[162] HIC, 'Risk, responsibility and human rights', p. 24.
[163] *Ibid.*, Annex II, p. 38.   [164] IFC/IBLF, *Guide*, p. 58.
[165] HIC, 'Risk, responsibility and human rights', p. 17.

Radon recommended that the UK government design tax incentives for companies that adopt and incorporate an HRIA tool into their corporate management, and support the creation of an independent board of human rights auditors to provide companies with reliable HRIAs.[166] PIFIs holding project sponsors to account could be a possible solution of the problem that project companies, which would be closer to the daily operations of a project and therefore in a better position to address upcoming human rights challenges, often lack the technical and financial resources to implement the human rights management measures.

The challenge is whether IFIs and ECAs will be able to effectively monitor and enforce compliance with these management plans throughout the life of a project.[167] The leverage a lender has will depend on the type of financial product offered, on its position within the financing structure of a project, and the point at which the lender becomes involved in the project cycle. Whereas the IFC may have certain leverage to encourage the inclusion of a human rights-based approach during the financing stages of a project,[168] judging from the current practice with ESIA and management plans, it does not seem to be able or willing to exert sufficient pressure on clients during the implementation stage to bring them back into compliance with standards.[169] NGOs are demanding that the IFC use its ability to influence project design, implementation and management through loan conditionalities that go further than what the IFC PS require; for example, introducing a compliance plan containing binding commitments regarding mitigation measures, resettlement and development entitlements mutually agreed on between the project sponsor and affected communities. More importantly, the IFC should actually hold borrowers accountable for their performance by threatening to withdraw the financing or by creating more favourable financing terms on satisfactory compliance with agreed targets.[170]

The Equator Banks' Best Practice Working Group picks these ideas up in a recently published guidance note for Equator Banks on incorporating environmental and social considerations into loan documentation.[171] This guidance note recognizes loan agreements as a key legal

---

[166] Drakos *et al.*, Evidentiary submission, above n. 72, recommendations.
[167] Crossin and Banfield, 'Conflict risk', pp. 17 and 21.
[168] *Ibid.* p. 22.   [169] HIC, 'Risk, responsibility and human rights', pp. 1 and 7.
[170] HIC, 'Risk, responsibility and human rights', pp. 31f.
[171] Equator Principles, *Guidance to EPFIs on Incorporating Environmental and Social Considerations into Loan Documentation* (August 2009), at: www.equator-principles.com/documents/EPLoanDocumentGuidance.pdf (accessed: 9 November 2009).

document providing Equator Banks with a formal opportunity to require the borrower to address environmental and social issues throughout the project cycle. It recommends that for all category A and B projects borrowers covenant in financing documentation: (a) to comply with all relevant host country social and environmental laws, regulations and permits; (b) to comply with the Action Plan during the construction and operation of the project; (c) to provide periodic compliance reports, prepared by in-house staff or third-party experts; and (d) to decommission the facilities in accordance with an agreed decommissioning plan. Furthermore, a set of preconditions can be used to require borrowers to make certain progress on environmental and social issues before disbursement. Material non-compliances with the covenants will normally constitute an event of default under the loan agreement. Although the lender will work with the borrower to bring it back into compliance to the extent feasible, if the borrower fails to re-establish compliance within an agreed grace period, the Equator Banks reserve the right to cancel a commitment, declare all amounts owed by the borrower to become immediately due and payable, and/or enforce security, as they consider appropriate.[172]

However, there is also the legitimate concern that if a financial institution withdraws from a project for reasons of non-compliance with human rights standards it loses all leverage to improve the project's impact and it could have negative consequences such as the resettled population not receiving adequate compensation.[173]

Concluding remarks

The current financial crisis poses a risk to the protection of human rights because economic actors and governments might be inclined to lower human rights standards to accelerate economic recovery. However, no sustainable recovery can be built on such a weak foundation and it would risk further decline of public confidence in business. Rather, the actual crisis shows that economic long-term prospects are tightly coupled with the well-being of society as a whole.[174] HRIAs have the potential to help bridge the gap between the interests of private companies and those of communities and at the same time yield economic returns in the medium and long term; they provide a sensible insurance policy and

[172] *Ibid.* pp. 1–3.   [173] UNHCHR, *Human rights and the financial sector*, para. 17.
[174] HRC, *Business and Human Rights*, paras. 118, 119.

an ethical and cost-effective tool for companies to assess and control the impact of their development activity in places where host governments are unable or unwilling to safeguard their citizens' rights; and although they initially require more time and money, they are win-wins for companies and lenders.[175]

The various stakeholders of a project finance investment, the sponsoring and operating companies, the lenders, the insurers as well as the affected local communities and NGOs that represent their interests, have come to realize that it is of crucial importance that the risks related to human rights that affect a project or its surrounding population and environment are effectively managed. NGOs as well as industry groups, the IFC or single companies have drafted impact assessment and management manuals and guidelines to address potential human rights challenges based on best practice from traditional ESIA. Compared to ESIA, however, these HRIAs have the added value that they assess human rights risks comprehensively and from a rights-based approach, taking into account not only risks that threaten the project itself but also the impacts that it has on the human rights situation in the host community. An HRIA is a tool that guides project participants not only in the assessment of potential human rights impacts of the project, but also in the management of identified risks in order to respect, protect and fulfil the human rights of all stakeholders.[176]

In this chapter several tension points between the demands of these HRIAs and the logic of project finance have been highlighted. First, it was argued that the restrictive stabilization and arbitration clauses of investment protection agreements concluded with host governments conflict with the aim of HRIAs to promote respect, protection and fulfilment of international human rights standards. The HRIA tools analysed should therefore include an assessment of the relationship between host government agreements (HGAs) and human rights impacts at a very early stage and provide recommendations to the project management teams. Second, it was found that the preference in project finance for compensation over avoidance of damage is incompatible with the preventive approach taken by all HRIA tools. Third, it became evident that the HRIA strategy for holding construction contractors and suppliers accountable for complying with human rights standards is

---

[175] Drakos *et al.*, Evidentiary submission, above n. 72.
[176] UNHCHR HRIA, Discussion Paper, para. 8; HIC, 'Risk, responsibility and human rights', pp. 16f.

difficult to reconcile with financial and time constraints of project finance. The same difficulties arise with HRIA demands to improve stakeholder consultation processes. HRIAs suggest that the participation of affected communities from the beginning of a project should be a key component of the assessment and management of human rights risks. This is particularly true in project finance where local communities have no voice in the risk-allocation and decision-making processes. However, taking such human rights management measures before the project starts to generate revenue means that the project sponsors will have to allocate funds for it from the planning stage onwards.

HRIA tools are only emerging and there is little information on how they will work on the ground. It remains to be seen if and how compliance with human rights management plans will be enforced. As HRIAs were developed on the basis of current practice of ESIAs and pursue a similar goal, although expressly grounded in international human rights, one could assume that HRIAs will run the same kind of risks in their implementation as do ESIAs. Therefore, it is appropriate to draw some conclusions from lessons learned from ESIA. Implementation of HRIA and management plans will remain problematic as long as the assessing companies do not strengthen their in-house capacity to deal with human rights challenges. Private lenders are under strong competition to acquire loan clients and tend to take short cuts. This competition undermines efforts of individual financial institutions to enforce compliance with common standards such as the EP. Public lenders have been criticized for giving their clients too much leeway in choosing between various alternatives to a project that is least damaging to human rights. Public and private lenders and insurers will need to hold the sponsors and project companies to account for implementing an HRIA and complying with the resulting management measures; otherwise, HRIAs risk being treated as a mere formality and will not have their intended outcome of promoting respect, protection and fulfilment of human rights in a project's host environment.

8

Project finance investments and political risk: an empirical investigation

CLAUDIA GIRARDONE AND STUART SNAITH

Introduction

In recent years project finance (PF) has become an increasingly popular method of funding long-term capital-intensive infrastructure projects worldwide, particularly in developing countries. The nature of modern project finance is to use limited or non-recourse syndicated loans to a special purpose vehicle (SPV), where such debt typically represents the lion's share of the capital structure. The vehicle usually has one objective, such as to build a dam or a pipeline, and therefore avoids some of the decision-making tensions common in the corporate finance literature.[1] In typical project finance syndication there tend to be several types of bank. It is not uncommon for multilateral development banks such as the International Finance Corporation (IFC) of the World Bank group to participate in the lending process; however, the biggest lenders are syndicates of large international banks. These institutions (e.g. Barclays plc and HSBC plc) are private sector entities that are characterized by the broad objectives of profit and shareholder wealth maximization.

Project finance lending techniques are often employed in developing countries to provide funding to various industrial sectors. Typically these tend to be asset-rich projects in sectors such as oil and gas, mining, utility and energy. Interestingly, as recently observed by Hainz and Kleimeier (2007), project finance loans are usually preferred if the economy of a country is poor, the corporate governance system is weak, and political risk and bank influence over the host government is high. Indeed, while in developed countries firms view project finance as just one financing alternative among many, in developing countries

---

[1] See e.g. Jensen and Meckling (1976).

this type of funding is sometimes preferred to on-balance sheet syndicated credits. Further, and perhaps more crucially, it can also be one of
the few sources of finance available in such countries. One view is that
this results in a weak negotiating position for developing-countries' host
governments when entering into contracts with project sponsors. This
can result in a larger degree of risk transference, vis-à-vis developed
countries, from the project to the host country.

From the lending banks' perspective the decision to invest is contin-
gent on the level of risk inherent in the project, and can be thought of as a
two-stage decision process. Initially there is the binary decision of
whether to pursue the investment or not. If the investment goes ahead,
this is followed by an assessment where the price of lending is set in
response to the project risk. Given the non-recourse nature of project
finance lending, a key driver of project finance is the minimization of
risk, and further, the allocation of risk to those parties best able to bear it.
This allocation of risk is often achieved via the complex set of interrelated contracts that form a project finance deal.[2] Esty (2004a) indicates
that a standard project contains forty or more contracts between the
input supplier and the output buyer involving more than fifteen different
parties in the process. In particular, project finance makes considerable
use of political risk guarantees and loan covenants that typically restrict
or encourage various actions to enhance the probability of repayment.
Additionally, banks are often organized in syndicates whose size has
been found to be directly associated to the level of risk involved in the
project (see e.g. Kleimeier and Megginson, 2000).[3]

Over the 1990s the rise in social and environmental damage and
human rights negligence derived from some project-financing operations has put increased pressure on the big lenders to set out a policy
framework dealing specifically with these issues. In 2003 a group of ten
large international financial institutions endorsed the Equator Principles
(EP), a voluntary set of rules aimed at the development of socially
responsible projects that reflect sound environmental management practices. These principles follow the environmental and social guidelines of
the IFC and have been restated and reviewed in a document published in
July 2006. In extreme cases EP signatory banks (in January 2011 there

---

[2] For example, host government agreements are designed to mitigate political risk stemming from host governments.
[3] Esty and Megginson (2002) refer to risk in this context as the risk of default. Other types
of risk could induce an inverse relationship to syndicate size.

were sixty-nine signatory banks) will avoid lending to borrowers that fail to comply with the EP. However, the purpose of the EP is to encourage those seeking funds to approach, from inception, projects in a way that it is consistent with the EP. Further, when such an approach is found to be deficient, the aim is to work towards appropriate changes to ensure compliance.[4] Despite these developments, the new policy framework has a number of non-trivial shortcomings and issues to be addressed, including free-rider problems and the need for improved implementation and compliance.

This chapter has two main contributions. On the one hand, it examines the recent trends in project financing and reviews the main finance literature with particular focus on the studies that account for political (or country/sovereign) risk. On the other hand, it carries out an empirical analysis in an attempt to gauge the degree of association between project finance and proxies for human rights. These proxies are gained using disaggregated political risk data. We use a sample of over 1,000 project finance loans from 1996 to 2003 and compare two different political risk indexes, derived from the International Country Risk Guide (ICRG) (in both its aggregate and disaggregate form) and the World Bank's Worldwide Governance Research Indicators Dataset. We also split the sample according to the World Bank's data on country development, yielding two datasets on developed and developing countries.

Based on our aggregate political risk measure, we find that, on average, low political risk levels are related to low loan spreads. With regard to our developing-country sample we find several interesting results. On the one hand we find a clear negative relationship between loan spreads and the quality and strength of the bureaucracy and the effectiveness, and strength of a country's legal and institutional systems. This implies that an improvement in either of these measures is associated with a reduction in the cost of a project finance loan. On the other hand, we find the opposite relationship with regard to government stability and democratic accountability: an improvement in either of these measures is associated with an increase in the cost of a project finance loan.

From Hainz and Kleimeier (2007) we know that project finance is often employed in countries where the corporate governance system is weak, and political risk and bank influence over the host government is

---

[4] While these principles are certainly laudable from a social and environmental standpoint, it is also important to realise that there is an element of risk reduction here.

high. Based on our developing-country sample, our findings point towards cheaper project finance loans for host countries that exhibit weakness in government stability/democratic accountability. Given the intrinsic link between risk and return, this implies that banks perceive less risk is inherent in such projects, hence in these developing countries we suggest that there is a larger degree of risk transference from the SPV to the host country. Given the wider concerns of social and economic justice, this suggests further scrutiny of host government agreements.

The remainder of this chapter is organized as follows: the next section identifies the recent key trends in project finance lending; the next reviews the main literature; then the data and the main methodological issues are presented; the final section discusses the main results, followed by our concluding comments.

Trends in project finance loans

Over the past twenty years project finance has experienced a considerable growth that was mainly brought about by the globalization of product markets, an extensive process of deregulation of key industrial sectors worldwide (e.g. power, telecommunications and transportation) and privatization of state-owned entities (Esty, 2004a; Sorge, 2004; see Figure 8.1).

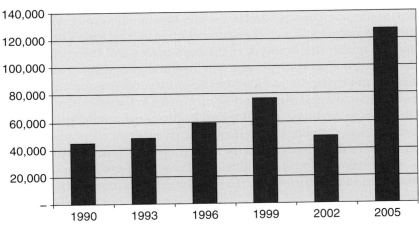

Figure 8.1   Main trends in PF lending (US$m.) (1990–2005)
        Source: Loan Analytics.

Overall, project finance loans have increased significantly over recent years, with the exception of 2002 when a fall in deal value volume was reported due to the slowdown in the global economy as well as regional and sector crises (Esty, 2004b).[5] Specifically, in this period emerging markets have experienced episodes of financial turmoil; the telecommunications and energy sectors encountered difficulties as did several high-profile projects such as the Euro Disney theme park and the Channel Tunnel linking the UK to the European continent.

Although in project finance deals financial institutions are typically organized in syndicates, it is illuminating to identify the absolute ranking of the lead banks by number of deals. Table 8.1 shows the top lenders from 2001 to 2005, all of which have endorsed the EP. Note that in the table the IFC is ranked 8th for number of deals, but the ranking in terms of deal values is relatively low (58th) which is in line with its inclusion on the grounds of political risk mitigation rather than a need for finance.

Project finance business is relatively well diversified across industrial sectors. However, it tends to be used primarily to fund tangible asset-rich and capital-intensive projects. Figure 8.2A and 8.2B illustrates the typical size of a project by sector and shows both the relative average size of a project in each sector, and the sum of the deal values in each sector (Panels A and B respectively).

From Figure 8.2A, it seems that some sectors tend to be (on average) involved in large projects e.g. transportation, but overall there is no clearly discernible time trend. A large average is indicative of a quantity of large projects in the absence of numerous smaller projects. Clearly, from 1990 to 1993 transportation shrank in average project size; this is what one should expect because of the Channel Tunnel loan of US $13,204 m., signed in 1990.

Looking at total value of project finance in Figure 8.2B, we can see that overall utility and energy and telecommunications display the largest proportion in most years. Moreover, while the relatively large 'Channel Tunnel effect' is clearly seen in Figure 8.2A, from Figure 8.2B the effect is clearly less defined. This is because transportation is a smaller sector in terms of number of deals, hence one large deal causes a large average deal size in Figure 8.2A. While at the same time the smaller number of deals yields a smaller sum vis-à-vis other sectors, hence transportation constitutes a smaller proportion of PF deals by sum.

---

[5] Overall PF lending as reduced since the recent financial crisis and the global recession.

Table 8.1 *Top 20 lenders in PF loans (2001–5)*

Lead bank	Deal value (US$m.)	No. of deals	% share	Ranking by deal value
BNP Paribas (France)	36,369.74	94	10.30	2
Royal Bank of Scotland plc (UK)	39,173.72	81	11.10	1
BBVA (Spain)	18,267.43	74	5.18	8
European Bank for Reconstruction and Development (EBRD)	4,153.36	57	1.18	59
Barclays (UK) plc	29,357.13	52	8.32	3
HSBC (UK) plc	24,606.27	52	6.97	4
Citigroup Inc. (US)	20,490.40	51	5.81	6
International Finance Corporation (IFC)	4,210.27	48	1.19	58
Sumitomo Mitsui Banking Corp. (Japan)	15,040.50	47	4.26	14
WestLB (Germany)	18,189.76	43	5.15	9
Calyon (France)	16,166.93	43	4.58	12
Bank of Tokyo-Mitsubishi Ltd (Japan)	13,407.03	43	3.80	16
Bank of Scotland (UK) plc	3,025.68	40	0.86	75
Banco Santander Central Hispano SA (Spain)	9,141.09	39	2.59	24
ANZ Investment Bank (Australia)	8,640.09	36	2.45	26
ABN AMRO Bank NV (Netherlands)	12,097.50	34	3.43	19
ING (UK)	8,632.66	32	2.45	27
SG (France)	15,219.83	31	4.31	13
SG Corporate and Investment Banking (France)	23,400.49	30	6.63	5
Citibank NA (Philippines)	18,010.87	29	5.10	10

Source: Loan Analytics.

Having established the market size, and the industrial distribution of PF loans, the next logical step is to examine the geographic distribution of such loans (see Table 8.2). Looking at the macro regions that attract PF lending, it seems clear that the majority of the business is conducted in Western Europe, the Indian subcontinent and North and South-East Asia.

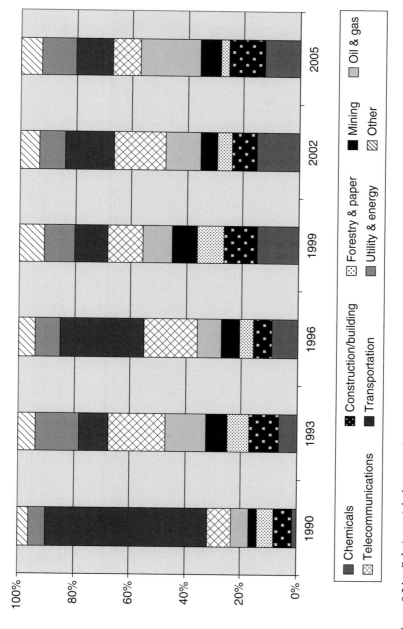

Figure 8.2A Relative weight by sector (averages) (1990–2005)

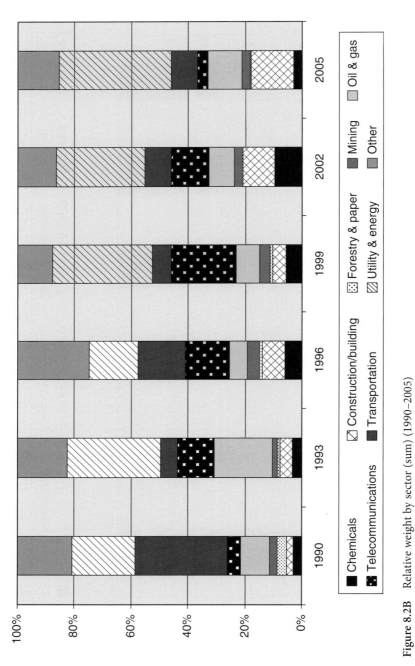

Figure 8.2B Relative weight by sector (sum) (1990–2005)
Source: Loan Analytics

Table 8.2 *PF lending by region (1990–2005, US$m.)*

Macro-regions	1990	1993	1996	1999	2002	2005	% change
North America	13,974	1,204	4,897	22,457	7,416	8,117	−42
Western Europe	19,929	8,575	18,828	19,482	17,148	46,072	+131
Australasia; Japan	325	3,161	1,657	7,408	6,231	11,321	+3,380
Middle East; Eastern Europe	1,112	4,745	5,536	8,297	4,230	33,978	+2,956
Indian subcontinent; North Asia; SE Asia	7,035	16,143	24,601	7,830	6,988	14,802	+110
Latin America; Caribbean	1,419	3,806	3,276	9,182	5,337	8,528	+501
Africa	755	730	238	1,872	1,458	4,072	+439

Source: Loan Analytics.

It is also noticeable that before the Asia crisis PF to developing countries surged, supported by a growing reliance on market economies in many countries during this period as a result of the increasing integration of global financial markets. In the Indian subcontinent and North and South-East Asia, it is possible to notice a drop in PF lending between 1996 and 1999 certainly due to the financial crisis that began in mid-1997 in East Asia.[6]

On the other hand, the smallest recipient of PF lending is North America. In this region PF lending peaked in 1999 and then dropped to levels significantly lower than those in 1990 (showing the sole negative percentage change over the last fifteen years). This reticence of US companies to engage with PF is interesting especially when considering that a large share of syndicated lending is financed by US banks (see Kleimeier and Megginson, 2000).

Figure 8.1 and Table 8.2 are useful insofar as they show us the trend and amounts of PF lending respectively. It is useful to look at the level of PF lending *relative* to all syndicated lending. Based on this metric we can then better appreciate the relative importance of such financing in a given region (see Figure 8.3).

---

[6] While overall PF lending has reduced since the recent financial crisis and the global recession, lending still continues to grow (based on first half-year figures, 2008 and 2009 comparison) in Asia and South America.

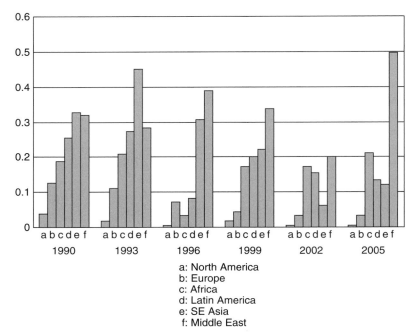

a: North America
b: Europe
c: Africa
d: Latin America
e: SE Asia
f: Middle East

Figure 8.3   PF lending (percentage of all syndicated loans)
Source: Loan Analytics.
Notes: PF lending (by deal value) as a percentage of all syndicated
lending for world regions.

Based on this figure it is noticeable that for North America and
Europe, PF represents a relatively small amount of syndicated lending,
which is interesting given that this is the origin of much of the PF capital.
What we do note is the important role of PF in Africa and Latin America
where such lending represents approximately 16–18 per cent of all
syndicated lending (on average).

However this relative measure is not as great as that found in South-
East Asia, and particularly in the Middle East. Figure 8.3 clearly suggests
that PF lending is, relative to all syndicated lending, utilized far less in
'western economies' than in regions of the world that contain a large
proportion of developing countries. It is noticeable that the consequence
of the East Asia financial crisis can be seen by the relative drop in PF
lending post-1997 in South-East Asia.

Literature review

Despite the growing international importance of PF to fund large-scale projects, there is a paucity of studies in this area. Esty (2004a) argues that the field of PF is 'relatively unexplored territory for both empirical and theoretical research'. The literature that offers an economic treatment of PF emphasizes a number of features that make it a 'special case' compared to alternative methods of financing. PF is generally used for longer-term, capital-intensive projects; the SPVs are legally independent and financed with equity from the sponsoring firm(s) and are also highly leveraged (the average debt–equity ratio is between 60 and 70 per cent) (see e.g. Gatti et al., 2007). PF makes considerable use of political risk guarantees and loan covenants that typically restrict or encourage various actions to enhance the probability of repayment. In this context, one of the main comparative advantages of PF is that it provides the means by which the allocation of specific project risks, such as operating risk and the risk of expropriation is placed upon those best able to handle it. Moreover, PF loans are generally characterized by larger syndicates compared to other syndicated credits. Finally, as recently highlighted by Esty and Megginson (2002) PF loans tend to be more international than other types of syndicated loans.

The extant empirical literature has examined PF lending from three perspectives. The first focuses on the determinants of loan pricing (e.g. Kleimeier and Megginson, 2000; Sorge and Gadanecz, 2008). The second examines what factors might affect the syndicate structure of the SPV (Esty and Megginson, 2002; Esty 2004b). Lastly, the final approach examines what factors might affect the PF proportion of syndicated lending (Altunbas and Gadanecz, 2004; Hainz and Kleimeier, 2007). A summary of key articles fitting these perspectives can be found in Table 8.3, while a more detailed discussion of the determinates on PF loan pricing now follows.

Kleimeier and Megginson (2000) represents an excellent early contribution to the debate on what variables are important in describing PF loan spreads. They find that PF loans have lower credit spreads over the London Interbank Offered Rate (LIBOR) than any other comparable non-project finance loan. Moreover, the main results generally suggest that PF loans should be considered separately from other types of syndicated loans because they have a longer than average maturity, are more likely to have third-party guarantees and to be extended to borrowers in riskier countries. In particular they find that the higher

Table 8.3 *Studies on PF loans and political risk*

Authors (year)	Aim of study	Measure of political risk	Main findings on political/country/ sovereign risk
Kleimeier–Megginson (2000)	Determinants of loan pricing for PF and non-PF loans	Measure of country risk rank provided by *Euromoney* magazine where low (high) risk countries have very low (high) risk ranks	– Lack of guarantees increases the spread – High country risk increases the spread
Esty–Megginson (2002)	Determinants of syndicate structure: relation between legal risk defined as the strength and enforcement of creditors' rights and debt ownership concentration	The 'Institutional Investor' country credit rating (II rating) prior to closing. The scale runs from 0 (high country risk) to 100 (low risk). It is a measure derived from a survey of international bankers	– Syndicate size is positively (negatively) related to the strength of creditor rights and the reliability of legal enforcement after controlling for loan size, sovereign risk and project risk
Esty (2004b)	How the differences in legal and financial systems affect the composition of loan syndicates and how the composition affects loan pricing	Five measures of legal enforcement are drawn from the ICRG database, namely effectiveness of the judiciary, rule of law, risk of contract repudiation, absence of corruption and risk of expropriation	– Legality is highly positively correlated with country risk – PF loan spreads are higher in countries with weak creditor rights and poor legal enforcement

Sorge (2004) and Sorge–Gadanecz (2008)	In-depth analysis of credit risk in PF with particular emphasis on the analysis of the term structure of credit spread compared to alternative methods of finance	– Separate political risk guarantees – Separate corruption index provided by Transparency International. It assigns a score of 0 to 10 to most countries in the world according to the level of corruption of the political system As in Sorge (2004)	– The availability of explicit or implicit forms of risk mitigation reduce the spread by almost one-third on average – Lenders financing projects in emerging markets charge a higher premium on borrowers from countries characterized by a more corrupt political system – The use of PF is correlated with high levels of host-country political risk. An important factor is the influence of the lender over political risk exposure
Hainz–Kleimeier (2007)	How PF lending uses PF loans to manage risks compared with other syndicated lending	World Bank Worldwide Governance Research Indicators Dataset and distinguish between six different measures (see Table 8.4 for these)	

maturity, the availability of third-party guarantees and the presence of collateralizeable assets reduce significantly the average PF loans spreads. Finally, PF loans involve more participating banks and are more likely to be extended to borrowers in asset-rich industries.

Kleimeier and Megginson's results were later confirmed by Altunbas and Gadanecz (2004) who investigate the micro-economic and macro-economic determinants of bank lending and find that PF loans have lower spreads than other forms of syndicated lending. The authors look at several types of syndicated loans, including PF, and take into account additional pricing factors such as fees that are typically charged in loan syndications. Overall, the results show an inverse relationship between the cost of borrowing and a country's economic strength, whereas *ceteris paribus* higher political risk results in larger loan spreads.

In a related study on the nature of credit risk in PF Sorge (2004) looks at the term structure of loan spreads using a set of micro-economics variables including maturity, loan guarantees and a measure of corruption as a proxy for political risk. Here the aim is to examine the nature of the relationship between maturity and the cost of the loan, namely whether it is a linear or non-linear relationship. The main finding is that the relationship between project loan spreads and maturity is hump-shaped. As one would expect, Sorge finds that while corruption increases the cost of borrowing, the involvement of multilateral development banks or export credit agencies decreases it. Sorge and Gadanecz (2008) extend the analysis by including both micro-economic and macro-economic factors in their estimation. The main conclusions are that for poorer countries in particular, political risk and political risk guarantees play an important role in PF, and the presence of the latter has a significant impact in reducing credit spreads. Other important factors are the host country's creditworthiness and the size of the syndicate.

Data and methodology

We employ the Loan Analytics database (formerly Loanware) from Dealogic which contains extensive information on loans made in the international syndicated loans market signed between January 1980 and the present date. Specifically, we use the financial information for a panel of over 1,000 project finance loans worth over US$205 billion, 1996–2003. All spreads are measured as the margin over LIBOR. Since our chosen time period covers some recent international financial crises

(South-East Asia, Russia, Brazil and Turkey) it is reasonable to expect that spreads have increased over the period of study as the availability of credit decreased particularly for the affected countries. Given the variables included in our model (see below), much of this effect should be captured by the changes in macro-economic conditions and political risk.

The dataset is split into two sub-samples: developed and developing countries, according to the World Bank's data on country development. Two proxies for disaggregated political risk are used: the ICRG political risk index and the World Bank's Worldwide Governance Research Indicators Dataset. The span of the dataset is dictated by data availability for both the World Bank's data on governance and on economic development. The latter uses gross national income per capita and defines 'high income' countries as developed and 'low income' and 'lower middle income' countries as developing.

The political risk rating included in the ICRG database is calculated for 140 countries and is based on 100 points. It includes 12 weighted variables covering both political and social attributes and can be broadly divided into two levels of risk: low risk (80–100 points) and high to moderate risk (0 to 79 points). The aim of this political risk rating is to offer a method of measuring the political stability of the countries covered by the ICRG on a comparable basis. Table 8.4 provides definitions of each variable.

Also included in Table 8.4 are the World Bank's aggregate governance indexes that specify six dimensions of governance that relate to political risk. Data are available for the years 1996, 1998, 2000, 2002 and 2004 for 209 countries and territories.[7] As with the ICRG index, high values are associated with low political risk.

Recalling that the higher the values, the lower the perceived level of political risk is important in interpreting the results of our statistical model below. This is straightforward for a measure such as the ICRG variable government stability. The more stable the government, the higher the rated measure. What is less intuitive are measures such as corruption. Here, a perceived improvement in the level of corruption is registered as a higher value for that measure, since political risk will be lower.

Our analysis of the data is based upon applying a statistical model to our sample of PF loans. In particular we aim to identify what factors are important in helping describe loan spreads once the effects of other

---

[7] Following the extant literature we interpolate to get data for 1997, 1999, 2001 and 2003.

factors are accounted for. The estimation procedure, a type of least squares regression,[8] will take all micro, macro and political risk factors, and assign values to the coefficients of these factors, β_i, γ_i and δ_i (and the constant term) that best describe the loan spread. By doing so, each variable will have its own coefficients:

$$Loan\ Spread = \alpha + \beta_i Micro + \delta_i Macro + \gamma_i Political\ Risk \qquad (1)$$

where micro factors include:

- Maturity: loan maturity in years.
- Deal value (US$m.).
- Guarantee: a dummy variable that takes the value of 1 if there is a third-party repayment guarantee and 0 otherwise. This refers to, say, an export credit agency providing some of the debt.
- Number of banks.
- Currency risk: a dummy variable that takes the value of 1 if a loan is exposed to currency risk and zero otherwise.
- Club or Bilateral: a dummy taking the value of 1 according to the type of deal.
- Environmental risk: a dummy taking the value of 1 if the industry of the borrower is high environmental risk and 0 otherwise.

This latter factor is relevant because it reflects the level of potential or actual environmental risks for each industrial sector included in our sample. A detailed description of this variable is given in Table 8.5.

Macro factors include:

- international reserves (% of GDP);
- investments (% of GDP);
- domestic credit to private sector (% of GDP);
- real GDP growth;
- current account balance (% of GDP);
- inflation (annual %);
- imports/exports; and
- PPP share of world GDP.

Finally, political risk is measured based upon the aggregate or disaggregate ICRG and World Bank measures.

---

[8] All regressions are cross-sectional using ordinary least squares, with White's (1980) corrected standard errors.

Table 8.4 *Political risk indexes and components*

ICRG	
Variable	Definition
Government stability	Government's ability to carry out its declared programmes and to stay in office. Sub-components: government unity; legislative strength; popular support
Socio-economic conditions	Socio-economic pressures at work in society that could constrain government action or fuel social dissatisfaction. Sub-components: unemployment; consumer confidence; poverty
Investment profile	Factors affecting the risk to investment not covered by other political, economic or financial risk components. Sub-components: contract viability/expropriation; profits repatriation; payment delays
Internal conflict	Political violence in a country and its actual and potential impact on governance. Sub-components: civil war/coup threat; terrorism/political violence; civil disorder
External conflict	Risk to the incumbent government from foreign action, from non-violent to violent external pressures. Sub-components: war; cross-border conflict; foreign pressures
Corruption	Corruption within the political system particularly in the form of excessive patronage, nepotism, job reservations, secret party funding and suspicious ties between politics and business
Military in politics	Involvement of military in politics even at peripheral level including the threat of military takeover
Religion in politics	Domination of society or governance by a single religious group that seeks to replace civil law by religious law and to exclude other religions from the political or social process
Law and order	Law is an assessment of the strength and impartiality of the legal system, while the order sub-component is an assessment of the population's observance of the law
Ethnic tensions	An assessment of the degree of tension within a country due to racial, nationality or language divisions
Democratic accountability	Responsiveness of government to its people: the less responsive, the more likely is it to fall
Quality of democracy	Institutional strength and quality of the bureaucracy refers to the ability to govern without drastic changes in policy or interruption of government services

Table 8.4 (*cont.*)

ICRG	
Variable	Definition
Political risk	< 50% very high risk; 50–59.9% high risk; 60–69.9% moderate risk; 70–79.9% low risk; 80%+ very low risk

World Bank	
Variable	Definition
Voice and accountability	Measures various political, civil and human rights e.g. these indicators measure the extent to which citizens of a country are able to participate in the selection of governments and the independence of the media
Political stability	The likelihood of violent threats to, or changes in, government, including terrorism e.g. acts having direct effect on the continuity of policies, and possibly undermining the ability of all citizens to select and replace peacefully those in power
Government effectiveness	The competence of the bureaucracy and the quality of public service delivery including the quality of the bureaucracy, the independence of the civil service from politics, and the credibility of the government's commitment to policies
Regulatory burden	The incidence of market-unfriendly policies, such as price controls or inadequate bank supervision, as well as perceptions of the burdens imposed by excessive regulation in areas like foreign trade and business development
Rule of law	The quality of contract enforcement, the effectiveness and predictability of the judiciary, the police and the courts, as well as the likelihood of crime and violence. It aims to measure the success of a society in developing an environment in which fair and predictable rules form the basis for economic and social interactions, including property rights protection
Control of corruption	The exercise of public power for private gain, including both petty and grand corruption and state capture

Source: World Bank and International Country Risk Guide.

Table 8.5 *Environmental impact by industry sector*

Greater environmental impact	Lesser environmental impact
Transportation	Aerospace
Utility & energy	Computers & electronics
Construction/building	Consumer products
Chemicals	Defence
Agribusiness	Dining & lodging
Forestry & paper	Finance
Oil & gas	Food & beverage
Mining	Government
Metal & steel	Holding companies
Auto/truck	Insurance
Health care	Leisure & recreation
Textile	Machinery
	Professional services
	Publishing
	Retail
	Telecommunications
	Real estate/property

The output from the regression model will yield coefficients that allow us to make statements on the magnitude to which a given factor can affect the price of a PF loan, *on average*. When conducting regression analysis the usual statistical caveat applies – that we are basing our inference on a sample of loans, i.e. not the whole universe of loans, and hence are subject to a certain degree of uncertainty.

Therefore, in addition to the magnitude/sign of the coefficients, and as a direct result of this uncertainty, we test to see whether a given factor is statistically significant. This allows one to say with a given degree of confidence that a variable is positive, negative or indeed not statistically different from zero. The latter is just as important as finding evidence of a positive or negative coefficient, as it implies that the variable in question does not help describe the loan spread.[9] Starting from the micro

---

[9] For example, the regression may yield a coefficient on 'law and order' of −2.5. If this is shown to be *statistically* different from 0 we posit, with a degree of confidence, that this negative relationship holds for the population of all loans. If however we cannot reject that the coefficient is 0, then it would not be appropriate to interpret our negative

variables, although one could expect that longer-term loans cost more, a linear relationship between spreads and maturity has usually not been found significant in PF loan studies.[10] On the other hand the loan size should be negatively related to spreads because only borrowers with a good credit history should be able to obtain large size loans. Concerning the guarantees, the expectation is that their availability will reduce the cost of borrowing.

Moreover, the number of banks in the syndicate is included to test to what extent syndicate structure affects the spread; it is meaningful to expect that a higher number of participants has a significant risk-mitigating effect. While this is certainly true in the case of strategic default, Esty and Megginson (2002) offer another possibility. They posit that a weakening of creditor rights, which would result in an increase in risk, would require a greater need for monitoring of cash flows and an increased need for recontracting resulting from economic distress. This type of risk they argue is best handled by a smaller syndicate. Concerning currency risk, this arises when the project takes place in a country that has a different currency from that in which the loan originated, and is therefore expected to affect the loan spread positively. Finally the expectations for the dummy variables that group deals by environmental risk and type of deal are mixed. Concerning environmental risk for example, since high-risk sectors have been assigned a 1, and low risk sectors a 0, the sign for this coefficient should be interpreted as indicating that if the environmental impact dummy is positive and significantly different from 0, the PF loan is on average more expensive in these industries.

Concerning the macro variables, for all indicators of actual or potential economic strength, expectations are for a negative relationship with loan spreads. These are: investments/GDP, domestic credit to private sector (percentage of GDP), real GDP growth, current account balance (percentage of GDP), and purchasing power parity share of world GDP. In contrast, inflation should be positively related with spread because it is likely associated with weaknesses associated with the country's finances. Similarly, a high imports–exports ratio could signal a strong dependence from abroad and thus is expected to be positively related with loan spreads. Finally, expectations for international reserves/GDP are mixed because while on the one hand if high they may signal a sort of

coefficient. Rather we would say that in the regression model, *ceteris paribus*, law and order do not affect the loan price.
[10] Sorge (2004) and Sorge and Gadanecz (2008) have tested logarithmic transformations and found that the relationship is indeed hump-shaped.

country's safety net, while on the other, it may mean the contrary as in various instances developing countries have preferred to rebuild their reserves rather than servicing their debts (see Altunbas and Gadanecz, 2004).

Results and discussion

Table 8.6 illustrates the regression results for several samples using the ICRG data on political risk. The table presents whether a result was found to be significantly positive, negative or insignificantly different from 0. Significance levels are indicated by the asterisks (*); and statistically the degree of association among dependent (loan spread) and independent variables (the various disaggregated political risk factors) is stronger where the number of asterisks is higher.

The first column shows the regression results using the aggregate measure of political risk. The second column is based on a developed country sub-sample, while the third is on based a developing country sub-sample. In both of these latter two columns the measure of political risk has been disaggregated into its constituent parts. Note that results of the variables used to control for micro-economic and macro-economic factors are not presented.

Recall that in every case the lower the risk point total, the higher the risk (and vice versa). For example, a high value for 'democratic accountability' means the democracy is rated as very accountable. Slightly less intuitively a higher value for 'ethnic tensions' implies a lower level of ethnic tension. So an increase in any political risk measure is indicative of a reduction in risk (for example strength of democracy, absence of corruption, or absence of the military in politics), while a low disaggregated value is seen as a measure of high risk (say, absence of law and order, presence of corruption).

Concerning the regressions' quality of fit, the adjusted R-squared (R^2) should be interpreted as a measure of how well the variation in the micro, macro and political risk variables describe the loan spread: the higher the R^2 percentage, the better the model fits the data.

In line with expectations, the first column in Table 8.6 shows that the aggregated measure of political risk as described by the ICRG is negative and significant. Although not reported in the table, the coefficient is about −2.4. This indicates that a 1 per cent reduction in the overall political risk (i.e. an increase in the index) results in a −2.4 basis point reduction in the loan price.

Table 8.6 *Regression results for political risk ICRG measures (1996–2003)*

	Aggregated political risk index	Disaggregated political risk	
		Developed countries	Developing countries
Political risk index	significantly negative (***)		
Government stability		insignificant	significantly positive (**)
Socio-economic conditions		insignificant	insignificant
Investment profile		insignificant	insignificant
Internal conflict		insignificant	insignificant
External conflict		insignificant	insignificant
Corruption		insignificant	insignificant
Military in politics		insignificant	insignificant
Religion in politics		insignificant	insignificant
Law and order		insignificant	significantly negative (***)
Ethnic tensions		insignificant	insignificant
Democratic accountability		insignificant	significantly positive (**)
Quality of democracy		insignificant	significantly negative (***)
Environmental risk	insignificant	significantly negative (***)	insignificant
Strength of regression (adjusted R²)	*15.1%*	*9.4%*	*36.7%*

Notes: ** *** indicate significant at 5 per cent and 1 per cent respectively. Column 1 shows the inference based on the regression using the aggregated measure of political risk. Columns 2 and 3 show the inference based on the disaggregated measure of political risk (environmental risk also shown). Note that for a given country each disaggregated measure of political risk assigns a higher value, the lower the risk. Inference based on micro-economic and macro-economic control variables not shown.

In the second and third columns of Table 8.6 the political risk index has been disaggregated and its relationship with loan spreads estimated for developed and developing countries. Concerning the former, it seems that political risk measures bear little or no importance for developed countries as all coefficients are insignificantly different from 0. Focusing on developing countries, we find four out of twelve coefficients are significantly different from 0: government stability, law and order, democratic accountability and quality of democracy. However, only two of these coefficients, namely law and order and quality of democracy have the expected negative sign.

In explaining the coefficient on law and order and quality of democracy, one can posit that many projects cause significant social and economic upheaval, especially in smaller or less-developed economies. Therefore the strength and impartiality of the legal system, the popular observance of the law as well as the institutional strength and quality of democracy will be significant factors in the pricing of a loan. In terms of developed countries it is fair to say that the 'level' of law and order has remained broadly constant and of a reasonable standard in recent times, negating the need to attach a premium to the cost of a loan. In the case of developing countries this is not so. Rather, issues of law and order are going to be far more likely to affect the cost of the loan in such countries, hence our negative coefficient implying that on average the cost of a loan will be less if there is an improvement in law and order.

In contrast to the previous negative coefficients, our findings for government stability and democratic accountability are significant and positive. This implies that an increase in government stability or democratic accountability will result in (on average) an increase in the cost of a loan. Conversely, a reduction in either of these measures seems to go hand in hand with lower loan spreads. Prima facie it is puzzling as to why there is a link between lower levels of stability and democracy of the host country and a lower cost of PF loans, though on reflection it can be seen to conform to our understanding of PF.

Some argue that, from a business point of view, the brokering of PF deals is best done in an environment of weak government, allowing the SPV to gain concessions that it would be unable to get in countries that are traditionally viewed as less risky. Indeed Hainz and Kleimeier (2007) find that PF loans are usually preferred in countries where the economy is poor, characterized by weak corporate governance, political risk and where bank influence over the host government is high. Using our PF loan sample we find, *ceteris paribus*, that the cost of PF loans is reduced when similar conditions exist in the host country.

Given that risk and return are intrinsically linked, the reduction in loan spread will be awarded when there is less risk inherent in the project. Our result therefore implies that there is a larger degree of risk transference in developing host countries that exhibit weaker levels of government stability and democratic accountability – in other words the reduction in the loan price is garnered by the developing host country taking on more risk than their developed country counterparts. This dovetails with our understanding of developing host countries agreeing to more stringent host government agreements.

An alternative interpretation follows from observing that the measures in question relate to changes in government. If we were to consider the governmental risk to an investment, we can break this down into two parts: (a) the risk of doing business in the country assuming there is no change in governmental risk (current risk); (b) the added risk resulting in a change in government.[11] From this, a change in government, even if for the better, can result in an increase in risk via uncertainty, especially if the risk of the latter is magnified by the risk of the former. From this definition we would expect to see positive coefficients on measures of governmental risk for those countries in the emerging and developing countries samples.

For example, developing-country X might suffer from certain weaknesses in government (current risk). This risk is known, and an attempt can be made to quantify this risk. However, if there is an expectation that there may be changes in the host country that may impact on this weakness of government, this may induce uncertainty as there is no guarantee that the stated or anticipated changes will materialize as planned, even if these changes are with a view to improving the situation in the host country. In this setting it seems logical for the banks to require additional return to compensate them for the additional risk they are bearing while the host government undergoes its adjustment.

Given the R^2 results in Table 8.6, there is evidence to suggest that when loans are priced for developed countries, the weighting placed on political risk will be lower, relative to less-developed countries. This is in line with the simple *a priori* assumption that these countries are on average characterized by a relatively low and often stable level of political risk. The micro and macro variables should be important in describing the loan price for both country sub-samples, but in conjunction with the differential treatment of political risk we would expect to see higher R^2 values in the higher-risk developing-countries samples, which is indeed the case.

Table 8.6 also reports the coefficients for a measure of environmental impact. This is a dummy variable, where 1 = high, 0 = low corresponding

---

[11] Such as a change in government stability.

to industrial sectors of high or low risk (see Table 8.4 above). We do not suggest that those labelled high-impact sectors will always have high environmental impact, and similarly for low-impact sectors. Instead this figure points to the fact that on average, projects in such sectors could have a larger impact on the environment.[12] The results from this dummy variable imply quite different conclusions for developed versus developing countries: while the coefficient is negative and significant for the developed countries sample, it is positive (though not significant) for developing countries. This suggests that in developed countries such PF loans are on average cheaper in the industries classified as having high environmental impact. One possible explanation for this is that the sectors classified as having high environmental impact might also be intrinsically less risky, possibly because they tend to deal more often with highly tangible, asset-rich projects, and thus attract a lower loan spread (see Table 8.5 for the definition of this dummy variable).

Our findings are broadly confirmed employing alternative measures of political risk from the World Bank's Worldwide Governance Research Indicators Dataset.[13] These results are shown in Table 8.7. While we consider this comparison an essential 'robustness test', the results should be interpreted with some caution because the data derive from a different source with definitions of variables making no two results directly comparable in the strictest sense.

Overall, Table 8.7 appears to confirm two main empirical findings. First, there exists a clear negative relationship between loan spreads and: (a) government effectiveness (that is associated with the ICRG definition of quality of democracy); and (b) the rule of law (law and order in the ICRG database). This implies that the availability of funds in PF is strongly related to the effectiveness, quality and strength of a country's legal and institutional systems. Further, we again find that our statistical model better describes our developing-country sample than our developed-country sample, once again pointing to the importance of political risk in the latter.

The second main result relates to the significant and positive coefficient for the corruption index that is found for developed and emerging countries. This implies that a reduction in corruption (an increase in the measure 'corruption') will mean that on average loans will be more

---

[12] We are grateful for the input from the International Institute for the Environment and Development in creation of this variable.
[13] See Table 8.4 above for the constituent definitions.

Table 8.7 *Regression results for political risk: WB measures 1996–2003*

Variable	Developed countries	Developing countries
Voice and accountability	insignificant	insignificant
Political stability	insignificant	insignificant
Government effectiveness	insignificant	significantly negative (***)
Regulatory burden	insignificant	significantly positive (**)
Rule of law	significantly negative (**)	significantly negative (***)
Control of corruption	significantly positive (**)	insignificant
Environmental risk	insignificant	significantly positive (***)
Strength of regression (adjusted R^2)	*10.4%*	*35.9%*

Notes: ** *** indicate significant at 5 per cent and 1 per cent respectively. Note that for a given country each disaggregated measure of political risk assigns a higher value the lower the risk.

expensive. However, the coefficient is not significant for developing countries and is not found significant using the ICRG definitions (Table 8.6). Such mixed results suggest that further examination of this specific variable in such regressions may be warranted.

Finally, we find a positive and significant coefficient on the environmental impact variable for our developing-country sample, and an insignificant result for developed countries.[14] This implies that projects categorized as having a high environmental impact will cost more in developing countries than projects perceived to have a lower environmental impact. One possible explanation for this contrast between developed and developing countries could be that many asset-rich projects have less environmental impact in developed countries because these are more likely to have governments that are able to enforce strict rules on environmental damage and are more effective in monitoring firms' behaviour. The positive coefficient for developing countries might be the banks' response to a lower level of monitoring in such countries, and therefore a higher perceived risk to the project's cash flows resulting from potential environment damage.

[14] Note using ICRG data we find a significant negative relationship for developed countries, and an insignificant relationship for developing countries.

Conclusions

In recent years the relative importance of PF investments for long-term infrastructure has increased remarkably. However, this lending technique is often employed in countries that are characterized by a relatively high level of political risk. In this chapter we considered the impact of PF loans on alternative measures of political risk disaggregated into proxies for human rights. We used a sample of over 1,000 PF loans over the 1996–2003 period and measures of political risk in both aggregate and disaggregate form. We then split the sample according to the World Bank's data on country development, yielding two datasets on developed and developing countries.

We control for micro- and macro-economic factors, and then examine the relationship between the aggregate and disaggregate measures of political risk with respect to the price of PF loans. With regard to the aggregated measure of political risk, we find a negative and significant relationship with loan spread. This means that on average low political risk levels are related to low loan spreads. This is an important baseline result that is in accord with economic intuition, but more detail is garnered when the relationship between loan spreads and political risk is analysed at a disaggregated level. With respect to the results for developed countries none of the disaggregate measures are found to be significant in describing loan price. This can be explained by the fact that political risk is unlikely to be a factor in such economies. However, on inspection of the developing-country results, there is evidence of a clear negative relationship between loan spreads and the quality of bureaucracy and the effectiveness of a country's legal and institutional systems. This is contrasted by the positive relationship between loan spreads and both government stability and democratic accountability. This implies that there is a tendency for more democratically accountable and stable developing host countries to pay more for a PF loan, or conversely when they are less so then PF are on average cheaper.

To explain the finding that loans may be cheaper to governments that have weak governmental stability and democratic accountability, we present a risk transference rationale. Given that PF SPVs are set up with the express purpose of transferring risk to interested parties, it is plausible that the weaker the government, the more risk can be transferred from the project to the host country via the host government agreement. This would result in there being less risk remaining to be priced in the project, and hence a lower spread offered.

References

Altunbas, Y. and B. Gadanecz (2004), 'Developing Country Economic Structure and the Pricing of Syndicated Credits', *Journal of Development Studies*, 40(5), 143–73.

Esty, B. C. (2004a), 'Why Study Large Projects? An Introduction to Research on Project Finance', *European Financial Management*, 10(2), 213–24.

Esty, B. C. (2004b), 'When do foreign banks finance domestic projects? New evidence on the importance of legal and financial systems', Harvard Business School, mimeo.

Esty, B. C. and W. L. Megginson (2002), 'Creditor Rights, Enforcement, and Debt Ownership Structure: Evidence from the Global Syndicated Loan Market', paper presented at Contemporary Corporate Governance Issues II: International Corporate Governance, Tuck School of Business, Dartmouth College, Hanover, NH, 12–13 July 2002.

Gatti S., A. Rigamonti, F. Saita and M. Senati (2007), 'Measuring Value-at-Risk in Project Finance Transactions', *European Financial Management*, 13(1).

Hainz C. and S. Kleimeier (2007), 'Project Finance as a Risk Management Tool in International Syndicated Lending', Governance and the Efficiency of Economic Systems Discussion Paper No. 183, University of Mannheim.

Jensen, M. C. and W. H. Meckling (1976), 'Theory of the Firm: Managerial Behavior, Agency Costs, and Ownership Structure', *Journal of Financial Economics*, 3(4), 305–60.

Kleimeier S. and W. Megginson (2000), 'Are Project Finance Loans Different from other Syndicated Credits?', *Journal of Applied Corporate Finance*, 13(1), 75–87.

Sorge M. (2004), 'The Nature of Credit Risk in Project Finance', *Bank for International Settlement Quarterly Review*, December.

Sorge M. and B. Gadanecz (2008), 'The Term Structure of Credit Spreads in Project Finance', *International Journal of Finance and Economics*, 13(1), 68–81.

White H. (1980), 'A Heteroskedasticity–Consistent Covariance Matrix Estimator and a Direct Test for Heteroskedasticity', *Econometrica*, 48(4), 817–38.

9

Insurance as a risk management tool: a mitigating or aggravating factor?

RASMIYA KAZIMOVA

Setting the background

The implications of non-recourse or limited recourse financing usually prompt potential project finance (PF) lenders to assess carefully all possible risks that might arise in a project to ensure that those risks are mitigated and controlled. The failure to do so might upset the schedule of cash flowing into the project, while the project revenues are the only source for repayment of the loan, with interest accruing on a daily basis.[1] In an extreme case, this might put the viability of the whole project at risk, thus triggering non-payment of debt owed to banks.

So lenders will typically look for the project to be sound at various levels: technically, environmentally and legally. Lenders will also look for the proof of demand for the project's output in different markets, as well as for the project's potential to penetrate those markets with the assumed percentage of sales and thus secure the assumed margins in each market. This will ensure that the project is feasible and complies with the lender's standards.

In theory, PF can be structured in such a way that there are no risks and lenders are content to rely solely upon the revenue-producing project contracts to service debt. In practice, however, this rarely happens and some form of credit support from a creditworthy party becomes an absolute necessity.[2]

Where there still remains an element of risk in a project, lenders ideally seek certain risk mitigants being in place, prior to granting PF.

---

[1] For further on PF structure, see Chapter 5.
[2] S. L. Hoffman, *The Law and Business of International Project Finance: A Resource for Governments, Sponsors, Lenders, Lawyers and Project Participants* (2nd edn, The Hague: Kluwer Law International, 2001), p. 382.

For example, if a project is to be carried out in a developing country with
a weak credit rating, and where the local client of the project does not
have enough experience and expertise in implementing the relevant type
of work, the involvement of experienced and creditworthy partners as
investors and engineering, procurement and construction (EPC) contractors, would mitigate against such risk, in addition to the other
prerequisite safeguards. When there is no participant in the project
that can take over a certain risk,[3] the other very important type of a
risk mitigant is procurement of insurance for a fee.[4]

PF lenders believe insurance provides a valuable risk mitigant. They
have focused their due diligence more on insurances over the recent
years and it has become the object of commercial negotiation – sometimes difficult – between lenders and sponsors.[5] This comes as no
surprise since the main aim of project insurance, which is 'to spread
risk and, if the risk materializes to spread the resulting loss',[6] is perfectly
in tune with what PF is all about: effective risk (and loss) allocation.[7]

Typically, lenders require sponsors to procure insurance against all
possible risks that are not borne by parties in the project and which could
negatively impact on the capacity of the project to meet its debt obligations in time, while having enough to cover operation and maintenance
expenses for an agreed period.

Some of the insurance packages required by lenders are very expensive, so sponsors try to persuade lenders to rely on less costly risk
mitigants. For example, the lenders may be content with evidence that
the project site is well secured against access by all those who might cause
damage to the assets, so that it is not essential that the special purpose
vehicle (SPV) procures a sabotage and terrorism insurance policy. But

---

[3] Excess risks between the participants should be redistributed in such a way as to lead
ultimately to a bankable project without burdening any single participant to the point
that PF is converted into recourse financing (see Hoffman, *Law and Business*, p. 382).

[4] An interview with an insurer conducted on 8 March 2007 revealed that on assessment the
risks are roughly divided into three categories: (a) those that the project participants can
deal with and eliminate; (b) those that they can manage; (c) those that they cannot
manage and for which a financial solution is required. Insurance or a financial bond is
considered to be better placed to deal with category of risks (c). Source requested
anonymity.

[5] An interview with a commercial PF lender conducted on 28 November 2008. Source
requested anonymity.

[6] M. Clarke, *Policies and Perceptions of Insurance Law in the Twenty-First Century* (Oxford
University Press, 2005), p. 251.

[7] Hoffman, *Law and Business*, p. 20.

this is something that would be decided on a case-by-case basis rather than a one-for-all-cases rule.[8] Despite the fact that insurance adds on the capital cost of the project, for certain business activities, not to have one in place would make PF unfeasible.[9] In general, lenders are not willing to be saddled with risks which they consider they are not fit to bear and will not grant PF to projects where the risk elements have not been covered off.

The risk aversion of lenders and their faith in insurance can be seen as positive, in that by making PF conditional on a particular type of policy being in place, banks ensure that a risk is assigned to an insurer, a party with knowledge and experience in mitigating that type of risk and with an interest in preventing that risk from materializing.

Insurers have developed expertise in risk prevention in some areas rather more than others. In Germany, the largest insurer has its own research centre with more than one hundred engineers providing technical reports, studies, tests, training and development.[10] In its turn, the results of this research help insurers to better understand the risks and the state-of-art ways to manage and mitigate them. This is reflected in the terms and conditions of an insurance policy and in the amount of premiums charged.[11]

Having access to insurance is also viewed as an advantage by various project counter-parties. As PF lenders' due diligence is focused on both the strength of the contracts and the parties behind those contracts, procurement of a relevant insurance policy with a reputable insurance company allows a project company to improve a lower credit rating; the insurance policy buttresses the contract, and it is on this that PF lenders will rely.[12]

---

[8] Interview as above, n. 5.

[9] At the same time, with the help of insurance some contested projects get 'the green light'. Two projects, gold mines in Guyana (Omai) and Irian Jaya (Freeport McMoRan), which later resulted in disasters, were supported by MIGA's insurance. For more information, see P. Chatterjee, 'Finance – Guyana: Backers of Gold Mine Have History of Disaster' (31 August 1998), accessible at the People's Paths Hope Page at www.yvwiiusdinvnohii.net/political/omaigold.htm (last accessed: 10 October 2009) and Down to Earth IFIs Factsheet Series, 'The Multilateral Investment Guarantee Agency (MIGA): Whose Interests are Served and at What Cost?' (No. 16, October 2001) at http://dte.gn.apc.org/Af16.htm (last accessed: 10 October 2009).

[10] Clarke, *Policies and Perceptions*, pp. 41–2.

[11] The insurer who spends little or nothing on loss prevention may be able to undercut other insurers. As many insurance markets are driven by price, those insured will buy cheap insurance today, rather than an insurance policy that at least in part subsidizes research for improvements in the future (*ibid.* p. 42).

[12] Interviews with a PF lender conducted on 28 November 2008 and a leading EPC contractor on 19 August 2009. Sources requested anonymity.

Furthermore, the fact that some types of insurance are mandatory under state law testifies to the fact that potential loss and damage to the community close to the site of a project is unacceptable.[13] In other cases insurance is made available and purchased in response to particular risk aversions.

As positive as this may be, one needs to acknowledge however that insurance policies which are not compulsory under the laws applicable to a project will often be purchased by a company at the insistence of or in response to expectations of PF lenders. In these cases, a company may feel that such policies are no longer necessary after a loan has been paid back. Loans are usually repaid well before the end of the project lifetime. So the positive impact of insurance on the PF arrangements may vanish with the loans being repaid.[14]

Were we to set aside the concern about the project being in operation longer than the term of a loan the advantages of having a project insured might tempt one to look at insurers through rose-coloured spectacles, were it not for the vivid lessons from the past. It is not long ago that non-governmental organizations attacked the official insurance agencies of the rich countries for supporting commerce – and sometimes corruption – over the needs of the poor.[15] And the complicity of greedy insurance companies in wartime human rights violations is still fresh in one's memory.[16]

---

[13] This, certainly, was the main consideration of the UK Parliament when it made insurance compulsory for drivers of motor vehicles under the Road Traffic Act 1930 (see Clarke, *Policies and Perceptions*, pp. 20–1). The following types of insurance are mandatory under the laws of the Republic of Azerbaijan: ecological; auditors' professional liability; fire; passengers'; civil servants'; service personnel's; civil liability of vehicle owners.

[14] Foreign sponsors may have an interest in extending the term of certain policies, such as PRI, after the loan has been paid, to insure themselves against the risk of expropriation of their property by host states.

[15] L. T. Wells and R. Ahmed, *Making Foreign Investment Safe: Property Rights and National Sovereignty* (Oxford University Press, 2007), p. 4. For more information on such incidents, see the ECA Watch website (www.eca-watch.org) and UNICORN (www.againstcorruption.com).

[16] Holocaust survivors have sued insurance companies for complicity in wartime human rights violations, and, with the aid of the US government, achieved several multimillion-dollar settlements. For further, see: S. D. Murphy, 'Nazi-Era Claims against German Companies', *American Journal of International Law*, 94 (2000), 682; G. D Feldman, *Allianz and the German Insurance Business, 1933–1945* (New York: Cambridge University Press, 2001); 'Denying History's Claims: Holocaust Survivors' Claims against Insurance Companies Doing Business in California: Information from the Office of Senator Tom Hayden' (Los Angeles, CA: Senator Hayden's district office, 1998); M. J.

Though this is definitely a reason to make us look for hidden problems in insurers' involvement in different deals, this chapter does not seek to analyse the motives of those issuing policies for particular projects. Instead, the aim here is more ambitious: it is to look into certain reasons for procuring insurance and to examine the procedures for issuing and claiming under insurance policies which could serve to create another layer of risk. This might happen at the same time that the insurance is intended to achieve the opposite: to help manage and mitigate risk.

A claim of moral hazard associated with insurance

The argument often articulated with regard to effectiveness of insurance to manage risks, and which is considered closely in this chapter, is that insurance carries with it the risk of moral hazard by taking away incentives to mitigate risks that once came to pass trigger payment under the insurance policy.[17]

Clarke masterfully described this risk by referring to Hecate's words in Shakespeare's play *Macbeth*: 'security is mortals' chiefest enemy'.[18] In the play, Macbeth becomes overconfident after being told by an apparition that no man 'born' of a woman can harm him. The play ends with his being surprised and put to the sword by a man born by Caesarean section, who, therefore, was not technically 'born' of a woman. So, it is believed, that on procuring insurance against particular risks, one becomes less careful to prevent them from occurring. Some may even be led to believe that by paying an insurance premium they earn the right to be careless; the higher the premium paid, the stronger is the belief.[19]

Sometimes third parties in a position to affect the risk may even get incentives to do so in order to be better off due to the insurer responding to the losses of the insured. Sometimes the terms and conditions of the

Bazyler and R. P. Alford (eds.), *Holocaust Restitution: Perspectives on the Litigation and Its Legacy* (New York University Press, 2006); S. Deborah, *A Status Report on Holocaust-Era Insurance Claims* (Report of the Washington State Insurance Commissioner, Washington State, December 2000).

[17] See for example, Wells and Ahmed, *Making Foreign Investment Safe*, pp. 201–2.
[18] William Shakespeare, *Macbeth* (III: 5), cited in Clarke, *Policies and Perceptions*.
[19] C. J. M. Schuyt, 'The Paradox of Welfare and Insurance', Geneva Papers 77 (1995), 430–8, in Clarke, *Policies and Perceptions*, p. 254. It could be alternatively argued that when one has to pay high premiums for insurance the insured tends to treat the terms of such a policy more seriously.

insurance policy and the nature of an insurer may affect the latter's attitude to the prospect of payment.

So, as such, the moral hazard associated with insurance could reveal itself on the part of the insured, the party able to affect the risk and the insurer. The moral hazard of concern to this author is that which influences the way environmental risks are being handled in a given project, not least because deterioration and contamination of the environment with consequential effects on the health and lives of workers and the host community are the most well-known side effects of certain projects that became feasible with the help of insurance. Considering this, all three sources of moral hazard in PF insurance will be considered to the extent necessary.

The arguments for and against

The impact of PF arrangements

PF and insurance focus on different risks to be managed and mitigated, which can, in principle, have an impact on how the risks covered by insurance per se are treated. PF is concerned with the risks that might upset the expected cash flow into the project and, thus, any resultant default on the loan, if for some reason the project becomes no longer viable or more expensive. This concern is reflected in how lenders view insurance, i.e. as a credit enhancement that is expected to inject the required funds into the project by compensating the loss sustained by the insured (if covered), and thus restoring the economics of the project. When it comes to insurance, though, it is concerned with compensating the loss in the first place, and has an ancillary role in managing the actual risks and preventing losses.[20]

So as long as insurance unequivocally backs up the project 'financially', the ways the risks covered by the insurance are managed and mitigated are, in principle, of no concern to lenders.[21] Although insurers

---

[20] ABI, UK Insurance – Key facts (2005), p. 8 at: www.abi.org.uk/BookShop/ResearchReports/Key%20facts%202005_LR.pdf (accessed: 23 February 2009).

[21] An interview with an SPV in an oil and gas project in a developing country conducted on 30 January 2008. The issue also surfaced in an interview with a credit rating agency conducted on 3 October 2007. The discussion was held around the tendency to accord higher scores to hell or high water contracts which secure the receipt of full revenue payments, despite the fact that projects may be technological/operational failures. The interviewee supported the hypothetical assumption that if a purely credit risk is not triggered by environmental and social risks presented by technical/operational shortcomings in the project, then retaining those in a project would not result in a lower project debt rating. Both sources requested anonymity.

prefer risks with a high frequency on a low scale,[22] almost any risk is insurable as long as its effects are reasonably predictable.[23] It is then the job of the insurers on the basis of their knowledge and experience of particular risks to balance potential gains and losses when considering whether or not to provide particular cover. Though, logically, it would not be in the best interests of insurers to retain risks in projects in return for some other benefit[24] real cases from the past lend force to the argument that nothing in principle prevents insurers from providing cover for a project with a heightened probability of risks materializing in the hope that the risks will not materialize for the lifetime of the cover or in the knowledge that they have nothing to lose if the risks do materialize.

It is alleged that in Indonesia numerous companies used the corrupt nature of the Suharto regime to their advantage and won lucrative orders for large, unnecessary and overpriced projects, particularly in the energy sector, the terms of which were against the interests of the people of Indonesia. Such projects were frequently insured by foreign export credits or guarantees in full knowledge of the situation. Overseas Private Investment Corporation (OPIC) was among the agencies to provide political risk insurance. When the economic crisis broke out in the autumn of 1997 the national energy company had to face expensive contracts for purchasing private power for which there was no demand. The moment it finally reneged on its contractual obligations and OPIC had to pay the claims of investors, pressure started being put on Indonesia by OPIC and the US government to reimburse OPIC. Indonesia finally had to pay the price, though OPIC had the option to void their guarantees for corrupt power plants and to hold the exporters accountable.[25] Investors, no longer interested in the region, used their

---

[22] A. J. Vermaat, 'Uninsurability: A Growing Problem', Geneva Papers, No. 77 (1995), 446–53; M. G. Faure, 'The Limits to Insurability from a Law and Economics Perspective', Geneva Papers, No. 77 (1995), 454–62, 458 referred to in Clarke, Policies and Perceptions, p. 39.

[23] Clarke, Policies and Perceptions, p. 40.

[24] In an interview with an insurer conducted on 8 March 2007 the discussion touched on limited recourse financing and the potential motivation of sponsors to reach the end of the construction phase as soon as possible to get themselves 'off the hook' even by cutting corners. The insurer supported the contention that insurers are inclined to refuse cover altogether rather than retain risks for higher premiums in cases when the planned schedule of construction would seem insufficient for them. Source requested anonymity.

[25] P. Bosshard, 'Publicly Guaranteed Corruption: Corrupt Power Projects and the Responsibility of Export Credit Agencies in Indonesia', ECA Watch, at: www.

access to the OPIC insurance as the means by which to walk away from the projects by being very confrontational, refusing to negotiate the terms of contracts and turning to arbitration.[26]

Thus, that which could be seen as an effective risk allocation for one (i.e. a PF lender) could still create a moral hazard for the other (in our case, an insurer and the insured), which finally rubbed off unfairly on the third party (i.e. a host government acting in public interest).

Although a PF lender, and particularly one which has agreed to be bound by the Equator Principles (EP),[27] will insist on the project meeting certain social and environmental standards before the loans are granted, it seems that such a bank's view of environmental risks is more simplistic, limiting them to those that might arise out of the fact that no standards or lower environmental standards are followed in a given project. This narrowness of view might prevent lenders from seeing that their arrangements may unintentionally aggravate the risks covered by insurance.

Among the arrangements preferred by PF lenders but which can potentially backfire on the quality of the environment are lump-sum turnkey contracts.[28] Lenders see these as an effective way to guarantee against cost and time overruns, as well as against complications arising out of defective designs, and also as a way of making sure that in a complicated project integration of different units has been successfully achieved. An insurer interviewed agreed that where contractors work on a lump-sum turnkey basis and are insured there is a possibility that under pressures of time and budget[29] they would be willing to cut corners.[30]

---

eca-watch.org/problems/corruption/bosshard_indon_nov2000.html (last accessed: 10 October 2009).
[26] Wells and Ahmed, *Making Foreign Investment Safe*, p. 171.
[27] A benchmark for the financial industry when determining, assessing and managing environmental and social risks in PF. For the full text of the Equator Principles, see: www.equator-principles.com/documents/Equator_Principles.pdf (last accessed: 10 October 2009).
[28] The size and the scope of some projects may not allow for a large enough range of qualified EPC contractors to accomplish a competitive bid for the entire construction work. Considering this, a number of lump-sum turnkey contracts for different parts of the project with a minimum interface risk is also a possibility not rejected by PF lenders. A guarantee for the minimum acceptable interface risk in such cases could be offered in the form of project management contractor involvement.
[29] Considering that the amount of profit a contractor would take under a lump-sum turnkey contract is in direct proportion to the sum the contractor actually saves in process of construction, a promise of a bonus to motivate a contractor to finish in time or ahead of time would heighten this concern.
[30] Interview with an insurer conducted on 8 March 2007. Source requested anonymity.

Although the examples considered above support the proposition that insurance gives rise to moral hazard, not least because PF is not concerned with each and every moral hazard that could potentially arise under insurance (but only that which could trigger default on the loan), to say that being insured per se takes away all incentives to prevent risks would be an inaccurate generalization. On close analysis of the requirements to be met before a policy is issued and clauses incorporated in a policy it becomes apparent that certain conditions imposed by insurers are in fact meant to protect them against the risk of moral hazard.

We will look at some of the precautions that are typical of most types of insurance policies.

Common mitigants of moral hazard

Before a particular risk can be insured, an insurer carries out due diligence to assess the risks already existing in the project and the probability of these and other potential risks materializing. The insurer will then require the insured to take all reasonable and available measures to significantly reduce the chances of such potential risks materializing.

The insurer must try to predict events and secure itself from moral hazard that could arise on both the part of the insured and on those that may affect the risk.[31] The results, subject to the risk being at all insurable, will be reflected in the policy's terms and conditions and in the premiums charged. Thus, terms and conditions and the amount of premiums are a means of imposing better risk management on the insured.

There may be different types of exclusion clause in the insurance. Some of them are express exclusion clauses providing that if certain conditions were to pass, the cover would not extend to them. For instance, the description of the peril covered could be very precise so that if the situation of an insured does not squarely fit into the description of the peril under the policy, it will not be covered. Some are covert: the policy may specify various obligations on the insured under the policy, such as the duty to disclose material information;[32] where the

---

[31] Clarke, *Policies and Perceptions*, p. 38

[32] See M. Kantor, 'Are You in Good Hands with Your Insurance Company? Regulatory Expropriation and Political Risk Insurance Policies', in T. H. Moran *et al.* (eds.), *International Political Risk Management: Needs of the Present, Challenges for the Future* (Washington, DC: World Bank, 2008), pp. 137–70, p. 164, citing from a sample PRI policy.

insured is found to be in breach of such clause, this can effectively be relied on by an insurer to refuse compensation for the losses.[33]

In some cases, insurers make policies subject to insurers having monitoring rights on the project which would allow them at any time to access the project premises when necessary to assess which mitigation measures are in place. Where the insured is found in or about to be in breach of a condition under the policy, the insured may be given some time to remedy the situation. Otherwise, the cover may be withdrawn.[34]

This, though, seems to be an exception rather than a rule.[35] Kantor suggests that in practice insurers do not carry out risk assessment. Instead they rely on the 'duty to disclose' clauses in the policy that require the insured to supply the insurer with all information that may influence the insurer reaching a decision to provide a particular cover and setting the premium.[36] This *uberrima fides* principle operates strictly in favour of the insurer and there is little scope for challenging it.[37]

For instance, the operational regulations of the Multilateral Investment Guarantee Agency (MIGA), the chief investment arm of the World Bank, state that:

---

[33] For more details on the lack of clarity of the difference between exception and warranty clauses in an insurance policy, see M. Clarke, *Policies and Perceptions*, pp. 160–1; M. A. Clarke, *The Law of Insurance Contracts* (4th edn, London: Informa Professional, 2002), p. 629. See also J. Lowry and P. Rawlings, *Insurance Law: Cases and Materials* (Oxford: Hart Publishing, 2004), ch. 8 on contractual terms, pp. 349–434, with accompanying references.

[34] N. Lockett, *Environmental Liability Insurance* (London: Cameron May, 1996), pp. 39–40. One form of insurance with very strong monitoring and remedial rights is the monoline wrap. Monoline wraps pay out the principal and the interest accrued on a debt when due if for some reason the insured borrower cannot do so. Thus, due to the nature or risks insured, monoline insurers get senior creditor rights against the borrower. This includes the right to get access to the project facilities for inspection and request the borrower to remediate the problems, if any. However, one should not overstate the importance of monitoring rights held by monoline providers as deterrents, since monoliners tend to insure very low (almost improbable) default risk assets. Source: interview with an insurer requesting anonymity, conducted on 8 May 2007. For more information on monoline wraps, see also: G. Russo, 'Overview of the Monoline or Financial Guaranty Insurance Business and Recent Events', Dwight Asset Management Company website: www.dwight.com/pubs/html/monoline_financialguaranty insurance.shtml (accessed: 10 October 2010).

[35] In an interview with an insurer conducted on 8 May 2007 it was stated that insurers do not usually provide continuous monitoring of the activities of the insured. Source requested anonymity.

[36] Kantor, 'Are You in Good Hands?', p. 165.

[37] Lockett, *Environmental Liability*, p. 34.

Compliance with host country laws and regulations normally will be confirmed through warranties and representation as per standard insurance industry practice.[38]

However the insurer does not rule out that in certain cases, especially in the cases of projects with potentially significant adverse impacts on environment, the compliance:

> will be verified by MIGA through requested monitoring reports, site visits, or other measures as necessary in addition to warranties and representations. Failure by the guarantee holder to respond to these requests or to abide by such laws, regulations, or specific requirements entitles MIGA to terminate the guarantee or to deny payment of a claim if the non-compliance is not corrected within a period set forth in the Contract of Guarantee.[39]

Be that as it may, were risks to materialize after the policy has been issued, a breach of a duty to disclose could be relied on by an insurer to declare the policy void.[40] Therefore, regardless of whether an insurer carries out an assessment or relies on the 'duty to disclose' clause in order to guarantee against risks already existing in the project or which may subsequently arise, it is not in the best interests of a prudent insured to cover up risks in the hope that insurers will not notice them. Thus, the existence of a duty-to-disclose clause in an insurance policy could, in principle, replace the need for an insurer to constantly monitor project activity.[41]

By paying the premium, the insured shares the costs of the risk against which it has been insured. The tendency to charge high premiums for higher risks[42] may serve as an incentive for companies to lower the

---

[38] Para. 13 of the Environmental Assessment Policy (EAP), at: www.miga.org/policies/index_sv.cfm?stid=1681 and para. 47 of MIGA's Environmental and Social Review Procedures (ESRP), at: www.miga.org/index.cfm?aid=27.

[39] Para. 13 of MIGA EAP and para. 48 of MIGA ESRP.

[40] For details of how this works, see Clarke, *Law of Insurance Contracts*, ss. 23-17 and 20-2A1, pp. 761–4 and 630–2, with accompanying references to supporting case law.

[41] This being said, it was indicated by one insurer that better monitoring is something that has recently started being insisted on by lenders. In cases likely to give rise to moral hazard, one insurer believed that there should always be somebody policing the project on behalf of an SPV or a consortium as to what is actually happening on the ground. Interview conducted on 8 May 2007. Source requested anonymity.

[42] 'Higher risks' in this context are defined to mean risks that are presented by the nature of activities rather than those deliberately retained in the project. A company with a history of no defaulting on insurance cover would be charged lower premiums as compared to, for example, one that has been found liable for damages in the past.

chances of risks materializing by, for example, having strong environmental risk management policy, employing state-of-the-art technology and following higher standards.[43]

Usually an insurance policy also imposes a cap on the amount to be insured. For example, for equity investments, MIGA can guarantee up to 90 per cent of the investment, plus up to an additional 50 per cent of the investment contribution to cover earnings attributable to and retained in the project. Regardless of the nature of the project, an investor is required to remain at risk for a portion of any loss.[44]

A limitation could be imposed on the amount that can be claimed in relation to any single incident covered, with an aggregate limitation on the whole policy per year. That would mean that if the risk came to materialize and lead to losses bigger than the amount insured, the insurer's exposure to the resultant expenses would be limited to the amount capped.[45]

Furthermore, as a rule, insurance policies specify a deductible, which is a certain amount of expenses that must be paid by the insured before an insurer will cover any expenses. The latter two types of safeguards are another way of making the insured share in the losses.

It appears that insurers usually do not look into the amount of contingency fund to be maintained by the SPV but rather concentrate on the risk culture of the company.[46] This approach could be argued to be effective, as the existence of the contingency fund is not a guarantee that the funds would be enough to cover the actual contingency, whereas the risk culture of the insured could be more effectively relied on to predict what would be the approach of the insured to the management of risks.[47]

General obstacles to the effectiveness of the mitigants

The above safeguards are only some of those available to mitigate the risk of moral hazard that could lead to environmentally unfriendly results.

---

[43] Clarke, Policies and Perceptions, p. 138.
[44] See MIGA, Investment Guarantee Guide at: www.miga.org/documents/IGGenglish.pdf (last accessed: 2 October 2009).
[45] This was not always so with environmental liability insurance but, rather, something that insurers took on board after having to pay out enormous sums in the absence of such limitation. Lockett, Environmental Liability, p. 36.
[46] Interview with an insurer conducted on 8 May 2007. Source requested anonymity.
[47] This assumption found its support by a rating agency in an interview conducted on 3 October 2007. Source requested anonymity.

This is not to say, however, that they support the argument that denies insurance creates another layer of risk. That would be too optimistic. As indicated earlier, PF lenders may insist on undertakings that may destroy the positive impact of safeguards in insurance policies against moral hazard. For instance, as positive as the exclusion or warranty clauses in insurance policies may seem, the PF lenders, by insisting on a non-vitiation clause, sweep away all that those safeguards are intended to achieve. A non-vitiation provision prevents the insurer from voiding a policy, or refusing to make a payment to the lender as loss payee, on the basis of misrepresentation, non-disclosure or breach of warranty by the insured or on the basis of mistake.[48] The reason for insisting on this is that each of these vitiating factors is very difficult for the PF lender to determine in its due diligence process, and impractical to monitor during the term of the loan.[49]

Imagine that the project company misrepresents the actual situation with environmental risks on the land plot where the infrastructure unit is to be built in order to be eligible for lower premiums or for insurance in general. If the covert environmental risk materializes and there is a non-vitiation clause, the insurer arguably will not be able to rely on the fact of misrepresentation to refuse paying to lenders for the loss under the policy. In its turn, this creates an inappropriate incentive for the insured and runs against the EP and what they expect of a signatory PF lender.

The law driving a particular insurance policy can equally help to prevent a moral hazard arising out of insurance as well as do a disservice by introducing one. The same could be said of the decisions made by insurers, adjudicators or arbitrators, as the case may be, to uphold or reject a claim by the insured for compensation. Those could act both as a deterrent to undesirable behaviour and an inspiration to such behaviour.

On top of that, the terms and conditions of an insurance policy, as well as the nature of the insurer together with subrogation rights[50] and the leverage the insurer may in certain circumstances have over the party to be compensated, are all factors that can help to answer the main question of this chapter in the affirmative or the negative.

In order to test the merits of each of these assumptions, let us turn to two different types of insurance, and consider their effects on environmental risk.

---

[48] Hoffman, *Law and Business*, p. 593.   [49] *Ibid.*
[50] For a definition of this term, see below p. 260.

The two types of policy are environmental liability insurance and political risk insurance. These are most relevant for present purposes since: (a) both can have an impact (be that direct or indirect) on the way in which environmental risks in projects are assessed, managed and mitigated; and (b) both are types of insurance that are typically required by PF lenders nowadays, with this requirement being almost uniformly complied with by investors. The second type of insurance, against political risk, becomes even more important if the project is being implemented in a developing country; and (c) they help to demonstrate how the existence or the lack of subrogation rights adds to the debate about whether or not project insurance aggravates moral hazard.

Political risk insurance (PRI)

In any project financing, whether domestic or transnational, the project is subject to governmental jurisdiction and action. This can entail additional risks, beyond the control of a project sponsor.[51] Though not unique in posing political risks to investors, emerging markets are nevertheless seen by investors as more likely to change laws unexpectedly, to impose currency controls or other unplanned-for regulatory changes, to breach contracts or even to expropriate property for inadequate compensation.[52] PRI has been introduced by the market to address this particular concern of investors.

Applying the same criteria for narrowing down the research as above, aspects of PRI cover that fall to be considered are those that may potentially be triggered by new laws. These may be passed by the host government in response to environmental concerns after an investment agreement has been signed and result in either increased expenses for development and operation of the project or make the project not viable.

A good starting point would be to emphasize that changes in law as such are not insured by the PRI market as this act of a state is not in violation of international law. As it is a basic tenet of PRI that it protects the existing rights of investors, not those ones they wish to have,[53] in

[51] Hoffman, *Law and Business*, p. 57.
[52] K. W. Hansen, 'An Introduction to Investment Insurance against Political Risks', in H. A. Davis (ed.), *Infrastructure Finance: Trends and Techniques* (London: Euromoney Institutional Investor plc, 2008), pp. 421–32, p. 421.
[53] F. E. Jenney, 'A Sword in a Stone: Problems (and a Few Proposed Solutions) Regarding Political Risk Insurance Coverage of Regulatory Takings', in Moran *et al.* (eds.), *International Political Risk Management*, pp. 178–9.

order to be able to underwrite a cover, a PRI insurer must later have a basis for a claim against the host government.[54] In turn, a host government is only liable for the consequences of its actions that are wrongful, as opposed to legitimate.[55]

Unfortunately for the PRI industry, it is extremely difficult to find an appropriate legal standard that distinguishes between 'wrongful' and 'legitimate' government regulatory actions.[56] Responding to the concern of investors and lenders about the potential negative impact of the application of new environmental laws by the host government to the previously agreed project, and keeping in mind the constraints of the PRI, the insurance industry has responded by extending certain of its already existing covers and has come up with new ones.

We now look at cover for regulatory takings and creeping regulatory expropriation,[57] breach-of-contract cover, and arbitral default cover for stabilization clauses.

Regulatory taking and creeping regulatory expropriation

The recognition of regulatory takings under international law has developed more recently as compared with the US. In the 1960s and 1970s, a

---

[54] See for example the MIGA's cover for expropriation which says: 'Compensation will be paid upon assignment of the investor's interest in the expropriated investment (e.g., equity shares or interest in a loan agreement) to MIGA', in Section on Types of Coverage, at: www.miga.org/guarantees/index_sv.cfm?stid=1547. This is fixed even procedurally: for instance, the host government and USExim (for example) must have in place a bilateral agreement that provides USExim with recourse to the host government if a political risk event results in a default in the USExim financing documents. For the OPIC Political Insurance Program, the US and the host country must enter into a bilateral agreement that relates to the OPIC programmes. Under a bilateral agreement, the approval of the host government must be obtained before the OPIC insurance is issued. See Hoffman, *Law and Business*, pp. 408 and 464.

[55] Jenney, 'Sword in a Stone', p. 171.   [56] *Ibid.* p. 173.

[57] Creeping regulatory expropriation and regulatory taking are sometimes used as synonyms since the creeping expropriation could be achieved by way of regulatory actions of host governments. However, some authors consider that there are differences: for creeping expropriation a series of actions would amount to expropriation whereas each one separately could be absolutely legitimate, or at least non-expropriatory in nature. See P. C. Choharis, 'Regulatory Takings under International Law: A Brief Legal and Practical Guide', in Moran *et al.* (eds.), *International Political Risk Management*, pp. 115–36, n. 2. For the purposes of this chapter 'expropriation' and 'taking' are used as synonyms, while the differentiation between 'creeping regulatory expropriation' and 'regulatory taking' as described is preserved.

few scholars argued that international law should recognize 'indirect' expropriations as well as direct seizures, but there were few authorities to buttress their arguments.[58] Eventually, however, scholars, arbitrators, bilateral treaties and then multilateral treaties began to recognize that governments may expropriate the property of foreign investors both by outright seizures and by indirect measures that were tantamount to a seizure.[59] While these treaties helped establish that a regulation, legislation or other government action may constitute an expropriation in violation of international law, it was far from clear when such a 'measure [was] tantamount to nationalization or expropriation'.[60] It has been said by one commentator that the attempt to define a 'taking' is like a physicist's search for the quark.[61]

'Creeping' expropriation is, perhaps, the most feared risk, by which the host government uses a combination of taxes, fees and other charges and devices to increase its share of the project's profits.[62] A series of acts (or omissions) by the host government that have the effect of an expropriation will qualify for a claim, even if no expropriation was declared or intended and no single government act alone would have constituted an expropriation. Whether the aggregate effects of individually legitimate – or at least non-expropriatory – governmental acts constitute an expropriation is the sort of thing over which the insurers and the insureds might disagree.[63]

---

[58] See, e.g., Burns H. Weston, '"Constructive Takings" under International Law: A Modest Foray into the Problem of "Creeping Expropriation"', *Va.J.Int'l.L.*, 16 (1975–6), 103; G. C. Christie, 'What Constitutes a Taking of Property under International Law?', *Brit.Y. B.Int'l L.*, 38 (1962), 307 referred to in Choharis, 'Regulatory Takings', p. 117, n. 7.

[59] See for example Article 1110 of NAFTA (1 January 1994), at: www.nafta-sec-alena.org/ DefaultSite/legal/index, which provides: 'no Party may directly or indirectly nationalize or expropriate an investment of an investor of another Party in its territory or take a measure tantamount to nationalization or expropriation of such an investment', unless the government's action is: (a) for a public purpose; (b) is non-discriminatory; (c) meets due process of law and minimum treatment accorded to the government's own nationals; and (d) pays compensation fully, promptly and in convertible currency. Energy Charter Treaty, 17 December 1994, art. 13(1), 34 ILM 360, 391 similarly requires compensation for investments 'nationalized, expropriated or subjected to a measure or measures having effect equivalent to nationalization or expropriation'.

[60] Choharis, 'Regulatory Takings', pp. 117–18.

[61] C. M. Haar and M. A. Wolf, *Land-use Planning: A Casebook on the Use, Misuse, and Re-use of Urban Land* (4th edn, Boston, MA: Little, Brown, & Co., 1989), p. 875, referred to in H. Mounfield, 'Regulatory Expropriations in Europe: The Approach of the European Court of Human Rights', *NYU Envtl. L.J.*, 11 (2003), 136, 137.

[62] Hoffman, *Law and Business*, p. 69.

[63] Hansen, 'Introduction to Investment Insurance', p. 423.

International law is used as guidance on what would constitute a regulatory taking or a creeping regulatory expropriation with no promising results, as it is vague, inconsistent, evolving and political.[64] Or, alternatively, the insurance policies use the language closely tracking the consensus standard for what is required for a particular act of state insured under PRI to be in violation of international law.[65] But once a PRI insurer, an adjudicator or an arbitrator finds the action(s) to amount to either of the two the failure to pay compensation will be considered a violation of international law. In turn, the standard of compensation is the most important, and historically the most contested requirement.[66]

It is possible to imagine the host government passing a single law or a series of laws imposing stricter environmental standards, which, though making it still possible to obtain a new permit meeting the requirements of the new law or laws, may nevertheless have a considerable impact on project capital costs, operating expenses and production and significantly reduce the return on investments. How would this be seen by the insurance market?

It is not uncommon for a PRI policy to exclude regulatory conduct that constitutes a bona fide non-discriminatory act. The MIGA contract explicitly carves out from its coverage any losses resulting from:

> a bona fide non-discriminatory measure of general application of a kind that governments normally take in the public interest for such purposes as ensuring public safety, raising revenues, protecting the environment, or regulating economic activities, unless the measure is designed by the Host Government to have a confiscatory effect.[67]

Leaving aside the fact that the language of these clauses may give rise to different interpretations,[68] the wording itself suggests that legislation has to meet certain criteria in order to allow the host government to avoid its action being framed a 'regulatory taking' or a 'creeping regulatory expropriation' which, once recognized as such, would be followed by a duty to compensate investors for losses.

---

[64] Jenney, 'Sword in a Stone', p. 176.
[65] *Ibid.* p. 179. It appears that lately commercial insurers waive the requirement that violation of international law should be established for contract frustration coverage to be triggered. See Hansen, 'Introduction to Investment Insurance', p. 425.
[66] A. Newcombe and L. Paradell, *Law and Practice of Investment Treaties: Standards of Treatment* (The Hague: Kluwer Law International, 2009), p. 369, with accompanying references, fn. 282.
[67] Hansen, 'Introduction to Investment Insurance', p. 427.
[68] Jenney, 'Sword in a Stone', pp. 179–80.

Court and arbitral decisions often hold that there is no regulatory taking or creeping regulatory expropriation when a sovereign acts to protect the public health, safety or environment. However, there are no international expropriation law cases that provide express guidance on when measures designed to protect these interests might justify non-compensation.[69] What is often emphasized though is that government action should be designed to minimize the intrusiveness of the property rights of foreign investors.[70]

There is a body of case law that has shown the readiness of judges to find regulatory action amounting to taking, and thus to rule on the duty to pay compensation, in cases when legislation had the effect variously expressed as 'appropriating or destroying property';[71] depriving the property owner of 'all economically viable' use;[72] depriving the owner, in whole or in significant part, of the use of reasonably-to-be-expected economic benefit of a property;[73] leading to 'substantial deprivation' of property rights;[74] or resulting in complete (or almost complete) deprivation of a claimant's property.[75] Judges have sometimes refused to find a taking in situations where the property owner's loss was less than total.[76] In other situations they have suggested that 95 per cent would likely qualify.[77]

Though these cases show a particular tendency, there is no internationally recognized rule that all value must be lost in order for an

---

[69] Newcombe and Paradell, *Law and Practice*, p. 361, with accompanying references, fn. 242.

[70] Choharis, 'Regulatory Takings', p. 125.

[71] *Pennsylvania Coal Co.* v. *Mahon*, 260 US 393, 415 (1922), cited *ibid.* 117.

[72] *Lucas* v. *South Carolina Coastal Council*, 505 US 1003, 1015 (1992), cited in Choharis, 'Regulatory Takings', p. 117.

[73] *Metalclad Corporation and United Mexican States*, ICSID. Case No. ARB(AF)/97/1, Award (30 August 2000), at para. 103, p. 195, available at: www.worldbank.org/icsid/cases/mm-award-e/pdf (accessed: 10 October 2010).

[74] Interim Award, *Pope & Talbot Inc. and the Government of Canada*, 26 June 2000, para. 102, available at: www.appletonlaw.com/cases/P&T-INTERIM%20AWARD.PDF.

[75] *S. D. Myers and Canada*, Partial Award, 13 November 2000, at paras. 281 and 282. Available at: www.dfait-maeci.gc.ca/tna-nac/documents/myersvcanadapartialaward_final_13-11-00.pdf (accessed: 10 October 2010).

[76] *Concrete Pipe & Prods. of Cal. Inc.* v. *Construction Laborers Pension Trust*, 508 US 602, 645 (1993) (declining to treat an interest in a pension plan as the entire property and finding no taking where the regulation allegedly resulted in a 46 per cent diminution in shareholder equity overall); *Keystone Bituminous Coal Ass'n* v. *DeBenedictis*, 480 US 470 (1987), 498–500 (no taking where regulation allowed property owner to mine 50 per cent of its coal).

[77] *Lucas* v. *South Carolina Coastal Council*, 505 US 1003, 1015 (1992).

expropriation under international law to occur. And indeed different courts and tribunals have repeatedly recognized partial takings.[78]

In our example, though, the project would still be able to function, the level of reduction in revenues[79] caused by passing environmentally friendly legislation – whether a single law or a series of discrete legislative acts – if significant, will invite a PRI insurer, an adjudicator or the arbitrator, as the case may be, to decide on whether the level and nature of interference with property rights of investors amounts to a regulatory taking or a creeping regulatory expropriation.

In its turn, the evidence suggests that certain factors may prejudice the success of finding in favour of state actions in public interest. We will look into these after briefly going through two other areas covered by PRI, touched on earlier.

Breach of contract

PRI insurers often seek to divide coverage into 'expropriation' and 'breach of contract'. A debate exists in international law as to whether breach of an investment agreement by a host government can constitute an expropriation and, if so, in what circumstances. Some PRI policies address this issue through interpretation of the general term 'expropriation' once a claim arises.[80] OPIC's cover for 'expropriation', for instance, mentions that 'under certain circumstances, OPIC is also able to cover the unlawful breach of specific contractual obligations of a subsovereign or a corporation owned or controlled by a foreign government'.[81] OPIC is also known to assure investors that a breach of contract by a state can, in some circumstances, rise to the level of an expropriation under international law. This happened in a well-known OPIC finding, *Ponderosa Assets*.[82]

---

[78] See e.g., *Florida Rock Industries, Inc.* v. *United States*, 18 F.3d 1560, 1567 (Fed. Cir. 1994) (implying that diminution of value of approximately 60 per cent might be compensable).

[79] Choharis listed profit or return to invest as one of the five basic property rights of investors and argued that the complete deprivation of one of the five property rights would be enough to amount to expropriation. However, he warned of the existence of cases proving otherwise. For further, see Choharis, 'Regulatory Takings', p. 123, with accompanying footnotes.

[80] Kantor, 'Are You in Good Hands?', p. 151.

[81] OPIC, Insurance: Expropriation at: www.opic.gov/insurance/coverage-types/expropriation (last accessed: 10 October 2009).

[82] See e.g. OPIC Memorandum of Determinations, Expropriation Claim of Ponderosa Assets, L P, Argentina – Contract of Insurance No. D733, at 7 (2 August 2005), available at:

Other PRI policies, however, expressly exclude breach of contract from 'expropriation' cover.[83]

Strong contracts backing the project are like an artery system supporting the life of a project. PF lenders will scrutinize these. Among those that are considered to be building blocks for a project are feedstock contracts, utilities contracts, land lease contracts, EPC contracts, operation and maintenance (O&M) contracts and off-take contracts.[84]

Suppose a host government passes a law banning the development and extraction of a particular mineral or natural resource in response to conservation concerns for future generations. Suppose that this particular mineral or natural resource is a feedstock which the government is under obligation to provide on a long-term basis to a given project. Compliance with this policy and laws would cause the government's default on the feedstock agreement which is a very important contract for the viability of the project. A breach-of-contract cover would be triggered by such a material default on the loan, once established in arbitration. As the effect of such a regulatory action by the state may amount to a complete deprivation of property rights of investors, it is possible that such a breach of contract arising out of passing a law by the host government may be recognized as amounting to expropriation. The finding of OPIC in the *Ponderosa* case would support this assumption.[85]

Arbitral default coverage for stabilization clauses

As we have seen, because the governmental action to pass new laws is not wrongful, political risk insurers do not typically insure against this risk. However, the host country may be willing to contract with the project sponsor that certain regulatory actions will not be taken. Stabilization clauses to that end are the usual way of dealing with this risk and may be found in most of the recent investment agreements. Indeed, in PF deals the inclusion of such clauses in investment contracts may be driven by positive treatment of these by rating agencies when rating a project debt.

---

www.opic.gov/sites/default/files/docs/Ponderosa_Assets_L.P._202005.pdf (last accessed: 10 October 2009).

[83] Kantor, 'Are You in Good Hands?', p. 151.

[84] Discussions with a PF lender and a major reputable EPC contractor in the oil, gas and petrochemical field, the latter with extensive experience of securing the support of ECAs for projects where the EPC services were provided by such a contractor.

[85] Expropriation Claim of Ponderosa Assets (above, n. 82). Though the application of the 'plain meaning' rule of contract interpretation would seem to exclude the cover. Kantor, 'Are You in Good Hands?', pp. 151–2.

In turn, the latter influences the decision of banks to provide lending and the terms and conditions on which the loans are provided.[86]

Lorenzo Cotula differentiates between different types of stabilization clauses usually found in investment contracts and treaties and emphasizes the chilling effect those may have on the regulatory power of host states.[87] Though some evidence suggests that breach of stabilization clauses more often than not leads to renegotiation of agreements,[88] rather than settling in arbitration, the availability of cover may put additional pressure on the host government to take needed action in the interests of its people.

Political insurance providers may be able to insure against the risk that the contract, especially the stabilization clause, is repudiated or abrogated, via an arbitral award default coverage.[89] Arbitral award default coverage (of a stabilization clause) is separate from expropriation coverage, and is designed to preserve for the insured the benefits of an agreement containing international arbitration as the dispute resolution mechanism. An arbitral award is much more easily insurable than a contractual promise to pay, or even a court judgment for payment, because an international arbitral award is more dependably enforceable against the host government. International arbitral awards have the force of law and are enforceable without judicial review, by virtue of the UN Convention on Recognition and Enforcement of Arbitral Awards (known as the 'New York Convention') and similar international treaties both in the host county and in other countries party to the same treaty. In other words failure to pay is a violation of international law.[90]

---

[86] *Standard & Poor's, 2007 Global Project Finance Yearbook: Project Finance Summary Debt Rating Criteria*, pp. 89–104, p. 101. The rating agency would nevertheless question whether a relevant public authority would stand by such a clause, if circumstances changed. In a nutshell, that would be put together with an overall risk assessment of the country. Interviews with rating agencies conducted on 29 September and 3 October 2007. Sources requested anonymity.

[87] Chapter 6.

[88] For more details see T. Waelde and A. Kolo, 'Renegotiation and Contract Adaptation in the International Investment Projects: Applicable Legal Principles and Industry Practices', *CEPMLP Internet Journal*, 5(3), at: www.dundee.ac.uk/cepmlp/journal/html/vol5/vol5-3.html (last accessed: 15 June 2007). With particular regard to environmental concerns, an interview with a representative of an SPV suggests that companies prefer to subsume reasonable extra environmental costs as part of capital expenses on the project rather than revert to arbitration in order to pass those costs onto the host government. Interview conducted on 30 January 2008. Source requested anonymity.

[89] Hoffman, *Law and Business*, p. 70.

[90] Jenney, 'Sword in a Stone', pp. 182–3.

In case of this cover it will be the arbitral panel, not the political risk insurer, who will determine that the host government has wrongfully breached a stabilization clause in an investment agreement and what the damages are.[91] Once an arbitral award is passed, the failure to pay the award by the host government will trigger the insurance cover concerned.

The concern about the chilling effect of inclusion of a stabilization clause in investment agreements is further heightened by the implications of insuring it. The risk arises from cases in which the losses sustained by the insured as a result of new laws passed to, for example, protect the environment are not considered an expropriatory interference with property rights. By procuring this cover, the insured is able to count on the fact that non-payment of compensation for losses arising from such new laws – as a stabilization clause typically requires – would set a chain reaction in motion leading to arbitral award against the host government and triggering the insurance. The fact that the PRI provider holds subrogation rights against the host government and that PRI providers may have significant leverage against the host government, as we will see later, could mean that if stabilization clauses do not persuade government to abstain from changing the legal regime or to pay the compensation for bringing about such changes, the PRI will make sure that the government pays the price. Let us now see how this works.

Subrogation rights

Subrogation arises as a consequence of the indemnity principle and refers to the right of an insurer, who has paid for a loss, to pursue the wrongdoer in the name of the insured. This would mean that, on receiving the compensation by the insured, whatever right the insured has against the wrongdoer passes to the insurer.[92] The existence of subrogation rights has a positive impact on premiums: the latter go down.[93]

As was already mentioned, PRI insurers underwrite the covers subject to having subrogation rights against the host government. By introducing such rights into insurance, insurers aimed to protect themselves against moral hazard on the part of the host government as the latter is

---

[91] *Ibid.* p. 184.
[92] Lowry and Rawlings, *Insurance Law*, p. 587, with supporting case law.
[93] *Ibid.* p. 621.

able to influence the risk of regulatory changes in anticipation of increasing its share of profits from the project. And the knowledge that the insured will be compensated and thus there will be no aggravation of relations between investors and host government could give inappropriate incentives to the latter.

What started as a good intention, though, turned out not to be so good, as what insurers, being shielded by subrogation rights, effectively did was introduce incentives for themselves to compensate easily for losses of investors even when host governments initiate changes in law for a public purpose. This is more so, when the PRI insurer is: (a) the one making a decision (rather than depending on a court judgment or determination by an arbitrator) on whether the cover has in fact been triggered; (b) an ECA interested in promoting the exporters from its country; and (c) has a certain leverage over the host government.

Leverage of public and private PRI providers over the host government

PRI was born and has spread in the public sector, but it has also flourished in the private sector.[94] Procuring PRI from either ECA or MIGA, rather than a commercial institution, would ensure that their corporate social responsibility mandates will restrict them in what they can do.[95] Not being aimed solely at creating profits could, on the other hand, allow them more flexibility in focusing on covers where the private sector feels that an investment is uninsurable.[96] Palmer observes that while the private sector also assesses environmental and other risks that fall into the realm of corporate social responsibility frameworks, public sector insurers embrace these principles as a necessity, regardless of the risk aspect. At the same time, he asserts that public sector insurers may be more effective in seeking subrogation-based recovery.[97]

Ansermino also believed that the deterrent role of private insurers is limited as compared with public sector agencies. If there is a role, that role would be for the private sector to go hand in hand with public

---

[94] Hansen, 'Introduction to Investment Insurance', p. 425.
[95] The lack of such restraints is argued to be on the plus side of commercial institutions providing PRI as they can move quickly to make covers available (see *ibid.*).
[96] G. Ansermino, 'The New Scramble for Commodities: Medium-Term Trends in Political Risk Insurance', in Moran *et al.* (eds.), *International Political Risk Management*, p. 228.
[97] J. Palmer, 'Looking Ahead: Will Political Risk Insurance Continue to Play a Meaningful Role in the Global Investment and Trade Environment?', *ibid.* pp. 221–2.

insurers.[98] Though Salinger, as a representative of the AIG private
insurance company, indicated that they had done very well in recoveries
and never had a case where they could not get access to relevant people,
he nevertheless admitted that access improves once they collaborate with
the public agency.[99]

This could turn out not to be a laudable thing as experience shows. In
the energy projects in Indonesia (referred to above), which were allegedly secured via corrupt influence on the host government and involved
OPIC support, in order to make the host government reimburse OPIC,
the US government warned the host government that it would invoke
the so-called Helms amendment. This would have led the US to vote
against Indonesian interests in all financial institutions as well as to take
other measures. Furthermore, the US government attempted to stop
further credit to the country from ADB. In the end, these and other
forms of pressure by the insurer and its country broke down the resistance of Indonesia to paying out.[100]

Inherent bias of ECAs

The ECA mandate requires it to support companies and promote the
purchase of goods of the ECA home country. Considering this, it is
doubtful that in acting as a PRI insurer and left in a position to judge
whether an investor from a home country is owed compensation ECAs
would be unbiased.

This gives reason to believe that determination of what is to constitute a regulatory taking or a creeping expropriation under international law and whether such an event takes place is better left to
arbitrators rather than PRI insurers. This belief has merit in that arbitrators should seek to arrive at an independent decision, as compared to
a PRI insurer.[101] It is therefore questionable whether it is a good thing
that a decision reached by a PRI insurer may influence the arbitral
process on the same issue. This is what actually happened in the
Ponderosa claim in Argentina: OPIC knew that the insured had a

[98] 'Discussion of the International Political Risk Insurance Industry in 2010', *ibid.* p. 245.
[99] *Ibid.*
[100] Bosshard, 'Publicly Guaranteed Corruption'. See also Wells and Ahmed, *Making Foreign Investment Safe*, pp. 174–9, 190–6.
[101] Though there could still be concern that the background of arbitrators may tip the balance in favour of protection of property rights of investors rather than uphold the mandate of the state to legislate new laws for the public benefit.

pending claim under the International Convention for the Settlement of Investment Disputes (ICSID), but made a determination that there had been an expropriation without waiting for the results of that process. Later an OPIC representative argued that 'a determination by a PRI insurer may actually influence the arbitral process in ICSID and give the investor a reason to find value in its political risk insurance coverage'.[102]

Confidentiality undertakings

A typical policy issued by a private insurer will provide that 'the Insured shall not disclose the existence of this insurance policy to any third party, with the exception of the Insured's bankers and other professional advisors on a confidential basis, without the prior written consent of the Underwriter'.[103] Moreover, most policies provide for the resolution of disputes in arbitration. Commonly used arbitration rules preserve the privacy of arbitral proceedings.[104] Among PRI insurers (whether public or private), only the US agency OPIC makes publicly available its claims determinations and arbitration awards relating to disputes with its policy beneficiaries.[105] Under the cover of confidentiality policy beneficiaries may offer exaggerated claims about a host state's conduct, confident that such allegations will not reach the ears of regulators, investors or the media.[106] This in itself may be relied on when making a decision against a host government.

Standard of compensation

As mentioned above, the standard of compensation for expropriation in customary international law has been one of the most contested issues, with standards espoused ranging from prompt and effective payment of full fair market value to those providing more flexibility in the amount, manner and timing of payment.

[102] E. Quintrell, OPIC, 'Commentary', in Moran *et al.* (eds.), *International Political Risk Management*, pp. 43–4.
[103] Quotations of policy language in this article are based on policy forms in Kantor's personal files. See Kantor, 'Are You in Good Hands?', p. 139.
[104] See AAA Commercial Rules, Rule R-23, AAA International Arbitration Rules, Article 20.4, LCIA Rules, Articles 19.4 and 30, ICC Arbitration Rules, Article 21.3 and MIGA Rules of Arbitration, Article 39.2.
[105] Kantor, 'Are You in Good Hands?', p. 139.   [106] *Ibid.*

Whereas the standard of 'prompt, adequate and effective compensation' is argued to capture the former meaning, the requirement of 'just' or 'appropriate' compensation is believed to support the contention that less than full fair market value may be awarded. The appropriateness of the distinction between 'full' and 'just' compensation however may be questioned.[107]

One may also argue that the implications of the words 'just', 'appropriate', 'adequate' and 'effective', besides having different implications depending on whether they are seen through the prism of foreign investors' interests or that of the state, are also subject to recent developments: what was just and appropriate yesterday may be unfair today if seen through the prism of sustainable development requirements.

The European Court of Human Rights (ECtHR), for instance, observed that there is no right to full compensation in all circumstances. Legitimate objectives of public interest may call for reimbursement at less than the full market value. And in certain circumstances the taking of property in the public interest without payment of compensation is treated as justifiable.[108]

When investors choose a developing country to develop a project it may be expected that the environmental laws of the country are not well developed and will continue to change, not least in order for the country to come into line with its international obligations. From this point of view, the argument of investors that the investment climate of the country should be predictable whereas the new environmental laws are not is far-fetched. Were we to leave aside the argument based on the reasonableness of passing new laws for public purpose from time to time and on a basis that is easily foreseeable, one has to emphasize that investors are not supposed to benefit from low environmental standards that compromise health and safety. So it is only reasonable that were the host government to pass new environmental laws in the public interest, and which could negatively influence the value of foreign investments,

---

[107] In *CME Czech Republic BV* v. *Czech Republic* (Final Award, 14 March 2003), the majority of the tribunal found that the standard of just compensation in the Netherlands' BIT practice is the same as full compensation under the Hull formula. Professor Brownlie, in dissent, however found that there was a distinction, with the just compensation standard being lower and based on subjective proof. Referred to in Newcombe and Paradell, *Law and Practice*, p. 379, fn. 352.

[108] *James* v. *UK*, Series A, No. 98, Application No. 8795/79, (1986) 8 EHRR 123, para. 54. For other case law supporting exceptions to the customary standard, see in Newcombe and Paradell, *Law and Practice*, p. 379, with accompanying references.

investors should be prepared to face that risk. The ECtHR seems to support this.[109]

A further issue with respect to the standard of compensation for expropriation is whether the requirement for reparation differs depending on whether expropriation is legal or illegal.

An expropriation is believed to be lawful if it satisfies certain conditions, which under customary international law are: (a) the requirement of a public purpose for the taking; (b) the requirement that there should be no discrimination; (c) payment of compensation; and (d) the requirement of due process.[110] Where the requirements or conditions for an expropriation are not satisfied, the expropriation is illegal.[111]

With regard to indirect expropriations and creeping expropriations, it was noted by Judge Brower:

> it is difficult to envisage a de facto or 'creeping' expropriation ever being lawful, for *the absence of a declared intention to expropriate* almost certainly implies that no contemporaneous provision for compensation has been made. Indeed, research reveals no international precedent finding such an expropriation to have been lawful.[112]

This is especially troublesome if we consider that the consequences of an illegal expropriation, according to the Permanent Court of International Justice (PCIJ) decision in the Chorzow Factory case,[113] are that reparation will not be confined to the making good of the loss actually sustained by the investor but additional factors such as loss of unrealized

---

[109] See *Fredin* v. *Sweden*, Series A No. 192, Application No. 12033/86 (1991 13 EHRR 784) and *Pine Valley Developments* v. *Ireland* (A/222), 29 November 1991. See also the arguments of Lorenzo Cotula on the compensation triggered by the breach of stabilization clause and the implicit exception of 'compliance with international law', in Chapter 6.

[110] For more details on each of the conditions, see Newcombe and Paradell, *Law and Practice*, pp. 369–77. See also UNCTAD, *Taking of Property, UNCTAD Series on Issues in International Investment Agreements* (New York and Geneva: UN, 2000), UNCTAD/ITE/IIT/15, pp. 12–13.

[111] Newcombe and Paradell, *Law and Practice*, p. 369.

[112] *Sedco, Inc.* v. *National Iranian Oil Co.* 10 Iran–US CTR 180 (1986) 25 ILM 629, 649 (my emphasis). Though the ECtHR seems to differentiate between wrongful failure to pay compensation and an inherently illegal expropriation (one that is discriminatory or lacks public purpose). Case of the *Former King of Greece* v. *Greece* judgment (28 November 2002), para. 78.

[113] *Factory at Chorzow (Germany* v. *Poland)*, 1928 PCIJ Rep Series A No. 17, 47 (13 September).

profits should be taken into account in calculating the damages owed to a foreign investor.[114]

In what way would it be troublesome for our case? Suppose that the state has agreed under the investment agreement not to change its laws, including environmental laws that are applicable to the project. Suppose at some point later the state reneges on its promise in order to pass in good faith and following a due process an urgently needed law for environmental purposes.

Though the *Methanex* arbitration can raise one's hopes that this action of the state would be considered non-compensatory,[115] a caveat in the decision that '*unless specific commitments had been given by the regulating government to the then putative foreign investor contemplating investment [then] the government would refrain from such regulation*',[116] still raises questions as to whether the fact that the state had earlier agreed to a stabilization clause would not bring its action within 'illegal expropriation' coverage.[117]

As we saw in the *Ponderosa* case[118] a breach of contract by a state can, in some circumstances, equate to an expropriation under international law. The latter would make the warning of Judge Brower valid and increase the risk that the state might be faced with an award, where the formula for calculation of compensation is 'investment plus unrealized profits'.

It is believed that excess awards in investment disputes, particularly when the formula for calculation is 'investment plus profits' can create

---

[114] See generally A. Sheppard, 'The Distinction between Lawful and Unlawful Expropriation', in C. Ribeiro (ed.), *Investment Arbitration and the Energy Charter Treaty* (New York: Juris, 2007); A. Reinisch, 'Legality of Expropriation', in A. Reinisch (ed.), *Standards of Investment Protection* (Oxford University Press, 2008); I. Marboe, 'Compensation and Damages in International Law: The Limits of "Fair Market Value"', *JWIT*, 7 (2006), 723.

[115] *Methanex* v. *US*, Final Award of the Tribunal on Jurisdiction and Merits (9 August 2005) at: http://naftaclaims.com/Disputes/USA/Methanex/Methanex_Final_Award. pdf. Though there is no guarantee that in similar arbitration cases in future the *Methanex* decision will be relied on, rather than the decision in *Metalclad* (above, n. 73), in which an opposite decision was reached: the state had to pay out compensation despite the claim that the action of local government was undertaken for environmental purposes.

[116] *Methanex* (above, n. 115), Final Award, Part IV, Ch. D, para. 7 (my emphasis).

[117] Professor Cameron notes that expropriation that breaches stabilization clauses of the parties' contract is unlawful (*International Energy Investment Law: The Pursuit of Stability* (Oxford University Press, 2010)), at p. 69, fn. 24.

[118] See e.g. Expropriation Claim of Ponderosa Assets (above, n. 83).

incentives for companies to apply to arbitration rather than renegotiate, so as to recapture their investment plus future profit without risk and work.[119] The existence of PRI provided by an ECA together with the fact that the ECA has a certain leverage and arguably an inherent bias to make the state pay the compensation can heighten this concern.

Let's now turn to another type of insurance to see what other moral hazards might ensue from it.

Environmental liability insurance

The liability insurance and the polluter-pays principle: is there a conflict?

Liability insurance is 'any insurance protection which indemnifies liability to third persons',[120] thus providing cover against a consequent depletion of the insured's assets.[121] Environmental liability arises not only by 'any injury to any person, and/or loss or damage to material property, and/or any nuisance, trespass, obstruction or other interference with any right of way, light, air or water resulting in financial loss occurring in connection with the Business',[122] but also 'pollution' or 'loss or damage as a result of impairment of the environment'.[123] In the latter case, the environment as a 'third party' is represented by the local authorities or sometimes by environmental interest groups who have the right to litigate on behalf of the damaged environment. Some of the policies can provide both covers under standard third-party insurance.[124] Some do expressly exclude the 'pollution' cover. The latter created the demand for a separate environmental impairment liability insurance, which the insurance industry has begun to offer. For the purposes of this chapter, environmental

---

[119] Wells and Ahmed, *Making Foreign Investment Safe*, pp. 211–12, Box 13.1, with accompanying endnotes.

[120] *Quinlan v. Liberty Bank Co.*, 575 So. 2d 336, 339 (La. 1990 – liability) referred to in Clarke, *Law of Insurance Contracts*, p. 494.

[121] *Ibid.*

[122] A typical environmental operative clause provided in Lockett, *Environmental Liability*, p. 34.

[123] Lugano Convention, Article 2§7c.

[124] As was the case with UK insurers until recently.

liability insurance will be used as an umbrella term designating a liability insurance policy triggered by injury to people and damage to property and generally the environment as a result of an industrial hazard.

Availability of environmental liability insurance in a world intensely concerned with the state of the environment, and the consequent threat to the livelihood of people, highlights the role for insurance in dealing with these concerns. Especially important here is the 'polluter-pays' principle.

The polluter-pays principle was first endorsed by the OECD in the early 1970s.[125] In order to encourage rational use of scarce environmental resources, the 1972 OECD Recommendation of the Council on Guiding Principles concerning International Economic Aspects of Environmental Policies (18) included recommendations that 'the polluter should bear the expense of carrying out the [control and prevention] measures decided by public authorities to ensure that the environment is in an acceptable state'.[126] That meant that 'the cost of these measures should be reflected in the cost of goods and services which cause pollution in production and/or consumption'.[127] The recommendation also advised against subsidies.[128] Since the UNCED Conference the polluter-pays principle for the first time secured international support as an environmental policy, by finding its reflection in Principle 16 of the Rio Declaration.[129]

It is strongly believed that that by internalizing the costs of pollution to polluting activities, the principle generates incentives for 'increased levels of prevention' of environmental harm. On the other hand, it is also

---

[125] OECD, Recommendation of the Council on Guiding Principles concerning International Economic Aspects of Environmental Policies, C(72) 128 of 26 May 1972; C(74) 223 (1974) and C(89) 88 (1988). See generally OECD, *The Polluter Pays Principle*, OCDE/GD(92)81 (1992).

[126] OECD, C(72)128, *ibid.* Annex, A(a)4.

[127] *Ibid.*   [128] *Ibid.*

[129] P. Birnie and A. Boyle, *International Law and the Environment* (2nd edn, Oxford University Press, 2002), p. 92 The principle is defined in broadly similar terms in the 1992 Paris Convention for the Protection of the Marine Environment of the NE Atlantic, Article 2(2)b; the 1992 Helsinki Convention on the Protection and Use of Transboundary Watercourses and Lakes, Article 2(5); the 1995 Barcelona Convention for the Protection of the Marine Environment and the Coastal Region of the Mediterranean, Article 4; and the 1996 Protocol to the London Dumping Convention, Article 3. See also 1991 European Energy Charter, Article 19(1). Other treaties simply refer to the 'polluter pays' principle without attempting to define it.

insisted that to be effective the regime of liability for harm to the environment needs to be supported by liability insurance.[130]

Indeed, the fact that a company has purchased a policy covering extra expenses arising out of its own legal liability for causing environmental harm could be interpreted both as the company being in compliance with the polluter-pays principle and falling out of it. On the one hand, if a company inflicts some environmental damage and is thinly capitalized to cover it, or becomes insolvent, the payment under the triggered insurance policy would guarantee that the polluter has met its obligations. On the other, the share of the polluter in compensating the damage could be limited to the level of insurance premiums actually paid, together with a certain deductible under the policy, if any, and a balance of expenses, if the insured amount is less than the outstanding clean-up cost. Other costs could be spread by the insurer within its whole pool of the insured. This raises a question: does availability of this type of insurance in the market, in fact, lead to dilution of responsibility of a potential polluter?

Negligence vs. recklessness argument for liability insurance

It is sometimes argued that the fact that liability insurance policies respond to harms caused in negligence makes companies less alert to risks. Whereas the first part of this statement is certainly true, the allegation as to the results is open to debate.

The opponents of this claim believe that 'were it not for the errant human element, the hazards insured against would be greatly diminished. It is in full appreciation of these conditions that [a man] seeks insurance, and it is after painstaking analysis of them that the insurer fixes his premiums and issues the policies. It is in recognition of this practice that the law [of the United States] requires the insurer to assume the risk of negligence of the insured.'[131]

In the UK the law does not 'require' cover against negligence but, unless negligence is expressly excepted, the cover against any hazard is presumed and construed to cover loss caused by the negligence of

---

[130] EU Commission White Paper on Environmental Liability of 9 February 2000, COM (2000) 66 final, at 29.

[131] Fire insurance cases: *Federal Ins Co. v. Tamiami Trail Tours Inc.*, 117 F 2d 794, 796 (5 Cir, 1941 – fire). *Mutatis mutandis, Columbia Ins Co. v. Lawrence*, 10 Pet 507, 517 *per* Story J (Sup. Ct 1836 – fire); *State Farm Fire & Casualty Co. v. Von Der Lieth*, 802 P 2d 285 (Cal, 1991-AR) referred to in Clarke, *Law of Insurance Contracts*, s. 192A, pp. 584–90, p. 584.

the insured[132] or its employees.[133] Loss negligently caused may be excluded directly and expressly, or indirectly by a positive requirement of diligence, but courts are inclined to interpret insurance contracts against that result.[134]

The argument that is articulated in order to negate the likelihood of moral hazard on the part of the insured and which could arise out of the very purpose of liability insurance is that policies are meant to respond to good faith omissions rather than create incentives for being reckless. The policies themselves may offer some mitigation of the risk of moral hazard. For instance, they may require the sponsors to act 'as if uninsured' or otherwise to mitigate losses. The courts also appear unwilling to compromise on this.

In a UK case, in the light of the contract to provide liability cover, Diplock LJ construed an exception of negligence very restrictively. Interpreted in isolation, a duty to take reasonable precautions might be seen as one breached by ordinary negligence, but this interpretation would defeat the purpose of a liability insurance contract:

> 'Reasonable' . . . means reasonable as between the insured and the insurer having regard to the commercial purpose of the contract, which is *inter alia* to indemnify the insured against liability for his (the insured's) personal negligence[135] . . . it is not enough that [the insured's] omission to take any particular precautions to avoid accidents should be negligent; it must at least be reckless, that is to say, made with actual recognition by the insured himself that a danger exists, and not caring whether or not it is averted. The purpose of the condition is to ensure that the insured will not, because he is covered against loss by the policy, refrain from taking precautions which he knows ought to be taken.[136]

---

[132] *Shaw v. Robberds* (1837) 6 Ad & E75, 84 *per* Lord Denman CJ (fire); *Cornish v. Accident Ins Co.* (1889) 23 QBD 453, 457 *per* Lindley LJ (CA–PA). But see Sir N. J. Mustill, 'Fault and Marine Losses' [1988] LMCLQ 310, at 333ff.

[133] See for example, *Leavell & Co. v. Fireman's Fund Ins Co.*, 372 F 2d 784.

[134] Clarke, *Law of Insurance Contracts*, s. 19-2A, pp. 584–90, 584.

[135] See also *Woolfall & Rimmer Ltd v. Moyle* [1942] 1 KB 66 (CA – employers' liability) where Goddard LJ observed (76) that, if the condition were seen in isolation 'it would follow that the underwriters were saying: "We will insure you against your liability for negligence on condition that you are not negligent," because, if the [insured] had taken all reasonable precautions to prevent accidents in the widest sense, they could not be liable in negligence' (*ibid.* p. 586, fn. 5).

[136] *Fraser v. Furman (Productions) Ltd* [1967] 1 WLR 898, 905–6 (CA), cited in Clarke, *Law of Insurance Contracts*, s. 19-2A, pp. 584–90, p. 586.

'Sudden and accidental'

The environmental liability policy tries to achieve this result by explicitly providing that the cover extends only to pollution that was 'sudden and accidental'. So, in order to reject the payment, the insurer would have to consider, among other things, whether the insured was aware of the likely consequences of such an event happening, whether the technology was available worldwide to lessen the degree of such a risk occurring, and whether the insured made all reasonable efforts to utilize such technology for mitigating the risks. The more dangerous the activities of the company, the stronger the duty of care owed by the company to potential plaintiffs.[137] This should induce in companies due diligence in relation to their environmental obligations in order not to fall out of the cover.

In addition, the courts are more likely to test negligence on a basis of knowledge of risk which ought to have been available anywhere worldwide and not only found at state or national levels. So this is likely to defeat a defence of the insured on grounds of the knowledge of risk not having been well developed at the time or standards becoming more stringent since the action.[138] This should logically motivate the insurers to insist on companies following the latest developments both in terms of standards imposed by law but also in terms of preventive measures.

No subrogation rights

Another fact – that in certain cases insurers will not have subrogation rights to recover the insurance proceeds they had paid to the insured (which, as we could see in the case of PRI above, might create wrong incentives for insurers themselves) – should serve as a positive sign.

As already mentioned, in general, upon payment, an insurer becomes subrogated for all the rights that its insured had against a third party. However, this is not the case when the only person whom the insurer would have to turn to in order to enforce its subrogation rights is the insured party. The insured has no right of action against itself (or against the co-insured) and nor does the insurer.[139]

---

[137] See Lockett, *Environmental Liability*, pp. 49–51.   [138] *Ibid.*, p. 28.
[139] For more details on the limits of the insurer's rights, see Clarke, *Law of Insurance Contracts*, s. 31–5, pp. 1036–51, with accompanying references to supporting case law.

Furthermore, a waiver of subrogation clause is customarily required in PF. The project lender does not want the insurer to pursue any such claims against the lender or the SPV.[140]

So the lack of subrogation rights in this specific case is supposed to make insurers more vigilant to spot potential moral hazards on the part of the insured and reflect this in the terms and conditions of the insurance policy, one of which could be reserving for themselves the right to access the premises of the insured at any time to assess the possibility of risks materializing. However, as we will see later, the courts' approach to interpretation of policies can potentially make this safeguard useless.

Legal liability

Insurers are only bound to pay the insured when the indemnity has been triggered by the insured being found 'legally liable' by a court for the payment of damages.[141] In turn, environmental liability losses can be incurred through torts, contractual obligations[142] or violation of statutes.[143]

Therefore the likelihood of insurers having to pay money at all and the extent of the risk insured depends not only on physical factors associated with the perils insured against and the 'state of the art' of ways to mitigate loss, but also and especially in the case of liability insurance, on the law, both liability law and rules of indemnity,[144] and the way courts approach the interpretation of the insurance policies.

Being guided by law and courts' decisions could be seen as positive, as it provides a forum and a benchmark for assessing actions or inactions independent of the insurer. However, both the law and courts can bring a negative side effect in the form of wrong incentives.

---

[140] Hoffman, *Law and Business*, p. 394.

[141] However, most insurers will try to settle the case first. Lockett, *Environmental Liability*, p. 34.

[142] See for example *Aswan (M/S) Engineering Establishment Co.* v. *Iron Trades Mutual Insurance Co.* [1988] ('liability at law' was deemed to include any liability assumed under contract) referred to in Lockett, *Environmental Liability*, p. 35

[143] American Risk Management Resources Network (ARMR Network), 'A User's Guide to Environmental Insurance', p. 1, at http://erraonline.org/usersguide.pdf (accessed: 10 October 2009).

[144] Clarke, *Policies and Perceptions*, p. 48.

State of the law

As driver of the liability insurance market, the law can have either a deterrent effect or give rise to moral hazard, depending on whether the legislator succeeds or fails in setting sanctions relative to potential polluters.

The laws of Azerbaijan may be used as an example to show how this works. On the one hand, the Law on Mandatory Ecological Insurance[145] provides that intended actions or inactions of the insured that bring about environmental pollution shall not be an insurable event, thus excluding recklessness from its cover.[146] On the other hand, the fines provided in law for polluting the environment above the limits permitted are insufficient to act as a restraining factor for a potential polluter.[147]

However, one also needs to recognize that laws which increase liability for environmental harms can scare insurers away.[148] An attempt of the legislator to find the right level of liability to motivate insurers can be fraught with another type of danger.

The EU Commission White Paper on Environmental Liability[149] is a good example of a policy-setting instrument which could potentially create wrong incentives while aiming to achieve the opposite result. The Commission suggested limiting liability for environmental harm in various ways in order to facilitate the provision of environmental liability insurance to back up the liability regime, which did not exist at the time of the Paper. Having proposed that, the Commission nevertheless acknowledged that such limitations of liability 'erode the effective application of the polluter pays principle' and, hence, weaken the incentive provided by the liability regime to prevent environmental damage.

Were an insurance policy provided to cover environmental liability as regulated by such laws, it could give rise to a heightened moral hazard by lowering the level of duty of care owed by the companies. What is the right balance when it comes to the level of liability is however an open question.

---

[145] No. 271-IIQ, dated 12 March 2002. Published in Azerbaijan newspaper, 21 April 2002, No. 90.
[146] *Ibid.*, s. 4.2.3.
[147] Interview with an insurer in Azerbaijan conducted on 23 May 2007. Source requested anonymity.
[148] For further, see Lockett, *Environmental Liability*, pp. 14–17 and 28–9.
[149] See above, n. 130.

Judicial interpretation of insurance policies

Judicial interpretation of insurance policies could be another reason for concern. It was noted, for example, that in the US and Canada judges are more politically sensitive and more easily swayed by public opinion and are therefore more willing to create insurance cover by reinterpretation to make sure that, after the environmental risks have materialized, an insurer is there to cover the negative consequences. And this is so despite the restrictive language of the policy and the exclusions that would have otherwise enabled an insurer to refuse cover.[150] Judges might be even more inclined to favour an interpretation against the insurer in cases where environmental insurance is compulsory and liability extends for clean-up costs on the basis that the insurer should not be able to exclude a risk that is imposed by statute.[151]

What is the danger then if judges are willing to reach an environmentally friendly interpretation of insurance policies?, one may ask. As positive as judicial innovation may seem at first blush, it reflects the preference (be that intentional or unintended) for post-factum remediation or compensation measures rather than preventive ones. What it effectively does is to void the restraining effect of exclusion clauses, thus taking incentives from the insured companies to apply reasonable efforts to prevent risks from materializing. This means that the positive effects of the lack of subrogation rights of insurers against the insured, as described above, would be lost. Which of the two approaches is more environmentally friendly though is again a difficult question to answer.

Conclusion

This overview of the impediments and safeguards inherent in most insurance policies, and particularly the PRI and environmental liability

---

[150] See for example *Keene Corp.* v. *Insurance Co. of N. America* 667 F.2d 1034, the decision of the Supreme Court of Canada in *Canadian Indemnity Co.* v. *Canadian Johns Manville Co. Ltd.*, referred to in Lockett, *Environmental Liability*, p. 18. For further on other judicial decisions to same effect see *ibid.* pp. 17–21.

[151] Lockett, *Environmental Liability*, p. 22, with supporting cases of *US* v. *Travelers Ins. Co.* (1983) and *Summit Associates Inc.* v. *Liberty Mutual Fire Insurance Co.* (1987) L-47287–84 NJ Sup. Crt Law Div. (Middx County). In the latter case the reason for rejection of the insurer's defence was that to impose clean-up costs on government agencies would impose an undue burden on the taxpayer, and that the health and safety of the population outweighed any express provision of the insurance policy.

insurance, leads one to believe that there is no straightforward answer as to whether insurance creates moral risk or not.

The risk of moral hazard could be introduced into insurance by the law driving a particular insurance market or the arrangements of PF which insurance is meant to make stronger.

Companies may fall foul of the insurance coverage due to a lack of understanding of the exact extent of the cover, and due to difficulty in predicting how the insurer, adjudicator or an arbitrator, as the case may be, would construct the terms of the policy and what decision may ensue. There is a good chance that the company's case will not fit precisely the definition of the insured peril or will fall under an exclusion or be found in breach of a warranty clause. In addition, the courts may strictly construe the terms of insurance policies so as to exclude the cover when they are concerned with long-term prevention of environmental risks and are thus convinced that the actual polluters must take the whole responsibility for the clean-up costs of environmental damage.

We have also seen that an insurer's having subrogation rights does not necessarily deter undesirable behaviour. And it is an inaccurate general-ization to say that their absence is an answer to a moral hazard. On the one hand, the case of environmental liability insurance has shown that while the lack of subrogation rights of insurers against the insured makes the former more alert to dangers of moral hazard on the part of the latter, the fact that courts sometimes decide cases on a short-term goal of *post factum* remediation or compensation could nevertheless expose the whole pool of the insured parties to paying for harm caused by the negligence of only one of them. On the other hand, the existence of subrogation rights in PRI policies, together with the leverage the insurers may have over the host government, can bring about moral hazard on the part of the insurers as they make the host government pay for enacting legislation passed for a legitimate public purpose. Subrogation rights are not therefore means of preventing undesirable behaviour.

Considering this, we see that Shakespeare's Macbeth was duped by the security he perceived was his, rather than what it actually was. Insurance does not provide surety that supports 'hopes' to get away with inflicting damages 'above wisdom, grace and fear'.[152] Rather one needs to look closely at the type of insurance and at the context in which that insurance exists.

---

[152] *Macbeth* (above, n. 18).

There is also a set of points that one has come to think of along the way to locate the insurance industry in the world economy, which is itself constantly changing under the influence of new developments.

As an offshoot of sustainable development, corporate social responsibility found its point of entry into the philosophy of many global corporations which have always considered themselves immune from any other concern than the need to increase profits.[153] The recent changes introduced by the UK Companies Act 2006, which have replaced a director's duty to act *bona fide* in the interests of the company by the duty to promote the success of the company for the benefit of its members, while giving due regard to a wider range of 'stakeholder' interests, in some way support this argument.[154]

A comparatively recent willingness within the financial industry to be ahead of legal regulation and agree on and further be guided by the EP, is another example of the continuing influence of this trend. What began as an initiative[155] of ten banks at the time has now become a global initiative with sixty-seven[156] PF lenders on board. As positive as this development may be, as was shown above, there is an urgent need to revise the perception of environmental risks by EP lenders as they search for ways to mitigate and control those risks. Exclusion of some project arrangements that might heighten environmental risks, a non-vitiation clause being an example, is well in tune with the spirit of the EP and should be required from EP lenders. It is what any fair interpretation of the EP calls for.

With particular reference to the insurance industry, one might ask: would the EP, applying as they do to PF loans, force an EP institution that has agreed to finance a project based on its compliance with the EP and is

---

[153] Milton Friedman, 'The Social Responsibility of Business Is to Increase Its Profits', *New York Times*, 13 September 1970, §6, 32.

[154] s. 172. The Institute of Chartered Accountants in England and Wales (ICAEW) emphasizes that directors will only be liable to the company or its shareholders for breach of this duty and if the company can demonstrate that is has suffered loss as a result of the breach. And though directors are not expected to document consideration of every mentioned factor when making business decisions, they might be expected to demonstrate that the wider consequences of decisions are routinely considered See: ICAEW, 'Modernising UK Company Law: Companies Act 2006', available at ICAEW's website.

[155] However one may argue whether it was in fact voluntary, as the EP appeared on 4 June 2003, in response to criticism from environmental and social pressure groups that bank loans had often contributed to the contamination and impoverishment of the developing world.

[156] ABSA became the 67th Equator Principle Financial Institution on 22 October 2009.

considering providing PRI, make express carve-outs in PRI covers in the interests of protection of the environment? Exclusion of PRI cover for stabilization clauses that have a chilling effect on the host government's ability to introduce stricter environmental laws in good faith could be a carve-out of the type concerned. The answer that first comes to mind is: they naturally should. However, the positive effect of this might be limited, as only one signatory to the EP – Export Development Canada – has a dual mandate of financing business and insuring against political risks.

Considering such new developments and the way they have been influencing different sectors, one may ask: what should be the insurance industry's standard for today? Do sustainable development and human rights requirements have something to contribute to an evaluation of the approach by the insurance industry to insuring risks? Is it the right time to impose strictly on the insurers the requirements for sustainable development, regardless of whether we are looking at a private or public institution? How would the sustainable development requirements if imposed on insurers respond to the moral hazard issues discussed above? Do we need another set of EP, but specifically targeted at the service provided by the insurance industry to PF? These are very difficult questions, having no single answers but rather inviting fresh debate.[157]

---

[157] The author's Ph.D. thesis (on file with the author) attempts to answer these types of questions.

10

Irreparable damage, project finance and access to remedies by third parties

JUDITH SCHÖNSTEINER

Introduction

Imagine an investment project in the extractive sector, such as an oil pipeline, during the construction phase. Assume as well that the investors, usually a consortium of companies, have opted for project finance (PF) and have made available considerable amounts of money for the overall project, including exploration and construction, that will later produce a revenue stream coming from oil, gas or minerals being marketed. Until the extraction begins, the investors run a heightened commercial risk: they have advanced their money, but cannot yet begin to recover return. Furthermore, they know that lenders most probably have, albeit limited, recourse to the sponsors' assets to service the loans, until the revenue phase begins. Sponsors therefore anxiously await the flow of crude oil or the start of mining, fearing any prior surge in costs, including those due to unexpected measures to protect human rights or the environment. Time is money, especially when investment costs have yet to be recovered. In that sense, projects that are quickly implemented tend to heighten the risk of worker accidents, death threats for community members resisting economic activity, spills and damages to the environment and irreversible health damages (see also Chapter 5 by Sheldon Leader). At the same time, the host state, in this situation, may be eager to create or maintain its reputation for an investor-friendly environment, and be more lenient on the implementation of social standards.

I am grateful to Sheldon Leader for his challenges to this argument throughout the process of drafting. Our discussions taught me a lot. I also thank Rasmiya Kazimova and Joo-Young Lee for their helpful comments, and David Ong and Martin Barr for their fine editing. All remaining errors are of course my own.

Imagine as well those individuals and communities living in proximity to the project. While these projects do not usually require their labour, as foreign specialists or workers are brought in, the people whose houses, fields, or fresh water sources are close to the project's installations fear that their rights to property, health, food etc. may be violated. Environmental and social impact assessment (ESIA) as well as human rights impact assessment (HRIA) (see Chapter 7 by Tamara Wiher) should prevent most of the damage from happening, and lenders in PF settings do usually require such assessments. What is more, the International Finance Corporation (IFC) Policy on Environmental and Social Sustainability requires its borrowers to consider the implementation of risk avoidance measures, 'whenever technically and financially feasible'. This provision constitutes a conditional preventive approach.[1] The IFC Policy does not, nevertheless, contain a recommendation to states to provide an adequate legal remedy to enforce these standards. This leaves the choice between avoidance and compensation entirely to the investor's discretion. Furthermore, compensation payment may be deliberately delayed or payable after a certain time, thus bridging the risky construction phase by paying out victims once revenues flow, rather than limiting the damage in the first place. This situation may lead to heightened human rights risk (see Chapter 5). Tying prevention to feasibility in this context does not coincide with the standards that international law requires for the prevention of damage to third parties' human rights. In that sense, four types of situations continue to generate concerns: (a) Impact assessments or policy recommendations are not carried out properly; (b) recommendations are not followed; (c) there are no complaint mechanisms available to call attention to dangers and damages; or (d) irreparable damage occurs. This chapter is concerned with the third and fourth problems. The claim made is sufficiently general to be applicable also to non-PF modes, but for the moment, let us maintain the assumption of PF being used to make some specific remarks on the human rights risks that are related to this mode of financing.

As tort law rightly states, for physical injury and similar damage, 'money compensation is often a poor equivalent of what has been lost'.[2] Nevertheless, in the current business and human rights discussion, the availability of remedies is usually a concern that kicks in *after* the

---

[1] IFC, Policy on Environmental and Social Sustainability, adopted 30 April 2006, Performance Standard 1, para. 14.

[2] D. Harris *et al.*, *Remedies in Contract and Tort* (2nd edn, London: Butterworths, 2002), p. 290.

damage has happened. Thus, the UN Secretary-General's Special
Representative (SRSG), John Ruggie, elaborated a framework for business and human rights that includes analysis of the availability of
reparation.[3] Other contributions to the debate focus on the availability
of damages or criminal suits in different jurisdictions.

There is a general omission, however: the need for provisional, precautionary or interim remedies has not been discussed.[4] In the framework
proposed by Ruggie, prevention is part of companies' 'duty to respect',[5]
which is based on the 'do no harm principle' and on the idea that in any
given society there are goods that are not amenable to a cost–benefit
analysis, as people would not accept the exchange at any price. For example,
people would generally not accept that their health be traded against a
certain sum of money, unless this money could allow them to achieve a
good they value more. The SRSG states that 'human rights are not merely
another topic' which could be set off against other interests.[6] This approach
finds its expression in the companies' obligation to apply 'due diligence',
meaning to 'become aware of, prevent and address adverse human rights
impacts'.[7] The duty to respect also encompasses access for victims to
'effective grievance mechanisms'.[8] If prevention of damage fails, there
need to be compensation mechanisms in place.

---

[3] See especially SRSG on the issue of human rights and transnational corporations and
other business enterprises, John Ruggie, *Protect, Respect and Remedy: A Framework for
Business and Human Rights*, A/HRC/8/5, 7 April 2008 (cited here as SRSG 2008
(Framework)).

[4] See for extensive overviews, for example, 'Oxford Pro Bono Publico, Obstacles to Justice
and Redress for Victims of Corporate Human Rights Abuse', 2008 (at: www.law.ox.ac.uk/
opbp/Oxford-Pro-Bono-Publico-submission-to-Ruggie-3-Nov-2008.pdf, last accessed 8
October 2009). See also International Commission of Jurists, *Expert Legal Panel on
Corporate Complicity and International Crimes*, vol. 3: 'Civil Liability 2008' (at http://
icj.org/IMG/Volume_3.pdf, last accessed 8 October 2009).

[5] SRSG 2008 (Framework).

[6] SRSG, 'Business and Human Rights: Towards Operationalizing the "Protect, Respect and
Remedy" Framework', A/HRC/11/13 of 22 April 2009 (cited here as SRSG Follow-up
2009), paras. 62 and 79.

[7] SRSG 2008 (Framework), para. 56. Ruggie highlights that there is no specific or even
restricted list of human rights that companies would have to respect, but that their duty
encompasses at least all human rights enshrined in the Universal Declaration of Human
Rights (UDHR) and the ICCPR, adopted 16 December 1966, entry into force 23 March
1976, and the ICESCR, adopted 16 December 1966, entry into force 3 January 1976. On
the duty of corporate actors to take into account human rights generally, see S. Leader,
'Collateral Protection of Rights in a Global Economy', *New York Law School Law Review*,
53 (2008–9), 806.

[8] SRSG 2008 (Framework), para. 82.

However, Ruggie's proposal does not address situations in which *prevention* would be the only means for states and companies to comply with the due diligence standard. A conceptual difficulty is that the SRSG seems to use 'remedy', 'redress' and 'reparation' interchangeably, while international human rights law understands the first in broader terms, as encompassing the second and third if damage has occurred.[9] However, a remedy need not be compensatory, it can also be preventive. The issue at stake is the following: if companies have a commercial interest in *choosing* compensation as an alternative to avoidance, rather than resorting to it only as a last resort in case prevention fails, international human rights law obliges the state to act upon its duty to protect human rights, and ensure that private actors do not infringe the human rights of others. I argue that this duty to protect encompasses the availability of preventive remedies that can address threats to human rights effectively before irreparable damage occurs. The chapter contributes to this important debate by analysing a series of prevention-related issues.

Prevention measures may generate more durable costs and other impacts on the economic viability and the course of a project than would having to pay compensation. Therefore, companies might prefer the compensation variant if no clear guidelines exist as to when prevention is the only viable solution in human rights terms. Generally, the law is more reluctant to grant preventive remedies, assuming that it should not interfere in the dealings of private citizens and organizations unless justified by a legitimate public goal.

This chapter makes the claim that the legal thresholds for awarding injunctive rather than compensatory remedies should be suitable to *prevent* violations of the core or essence of human rights. In other words, the argument seeks to link a substantive characteristic of human rights law with the request for a certain procedure for implementation. In that sense, it is argued that a business and human rights framework should not (tacitly or explicitly) choose between prevention and compensation solely by comparing the economic merits of each approach.[10] While there might be an argument for preferring damages to specific performance in contract

---

[9] In this context, the SRSG distinguishes the obligation of states to provide access to an effective remedy from the question whether there is an individual right to a remedy directly against a corporate actor, for example, through civil law action. See SRSG Follow-up 2009, para. 88.

[10] See for example R. A. Posner, *Economic Analysis of Law* (2nd edn, Toronto: Little, Brown and Company, 1997). For a discussion of this 'economic theory of efficient breach', see: D. Laycock, *The Death of the Irreparable Injury Rule* (New York: Oxford University

law,[11] such an approach is not suitable for situations that affect human rights. Simply put, we would not be ready to receive money for the violation of a human right if the alternative was that the violation could be avoided in the first place.

This chapter highlights the problem of remedies for third parties, especially the right to an effective remedy, making the case for an obligation to provide for preventive measures in certain cases of threatened human rights violations. Within this context, it then examines a cross-section of cases from Latin American countries.

The chapter concludes by analysing whether a claim for preventive remedies would be likely to find success under international human rights law.[12]

The problem of remedies for third parties

Individuals and communities whose human rights might be affected by corporate activity are usually not in a contractual relation with the investors. Exceptions are for example labour contracts or leasing contracts of property.[13] This setting implies that contract damages are usually unavailable to the affected communities who are not parties to the concession contract or host government agreement. Although some jurisdictions allow the principle of privity of contract to be limited by third party claims in certain situations where the contract awards benefits to them,[14] it is often only tort claims that can be brought against a

---

Press, 1991), p. 260; G. Alexander, 'The Social-Obligation Norm in American Property Law', *Cornell Law Review*, 94 (2009), 745.

[11] See H. Lando and C. Rose, 'On the Enforcement of Specific Performance in Civil Law Countries', *International Review of Law and Economics*, 24 (2004), 473.

[12] For a discussion of the availability of interim injunctions for damage threatened to the environment, in both civil and common law systems, see C. Martin, 'Interlocutory Injunctions and the Environment: Comparing the Law between Quebec and the Other Provinces', *J. Env. L. & Prac.*, 13 (2004), 359.

[13] Situations may occur in which individuals, due to their dependence on an employer, consent to a limitation of their rights that they would otherwise not have agreed to. Such situations may be exacerbated in remote areas where the foreign investor's project is the only potential source of employment. See for example D. R. Namuncura, *Represa o Pobreza?* (Santiago: LOM Ediciones, 1999), discussing land conflicts in relation to the Ralco hydroelectric power station in indigenous territory in southern Chile.

[14] See for example the English Contracts (Rights of Third Parties) Act 1999. See also: E. McKendrick, *Contract Law* (7th edn, Basingstoke: Palgrave Macmillan, 2007), p. 155; Harris *et al.*, *Remedies*, p. 177. In Ireland, the Law Commission has been considering reforming privity rules to allow third parties to sue under a contract in certain circumstances; see discussion in *Judicial Studies Institute Journal*, 1 (2008). The exception established in *Jackson* v. *Horizon Holidays Ltd* [1975] 1 WLR 1468, allowing third

contracting party with respect to any effects of the contractual agreement (other than benefits) on third parties.[15] Generally, remedies for third parties may be available at tort, in constitutional or in administrative law, or in international human rights law.

A second issue involves the state's role in a globalized economy. The state is endowed to act in the public interest, and in this context also regulates the public and private spheres. As Gus van Harten points out, since the 1990s, states have given considerable power to investors and private arbitrators to challenge states' policy choices through investment treaty-based international litigation.[16] The right to bring international claims under investment treaties and contracts allows investors and arbitrators to join forces against the state, engaging in a process akin to judicial review by private actors.[17] Public policy decisions – even the granting of a remedy in favour of a third party that causes adverse effects on the balance sheet of a foreign investor[18] – may in some cases be

---

parties on whose behalf a contract has been concluded to sue under the contract, has not been repealed by the Contracts (Rights of Third Parties) Act 1999; see C. Turner, *Unlocking Contract Law* (2nd edn, London: Hodder Arnold, 2007), p. 380. In civil law jurisdictions, benefits that two parties bestow on a third party through a contract can be claimed by the beneficiary; see for example Article 1449 of the Chilean Civil Code, DFL No. 1, promulgated 16 May 2000, in the version of 24 September 2009. In Germany, the Civil Code (BGB Article 328(1)) provides for a similar rule. In Argentina, the general rule is that contracts may not generate any prejudice to third parties (Article 1195 of the Civil Code of the Republic of Argentina, adopted through Law 340, entry into force 1 January 1871), and cannot be invoked by them (Article 1199). However, as in Chile and Germany, benefits that a contract bestows on a third party can be invoked under Article 504 of the Civil Code.

[15] See M. G. Bridge, 'Legislative Comment: Privity of Contract, Third Parties', *Edinburgh Law Review*, 5(1) (2001), 85–102, 94. The author highlights that the doctrine of privity does not apply without restrictions to state contracts, as the state is allowed to impose certain justified burdens on its citizens. By way of example for the many civil law jurisdictions, Chilean law provides for the use of non-contractual remedies in this case; see Civil Code, Book IV, Title 35 (on delicts and quasi-delicts).

[16] G. van Harten, *Investment Treaty Arbitration and Public Law* (Oxford University Press, 2007), chs. 3 and 6.

[17] *Ibid.* ch. 4.

[18] Stabilization clauses may encompass judicial decisions. For example, consider Convention de Collaboration, République Démocratique du Congo et China Railways Group *et al.*, adopted 22 April 2008 (at: www.lesoftonline.net/phil.php?id=1155, last accessed 7 October 2009). The stabilization clause in Article 14(4) stipulates that 'all new legal and regulatory requirements which put them at a disadvantage will not be applied' (cited here as DRC – China Railway Group). This example fits with the conclusions drawn in a special report for the SRSG and IFC, A. Shemberg, *Stabilization Clauses and Human Rights*, May 2009 (at: www.ifc.org/ifcext/sustainability.nsf/Content/Publications_LessonsLearned)

interpreted as expropriation because of the degree to which it thwarts an investor's reasonable expectations of profit. International investment law expands state liability for activities it undertakes *jure gestionis* to traditional areas of sovereign decision making *jure imperii*.[19] In that sense, arbitrators can, defending investor rights, intervene in the regulatory function of states. This may have considerable impact on the availability of remedies for the protection of human rights and the environment.

In such a situation, remedies for third parties are often additionally barred because specific provisions in the contract divert contract-related litigation to the international sphere (for example, through arbitration clauses).[20] Pursuant to the New York Convention, an arbitral award takes priority over domestic law and jurisprudence, unless the award would fall into the usually narrowly defined 'public policy' exception.[21]

Thus, a third party who may have sued a governmental entity in public law could meet reluctant judges who know that a decision hampering the investor's revenue expectations may lead to a claim in arbitration, especially if stabilization clauses in the contract are deemed comprehensive.[22] For example, the investor in the Chilean Campiche energy project was considering taking the case to the ICSID tribunal to obtain an arbitral award that would reinstate the Environmental Agency's decision that had granted the permit.[23] The issue concerns a coal-fired energy plant that saw its licence to operate withdrawn by the Supreme Court for

---

[19] van Harten, *Investment*, ch. 3.

[20] DRC – China Railway Group, Arbitration clause Article 20(1–2).

[21] Article 2(f) of the Convention on the Recognition and Enforcement of Foreign Arbitral Awards, the 'New York Convention', adopted 10 June 1958, entry into force 7 June 1959. It should be noted that the equally authentic Spanish and French versions of the treaty speak of 'public order' instead of 'public policy', and reflect this in the respective laws. See, for example, Republic of Chile, Ley 19.971, Article 36(b.ii). To the author's knowledge, research into this idiomatic difference remains to be undertaken, despite recent attention to the public policy clause. See: J. Fry, 'Désordre Public International under the New York Convention: Whither Truly International Public Policy?', *Chinese J. Int'l L.* 8 (1) (2009), 81–134; C. Gibson, 'Arbitration, Civilization and Public Policy: Seeking Counterpoise between Arbitral Autonomy and the Public Policy Defense in View of Foreign Mandatory Public Law', *Penn. St. L. Rev.*, 113(4) (2009), 1227–68.

[22] See also Shemberg, *Stabilization Clauses*.

[23] 'AES Gener estudia demandar a Chile ante el CIADI por Central Campiche', *El Mostrador*, 22 October 2009 (at: http://old.elmostrador.cl/index.php/noticias/articulo/aes-gener-estudia-demandar-a-chile-ante-el-ciadi-por-central-campiche). The company is planning another project which has been critically studied by the Chilean House which adopted its report on 15 January 2010 (see: www.fima.cl/2010/01/15/aes-gener-en-la-mira-del-parlamento/).

not complying with the proper approval process for the change in use of lands from a green to an industrially used area.[24] For third parties affected by investment projects, however, the possibility to sue in foreign courts or international tribunals is usually unavailable due to lack of standing, *forum non conveniens* or due to practical and financial obstacles.[25]

In sum, the state may find itself torn between the competing interests of a third party seeking an injunction and investors seeking their return on the investment, these investors sometimes being supported by other interest groups in that society. The state might be expected to have more to gain from pleasing investors[26] due to unevenly distributed bargaining powers: for example, higher awards are to be expected from arbitrators than from domestic judges in public law or international human rights law. States know that while investors have international remedies against the state, this is not so for third parties in such scenarios.

Finally, even if domestic remedies were available, there is another problem in PF settings: the occasionally low level of assets available to compensate successful damages claims. As investors usually withdraw revenues immediately from the special purpose vehicle (SPV), either to pay back a loan or to transfer the revenues to their shareholders, third parties may well see their efforts to obtain compensation frustrated. This may even be the case where they obtain a favourable judgment; especially in cases where the SPV goes into liquidation, as repayment of the related loans will be the overriding consideration in terms of the contract, which will set out priorities among the parties to the contract.[27] Greater liquidity of sponsors is to be expected during the construction phase, when recourse to the sponsors' assets is usually available. Sponsors and lenders perceive this greater access to assets as a risk, and sometimes seek to have

---

[24] Ricardo Gonzalo Dubric/Comisión Regional del Medio Ambiente de Valparaíso, Judgment of the Third Chamber of the Supreme Court, Rol 1219-2009, of 22 June 2009. COREMA, the environmental agency, had granted its permit on 9 May 2008. See also 'Suprema cuestiona a Corema por autorizar termoeléctrica de carbon', El Mercurio Valparaíso, 22 June 2009 (at: www.mercuriovalpo.cl/prontus4_noticias/site/artic/20090622/pags/20090622152059.html).

[25] See also Oxford Pro Bono Publico (above n. 4).

[26] See for example E. Mujih, '"Co-deregulation" of Multinational Companies Operating in Developing Countries: Partnering against Corporate Social Responsibility?', AJICL, 16 (2008), 249.

[27] See generally on the risk lenders want to reduce, S. Hoffman, The Law and Business of International Project Finance (2nd edn, The Hague: Kluwer Law International, 2001), p. 19 and specifically, p. 511.

the construction speeded up, which, in turn, augments the risk of damage, moving away from an avoidance preference. Responding to a similar concern about the problematic volatility of capital while a suit is pending, a UK court has recently granted an injunction to prevent a mining company with activities in Peru from removing its capital from the UK, so that compliance with any eventual award is not prejudiced. The merits of the case deal with torture allegations against Monterrico Metals and its Peruvian subsidiary in relation to the Rio Blanco mining project.[28]

Taking these problems into account, I now explore what international human rights law has to say about the availability of an effective remedy *before* damage actually occurs. In this context, I briefly touch upon conflicts of treaty obligations that a state may be confronted with in such situations.

Why the state cannot suspend the right to a remedy

There is an argument that the state, due to its sovereignty, is free to buy into any international treaty or agreement the government in power would choose to, without restrictions in principle or law.[29] There are only two generally accepted restrictions to this freedom: first, a treaty, which contains provisions that run counter *ius cogens* norms, is void.[30] Second, in the case where a UN member has engaged in an agreement that generates obligations which conflict with obligations that stem from the UN Charter, the latter will prevail (Article 103 of the UN Charter). With the 'fragmentation' of international law,[31] the formation of specific

---

[28] Freezing injunction against Monterrico Metals in the UK, requested 2 June 2009, granted on 16 October 2009; see *Guerrero* v. *Monterrico*, [2009] EWHC 2475 (QB). A similar injunction was granted on 5 September 2009 in Hong Kong, where the company is headquartered after a Chinese takeover. As counsel Richard Meeran, Leigh Day & Co., commented on the UK decision: 'Without this freezing injunction, access to justice would effectively have been denied' (press release of 19 October 2009, at: www.leighday.co.uk/news/news-archive/leigh-day-co-issue-proceedings-against-british).

[29] See for an analysis, S. Leader, 'Human Rights, Risks and New Strategies for Global Investment', *JIEL*, 9 (2006), 657, 662.

[30] Vienna Convention of the Law of Treaties, Article 53, adopted 23 May 1969, entry into force 27 January1980.

[31] International Law Commission (ILC), *Conclusions of the Work of the Study Group on the Fragmentation of International Law: Difficulties Arising from the Diversification and Expansion of International Law*, adopted by ILC at its 58th session, 2006, and submitted to the General Assembly as a part of the Commission's report covering the work of that session (A/61/10, para. 251).

'regimes' of international law that are considered *lex specialis*,[32] and the unsuitability of the *lex posterior derogat legi priori* rule of Article 30 of the Vienna Convention on the Law of Treaties in modern international law,[33] the difficult question to answer is which of two (or more) conflicting obligations prevails. Certain commentators assert that Article 103 suggests that the aims and purposes – not only explicit obligations listed in the Charter – 'constitute an international public order to which other treaty regimes ... must conform'.[34] This was also the view of the European Court of Justice (ECJ) in *Kadi*.[35] With respect to those obligations that a state cannot honour because of this conflict, the law of international state responsibility would usually establish the legal consequences and require the state to make reparations. The most difficult question in this context arises in relation to the obligations of cessation and non-repetition,[36] which bring the state back to the initial conflict.

Despite the important issues raised, the issues of treaty and norm conflicts in international law are not the focus of this chapter. They are, however, the background to the question that is asked here. Neither human rights treaties nor bilateral investment treaties typically include general clauses on the question of conflicting obligations. Most conflicts between international investment law and international human rights law cannot be satisfactorily solved through the current rules of

---

[32] J. Klabbers, *Treaty Conflict and the European Union* (Cambridge University Press, 2009).

[33] See ILC, *Fragmentation of International Law: Difficulties arising from the Diversification and Expansion of International Law, Report of the Study Group of the International Law Commission*, finalized by Martti Koskenniemi on 13 April 2006, A/CN4/L682; Klabbers, *Treaty Conflict*, p. 112; C. Borgen, 'Resolving Treaty Conflicts', *Geo. Wash. Int'l L. Rev.*, 37 (2005), 573, 577.

[34] D. Shelton, 'Hierarchy of Norms and Human Rights: Of Trumps and Winners', *Sask. L. Rev.*, 65 (2002), 301, 307. See also the discussion of Kadi in D. Shelton, 'Normative Hierarchy in International Law', *AJIL*, 100 (2006), 291, 311–12. For a similar argument, see: B. Fassbender, 'The United Nations Charter as a Constitution for the International Community', *Colum. J. Transnat'l L.*, 36 (1998), 529, 573; and C. Tomuschat, 'The Lockerbie Case before the International Court of Justice', *Rev. Int'l Comm'n Jurists*, 48 (1992), 43–4. But see also: M. Milanović, 'Norm Conflict in International Law: Whither Human Rights?', *Duke J. Comp. & Int'l Law*, 20 (2009), 69.

[35] Case T-315101, *Kadi v. Council* (ECJ, 21 September 2005), para. 288.

[36] Draft Articles on State Responsibility for Internationally Wrongful Acts, adopted by ILC at its 53rd session, 2001, and submitted to the General Assembly as a part of the Commission's report covering the work of that session (A/56/10) (cited here as Draft Articles 2001). Specific questions are expected to arise in relation to internationalized contracts. This issue cannot be dealt with here.

international law. The argument of this chapter is thus being made 'from within' international human rights law, pointing occasionally to recent developments on the issue of conflicting norms.

With this caveat in mind, international human rights law binds the state for all of its activities.[37] Thus, for example, Article 2(1) of the International Covenant on Civil and Political Rights (ICCPR) stipulates:

> Each State Party to the present Covenant undertakes to respect and to ensure to all individuals within its territory and subject to its jurisdiction the rights recognized in the present Covenant.

With respect to a similar provision in the American Convention on Human Rights (ACHR), the Inter-American Court of Human Rights (IACtHR) held in 2006 that this is also true for situations in which the reason for non-compliance with the ACHR is a bilateral investment treaty.[38] While international human rights law concedes to the state that it can limit certain rights in light of other interests, such as national security or public health, a wholesale waiver of such rights by the state is quite a different matter.

The right to an accessible and effective remedy is considered a non-limitable right in international human rights law, given its crucial role in enforcing of all other rights. It is true that the state does not usually, by ratifying an investment treaty or by signing an investment contract, restrict a fundamental right. However, if the treaty, contract or law establishes that remedies against the investor are barred in national law, and that all disputes are to be submitted to arbitration, the enjoyment of any individual or community right may become futile. Without an effective remedy, human rights cannot be enforced.

The 'right to an effective remedy' has a crucial role in several international human rights treaties. It is even considered non-derogable during a state of emergency, the IACtHR has observed.[39] The Human Rights

---

[37] Both international covenants cede priority to Charter provisions; see Article 46 of the ICCPR and Article 24 of the ICESCR.

[38] IACtHR, *Case of the Sawhoyamaxa Indigenous Community* v. *Paraguay*, Merits, Reparations and Costs. Judgment of 29 March 2006, Series C. No. 146. The case involved violations to the right to life due to lack of medical care as a consequence of concessions granted in indigenous territory pursuant to the German–Paraguayan Bilateral Investment Treaty, para. 197.

[39] The has determined that the right to an effective remedy is a prerequisite for the protection of these non-derogable rights, and therefore, is to be also understood as non-derogable. See IACtHR, *Judicial Guarantees in States of Emergency* (Arts. 27(2), 25 and (8) of the ACHR). Advisory Opinion OC-9/87 of 6 October 1987. Series A. No. 9.

Committee held with respect to the duties arising, in all situations, under Article 2(3) of the ICCPR:

> Article 2[(3)] requires that in addition to effective protection of Covenant rights States Parties must ensure that individuals also have accessible and effective remedies to vindicate those rights . . . The Committee attaches importance to States Parties' establishing appropriate judicial and administrative mechanisms for addressing claims of rights violations under domestic law. [States are] required to give effect to the general obligation to investigate allegations of violations *promptly, thoroughly and effectively* through independent and impartial bodies.[40]

The Siracusa Principles, adopted by a group of experts in the pursuit of spelling out the limitation and derogation provisions of the ICCPR, observed in this context: 'Every limitation imposed [on the rights protected in the Covenant] shall be subject to the possibility of challenge to and remedy against its abusive application.'[41]

The International Covenant on Economic, Social and Cultural Rights (ICESCR) does not contain a remedy provision similar to that of the ICCPR. The Committee on ESCR has, however, determined that a state party to the Covenant needs to show that a judicial remedy is not an 'appropriate means' according to the obligations in Article 2(1) or 'unnecessary'.[42] In most cases, the Committee considers that a remedy is necessary.[43] This assumption in favour of judicial remedies to enforce economic, social and cultural rights (ESCR) is complemented in Article 4 of the ICESCR by a list of requirements that have to be fulfilled before a state can impose any limitations to the enjoyment of ESCR. In that sense, a state will have to argue that any infringement of these rights, even if it were stemming from obligations contracted into through international investment treaties or internationalized contracts, is 'determined by law [and] compatible with the nature of these rights and solely for the purpose of promoting the general welfare in a democratic society'.

---

[40] Human Rights Committee (HR Comm.), General Comment No. 31, Nature of the General Legal Obligations of the Parties to the Covenant, UN Doc. CCPR/C/21/Rev.1/Add.13 (2004), para. 15 (emphases added).

[41] Siracusa Principles, Principle 8; see *HRQ*, 7 (1985), 3, 4.

[42] UN ESCR, General Comment No. 9, The domestic application of the Covenant, UN Doc. E/C.12/1998/24 (1998), paras. 2–3.

[43] See for an overview, SRSG, *State Obligations to Provide Access to Remedy for Human Rights Abuses by Third Parties, Including Business: An Overview of International and Regional Provisions, Commentary and Decisions*, A/HRC/11/13/Add.1 of 15/5/2009, paras. 23–26 (cited here as SRSG 2009 (states)). See generally A. Clapham, *Human Rights Obligations of Non-State Actors* (Oxford University Press, 2006).

The European Convention on Human Rights (ECHR) and the ACHR also provide for the right to an effective remedy, in Articles 13 and 25 respectively.

It is interesting in this context to take note of a decision by the House of Lords, which was called to consider a conflict of norms between the UN Charter and ECHR in *Al-Jedda*, concerning the detention of a terror suspect in Iraq by British troops.[44] Their Lordships held that despite the fact that the obligations imposed by the UN Security Council in a Chapter VII resolution enjoyed priority over the obligations arising under Article 5(1) of the ECHR, the government was obliged to intrude into the applicant's right to personal liberty to the least degree possible, meaning that 'a kernel of Article 5(1) remain[s]'[45] and especially, the government 'must ensure that the detainee's rights under article 5 are not infringed to any greater extent than is inherent in such detention'.[46] This includes that the detained must continue to have access to judicial review as a remedy to challenge his detention. Taking the essence of this argument, the House of Lords considered that the right to an effective remedy was not affected by otherwise superseding UN Charter obligations. From this one may conclude, subject to further research, that conflict of human rights norms with international investment law should not lead to suspension of the right to a remedy. As international investment law cannot supersede UN Charter obligations due to Article 103, unlike a Security Council resolution under Chapter VII, international investment law therefore cannot encroach further on the Charter-based human rights guarantees. Rather, it will be worthwhile to explore, building on Dinah Shelton's argument, *to what extent* human rights norms directly stem from the object and purpose of the UN Charter and therefore may be vested with greater authority than bilateral or multilateral investment treaties, which may at most claim a subsidiary role to the aims of the UN.

What kind of remedy? An argument for prevention

When a state ratifies a human rights treaty, that state has a general duty to respect, protect and fulfil the human rights obligations of the treaty; this will be binding on the state. This duty includes the obligation to

---

[44] *R. (on the application of Al-Jedda) (FC) (Appellant)* v. *Secretary of State for Defence (Respondent)*, decision of 12 December 2007 [2007] UKHL 58, esp. paras. 26ff.

[45] Milanović, 'Norm Conflict', 82.

[46] *Al-Jedda*, paras. 39 and 126, stating: 'The right is qualified but not displaced'; and para. 130, calling for regular review of the detention.

protect inhabitants of their territory from interference with their human rights by third parties.[47] As was shown in the previous section, state obligations are accompanied by the duty to provide effective remedies for any violation of rights that are protected by human rights treaties.

Procedurally, this aim can be achieved through various means, among them deterrence through the threat of damages or the threat of criminal law sanctions. Additionally, there are injunctive remedies, both inter-locutory and permanent, and *quia timet* injunctions in different areas of law. The specificity of injunctive remedies is that they are reinforced through rules on contempt of court, and can usually not be replaced by damages. Non-repetition, and generally, prevention, is especially impor-tant if the harm caused by the violation of a right cannot be compensated by monetary means, as is the case for many human rights violations.[48] As shall be seen, the right to property presents an exception in most situations. Non-repetition guarantees are a recognized remedy also in general international law.[49]

In the following, I argue that a remedy is effective, ideally, if it achieves the prevention or non-repetition of certain human rights violations.[50] The general obligations established in international human rights trea-ties point in this direction when they establish, as does Article 1(1) of the ACHR, that '[t]he States Parties to this Convention undertake to respect the rights and freedoms recognized herein and to ensure to all persons subject to their jurisdiction the free and full exercise of those rights and freedoms.'[51] What, however, does this general duty to establish an effective remedy mean in a corporate context? Due to the financial

---

[47] For a summary of the respect, protect and fulfilment framework in the context of international corporate activity, see SRSG Framework 2008.

[48] The IACtHR has consistently held that restitution is the preferred remedy. See for example *Case of Herrera-Ulloa v. Costa Rica*, Preliminary Objections, Merits, Reparations and Costs. Judgment of 2 July 2004. Series C. No. 107, a freedom of expression case, para. 192. The Court has not referred to the principle in recent decisions, but refers to it citing its case law; see for example *Case of Escher et al. v. Brazil*, Preliminary Objections, Merits, Reparations and Costs. Judgment of 6 July 2009, paras. 221 and 222.

[49] Draft Articles 2001, Article 30b.

[50] See for a similar argument, L. Laplante, 'Bringing Effective Remedies Home: The Inter-American Human Rights System, Remedies and the Duty of Prevention', *NQHR*, 22 (2004), 347, esp. 348 and 358–9.

[51] Similarly, Article 2(1) of the ICCPR. Article 1 of the ECHR, adopted 4 November 1951, entry into force 3 September 1953, calls upon states to 'secure' the rights and freedoms enshrined in the Convention.

power held by some transnational corporations, the threat of having to pay reparation may be an insufficient deterrent. It may be cheaper to violate human rights if the trade-off means earlier revenues. Also, criminal remedies against companies or their directors are limited in many countries.[52] In order to ensure that human rights violations cannot be 'bought', a suitable juridical tool would be the provision of remedies that do not allow a private actor to pay compensation *instead of* performance or a cessation promise. What does settled human rights law have to say on the issue of duties to prevent?

International human rights courts have held consistently that a state cannot prevent all crimes from happening. What due diligence obligations entail is providing an effective *ex post* remedy to identify and thereafter sanction the perpetrators; it also seeks to provide a mechanism for victims to obtain adequate compensation. However, in certain circumstances, international human rights law requires states to take measures to prevent certain acts from happening. Thus, the duty to prevent is part of settled international human rights law, although its scope varies depending on the interpretation the respective international organs have given to the concept. In the European Court of Human Rights (ECtHR), the duty to prevent a violation of the ECHR relates to threatened violations of the right to life and the right to personal integrity. In *Osman* v. *United Kingdom*, the Court established that the authorities have to take preventive measures beyond establishing an effective criminal law system if private actors impose a 'real and immediate risk' to the life of a person, which is known or ought to have been known by the authorities. They have to do what can be 'reasonably expected', i.e. that which does not pose an 'impossible or disproportionate burden' on the state.[53]

In the *Osman* case, the Court did not find a violation; it did, applying the same principle, in the *Öneryildiz* case. The Court observed that the positive obligation to safeguard the right to life extends to public and private activity, and '*a fortiori* to ... dangerous' industrial activities.[54]

---

[52] For an overview, see International Commission of Jurists, *Expert Legal Panel on Corporate Complicity and International Crimes, Corporate Complicity and Legal Accountability*, vol. 2: 'Criminal Law and International Crimes 2008' (at: http://icj.org/IMG/Volume_2.pdf, last accessed 8 October 2009). See also R. Hartley, *Corporate Crime* (Santa Barbara, CA: ABC-Clio, 2008), esp. p. 51.

[53] ECtHR, *Osman* v. *United Kingdom* (1998), Grand Chamber, 29 EHRR 245, para. 116.

[54] ECtHR, *Öneryildiz* v. *Turkey* (2004), Grand Chamber, 41 EHRR 20, para. 71. See also ECtHR, *Guerra et al.* v. *Italy* (1998), Grand Chamber, 26 EHRR 357, paras. 60–2.

The Grand Chamber specified that the duty to protect implies that the state establish a legislative and administrative framework for deterrence of violations of the right to life.[55] The Court did not explain whether such a framework also has to encompass preventive remedies. In this case, possibly, the issue did not arise, since the main problem was a lack of information by state authorities as to the risk that emanated from a publicly run rubbish tip. Nevertheless, the Court concluded that the 'lack of appropriate steps to prevent the accidental death of nine of the applicant's close relatives' constituted a violation of Article 2 of the ECHR.[56] In the recent *Opuz* decision, a case of domestic violence, the Court found that the measures taken by the judicial authorities revealed a 'lack of efficacy . . . and had no noticeable preventative or deterrent effect on the [perpetrator's] conduct'.[57] They should have provided 'protective measures in the form of effective deterrence'.[58] The Court found a violation of Articles 2 and 3 of the ECHR, however, but left it to the state to determine the means by which it chooses to achieve compliance in such cases.[59]

The IACtHR, like its European counterpart, bases the duty to prevent on due diligence requirement.[60] However, the IACtHR does not explicitly restrict the duty to prevent to right to life and personal integrity cases. Rather, it employs a general due diligence and prevention standard that stems from the general obligation to respect and guarantee the rights set forth in the ACHR (Article 1(1)). The Court explained in the *Godínez Cruz* case:

> An illegal act which violates human rights and which is initially not directly imputable to a State (for example, because it is the act of a private person or because the person responsible has not been identified) can lead to international responsibility of the State, not because of the act itself, but *because of the lack of due diligence to prevent the violation or to respond to it* as required by the Convention.[61]

The IACtHR interprets the right to life widely, and the duty to prevent extends to the right to property and to the right to health if they are affected in such a manner that the survival of an indigenous or tribal

---

[55] *Öneryildiz*, para. 89. [56] *Ibid.* operative para. 1.
[57] ECtHR, *Opuz* v. *Turkey* (2009), Application No. 33401/02, para. 170.
[58] *Ibid.* para. 177. [59] See for example, *ibid.* para. 165.
[60] IACtHR, *Case of Velásquez-Rodríguez* v. *Honduras*, Merits. Judgment of 29 July 1988. Series C. No. 4, paras. 172 and 174.
[61] IACtHR, *Case of Godínez-Cruz* v. *Honduras*, Merits. Judgment of 20 January 1989. Series C. No. 5, para. 182 (emphasis added).

group or its members is at stake.[62] In right-to-property cases that affect
the *survival* of an indigenous or tribal group, payment of compensation
permits the state to engage only in partial expropriation (amounting to
shared use of the territory). This is in turn subject to the condition that
the indigenous landowners are consulted, receive a share in the benefits
of the project and an environmental and social impact assessment
(ESIA) is carried out.

The UN treaty bodies put forward that the duty to prevent applies to a
wider range of rights. Thus, the Committee observes generally that 'failing to take appropriate measures or to exercise due diligence to prevent,
punish, investigate or redress the harm caused . . . by private persons or
entities'[63] can give rise to a violation of Article 2 of the ICCPR. It
mentions in this context the rights to privacy, freedom from torture,
and to non-discriminatory access to housing and work. While the
Committee therefore does not indicate that prevention of a violation is
the preferred means to comply with Article 2 of the ICCPR, the
Committee is clear in recalling that '[i]n general, the purposes of the
Covenant would be defeated without an obligation . . . to prevent recurrence of a violation'.[64] Most importantly, the Committee holds that:

> the right to an effective remedy may in certain circumstances require
> States Parties to provide for and implement provisional or interim
> measures to avoid continuing violations and to endeavour to repair at
> the earliest possible opportunity any harm that may have been caused by
> such violations.[65]

The Human Rights Committee does not specify in which situations such
remedies should be available. Nevertheless, and here all international
human rights courts and bodies concur, the '[c]essation of an ongoing
violation is an essential element of the right to an effective remedy'.[66]
This duty of cessation stems from the law of state responsibility and
applies to all human rights violations without distinction.

The UN Committee on Economic, Social and Cultural Rights
(CESCR) explains the implications of the duty to prevent especially in

---

[62] IACtHR, *Case of the Saramaka People* v. *Suriname*, Preliminary Objections, Merits, Reparations and Costs. Judgment of 28 November 2007. Series C. No. 172, para. 121, referring to *Sawhoyamaxa*.

[63] UN HR Comm., General Comment No. 31, Nature of the General Legal Obligation on States Parties to the Covenant, UN Doc. CCPR/C/21/Rev.1/Add.13 (2004) (cited here as GC 31), para. 8.

[64] *Ibid*. para. 17.   [65] *Ibid*. para. 19.   [66] *Ibid*. para.15.

relation to the rights to health, food and water. It states that violations may occur if states fail 'to regulate activities of individuals or groups so as to prevent them from violating the right to food of others'.[67] It calls upon states to 'give particular attention to the need to prevent discrimination in access to food', and stipulates that framework laws to ensure the right to food include 'recourse procedures'.[68] The Committee does not pronounce on the necessity to establish remedies that are actionable upon the threat to the right to food.

In its General Comment on the right to water, in contrast, the Committee calls upon states to make 'legislative and other measures' available to 'prevent private parties from interfering in any way with the enjoyment of the right to water'.[69] It urges the establishment of an 'effective regulatory system' and holds that *before* the right to water is affected, the state must ensure the opportunity for 'legal recourse and remedies for those affected'.[70] This formulation is the strongest that can be found in the General Comments, pointing towards the necessity of preventive rather than compensatory remedies.

When should preventive remedies be available, then? I submit that there is a state duty to prevent by law and regulation of business activity any damage that might occur at the core, or the 'essence', of each human right. This core is what international human rights law does not allow to be limited or balanced against other considerations or other rights. For each right, the core has to be defined specifically, and no general formula is likely to be found.[71] For example, for ESCR, this core consists in the 'minimum essential level ... of each of the rights', which has been defined by the CESCR for several rights protected under the ICESCR, listing a series of 'core obligations'.[72]

For civil and political rights, limitations are possible to the extent they are explicitly permitted in the respective treaty. We might therefore

---

[67] UN Committee on ESCR, General Comment No. 12: The Right to Adequate Food (Article 11), UN Doc. E/C.12/1999/5, adopted 12 May 1999, para. 19.

[68] *Ibid.* paras. 26 and 29.

[69] UN Committee on ESCR, General Comment No. 15: The Right to Water (Articles 11 and 12), UN Doc. E/C.12/2002/11, adopted 20 January 2003, para. 23.

[70] *Ibid.* paras. 24 and 56.

[71] For an overview and discussion on the complexity of the concept in the area of ESCR, see K. Young, 'The Minimum Core of Economic and Social Rights: A Concept in Search of Content', *Yale Journal of International Law*, 33 (2008), 113.

[72] UN Committee on ESCR, General Comment No. 3, The Nature of States Parties Obligations (Article 2(1) of the Covenant), adopted 14 December 1990, UN Doc. E/1991/23 Annex III, para. 10.

speak of the core of these rights referring to the non-limitable content of, for example, the right to freedom of expression, the right to privacy or the right to personal liberty. The right to property is similar to civil and political rights in the sense that it can only be restricted in the circumstances explicitly provided for in the treaties.[73]

The CESCR deals with the core of ESCR in the context of the Article 2(1) provision on 'progressive realization' of the Covenant rights, stating that there are certain obligations to be fulfilled with immediate effect.[74] In countries with resource constraints, the state must 'demonstrate that every effort has been made to use all resources that are at its disposition in an effort to satisfy, as a matter of priority, those minimum obligations' in order not to violate its commitments under the Covenant.[75] The Committee held in two General Comments that the minimum core is 'non-derogable' saying that 'a State party cannot, under any circumstances whatsoever, justify its non-compliance with the core obligations . . . which are non-derogable'.[76] It may be criticized that the Committee extends the application of the derogability concept to situations which are not emergencies in the reading of the ICCPR.[77] It has to be taken into account, however, that the ICESCR does not contain a provision on states of emergency,[78] allowing the presumption that the Committee was highlighting a certain characteristic of the core of rights rather than referring to the implications that the derogability scheme has in the ICCPR.[79] Such a reading is confirmed in the Committee's statement on poverty and ESCR in 2001, when it emphasized that 'because core obligations are non-derogable, they continue to exist in situations of conflict, emergency and natural disaster'.[80] Actually, the Rapporteur for the Siracusa Principles on the Limitations Provisions, Alexandre Kiss, argued that non-derogable

---

[73] Article 21 of the ACHR, adopted at the Inter-American Specialized Conference on Human Rights, San José, Costa Rica, 22 November 1969, entry into force 18 July 1978, and Article 1 of Protocol 1 to the ECHR, adopted 20 March 1952.

[74] Committee on ESCR, GC 3, paras. 1 and 10.   [75] Ibid. para. 10.

[76] Committee on ESCR, GC 14, para. 47, and GC 15, para. 67.

[77] On the different schemes applicable to limitations and derogation with respect to the ICCPR, see: 'Siracusa Principles', HRQ, 7 (1985), 3; A. Kiss, 'Commentary by the Rapporteur on the Limitation Provisions', HRQ, 7 (1985), 15.

[78] For an argument on derogation and limitation in the ICESCR, see A. Müller, 'Limitations to and Derogations from Economic, Social and Cultural Rights', Hum. Rts L. Rev., 9 (2009), 557.

[79] See also for this use of derogability Young, 'Minimum Core', 167.

[80] UN Committee on ESCR, Poverty and the International Covenant on Economic, Social and Cultural Rights, Statement adopted on 4 May 2001, E/C12/2001/10, para. 18.

civil and political rights protected under the ICCPR warranted greater protection when it came to *balancing* them with the rights and freedoms of others (thus a context that is not covered by the derogability scheme), as they are 'absolute'.[81] It should be noted, additionally, that two absolute rights might also conflict.

In that sense, the ESCR Committee's reading tells us something important: while there are different mechanisms operating with respect to limitation, derogation and non-retrogressive interpretation, there seems to be an overlap among those rights and those core elements of human rights that require 'stricter' protection with respect to most or all of these mechanisms. In the following, some typical conflicts of investor property rights with human rights are sketched to illustrate these points.

Balancing investor property rights and human rights

The financial feasibility exemption in the IFC guidelines suggests that in cases of hard conflict, investor property rights will trump social concerns and human rights. The subtext seems to be that there is something 'irreparable' in the investment project that the investor cannot be asked to renounce. In the language used so far, this would mean that there is something like a core investor property right that could win out in a balancing exercise against human rights that are affected only at their periphery. How should we assess this assumption from a human rights perspective?

Even if the right to property were considered a human right in all its dimensions – and there is doubt on this point[82] – it would have to enter into the balance with other human rights. The limitations that are allowed to encroach upon the ownership and use of property for reasons of public utility have to be duly taken into account.[83] In addition, there

---

[81] Kiss, 'Commentary', 22.

[82] American Declaration of the Rights and Duties of Man, Adopted by the Ninth International Conference of American States, Bogotá (1948), Article XXIII reads 'everyone has the right to own such private property as meets the essential needs of decent living and helps to maintain the dignity of the individual and the home'. The ACHR only protects property rights of natural persons, see Article 21 ACHR. For an argument that the ECHR scheme is the exception rather than the rule, T. Allen, 'Compensation for Property under the European Convention on Human Rights', *Mich. J. Int'l L.*, 28 (2007), 287.

[83] Article 1 Protocol 1 of the ECHR and Article 21 of the ACHR. The right to property has not been enshrined in the Covenants, especially due to disagreement on limitation clauses and compensation provisions; see C. Krause, 'The Right to Property', in A. Eide *et al.* (eds.), *Economic, Social and Cultural Rights. A Textbook* (2nd edn, Dordrecht: Martinus Nijhoff Publishers, 2001), pp. 191–209, p. 194.

are difficult questions on both the requirement and level of compensation to be paid 'the most disputed aspect of property expropriation'[84]
which have to be left to further inquiry. The question is: is there such a
thing as a core right to property, and are the investor's property rights
likely to fall within this core? It is useful to remind ourselves of the
'interaction of human rights'[85] when answering this question. The thrust
of this idea is that the right to property is essential to enjoy other human
rights, and deserves greater protection than if it merely serves profit-
generating purposes.[86] Consequently, a carpenter would be entitled to
receive greater protection for his shop because his right to work is
involved, or the right of a subsistence farmer to her plot would override
an agri-industry property interest over the same land, on the basis that,
for the subsistence farmer, her right to food and perhaps even her right to
life is at stake. Thus, it is submitted that the threatened insolvency of a
private investor's SPV would not qualify as a more important right to be
protected through the right to property, according to this line of argument. Certainly, there would be difficulty in arguing that investor losses
fall under a defined core of property rights, according to the IFC's
financial feasibility standard. Taking things a bit further, it might well
be that this lack of interaction with other human rights puts the invest-
or's property interests outside the core of a human right to property.

   More concretely, and to return to the pipeline scenario outlined above,
it is possible to identify three situations of conflicts between investor
property rights and human rights. The project director, facing insolvency of the SPV, decides to do away with a second layer of coating for
the pipeline in less densely populated areas, so that the construction
phase can finish in time. The risk he runs is that the crude will most
surely begin to leak in several areas across the country, which the ESIA
indicated as essential for the state's capacity to provide the population's
potable water. Providing potable water to the population is one of the
core obligations the state is due to comply with under the ICESCR.[87]
State regulation and the system of remedies available must ensure that
'under any circumstances whatsoever'[88] it complies with this core obligation. Certainly from a human rights perspective, the water concern
should trump that of the insolvency of the SPV, as the property rights
involved are not at their core. In this situation, however, the director

---

[84] *Ibid.* pp. 200–1.
[85] T. van Banning, *The Human Right to Property* (Antwerp: Intersentia, 2002), pp. 199–209.
[86] *Ibid.* p. 210.   [87] UN Committee on ESCR, GC 14, para. 43c.   [88] *Ibid.* para. 47.

might be tempted to proceed to save the SPV rather than being concerned with the population's water rights. If the state allows this, it would violate its said duty to protect under the ICESCR.

In a second situation, the project director decides to speed up the construction process by adding a third shift from 10 p.m. to 6 a.m. in the vicinity of residential areas. This measure is usually prohibited by legislation to protect the right to privacy of nearby residents, which would be affected by the increased noise during the night. Here, the investor's property rights arguably conflict with a human right, which can be limited for a series of reasons if certain safeguards are met. In cases of such non-absolute rights, therefore, the state may be allowed under international human rights law to balance the rights at stake in favour of the investor.[89]

The most difficult situation seems to arise for the legislator, or for a judge in a case brought before a court, in the following situation: where it is shown that the pipeline investment was substantially contributing to the fulfilment of a state's core obligation, for example through considerable amounts of tax or royalties that the host state agreement reserved for providing basic health services[90] or primary schooling[91] in the country, then there is an argument to be made that interaction with other rights is presumed, and the balancing exercise will have to take this into account. The difficult choice now would be between the loss of the tax on revenues if the SPV went into insolvency, and the pollution of the water resources. Both elements affect its ability to comply with its core obligations under the ICESCR. No trump can be envisaged in this situation, and a judge would probably assign the financial responsibility to pay for the extra coating to the state, so that it can comply with the two obligations it has. This scenario shows how a public interest might come to 'save' an SPV.

From this the following question ensues: how should the state shape its remedies system in such a way that this kind of situation can indeed be dealt with adequately? Assuming that there is a system of ESIA in place, which is a suitable *policy* measure for prevention, the question is: how to enforce respect for human rights throughout the operation of the project? Bringing together the arguments on prevention and core

---

[89] ECtHR, *Hatton and others* v. *United Kingdom* (Application No. 36022/97), Grand Chamber decision, 8 July 2003.

[90] UN Committee on ESCR, GC 14, para. 43a.

[91] UN Committee on ESCR, GC 11, para. 57.

obligations, a state needs to include, in the range of juridical remedies available, effective preventive remedies. As such, it avoids incompliance with its core obligations, and ensures protection of human rights up to the extent that they cannot be limited under international human rights law. I argue that while legal systems, including the international human rights systems, generally do provide for preventive remedies mechanisms, the threshold of irreparability of the damage that has to be shown in these cases tends to be too onerous in the jurisdictions examined. It is suggested that drawing from the concept of core of a human right can assist in getting these thresholds in line with international human rights obligations. Such a legal standard would then show to investors where 'financial feasibility' cannot be invoked against compliance with social obligations, and where compensation is therefore not an adequate option, even if the IFC standards allow for it.

Preventive remedies in domestic and international procedures

This section will examine to what extent preventive remedies that are available in a cross-section of jurisdictions, including international human rights bodies, are suitable as 'adequate and effective remedies' according to international human rights law.[92] It will especially address how these remedies resolve the challenges posed by irreparability thresholds and cross-undertakings. Finally, I briefly highlight two external problems, which may negatively affect the availability of suitable preventive remedies: issues of rule of law; and the enforcement of the state's duty to prevent in direct negotiations between companies and affected individuals or communities.

   The choice of cases is admittedly incomplete and unsystematic, but unites some of the internationally discussed situations of the Americas. The cases have illustrative value only; an in-depth review of national legislation or case law is not the purpose of this chapter. Rather, I argue that the law as it stands does not always seem able to address the preference for avoidance advanced by international human rights law, and as recommended by the IFC.

---

[92] In the argument I am making in what follows, I assume that at least some aspects of economic, social and cultural rights are justiciable. For a discussion on this point, which I cannot address in the limited space here, see F. Coomans (ed.), *Justiciability of Economic and Social Rights: Experiences from Domestic Systems* (Antwerp: Intersentia, 2006).

Thresholds of irreparability

Responsibility for damage is usually allocated in different jurisdictions pursuant to an evaluation of fault, recurring to concepts such as intent or negligence. Another usually exceptional possibility is strict liability, which only considers remoteness of damage and factual causation.[93] Most civil law regimes consider that the more serious a risk is, the more difficult it becomes for a company to argue that it did not know of the risk. This weakens its defence that it could not have taken precautionary measures to avoid the harm.[94] There is an argument that human rights risk should always fall under a strict liability scheme.[95] The reason is that in human rights cases it is very important that the gravity of damage, and not only the likelihood that it will occur, is factored into the test.[96]

The award of preventive remedies follows similar patterns and criteria both in different jurisdictions and in different areas of law. This is certainly true for the substantive tier of the relevant tests: there must be some kind of urgency with respect to possible harm as well as the possibility of violation of a right or entitlement. Differences arise between some tests that introduce the gravity of the violation as a second criterion, and others, which measure the risk that (any) violation might occur. There are also tests that combine urgency, risk and gravity. There is divergence between jurisdictions as to the level of the applicable threshold, especially with respect to different evidence requirements to substantiate a risk. Within a single jurisdiction, tests for precautionary measures are often similar for all areas of law since they are taken from equity or civil law and applied across the board. As we shall see, there may be differences for constitutional remedies.

The award of equitable (non-compensatory) remedies in common law has been in theory determined by the 'irreparable injury rule', meaning that these remedies were considered available only if compensation was inadequate to remedy the wrong.[97] In practice, however, judges who were asked to decide on permanent injunctions would *cite* the rule faithfully, only to disregard it when *deciding* the case. Actually, they

---

[93] International Commission of Jurists, 'Civil Liability 2008', pp. 22–5. [94] *Ibid.* 14–17.

[95] See for a brief conceptual analysis with respect to international human rights law, IACtHR, *Case of El Amparo* v. *Venezuela*, Interpretation of the Judgment of Reparations and Costs. Order of the Court of 16 April 1997. Series C. No. 46, Opinion of Judge Cançado Trindade, paras. 15–21.

[96] With respect to the likelihood that damage would occur, see International Commission of Jurists, 'Civil Liability 2008', p. 19.

[97] See, for example, Laycock, *Death*, p. 4.

applied this rule only in sales cases. In all other cases, especially involving civil rights, US courts generally considered injury to legal rights irreparable, principally granting injunctions.[98] In that sense, Laycock declared in 1990, after examining judicial practice in the USA, 'the irreparable injury rule is dead'.[99] This development would conform to human rights concerns; however, as Laycock shows, preliminary injunctions – which would be suitable to address the need for prevention in scenarios such as the pipeline-coating scenario – do not follow this same logic.

Generally, those who fear that their rights could be irreparably violated have a clear interest in making their case *before* any damage occurs. In equity, *quia timet* injunctions are the remedy that at first glance seems to provide the greatest chance of obtaining the desired result, as an award is based on risk and not proof of damage. Generally, *quia timet* injunctions are granted if there is 'a strong case of probability', 'proof of imminent danger' and 'proof that the apprehended damage ... is substantial'.[100] However, *quia timet* injunctions are less likely to be granted than other injunctions.[101] Since the standard of proof is higher for a *quia timet* injunction, courts usually require a high risk to be proved, and an assurance of damages (cross-undertaking) in the case that the defendant should be found right on the merits. The same problem exists for interlocutory injunctions. Laycock observes:

> [C]ourts at the preliminary relief stage routinely find that damages will be an adequate remedy for injuries they would consider irreparable after a full trial [and he concludes that] [p]reliminary injunctions are hotly contested and often denied in substantive areas where all injury is irreparable and permanent injunctions are routine, such as intellectual property, civil rights and civil liberties, and environmental law.[102]

An interesting case on corporate interests showing the different standards of irreparability to be proved in interlocutory and permanent relief comes from Belize, where a hydroelectric power project was allowed to go ahead, although counsel argued that there were serious doubts about

[98] *Ibid.* pp. 100–10.   [99] *Ibid.*
[100] J. Martin, *Hanbury & Martin Modern Equity* (17th edn, London: Sweet & Maxwell, 2005), pp. 801–3.
[101] *Ibid.* 802. Harris reports: '[i]f there is doubt, [the] balance of convenience test compares 'the extent of the uncompensatable disadvantage to each party' (Harris *et al.*, *Remedies*, p. 609). US law continues to use a test which gives heavy weight to the question of a prima facie case on the merits, as was English law previously; see Laycock, *Death*, p. 118.
[102] Laycock, *Death*, pp. 113 and 116 (fns. omitted).

the appropriateness of the EIA carried out prior to the project's commencement. Both majority and minority reasoning of the 3:2 decision of the Privy Council on a permanent injunction in 2004 are interesting for our purposes.[103] For the majority, Lord Hoffmann noted that Belize is a sovereign country with a democratic Constitution. The government, accordingly, could freely make policy decisions such as the construction of a hydroelectric power plant, even in an ecologically sensitive area. For Lord Hoffmann, the question did not 'raise issues of human rights'[104] and therefore the Belizean government could go ahead and grant the licence.[105]

The case shows that judges do take into account human rights considerations when assessing a claim for an injunction, pursuant to s. 12(3) of the Human Rights Act 1998, which prescribes a specific test for the granting of interlocutory injunctions in human rights cases. The Act requires a judge to consider first the strength of the case before turning to the balance of convenience. In that context, a lesser likelihood of succeeding at trial can be outweighed by the specific gravity of the feared damage.[106] Potentially, therefore, if human rights protected through the 1998 Act are at stake, a preventive remedy could be more readily available than in other cases.

The minority observed that the appeal should have been allowed based on serious errors in the EIA. The two judges would have ordered a new EIA, with prior consultation of the population. Lord Walker of Gestingthorpe concluded that

> [t]he rule of law must not be sacrificed to foreign investment, however desirable (indeed, recent history shows that in many parts of the world respect for the rule of law is an incentive, and disrespect for the rule of law can be a severe deterrent, to foreign investment). It is no answer to the erroneous geology in the EIA to say that the dam design would not necessarily have been different. The people of Belize are entitled to be properly informed about any proposals for alterations in the dam design before the project is approved and before work continues with its construction.[107]

---

[103] Claimants had filed for an interlocutory injunction, decided in 2003, and a permanent injunction, decided in 2004. Here, I refer to the 2004 decision, Privy Council, *Belize Alliance of Conservation Non-Governmental Organizations* v. *Department of the Environment and Belize Electric Company Ltd*, Privy Council Appeal No. 47 of 2003, decision adopted 29 January 2004 (cited here as Belize Privy Council 2004).

[104] *Ibid.* para. 9.   [105] *Ibid.* para. 10.   [106] Martin, *Hanbury & Martin*, p. 795.

[107] Belize Privy Council 2004, para. 120.

This perspective coincides with an argument that can be made in international human rights law that there are situations in which the core of the right to participation cannot be balanced against other interests.[108] In that sense, the interpretation that Lord Hoffmann gave to the term 'human rights' may be considered too restrictive nowadays.

It is interesting for our purposes that one of the dissenting Lords had earlier declined an *interlocutory* injunction, arguing that the balance of risk tilted towards the defendants; he suggested that it would be adequate to deal with the possible damages arising from continued construction should the claimants win on the merits.[109] Here, the judge upheld a compensation preference, although he clearly showed sensitivity for human rights concerns on the merits. According to the argument presented above, he would be justified in doing so if this only restricts the right to information at its periphery.

Following a logic similar to the argument presented in this chapter, in an analysis of English tort law, Murphy suggests that mandatory *quia timet* injunctions should be more readily granted in cases of threat or risk of physical injury.[110] He criticizes the fact that non-monetary damages for infringements of property-like rights are available 'unless, exceptionally, a monetary remedy would be adequate', whereas other interests are remedied through damages 'only if a monetary remedy would not be adequate'.[111] Greater readiness to grant *quia timet* injunctions would thus restore the hierarchy of values in tort law.

---

[108] The ECHR and the HRA 1998 do not recognize a non-derogable right to participation; however, the Parliamentary Assembly of the Council of Europe recommends enshrining a right to participation with respect to the right to a healthy environment (see: http://assembly.coe.int/Documents/WorkingDocs/Doc09/EDOC12003.pdf). The recommendation makes reference to the Convention on Access to Information, Public Participation in Decision-making and Access to Justice in Environmental Matters signed in Aarhus on 25 June 1998, of which Article 1 recognizes a right to public participation in environmental decision making. With the ratification of the Convention in 2005, the UK clearly recognizes this as a legal right (see Declaration at the moment of ratification). No territorial restriction applies and it may well be that the term 'human rights' would have to be interpreted in the light of this Convention if the Belizean case were decided today. The UK had signed the Convention in 1998, accepting thus the obligation not to contravene the object and purpose of the Convention, arguably expressed in Article 1. The decision in the Belizean case does not reflect this.

[109] See Privy Council, *Belize Alliance of Conservation Non-Governmental Organizations* v. *Department of the Environment and Belize Electric Company Ltd*, Privy Council Appeal No. 47 of 2003, decision adopted 13 August 2003, para. 30.

[110] J. Murphy, 'Rethinking Injunctions in Tort Law', *Oxford J. Legal Stud.*, 27 (2007), 509.

[111] *Ibid.* 515.

Preventive remedies should be readily available in constitutional law. Since an exhaustive or even a systematic account of constitutional systems is not possible here,[112] the basic principles will be illustrated by the Colombian example.

In Colombia, constitutional rights and the 'constitutional block'[113] are protected through the *tutela* writ, which according to Article 86 of the Colombian Constitution, allows for a summary decision, in a maximum of ten days,[114] on alleged infringement of or threat to constitutional rights by any public authority. Private actors may be sued through a *tutela* writ in certain situations, especially if the alleged victim is in a relation of 'subordination or defencelessness' with respect to the person against whom the *tutela* is sought.[115] The *tutela* is available whenever a constitutional right is violated or threatened by public authorities, and there is no specific standard of irreparability to be met to access the remedy. Additionally, Colombian law provides for interlocutory measures for constitutional rights (*tutela transitoria*) where an irreparability threshold *does* apply. Colombian constitutional judges have been willing to award *tutela* protection against hydroelectric power projects and extractive industries such as mining and drilling.

For example, in the case of the U'wa Indigenous People, the Constitutional Court of Colombia decided that an incomplete consultation carried out before granting an exploitation permit in the U'wa territory violated their constitutional rights and was contrary to Colombia's obligations under ILO Convention No. 169.[116] The Court granted this

---

[112] A general comparative analysis has been provided by M. González, *Medidas Cautelares en el Derecho Procesal Civil* (Santiago: Editorial Jurídica, 2004). See generally on *amparo* and *habeas corpus* proceedings in Latin America, H. Nogueira Alcalá, *Acciones Constitucionales de Amparo y Protección: Realidad y Prospectiva en Chile y América Latina* (Editorial Universidad de Talca, 2000). See also E. Paillas, *El Recurso de Protección Ante el Derecho Comparado. Una Acción en Busca de Una Justicia Rápida y Eficaz* (3rd edn, Santiago: Editorial Jurídica, 2002).

[113] Constitutional Court of Colombia, C-225 of 1995. The block of constitutionality encompasses international human rights treaties and ILO conventions ratified by Colombia. See also M. Arango Olaya, 'El Bloque de Constitucionalidad en la Jurisprudencia de la Corte Constitucional de Colombia', *Precedente* (2004), 79–102 (at: www.icesi.edu.co/esn/contenido/pdfs/C1C-marango-bloque.pdf, last accessed 7 October 2009).

[114] See Constitutional Court of Colombia, SU-039 of 1997, citing its decision T-203 of 1993.

[115] Article 86 Constitution of Colombia of 1991, and Decree 2591 of 1991.

[116] International Labour Organization, Indigenous and Tribal Peoples Convention, adopted 27 June 1989. With Colombia's ratification on 7 August 1991, the Convention entered into force on 5 September 1991.

action, which was allowed to proceed in parallel to a suit at administrative law, and ordered that a proper consultation had to be carried out within thirty days. This transitory *tutela*[117] has interlocutory effects. Decree 2591/91 stipulates:

> When a judge considers it explicitly necessary and urgent to protect a right, he will suspend the application of the concrete act that threatens or violates the right.[118]

The remedy is granted when there is a threat of irreparable damage (*perjuicio irremediable*).[119] The Constitutional Court has explained that the threshold for granting such a suspension is the threat or existence of irreparable harm. In short, the threat must be imminent, urgent, serious (*grave*), and must be such that the remedy cannot be postponed.[120] According to the Court, imminent means that the damage will happen soon (*prontamente*) and that it does not constitute a mere 'hypothetical speculation'. Seriousness refers to the 'importance that the legal order concedes to certain protected goods'.[121] Néstor Correa criticizes the fact that the Court confuses imminence, which is a purely temporal criterion, with probability. Furthermore, he observes that the focus of 'seriousness' should be on irreparability, which according to him is given when restitution is not possible.[122] His point seems to coincide with what I have deduced from international human rights law above. In general, Colombian constitutional procedures seem to allow for prevention in the sense advocated above. As we shall see below, the decisions meet with an important implementation problem.

Since the availability of suitable preventive remedies in cases that concern core human rights issues seem to be de facto or de jure relatively scarce in domestic legal systems, one would like to turn to the international human rights bodies to achieve the protection that was not obtained in domestic proceedings. Surprisingly, however, the requirement of irreparability also applies in the procedures of most international human rights

---

[117] See for details also E. Cifuentes Muñoz, 'La Acción de Tutela en Colombia', *Nogueira* (2000), 297–305, 302.

[118] Article 7 of Decree 2591/91, cited according to Constitutional Court of Colombia, SU-039 of 1997 (author's translation).

[119] Article 8 of Decree 2591/91 and Constitutional Court of Colombia SU-039 of 1997, s. 4.1.

[120] See Constitutional Court of Colombia, T-225 of 1993.   [121] *Ibid.*

[122] The remaining two criteria refer to the suitability of the remedy, and have been considered unhelpful. See N. Correa Henao, *Derecho Procesal de la Acción de Tutela* (2nd edn, Bogotá: Pontificia Universidad Javeriana, 2005), pp. 143–4.

bodies.[123] Here, the focus will only be on the Inter-American system of human rights, which uses standards that come closest to the preventive argument presented above.

The IACtHR has been generally amenable to granting provisional measures. Provisional measures have a conventional basis in Article 63(2) of the ACHR, which provides that they can be awarded in cases of 'extreme gravity and urgency, and when necessary to avoid irreparable damage to persons'. In practice, this has meant that the Court has repeatedly issued provisional measures in cases in which public or private (or unknown) actors have threatened the right to life and physical integrity of the beneficiaries. For example, in the case of the Afro-Colombian Jiguamiandó and Curbaradó communities, the Court reiterated its provisional measures in February 2008,[124] making explicit reference to threats these communities had received from persons linked to the palm-oil industry.

Furthermore, the Court issued an order unprecedented in international law in an Ecuadorian case where an extractive industry threatened to interfere with the right to free movement of indigenous communities.[125] The Court specifically requested the state to ensure:

> the freedom of movement of the members of the Indigenous People Sarayaku, especially on the Borbonaza river [in Ecuador]; [and to] repair

---

[123] See generally J. G. Naldi, 'Interim Measures in the UN Human Rights Committee', *International and Comparative Law Quarterly*, 53 (2004), 445–54. For case law, see esp. HR Comm., *Länsman* v. *Finland*, Communication No. 511/1992, UN Doc. CCPR/C/52D, 5 November 1992, opinion approved 8 November 1994. Interim protection was not granted in this case, and no violation was found, only exploration activities for quarrying had been undertaken. Most importantly, HR Comm., *Chief Ominayak and Lubicon Band* v. *Canada*, Communication No. 167/1984, UN Doc. CCPR/C/38/D/167/1984, opinion approved 10 May 1990, where the Committee granted interim measures that the applicants were repeatedly denied at domestic level.

[124] The IACtHR issued two resolutions on provisional measures in this case, both on 5 February 2008. They are not distinguished in title, date or numbering. The resolution of interest here is the one that refers to a public, not private hearing on that same day; see Issue of the Communities Jiguamiandó and Curbaradó and Colombia (A), Resolution on Provisional Measures of 5 February 2008, in the third paragraph of this document. The resolution issued after a *private* hearing refers exclusively to procedural issues regarding the number of beneficiaries of the provisional measures, Issue of the Communities Jiguamiandó and Curbaradó and Colombia (B), Resolution on Provisional Measures of 5/2/2008, in the sixth paragraph of this document.

[125] IACtHR, Issue of the Indigenous People Sarayaku and Ecuador, Resolution on Provisional Measures of 6 July 2004, reiterated in Resolution on Provisional Measures of 17 June 2005, operative para. 1a. See also Issue of the Indigenous People Kankuamo and Colombia, 5 July 2004, operative para. 3.

the airfield located in the territory where the ... Sarayaku are living, in order to guarantee that this means of transport is not suspended.[126]

The Court therefore seems to consider that the irreparability threshold is reached even if it is not the life or personal integrity of the beneficiary that is in danger. The link made in the provisional measures between these different rights suggests that irreparability should be interpreted more broadly. Nevertheless, the evidence does not support the putative argument that has been made above with respect to preventive protection for the core of 'any' human right. This argument remains a theoretical quest, therefore.

The Commission has issued precautionary measures in a great variety of cases; like the Court, it awards interim measures when there is a threat to life or physical integrity, which includes serious threats to the right to health; the definition of this threat being broadly interpreted. Measures in the Commission were ordered against pollution in the Peruvian city La Oroya where the metallurgical industry is operating without adopting sufficient environmental standards;[127] furthermore, the Commission ordered precautionary measures against illegal logging in their territory for indigenous communities who live in voluntary isolation;[128] and the Commission ordered the immediate suspension of works on a hydroelectric plant and any activity related to the respective concession, in order to protect the rights of the indigenous Ngöbe people.[129] The Commission has granted various precautionary measures in favour of NGO members or individuals who receive threats because of their opposition to investment projects or for their lobbying for environmental protection.[130]

---

[126] Sarayaku 2004 and 2005, operative paras. 1d and e.
[127] IACHR, *La Oroya* v. *Peru*, decision of 31 August 2007, reported in Annual Report 2007, Chapter III.C.1, para. 46 (at: www.cidh.org).
[128] IACHR, Indigenous peoples of Mashco Piro, Yora and Amahuaca in voluntary isolation and Peru, Precautionary Measures of 22 March 2007.
[129] IACHR, PM56/08, Ngöbe Indigenous Communities and Panamá, Precautionary Measures of 19 June 2009 (summary at: www.cidh.oas.org/medidas/2009.eng.htm, last accessed 8 October 2009). The Court did not grant provisional measures that were requested by the Commission; The decision was especially based on the lack of urgency the Court deduced from slow processing at the Commission; see IACtHR, Ngöbe Indigenous Communities and Panamá, Order on provisional measures of 28 May 2010, considering paras. 12; 16.
[130] IACHR, Trade unionists at the Empresa Portuaria Quetzal and Guatemala, Precautionary Measures of 31 August 2007; *Marco Arana, Mirtha Vásquez et al.* v. *Peru*, Precautionary Measures of 23 April 2007, referring to death threats in relation to their opposition to mining projects.

Contrary to other international human rights organs, the Inter-American Commission and Court of Human Rights interpret the rights to life and physical integrity widely, encompassing serious threats to the right to health.[131] This is reflected in the type of provisional and precautionary measures the organs order. However, the bodies do not award measures to protect the core of all Convention rights. As the Commission does not publish any records of rejected requests for precautionary measures, it is not possible to verify if there were other requests that the Commission considered insufficiently 'grave and urgent' for not consisting in a threat to the life and physical integrity of a person.

In sum, all tests in international human rights law take into account the gravity of the damage that is likely to occur. In that sense, these tests are, from a human rights perspective, preferable to tests that mainly consider the degree of risk. It may be due to the subsidiary character of these international bodies, which do not want to replace domestic mechanisms, that they only grant provisional or protective measures for threats to the right to life, to the right to physical and psychological integrity, and to the right to personal liberty. The jurisprudence of the IACtHR indicates, nevertheless, that the threatened or actual violation of other rights may also meet the gravity test.

Cross-undertakings

Cross-undertakings may constitute an important obstacle to obtaining preventive remedies. The Belizean case mentioned above provides interesting insight into this issue. Cross-undertakings are usually ordered in exchange of an interlocutory injunction. In situations like the Belizean, the interest engaged is not of an economic nature (that is exactly why it cannot be compensated for). Since the claimant's interest is in a human right and not an economic right, s/he cannot be expected to dispose of the economic resources another claimant would have in a case where economic interest stands against another economic interest (i.e. a classical sales of goods case). The guarantee of damages, or

---

[131] IACtHR, *Case of the Sawhoyamaxa Indigenous Community* v. *Paraguay*, Merits, Reparations and Costs. Judgment of 29 March 2006. Series C. No. 146; and *Case of the Yakye Axa Indigenous Community* v. *Paraguay*, Merits, Reparations and Costs. Judgment of 17 June 2005. Series C. No. 125.

cross-undertaking, which most jurisdictions require when granting preliminary (or interlocutory) injunctions, potentially causes problems with
respect to poor or indigent claimants. Canada takes a different approach:
the Canadian Quebec Act, s. 19.4, sets the maximum guarantee for interim
awards in environmental law to C\$500.[132] A cross-undertaking should not
have to back the undue economic loss that a defendant investor would have
incurred in case s/he wins the case on the merits. Even if the claimants were
not poor, they can hardly be expected to have the money to compensate a
transnational corporation for loss of revenues.

Support for this point can be found in other UK decisions. Lord
Denning, for the Court of Appeal argued in *Allen* v. *Jambo Holdings*
that '[he does] not see why a poor plaintiff should be denied a Mareva
injunction just because he is poor, whereas a rich plaintiff would get
it'.[133] The Privy Council had to decide in 2003 on an application for an
interim injunction with respect to the Belize hydroelectric power station.
The Lords did not think that the *Allen* v. *Jambo Holdings* reasoning
applied to the Belizean non-governmental organization (NGO) that had
requested the interim injunction. The lack of a cross-undertaking was a
major reason why the injunction was not granted.[134] In that sense, a
remedy was not available in this case, although this ruling does not imply
that the decision on the merits would have been the same. In *Guerrero* v.
Monterrico, the single judge decided that in principle, poverty does not
exempt from providing cross-undertakings. However, in this specific
case, the judge ordered a freezing injunction against the company and
relegated the order of a cross-undertaking to a future hearing.[135]

Leubsdorf argues, in line with the concerns submitted here, that providing a bond is not and should not be the decisive factor in awarding interim
injunctions.[136] His argument finds important support in international
human rights law. A remedy would not be 'effective' if poor applicants

[132] Martin, 'Interlocutory Injunctions', 401.
[133] *Allen* v. *Jambo Holdings* [1980] 1 WLR 1252, at 1257. The two other justices agreed.
[134] Belize Privy Council 2003, paras. 47 and 39.
[135] *Guerrero* v. *Monterrico* [2009] EWHC 2475 (QB), paras. 43–4. See for further developments, *Guerrero* v. *Monterrico* [2010] EWHC 3228 (QB).
[136] From an economic analysis of law, R. W. Brooks and W. F. Schwartz proposed that
interim injunctions should exclusively depend on the undertaking by the claimant, so
that the defendant's inconvenience can be paid off in case the claimant loses on the
merits (see 'Legal Uncertainty, Economic Efficiency, and the Preliminary Injunction
Doctrine', *Stanford Law Review*, 58 (2005), 381–410). J. Leubsdorf criticizes the
approach and among other arguments adduces that it would be difficult for a 'prevailing defendant' in environmental or civil rights injunctions to recover a monetary bond

could not have access to it because of their financial situation. This could be achieved if cross-undertakings were not calculated on the material damage that might occur through the granting of the provisional measure.

Rule of law

While this chapter is primarily concerned with legal obstacles to obtaining preventive remedies, it cannot omit a brief comment on extra-legal obstructions of the right to an effective remedy. If the rule of law is not guaranteed in a country, be it due to corruption, violence, or for any other reason, the right to an effective remedy remains as illusionary as if the law had a structural problem on the irreparability threshold.

Lacking rule of law is evidenced, for example, by the lack of response to the decision of the Colombian Constitutional Court in the Urrá hydroelectric dam case. The Embera Katío filed a *tutela* writ for protection of their constitutional rights. While the decision on appeal was pending, provisional measures from a lower court halted the filling of the reservoir. On the merits, the Court awarded a series of compensatory remedies, payable by the operating company, for damage already caused. Additionally, the Court awarded preventive remedies to protect the rights of the indigenous people in the future, drawing a balance between opposed interests: corporate, indigenous, and locals who did not oppose the project as they received benefits and work opportunities from the project. Especially, the Court ordered protection of the 'fundamental rights to survival, to ethnic, cultural, social and economic integrity, to participation and to due process' specified in the rules of prior consultation, and ordered the company to resume the implementation of all development agreements until a second consultation process would yield its results with respect to further development and compensation programmes.[137]

However, the company did not comply with the decision of the Constitutional Court, and several members and leaders of the Embera Katío have been disappeared after their protests intensified in 1999. The Inter-American Commission on Human Rights issued precautionary measures in their favour;[138] the measures have been extended for the

(see 'Preliminary Injunctions: In Defense of the Merits', *Fordham L. Rev.*, 76(2007), 33, 41–2).
[137] Colombian Constitutional Court, T-652 of 1998, operative paras. 1, 5 and 9.
[138] The Inter-American Commission on Human Rights granted precautionary measures for several abducted members of the Embera indigenous people; see IACHR, Annual Report 2001, para. 19.

community leader who was not released like the others.[139] The complex questions arising from the lack of rule of law and violent pressures on law enforcement authorities cannot be dealt with in the limited scope of this chapter. The example shows, nevertheless, how a relatively favourable award may remain without effect. Were the case sent to the Inter-American Commission on Human Rights, this could entail a condemnation of the state for the violation of Articles 8 and 25 ACHR.

Direct negotiations between companies and affected individuals and communities

This analysis has focused principally on public authorities as the responsible actors to respect and protect the human rights of communities and individuals possibly affected by investment activity. In international human rights law, the duty to prevent is a state duty that has to be guaranteed through the different legal provisions in domestic law. A precondition for compliance is the faculty and willingness by governments to regulate private activity if international economic interests are involved. In many situations of large-scale investment, human rights issues, such as the right to subsistence property and the right to health affected by residues and trespass, arise when investors negotiate directly with potentially affected individuals and communities. Discrepancy in bargaining power appears especially if the investor promises jobs in remote areas, and thus possesses an additional tool for pressure, or if community members are illiterate. This situation may lead to the signing of compensation agreements, either for leasing or selling of land or after damage has occurred, which are not in conformity with international human rights law.

In the Chilean Pascua Lama gold mine project, carried out by a subsidiary of Barrick Gold, the subsidiary signed a protocol with the directory of the local 'Vigilance Committee' established under the Chilean Water Law.[140] The protocol contained a commitment to environmental precautions by the subsidiary and compensation to owners of water rights in the valley where the mining project would be undertaken. An administrative suit was filed, including a request for precautionary

---

[139] IACHR, Report on the Situation of Human Rights Defenders in the Americas, OEA/Ser.L/V/II.124, adopted 7 March 2006, para. 149.

[140] Article 186 of the Chilean Código de Aguas, Decreto con fuerza de Ley 1.122, adopted 13 August 1981.

measures, in the name of indigenous communities and individual members of the Committee who did not feel represented by the directory. In Chile, water rights are bought and sold by individuals, legal persons and communities, and they cannot be waived without consent.[141]

The government may argue that no human rights issues are involved since the contracts are between private parties. At a minimum, however, the law needs to provide effective remedies to address human rights abuse in such situations. The state's duty to protect and fulfil human rights also encompasses some form of oversight of negotiations to ensure the protection of constitutional and human rights. While out-of-court settlements may be beneficial in many cases, there needs to be some form of control assuring that the avoidance preference and duty to prevent are taken into due account. Usually, civil law provisions on negligent behaviour, administrative law or criminal law are suitable to exercise this control. Here again, however, it will depend on the relevant thresholds of irreparability, burden and standard of proof and whether this remedy is sufficient deterrence such that the state does not incur international responsibility for violations of its human rights obligations.

Conclusions and recommendations

The argument put forward in this chapter addressed the tension between avoidance or prevention and compensation for damage in situations where the enjoyment of human rights could be threatened by investment activity. While the analysis claims to have more general value, it has been considered especially pertinent in a PF context, in which pressure to move to the non-recourse stage of a project makes it more likely that sponsors would not deem the avoidance of damage 'financially feasible', preferring to pay compensation to waiting any longer for the revenue flow and the possibility of paying back the lenders.

International human rights law, pointing in a different direction, supports the case for making the duty to prevent enforceable in certain cases. An argument was made that preventive remedies should in that sense be available when the core of human rights would be affected – the reason being that it is just this core of a human rights that we would not

---

[141] Application for administrative review of the underwriting of a protocol on 30 June 2005 by the Junta de Vigilancia de la Cuenca del Río Huasco y sus Afluentes and Compañía Minera Nevada, Applicants: Comunidad Diaguita de los Huascoaltinos (on file with the author).

agree to trade against a sum of money. The focus of analysis therefore has been on procedural issues, which were tied in with an arguably suitable test for balancing investor rights and individual or community rights. A selective overview of legal provisions and case law showed several difficulties involved when adjusting available preventive remedies to such a standard. It has been found that countries with strong constitutional rights protection, which can be invoked against private parties, seem to be best suited to provide these remedies, except when the term 'irreparability' is interpreted in restricted terms as involving only threats to the right to life or physical integrity. If the rule of law is weak, however, such favourable jurisprudence cannot necessarily make a difference on the ground, due to the lack of implementation.

If this argument is accepted, several needs for reform can be identified. Some jurisdictions may already have adequate systems for preventive remedies, and just need to assure that they are duly implemented. While extraterritorial applicability of domestic law raises complex questions by itself,[142] home states should revise their legislation and jurisprudence in order to examine whether suitable preventive remedies are available for alleged victims of human rights violations that may be caused by companies headquartered in these states. Host states should take into consideration the fact that lenders, independently of the mode of finance used, will want to move ahead quickly with the building and operation of a project. This heightened interest in moving ahead quickly can lead to a calculation that any damage arising should be paid off through damages. Host states that are aware of their duty to prevent damage to human rights will not give in to such preference, insisting on higher levels of protection for their populations when the non-limitable core of rights would be affected.

In that sense, host states should make effective remedies available for third parties at the national level by accepting that state contract or investment treaty clauses cannot override core human rights treaty obligations. Human rights bodies and the respective domestic courts should consider whether it is only threats to the rights to life and physical integrity that may constitute situations of urgency and gravity. The lower threshold that was advocated in this chapter could apply to all situations in which the non-limitable core of human rights is threatened.

---

[142] See: M. Kamminga and F. Coomans, *Extraterritorial Application of Human Rights Treaties* (Antwerp: Intersentia, 2004); N. Jägers, *Corporate Human Rights Obligations: In Search of Accountability* (Antwerp: Intersentia, 2002).

Second, low or only nominal cross-undertakings should be requested from public interest NGOs or poor individuals when they file for an interim injunction on alleged human rights violations. The inability to give a cross-undertaking should never be the decisive reason for not awarding a preliminary injunction to protect the core of a human right. This concern is especially acute considering that project sponsors, along with the SPV, will seek to generate revenues that far outweigh the financial capacity of civil society actors or individual right holders to defend the core of human rights threatened by the project.

Admittedly, this argument leaves more questions than answers. Procedural obstacles to the availability of remedies generally should in particular be fully addressed. It might well be that in practice, legal standing issues for civil society actors against multinational companies in a globalized economy turn out to be a greater obstacle to obtaining a (preventive or compensatory) remedy than the irreparability threshold. However, addressing the specific question of prevention, this chapter aimed at contributing to the discussion on enforcement of corporate recommendations, so as to make the prevention preference of the OECD Guidelines more effective on the ground.

PART III

Case studies

11

The implications of the Chad–Cameroon and Sakhalin transnational investment agreements for the application of international environmental principles

DAVID ONG

Introduction

This chapter will assess the implications of two 'transnational' investment agreements (TIAs) involving both international and 'transnational' actors within two different geographical situations in terms of their application (or otherwise) of accepted international environmental principles. The first TIA involves two, sub-Saharan, west African developing countries (Chad and Cameroon), and the second TIA applies within a Eurasian transitional economy (Russian Federation). The term 'transnational' is used here to denote those agreements, organizations or institutions that are undoubtedly international in their scope but involve non-state actors, such as multinational/transnational corporations (MN/TNCs), acting in concert with states. The type of transnational agreements discussed here are TIAs involving MNCs/TNCs and their host states regarding the terms of their investments within the host state concerned.[1] Within this context, two specific examples will be examined. These are first, the Chad–Cameroon Oil Development and Pipeline Project;[2] and second, the Sakhalin II Petroleum Development and Pipeline Project,[3] located on the island of Sakhalin in the far-eastern

---

[1] See pp. xx–x of my earlier contribution to this volume, Chapter 4, for a proposed taxonomy of the different types of international and transnational agreements and actors examined within this book.

[2] For general information on the public International Financial Institutions' (IFIs') involvement in this project, see World Bank website, at: www.worldbank.org.

[3] For general information on the Sakhalin II project, see Sakhalin Energy Corp. website, at: www.sakhalinenerg.ru/ru. For the latest information on the financing aspects of this

corner of the Russian Federation. These TIAs providing the regulatory and contractual framework governing the petroleum development and transportation activity in each of the two case studies examined here will be the focus of this contribution, in terms of the different legal relationships they have engendered between states, transnational corporations, civil society groups and other international and transnational actors.

Following on from my earlier contribution (Chapter 4) on the application of important environmental principles to TIAs and transnational actors such as the private banks that provide the project finance (PF) for activities regulated by these TIAs, the present case studies will examine how far these internationally accepted environmental principles have been either applied, or, conversely, transgressed against within these TIAs and actors. In doing so, this chapter will also highlight the enduring role of the governments of the host states within which these projects are located. In both the case studies considered below, it may be seen that despite the best efforts of the public international financial institutions involved such as the World Bank, or International Bank for Reconstruction and Development (IBRD), in the case of Chad, and the European Bank for Reconstruction and Development (EBRD) in the Russian case study on Sakhalin, the 'best-practice' application of relevant international environmental principles has not necessarily materialized. Indeed, with the Sakhalin project, we shall see that environmental protection was utilized by the Russian federal government as a political and legal tool for leveraging the shareholding participation of the Russian state-owned Gazprom company,[4] within the original consortium of partners that owned the operating company concerned, namely, Sakhalin Energy.

Case studies of the Chad–Cameroon and Sakhalin II projects

The Chad–Cameroon Oil Development and Pipeline Project

The Chad–Cameroon Oil Development and Pipeline Project consists of oil production from around 250 wells in three oilfields in the Doba

project, see BankTrack website, at: www.banktrack.org/. Information on the environmental issues arising from this project can also be accessed at the World-Wide Fund for Nature (WWF) website at: www.wwf.org and Pacific Environment website at: www.pacificenvironment.org/

[4] According to a recent news report, the Russian federation government holds 50.002 per cent of Gazprom shares. See Dan Roberts, 'Russian energy group with power to turn off the lights in Europe', *Guardian* newspaper (UK) 11 January 2010, at 27.

basin, in southern Chad, as well as the construction and operation of a 1,050 kilometre long transboundary pipeline to transport the oil from Chad through Cameroon for export from the Cameroon port of Kribi on the Atlantic coast of west Africa. The project is run by a consortium of three multinational/transnational oil companies, namely Exxon-Mobil (US), Chevron-Texaco (US) and Petronas (Malaysia). It has been pumping more than 200,000 barrels of oil a day from Chad since July 2003. It is the largest single project of its kind in the sub-Saharan African region, being valued at US$4.2 billion. More than half of this total project cost has been borne directly by the three MNC/TNC consortium partners. A further US$334 million in loans was provided by public international financial institutions (IFIs) such as the World Bank group (specifically, from the IBRD and the International Finance Corporation (IFC) and the European Investment Bank (US$41.5 million). State-backed export credit agencies from the USA (US Ex-Im Bank), France (COFACE) and Africa (African Ex-Im Bank) contributed a further US$900 million, bringing the total amount of state/public-funded support to around US$1.234 billion.[5] The remaining sum of around US$700 million or so was provided through private PF arrangements involving ABN-Amro (Netherlands) and Crédit Agricole Indosuez (France) respectively. Both these private PF partners are signed up to the Equator Principles (EP) (analysed above in my Chapter 4) but there is little evidence to suggest that the EP had any impact on the management and operation of the Chad–Cameroon project in light of the World Bank's extensive and ultimately unsuccessful involvement with it. Indeed, as an authoritative non-governmental organization (NGO) report observes, the participation of the World Bank and other public IFIs provided 'crucial political cover for private sponsors and lenders',[6] so that the political risks of this initial petroleum production and export venture in Chad and the transboundary transportation of the product through Cameroon would be mitigated over the term of the project, in order to both recoup and profit from the respective

---

[5] Information obtained from the World Bank Group, Western national export credit agencies, the Afreximbank and the NGO, Environmental Defence, cited in 'Chad–Cameroon: Against All Odds', *Petroleum Economist*, 16 February 2004.

[6] See Ian Gary and Nikki Reisch, *Chad's Oil: Miracle or Mirage? Following the Money in Africa's Newest Petrol State*, Catholic Relief Services Report (2005) at 8, fns. 19 and 20, citing the World Bank, Chad–Cameroon Petroleum Development and Pipeline Project, Project Appraisal Document, 13 April 2000.

equity and debt investments of these private entities, namely, the MNC/ TNC oil companies and their related PF banks.

The Chad–Cameroon project, like the Baku–Tbilisi–Ceyhan (BTC) pipeline project considered below in Chapter 12, raises interesting questions regarding the application of international environmental principles and standards in transboundary infrastructure development projects that also require extensive domestic contractual arrangements and legislation to be implemented properly. The transboundary nature of this bilateral infrastructure development project gives rise to both positive and negative implications for the application of the international environmental principles (described in Chapter 4 above). On the one hand, the bilateral character of this project clearly requires the application of international environmental principles and standards to ensure the harmonization, if not uniformity, of implementation within both states concerned. On the other hand, ensuring such uniformity between two different jurisdictions and legal systems serves to highlight a perennial problem afflicting international law and especially international environmental law: how to ensure its effective implementation at the domestic level within states that operate in different legal and political systems, as well as being diverse in their economic, social and cultural standing.

The legal framework governing the Chad–Cameroon project consists of a single bilateral treaty between the two states and a couple of TIAs between the individual host-state governments and the consortium of investing MNCs/TNCs, respectively, as well as other related domestic instruments. These instruments will be analysed in turn to see whether the international environmental principles described in Chapter 4 above have been included for application within the project; and, if so, the extent to which these principles have been so applied. The first of these is the bilateral 1996 agreement between the two republics relating to the construction and operation of a transportation system of hydrocarbons by pipeline running from Chad into Cameroon.[7] This bilateral agreement lays down the international legal framework for the whole pipeline

---

[7] Full title: Agreement between the Republic of Chad and the Republic of Cameroon relating to the Construction and Operation of a Transportation System of Hydrocarbons by Pipeline. Adopted: 8 February 1996. Ratified by the Republic of Chad by Law No.20/PR/96 of 23 August 1996 and the Republic of Cameroon by Law No.96/13 of 5 August 1996.

project. Several provisions within it relate to environmental protection, and these are binding on both states parties to the agreement.

However, the focus here is on the subsequent TIAs made between the two states concerned and the consortium of multinational oil companies investing in the construction and operation of the oil pipeline project. It is the impact of these TIAs that forms the main subject of enquiry here. We can now turn to an examination of these transnational legal instruments agreed between the respective governments and their purposefully established domestic corporate entities charged with implementing this oil development and pipeline project. These are, respectively, the Conventions of Establishment between the Republic of Chad and the Tchad Oil Transportation Company (TOTCO)[8] and that of the Republic of Cameroon and the Cameroon Oil Transportation Company (COTCO).[9] Although called 'Conventions', these are in fact domestic contractual instruments made between the respective governments of the states concerned (Chad and Cameroon, respectively) and the domestic corporations (TOTCO and COTCO, respectively) established by the consortium of MNC/TNC oil companies investing in this project.

As noted above, the three MNC/TNC oil companies that form the consortium which in turn wholly owns the domestic oil transportation companies established by these conventions, namely, TOTCO and COTCO, are Exxon-Mobil and Chevron-Texaco, both of which are US based, and Petronas, the Malaysian state oil company.[10] The fact that one of the multinational consortium partners hails from a fellow developing country raises interesting issues. Until now, an unwritten presumption of the analysis presented here has been that the usually Western (or other developed country) origin of the investing MNCs would mean that they were both more familiar with, and in many cases, actually applying the important environmental principles described above within their domestic operations. While Malaysia is without question one of the most highly developed of the many developing countries around the world, its domestic environmental protection record remains problematic and thus the Petronas state oil company should not necessarily be expected to uphold such high environmental standards as its Western

---

[8] Hereinafter called the Chad–TOTCO convention, 10 July 1998.
[9] Hereinafter called the Cameroon–COTCO convention.
[10] Exxon-Mobil is the largest shareholder in the concession (45 per cent) and lead operator, with Chevron-Texaco holding 35 per cent, and Petronas having a 25 per cent share. The consortium was originally composed of Exxon, Total (now TotalFinaElf) and Shell.

counterparts. On the other hand, the burgeoning role of MNCs from developing countries within the international investment arena suggests that such an application of the common but differentiated responsibilities principle that usually pertains only to developing countries under international environmental law may result in rent-seeking behaviour from these usually well-funded and well-managed MNCs/TNCs that are nominally based in these developing countries.[11]

The highly unbalanced nature of these essentially 'private' contracts between this consortium of MNC/TNC oil companies and the host state or government concerned has already been noted by commentators. In particular, as Leubuscher notes, these TIAs grant their corporate parties private, contractually based rights, while leaving the host state or government hamstrung or straddled between its contractual duties to the consortium and its continuing human rights and environmental obligations under general international law.[12] Moreover, as so-called 'private' contracts, TIAs are not subject to the requirements of disclosure and transparency that would normally be expected when a public body is involved. Thus, their inherent inequality is hidden from public scrutiny and this perpetuates the perception, if not the reality, of the lack of accountability of TNCs in their activities within developing and transitional economies. Possible justifications for the asymmetric nature of TIAs, especially within the African context rely, *inter alia*, on the fact that due to its particularly acute set of circumstances, Africa is regarded as an especially risky investment environment. For example, Guest notes that 'Multinationals hesitate to do business in Africa because it seems too difficult and risky',[13] although this has arguably improved of late.

The first observation regarding these TIAs that can be made from the environmental perspective is that there is no specific titled provision

[11] Petronas, for example, now operates in thirty-two countries outside Malaysia and appears to specialize in joint ventures within countries that its international rivals have either shunned, or are barred from entering. It has built a portfolio of overseas assets that contribute to more than 75 per cent of its revenues. See: 'Petronas: A Well-Oiled Money Machine', *Far Eastern Economic Review*, 13 March 2003, at 40–3.
[12] Susan Leubuscher, 'Obligations and Possible Liabilities Resulting from the COTCO Convention of Establishment', in S. A. Bronkhorst (ed.), *Liability for Environmental Damage and the World Bank's Chad–Cameroon Oil and Pipeline Project*, Selected papers of the Netherlands Committee of the International Union for the Conservation of Nature (NC–IUCN) Symposium, The Hague, Netherlands, 25 February 2000. Amsterdam: NC–IUCN, pp. 35–41, p. 36.
[13] Robert Guest, *The Shackled Continent: Africa's Past, Present and Future* (London: Pan Books, 2004), p. 182.

within either of these conventions dealing with either the procedural requirements for the necessary bilateral cooperation towards ensuring effective environmental protection from the pipeline impacts or the substantive obligations for such environmental protection within each individual state. In the Chad–TOTCO convention, for example, the only allusion to the substantive environmental laws applicable to this project is in Article 14. Here it is provided that TOTCO shall take all reasonable measures in order to, *inter alia*, 'safeguard the environment and avoid wastage of, or pollution of aquifers by hydrocarbons, as well as any mud or any other product used in the Transportation Activities' (Article 14.1(b)).

Moreover, the application of these domestic environmental laws to TOTCO, including the environmental management plan of the EIA requirement approved by both the Chad government and the World Bank, is simultaneously undermined and superseded by the applicable law and stability provision in this convention. Article 21 provides, *inter alia*, that while TOTCO is required to comply with the laws and regulation of Chad, *any* reference to such laws shall *not* in any way be interpreted to increase, either directly or indirectly, the obligations imposed upon TOTCO under this convention.[14] Chad has also guaranteed that no governmental act taken after 19 December 1988 will be applied to TOTCO.[15] This clearly implies that any improvements to the environmental laws applicable to the Chad segment of the project shall not apply to TOTCO and effectively freezes TOTCO's obligations under the applicable Chad laws, including its environmental obligations, to those that were in force prior to 19 December 1988. Finally, Article 21.5 provides that in case of contradiction or inconsistency between the Chad–TOTCO convention and the laws and regulations of Chad, the provisions of the convention shall prevail, unless the parties decide otherwise. The legal consequence of the applicable law provision that effectively freezes the applicable domestic environmental provisions to those which were in force in 1988 is to relieve Chad of its obligation to apply the evolving international environmental principles and standards to its domestic environmental laws, where they might apply to TOTCO. Such enforced discriminatory behaviour by Chad in respect of the domestic laws applicable to TOTCO is also clearly inimical to the notion of a progressively developing international environmental law that states continuously apply to their domestic situations. Chad here is effectively

---

[14] Article 21.2 of the Chad–TOTCO convention.   [15] *Ibid.* Article 21.3.

withdrawing from this continuing obligation, at least in respect of the domestic environmental laws applicable to TOTCO.

In the Cameroon–COTCO convention too, there is no separate and explicit environmental protection clause, with Article 13 providing for COTCO's obligations to comply with the 'international technical and safety standards prevailing in the petroleum industry' relating to the *management and protection of the environment* and the population, in accordance with the Cameroon national legislation in these areas referred to under Article 30 of the convention (emphasis added). Disquietingly, it may be noted that this clause appears to render COTCO the sole arbitrator in the interpretation and application of the international petroleum industry standards referred to here. On the whole, however, unlike the Chad–TOTCO convention, there is here at least some evidence of the environmental principle of integration being applied, taking into account the need for environmental protection in the running of the project. In this respect, Article 13 also provides that 'COTCO is bound to regularly monitor the effects of all the activities it authorizes or carries out, in order to ensure that said activities are not dangerous for the population and *do not pollute environment or the sea*' (emphasis added). Article 14.1 further concretizes COTCO's commitment to undergo continuous environmental vigilance by providing that '[D]uring the construction, operation and maintenance of the Cameroon Transportation System, COTCO is subject to administrative monitoring regulations and technical inspections relating to the safety as well as to *the protection of the environment* and the population provided for by the Cameroon legislation referred to in Article 30' (emphasis added). For these purposes, COTCO also undertook to allow designated Cameroon personnel to have access to all works, installations and sites subject to its control.[16] Finally, Annex II of the convention covering 'Infrastructure Improvement and Construction Works' provides that COTCO shall 'comply with and apply Cameroonian legislation referred to in Article 30 as well as the provisions of the Environmental Management Plan referred to in Article 13'. Under paragraph 1.1.4 of Annex II, 'COTCO undertakes to eliminate or limit the adverse impact on the population and the environment'. In this regard, COTCO shall, *inter alia*, under paragraph A, 'take responsibility for and bear the cost of all preventive actions and measures required by industry standards for construction adapted to local conditions to protect the neighbouring properties and communities and the

[16] Article 14.2 of the Cameroon–COTCO convention.

environment and to prevent the occurrence of abnormal disruptions'. This is a welcome application of the preventive principle described above in Chapter 4, although it should be noted that this undertaking on the part of COTCO apparently applies only to the construction phase of the pipeline and any improvements to the infrastructure, rather than its actual operation.

On the other hand, similarly stringent and anachronistic applicable law and stability provisions can be found in the Cameroon–COTCO convention. Under Article 3, this convention is to remain in force for at least twenty-five years from its operations commencement date,[17] and will be renewed automatically at COTCO's request for a second period of twenty-five years, under the same terms and conditions, and thereafter for possible further twenty-five-year periods, on terms to be agreed between the parties. The potential longevity of the convention is highly significant for our purposes here because under the stability clauses for the legal and taxation regime applicable to COTCO, Cameroon has agreed not to modify, *inter alia*, the applicable legal regime in such a way as to affect adversely the rights of COTCO for the whole duration of this project.[18] Moreover, it is provided that 'no legislative, regulatory or administrative measure contrary to the provisions of this Convention shall apply to (COTCO, etc.) ... without COTCO's prior written consent'. As if the above provisions were not considered sufficient for the COTCO consortium's investment protection, a further, even more subjectively worded clause is provided on COTCO's behalf for the lifetime of the convention, to the extent that where COTCO is of the opinion that a legislative, regulatory or administrative measure which has been taken by the Republic of Cameroon adversely affects the rights and obligations of COTCO, then 'COTCO has the right to request that such measure does not apply to (COTCO etc.) ... with respect to activities undertaken under this Convention'.[19] Such laws would clearly include environmental laws purporting to improve environmental protection.

This diminution of Cameroonian sovereignty to determine the applicable environmental laws, principles and standards for all entities within its jurisdiction can be contrasted with the provision under Article 9 of the Cameroon–COTCO convention that provides COTCO with the 'Right to Transport Hydrocarbons' but specifically allows the Republic of Cameroon to limit or even suspend, although apparently not to halt

[17] *Ibid*. Article 3.1. Subject to the right of renunciation available to both Parties under Article 39 of the Cameroon–COTCO convention.
[18] *Ibid*. Article 24.2. [19] *Ibid*. Article 24.3(a).

indefinitely, the transit of hydrocarbons through the designated pipeline. This expression of the host-state's right to limit or even suspend hydrocarbon transit through the pipeline, as an affirmation of its full sovereignty, can be undertaken for the following reasons, *inter alia*, to safeguard its legitimate interests in matters of territorial integrity, public safety, civil safety, or *protection of the environment*, or in order to comply with its international obligations. Article 9.4 of the Chad–TOTCO convention provides for the same possibility of the exercise of sovereignty by Chad in similar circumstances. It should be emphasized however that even here the exercise of Cameroon and Chad's sovereignty is limited only to situations where the hydrocarbons concerned originate from, or are destined for countries with which commercial relations are prohibited, for example, as a result of UN sanctions. Indeed it can be argued plausibly that this limited exception to Cameroon's exercise of its sovereignty in such cases, merely serves to highlight the more general reduction of its ability to act as a sovereign state in nearly all other matters relating to COTCO's activities under the convention.

Further evidence of Cameroon's loss of sovereign autonomy is manifested by the voluntary withdrawal by Cameroon of its domestic court jurisdiction over disputes involving COTCO even in matters that would normally be considered beyond the usual requirement of stability clauses for foreign investment protection purposes. This is clearly implied by the dispute settlement provisions under Article 36 of the convention that nowhere provide for the possibility of any legal dispute arising between COTCO and Cameroon being adjudicated by a Cameroon court. Specifically, in the case of environmental protection, by allowing COTCO a large measure of legal autonomy in determining its own compliance standard with respect to the environmental principles and standards adopted by the petroleum industry,[20] the Cameroon–COTCO convention undermines Cameroonian sovereignty on at least two levels: first, and most obviously by not allowing any disputes over COTCO's environmental compliance with the industry standards to be adjudicated before domestic Cameroonian courts. Second, and more subtly, by allowing COTCO to take Cameroon to international arbitration,[21] on the basis of the alleged unreasonableness of its (Cameroon's) actions impinging on COTCO, even though the scope of such allegedly unreasonable behaviour is undefined and can easily be invoked against Cameroon, for example, by the mere adoption by

[20] *Ibid.* Article 13.
[21] Using the dispute settlement procedure established by *ibid.* Article 36.

Cameroon in its domestic environmental laws of the very same international petroleum industry standards for environmental protection that COTCO has explicitly agreed to uphold under the convention.

Other observations that can be made at this juncture concern the adequacy and efficacy of the domestic environmental law systems in both Chad and Cameroon to implement the applicable environmental principles and standards (noted in Chapter 4 above), which are inadequately included in the TIAs examined here. The allusions to the applicable domestic laws within both these conventions turn the spotlight on the substantive environmental laws promulgated in both countries and the national legal systems in place for their application and enforcement.

In this respect, concerns have been raised over the inadequacy of Chad's environmental laws, as well as the efficacy of its legal system in respect of the application and enforcement of those laws that have been promulgated. According to a domestic legal expert, for example: '[I]t should be underlined from the start that the Chadian legal system lacks suitable legal instruments.'[22] Of these few applicable laws, Law No. 014/ PR/98 of 17 August 1998 lays down general principles of environmental protection, including the polluter-pays principle under s. 101, which stipulates that any person or entity found guilty of an offence that resulted in environmental degradation may be subject to criminal sanctions and civil liability actions as well as being required to pay the appropriate state authority for the restoration of the damaged environment. This law is however subject to implementing decrees and concern has been expressed over the Chad government's willingness to enforce these offences upon TOTCO.[23] An earlier, 1988 convention between the consortium of investing multinational oil companies and TOTCO also provides for the consortium to be bound to pay compensation to any person, including the State of Chad, for damage suffered but it is unclear within both these instruments what type of damage can be compensated for, in particular whether it includes 'pure' environmental or ecological damage to wildlife and their habitats.[24]

In relation to Cameroon, where the environmental laws are relatively speaking more comprehensive in their coverage than in Chad,[25]

---

[22] Deokoubou Christophe, 'The Chad–Cameroon Oil and Pipeline Project: Liability for Environmental Damage under the Laws of Chad', in Bronkhorst, *Liability*, pp. 24–9, p. 25.
[23] *Ibid.*   [24] *Ibid.* p. 26.
[25] Samuel Nguiffo, 'Regulations Governing Liability for Environmental Damage in Cameroon: An Analysis in the Light of the Chad–Cameroon Oil Project', in Bronkhorst, *Liability*, pp. 30–4.

concerns in this area have mainly focused on the efficacy issue, i.e.,
ensuring that the relatively well-developed substantive environmental
laws promulgated by Cameroon are being properly applied and
enforced. Thus, although Cameroon's Framework Law on the
Environment[26] is underpinned by the provision of a constitutional
right to a healthy environment in the Preamble to the 1996 Cameroon
Constitution, and applies several of the environmental principles discussed above,[27] there are still questions as to how these generalized
obligations will be enforced in the Cameroon legal system.[28] In particular, even the existence of a theoretical provision for local communities
and 'approved associations' to take legal action for harm to natural
elements of the environment founders due to their lack of formal legal
status, thus only allowing actions on traditional legal bases such as
personal injury and thereby prompting Nguiffo to note their lack of
utility in cases of natural wildlife damage rather than to humans.[29]

Finally, it should be noted that both the Chad–TOTCO and
Cameroon–COTCO conventions have opted for indemnification or
compensation as the means for remedying damage caused by either of
the two consortium companies, TOTCO and COTCO. In the former
convention, TOTCO's 'inexecution' of obligations under the convention
or its 'non-compliance with industry practices generally recognised in
the international petroleum industry' would trigger the obligation to
indemnify the Republic of Chad and also 'any person' in case of damage
caused to it.[30] This indemnification by TOTCO even extends to include
situations where the Republic of Chad would be subject to a liability
claim from a third party, whereby TOTCO would indemnify the
Republic for any claim relating to said damages. Under the
Cameroon–COTCO convention, Article 17 also provides for COTCO
to be bound to make reparations 'for the damages incurred by any
person, due to the construction, operation and maintenance of the
Cameroon Transportation System (to be built and operated by
COTCO)'. However, these provisions can be criticized on at least two
fronts: first, they do not appear to consider indemnifying damage to
property, let alone 'pure' environmental or ecological damage such as

---

[26] Cameroon Law No. 91/12 of 5 August 1996.
[27] Notably, the precautionary and polluter-pays principles, as well as the principle of access
   to environmental information; see Nguiffo 'Regulations', in Bronkhorst, *Liability*,
   pp. 30–1.
[28] *Ibid.* p. 31.   [29] *Ibid.* p. 33.   [30] Article 20.2 of the Chad–TOTCO convention.

wildlife and their habitats. Second, they represent an *ex post facto* solution where progressive environmental laws would always favour an a priori, proactive solution that, as far as possible, would prevent pollution and harm from occurring in the first place.[31]

A further perspective that should be borne in mind is the asymmetrical legal relationship between the host state and the consortium of investing MNCs/TNCs embodied by the TOTCO and COTCO instruments. The undoubted concern of many developing countries such as Cameroon and Chad is the potentially damaging impact of the international arbitration of disputes arising under these instruments on the vital foreign investment risk rating of these countries. This will undoubtedly function as a clear disincentive for Cameroon to act in any other way but complacently in the face of a possible threat by COTCO to take it to international arbitration. There is simply too much to lose from the host country's perspective. As Stevens notes, when charting the history of international transit pipelines, a 'cavalier approach to contracts risks a reputation for unreliability, thereby inhibiting others from signing contracts'.[32]

The most recent TIA to be adopted on this project regulates the relationship between Chad and the consortium of MNCs/TNCs undertaking the oilfield development on its territory. This is the 2004 Chad–Esso/Chevron/Petronas Petroleum concession convention. According to an unofficial translation of the original legal document in French, Article 4.3 of this convention provides that the consortium will indemnify the state in the event that it causes damage due to the non-observance of this convention, or more significantly for our purposes here, by any failure of the consortium to respect standards generally accepted in the international petroleum industry. This is very similar in effect to Article 20.2 of the Chad–TOTCO convention. Again, however, what may be seen as an explicit undertaking to provide compensation for damage, including environmental damage, although this head of liability is not explicitly provided, can on closer inspection be criticized as follows. First, even if environmental damage is encompassed within the scope of the damage for which the consortium will indemnify the state, there is continuing uncertainty as to whether this will also cover 'pure' environmental or ecological damage to wildlife species and their habitats, for example.

---

[31] For further treatment of this distinction, see Chapter 10.

[32] Paul Stevens, 'A History of Transit Pipelines in the Middle East: Lessons for the Future', in Gerald Blake *et al.* (eds.), *Boundaries and Energy: Problems and Prospects* (The Hague: Kluwer International Law, 1998), pp. 215–32, p. 229.

Second, as noted previously, this undertaking to indemnify rather than a commitment to prevent damage in the first place can be seen as over-turning the fundamental premise of environmental law to prevent rather than mitigate and compensate for pollution damage. Third, the under-taking to indemnify by the consortium is limited solely to the state as a possible claimant. There is no corresponding provision, at least within this instrument, and therefore no guarantee, that the state will allow claims from individual citizens who suffer personal injury, loss or prop-erty damage, let alone claims from those concerned with wildlife dam-age, to receive the benefits of such compensation. Indeed, should the state decide, for reasons of the greater public interest of the nation, for example, not to claim the indemnity offered by the consortium for any damage arising from its activities, then no compensation will be forth-coming at all, short of any ex gratia payments made by the consortium without admissions of fault or liability, to the impoverished local com-munities. The likelihood of NGOs receiving such payments on behalf of any damage to wildlife is correspondingly lower.

Moving onto the dispute settlement procedures laid out in Article 33 of the 2004 Chad–Esso/Chevron/Petronas Consortium Convention, Article 33.4 provides that in any arbitral proceedings between the parties to the agreement, the arbitrators must reach their decisions by applying, *inter alia*, general principles of international law. While this provision may allow the widely accepted, if not well-implemented, environmental principles highlighted above to be invoked by the Chad government in defence of actions that the consortium choose to construe as some form of 'regulatory taking' or even in breach of the stabilization clause, it is noticeably hemmed in by the other, more specific laws that can be deemed to apply in such cases. Thus, Article 34 providing for the applicable law in such instances, specifies in Article 34.1 the prevalent application of the petroleum code within the convention, save for incompatibility with the terms of the convention, in which case the latter prevails. Moreover, Article 34.2 in common with similar provisions found elsewhere in the BTC and Sakhalin II Project TIAs (examined above and below), establishes that the rights and economic advantages of the consortium provided by the convention shall prevail over any incompatible Chad domestic laws in the sense that such domestic laws cannot be interpreted so as to add to the obligations of the consortium, or otherwise be allowed to negatively affect its rights. The limiting effect of this provision for the progressive development of Chad environmental laws that might be so construed by the consortium is clear.

Having undertaken a thorough analysis of the detrimental effects of the Chad–Cameroon TIAs from an environmental protection perspective, especially in terms of the apparent constraint on the ability of the host governments concerned to improve unilaterally the local environmental standards as against the multinational oil companies involved with this project, it is significant to note that the host Chad government was nevertheless able to turn the tables and reassert its sovereignty against the conditional strictures maintained by the World Bank in relation to the utilization of the oil revenues from the oil pipeline project. In 2001, the World Bank provided financing to Chad to support development of the Chad oilfields involved in this project through a specific agreement which required that substantial oil revenues be directed towards poverty reduction. These revenues were to be subjected to spending constraints within priority public sectors such as education, health and housing, rather than other types of government outlay, notably, military spending. In order to ensure that these constrained public-spending requirements placed on Chad were in fact implemented, Chad had to enact a revenue management law in 1999. This stipulates that 80 per cent of the Chad oil revenues from the three specific fields in Doba that are associated with the Chad–Cameroon project will be expended on education, health, rural development, infrastructure, water and environmental resources. Five per cent was to be spent on the communities directly affected by the oilfields development and pipeline construction and operation. Moreover, an independent government/civil society committee, namely, the Revenue Oversight Committee – or in French, the Collège de Contrôle et de Surveillance des Ressources Pétrolières – is authorized to oversee expenditure from both the direct revenues and dividends from these oilfields. The Committee/Collège is composed of nine members, drawn from the judiciary, legislature, civil service and also four representatives of civil society.[33] The complex and restrictive rules placed on the revenues realized from the pipeline made some activists, concerned with infringements by the World Bank on national sovereignty, uncomfortable, but representation from Chadian civil society in the Committee/Collège, as well as awareness of the autocratic nature of President Déby's government, led to a general consensus to support the controls instituted by the revenue

[33] Yinka O. Omorogbe, 'Alternative Regulation and Governance Reform in Resource-Rich Developing Countries in Africa', in B. Barton et al. (eds.), Regulating Energy and Natural Resources (Oxford University Press, 2006), pp. 39–65, pp. 62–3.

management law made in agreement with the World Bank. Over the years, however, Chad failed to comply with certain key requirements of this law, in particular to devote most of its revenue from oil production royalties to poverty alleviation and to maintain a 'future generations fund' for the post-oil era. For example, since the law only covered the three fields in Doba, petroleum revenue from other fields was channelled away from the designated priority areas. Also, the specific 5 per cent provision for directly affected communities of the project was susceptible to change after five years.[34]

The World Bank then entered into an embattled relationship with the Chad government over the control of the revenues from the Exxon-Mobil-led project. For example, soon after the contract with Exxon-Mobil was finalized in 2000, President Déby of Chad took US$25 million of the initial signing bonus and used it to purchase arms – a move that was eventually excused on the grounds that the money was not from direct oil profits. In December 2005, President Déby then orchestrated an amendment to the country's oil revenue management law that allowed it to redirect funds to security spending to quell increasing unrest in the country. In response, the World Bank suspended its loans to Chad in January 2006, triggering a freeze of the offshore escrow accounts holding oil revenue payments. Facing a stand-off in which the Chad government threatened to halt oil production, the World Bank reopened negotiations with Chad leading to an agreement being signed that allowed the resumption of World Bank lending and granting the Chad government an arguably even greater discretion over its oil revenues than before. NGOs and related civil society representatives had long raised questions about whether the World Bank could hold Chad to its commitments to spend on priority sectors.

The government of Chad and the World Bank signed a memorandum of understanding (MOU) on 14 July 2006 regarding the use of the country's oil revenues. This agreement, by which the Chadian government has committed to direct 70 per cent of the national budget to priority public sector spending, especially on poverty reduction programmes, and provided for long-term growth and opportunity by creating a stabilization fund. Priority programmes are in the areas of health, education, agriculture, infrastructure, environment, rural development,

---

[34] *Ibid.* p. 63, citing Ian Gary and Terry Lynn Karl, 'The Chad–Cameroon Oil Experiment: Rhetoric and Reality', in *Bottom of the Barrel: Africa's Boom and the Poor*, Catholic Relief Services Report (2003), pp. 67–70.

de-mining and good governance. To map out poverty reduction priorities and provide a permanent framework for spending, the World Bank,
other donors and civil society groups will support the government in
preparing a poverty reduction strategy paper. This strategy was to be
completed within a year and implemented in law. The government also
pledged to enhance transparency and accountability with a new pledge
of support for the role of the Collège de Contrôle et de Surveillance des
Ressources Pétrolières, Chad's independent oil revenue oversight
authority, established under the revenue management law. Under the
new agreement, government revenues in excess of the projections of the
expenditure framework were to be set aside in a reserve stabilization
fund for future use.[35] However, the commitments in the MOU remained
voluntary, as no changes were made to the Chad legal framework
governing the management of the country's oil wealth since it was
modified in December 2005. While the agreement has been heralded as
a resolution to the protracted dispute over oil revenue management
between the two parties, some civil society observers remained sceptical
that the Chad government was exhibiting any more will or capacity to
deliver on promises to use oil money for the poor than it did when the
World Bank suspended lending to Chad in January 2006. The MOU,
which was in effect during 2007, left many questions unanswered and
key details about oversight of spending and management of windfalls
were not clarified. While the inclusion of all revenues, including income
taxes and duties from the oil sector which are expected to reach US$1.5
billion, represents a significant increase in the funds that the government
has committed to spend on priority sectors, the definition of 'priority
sector' in the MOU is extremely broad, including practically everything
but security spending. The MOU is silent on oil sector transparency,
especially regarding the disclosure of tax revenues from the oil sector or
production figures from new oilfields. The World Bank also offered to
strengthen the Collège de Contrôle et de Surveillance des Ressources
Pétrolières, the joint government–civil society oversight body responsible for tracking the investment of oil revenues in poverty reduction
schemes. However, the MOU did not specify how the role of the
Collège would change, given the recent modifications to the revenue
management system, or what would be done to ensure that action is
taken on findings of irregularities in oil-revenue spending – a problem in

---

[35] See 'World Bank, Govt. of Chad Sign Memorandum of Understanding on Poverty
Reduction', World Bank Press Release No.2009/073/AFR; at WB's website.

the past. Furthermore, the 2006 MOU refers to the creation of a special account for surplus oil revenues, beyond those budgeted, but the details of these modalities remained to be defined.

The turbulent experiences to date with the oil project in Chad raise fundamental questions about whether public financial institutions, such as the World Bank, should support extractive industries in unstable countries without functioning democratic institutions. Will another promise from the Chadian government be enough to ensure that future oil revenues are utilized for the benefit of the country's desperately poor population? The proof lies in the implementation of the agreement, but the track record to date suggests good reason for continued concern about the fate of the World Bank's 'model' oil project.[36] The civil society concerns expressed above evidently came to pass and the World Bank finally ended its involvement in this project following the repayment of its pipeline-related financing loans by the Chad government. As the World Bank itself concluded, a new agreement was signed in 2006, but once again the government did not allocate adequate resources critical for poverty reduction in education, health, infrastructure, rural development and governance. Regrettably, it became evident that the arrangements that had underpinned the World Bank's involvement in the Chad–Cameroon pipeline project were not working. The World Bank therefore concluded that it could not continue to support this project under these circumstances. During discussions held with the government of Chad in N'Djamena in the week of 25 August 2008, the Chadian government agreed to prepay the World Bank for pipeline-related financing. Chad fully prepaid both the World Bank (IBRD) and International Development Association (IDA) components of the loan, as of 5 September 2008. While this payment effectively ended the World Bank's involvement in the Chad–Cameroon project,[37] the Bank held out an olive branch to the Chad government by recognizing that the country's significant development problems had been exacerbated by regional instability and the flight of refugees, mainly from the neighbouring Sudan conflict. The World Bank noted that it was willing to work with Chad again if the Chad government wished to focus its energies on a

---

[36] Accessed from Bank Information Center (BIC) website, at: www.bicusa.org/en/Article.2892.aspx.

[37] Although the World Bank's associated body, the International Finance Corporation (IFC), is still involved with the project through its loans to the oil MN/TNCs involved in the consortium with Chad.

programme to support inclusive development to overcome poverty, assist displaced people, and improve governance and effectiveness to achieve results.[38]

The Sakhalin II petroleum development and pipeline project

The focus in this second case study will be on the so-called Sakhalin II petroleum development and pipeline project (hereinafter, Sakhalin II project) on Sakhalin Island in the Russian Far East. There are in fact at least five oil and gas projects at different stages of development on Sakhalin Island and its surrounding waters off the North Pacific coastline, in the Russian Far East region.[39] As Dean and Barry note, the 'Sakhalin oil and gas projects, which have grown into one of the largest direct investments into the Russian economy, involve the participation of a large number of Russian and foreign energy companies'.[40] The Sakhalin II project was initially developed by Shell, Matsushita and Mitsui, involving the development of Russia's first liquefied natural gas (LNG) facility, to be built on the southern tip of Sakhalin Island, near the town of Prigorodnoye. Like the Chad–Cameroon project, the Sakhalin project also encompassed the building and operation of extensive production and pipeline transit infrastructure. However, the circumstances of this project and consequently certain aspects of the applicable international environmental law are different from those of the Chad–Cameroon project. First, it lacks the transboundary element found in the former, in that both the production and pipeline facilities are within the sole territorial and maritime jurisdiction of the Russian Federation. Second, at least part of the pipeline passes through Russian maritime jurisdiction. And finally, the Sakhalin project consists of both oil and natural gas production and transportation.

The Sakhalin II project is the largest integrated oil and gas project in the world according to its sponsor, Sakhalin Energy Investment

---

[38] See 'World Bank Statement on Chad–Cameroon Pipeline', World Bank Press Release No: 2009/073/AFR, released in Washington on 9 September 2008 (as above n. 35).

[39] For example, the Sakhalin I project is operated by ENL, a consortium including Exxon-Mobil, Rosneft, Sakhalin Oil and Gas Development Co. Ltd (SODECO), ONGC Videsh Ltd, Sakhalinmorneftegas-Shelf and RN-Astra.

[40] Richard N. Dean and Michael P. Barry, 'A Conflict of Interest for Russia: Offshore Oil vs. the Problems of Environmental Regulation', in Myron H. Nordquist, John Norton Moore and Alexander S. Skaridov (eds.), *International Energy Policy, the Arctic and the Law of the Sea* (Leiden: Martinus Nijhoff, 2005), pp. 213–46, p. 215.

Company Ltd (SEIC, also known as Sakhalin Energy). At a cost of over
US$25 billion, the Sakhalin II project includes three large offshore plat-
forms, 165 km of sub-sea pipelines to shore, 800 km of onshore pipeline,
one of the world's largest LNG plants, and oil and gas export terminals.
Oil and gas from beneath three platforms off the island's north-east coast
will be pumped onshore by pipeline and sent 800 km south to the tip of
the island. There the oil will be loaded into tankers and the gas super-
cooled in giant LNG plants, to be shipped to energy-hungry Japan and
South Korea, and probably to China. Some gas will also pass through a
terminal in Baja California, Mexico and onto the US West Coast. This
project has confirmed Sakhalin's stature as a major new energy province
and transformed Russia into a key supplier to Asia, and especially the
burgeoning East Asian markets.

In April 1994, Royal Dutch Shell plc, Mitsui & Co., Ltd and Mitsubishi
Corporation established Sakhalin Energy, aimed at developing the
Piltun–Astokhskoye oilfield and the Lunskoye gasfield in the northeastern shelf of Sakhalin Island within the framework of the Sakhalin
II project. In June 1994, Sakhalin Energy and the Russian state on behalf
of the government of the Russian Federation and the Sakhalin Oblast
administration signed a production-sharing agreement (PSA).[41] This
PSA provides for all the relevant issues involved, namely, investor
protection, host-state regulatory framework, and international industry
standards applicable to this project and is therefore the governing TIA
for this project. According to Dean and Barry, the Sakhalin Island projects
were the first in Russia to employ PSAs.[42] The Sakhalin II project was
the first PSA to go into operation in Russia. Phase 1 of this project was
launched in 1996. The Sakhalin II project was also the first to secure a PF
loan in the oil and gas industry in the Russian Federation. The first Sakhalin
II phase 1 financing agreement was signed in 1998 and the Japan Bank for
International Cooperation (JBIC) (then the Export-Import Bank of Japan)
was one of the project lenders. In 1999, the first oil was produced at the

---

[41] Full title: Agreement on the Development of the Piltun-Astokhskoe and Lunskoe Oil
and Gas Fields on the Basis of Production Sharing between the Russian Federation and
Sakhalin Energy Investment Company, Ltd, adopted on 22 June 1994. An unpublished
and unofficial translated copy of this agreement is on file with the author. The main
Western MNC/TNC involved in the Sakhalin II project is the Royal Dutch/Shell 'super
major' oil company. However, its shareholding participation in this project has been
more than halved by Russian federal government intervention, although it still acts as
the operator for this project (see discussion below).
[42] Dean and Barry, 'Conflict of Interest', p. 215. The Sakhalin I project involving Exxon-
Mobil was also the subject of a PSA.

Piltun–Astokhskoye oilfield. In 2001, the then shareholders of Sakhalin Energy – Shell, Mitsui and Mitsubishi – had asked the EBRD to partially finance Sakhalin II, which will produce offshore gas and oil from Russia's far-eastern coast. Much collaborative work was undertaken with Sakhalin Energy to ensure the project could meet the expectations – especially environmental standards – of EBRD financing, but the EBRD had not taken a decision on whether to make the investment when Gazprom took over the majority shareholding within the consortium of companies that own Sakhalin Energy. Shell had previously held a controlling 55 per cent stake in Sakhalin Energy, while Japan's Mitsui and Mitsubishi own 25 per cent and 20 per cent, respectively. The EBRD had declared that the project met sufficient requirements for it to seek the views of the public and conducted an intensive consultation process in Russia, Japan and London. Pending the decision on whether to finance, the EBRD has continued to monitor construction and encouraged the adoption of long-term safeguards, especially relating to environmental and social aspects of the US$20 billion project.

The EBRD saw its potential role in the Sakhalin II project as a financial partner to encourage the highest standards of environmental protection in the design and construction phases of the project, which included offshore drilling and underwater pipelines to Sakhalin Island, land pipelines for oil and gas, an LNG plant and oil and gas export terminals. Through its engagement in the development of the project, the EBRD had helped to introduce commitments to consultation and transparency and on the treatment of indigenous peoples. The EBRD had worked with Sakhalin Energy on many enhancements during the construction phase: Sakhalin Energy rerouted pipelines to accommodate the rare western grey whale that feeds in the region; a panel of recognized whale experts was established to monitor and advise on operations; significant improvements were introduced to the strategy for on-land pipeline construction, especially the environmentally sensitive crossings of some 1,000 rivers; and Sakhalin Energy adopted a standard-setting plan for treatment of indigenous peoples as well as transparency and consultation. However, in August 2007, after Gazprom joined the consortium, the EBRD announced that it 'will not resume negotiations on financing the Sakhalin II project'.[43]

Altogether, Sakhalin II boasts 4.5 billion barrels of reserves. Shell expected to be producing 185,000 barrels a day of oil plus condensates

[43] Information accessed from the EBRD website: www.ebrd.com/new/pressrel/2007/070111.htm.

from gas and 467 billion cubic feet per year of gas by 2008.[44] However, the Sakhalin II project is also the most infamous of the Sakhalin projects, well known for both its environmental standards violations and for the Russian federal government's pressure on Royal Dutch Shell to transfer the controlling share of the project to the Russian state-owned Gazprom corporation. Indeed, the Sakhalin II project has been implicated in several issues involving severe environmental impacts and risks, namely: (a) 800 km of the project's onshore pipelines have created severe erosion that has damaged hundreds of wild salmon rivers and tributaries and threatens future damage from poorly designed crossing of manifold geohazards, including twenty-two active earthquake fault crossings and landslide-prone areas; (b) LNG terminal dredging and the dumping of dredging wastes damaged the fisheries-rich Aniva Bay. Associated construction activities disrupted local fishermen and fishing companies' activities, adversely affecting the quality and quantity of fish caught, leading fishermen to bring a claim to the Independent Recourse Mechanism of the EBRD in 2005. After a massive die-off of herring in 1999 at Piltun Bay, independent lab tests conducted by environmental groups showed herring contained pollutants of the kind used in Sakhalin II drilling; (c) The project's offshore platforms and sub-sea pipelines threaten the critically endangered western grey whale population. SEIC has failed to follow many of the recommendations of the Western Gray Whale Advisory Panel (WGWAP), violating a condition of several public and private lenders; (d) The project poses unacceptable long-term risk of oil spills in treacherous weather and ice, given the fact that the oil industry, including SEIC, has no successful experience of responding to oil spills in frozen conditions. Meanwhile, SEIC's complete oil spill response plans have been concealed from the public. SEIC has also claimed its Sakhalin Indigenous Minority Development Plan (SIMDP) is an example of best practice, yet it was developed only after the project was far into the construction phase, damage to indigenous peoples' resources had already occurred, and local indigenous people had blockaded the project. Moreover, from a social perspective, all gas is exported while local people burn dirty coal for their energy needs. Most jobs created were filled by workers from elsewhere in Russia and foreign countries, and were associated with the construction phase, creating a

---

[44] 'Sakhalin Island: Journey to Extreme Oil', *Business Week*, 15 May 2006, at: www.businessweek.com/magazine/content/06_20/b3984008.htm.

boom–bust cycle. The huge influx of workers from outside inflated housing costs to levels that rivalled those in Moscow, and also created heavy pressure on community infrastructure, which increased violence and the spread of sexually transmitted diseases.[45]

Throughout the life of the Sakhalin II project, SEIC sought both public financial backing from taxpayer-supported banks such as the US Export-Import Bank and EBRD, and PF from private banks such as Credit Suisse First Boston, but environmental violations forced the Western public IFIs to deny funding to the massive project. These chronic violations of public and private bank environmental policies contributed to the 2007 decision by the EBRD not to finance the project and led SEIC to abandon its attempt to obtain nearly US$1 bn in public financing from the US Export-Import Bank and UK Export Credit Guarantee Department. Alone among the many potential public IFIs, only the JBIC has so far decided to fund the Sakhalin II project. The project thus became the first to secure a PF loan in the oil and gas industry in the Russian Federation. The initial Sakhalin II phase 1 financing agreement was signed in 1998 and JBIC (then the Export-Import Bank of Japan) was one of the project lenders. According to SEIC's 2008 Annual Report, JBIC's involvement in and support for this project over the years has encouraged Sakhalin Energy to set world-class standards for social and environmental performance and transparency in both the construction and production phases of the project.[46] However, the negative response to these PF arrangements can be gauged from the pronouncements of environmental NGOs and other civil society interest groups against the JBIC and against the decision of four private banks to provide approximately US$5.3 billion in financing for the problematic Sakhalin II project. According to these groups, JBIC (the Japan government's official export credit agency), Bank of Tokyo-Mitsubishi UFJ (Japan), Mizuho Corporate Bank Ltd (Japan), Sumitomo Mitsui Bank Corp. (Japan) and BNP Paribas (France) have violated their own environmental policies and standards by agreeing to finance the project.[47] These concerns had previously been expressed in a formal letter by these civil society interest organizations to JBIC when this Japanese public IFI was

---

[45] Information obtained from the 'Sakhalin Watch' website, at: www.sakhalinwatch.org/.
[46] Sakhalin Energy Corporation, 2008 Annual Report, at: www.sakhalinenergy.com/en/documents/Sakhalin_Energy_2008_Engl_New.pdf.
[47] For example, see remarks attributed to Naomi Kanzaki, Development Finance and Environment Program Director, Friends of the Earth, Japan, at: www.foejapan.org/.

actively considering its decision to finance the project. The letter cited, *inter alia*, documentation demonstrating that the principal design of the project and its primary technical decisions did not comply with the JBIC Guidelines for Confirmation of Environmental and Social Considerations (JBIC Environmental Guidelines).[48] Specifically, the JBIC Environmental Guidelines which require the project to comply with the environmental laws and standards of the host national and local governments had not been followed. Moreover, SEIC's failure to release its oil spill response plan was a direct violation of Russian citizens' legal and constitutional rights to environmental information, as well as international rights and norms guaranteeing people's rights to access to information. The letter concluded by alleging that:

> Sakhalin Energy has failed to design and construct a project that meets basic social and environmental standards; clearly, Sakhalin-2 cannot be considered to be a project that meets international standards. Most importantly, Sakhalin Energy's failures to properly design and construct the Sakhalin-2 project greatly increase the likelihood of major accidents in the future that could lead to significant pollution of both Sakhalin and Japan's shorelines and fisheries resources. The Sakhalin-2 project clearly does not meet the common approaches to social and environmental standards agreed to by (national) Export Credit Agencies and (also) did not meet the social and environmental standards of the Japan Bank for International Cooperation. The current problems with construction of the Sakhalin-2 project demonstrate that Sakhalin Energy is not capable of minimizing its negative impacts and that the company continues to violate Russian environmental legislation and requirements as well as the policies of your bank. The failure of Sakhalin Energy to resolve its severe environmental and social problems led to the withdrawal of the European Bank for Reconstruction and Development from the project. Given the above, it is clear that a decision by the Japan Bank for International Cooperation to support the Sakhalin-2 project in its current form would represent a dramatic violation of the Bank's policy and significantly harm the respected reputation of your bank.[49]

---

[48] Under these JBIC guidelines, the project operator (Sakhalin Energy) is required to examine derivative, secondary and cumulative impact as part of the overall scope of the project's impact. The guidelines also say that it is desirable that impacts which can occur at any time during the duration of the project be continuously considered throughout the life cycle of the project.

[49] Letter from fourteen Environmental and Social Interest NGOs to Koji Tanami, Governor, JBIC, re: 'Review of Environmental and Social Standards of Sakhalin-2 and NGO Concerns about Project Financing', 11 October 2007, at Friends of the Earth (Japan) website: www.foejapan.org/.

However, in 2008, the publicly owned JBIC, three private Japanese banks and three European private banks provided an estimated US$5 billion in financing for phase 2 of the Sakhalin II project.[50] According to civil society interest groups, the decision of the private Japanese and French banks to finance the project ignored its severe violations of these banks' own environmental and social policies, as has been documented over several years by a diverse array of professional experts appointed by SEIC, various public and private banks, international and Russian scientific institutions and the Russian government authorities.

The Sakhalin II project is therefore yet another clear indication of the distance that remains to be travelled before effective domestic implementation of international environmental principles can be achieved. In 2002, it was noted that:

> [A]fter the collapse of the USSR, many democratic principles were adopted in the Newly Independent States (NIS), including access to information and public participation in environmental and natural resource usage decision-making ... Unfortunately, little has been done to transform legal provisions into actual practice.[51]

More than a few years on from that comment, the Russian environmental situation remains parlous today. The Russian Federation, in whose territorial jurisdiction the Sakhalin Project resides, has promulgated several pieces of legislation on environmental protection, such as the 1991 law on environmental protection. Even if it is assumed that this general environmental legislation purports to implement at least some of the applicable international environmental principles described above, it is the specific implementation of these principles and the equally well-accepted international industry standards that are in question here.

Phase 1 of the Sakhalin II project consisted of an offshore oil platform that began production in 1999. In 2003, the much larger phase 2 of the project was launched, involving another offshore oil and associated gas platform, a further gas platform, offshore and onshore pipelines, an onshore processing facility, an LNG facility and an oil export terminal. Phase 2 of this project therefore aimed to both expand oil production and add gas production from offshore Sakhalin deposits,

---

[50] Information at: www.pacificenvironment.org/article.php?id=2875.

[51] Svitlana Kravchenko, 'New Laws on Public Participation in the Newly Independent States', in D. M. Zillman *et al.* (eds.), *Human Rights in Natural Resource Development: Public Participation in the Sustainable Development of Mining and Energy Resources* (Oxford University Press, 2002), pp. 467–503, p. 467.

but concerns were once again expressed about the risks of this phase
of the project, *inter alia*, to the western grey whale. A report assessing
these risks was produced by an Independent Scientific Review Panel
(ISRP) convened by the World Conservation Union (IUCN –
International Union for Conservation of Nature) at the request of
SEIC. The ISRP eventually evolved into the WGWAP. The WGWAP
was asked to evaluate the science around the conservation of the
western grey whale and related biodiversity. However, it was not asked
to develop prescriptive recommendations, but rather to provide
evidence-based analysis and conclusions about the relevant issues.
Nevertheless, both the ISRP and now the WGWAP have been compelled
to include several criticisms of the Sakhalin II project impacts on the
western grey whales in its reports.[52] This has led to continuing civil
society criticism that the project still violates Russian law in several
instances, for example, in respect of pipeline construction standards;
and also that the project continues to represent a serious threat to the
environment, including to rare and endangered species such as the
western grey whale, as well as to the fisheries resources of Sakhalin
and Hokkaido.

The environmental violations reportedly committed by Sakhalin
Energy led to major Russian government action in 2006 to require
Sakhalin Energy to improve its behaviour and, ultimately, to a change
in the majority shareholder of the project. This is because at around this
time, both the Eastern Siberia and the (Russian) Far East regions became
higher priority regions for Gazprom in its long-term strategy perspective
for the future development of Russian energy supplies to its booming
East Asian neighbour economies, notably, China, Japan and Korea. This
increasing Gazprom interest coincided with the rising concerns of the
Russian environmental ministry/agency, Rosprirodnadzor,[53] over the
environmental impacts of the Sakhalin Island-based projects. The company came under the scrutiny of federal authorities in September 2006
when the Natural Resources Ministry said the operating company was in
breach of environmental laws, and ordered an investigation. Analysts
however linked the probe with Shell's decision to double the project costs

[52] See, for example, 'Impacts of Sakhalin II Phase 2 on Western North Pacific Gray Whales and
Related Biodiversity', Report of Independent Scientific Review Panel (December 2004), at
IUCN website: http://cmsdata.iucn.org/downloads/isrp_report_with_covers_high_res.pdf.
[53] The (loosely translated) full title of this Russian government agency is the Federal
Service for the Supervision of Natural Resource Use.

to US$22 billion, thereby putting off the date on which the Russian government will receive its share of the profits. Following on from the Russian Federal Service for the Oversight of Natural Resources' inquiry into alleged violations in implementing the Shell-led Sakhalin II energy project, Russia's natural resources minister, Yury Trutnev, held that they were punishable under at least five statutes of Russia's Criminal Code, and also accused regional regulators of failing to perform their oversight duties properly to ensure compliance with environmental legislation. The Sakhalin II project operator, Sakhalin Energy, admitted to damaging the ecosystem of the country's largest island, off the Pacific Ocean coast. Following a meeting with Trutnev, the Sakhalin Energy CEO, Ian Craig, announced that they had agreed to draw up a joint plan of action to rectify the environmental damage inflicted by the project. Craig said Sakhalin Energy would be willing to compensate for the damage, although he expressed doubt the ministry's preliminary estimates, putting it at 10 billion rubles (US$371.33 million), were accurate.[54] On the other hand, the environmental and social conditions associated with the Sakhalin II project have not improved or come into compliance with Russian law, and both the Russian federal and provincial (Sakhalin) government agencies are reportedly continuing with their inspections.

Following the 2006 audits by Rosprirodnadzor, Sakhalin Energy compiled an environmental action plan in 2007. The environmental action plan has a special focus on river crossings, erosion control and land reinstatement. The multi-billion dollar project, led by Royal Dutch Shell, has been accused of inflicting large-scale damage on Sakhalin's ecosystem, including illegal deforestation, the dumping of toxic waste and soil erosion. However, the PSA allowed Shell to recoup all its expenses before sharing any of its profits with the Russian state, and therefore is hugely unpopular with the Russian government. Moreover, as *The Economist* notes, these PSA-type TIAs were also 'designed to insulate big investors from legal and taxation changes, but are now seen [by Russian officials] as anachronistic relics of a humiliating era'.[55] Thus, under Putin's presidency, the Russian state had slowly turned away from the laissez-faire approach of the Yeltsin era and instead embarked on a policy of

---

[54] Minister orders report on Sakhalin II eco-damage, operator admits guilt, 25 October 2006, on Rianovosti, Russian news website, at: http://en.rian.ru/russia/20061025/55127992.html.

[55] See 'Russian Energy: hardball: would the Kremlin really renege on Russia's biggest foreign investments?', *The Economist*, 16 September 2006, at 86.

reasserting its role within the economic control and regulation of the Russian oil and gas industry, especially for political and strategic purposes. Dixon, for example, observes the impact of this new interventionist approach with regard to previously privately owned Russian oil companies such as Yukos and TNK-BP.[56] The latter consortium is particularly apt for our own case study on Sakhalin II, as it also involves the participation of a major Western oil company, British Petroleum (BP). Indeed, a recent report that Rosprirodnadzor was recommending the withdrawal of the TNK-BP licence to develop the Kovykta gas condensate field fuelled speculation that similar tactics were being adopted in this case as with the Sakhalin II project.[57]

This new interventionist approach has been taken despite the fact that the privatization of the Russian petroleum industry had increased output by the end of the 1990s, whereas the growing presence of both the Russian federal government and Russian state-owned or controlled companies within the industry of late is actually resulting in a reduction of oil and gas output.[58] According to Perovic and Orttung, the Kremlin was able to utilize a number of tools to achieve its goals in this respect, including its 'tight control over the regulatory environment, the taxation regime, transportation monopolies (through state-owned pipeline company – Transneft) as well as licenses and the operating environment'.[59] On the other hand, increasing Russian state intervention on the ownership and regulatory fronts has perhaps predictably had a detrimental effect on foreign investment within the petroleum sector, especially in remote regions such as Eastern Siberia and Sakhalin Island. While Russia's key state-owned and controlled companies have gained control over many private projects and companies, they urgently need access to private capital and sophisticated technology in the hands of the oil MNC/TNCs to realize fully the oil and gas potential of these remote areas. At the same time, these MNC/TNCs are increasingly reluctant to invest in risky and expensive projects without the required tax incentives

---

[56] Sarah Dixon, *Organisational Transformation in the Russian Oil Industry* (Cheltenham: Edward Elgar, 2008), p. 82 (epilogue to Yukos case study) and p. 209 (postscript).

[57] See: Catherine Belton, 'Threat to TNK-BP gas licence', *Financial Times* (UK) newspaper , 18 February 2010, at 17.

[58] Jeronim Perovic and Robert W. Orttung, 'Russia's Role for Global Energy Security', in Andras Wenger, Orttung and Perovic (eds.), *Energy and the Transformation of International Relations: Towards a New Producer–Consumer Framework* (Oxford University Press, 2009), pp. 117–57, p. 123.

[59] *Ibid.* p. 124.

and contractual protection for their investment.[60] Within this context, it should perhaps have come as no surprise to find that the Russian Federation's proposed solution to these environmental concerns was to pressure Shell into giving up its majority share in the Sakhalin II project to the Russian state-owned Gazprom company. More specifically, this move was in line with the Russian Federation's evolving state policy on the gas infrastructure development in the (Russian) Far East region, as stipulated in the Development Programme for the Integrated Gas Production, Transportation and Supply System with due regard to the possible exports to the China and Asia-Pacific markets approved by the government of the Russian Federation on 15 June 2007.[61] Gazprom was then appointed a coordinator of the programme execution. The programme defines the priority order of the regional gas reserves development aimed at achieving the settled goals. Industrial gas production in Eastern Siberia and the (Russian) Far East was to begin with the fields that had already been prepared for utilization on the Sakhalin Shelf (Sakhalin I and Sakhalin II projects).

These Russian government and Gazprom moves to increase the Russian state-owned company's involvement were initially resisted by Shell. However, the pressure on Shell increased with the EBRD's delays in approving (and eventual refusal to approve) financing support for the Shell-led consortium's investment in the project, which was at least in part due to the alleged environmental violations being investigated by Rosprirodnadzor. This setback in relation to the public financing support aspect of the project resulted in negotiations between the Shell-led consortium and Gazprom. These negotiations ultimately led OAO Gazprom, Royal Dutch Shell plc, Mitsui & Co., Ltd and Mitsubishi Corporation to sign a protocol on Gazprom's joining the consortium owning SEIC (Sakhalin Energy) as the main shareholder, in December 2006. Under this protocol, the original consortium of (private) shareholders agreed to dilute their shares by half and sell a majority share of the project to Gazprom. Thus, the Russian government threats against the project due to alleged environmental violations have at least indirectly resulted in Shell reducing its stake in the project from 55 per cent to 25 per cent. Japanese minority shareholders Mitsui and Mitsubishi, initially holding 25 and 20 per cent respectively,

---

[60] *Ibid.* p. 125.

[61] By Order No. 340 of the (Russian) Ministry of Industry and Energy as of 3 September 2007.

reduced their stakes by 10 per cent each. Gazprom needed an additional share to make its majority hold official. After months of strained negotiations, Shell and its partners gave Gazprom a 50 per cent plus one share control of the controversial oil and gas project. In accordance with the protocol terms, Gazprom purchased a 50 per cent stake plus one share in Sakhalin Energy. In April 2007, the shareholders of SEIC including Gazprom signed the PSA that was previously applicable between the original consortium and the Russian state. As from 18 April 2007, Sakhalin Energy (or SEIC) is still the operator of the Sakhalin II project, and the shareholder companies and their percentage of shareholdings are as follows: OAO Gazprom, 50 per cent, plus one share; Shell Sakhalin Holdings B.V., parent company Royal Dutch Shell plc, the Netherlands, 27.5 per cent minus one share; Mitsui Sakhalin Holdings BV, parent company Mitsui & Co., Ltd, Japan, 12.5 per cent; Diamond Gas Sakhalin BV, parent company Mitsubishi Corporation, Japan, 10 per cent.[62] Shell initially held the controlling share of the Sakhalin II project, but as noted above, the Russian state-owned Gazprom is now the majority stakeholder. However, Shell continues to be the main operator in the project and all the high-ranking positions in the SEIC consortium are still held by the same Shell personnel. The four shareholders work together under a PSA to finance and manage the construction of the project's oil and gas extraction and transportation facilities and share the income from sale of oil and LNG proportionally. The available information indicates that all extracted materials are to be exported (LNG to Japan, (South) Korea and North America).

In earlier negotiations, Gazprom would have received a 25 per cent stake in Sakhalin in exchange for giving Shell a 50 per cent hold on Zapolyarnoye, a smaller field in Western Siberia. However, negotiations came to a quick end when Shell more than doubled Sakhalin's estimated costs from US$10 bn to US$22 bn, and Gazprom withdrew. Now, with Gazprom gaining control of Sakhalin, the upside for Shell may be not only a stake in the Zapolyarnoye field, but also a cash payment, although all this is unconfirmed. The effect of this change in shareholders within the consortium owning Sakhalin Energy (SEIC) has worried wider stakeholder groups and interests, with the suspicion that the Russian (federal) environmental agency, Rosprirodnadzor's

---

[62] Information from Gazprom website at: www.gazprom.com/production/projects/deposits/sakhalin2/.

crackdown on Sakhalin Energy's ecological abuses may end now that Gazprom has taken control of the project. Oleg Mitvol, the deputy head of the agency, claims there will no be favourites when it comes to environmental violations.[63] That remains to be seen, although it was recently reported that in early August 2009 the (local) Sakhalin Rosprirodnadzor had inspected the Sakhalin II project pipeline and identified a number of violations, resulting in an injunction requiring Sakhalin Energy to address these violations, which had still not been resolved by the time of the next public environmental inspections, two months later.[64] Neither did Shell threaten to invoke the stabilization clause under s. 24 of the 1994 PSA with Russia for the Sakhalin II project. Suspicion that Shell had been either warned or bought off this possible course of action, or both, is heightened by the news that Shell is being retained by Sakhalin Energy as the actual operator of phase 2 of the Sakhalin II project on a service contract basis.

Following this significant change in the ownership of the SEIC, the EBRD announced that it would no longer consider the financing package of the Sakhalin II project that it had been considering for the past five years. With the acquisition by Gazprom of a majority stake in Sakhalin Energy, there was a significant material change to the project which the EBRD had been considering. The shareholders and the structure of the company had changed and the approach to financing had by then yet to be decided by the new shareholders. This meant that it was not feasible for the EBRD to continue with its deliberations for possible financing support of the current phases of the project. The closer the project comes to completion, the less value EBRD financing would have added to this project, and, ultimately, the partial takeover of Sakhalin Energy/SEIC by Gazprom ensured the end of the EBRD's involvement. However, the EBRD did note that if the new group of shareholders were to request it and make a case that the project could be eligible for EBRD investment, the EBRD might consider financing it in the future. In other words, the EBRD door has not been completely closed on financing support for this project. Along with this shareholding restructuring process, new PF-based arrangements were also put into place. In Tokyo, on 16 June 2008,

---

[63] See: 'Shell and partners cede control of Sakhalin II to Gazprom', Bank Information Center, 12 December 2006, at: www.bicusa.org/en/Article.3046.aspx.

[64] See: 'Sakhalin-II has pumped oil and gas for a year without proper approval for the main pipelines', Sakhalin Environment Watch, Press Release, 20 October 2009, at: www.ecosakh.ru/.

Sakhalin Energy, the JBIC and an international consortium of commercial banks signed a US$5.3 billion agreement to finance phase 2 of the
Sakhalin II project.

As noted above, PF is frequently used in the world's oil and gas
industry for the development of major infrastructure assets. Repayment
of the debt comes from the cash flow generated by the financed asset. By
signing this financing agreement, Sakhalin Energy set a new record for
Russia in terms of the amount raised and established new benchmarks for
future Russian and international oil and gas developments. Japan's leading financial institution, JBIC, gave strong support to Sakhalin Energy,
providing US$3.7 bn. The consortium of commercial banks contributed
an additional US$1.6 bn. Previously, Sakhalin Energy had funded the
cash needs for phase 2 of the project from shareholder financing and oil
revenues. The PF loan will be used primarily to replace shareholder
finance for the phase 2 final construction stage and start-up costs, on a
45 : 55 debt to equity ratio, that is to say, PF will be relied upon to fund
45 per cent of the overall Sakhalin II project initiation costs. Direct
lenders to phase 2 of the Sakhalin II project include JBIC, Bank of
Tokyo-Mitsubishi, Mizuho Corporate Bank, Sumitomo Mitsui Banking
Corp., Credit Suisse, BNP Paribas and Standard Chartered – together
providing US$5.3 billion in PF.[65] According to Reuters, ABN-AMRO,
Morgan Stanley and Société Générale provided an additional US$4.5
billion for Gazprom's 2007 to 2008 majority shareholding acquisition
of the Sakhalin II project.

On 11 June 2008, seventeen environmental groups sent the banks
involved a further fourteen-page letter citing a litany of these examples
of violations and stressing that financing for Sakhalin II by JBIC and
other banks conflicts with decisions against financing by the broader
international banking community, as follows:

> Sakhalin II never achieved environmental clearances from the European
> Bank for Reconstruction and Development, UK Export Credit Guarantee
> Department and the US Export-Import Bank. The project's fundamental
> environmental and social shortcomings contributed to the ultimate
> unwillingness of these public banks to finance the project.[66]

---

[65] 'Sakhalin II: whale wars, project finance', posted 29 July 2008, Pacific Environment
website, at: http://pacificenvironment.org/article.php?id=2877.
[66] Text of letter accessible from Friends of the Earth (FoE), Japan website, at: www.
foejapan.org/aid/jbic02/sakhalin/pdf/20080611JBIC%20letter.pdf.

The NGOs' letter further noted:

> We recognize that JBIC has tried to lessen the environmental damage in
> some limited areas of the project. However, this incomplete progress is
> largely overshadowed by a far larger number of environmental failures
> and fundamental violations of internationally accepted practices as
> well as JBIC's Environmental Guidelines. We believe that JBIC's
> Environmental Guidelines were adopted with the intention that they be
> followed, and we believe that JBIC must therefore honor this commit-
> ment by not financing Sakhalin II. However, we have informed JBIC
> on many occasions that Sakhalin II has committed fundamental and
> irreversible violations of 'JBIC Guidelines for Confirmation of
> Environmental and Social Considerations,' international commitments,
> as well as Russian law. Given the project's many irreparable policy
> breaches and Sakhalin Energy's chronic unwillingness to correct repair-
> able damage, financing by JBIC will eviscerate your Bank's environmen-
> tal and social credibility, increase risks to the Japanese government, and
> damage the larger international effort to maintain ecological safeguards
> through the OECD Common Approaches[67] and the Equator Principles.

Apart from the furore surrounding the provision of funding from a
public IFI in the form of the JBIC, it should be noted that a number of
private IFIs have also provided PF for the Sakhalin II project, in the
amounts as follows: (a) Bank of Tokyo-Mitsubishi UFJ, corporate loan:
US$358 million, as well as participation in a loan of US$1.6 billion
provided by a consortium of private IFIs, namely, Bank of Tokyo-
Mitsubishi UFJ, Mizuho Corporate Bank, Sumitomo Mitsui Banking
Corp. and BNP Paribas, in addition to a US$3.7 billion loan provided
by JBIC. (b) BNP Paribas, corporate loan: US$125 million, as well as
participation in the US$1.6 billion provided by the private IFI consor-
tium. (c) Credit Suisse, corporate loan: US$100 million, as well as
participation in the US$1.6 billion loan; Mizuho, corporate loan: US
$358 million, as well as participation in the private IFI consortium loan.
(d) Royal Bank of Scotland and (e) Société Générale, joint corporate
loan: US$2 billion to finance Gazprom from an international banking
syndicate, of which ABN-Amro Bank (the Netherlands) was the lead
arranger. This part of ABN-Amro is now part of Royal Bank of Scotland
(RBS) and Société Générale. (f) Standard Chartered, corporate loan: US
$300 million, as well as participation in the private IFI consortium loan
of US$1.6 billion. (g) Sumitomo Mitsui Banking Corporation, corporate

---

67 OECD Recommendation on Common Approaches on the Environment and Officially
Supported Export Credits, OECD website, at: www.oecd.org/.

loan: US$358 million, as well as participation in the private IFI consor-
tium loan. All of these private IFIs have accepted the EP in the following
order: RBS (4 June 2003), Credit Suisse (4 June 2003), Standard
Chartered (8 October 2003), Mizuho (27 October 2003), Bank of
Tokyo-Mitsubishi UFJ (22 December 2005), Sumitomo Mitsui Banking
Corporation (27 December 2005) and Société Générale (3 September
2007). Finally, BNP Paribas adopted the EP on 24 October 2008 and is
currently not yet obliged to meet the reporting standards required of
EPFIs (Equator Principles Financial Institutions).[68]

The individual decisions in favour of PF provision for the Sakhalin II
project made by these private IFIs, all of which are also EPFIs, do not
appear to have paid sufficient heed to the environmental and social
concerns raised by the increasingly large group of international and
local (Russian and Sakhalin) civil society interest organizations working
on Sakhalin Island issues. Indeed, in anticipation of the Sakhalin II
project consortium efforts to obtain project financing, this civil society
group organized itself as a single body called 'PLATFORM' to collaborate on this issue. The conclusion of their jointly drafted report is that
Sakhalin Energy had failed to fulfil the required criteria for compliance
with the EP to allow the EPFIs to provide PF for phase 2 of the project.[69]
Specifically, the following deficiencies in relation to the EP were highlighted: First, the environmental aspect of the environmental, social and
health impact statement required by EP 2 and 3 is not adequately
addressed. For example, major elements of the biological diversity baseline facts (such as information about endangered species) and the geo-
physical baseline (such as seismic behaviour at pipeline crossings) are
not assessed in the required EIA statement. Second, mitigation measures
related to assessed biodiversity impacts, such as those affecting the
western grey whale migration, feeding and breeding habits, had not
been implemented. Third, despite reports of environmental action
plans being implemented (see above), no Environmental Management
Plan has been published, *prior to* PF consideration as required by EP 4.
Fourth, in relation to EP 5 on consultation with project-affected groups,
the criticism is that the consultation mechanism was inadequate and not
subject to an independent expert review, as required for Category A
projects, such as Sakhalin II.

[68] Information accessed from the Bank Information Centre website, at: www.bic.org/.
[69] PLATFORM, 'Principal Objections: Analysis of the Sakhalin II oil and gas project's
compliance with the Equator Principles on responsible lending' (May 2004).

In February 2009, the first Russian LNG plant was launched on Sakhalin Island under phase 2 of the Sakhalin II project. However, this was followed by a critical report by the WGWAP, established under the IUCN to replace the ISRP. The fifth WGWAP report suggested that the unexpectedly low numbers of the already endangered species of western grey whales observed offshore Sakhalin in the summer of 2008 could have been related to the significant oil industry activity being undertaken in the vicinity of the known habitat of these whales. A further recent example of the continuing environmental sensitivities associated with the Sakhalin II project may be discerned from the announcement of Sakhalin Energy's decision to postpone a 4D (four-dimensional) seismic survey at the sixth meeting of the WGWAP on 24 April 2009.[70]

Throughout this controversy, it is notable that none of the stake-holders involved, whether the primary parties to the contractual arrangements and the legal framework regulating this relationship, or the secondary parties involved, including the public and private IFIs funding this venture, as well as the social and environmental NGO interest groups concerned, have alluded to the central legal document governing the Sakhalin II project, namely, the 1994 PSA. As mentioned above, this PSA between the Russian Federation and the SEIC is the TIA which applies to the project, albeit with the addition of the new majority corporate shareholder in the form of Gazprom. A short analysis of the relevant TIA is in order, paying particular attention to the scope for the application of the evolving international environmental principles within the legal relationship established between the host (Russian) state and Sakhalin Energy.

To begin with, s. 24(a) of the 1994 PSA provides that the Sakhalin project shall be carried out 'in accordance with' the laws, bylaws and other acts of (Russian federal and Sakhalin Oblast provincial) government bodies 'that have been officially brought into effect' on Russian territory and are publicly available. However, s. 24(b) then commits all the Russian (federal and provincial) government bodies involved to ensure the necessary decisions for the implementation of the PSA are approved and that their (Russian government) obligations under this TIA will be met, including the rights and exemptions (for Sakhalin Energy) specified in Appendix E. This last clause is significant from an environmental protection perspective, as within Supplement 7 of Appendix E of the

---

[70] Accessible at IUCN website, at: www.iucn.org/.

PSA, entitled 'General Issues', paragraph 4 provides that: 'After proper treatment and processing, drilling agents, cuttings, and liquid produced in the wells may be dumped into water from the offshore platforms and shall not be considered as waste or sewage prohibited for dumping into sea.' This clear exemption from the otherwise applicable definition of waste or sewage to be prohibited from dumping into the sea under Russian laws is especially pertinent when we consider that s. 25 of the PSA then provides that the 'Company' (SEIC or Sakhalin Energy) is regulated by Russian Federation and Sakhalin Oblast legislation, *inter alia*, on environmental protection and shall take measures in accordance with the PSA and 'Standards Generally Accepted in the International Oil and Gas Industry'. On the face of it, this commitment on the part of Sakhalin Energy to both the host country's environmental legislation as well as international petroleum industry standards appears to be insufficient to ensure adequate environmental protection when such clear exemptions are written into the PSA.

Neither does the undertaking by Sakhalin Energy in s. 24(e) of the PSA to 'take every reasonable measure to restrict pollution and prevent damage', *inter alia*, to air, water, flora and fauna, overcome the specific exemptions located elsewhere in this legal document. Moreover, within s. 30(a) on the 'Applicable Law and Regulators' provision of the PSA, the so-called 'Operations' of the Sakhalin Project, defined generally under s. 1 (Definitions; Interpretation) as including all operations and activities stipulated by the TIA, are reiterated as being subject to Russian (federal and provincial) laws and government acts, including any exemptions mentioned there. Although this is stated to be 'without limitations' to the actual 'Applicable Law' of the TIA, namely the State of New York (US) legislation, it would be difficult in the extreme to envisage how the New York State laws and standards on, *inter alia*, environmental protection, could be held to apply to the Sakhalin II project, pre-empting the applicable Russian laws and standards on this issue.

These general commitments by Sakhalin Energy to observe the applicable Russian and local environmental rules, as well as international petroleum industry standards, are further undermined (as noted in the Chad–Cameroon case study above) by their static nature. Under s. 24(d), the Russian 'Party' undertakes to 'work diligently' to keep the Sakhalin project exempt from any amending Russian federal or provincial legislation and official government acts, including any changes in their interpretation and application procedure, after 31 December 1993.

Additionally, under s. 24(f) of the PSA, the Russian party undertakes to compensate the company for *any* damage sustained due to 'unfavourable' changes to the Russian federation and other laws applicable to the project's activities. This includes changes in the interpretation or application procedure by Russian federal and provincial government bodies, as well as Russian 'judicial authorities', thereby significantly expanding the potential scope for compensation claims beyond the initial exemption from (Russian) federal and provincial legislative amendments and the interpretation and application thereof.

This compensation undertaking was applicable from 31 December 1993, that is to say, nearly six months prior to the PSA itself being adopted on 22 June 1994. Thus, both the 'applicable domestic law' provision under s. 24(d) and the compensation provision under s. 24(f) in effect 'freeze' the legal obligations by which the company is bound to those laws and standards applicable up to 31 December 1993. The implication of the Russian undertaking to compensate for any damage suffered by Sakhalin Energy due to 'unfavourable changes' in the applicable laws (including changes in their interpretation and application) beyond 31 December 1993, is that it arguably prevents these laws from being improved upon, if such improvement could be deemed to constitute an 'unfavourable change' causing damage to the company. At the very least, it certainly acts as a disincentive for both the Russian federation and the regional/local Sakhalin government/legislature to amend or introduce more progressive environmental laws based on positive developments in the evolution of international environmental principles and/or international standards for the petroleum extraction industry. For example, Sakhalin Energy could interpret the imposition of new and/or amended environmental laws applicable to its activities that are more stringent than those which obtained previously as constituting an 'unfavourable change'. This would then allow the company to claim compensation from the Russian federation, even if the new or amended environmental laws are designed to apply more progressive interpretations of international environmental principles and standards. It also remains to be seen whether the company is constrained to improve its compliance in line with the progressive evolution of the applicable international standards for the industry concerned; given that any new, improved industry standards could be construed as a 'change in interpretation' of the previously applicable international standard that the company had pledged to have regard to and therefore also entitle it to compensation under s. 24(f) of the 1994 PSA.

An opportunity to test the alleged protection of Sakhalin Energy's interests under these legal provisions arose when the Russian federal agencies began to conduct more stringent environmental investigations into Sakhalin Energy operations at around the same time Gazprom indicated its interest in becoming involved in the Sakhalin II project. Given the twin benefits accruing to Sakhalin Energy in terms of the law 'freeze' and compensation clauses dating back to 31 December 1993, it would have been possible for the company to contemplate suing the Russian government for its ostensibly pre-emptive and arguably discriminatory actions. However, despite these PSA clauses being ostensibly applicable against the Russian federal government's perceived pressure to engineer the Gazprom involvement within the Sakhalin II project, there was little sign that Sakhalin Energy and its (then) main shareholder and (still) operator, Shell was prepared to refer to them in its initial dispute over environmental violations with the Russian federal environmental agency. This would have entailed resort to arbitration in Stockholm, Sweden in compliance with UN Commission on International Trade Law (UNCITRAL) Arbitration Rules, and for which the Russian federation has relinquished its sovereign immunity, under s. 30(c) of the PSA. Media speculation has suggested that an informal agreement was reached between the Russian authorities and Shell, whereby Sakhalin Energy declined the opportunity to rely on the dispute settlement provisions under s. 30(b) of the 1994 PSA, in return for Shell being allowed to continue as the main operator of the Sakhalin II project, and retain good working relationships in both other and future Russian oil- and gasfield developments. Notwithstanding the unsubstantiated claims on this issue, the lack of any legal challenge on the part of the operating company in this respect does at least point to the significant role of the host state (Russia) in this dispute, which as with the Chad government in the previous case study (above), was able to overcome perceived contractual limitations on its actions by asserting its underlying sovereignty through its regulatory enforcement actions, ostensibly on behalf of environmental protection. However, as Perovic and Orttung have presciently observed: 'Contract sanctity is an important issue and the breaking of the Sakhalin-2 Project PSA with Shell has created uncertainty for all future investors, with no guarantee that large investments in new greenfield developments will be secure.'[71]

[71] Perovic and Orttung, 'Russia's Role', p. 125.

The implications of the Chad–Cameroon and Sakhalin II projects for the application of international environmental principles in TIAs

This study of the TIAs in both the Chad–Cameroon and Sakhalin projects is revealing in its implications for the domestic implementation and enforcement of international environmental principles within the host states of these projects. It is also at least arguably symptomatic of the detrimental effects of the investment protection practices of MN/TNCs through the vehicle of TIAs in general. TIAs are currently designed to operate within an artificially created and maintained legal lacuna, with the only exception being the laws and standards that the TNCs themselves are comfortable with. In this respect, they exploit the uncertain legal status of TNCs under international law and take advantage of the foreign investment needs of developing and transitional economies to ensure that they raise as little commercial risk as possible for these corporations. In this sense, the inclusion of such regressive environmental protection clauses within the TIAs examined here neatly encapsulates what Braithwaite and Drahos have nominated as the most important contest between competing principles within the process of globalization of environmental regulation. This is the contest for TNCs to choose between the principle of lowest-cost location and the principle of world's best practice, where the principle of lowest-cost location leads to a race-to-the-bottom scenario for environmental and other types of regulation standards globally, while the principle of adopting world's best practice can lead to the opposite scenario, namely a race to the top by TNCs eager to gain and maintain a competitive edge by promoting and adhering to higher environmental standards.[72] There can be little doubt from the above exegesis that the investing TNCs/MNCs have opted to apply the former, rather than the latter globalization principle in the TIAs examined here.

The observed trend in TIAs showcased here also represents an arguably perverse application of the doctrine of 'internationalization' of contracts between foreign investors and host states.[73] The

---

[72] J. Braithwaite and P. Drahos, *Global Business Regulation* (Cambridge University Press, 2000), p. 279.

[73] This doctrine suggests that TIAs, although agreed between private investors and host states as contractual instruments, are nevertheless governed by reference to principles of international law. It was formally applied by Professor Dupuy, the sole arbitrator in *Texaco* v. *Libya*, 17 ILM 1 (1978), whose judgment forms the high watermark for the

'internationalization' of TIAs was driven by these foreign investors and supported by their home countries with a view to protecting such investment from the vagaries of the traditionally wide, even unlimited, discretion of host states to regulate the activities of foreign investors.[74] The perceived need for international minimum standards of protection for foreign investments was in order to regulate the scope and extent of the host state's discretion. A further corollary of the 'internationalization' of TIAs is the use of 'stabilization' clauses to restrict and even exclude the application of the host-state's domestic laws where these are used to threaten the primary object of the TIA. However, the pendulum now appears to have swung fully over to the other side so that the protection imposed through the 'internationalization' of TIAs is now comprehensive in scope, going far beyond the original aim of the investment. At least in the environmental field, these 'stabilization' clauses ostensibly introduced to protect foreign investment can be utilized to discourage the implementation of progressively developing international environmental principles within these host states. Indeed, the inducement of 'regulatory stasis' in respect of the applicable domestic environmental laws because of the TIA provisions on the applicable law in the event of a dispute reveals an anachronistic preference on the part of the domestic entity established by the investing transnational companies for the arguably discredited 'rule compliance' model over that of the 'continuous improvement' business model in their overall corporate strategy.[75]

All this is notwithstanding apparently progressive developments in the jurisprudence of the international case law on 'stabilization clauses', and more recently, 'regulatory taking', noted in Lorenzo Cotula's contribution (in Chapter 6) to this volume. These developments suggest that regulatory change by host states that is claimed to be induced by the adoption of new or improved environmental principles and standards at the international level should constitute an acceptable practice by the host state that falls short of the usual requirements of compensation to the investing companies concerned. As Higgins noted more than a decade ago, '[I]n particular, [stabilization] clauses that seek to "freeze" the situation at the moment of contracting are being accorded

doctrine of 'internationalized' contracts, against which the tide has ebbed and flowed in subsequent cases.

74 Peter Muchlinski, *Multinational Enterprises and the Law*, updated 1st edn (Oxford: Blackwell, 1999), p. 173, citing C. D. Wallace, *Legal Control of Multinational Enterprises* (Leiden: Martinus Nijhoff, 1983), p. 84.
75 Braithwaite and Drahos, *Global Business Regulation*, p. 280.

less and less efficacy by tribunals ... Attempts to secure negotiated change will today be tolerantly regarded.'[76] More recently, within the specific context of environmental regulatory taking, Waelde and Kolo observe that '[O]ne cannot postulate that the environmental regime should be absolutely frozen, especially in the case of large-scale economic development projects and of technical innovation and consequent changing environmental expectations and accepted standards.'[77] As Dashwood notes in the context of international law generally, 'if corporations expect to be able to enjoy rights (for example, a stable investment climate), then they must also be prepared to accept corresponding duties. The question then becomes what should be the extent of those duties, and to whom do those duties relate.'[78] Within the environmental context, it is suggested here that this should include the extension of potential corporate liability to include ecological or 'pure' environmental damage to wildlife, as well as the acceptance of the legal standing of competent environmental NGOs to both lobby and claim damages on behalf of the non-anthropocentric elements of the natural environment.

Moreover, while reducing exposure levels is a commendable goal for any investing transnational company, especially in relation to the ever present threat of expropriation of corporate assets by the host state, the current fully comprehensive, 'blunderbuss'-type, approach to protection against such risks embodied by the present case studies will ultimately threaten the long-term security of the company's investment. This is especially true in respect of environmental protection as the wholesale withdrawal of this subject from the applicable laws of the host state, coupled with the eschewing of best practice notions in favour of the more ambiguously phrased 'generally accepted industry standards' merely encourages a lack of proper scrutiny in the environmental management of the infrastructure project that is the subject of the TIA. This lack of scrutiny in turn increases the risk of another major pollution incident

[76] R. Higgins, *Problems and Process: International Law and How We Use It* (Oxford University Press, 1994), p. 142.

[77] T. Waelde and A. Kolo, 'Environmental Regulation, Investment Protection and Regulatory Taking in International Law', *ICLQ* 50 (2001), 811–48, 824, citing Petersmann in support; see Ernst-Ulrich Petersmann, 'National Constitutions and International Economic Law', in Meinhard Hilf and Ernst Ulrich Petersmann (eds.), *National Constitutions and International Economic Law* (Deventer: Kluwer, 1993).

[78] Hevina S. Dashwood, in John J. Kirton and Michael J. Trebilcock (eds.), *Hard Choices, Soft Law: Voluntary Standards in Global Trade, Environment and Social Governance* (Aldershot: Ashgate, 2004), pp. 189–202, p. 191.

such as those that occurred in Bhopal, Seveso or even Chernobyl, with
potentially serious consequences for both humans and the wider natural
environment that they live in. Indeed, instances of delays and cost
overruns due to environmental issues apparently unforeseen by the
investing companies can already be cited in respect of the case studies
presented here. For example, the unilateral temporary suspension of
work on the BTC pipeline by the Georgian government because of its
prospective passage through a national park,[79] and the recent admission
by Shell that the costs of its Sakhalin II project will be more than double
initial estimates due to its failure to take into account, *inter alia*, environmental issues such as the fact that the waters between Sakhalin Island
and the Russian mainland are the feeding/breeding grounds for an
endangered species of the western grey whale.[80]

Even when serious environmental risk from the activities of the
investing companies is initially identified, it is arguably defined and
responded to in a reactive manner, i.e., only on the basis of the 'probability that the cost of any environmental degradation of the natural
environment caused by the operation of a project facility will be imposed
upon the stakeholders in that facility (usually narrowly defined to mean
only the investing MNCs/TNCs) by public law, private law, or by other
means'.[81] Relatively little effort is thus expended to introduce preventive,
or even precautionary measures against the possibility of such natural
environmental degradation, beyond what is strictly required by the
applicable industry standards. Moreover, as noted in the above TIA
examples, such 'environmental degradation' is almost invariably compensated for only in terms of traditional tortious liability for human
physical injury, property damage and possibly economic loss, rather
than the more far-reaching but problematic to value in strict cash
terms liability for 'pure' environmental or ecological damage, such as
damage to wildlife habitat. This general restriction of the available heads
of liability to matters of personal health and safety as well as property
damage occurs despite the fact that both 'environmental risk' and 'environmental impact' assessment procedures usually include categories for

---

[79] See N. Mathiason, 'BP's pipeline to nowhere: Georgia halts oil giant's £2.4 bn project',
The Observer, Business section, 25 July 2004, 1.

[80] Ashley Seager, 'Shell costs double at Sakhalin', *Guardian* newspaper (UK), 15 July 2005,
at 19.

[81] Rumu Sarkar, *Transnational Business Law: A Development Perspective* (The Hague:
Kluwer Law International, 2003), p. 135, citing Albert Wilson, *Environmental Risk:
Identification and Management* (Chelsen, MI: Lewis, 1991), p. 24.

damage to wildlife and their habitats, resulting in a reduction in biological diversity.

Recent literature on transnational investment law recognizes an increased focus on environmental protection in PF undertakings but denotes this trend as an acceptance of environmental liability,[82] rather than a proactive duty to actively implement accepted environmental principles within the energy and transportation infrastructure development projects involved. This is apparently in keeping with the traditional notion of there being only two basic types of environmental law risks, namely, administrative regulatory risks and civil liability risks.[83] Future TIAs must therefore be prevailed upon to either implicitly or explicitly incorporate applicable international environmental principles and standards as well as ensure that these are not either frozen in time or otherwise rendered inapplicable to the activities of these investing companies. Many of these principles are in any case now increasingly implemented within the domestic legislation of both developed and developing countries, such that Young has observed that '[M]ultinational companies are well advised to be concerned with a number of trends wherever they operate', including, *inter alia*, 'the development of citizen and environmental group participation in the administrative process and litigation ... (and) ... civil liability schemes for environmental harms'.[84]

How can this integration of environmental principles and standards take place within future TIAs? Realizing that this will be an uphill struggle, what is suggested here is a stepped pathway that begins with basic, imperative requirements to ensure an international minimum environmental standard is set for all TIAs, before progressing to an ideal situation whereby TIAs will include an explicit reference to either the relevant industry's environmental best-practice standard, or the transnational investor's home country environmental standards, or the domestic environmental standards of the host state, whichever is the highest of the three.

---

[82] *Ibid.* p. 143.

[83] Steven Scott Young, *International Law of Environmental Protection* (Des Plaines, IL: Cahners Publishing, 1995), p. 383.

[84] *Ibid.* p. 389, citing Janis L. Kirkland, Nancy G. Simms and Turner T. Smith, Jr, 'An International Perspective on Environmental Liability', in David A. Carpenter, Robert F. Cushman and Bruce W. Roznowski (eds.), *Environmental Dispute Handbook: Liability and Claims*, vol. 1 (New York: John Wiley & Sons, 1991), p. 177.

First, as suggested above, an international minimum set of environmental principles and standards must be presumed to be part of the implied terms accepted by all parties to the TIA and therefore applied by the investing MNCs/TNCs within the project concerned, whether or not they are in fact required by the domestic environmental laws of the host state, unless these domestic laws are in actual fact more stringent than the international minimum environmental principles and standards. This should act to reduce the temptation for investing MNCs/TNCs to adopt a 'race to the bottom' approach by targeting developing countries whose environmental laws are not sufficiently well established, in order to gain a competitive edge from lower environmental standards in these countries. In any case, such international minimum environmental principles and standards will in all probability already be applicable and be practised by the investing MNCs/TNCs within their own home states. The enforcement of such implied international minimum environmental principles and standards upon the investing MNCs/TNCs by the host or home states might still be legally problematic if these principles and standards are not yet at least equivalent to the domestic standard due to the prevailing jurisdictional lacunae under international law when dealing with MNC/TNC activities around the world. Given that the current legal impasse is likely to continue, the implied inclusion of these environmental principles and standards within the TIA is an attempt to bypass this difficulty. Their invocation within the TIA would require the MNCs/TNCs concerned to show exactly how these environmental principles and standards are being implemented in the TIA project concerned and thereby allows for a more structured, audit-type accountability of the investing MNC/TNC activities by global civil society than is currently the case.

Second, the applicable law provisions of the TIA should contain explicit references to domestic environmental laws, with no temporal or operational limitations as to their application to the domestic entity established by investing multinational firms. Thus, on the assumption that domestic environmental laws in developing countries initially embody lower standards which are progressively improved upon over time, eventually achieving the international minimum standard already implied within the TIA (see above), such a clause should provide the host developing country concerned with the flexibility to 'catch up' with the internationally accepted principles and standards applicable to the particular development activity funded by the TIA concerned through the progressive amendment of its environmental laws and promulgation of new legislation. At the same time, this should also prevent the developing host country from employing the threat of discriminatory environmental regulation as a legitimizing cloak to cover indirect expropriation. It will also give the host state every incentive to legislate for the inclusion of the international minimum environmental principles and standards within its domestic laws so as to be able to enforce these laws upon the investing MNCs/TNCs concerned, thereby also ensuring that it does not breach the national treatment principle under the Trade-Related Investment Measures (TRIMs) Agreement within the World Trade Organization (WTO) regime.

Third, the stability clauses that provide recourse to international arbitration procedures should be limited to the primary concern of the investing MNCs, namely, that of expropriation or nationalization of the domestic entity established by these investing firms. In any case, this is arguably in line with the jurisprudential trend already being adopted by international arbitral tribunals on the subject of nationalization. Disputes arising from the application of domestic environmental laws should be made subject to the principle of subsidiarity and therefore adjudicated before the domestic courts of the host state. In any case, if the environmental standard which is being applied to the project is the highest possible standard, whether or not it is based on either the industry's best practice, or the environmental standard of the transnational investor's home state, or the domestic environmental standard of the host state, then there should be little likelihood of a dispute arising between the investing companies and the host state on this basis.

12

Project finance arrangements for the Baku–Tbilisi–Ceyhan project: human rights and sustainable development implications

ANNIE DUFEY WITH CONTRIBUTION FROM
RASMIYA KAZIMOVA

Introduction

The research questions

The basic research questions addressed in this case study are as follows: what are the links between project-financed foreign direct investment, and sustainable development and human rights issues? To what extent does the use of project finance (PF) accentuate the positive and negative impacts of foreign direct investment on sustainable development and human rights and how?

Two main sets of issues were analysed in relation to these research questions. A first set of issues refers to contractual arrangements that are an essential part of PF, and their possible effects on foreign investment in the host country and on sustainable development and human rights issues. Because the revenue flows of the projects are the main/only source for loan payments under PF, predictability of the project revenue is crucial to lenders. This creates incentives for project sponsors to enter into contractual arrangements to provide a framework for project viability and allocate risk between parties.[1] The hypothesis of this chapter is that these contracts, as part of risk allocation between partners, may include financial and other arrangements that interfere with the achievement of sustainable development goals in the host country.

An earlier version of this case study was prepared by Annie Dufey for the International Institute for Environment and Development (IIED) (April 2009). Available at: www.iied.org/pubs/display.php?o=G02486 (last accessed 30 January 2010).

[1] S. L. Hoffman, *The Law and Business of International Project Finance: A Resource for Governments, Sponsors, Lenders, Lawyers and Project Participants* (2nd edn, The Hague: Kluwer Law International, 2001), p. 7.

A second set of issues refers to the links between the due diligence process of PF institutions involved in the financial arrangements and sustainable development and human rights issues. 'Due diligence' is an interdisciplinary process involving analyses of legal, technical, environmental, social and financial risks designed to detect events that might result in total or partial project failure. A claim which is examined closely here is that financial institutions can affect the sustainable development impacts of a project by making loans or guarantees conditional on a borrower's compliance with certain environmental, social and/or human rights standards.

The case study: the Baku–Tbilisi–Ceyhan pipeline project

This case study analyses these two sets of issues by looking at the Baku–Tbilisi–Ceyhan (BTC) pipeline project: a project for a 1,768 km oil pipeline to connect the Caspian and Mediterranean seas, led by British Petroleum (BP). Key reasons for the selection of this project as a case study are:

- Information availability: access to information about contractual arrangements and the procedures followed by financial institutions involved in the loan is a key factor. This type of information is usually considered sensitive by both the project sponsors and the financial institutions involved, which means information usually remains confidential. However, in the case of the BTC pipeline, the International Finance Corporation (IFC), the private-sector arm of the World Bank Group, was involved in the financial arrangement. IFC has a disclosure policy that requires that important information regarding the due diligence process for the project – in particular environmental and social assessments, monitoring plans, etc. – is disclosed to the public.
- There are three legal contracts (host government agreements, or HGAs) between each of the host governments and project sponsors (later succeeded by the project company, BTC Co.). These BTC HGAs are considered some of the most high profile agreements of this type to date and constitute one of the core points in civil society's opposition to the project. Though agreements of this type usually remain confidential, in the case of the BTC pipeline the IFC also requested the project sponsors to make them public.
- In addition, because the BTC pipeline is one of the largest foreign private investments to date – over US$4 billion – it has been under

global scrutiny. There is a large amount of information on the project produced by many different institutions ranging from civil society groups to the multilateral financial institutions involved, other than the IFC.

- It was the first project classified as category A under the Equator Principles (EP).[2] The EP are an industry standard adopted in June 2003[3] and which provide a framework for commercial banks to evaluate projects they intend to project-finance, in terms of environmental and social impacts and risks.

Methodology

This primarily entails a review of the main literature on the BTC project and its related financing. Special attention was given to contracts between the project sponsors and the HGAs, contracts between the project sponsors and contractors as well as commentaries on them. Information produced by the financial institutions regarding their own environmental and social due diligence processes or reviews of these processes conducted by other stakeholders was another important source of data. This was complemented with interviews with key stakeholders involved in the process.

Structure of the case study

The case study is structured as follows. This brief introduction is followed by background information on the project and its PF. Then the contractual arrangements and their links with sustainable development and human rights issues are considered, before focusing on the lenders' approach to sustainable development. In particular the focus is on the environmental and social due diligence processes conducted by the main multilateral financial institutions involved – IFC and the European Bank for Reconstruction and Development (EBRD) – and then on those followed by the commercial banks. Finally, the chapter concludes with a critical analysis of the main links between the PF arrangements and

---

[2] Equator Principles (EP), 'BTC is the First Major Test of the Equator Principles' (27 February 2004), at: www.equator-principles.com/btc.shtml.
[3] ABSA became the sixty-seventh Equator Principle Financial Institution on 22 October 2009. For more details, see www.equator-principles.com/documents/AbsaPressRelease 22October2009.pdf.

sustainable development by looking at both the opportunities and challenges that need to be addressed.

About the BTC project and the PF

General description

Location

The BTC project is a 1,768 km oil pipeline that connects the Caspian and Mediterranean seas. This pipeline project transports oil from the port of Baku in Azerbaijan, through Tbilisi in Georgia to the port of Ceyhan in Turkey. The oil originates from the Azeri–Chirag–Gunashli (ACG) offshore oilfield complex as well as other Azeri oilfields.[4] From the Ceyhan terminal and its Yumurtalik port on the Mediterranean coast of Turkey, supertankers ship the Azerbaijani oil to consumer markets. The pipeline is anticipated to have a lifespan of at least forty years.[5] At full capacity BTC was expected to deliver 1 million barrels of oil per day. Since its operation, the capacity of the pipeline has increased by 20 per cent.[6]

The BTC pipeline is part of a large-scale attempt to create alternative oil routes and ease dependence on Middle East oil and Russian pipelines as well as avoid having to deal with Iran. As such the project is a major component of the Azerbaijan–Georgia–Turkey (AGT) projects, of which there are four; BP is the operator and largest shareholder in all four AGT projects.[7] These are the:

---

[4] The Azeri, Chirag and deepwater Gunashli (ACG) fields operated by BP Exploration (Caspian Sea) Limited have been developed in four separate phases, the first of which, the Early Oil project, was financed by IFC and EBRD in 1998. The second stage, called Phase 1, was sanctioned in August 2001 and was financed by IFC and EBRD. The financing of the Phase 1 project was conducted in parallel with the BTC project. Phase 2 was sanctioned in September 2002, and Phase 3 in September 2004. Following the completion of all of the phases in 2009, the ACG field peak production of crude is expected to be over 1 million barrels of oil per day based on proven plus probable reserve estimates.

[5] Article 3 of the Azerbaijani HGA provides: 'This Agreement shall be effective and binding from the date it has been fully executed by all Parties hereto (the "Effective Date"), shall continue for a primary term of forty (40) years from the date of first shipment of Petroleum through the custody transfer meter at the Point of Terminus (the "Primary Term") and, subject to all other provisions of this Agreement, shall continue in full force and effect after the Primary Term for two (2) successive ten (10)-year rollover terms.' Identical articles are incorporated into the other two HGAs.

[6] 'Baku–Tbilisi–Ceyhan Pipeline Capacity Increases by 20 pct', Today's Zaman, 13 November 2009, at: www.todayszaman.com/tz-web/news-192777-baku-tbilisi-ceyhan-pipeline-capacity-increases-by-20-pct.html.

[7] For details on the parties to these projects, see: www.bp.com/managedlistingsection.do?categoryId=9007996&contentId=7014981.

- Azeri–Chirag–Gunashli offshore oilfield development;
- Baku–Tbilisi–Ceyhan oil pipeline;
- Shah Deniz offshore gasfield development; and
- South Caucasus gas pipeline.

The construction of the BTC pipeline was also intended to ease the heavy traffic in the Bosporus by carrying some of the Russian and Kazakh oil that is currently transferred by oil tankers entering the Turkish Straits.[8] As a result of this, the pipeline was expected to reduce the risk of environmental catastrophes in the Bosporus by reducing the traffic of ships with hazardous cargo.[9]

Construction

Project construction (the Baku portion) started in April 2003[10] in accordance with the development and production schedule at the three oilfields. The pipeline was originally expected to be completed in the third quarter of 2005.[11] However, engineers only started final tests to the pipeline in June 2006 and it formally opened on 13 July 2006, a year behind schedule.[12] The delay in completion of the project was explained by 'rigorous testing and commissioning activities designed to ensure the integrity and safety of each section of the pipeline prior to introducing oil, that took longer than expected but were necessary to make sure that the link operates efficiently and safely for the next 40 years or more'. Other factors contributing to the delay were claimed to include 'poor winter weather conditions and contractor performance, particularly on the Turkish section of the line'.[13]

---

[8] Tuncay Babali, 'Implications of the Baku–Tbilisi–Ceyhan Main Oil Pipeline Project', *Perceptions* (winter 2005), at: www.sam.gov.tr/perceptions/Volume10/winter2005/TuncayBabali.pdf.

[9] M. Gidney and A. Chavarot, 'Financing the James Bond Pipeline', features BTC, *Project Finance International*, 285 (17 March 2004), 47; interview with Mithat Rende, a senior Turkish diplomat in charge of energy issues at the foreign ministry. Accessible from: http://en.trend.az/ (10 July 2006).

[10] BP in Azerbaijan: Sustainability Report 2005, History, p. 8 at: www.bp.com/liveassets/bp_internet/globalbp/STAGING/global_assets/downloads/A/Azerbaijan_sustainability_report_2005_ENGLISH.pdf.

[11] V. Socor, 'Baku–Tbilisi–Ceyhan Oil Pipeline Inauguration', *Eurasia Daily Monitor*, 2(105) (30 May 2005), at: www.jamestown.org/single/?no_cache=1&tx_ttnews%5Btt_news%5D=30462.

[12] BP Press Release, 'BTC celebrates full commissioning' (13 July 2006), at: www.bp.com/genericarticle.do?categoryId=9006615&contentId=7020655.

[13] BP in Azerbaijan Sustainability Report 2005, p. 15.

In Azerbaijan and Georgia, BP and BTC Co. were directly managing all aspects of pipeline construction,[14] hiring two prime contractors: Consolidated Contractors International Company (CCIC) who were responsible for the pipeline construction and valves, and Spie–Capag Petrofac Joint Venture (SPJV) who were in charge of the main above-ground installations (AGIs).[15] In Turkey, BOTAŞ (a Turkish state-owned company) served as managing contractor.[16]

Costs

At the time of its commencement the BTC pipeline was the largest cross-border infrastructure construction project in the world[17] and is still the largest foreign investment in any of the three host countries.[18] Original total construction costs for the BTC pipeline were estimated to be US$3.6 billion,[19] including financing costs. Without financing costs this estimate was US$2.95 billion. However, costs increased during the construction phase by 32 per cent of the original budget and went over US$4 billion.[20] This increase was due to higher than expected costs for contractors and materials, as well as construction delays, especially in the Turkish portion of the pipeline. An additional US$600 million was needed for filling the pipeline with oil.[21]

---

[14] Caspian Development Advisory Panel (CDAP), Report on Turkey and Project-related Security and Human Rights Issues in Azerbaijan, Georgia, and Turkey (December 2003), p. 9, at: http://subsites.bp.com/caspian/MediaLibrary/Download/59/CDAP%20Turkey%20Report%20Final.pdf.

[15] EBRD, 'Independent Recourse Mechanism – Eligibility Assessment – Report Complaint: BTC Pipeline Construction – Damage to Property in Gyrakh Kesemenli Village, Azerbaijan' (2005), p. 2, at: www.ebrd.com/about/integrity/irm/0502ear.pdf.

[16] CDAP, Report on Turkey, p. 9.

[17] IFC, 'Lessons of Experience: The Baku–Tbilisi–Ceyhan (BTC) Pipeline Project', September 2006, No. 2, p. 1 at: www.ifc.org/ifcext/enviro.nsf/AttachmentsByTitle/p_BTC_LessonsLearned/$FILE/BTC_LOE_Final.pdf.

[18] Overseas Private Investment Corporation (OPIC), 'OPIC provides $100 million in insurance for loans to Caspian pipeline project', OPIC press release, 4 February 2004, at: www.america.gov/st/washfileenglish/2004/February/20040205133825BTruevece R0.1443445.html.

[19] IFC, 'Baku–Tbilisi–Ceyhan Oil Pipeline Project', at: www.ifc.org/btc.

[20] Platform, 'Oil addicts find new veins as BTC pipeline finally opens', press release, 12 July 2006, at: www.platformlondon.org/carbonweb/showitem.asp?article=170&parent=9; Bank Information Center, 'Explosion Along the BTC Pipeline Confirms Civil Society Concerns' (7 August 2008), at: www.bicusa.org/en/Article.3867.aspx.

[21] 'BTC Pipeline Construction to Cost 30% above Original Estimate', Alexander's Gas and Oil Connections, 11(9) 2006, at: www.gasandoil.com/goc/company/cnc61818.htm. See also BP press release, 3 February 2004 (available at: www.bp.com).

Project sponsors

The BTC oil pipeline was developed and is currently run by the Baku–Tbilisi–Ceyhan Pipeline Company, also known as BTC Co. The company was incorporated in the Cayman Islands and owned by the following oil companies:[22]

- BP, United Kingdom (30.10 per cent);
- State Oil Company of Azerbaijan (SOCAR), Azerbaijan (25 per cent);
- Unocal, United States (8.90 per cent);
- Statoil, Norway (8.71 per cent);
- Turkiye Petrolleri Anonim Ortakligi (TPAO), Turkey (6.53 per cent);
- ENI/Agip, Italy (5 per cent);
- TotalFinaElf, France (5 per cent);
- Itochu, Japan (3.40 per cent);
- Inpex, Japan (2.50 per cent);
- ConocoPhillips, United States (2.50 per cent); and
- Amerada Hess, United States (2.36 per cent).

As well as being the largest shareholder in the project, BP is also the project operator.

Stakeholders' perspectives on the project

The range of stakeholders includes project sponsors, host governments, affected communities, home governments, financial institutions and civil society.

As such, it is a complex and polemic project with stakeholders polarized between two views.

On the one hand, those supporting the project include the project sponsors, host governments and financial institutions involved, i.e. development banks – especially IFC and EBRD – and a set of fifteen commercial banks involved supported by export credit agencies (ECAs). Key arguments backing the project are based on the project's contribution to the economic development of this part of the world. Opportunities for the region were claimed to be the following:

- Azerbaijan would benefit from both the BTC pipeline and the Azeri–Chirag–Gunashli (ACG) Phase 1 projects, through the initial investment, oil revenues, taxes and equity returns to a total of some US$40 billion. Georgia would gain from an income of US$1 million in

---

[22] Gidney and Chavarot, 'Financing the James Bond Pipeline', 49.

investment and US$580 million in transit fees. The latter could reach US$50 million per year, equivalent to 2 per cent of Georgia's GDP (gross domestic product).[23] Turkey would also benefit (though to a much lesser extent in terms of GDP per capita): the Turkish government would receive an estimated US$1.2 billion to US$1.8 billion in pipeline transit fees, while BOTAŞ would receive an estimated US$70 million annually in operating fees for its role as operator in Turkey.[24] The pipeline would be transferred to the ownership of Azerbaijan at no cost after the investors in BTC Co. achieve a 12.5 per cent rate of return over a twenty-year period.[25]

- The project would create employment, in particular during the construction phase (over 10,000 jobs) and 850 permanent jobs.[26]
- Indirect benefits in the form of new infrastructure and technology transfer.[27] The project has had and will continue to have a positive impact on cooperation between the three countries involved.[28]
- The project would also bring environmental benefits by helping to relieve growing pressure on the environmentally sensitive Bosporus Straits from increasing tanker traffic[29] and through the transfer of higher environmental (and social) standards.[30]
- Other environmental and social benefits would come from the project's community investment programme in all three countries. BTC Co., together with the South Caucasus Pipeline (SCP) Company, would spend some US$30 million (including US$5.5 million already

---

[23] EBRD's business group director of energy, letter to CEE Bankwatch and Platform on the Claros financial report.
[24] CDAP, Report on Turkey, pp. 28–37.
[25] No author, 'The BTC Intergovernmental and Host Government Agreements', available at: www.bakuceyhan.org.uk/correspondence/BP_re_legals_sept_02.pdf.
[26] BMT Cordah Ltd, *Compliance Review of the Environmental Assessment of the Baku–Tbilisi–Ceyhan (BTC) Pipeline*, Report to DFID (30 October 2003), at: http://webarchive.nationalarchives.gov.uk/+/www.dfid.gov.uk/pubs/files/baku-pipeline-report.pdf.
[27] ABN AMRO, 'ABN AMRO's Explanation to its Participation in the BTC Pipeline Project' (10 December 2003), available at: http://files.shareholder.com/downloads/ABN/0x0x145138/b89c6b34–8b0a-4ebf-b2b3–6d149edfe949/abnamro_btcpipeline.pdf.
[28] *Ibid.* [29] *Ibid.*
[30] *Ibid.* The interim report of CDAP on Azerbaijan and Georgia of August 2003, at: http://subsites.bp.com/caspian/CDAP/CDAP%20Interim%20Report%20Final%20-%20Aug03.pdf also points out that making the project subject to European and international standards is much more effective than if it were regulated by national legislation, since forty years is a long term for a domestic law, which varies at the same time from country to country.

awarded in Azerbaijan) on community and environmental investment in Azerbaijan, Georgia and Turkey.[31] Nonetheless, supporters also recognize that it is a unique project that imposes several challenges, especially in the environmental and social fields.

On the other hand, national civil society groups and project-affected communities, along with several international non-governmental organizations (NGOs), have heavily criticized the project. Main criticisms refer to the project's links with undemocratic regimes, exacerbation of tensions in the region and its potentially negative environmental and human rights impacts during construction and operation of the pipeline. More specifically, these concerns arise out of the following:

- The HGAs between project sponsors and each of the host governments (later succeeded by BTC Co.) exempt the project from all relevant local environmental, social and human rights law (apart from the one that was in force at the time of signing of the HGA and not in conflict with the HGA regulatory regime) bar national constitutions. The HGAs oblige governments to maintain the 'economic equilibrium' or profitability of the project, guaranteeing BTC Co.'s initially assumed profits, thus externalizing additional expenses that could arise out of a state act that would impact on the profit margin for this project.
- The BTC pipeline route runs through different areas including areas of crucial environmental importance, such as: zones with protected and endangered birds; a national park in Georgia, which is the source of Borjomi mineral water – Georgia's largest export product; and areas of high seismic activity, landslides and avalanches.
- The pipeline runs through areas inhabited by the Kurdish population that has suffered decades of human rights abuse from the Turkish government.
- The use of inadequate coating material along some parts of the pipeline could result in corrosion, widespread leakage and, potentially, massive explosions.
- The potential of militarization in the region due to the need to provide for the security of the pipeline.

---

[31] BP Press Office in Baku, 'BTC signs project finance agreements', press release, 3 February 2004, at: www.winne.com/news/2004/february/btc_signs_project.php.

Project financing

Background

BTC is as complex as any financing undertaken by the PF community.[32] The financing phase took over two and a half years (July 2001–February 2004). The initial estimate of construction costs for the BTC pipeline was US$2.95 billion. With financing costs and the interest to be paid during construction this figure rose to US$3.6 billion. Finally, due to a 32 per cent increase in the construction phase expenses from the original budget, the final cost of the pipeline was over US$4.0 billion.[33]

Project financing are complex transactions involving many participants with diverse interests. The complexity of risk allocation linked to PF[34] implies that developing countries rarely have an unlimited ability to accept allocation of risk, so they have to secure their positions with credible assets and/or payment guarantees from other parties. This necessitates the involvement of multilateral (public) financial institutions such as the IFC ECAs that have been institutionally designed to accept some of the risk in order to make projects financeable.[35] Indeed, after the recent financial crisis, the role for multilateral financial institutions within project-financed investment projects has become even stronger.[36]

In the case of BTC, a preliminary informative memorandum on its PF requirements was sent to the IFC, EBRD, a dozen ECAs and several private lenders in October 2001.[37] In July 2001 the investment bank Lazard Brothers (UK) was appointed by BP as financial adviser to set up the most suitable financing structure. The law firm Sullivan & Cromwell (US) was appointed at the same time to advise on the legal side of the financing structure. EBRD and IFC were advised by Allen & Overy.[38] Later, in April 2002 ABN AMRO Bank (Netherlands) and Société Générale (France) were to review the financial structure proposed by

---

[32] J. Watkins, 'BTC – Reaching First Drawdown', BTC features, *Project Finance International*, 298 (29 September 2004), 48.

[33] 'BTC Pipeline Costs Rise', *Oil Daily* (20 April 2006), at: http://goliath.ecnext.com/coms2/gi_0199–5580080/BTC-pipeline-costs-rise-Baku.html.

[34] On risk allocation, see Chapter 5 in this book by Sheldon Leader.

[35] Hoffman, *Law and Business*, sect. 21.

[36] 'Back in the Funding Mix: Multilaterals Report 2009', *Project Finance International*, at: www.pfie.org.

[37] 'Timeline for a Pipeline (Past & Future)', available at: www.foe.co.uk/resource/reports/common_concerns_timeline.pdf.

[38] Gidney and Chavarot, 'Financing the James Bond Pipeline', 50.

Lazard Brothers, after which the company would be able to make a definitive decision.

Meanwhile, in August 2002 the BTC sponsors signed the required agreements in London to formally create the Baku–Tbilisi–Ceyhan Pipeline Company (BTC Co.). BTC Co. planned to secure financing before the end of 2002. However, in December 2002 BP announced that finding finance for the pipeline would be delayed by six months to the third quarter of 2003 because of the complexity of talks with international lenders. Among the key issues that have been highlighted as delaying the financing were: the IFC and EBRD's need to evaluate 'the project on a number of grounds, including environmental and social, as well as financial and economic'; and the Georgian government's late approval of the pipeline's route because of concerns about its environmental impact.[39]

In April 2003, Lazard sent invitations for expression of interest to forty banks. A shortlist was drawn up by late July 2003 and the information package was sent out in late August 2003. The IFC and the EBRD finally approved the financing for the BTC project on 4 and 11 November 2003, respectively. This was of crucial importance to the success of the whole PF, since IFC and EBRD involvement provided the political risk insurance required. Their participation mobilized the additional financing. The final financing package was signed in February 2004 and includes 208 finance documents, with over 17,000 signatures from 78 different parties. It represents a major milestone in the implementation of the financing arrangements for the pipeline.[40] Approximately 30 per cent of BTC costs were funded by equity contributions (US$1.01 billion). The remaining 70 per cent of the total was provided in the form of financing by third parties including multilateral development banks, ECAs and political risk insurers from seven different countries and a syndicate of fifteen commercial banks.[41] The group

[39] AFX, 'BP sees BTC pipeline finance delayed until Q3' (13 December 2002); D. Stern, 'Protests Threaten Caspian Pipeline Funding', *Financial Times* (6 February 2003); delay on EBRD financing, due to environmental problems, has been reported in Agence France Presse (19 April 2003), 'EBRD delaying financing of BTC pipeline: Azeri official'. IFC delay reported in meetings of IFC staff with NGOs, April 2003.
[40] Watkins, 'BTC', 49; BP Press Office in Baku, 'BTC signs project finance agreements', press release, 3 February 2004, at: www.winne.com/news/2004/february/btc_signs_project. php.
[41] BP Press Office in Baku, 'BTC signs'.

providing the credit, ECA-supported loans and risk insurance to BTC comprises the:[42]

- Multilateral lending agencies: the IFC and the EBRD.
- ECAs and political risk insurers from seven countries: the Japan Bank for International Cooperation (JBIC); Nippon Export and Investment Insurance (NEXI – Japan); the Export-Import Bank of the United States of America (US Ex-Im); the Export Credits Guarantee Department (ECGD – UK); the-Overseas Private Investment Corporation (OPIC – USA); Compagnie Française pour le Commerce Extérieur (COFACE – France); Euler Hermes Kreditversicherungs-AG (HERMES – Germany); and SACE SpA – Servizi Assicurativi del Commercio Estero (SACE – Italy).
- A syndicate of fifteen commercial banks led by ABN AMRO (leading institution) Citibank, Mizuho and Société Générale with Banca Intesa, BNP Paribas, Crédit Agricole Indosuez,[43] Dexia, HypoVereinsbank, ING, KBC, Natexis Banques Populaires, San Paolo IMI, WestLB and Royal Bank of Scotland.
- Loans provided by BP, Statoil, Total and ConocoPhillips as senior sponsor lenders.

The loan–debt characteristics

The BTC project was financed by a PF structure. 'Project finance' is used to refer to a non-recourse or limited recourse structure, in which debt, equity and credit enhancement are combined for the construction and operation of the refinancing of a particular facility in a capital-intensive industry, in which lenders base credit appraisals on the projected revenues from the operation of the facility, rather than the general assets or credit of the sponsor of the facility, and rely on the asset of the facility, including any revenue-producing contracts and other cash flow generated by the facility, as collateral for the debt.[44]

BTC financing corresponds to a limited-recourse PF model. For sponsor guarantees to fall away, a number of specifications had to be met, one of which was pipeline operations. This relates to evidence that the BTC Co. could operate the pipeline to the planned capacity for a period of time, i.e., that the company could reach peak capacity. This extended further to whether the pipeline was complying with

---

[42] *Ibid.* See Table 12.1 for details on the loans.
[43] Crédit Agricole Indosuez and Crédit Lyonnais merged to form Calyon on 30 April 2004.
[44] Hoffman, *Law and Business*, pp. 4–5.

environmental and social standards, and that there were no material breaches of BTC Co. obligations. This was dealt with through environmental and social audits by lenders' consultants, which took place in May and June of 2007, and the certification was completed after dealing with various issues that arose from that process in September of the same year. Until then the lenders had recourse to the sponsors' assets. Thereafter, the loan became non-recourse.[45] However, as BP is both the operator and also a strategic partner of the project, liability may still arise from contractual undertakings, guarantees or other obligations of BP under the project.[46]

Table 12.1 presents a summary of the total debt as of February 2006, as derived from the Dealogic ProjectWare. The financing comes from a US$2.589 billion debt package. The debt package consists of US$500 million in A/B loans, arranged equally by the IFC and the EBRD;[47] a US$100 million OPIC-covered loan; a US$300 million JBIC overseas investment facility; and US$766 million of ECA-covered facilities. Of the ECA guaranteed debt, US$180 million is covered by JBIC; US$120 million by NEXI; US$150 million by US Ex-Im; US$106 million by ECGD; COFACE and Hermes both US$90 million and SACE is providing a guarantee for US$30 million. The tranches are priced differently with the weighted average pricing of the deal being L+300bp.

The commercial debt is accompanied by US$923 million in sponsor loans, the conditions of which mirror the commercial debt.[48] The project's shareholders have invested about US$1 billion in equity. It was also suggested that the shareholders were asked to allocate an additional US$333 million for a cost overrun on the Turkish side.[49]

---

[45] Interview conducted on 30 January 2008. Source requested anonymity. Interview with Thomas Dimitroff, British Power, conducted on 27 May 2006.

[46] Hoffman, *Law and Business*, p. 14.

[47] An 'A' loan is financed by the multilateral financial institution's own sources. A 'B' loan is a loan made available by the multilateral financial institution and then syndicated (i.e. participation interests in the loan are sold) to commercial banks but treated in the same way as the 'A' loan (i.e. the multilateral financial institution documents and administers the loan, and collects and distributes payments and collateral pro rata between itself and the 'B' loan lenders).

[48] Gidney and Chavarot, 'Financing the James Bond Pipeline', table 48.

[49] 'BP-led Baku–Ceyhan consortium to pay BOTAS oil USD 333 million for cost overruns', AFX News (6 June 2006), at: www.iii.co.uk/investment/detail/?display=news& code=cotn:BP-.L&action=article&articleid=5666817. This amount is outside the 30 per cent cost overrun on the whole project that led to the final estimation of expenses at the level of US$3.9 billion.

Table 12.1 *Summary of the debt*

	Characteristics	Margin (base points)	Mandate arrangers	Lead managers	Guarantor
1	US$125m. 12 years (A Loan)		IFC	IFC	
2	US$125m. 10 years (B Loan)	LIBOR 200–300bp	IFC + the 15 commercial banks*	The 15 commercial banks	
3	US$125m. 12 years (A Loan)		EBRD		
4	US$125m. 10 years (B Loan)	LIBOR 200–300bp	EBRD + the 15 commercial banks	The 15 commercial banks	
5	US$300m. 12 years (Term Loan)		JBIC	JBIC	
6	US$180m. 12 years (Term Loan)		The 15 commercial banks	The 15 commercial banks	JBIC (Japan)
7	US$120m. 12 years (Term Loan)	LIBOR 65bp	The 15 commercial banks	The 15 commercial banks	NEXI
8	US$150m. 12 years (Term Loan)		The 15 commercial banks	The 15 commercial banks	US Ex-Im Bank
9	US$90m. 12 years (Term Loan)	LIBOR 50bp	The 15 commercial banks	The 15 commercial banks	Hermes AG (Germany)
10	US$90m. 12 years (Term Loan)	LIBOR 75bp	The 15 commercial banks	The 15 commercial banks	COFACE (France)
11	US$30m. 12 years (Term Loan)	LIBOR 75bp	The 15 commercial banks	The 15 commercial banks	SACE SpA (Italy)

Table 12.1 (*cont.*)

Characteristics	Margin (base points)	Mandate arrangers	Lead managers	Guarantor
12 US$100m. 12 years (Term Loan)	LIBOR 65bp	The 15 commercial banks	The 15 commercial banks	OPIC
13 US$106m. 12 years (Term Loan)	LIBOR 25bp	The 15 commercial banks	The 15 commercial banks	ECGD (UK)
14 US$923m. 12 years (Term Loan)		BP Amoco plc; Total SA; Statoil ASA; ConocoPhillips	BP Amoco plc; Total SA; Statoil ASA; ConocoPhillips	

Source: elaborated from Dealogic projectware database

*The syndicate of 15 commercial banks includes ABN AMRO, Citibank, Mizuho and Société Générale as leading institutions with Banca Intesa, BNP Paribas, Crédit Agricole Indosuez, Dexia, HypoVereinsbank, ING, KBC, Natexis Banques Populaires, San Paolo IMI, WestLB and Royal Bank of Scotland.

The legal framework and its links with PF and sustainable development

As the ability of a project company to generate revenue from a project's operations is the foundation of PF, the contracts form the framework for the viability of the project and control the allocation of risks.[50] Contracts must not interfere unduly with the expectation for debt repayment from project revenues. They are particularly designed to anticipate regulatory problems unique to the project and the environment in which the project will exist.[51] However, in their aim to reduce or allocate risk between the partners, these contracts may include stabilization clauses or financial arrangements that may interfere with the achievement of sustainable development goals in the host country.

The relationship between BTC Co. and each host government is governed by four core documents. The foundation of the structure is an intergovernmental agreement entered into between Azerbaijan, Georgia and Turkey (the IGA). Annexed to the IGA are, among other documents, the texts of three separate host government agreements between BTC project sponsors and each host government (the HGAs), later succeeded by BTC Co. The IGA was entered into on 18 November 1999 and each HGA was entered into in October 2000. These contracts and their implications for sustainable development are discussed below.

The intergovernmental agreement

The IGA is an international treaty, through which the host states formally agree to ensure the safety and security of project personnel, facilities, assets and in-transit petroleum. It creates, therefore, a binding obligation between each host government, enforceable under public international law.[52] Key terms of the IGA are:

- a commitment from each host government to present the IGA, including the HGAs and other documents included in the annexes, for ratification so as to make all those terms the prevailing legal regime applicable to its state;[53]

---

[50] Financial strength and reliability of parties behind the contracts is not the least important factor. In fact both factors go hand in hand.

[51] Hoffman, *Law and Business*, p. 7.

[52] For IGA, see: http://subsites.bp.com/caspian/BTC/Eng/agmt4/agmt4.PDF.

[53] *Ibid.* Article II(1).

- a general commitment from each host government to support the project, including: ensuring freedom of petroleum transit, guaranteeing the performance by state entities of certain project contracts[54] and granting land rights to the project;[55]
- a commitment from each host government to provide security for the pipeline;[56]
- an agreement as to the applicable technical, safety and environmental standards for the project.[57] This was an important provision for much of the subsequent debate; and
- confirmation that the only taxes imposed on the project would be those set out in the HGAs and an agreement on how to allocate taxable profits between the project states.[58]

Host government agreements

HGs are legal contracts between the state and affiliates of project sponsors that identify both parties' rights and obligations to ensure the success of the proposed project. BTC Co. succeeded to the rights of these affiliates under the HGAs on 1 August 2002. The BTC's HGAs are considered some of the most high profile agreements of this type to date and constitute one of the core/central points in civil society opposition to the project.[59] The three HGAs are drafted in very similar terms. They are long and complex documents, with more than seventy pages each with several annexes. Essentially, under the HGA, each host government grants project sponsors a right to build and operate the pipeline and agrees to provide various forms of support for the project. On their side, project sponsors commit to a certain set of standards while carrying out the project and also to pay specified tax or tariff amounts to the host government. Each HGA provides for a certain dispute resolution procedure – arbitration with no need to exhaust local remedies – and stipulates the law – English law – applicable to

---

[54] *Ibid.* Article II(4)(ii) and (iii).   [55] *Ibid.* Article II(4)(iv).
[56] *Ibid.* Article III(2).   [57] *Ibid.* Article IV.
[58] *Ibid.* Article V(1). For a summary of the key terms, see also B. H. Carpenter and W. Labadi, 'Striking a Balance: Intergovernmental and Host Government Agreements in the Context of the Baku–Tbilisi–Ceyhan Pipeline Project', available at: www.ebrd.com/pubs/legal/lit042.pdf.
[59] USAID, 'Multilateral Development Bank Assistance Proposals Likely to Have Adverse Impacts on the Environment, Natural Resources, Public Health and Indigenous Peoples' (September 2002–October 2004), at: www.bakuceyhan.org.uk/USAID_MDB_report_Sept02-Oct04.pdf, 28.

the agreement.[60] Each HGA also specifies certain events the occurrence of which would relieve parties of their duties under the agreement or rather trigger their liability.[61]

The BTC's HGAs and their links with sustainable development

Civil society legal analysis of the HGAs[62] revealed several concerns. One of the claims was that the host countries had agreed to exempt the project from application of the local laws, except from obligations arising under the Constitution,[63] and given up their right to impose more stringent environmental and social standards throughout the forty-year term of the HGA, which could be extended for a further twenty years.[64] Thus, this undertaking was claimed to transfer the financial burden from the investor to the government if the government instituted more stringent legislative standards with a negative impact on the project.[65]

The economic equilibrium clause incorporated in the HGAs to this end also alarmed civil society groups as it was seen to enable BTC sponsors to contract out of the rule of law. It would prevent the government from delaying the project implementation through any action based on environmental and social (e.g. health) concerns except in the case of an 'imminent, material threat to public security, health safety or the environment'.[66] Moreover, being faced with the threat of punitive costs for protecting the human rights of those affected by the pipeline is likely to have a chilling effect on a government's ability to improve its general human rights record and environmental conditions.[67]

A second type of concern relates to the project agreements' privileged legal status. This establishes the IGA and each of the HGAs as the prevailing legal regime under international law and the laws of each of the three countries, overriding all conflicting domestic law, present and

---

[60] See Article 17 of the Azerbaijani HGA, at: http://subsites.bp.com/caspian/BTC/Eng/agmt1/agmt1.PDF.

[61] The three HGAs can be accessed at: www.bp.com/sectiongenericarticle.do?categoryId=9029334&contentId=7053632.

[62] See Amnesty International (AI), 'Human Rights On the Line: the Baku–Tbilisi–Ceyhan Pipeline' (May 2003), available at: www.amnestyusa.org/business/humanrightsontheline.pdf.

[63] Preamble to the Azerbaijani HGA (above n. 60).

[64] Articles 7.2 (x) and 9.1 (iii) of the Azerbaijani HGA: Articles 7.2 (x) and 9.1 (iii) of the Georgian HGA; Articles 7.2 (xi) and 10.1 (iii) of the Turkish HGA (above n. 61).

[65] USAID, 'Multilateral', 29.   [66] Article 5.2 (iii) of the Azerbaijani HGA (above n. 60).

[67] AI, 'Human Rights', 5 and 16.

future, bar the Constitution. Concerns were expressed that the social and environmental provisions of HGAs would take precedence over existing and future environmental and social laws to the extent that such local laws would conflict with HGA standards.[68] For instance, in the case of Georgia, the HGA was invoked to override its national Water Act in areas where such overriding was needed in order to develop the pipeline right of way (ROW).[69] A third area of concern was the scope for individual citizens to enforce the obligations assumed by BTC Co.: while host governments could, if they wished, enforce a rigorous environmental and social regime upon the project, a local citizen could not.[70]

Due to the controversy surrounding these issues, and because the standards to which the project is subject were not explicitly set out in the HGAs, the project sponsors subsequently issued several clarifying legal documents including:

- A joint statement,[71] set up in May 2003, responds to NGO concerns about the potential impact of the project's legal framework on the autonomy and policy-making discretion of the host states. It says that those concerns are groundless and clarifies and restates the parties' interpretation of the IGA, HGAs and other project agreements focusing on the standards to which the project is subject. Particularly, it emphasizes that the process leading to the conclusion of the IGA, HGA and other project agreements was in compliance with relevant national law. When it comes to the standards binding on the project, they are required to be 'no less stringent' than those generally applied within member states of the European Union (EU), including the evolving standards and practices within the petroleum industry. The statement also highlights the parties' commitment to the relevant international human rights and environmental norms and standards.
- The Protocol Relating to the Provision of Security for the East–West Energy Corridor (the Security Protocol),[72] executed on 23 July 2003, formally commits the host governments to a cooperative security

[68] World Wide Fund for Nature (WWF), 'BTC Applications to IFC and EBRD for Finance: WWF Comment' (October 2003). Available at: www.wwf.org
[69] USAID, 'Multilateral', 28–9.
[70] Amnesty International, 'Human Rights', 14–15; Carpenter and Labadi, 'Striking a Balance'. See Chapter 10 of this book.
[71] Available at: http://subsites.bp.com/caspian/Joint%20Statement.pdf.
[72] Available at: http://subsites.bp.com/caspian/Security%20Protocol.pdf.

scheme. It deals with the manner in which the host governments propose to meet their security commitments under the HGAs.

- The BTC Human Rights Undertaking:[73] is a legally binding unilateral deed under English law executed by BTC Co. in September 2003. It clarifies aspects of BTC's legal framework and confirms the commitment of the parties to see the project regulated by evolving health, safety and environment (HSE) and human rights standards under domestic law, including without limitation international law as implemented by domestic law. It seeks to annul the compensation claims in the HGA in the event of new laws being introduced for these reasons.

However, there are mixed views about the impacts that these additional instruments may have. On the one hand, additional NGO analysis states that the documents have been drafted from a blinkered perspective and do not appear to resolve the deficiencies in the HGAs. There were also concerns about whether the Human Rights Undertaking will be binding on BTC Co. when SOCAR increases its proportional ownership of BTC.[74] Moreover, even though the Caspian Development Advisory Panel recognizes BP's efforts, these documents are only seen as a first step towards supporting human rights in the area. On the other hand, analysis conducted by EBRD states that when the HGAs are read in this light (i.e. from the perspective of commitments set down in the joint statement) what emerges is a commitment, in the key areas of concern, to standards that should be acceptable throughout the life of the project.[75]

Construction agreements

Other key documents for PF initiatives are the construction agreements. According to Hoffman, the construction contract in PF must serve to provide the project company with a finished facility that satisfies certain agreed-upon performance criteria for a fixed or reasonably predictable price on a defined date.[76]

Unless the contract price is extremely attractive, the three main objectives of the contractor in contract negotiation are to limit the risk

---

[73] Available at: http://subsites.bp.com/caspian/Human%20Rights%20Undertaking.pdf.
[74] AI, 'Human Rights'; WWF, 'BTC Applications'; USAID, 'Multilateral'; CDAP, Report on Turkey, p. 96.
[75] Carpenter and Labadi, 'Striking a Balance'.   [76] Hoffman, *Law and Business*, pp. 48–9.

of any change in the cost of the project, to ensure there is sufficient contractual excuse for late delivery, and to provide sufficient time to satisfy performance guarantees.[77] It is suggested that if the contract involves a fixed price and fixed date and provides for liquidated damages for delays, then the contractor has the incentive to cut corners on environmental, social and technical standards in order to remain on schedule and/or stay under budget. The promise of a bonus payment for finishing the construction ahead of schedule is also believed to heighten this concern.[78]

In Azerbaijan and Georgia, BTC Co. and BP as an operator directly managed all aspects of pipeline construction, i.e. hiring and supervision of contractors handling the construction.[79] As noted above, two main contractors were hired: CCIC who were responsible for the pipeline construction and valves, and SCPV who were responsible for the main above-ground installations (AGIs).[80] In Turkey BOTAŞ – a Turkish government body – served as managing contractor. The relationship between BOTAŞ and BTC Co. was set out in a lump sum turnkey agreement (LSTA) included in Appendix 2 to the Turkish HGA.[81] Under the LSTA, BOTAŞ agreed to design, engineer, procure, construct, start up, demonstrate, test and put into operation the BTC facilities in Turkey[82] for a fixed price of US$1.3 billion.[83] The LSTA and HGA also established BOTAŞ as responsible for land acquisition and compensation activities for which a lump sum of US$99 million was set aside.[84]

[77] *Ibid.* p. 49.
[78] CDAP, Report on Turkey, p. 9; see Chapter 5 in this book. Interview with an NGO working in the area of engineering and development conducted on 23 July 2007. Source requested anonymity.
[79] CDAP, Report on Turkey.
[80] EBRD, 'Independent Recourse Mechanism'.
[81] Available at: http://subsites.bp.com/caspian/BTC/Eng/agmt5/agmt5.PDF.
[82] Article 3.1 of the LSTA.
[83] *Ibid.* Article 5.1. The exact lump sum fixed price is US$1,307,610,000. Agreement provided for a possibility to renegotiate both the amount of the fixed price and the completion dates in case of delay on the part of MEP participants to give notice to proceed with land acquisition and the construction phase, as a result of which price and date details in BOTAŞ's bid would no longer be realistic (*ibid.* Articles 5.1.1 and 5.1.2).
[84] Section 7.2 (vii) (1) of the Turkish HGA and Article 3.1.2.2 of the LSTA. However, the LSTA also provides that if MEP participants delay in giving BOTAŞ notice to proceed with land acquisition and the construction phase as of the date falling thirteen months after the provisional rights to the permanent land have been obtained by the state authorities they 'will become obligated to pay an additional amount in respect to such rights to land, such additional amount to be 3% of $72,250,000 multiplied by a fraction,

BOTAŞ was also responsible for producing an environmental impact assessment (EIA) report within the lump sum fixed price,[85] and was under the duty to undertake all environmental planning, mitigation and monitoring in Turkey within the lump sum fixed price, particularly by implementing the provisions of the environmental management and monitoring plan (EMMP) and the social management and monitoring plan (SMMP) and supporting plans. Contractors were to be responsible for the implementation of, and adherence to, all the mitigation measures outlined in the EIA, EMMP and SMMP. BTC Co. was to ensure that the management plans would be implemented.[86]

The Turkish government guaranteed performance of all designated duties by BOTAŞ under the turnkey agreement, including payments of amounts payable by the company under the agreement.[87] The Turkish treasury provided a Turkish government guarantee for payments to be made by BOTAŞ under the LSTA. With regard to the cost overruns the LSTA provided that the cost overrun amount 'shall not exceed 300 million plus the aggregate amount of Turnkey Contractor Additional Funding Requirements'.[88] To the extent costs go beyond the US$300 million governmental buffer in satisfying commitments that are appropriately attributable to the LSTA, the amounts generally would have been withheld from transit fees and other amounts owing to BOTAŞ (subject to a cap of 30 per cent of the overall LSTA budget).[89] The LSTA also contained separate provisions on liquidated damages in the event that BOTAŞ delayed handing over the ready facilities on time.[90]

---

the numerator of which shall be the number of days beyond the above mentioned 13 months the Notice of Proceed is given, and the denominator of which is 365' (Article 5.1.3). Additionally, in case of scope change, the turnkey contractor would have the right to additional compensation for acquisition of provisional right to the permanent land in relation to the additional portion of work, with a cap being agreed at the level of US $8,500,000 (Article 5.1.4).

[85] Non-Technical Summary of the Environmental Impact Assessment of the Turkish section of the Baku–Tbilisi–Ceyhan Crude Oil Pipeline Project (September 2002), 41 available at: www.bp.com/liveassets/bp_internet/bp_caspian/bp_caspian_en/STAGING/local_assets/downloads_pdfs/xyz/BTC_English_ESIAs_Executive_Summary_Turkey_Content_BTC_EIA_Executive_Summary.PDF.

[86] Section 17 of the BTC Project EIA for the Turkish section, Final EIA, available at: www.bp.com/genericarticle.do?categoryId=9006630&contentId=7013653.

[87] Article 8 of the Turkish HGA, available at: www.bp.com/sectiongenericarticle.do?categoryId=9029334&contentId=7053632. Section 1.01 of the governmental guarantee, Appendix 3 to the HGA.

[88] LSTA Articles 10.4.4(a) and 10.4.5(b).

[89] CDAP, Report on Turkey, pp. 25–6; LSTA Article 25.6.   [90] LSTA Article 8.2.

It should be noted that there is some evidence suggesting that the fixed price agreed by BOTAŞ might be underpriced.[91] Claros Consulting, by comparing the Turkish section with the other sections, affirms that it does look cheap considering that this section only accounts for 47 per cent of the contract costs but 61 per cent of the pipeline length (and none of it with the advantage of using an existing route). Claros Consulting suggested that the contract is underpriced by some US$600 million.[92] The report compares BTC with pipelines in the UK and Alaska, where the respective cost is respectively two and ten times more than their original estimates.[93] Moreover, the price of the agreement fixed in the turnkey agreement that was negotiated nearly two years before the EIA was approved by the Turkish government,[94] hence any findings of the EIA that could result in significant additional project costs were not be included in this initial budget. Indeed, another source suggests that the Turkish portion was underpriced, as BOTAŞ filed compensation claims for US$400 million against BTC Co. due to increased construction costs.[95] Lawyers and financial experts of both parties negotiated the allocation of an additional US$330 million as compensation to BOTAŞ. Additional costs, however, arose in all three countries. Increased costs were partly attributed to construction delays due to environmental and social concerns raised by civil society but also to a world trend for increases in labour, electric power and fuel costs.[96]

BTC construction agreements links with sustainable development and human rights

Several concerns have been raised with relation to the terms of the LSTA. These arose initially because the LSTA was not in the public domain

---

[91] No author, 'BTC Intergovernmental and Host Government Agreements'.

[92] Claros Consulting, 'The Baku–Tbilisi–Ceyhan Pipeline and BP: A Financial Analysis. Building Tomorrow's Crisis?', by Mark Mansley (May 2003) at: http://bankwatch.org/documents/financial_analysis_03_03.pdf. Information as of June 2006 suggests that BOTAŞ asked for an additional US$400 million to complete the project and a final amount of US$333 million was agreed. This was confirmed by the official of the Foreign Investment Department of SOCAR, but BP declined to confirm or reject this.

[93] *Ibid.*

[94] In fact, the construction started before the EIA was approved. Corner House, 'The Baku–Tbilisi–Ceyhan (BTC) Pipeline Project: A Note on Potential Breaches of the EC Directive on Environmental Impact Assessment', available at: www.bakuceyhan.org.uk/publications/breaches_of_eu_directive_final.rtf.

[95] AFX News, 'BP-led Baku–Ceyhan consortium'.

[96] See 'BTC Pipeline Has Been Constructed for 90%', exclusive interview with SOCAR president, Natig Aliyev, *Caspian Energy*, 6(28) 2004, at: http://caspianenergy.com.

until very late in the process. Additionally, it was argued that low price, financial penalties involved and the Turkish government guarantee backing BOTAŞ's performance made intervening in the project on environmental and social grounds complicated. Indeed, financial penalties for delay in project completion provide a greater incentive for project parties to avoid substantively changing dynamics to eliminate or mitigate adverse environmental or social impact.

All these issues raised concerns about the capacity and incentives for BOTAŞ – and the Turkish government in general – to comply with adequate environmental and social standards. These concerns were not only voiced by civil society groups but also raised by the Caspian Development Advisory Panel (CDAP) – a BP-established independent external advisory panel to study the BTC project. Indeed, the CDAP noted that BOTAŞ's central role under the HGA and LSTA presents BP with perhaps the most significant challenge in Turkey. The financial challenges raised by the LSTA, coupled with a weak but evolving environmental and social compliance culture in BOTAŞ and its contractors, raised questions for the CDAP over whether the various environmental and social commitments made in the EIA and the health and safety commitments made in other project documents would be met. In particular, it was concerned that BOTAŞ and its contractors might feel pressure to cut corners on environmental, social and technical standards in order to remain on schedule and/or under budget vis-à-vis the LSTA. Moreover, they further argued that BP and BTC personnel lacked the authority to stop work or to exercise other severe contract remedies, to ensure that BOTAŞ and its contractors met BTC's EIA commitments.[97] These fears were reinforced by meetings between the CDAP and key senior Turkish government officials who demonstrated little appreciation of the need for such standards and instead voiced complaints about BP's insistence on maintaining its environmental, health and safety standards and suggested that a relaxation of these standards would better enable BOTAŞ to complete construction on time and under budget.[98]

In addition, the terms of the LSTA, and particularly the need for BOTAŞ to keep under or within budget and to deliver on time could also explain the way in which BOTAŞ conducted the land acquisition and compensation process. Under the HGA BOTAŞ was responsible for the resettlement plan to which US$99 million was allocated. In Turkey,

[97] CDAP, Report on Turkey, sec. VII.   [98] *Ibid.* p. 40.

land may be held by private owners in one of two ways: (a) by registration of the ownership and the issuance of a deed reflecting title to the land (registered ownership); or (b) by customary use and occupation of land (customary ownership). Compensation should be provided for both categories of owners. Of the private lands to be acquired along the pipeline ROW, BOTAŞ identified 2,748 parcels subject to customary ownership and 6,358 registered parcels. Determination of the ownership of registered land was complicated by factors such as multiple ownership, out-of-date deeds, and conflicting customary and registered ownership claims. Additionally, villages typically had usage rights over common lands (particularly over pasture lands) although the legal owner of the land was a state agency such as the Treasury. On average, each of the 6,300-plus privately owned registered parcels of land along the pipeline ROW had six owners.[99]

Given that the terms of BOTAŞ's contract were negotiated well before the identification of all the aforementioned complexities and that BOTAŞ needed to conduct the land acquisition plan on time and to keep within budget, BOTAŞ decided to make use of Article 27 of the reformed code for its land acquisition along the pipeline rather than Article 10. This raised several human rights concerns among civil society. Article 10 is the ordinary process for land expropriation processes, which provides for significant periods of time for owners to be identified, for negotiations to occur and for appeals of expropriation decisions to be lodged. Article 27 is an expedited alternative to Article 10 by which courts are required to make property valuation decisions within seven days, and the expropriation is effective immediately upon deposit of the appraised amount in a trust for the owner or owners, even if the valuation is appealed.[100] Finally, in response to concerns expressed by international NGOs and other opposition groups as to the use of Article 27, BTC Co. and BOTAŞ modified the Article 27 process to provide, among other safeguards, more time for identification and notification of landowners and valuation of private parcels based on market surveys. Another issue is that BOTAŞ was accused of offering far less compensation to landowners than promised and NGOs said there were cases of landowners being threatened for refusing to accept offers of compensation.[101]

---

[99]   *Ibid.* pp. 58–60.   [100]   *Ibid.* p. 65.
[101]   *The Guardian*, 'Q&A: The Baku–Tbilisi–Ceyhan pipeline', by Mark Tran (26 May 2005), available at: www.guardian.co.uk/oil/story/0,11319,1492872,00.html.

Finally, it seems the pressure to keep activities on schedule and within budget due to the contractual terms on the BTC pipeline[102] gave rise to compliance problems on environmental issues, quite apart from those affecting the Turkish portion of the pipeline. At least this is what is implied by the letter sent from BTC Co. to the Georgian government asking for expedited approval of the ESIA EIA (see Box 12.1).

BOX 12.1 **The Georgian ESIA approval process**

In Georgia, given the volume and complexity of the material to review for the ESIA, the minister of the environment requested and received technical assistance from the Dutch Commission on Environmental Impact Assessment. By November 2002, BP wrote to the president of Georgia demanding that Georgia approve the EIA for the project so as not to upset the consortium's commercial timetable, despite major outstanding issues with regard to the pipeline. As the letter puts it: 'Without ... timely approval we cannot move forward with the construction phase and we will halt work in Azerbaijan and the Lump Sum Turnkey Contract in Turkey. This will have an immediate knock on effect on the upstream investment and the Shah Deniz project and destroy the benefits detailed in the Declaration of Intent signed between BTC Co. and Georgian International Oil Corporation (GIOC) on October 30th in your presence.'[103] The Georgian ESIA was finally approved on 30 November 2002.

The USAID report suggests that at the time the Georgian minister of environment signed the environmental permit for construction to proceed, a number of conditions were attached in order to remedy deficiencies in the ESIA such as requesting additional analyses of a series of potential landslide zones along the route and another route alternative. Later, in 2004, the government of Georgia imposed a two-week suspension on construction of the BTC pipeline in the Borjomi region which is a sensitive site for both environmental and security reasons. The government wanted independent experts to conduct safety tests. The

---

[102] In the case of BTC the concern about staying within the initially assumed and agreed schedule was explained also by the parallel upstream project – the development of the Azeri–Chirag–Gunashli offshore oilfield. The BTC pipeline was supposed to take the oil from that field once it is ready and the schedules of both projects, i.e. the point of completion, should have overlapped. Interview conducted on 30 January 2008. Source requested anonymity.

[103] 'Developmental, Human Rights and Environmental Impacts of the Baku–Tbilisi–Ceyhan Oil Pipeline', memorandum from concerned NGOs to Department for International Development, Foreign and Commonwealth Office, HM Treasury and UK ECGD (November 2002), at: www.ilisu.org.uk/DflDmemo.doc.

BOX 12.1 (cont.)

minister of environment expressed continued concerns about the environmental impact stating that some of the conditions of the environmental permit had not been met. However it is not clear how effectively the government's concerns were addressed due to the contractual deadline and its financial responsibility for any substantial delays in project completion.[104]

Not surprisingly, given the potential sums involved, most pipeline protests in Azerbaijan have focused on compensation, rather than on environmental or other concerns. One activist argued that BP shared much of the blame along with local officials. Mais Gulaliyev, president of the Civil Initiatives Center, a Baku-based NGO claimed that the company did not respond adequately to disputed compensation claims. Despite '56 meetings with BP representatives', he said, '[t]hey always promised to find out [what was wrong], but did not solve a single problem'. BP representatives did not offer its side of the story.[105]

Legal action against BTC and other stakeholders

As a result of these concerns, civil society has pursued several legal actions against BTC Co. There were (at least) three sets of legal actions initiated against BTC Co.

On 2 January 2004 Cemender Korkmaz, the Corner House and the Kurdish Human Rights Project (KHRP) applied to the Court of First Instance (CFI) for the annulment of the European Commission's Regular Report of 5 November 2003 concerning Turkey's progress towards accession, insofar as it contained a European Commission decision refusing to make a recommendation to the European Council to freeze pre-accession aid granted to Turkey until it complied with the Copenhagen criteria by modifying or terminating the BTC project, and, in the alternative, for a finding of failure to act in that connection, and, in any event, for an injunction in that regard. The applicants claimed that Turkey's involvement with the BTC project was in breach of pre-accession criteria which centre on respect and protection of human

[104] USAID, 'Multilateral', 19.
[105] EurasiaNet Business & Economics, 'Life Along the Pipeline: BTC's Impact on Azerbaijan', by Rovshan Ismayilov, 15 March 2007, at: www.eurasianet.org/departments/insight/articles/eav031507.shtml.

rights.[106] By its order, the CFI has declared the application inadmissible thus preventing judgment on the substance.[107]

In January 2004, KHRP also filed cases with the European Court of Human Rights (ECtHR) on behalf of 38 affected villagers along the route, alleging multiple violations of the European Convention on Human Rights including Article 1 of Protocol 1 (the right to peaceful enjoyment of property), Article 8 (the right to respect for private and family life), Article 13 (the right to an effective remedy) and Article 14 (rights to be secured without discrimination).[108] The Georgian environmental group Green Alternative alleged that the pipeline consortium and the Shevardnadze government violated Georgian environmental law in sending the pipeline through the Borjomi-Kharagauli National Park. The legal action was originally filed with the ECtHR on 29 May 2003. On 27 June 2003 the Georgian District Court granted Green Alternative the right to commence a legal action in connection with the pipeline. The legal action was brought against the Georgian Ministry of Environment and Natural Resources, the Georgian branch of the Baku–Tbilisi–Ceyhan Pipeline company, the Ministry of Foreign Affairs and the Parliament Office of Georgia.[109] Houston-based ConocoPhillips was also named among the defendants in the lawsuit, as well as other members of the BP-led pipeline consortium, including Statoil ASA, Unocal, Inpex and Delta Hess.[110] The group is appealing an unfavourable ruling on this case.[111]

---

[106] Case T-2/04, *Cemender Korkmaz, Corner House Research and the Kurdish Human Rights Project* v. *Commission of the EC* (2004/C71/60), OJ (EC) (C 71/32, 20 March 2004), at: http://eur-lex.europa.eu/LexUriServ/site/en/oj/2004/c_071/c_07120040320 en00320033.pdf.

[107] Case T-2/04, *Order of the Court of First Instance of the European Communities* (Fourth Chamber, 30 March 2006) at: http://eur-lex.europa.eu/LexUriServ/LexUriServ.do? uri=CELEX:62004B0002:EN:HTML.

[108] A. Lustgarten, 'The Baku–Tbilisi–Ceyhan pipeline: exporting an "environmental time bomb"', European ECA Reform Campaign, project factsheet, issue 1, April 2005. Available at: www.fern.org/sites/fern.org/files/media/documents/document_2651_2652. pdf.

[109] Baku–Ceyhan Campaign, 'BP pipeline faces court challenge in Georgia' (Tbilisi, 27 June 2003), at: www.bakuceyhan.org.uk/press_releases/news07.htm.

[110] 'ConocoPhillips Named as a Defendant in Environmental Lawsuit', *Houston Business Journal* (27 June 2003), available at: http://houston.bizjournals.com/houston/stories/ 2003/06/23/daily53.html.

[111] BankTrack, 'Principles, Profits or Just PR? Triple P investments Under the Equator Principles: An Anniversary Assessment' (4 June 2004), 17, available at: www.banktrack. org/show/focus/the_equator_principles.

Moreover, in April 2003 a consortium of NGOs including Friends of the Earth (FoE), Milieudefensie (FoE Netherlands) and the Corner House filed a complaint against BP that the HGAs would be breaching the OECD Guidelines for Multinational Enterprises.[112] Following the submission of the complaint to the National Contact Point in the UK the host governments and BTC signed the joint statement on the interpretation of the HGA in June 2003.[113]

In October 2003, a complaint alleging non-observance of the Guidelines in the areas of environment, 'contractual' and respect of human rights by three French companies involved in the BTC pipeline construction was submitted to the French National Contact Point.[114] In 2004 complaints alleging non-observance of the Guidelines' recommendations on human and labour rights and the environment by the Italian companies involved in BTC were also submitted to the Italian National Contact Point.[115]

The banks have also been under direct attack for their failed due diligence on the BTC pipeline. A Belgian NGO, Proyecto Gato, made a formal complaint against three Belgian banks (Dexia, KBC and ING – all three signatories to the EP) through the OECD's Guidelines mechanism. The complaint centred on the pipeline-coating issue and on the undue constraint over the host governments' ability to regulate as imposed by the project's legal agreements.[116] All the OECD specific instances are still pending.[117]

In Azerbaijan the most serious of the outcries concerned fourteen families from the village of Hajali, located in western Azerbaijan. These families claim that they were never paid for use of their land, and accuse local officials of fraud. Hajali villager Mehman Hasanov, a 40-year-old, claims that when compensation was being paid for land use, his land was illegally registered in the name of a relative of the then chairman of the regional executive committee. After losing a case before the Azerbaijani Supreme Court, the village's fourteen families applied to the ECtHR in Strasbourg.[118]

---

[112] FoE *et al.*, 'Complaint under the OECD's Guidelines on Multinational Enterprises', FoE, Milieudefensie (FoE Netherlands) and the Corner House (29 April 2003), available at: www.bakuceyhan.org.uk/publications/oecd_complaint_final_uk.doc.

[113] EBRD, 'The Baku–Tbilisi–Ceyhan Pipeline Project: NGO comments and EBRD response' (2003), at: www.ebrd.com/projects/eias/18806ngo.pdf.

[114] OECD Guidelines for Multinational Enterprises: Specific Instances Considered by National Contact Points (7 October 2009), at: www.oecd.org/dataoecd/15/43/33914891.pdf

[115] *Ibid.*   [116] *Ibid.* See also BankTrack, 'Principles, Profits or Just PR?', 17.

[117] OECD Guidelines (2009).

[118] EurasiaNet Business & Economics, 'Life Along the Pipeline'.

Lenders' approach to risk and sustainable development

The level of due diligence undertaken involves considerations of time available, cost and project type.[119] The environmental and social due diligence conducted in PF also depends on the requirements of the financial institutions involved, the nature of the project and the size of the loan. For example, multilateral development institutions such as the IFC require due diligence processes for all the projects they fund. The level of its due diligence will depend on the categorization of the project according to potential adverse impacts (A, B or C).[120] In the case of commercial banks, as noted above, since July 2003 the large majority are committed to the EP, which provide a framework for banks to review, evaluate and mitigate or avoid environmental and social impacts and risks of PF-financed projects. The EP are based on the IFC's environmental and social safeguard policies and apply to PF transactions over US$10 million.

Therefore, financial institutions might affect the sustainable development impacts of a project by making loans or guarantees conditional on a borrower's complying with certain environmental, social and/or human rights standards. The due diligence processes conducted by the main financial institutions involved in the BTC pipeline are described below. The first section concentrates on the process followed by the multilateral financial institutions, notably the IFC and EBRD. However, the analysis also provides examples of other multilateral financial institutions involved where relevant. The final section concentrates on commercial banks' due diligence processes.

Multilateral financial institutions' environmental and social due diligence: IFC and EBRD

The environmental and social guidelines applied

The IFC expects clients to assess and manage the social and environmental risks and impacts of their projects and to implement measures to meet the IFC standards. The IFC's role is to review the client's assessments; to assist the client in developing measures to avoid, minimize, mitigate or compensate for social and environmental impacts

---

[119] Hoffman, *Law and Business*, p. 85. For definition and discussion of the due diligence process, see above, pp. 365–6.

[120] In February 2006 IFC released a new set of standards for conducting environmental and social reviews of the projects.

consistent with IFC standards; to categorize the project in order to specify the IFC's institutional requirements to disclose project-specific information to the public; to help identify opportunities to improve social and environmental outcomes; and to monitor the client's social and environmental performance throughout the life of the IFC's investment.

According to the 1998 IFC Environmental and Social Review Procedure, the BTC pipeline corresponds to a category-A project – with potential significant adverse environmental or social impacts that are diverse, irreversible or unprecedented.[121] The following are the policies and guidelines that were considered in IFC due diligence for BTC as a category-A project:[122]

- IFC environmental and social review procedure (December 1998);[123]
- Safeguard policies, such as the IFC's OP 4.01 policy on environmental assessment (EA) (October 1998); natural habitats (OP 4.04, November 1998); indigenous peoples (OD 4.20, September 1991); involuntary resettlement (OD 4.30, June 1990), etc.;[124]
- IFC's policy on disclosure of information (September 1998) describing materials to be made available to the public; and[125]
- the sector-specific Environmental, Health and Safety Guidelines within the Pollution Prevention and Abatement Handbook (1999).[126]

The EBRD also applied World Bank and IFC environmental and social safeguard policies and guidelines as the project is jointly financed by

---

[121] Projects are classified according to three categories: category A: projects with potentially significant adverse environmental or social impacts that are diverse, irreversible or unprecedented; category B: projects with potentially limited adverse environmental or social impacts that are few in number, site-specific, largely reversible and readily addressed through mitigation measures; and category C: projects with minimal or no adverse environmental or social impacts.

[122] These policies and guidelines have been updated or replaced since then, but were in effect during the period of BTC due diligence. For the archived version, see: www.ifc. org/ifcext/sustainability.nsf/Content/Policies_Archived. New environmental and social standards applicable to IFC-financed or -supported projects are available at: www.ifc.org/ifcext/sustainability.nsf/Content/EnvSocStandards.

[123] Replaced by the revised Environmental and Social Review Procedure in April 2006, which was again updated in July 2007.

[124] Replaced by the policy on social and environmental sustainability and the performance standards in February 2006.

[125] Replaced by the revised IFC policy on disclosure of information in February 2006.

[126] Replaced by new versions of the World Bank Group Environmental, Health and Safety (EHS) Guidelines in April 2007.

these institutions. In addition, the EBRD 1996 Environmental Policy and Environmental Procedures and the 2000 Disclosure of Information Policy[127] have been applied to this project, requiring the application of pertinent EU environmental standards.

IFC financing to the BTC pipeline covers the operations in Azerbaijan, Georgia and Turkey, while the EBRD only covers those in Azerbaijan and Georgia, as it does not operate in Turkey.

The due diligence process

IFC and EBRD due diligence on the BTC project officially commenced with the signing of the joint mandate letter in December 2001.[128] However, both multilateral development institutions suggested that even prior to that they provided inputs into the scoping document for the draft ESIA.[129] According to the IFC guidelines for category-A projects, the banks required project sponsors to prepare separate ESIAs for Azerbaijan and Georgia and EIA for Turkey to comply with each country's requirements. Preparation of the ESIAs/EIA commenced in 2001 with initial scoping meetings with affected communities, and interaction continued in the form of a number of environmental and socio-economic baseline surveys. The draft ESIAs and the EIA were released in May and June 2002 respectively, as part of the host country disclosure process.[130] The main issues covered by the ESIAs included: temporary economic disruption (mainly cropping and grazing) and limited permanent use of land (no physical resettlement); compensation measures for displaced fishermen near the Ceyhan terminal and other informal users of common property resources; potential impacts on various vulnerable groups (e.g. the elderly and ethnic minorities); alternative analysis of pipeline corridors and pipeline alignment within the preferred corridor; impacts on biodiversity; oil-spill prevention and response planning; and worker and public health and safety.

The ESIA/EIA release was followed by a sixty-day consultation period with national governments, affected villages, NGOs and civil society along the pipeline. This process generated numerous comments that were incorporated into the draft ESIAs/EIA that were finalized for host

---

[127] New policies and guidelines are now in place. See: www.ebrd.com/enviro/policy/index. htm

[128] IFC, 'BTC Pipeline and ACG Phase 1 Projects Environmental and Social Documentation – IFC Response to Submissions Received During the 120-day Public Comment Period' (27 October 2003), available at: www.ifc.org.

[129] *Ibid*, p. 36. EBRD, 'Baku–Tbilisi–Ceyhan Pipeline Project'.   [130] IFC, 'BTC Pipeline'.

government purposes.[131] Moreover, in addition to the public consultations held by BTC, the IFC together with EBRD also decided to meet
formally with project stakeholders so that they could validate the sponsors' consultation efforts and also ensure the respective board would be
well informed about public responses. In August/September 2003 a
series of six multi-stakeholder forums (MSFs) run by independent facil-
itators was held along the pipeline route (two in each country) and were
attended by over 800 people. There have also been over eighty NGO
meetings between the IFC and NGOs over the period 2001 to 2003,
making this project one of the most community/NGO-interactive projects completed to date.[132]

Then, in response to specific questions raised by the lenders following
the review of the ESIAs and the HGAs, BTC Co. was also asked to
prepare supplemental documentation to demonstrate that the project
adhered to IFC safeguard policies and guidelines. This included the
supplementary lender information pack (SLIP) which contained detailed
information on environmental and social matters related to the BTC
project including: a discussion of the environmental standards that apply
to the project such as standards on air emissions, water discharge and
noise emissions; an analysis of the power generation option; an approach
to groundwater protection; a summary of project benefits; the project
environmental investment plan; the project community investment
plan; an analysis of compliance regarding IFC Policy OP 4.04 on natural
habitat and OPN 11.03 on cultural property; and detailed information
on issues specific to each country.[133]

On the basis of the findings of the ESIAs and EIA, an environmental
and social action plan (ESAP) was prepared for the project detailing how
impacts would be avoided, mitigated or compensated, including numerous contractor control plans (CCPs) and BTC Co. management plans.
The CCPs set forth the potential risks posed by the project, the details of

---

[131] *Ibid.* pp. 18–21. Each in-country approved ESIA was subject to a 60-day in-country
public disclosure period, during which governments and regulators had an opportunity
to review and comment on the documents. The Azerbaijani, Georgian and Turkish
governments provided ESIA comments after which addenda to the Azerbaijani and
Georgian ESIAs and an amended Turkish EIA responding to the comments were
prepared. The amended Turkish EIA and the Azerbaijani and Georgian addenda
were publicly disclosed and reviewed by the relevant government, each of which
subsequently approved the applicable in-country ESIA package. The ESIA/EIA for
Azerbaijan, Turkey and Georgia were finally approved by the respective governments
in September, October and November 2002, respectively.
[132] *Ibid.*   [133] SLIP documents available at: www.bp.com.

mitigation measures to be implemented and the monitoring that would be undertaken to ensure that the mitigation measures were being adequately implemented. The IFC and EBRD established procedures for monitoring the implementation of these mitigation measures.[134]

The framework and procedures to be followed to address land acquisition, compensation and measures for restoration of livelihood for populations affected by construction of the BTC pipelines were detailed in guides to land acquisition and compensation (GLAC) and the resettlement action plan (RAP). Copies of the GLAC (which are user-friendly summaries of the full RAP) were distributed to affected communities in September 2002. The full RAPs were released in December 2002. Finalization of some land acquisition agreements commenced in early 2003 and by September 2003, 99 per cent, 69 per cent and 77 per cent of land required had been acquired in Azerbaijan, Georgia and Turkey respectively.[135] The IFC also required the development of an updated public consultation disclosure plan (PCDP), a Georgia-specific route study, a regional review and various other supplemental studies,[136] and that the sponsors release the HGAs between the project sponsors and the host governments to the public.[137]

Given the exceptional nature of the BTC project, the sponsors agreed to a programme of pre-financial close construction monitoring to enable the IFC and EBRD to monitor compliance closely during early stages of construction. The monitoring was carried out through visits by the IFC and EBRD supported by independent advisers[138] and followed by post-financial monitoring. For the purposes of the latter the companies D'Appolonia SpA and WorleyParsons were appointed in early 2004 as the post-financial close independent environmental consultants (IECs) to the lender group. The overall role of the IECs was to assess and report to the lender group on the compliance of the project with the environmental and social provisions contained within the respective project ESAPs, the associated CCPs and BTC (and ACG) management plans and with HSE management systems over the duration of the loan.[139]

The environmental and social assessment package produced for the IFC and EBRD due diligence process was released on 11 June 2003 and allowed for a 120-day comment period. The package included 46 volumes

---

[134] EBRD, 'Baku–Tbilisi–Ceyhan Pipeline Project'.   [135] IFC, 'BTC Pipeline'.
[136] See IFC website on the project at: www.ifc.org/ifcext/btc.nsf/Content/Project_Documents.
[137] IFC, 'BTC Pipeline'.   [138] EBRD, 'Baku–Tbilisi–Ceyhan Pipeline Project'.
[139] EBRD, 'Independent Recourse Mechanism'.

of more than 11,000 pages. According to the IFC this is 'the largest environmental and social document ever released'.[140] Finally, the boards of both the IFC and EBRD approved the financing for the BTC project on 4 and 11 November 2003 respectively.[141]

Main criticisms of the multilateral financial institutions' environmental and social approach to the projects

Both the IFC and EBRD received several comments from civil society including national and international NGOs, local communities and other institutions such as the Netherlands Commission for Environmental Impact Assessment (NCEIA).[142] They argued that the due diligence processes conducted by the institutions were inadequate when assessing several of the environmental and social impacts of the project and also breached several key institutional policies. Project implementation was also particularly critical for the BTC Co., especially if it did not fulfil the obligations assumed in the ESIA and the RAP. This is because these multilateral financial institutions had been relying to a large extent on information provided by the project sponsor (not BTC Co. itself) during due diligence instead of having to conduct independent investigations in order to be assured. Main criticisms are summarized in Box 12.2.

BOX 12.2 Summary of key criticisms made of IFC/EBRD's due diligence

- Violation of IFC Policy OP 4.01 on environmental assessment/EBRD environmental policy and environmental procedures due to:
  - inadequate assessment of route alternatives for the pipeline;
  - failure to take into account the impacts of the pipeline routing in Georgia, in particular the area of Lake Tsalka and area near the Borjomi National Park – source of Borjomi mineral water, one of Georgia's main exports;
  - claim that the BTC pipeline and ACG Phase 1 projects had not been properly planned; nor had cumulative impacts been adequately assessed; nor had a strategic environmental assessment (SEA) been conducted;

---

[140] All the documents are available in Azerbaijani, English, Georgian, Russian and Turkish languages.
[141] IFC, 'BTC', at: www.ifc.org/btc; EBRD, 'EBRD board approves BTC Pipeline Financing', press release, 11 November 2003, at: www.ebrd.com/new/pressrel/2003/142nov11.htm.
[142] For a list of civil society submissions to the IFC, see: www.ifc.org/ifcext/btc.nsf/Content/Correspondence; for a list of civil society submissions to EBRD and EBRD responses, see: EBRD, 'Independent Recourse Mechanism'.

- construction of the BTC pipeline began before EIA approval;
- inadequate assessment of impacts on flora and fauna;
- failure to complete an adequate baseline study;
- inadequate treatment of seismic risks;
- failure to reduce or remedy risk of oil spills at Ceyhan and of decommissioning;
- insufficient analysis of species;
- failure to present original data;
- methodological gaps not indicated in the EIA;
- inadequate consultation with affected villagers;
- independence of the EA experts called into question;
- failure to address transboundary impacts of tanker traffic; and
- failure to address indirect impacts on climate change.
- Violation of IFC Policy OP 4.04 on natural habitats due to:
  - consultation process began too late and construction of pipeline began too early to permit project sponsors to tap into knowledge of local communities with regard to natural habitats;
  - project sponsors failed to provide adequate information to affected people with regard to protection of natural habitats, and to their rights in relation to that; project sponsors underreported likely negative impacts of project;
  - views of local communities or NGOs were insufficiently taken into account regarding impact of project on natural habitats;
  - project sponsors failed to conduct sufficient research into local ecosystems to understand or accommodate local communities' roles in relation to natural habitats;
  - local communities had not been given a significant role in planning, designing, implementing or monitoring project in relation to natural habitats.[143]
- Violation of World Bank Policy OD 4.30 on involuntary resettlement due to:
  - displacement took place before compensation was completed;
  - insufficient level of compensation;
  - inadequate consultation with affected communities on land expropriation and compensation;
  - affected communities not properly informed of their rights with respect to land expropriation;
  - no consultation on resettlement alternatives;
  - not adequately considering specific impacts of land expropriation on vulnerable groups and ethnic minorities;

---

[143] Baku–Ceyhan Campaign, 'Evaluation of Compliance of the Baku–Tbilisi–Ceyhan (BTC) pipeline with the Equator Principles: Supplementary Appendix to EIA Review – BTC pipeline' (Turkey section), 11, available at: www.bakuceyhan.org.uk/publications/Equator_Principles.doc.

BOX 12.2 (cont.)

- failure to treat customary land users equally or fairly; and
- RAP approved by IFC staff as 'fit for purpose' prior to its completion – for example, the resettlement plan for fishing communities was not finalized.
- Violation of the World Bank Policy OPN 11.03 on cultural property due to:
  - failure to acknowledge links between local people and cultural heritage;
  - failure to obtain comprehensive inventory of cultural heritage resources before construction;
  - failure to predict or adequately prevent likely impacts of construction on cultural resources;
  - failure to consult local people with regard to cultural heritage and route planning;
  - failure to engage local people as stakeholders in preservation of cultural resources;
  - inadequate mitigation measures;
  - survey methods had been cursory and superficial; and
  - ongoing destruction of cultural resources.
- Violation of the World Bank OD 4.20 policy on indigenous peoples:
  - serious concerns were expressed due to the IFC's decision not to apply this policy to the affected Kurdish population in Turkey.
- Violation of IFC policy on public disclosure/EBRD policy on public disclosure:
  - inability of vulnerable groups (especially Kurds) to express their views freely in the socio-political context of Turkey and specifically, when representatives of the central government authority had been present during consultations;
  - language used for consultations (specifically scarce use of Kurdish-language media, particularly with reference to women);
  - lack of comprehensiveness of the groups identified and selected for consultation (some potentially relevant consultees apparently omitted);
  - inappropriate choice of consultation or mechanisms for certain groups; and
  - in general, consultation procedures took place too late in the process.
- Regarding the legal regime:
  - several NGOs hold the view that although BTC has resolved some of the problems raised by the HGAs (see above, pp. 389–90) there are still some problems in protecting the rights of affected people, issues that need to be resolved;
  - conflicts between the HGAs and Turkey's accession agreements; and
  - in Turkey, there were accusations of massive use of emergency powers normally reserved for national disasters to acquire land without compensation being agreed.

In some cases, civil society organizations and communities addressed formal complaints to the ombudsman bodies of the banks – the CAO in the case of the IFC and the Independent Recourse Mechanism (IRM) in the case of EBRD – complaining that BTC was not fulfilling the obligations assumed in the ESIA and RAP.[144]

Both the IFC[145] and EBRD[146] addressed comments received from the civil society organizations during their due diligence process. In general they dismissed the criticisms and argued that after careful review of all comments received they determined that the environmental and social documentation was compliant with all their institutional safeguard policies, procedures and guidelines. According to the banks, the sponsors, using IFC guidance and policies, conducted 'world class' ESIAs and mitigation measures (including resettlement/compensation) and public consultation processes.[147] In many cases they argued the project sponsors had gone beyond the multilateral banks' policies. These included, for example, arranging for a 120-day consultation period instead of 60 days or the use of NGOs to assist in the land acquisition and compensation process and initiation of national Community Investment Programmes (CIPs) for communities affected by the pipeline. Moreover, the IFC also noted that the preparation of the RAPs and GLAC was not a requirement of any of the three governments involved, and preparation of the GLAC is not an IFC requirement either but another example of an 'above and beyond' measure taken to ensure landowners were well informed and had easy-to-use information at their disposal.[148]

However, the multilateral banks also recognized that there were numerous implementation challenges as the project progressed that would require ongoing monitoring, supervision and adjustments/improvement where needed.[149] Examples of where challenges arose include the involuntary resettlement proceedings considering the complex land acquisition process involving over 17,700 parcels of land.[150] Regarding the legal framework of the project and the HGAs, the IFC argued that while they themselves did not participate in the HGA negotiations and required project sponsors to disclose the HGAs to the

---

[144] For a summary of complaints lodged with the IFC CAO during the years 2003 to 2006, see: www.cao-ombudsman.org/cases/; for a list of complaints filed with the EBRD IRM on the BTC project, see: www.ebrd.com/about/integrity/irm/register.htm.
[145] IFC, 'BTC Pipeline'.   [146] EBRD, 'Independent Recourse Mechanism'.
[147] IFC, 'BTC Pipeline'.   [148] *Ibid.*   [149] *Ibid.*   [150] *Ibid.*

public, it believed the HGAs conformed to the laws of the countries concerned, as passed by their parliaments. These types of arrangements in projects of this nature were claimed to be necessary in order to provide a reasonable framework for their implementation where none existed before.[151]

On the other hand, external reviews of the due diligence process conducted by IFC/EBRD highlighted some shortcomings. For instance, a review of compliance of the EAs with IFC and EBRD policies commissioned by the UK Department for International Development (DFID)[152] concluded that for the environmental assessment policies, consultation processes with respect to 'draft' and final ESIA reports and to the ESAP were not held in time. Moreover, construction activities had commenced without full completion and acceptance by all governments and members of the lender group, of environmental and social management documents, systems and procedures. Though this situation was not contrary to any of the IFC/EBRD policies, procedure, and guidelines, it was certainly not consistent with good international ESIA practice.

Regarding PCDP policies, the report pointed to two main problems. First, PCDPs were not put in place straight after completion of the scoping stage. For instance, the Azerbaijan PCDP was issued as a draft in April 2003 at the end of the ESIA process which overlapped with the start of construction works. Second, the PCDPs had not demonstrated consultation techniques sufficient to deal with differences across vulnerable groups – living along the pipeline route – and their access to power and knowledge.[153]

Regarding policy OD 4.20 on indigenous people, the report argued that the IFC decision not to apply this policy to the Kurdish population was the result of a conscious decision and it is within the IFC's rights to decide which policies apply to a project. This is claimed to be a contentious decision. The IFC considered that the Kurds are not sufficiently dependent on subsistence agriculture or alienated from wider socio-political processes to be classed as 'indigenous' even though they meet the other key criteria as set out in OD.4.20. Many NGOs take the opposite view. The report concluded that based on this analysis a case can be made for and against the application of OD 4.20 and therefore it was not a clear-cut issue.

---

[151] Jasmin Tayyab, civil society coordinator of IFC in a letter to Platform and CEE Bankwatch; available at: www.carbonweb.org/documents/ifc.pdf.
[152] BMT Cordah Ltd, *Compliance Review.*   [153] *Ibid.*

Furthermore, a review of IFC/EBRD's environmental and social due diligence process, conducted by USAID in October 2003 under the framework of its own due diligence process, also questioned some elements. This included an analysis of route alternatives that was not conducted according to standard EIA practices and did not meet USAID internal standards. The review also claimed that inadequate critical baseline information and impacts analysis was used to determine necessary mitigation measures. In addition the review identified other environmental and social issues detailed in Box 12.3.[154]

USAID review of the ESIA process for the BTC pipeline[155]

The USAID review of the Georgian ESIA for the BTC project revealed that the analysis of alternatives and key baseline data associated with the project were insufficient, and did not meet USAID internal standards (22 CFR 216). The review revealed key elements that were missing in project documents including the ESIA, addendum and CCPs:

- An analysis of route alternatives was not conducted according to standard EIA practices:
  - At regional level, the final ESIA discussed five strategic route options and concluded that the 'Baku–Tbilisi–Ceyhan route represented the lowest environmental risk option'. However, the assessment lacks transparency since documents supporting this conclusion were not available to the public to review. Therefore, it is unclear how environmental and social impacts were factored into the risk assessment and decision-making process for selecting the final strategic route. For the strategic and national levels of corridor selection the analysis needed to provide a thorough description of alternatives that facilitated a side-by-side comparison in terms of their technical, social, environmental, economic and security risks and benefits. The same information was also needed for segments of the preferred 500-metre ROW.
- Critical baseline information, impact analyses for determining to what extent impacts can be mitigated and mitigation measures were absent:
  - Hydrogeology in the Borjomi region: additional research was necessary to bridge the information gap highlighted by Georgian and other scientists. Additional research was needed to carry out a proper assessment of the risks of pollution of groundwater springs and mineral water aquifers to determine if the pipeline route presented an acceptable risk and, if so, to develop mitigation measures using the most precise and accurate information possible.

---

[154] Transmittal letter from USAID to the Department of Treasury, 29 October 2003, available in USAID, 'Multilateral Development Bank', Appendix C.
[155] *Ibid.*

- New and/or improved access roads: prior to additional road construction/ improvements, complete analysis of the entire road development in conjunction with the pipeline ROW development needed to be undertaken to determine the extent of impacts (direct, indirect and cumulative) and to identify proper avoidance and mitigation measures.
- Outstanding biodiversity data issues: prior to additional construction, key deficiencies in data collection for endangered species along the pipeline ROW needed to be obtained. This data should have included estimates of population size and habitat use, i.e. feeding and nesting sites. A clear methodology and decision-making process were needed for determining when pre-clearance surveys were required to be delineated within the context of biodiversity impact and adequate time allotted to conduct surveys and develop mitigation measures and monitoring plans. A biodiversity-monitoring plan needed to be developed and implemented for the entire project. Examples of missing data include, for the Georgian ESIA for instance: no identification of all sections of the pipeline where species are protected by Georgian law; no inclusion of a quantitative evaluation of endangered species to help determine impacts, mitigation measures and monitoring programmes. Specific examples include the treatment of the endemic Caucasus black grouse and grey partridge, as well as aquatic species. In the case of Turkey, inadequate attention was given to critical wetlands, bird assessments and endangered species. The latter is something the BTC's document acknowledges when it states 'Turkey is relatively under-surveyed', but it appeared to have made no effort to improve data gaps.
- Blind faults: the presence of blind faults should have been assessed through seismic surveys. This would have provided the missing information required to review the various routes thoroughly and improve pipeline alignment along environmentally sensitive areas of the route.

In addition to these concerns about the ESIA, USAID's review identified the following substantive environmental and social issues under Title XIII of the International Financial Institutions Act:

- lack of government capacity to oversee and monitor construction and operation phases of project, including interaction between affected communities and project sponsor;
- lack of definition of mechanisms for transparent revenue management from oil production/transit proceeds;
- potential cumulative negative impacts of non-ACG oil (which may not be produced following relevant MDB and/or international environmental and social standards) transported via BTC pipeline; and
- absence of a decommissioning plan and of designated resources for pipeline decommissioning.

The issue of pipeline coating has also led to questioning of the adequacy of the multilateral banks' due diligence processes but that appeared in the public domain after IFC/EBRD had approved the loan. The issue is basically about shortcomings in the selection of the material for the anti-corrosion coating of the pipeline, leading to the use of inadequate material. The issue raised significant concern over the safety of the pipeline as well as additional criticisms of the due diligence process conducted by multilateral financial institutions. In particular, the issue was raised by the UK Parliament in the context of an inquiry as to the adequacy of the due diligence processes conducted by the UK Export Credit Guarantee Department (ECGD) – a junior partner in the lender group of banks in the BTC project.[156]

The UK Parliament's House of Commons Trade and Industry Select Committee asked the ECGD to report on the coating issue after revelations in the *Sunday Times* newspaper on 15 February 2004[157] that BP, the operator of the project, decided to ignore internal warnings that its coating would fail to seal the pipeline's welds from corrosion and also that BP failed to disclose this information to the lenders so as not to jeopardize the lending. The article maintained that the information was available in a critical internal BP report, dating from November 2002. Though at the beginning of the enquiry ECGD maintained the 'pipeline was safe', after further MPs' allegations and enquiries, ECGD finally admitted to Parliament that there were problems with the coating selection as the coating system had no track record and the pipeline was likely to fail some time during its forty-year operational life.[158]

On the other hand, there is no evidence suggesting any other major reaction from the other multilateral financial institutions involved in financing the project. The IFC response to the issue was that they themselves and some other lenders were now satisfied with 'corrective actions' on the pipeline taken by BP.[159]

[156] The original enquiry focused on whether breaches of the World Bank Policy OD 4.30 on involuntary resettlement represent a breach of the ECGD loan agreement for the BTC project.

[157] 'BP accused of cover-up in pipeline deal', *Sunday Times*, 15 February 2004, at: www.timesonline.co.uk/tol/news/uk/article1020361.ece.

[158] UK Parliament, House of Commons, Trade and Industry Committee: Implementation of ECGD's Business Principles (Ninth Report of Session 2004–5 (8 March 2005)), available at: www.publications.parliament.uk/pa/cm200405/cmselect/cmtrdind/374/374.pdf

[159] J. Monahan, 'Principles in question', *Banker*, 7 March, 2005, 60, available at: www.equator-principles.com/documents/Principles_in_question.pdf#search=%22bank track%20BTC%22.

ECGD due diligence process

The due diligence process

The project was assessed in accordance with ECGD's underwriting procedures including an appraisal of the risks to ECGD of providing cover for the project and a review of the environmental, social and human rights impacts of the project carried out in accordance with ECGD's case impact analysis process. Under ECGD's public disclosure procedures a brief account of the project was published on its website over the period 19 May to 10 November 2003. In determining the acceptability of the impacts of the project, ECGD followed its case impact analysis process, regarding the relevant directives, policies and guidelines of the World Bank Group including the Safeguard Policies, the Pollution Prevention and Abatement Handbook and the equivalent environmental guidelines of the IFC. On the basis of this documentation the Departmental Business Principles Unit (BPU) produced a report that constituted a major element of the information considered by the Department's Underwriting Committee prior to its decision to authorize support for the project. On 17 December 2003 the Department published a 'Note of Decision' on its website generally describing the factors that were taken into account in ECGD's decision to support the BTC project. The note stated the ECGD cover for the project was subject to: ECGD's prior approval of the project's ESAP, the general oil spill response plan and the general hydrostatic testing plan; and ECGD's approval of the final project documentation.[160]

Main criticisms

Key critics include civil society groups and UK parliamentarians who questioned compliance with ECGD business principles as they relate to the government's objectives for sustainable development, environmental protection, the protection of human rights and the prevention of corruption. Main criticisms refer to ECGD reluctance to put the BPU report into the public domain, particularly as this would have provided essential insight into ECGD's decision-making process, and enhanced transparency. Critics also pointed out that the 'Note of Decision' was too general in describing the factors taken into account in ECGD's decision to support the BTC project, and therefore fell a long way short of the assessment of the project produced by the BPU. Moreover, it was also noted that ECGD reluctance to make public its own assessment of the project ran counter to the Department's professed commitment to transparency in its business.

Other critics argue that ECGD relied to a large extent on information provided by the project sponsor during the evaluation of the project and in the decision-making

---

[160] ECGD 2003, 'Note of Decision on the Baku–Tbilisi–Ceyhan Pipeline Project' (17 December 2003), available at: www.ecgd.gov.uk/btc_-_note_of_decision.doc

process and that it was too quick to accept companies' assurances that the required environmental and social standards were being observed, rather than undertake independent investigations to verify those assurances.[161]

Another set of criticisms called into question ECGD's ability to monitor the implementation of the project effectively and suggested that quality control failures in the implementation of the pipeline construction were partly due to inadequate supervision by ECGD.

ECGD response

ECGD pointed out the fact that it carried out an assessment of the financial, social, technical and environmental risks associated with the project prior to taking the decision to support the project. In arriving at its decision, ECGD was advised by a number of independent experts and was not, as was alleged, over-reliant on information provided by the project sponsors. The Department explained that, in line with normal practice for projects of this size, ECGD had, together with the other lenders, carried out a wide-ranging consultation with NGOs and other stakeholders about BTC, including NGOs in the three host countries. Where NGOs raised specific issues ECGD investigated them properly, taking advice from the independent consultants appointed by the lender group to assess the project application and monitor the implementation of the project. The ECGD's business principles adviser conducted field visits in order to clarify specific issues and to verify the findings of the Department's consultants. The BPU's report to ECGD's Underwriting Committee reviewed the concerns expressed by the NGOs during the consultation process. Where he found those concerns to be justified, he recommended that ECGD support for the project should be conditional upon action being taken by the applicant to provide a remedy to the problem. The Department accepted these recommendations and ECGD support was given to the project subject to a number of conditions, compliance with which was monitored by BPU and ECGD's consultants. On project monitoring, ECGD argued the construction phase of the project was subject to regular inspection and monitoring by the lender group's independent consultants, WorleyParsons, supplemented by less frequent site inspections by the BPU. The Department was satisfied that the regime of inspection and auditing that had been put in place would be successful in maintaining best practice during the construction of the pipeline. ECGD's business principles adviser, David Allwood, was satisfied that the construction defects identified (the pipeline coating) had been remedied by the company, which had discovered the problem with defective welding during its own quality assurance procedures and had rectified the fault before the engineering consultants visited the site.[162]

---

[161] UK Parliament, *Implementation of ECGD's Business Principles.*   [162] *Ibid.*

Commercial banks' due diligence

Over recent years a growing number of commercial banks have been adopting policies to conduct environmental and social risk assessment of the projects they are involved in. Notably, in June 2003, ten of the major commercial banks endorsed the EP, which provide a framework for banks to review, evaluate and mitigate or avoid environmental and social impacts and risks associated with projects they finance through PF. The EP are based on the IFC's environmental and social safeguard policies and apply to PF transactions over US$10 million. As of February 2006, the number of signatories to the EP grew to forty banks, which collectively represent some 80 per cent of global project finance. The EP are therefore considered the industry standard for conducting environmental and social due diligence on PF transactions.

For the BTC project, ten of the fifteen commercial banks involved in the loan were committed to the EP at the time the loan was approved (February 2004). The other five were Société Générale, BNP Paribas, Banca Intesa, Natexis Banques Populaires and San Paolo IMI.[163] The BTC project was the first category-A project under the EP and was thus considered a major test for them.[164] Similar to multilateral financial institutions supporting the pipeline, commercial banks, especially EP signatories, were targeted by civil society groups as not being in compliance with the EP. In particular, they argued there were several specific violations of the EP, for example the clauses on content of the EIA report and the clause on consultation, plus several violations of IFC standards (OP 4.01 on environmental assessment; OP 4.04 on natural habitats; OD 4.20 on indigenous peoples; OP 4.30 on involuntary resettlement; and OPN 11.03 on cultural property), with which the EP require compliance.[165] Moreover, they argued that the banks did not require improvements from BP to ensure compliance.

Commercial banks addressed some of the criticisms, providing some general information about their due diligence and their decision making relative to the project. Among the key issues highlighted by the banks as

---

[163] Except for the Natexis Banques Populaire, the rest have since adopted the EP. San Paolo IMI merged with Banca Intesa to create Intesa Sanpaolo.

[164] EP, 'BTC is the First Major Test of the EP'.

[165] Platform, 'Evaluation of compliance of the Baku–Tbilisi–Ceyhan (BTC) pipeline with the Equator Principles Supplementary Appendix to EIA Review – BTC pipeline' (Turkey section) (2003), 3, available at: www.platformlondon.org/carbonweb/documents/Equator_Principles.pdf.

influencing this decision making were: the due diligence conducted by the IFC and EBRD since they each have extensive environmental and social policies and staff experienced in environmental and social issues evaluation; and the appointment of independent environmental consultant Mott MacDonald to conduct due diligence and assess compliance with the EP. In particular, there were three banks that released public notes addressing the criticisms:

- ABN AMRO, the leader arranger of the syndicated loan noted that the bank's due diligence included: an assessment of all relevant BTC project documentation; reports by multilateral development banks; reports by independent advisers and other related institutions; and reports by NGOs. They also conducted several meetings with NGOs in relation to the project. According to the bank's own assessment, the BTC pipeline project was compliant with the EP. Moreover, the bank included an analysis of its application of the EP to the BTC project.[166]
- The Royal Bank Group highlighted the fact it worked closely with the IFC to ensure that the IFC met the social and environmental criteria enshrined in the EP and the Group would not participate in the transaction unless satisfied that the social and environmental criteria set by the EP were met by BTC.[167]
- In the case of Crédit Agricole Group, the bank highlighted the fact that it commenced its social and environmental due diligence from the outset of its involvement and it relied heavily on the work undertaken by the sponsors, IFC/EBRD and the IECs. The bank also noted that it was confident that the project was compliant with the EP.[168]

Moreover, lenders noted that BTC was a complex project and there might be diverging views on whether it was compliant with the EP. They argued that because the safeguard policies referenced in the EP were processes, and because questions needed to be asked, they required significant judgement on the part of the banks. This meant that, in spite of intensive work and good faith by all parties, people could differ on their conclusions. In this case, while some NGOs had a different view, the private-sector banks, the multilateral and bilateral agencies, the

---

[166] ABN AMRO, 'Explanation'.

[167] Email sent by RBS Investor Relations Group to Platform, 19 November 2003, available at: www.platformlondon.org/carbonweb/documents/RBS_reply.pdf.

[168] Crédit Agricole, letter to Platform, 2 February 2004, available at: www.platformlondon. org/carbonweb/documents/credit_agricole_reply.pdf.

sponsors and the host governments all believed that this project incorporated significant measures to respect the environment and social concerns, and as such it should proceed.[169]

After disclosure of the problem of the inadequate pipeline coating and the fact that the project sponsor tried to conceal this information from the lenders, it seems the vast majority of the banks did not take further measures. Indeed, all the commercial banks, including both signatories to the EP and non-signatories, refused to comment on the issue at all, citing 'commercial confidentiality'.[170] Later, the IFC commented on the issue to the effect that it and some other lenders were satisfied with the 'corrective actions' on the pipeline taken by BP. However, there is no information on whether lenders placed additional requirements or conditions on the loan, or whether any other type of action was taken. On the other hand, only one bank, Banca Intesa, decided to pull out of the loan agreement presumably over concerns about safety flaws and reputation risk.[171] The bank agreed to invest in BTC because of the involvement of the IFC. However, when major problems came to light in 2004 regarding the selection of the pipeline corrosion protection system, the bank decided to pull out, selling out its quota in the consortium.[172]

The commercial banks have been under direct attack for their alleged lack of due diligence on the BTC pipeline. NGOs have warned the banks that a financial risk may arise from their being sued for their part in the environmental and social damage if the pipeline should leak and it could be proved they knew about the issue. The warning to the boards and legal departments of the banks came in a letter from British, Georgian and Azeri campaign groups who have been monitoring the pipeline's impacts. The banks, including the Royal Bank of Scotland and ABN AMRO, would be liable to Turkish, Georgian and Azeri claimants if they had prior knowledge of a potential cause of pipeline failure yet failed to act to remove the risk of pollution.

---

[169] Monahan, 'Principles', 60.
[170] G. Muttitt, 'Disaster in the pipeline: Baku–Tbilisi–Ceyhan' (May 2004), Platform, available at: www.carbonweb.org/documents/disaster.pdf
[171] M. Gillard, 'The Contract of the Century', Spinwatch (29 November 2004), available at: www.spinwatch.org/reviews-mainmenu-24/61-oil-industry/118-con-tract-of-the-century.
[172] Baku–Ceyhan Campaign, 'Major Private Backer Pulls out of Embattled BP Oil Pipeline. Italy's Largest Bank Selling its $60 Million Stake in Baku–Ceyhan Project' (1 December 2004), available at: www.bakuceyhan.org.uk/press_releases/intesa.htm. See also Monahan, 'Principles'.

In the same vein, a Belgian NGO, Proyecto Gato, lodged a formal complaint against three Belgian banks (Dexia, KBC and ING – all three signatories to the EP) through the OECD's guidelines on multinational enterprises. The complaint also centred on the pipeline-coating issue and on the undue constraint that the project's legal documents had on host governments' regulating powers.[173] The case is still pending.[174]

Critical analysis of the links between PF, sustainable development and human rights

Sustainable development opportunities that arise from PF institutions' environmental and social due diligence

There are some positive links that can be expected where the IFC and other multilateral financial institutions are involved in the PF arrangement:

- IFC environmental and social procedures act as bait to encourage positive sustainable development impacts. They send a strong signal to other financial institutions regarding the environmental and social 'health' of the projects: the IFC has a comprehensive set of procedures for conducting environmental and social assessments, which it applies – though not without shortcomings – to all the projects it funds. It also has the mandate to increase the development contribution of the projects it funds.[175] Since IFC participation in the loan is essential for its political risk mitigation effect, the corporation's decision on whether or not to finance the project/or to ask for additional requirements on environmental and social grounds sends a strong signal to the rest of the financing institutions involved including other multilateral financial institutions and commercial banks.
- IFC involvement ensures an EIA process more open to public scrutiny: the IFC has a disclosure policy which means its due diligence processes are more open to public scrutiny than, for example, the policies of commercial banks. IFC disclosure policy provides an

[173] Muttitt, 'Disaster'.   [174] OECD Guidelines (2009).
[175] For a critical analysis of IFC procedures, see Chapter 7 in this book, on human rights impact assessments and PF, by Tamara Wiher. For 'avoidance over compensation' priority in IFC approach argument see Chapter 5 in this book.

opportunity for other stakeholders to have an influence on the process. This can be realized either by providing insights on unaddressed or poorly addressed areas or by being vigilant over whether the IFC is sticking to its own policies for conducting environmental and social assessments. In the specific case of the BTC pipeline, one example is when the IFC required the project sponsors to disclose the HGAs. This provided the opportunity for civil society groups to comment on the contracts and to highlight areas that conflicted with sustainable development and human rights goals.

- Additional positive links associated with multilateral financial institutions' involvement in the loan: the BTC, EBRD and BP agreed to establish a programme of sustainable socio-economic development activities that will be undertaken once economic activity declines following the completion of the BTC construction phase in 2005. This initiative aims to stimulate long-term sustainable development in the non-oil sector in the region through provision of financing and grants. BP is ready to commit some US$25 million to the programme, with EBRD having agreed to match BP's commitment. EBRD and BP hope to be able to attract further commitments to this facility raising a total amount of up to US$100 million to be invested over the first ten years of operations, commencing in 2005.[176]

- Commercial banks' commitments to the EP provide opportunities to improve sustainable development impacts of the projects: the EP are a set of guidelines to conduct environmental and social assessments according to the IFC guidelines, which only apply to PF transactions. At the time the loan was agreed, ten of the fifteen commercial banks involved in the BTC loan were committed to the EP. As noted above, the BTC project was the first category-A project under the EP and therefore considered a major test for the EP.

- EP provide a window of opportunity to scrutinize commercial banks' practice: since EP are a public commitment made by the banks endorsing them, and the EP are linked to familiar procedures such as the IFC guidelines, they provide a window of opportunity for civil society to intervene in the process and to promote/advocate better practice where non-compliance is suspected.

- Reputation matters: one of the key motivations of the banks to engage with better environmental and social practice is to have some assurance that their financing actions will not become subject to negative

---

[176] EBRD, 'Baku–Tbilisi–Ceyhan Pipeline Project'.

publicity.[177] Indeed, the decision of Banca Intesa to sell its part of the loan due to concerns about safety flaws and reputation risk may illustrate this point.

Sustainable development and human rights challenges arising from PF

There are several issues arising from the financing process of the BTC pipeline case study that highlight a number of points that need to be addressed so as to improve the sustainable development impacts of the project:

- Financial institutions rely too heavily on the due diligence process conducted by the IFC: both multilateral financial institutions such as EBRD and ECGD as well as commercial banks have relied heavily on the due diligence process conducted by the IFC, rather than undertake their own independent processes. This provides less room to identify additional project gaps, as opposed to each institution conducting an independent process. One example where gaps were not detected by the IFC was the issue of the wrong selection of the pipeline coating. The issue was not detected during the IFC due diligence process, nor by any of the other institutions because they relied on the information provided by the IFC, the project sponsors and the IECs jointly appointed by the lender group. This issue also leads to the next point.
- Too much reliance on the information provided by the project sponsor and very little independent verification: this applies to both multilateral financial institutions such as the IFC and EBRD, commercial banks and the IECs. In general, there is a marked tendency for the financial institutions involved in the loan to rely on the information provided by the project sponsor and not to conduct an independent verification of the information. In the case of BTC, though lenders did hire an IEC to conduct the environmental and social due diligence and the monitoring processes, the evidence also shows that the IEC, at least in the case of the coating issue, only conducted a desk review which mostly relied on the information provided by the project sponsor.[178]

---

[177] M. Spek, *Financing Pulp Mills: An Appraisal of Risk Assessment and Safeguard Procedures* (Bogor: Center for International Forestry Research, 2006), p. 54, available at: www.cifor.cgiar.org/publications/pdf_files/Books/BSpek0601.pdf.

[178] Baku–Ceyhan Campaign, 'Government Admits Failing BP Pipeline Was Experimental Engineering', by Michael Gillard (24 November 2004), available at: www.bakuceyhan. org.uk/publications/corrosion.pdf

- Need for more standardization in reporting on how implementation and compliance with environmental and social procedures are measured: as noted by the commercial banks themselves, policies referenced in the EP are processes, and questions need to be asked; they require significant judgement on the part of the banks. This means that different institutions can differ in their conclusions on the same project. This point could be improved through the integration of an independent compliance mechanism similar to the CAO or the IRM in the IFC and EBRD respectively.
- Need for information disclosure from commercial banks: commercial banks often cite 'client confidentiality' as a barrier to avoid disclosure of their involvement in PF transactions. Commercial banks do not have disclosure policies that oblige them to disclose how they are conducting their social and environmental due diligence processes or how they guide their decision-making processes. Indeed, as illustrated above, IFC disclosure policy provides some opportunities to improve the sustainable development impacts of the BTC pipeline. Improved transparency from commercial banks would also serve to improve levels of trust and relationships with civil society.
- Need for financial institutions to be more proactive in situations of negligence: the behaviour of the majority of financial institutions is called into question by their apparent lack of reaction to evident shortcomings such as in the selection of the pipeline coating, where the project sponsor covered up the information to avoid jeopardizing the financing of the project. On the one hand, improvements must be made to how the banks conduct their due diligence process (i.e. extensive and independent verification as highlighted in the point above) so as to increase the possibilities of detecting problems early in the process and minimize the likelihood that problems of this nature appear after the loan is agreed. On the other hand, financial institutions have a responsibility towards the projects they fund and according to the IFC guidelines and the EP, they are committed to monitoring the project to verify compliance. However, it seems they make no provisions for when flaws of this nature (i.e. serious negligence from the project sponsors) do happen. This points to the need for financial institutions to be proactive in a situation when there is strong evidence of negligence by imposing, for example, conditions/penalties on the project sponsors beforehand so as to avoid/ minimize the likelihood of this type of situation.
- Timing: this is important in order to have the opportunity to influence the sustainable development impacts of the project. In the case of the

BTC pipeline, the sponsor commenced with construction activities before the financial institution had finalized its due diligence processes and even before the release of the final EIA for public comment. Commencing construction activities before any thorough review has been made of the final EIA by the respective financial institutions, civil society and the affected communities makes it extremely difficult to change the dynamics of the project to avoid, eliminate or mitigate any potentially adverse impacts, especially when this involves modifications in the design, construction and operations phases. Though this is consistent with IFC policy, it goes against good international ESIA practice. This points to the need to align IFC policy with good ESIA international practice by commencing construction activities only once the due diligence activities have finished and produced results in support of further development of the project and all concerns arising out of the ESIA report have been duly addressed.

- Period of coverage: financial institutions should be responsible for the whole life of the projects they fund and not only until the repayment of the loan has been completed. In the BTC pipeline, financial institutions provided for pre-financial close construction monitoring and also for post-financial monitoring activities during the construction phase. However, there are several impacts that might occur during the pipeline operation or even during the pipeline closure which also require monitoring. However, at present there is no evidence of monitoring activities or any leverage point on the part of financial institutions after the loan is repaid. These measures are important to give the lender the incentive to comply with the environmental and social commitments contained in the ESIA and the ESAP. Moreover, there is evidence suggesting that such post-loan measures might be needed. Indeed, USAID noted the lack of a detailed decommissioning plan for any of the three countries. The handover of facilities to state-owned SOCAR (Azerbaijan's state-owned oil and gas company) and GIOC (Georgian International Oil Corporation) will occur after twenty years when the oilfield productivity is below profitable rates unless supplemented with oil from other sources. Therefore, the source of financial resources that would be ultimately required for decommissioning is uncertain. This is particularly worrying considering that SOCAR does not have a sound environmental performance record with other oilfields under its management regime.[179]

---

[179] USAID, 'Multilateral Development Bank', 30.

13

The Orion and CMB pulp plants in Uruguay

ANNIE DUFEY WITH CONTRIBUTION FROM
DIANA MORALES

Introduction

The research questions

What are the links between project finance (PF), foreign direct invest-ment and sustainable development and human rights issues? To what extent does the use of PF accentuate the positive and/or negative impacts of foreign direct investment on sustainable development and human rights and through which channels?

The question can be answered in part by looking, as this chapter does, at links between the due diligence process of PF institutions involved in the financial arrangements and examining their potential impact on sustainable development and human rights issues. The 'due diligence' process is an interdisciplinary process of analysing legal, technical, environmental, social and financial risks designed to detect events that might result in total or partial project failure. Financial institutions therefore might affect the sustainable development impacts of a project by making loans or guarantees conditional on a borrower's compliance with certain environmental, social and/or human rights standards.

The case study: the Orion and CMB pulp mills

This chapter analyses these issues by looking at the Orion and CMB pulp mills located on the Uruguayan–Argentinian border. The pulp mills are sponsored by the Finnish company Botnia and the Spanish Group ENCE, respectively. The two plants together constitute the largest

Thanks to Maryanne Grieg-Gran from IIED and Sheldon Leader and Judith Schönsteiner from the University of Essex for their comments and advice on earlier versions of this chapter.

foreign investment ever in Uruguay. Key reasons for the selection of the pulp mills as a case study include:

- Institutions and the borrower are generally confidential; in the case of the two pulp mills, the International Finance Corporation (IFC), the private-sector arm of the World Bank Group, is involved in the financial arrangement. The IFC has a disclosure policy in which important information regarding the due diligence process of the projects – in particular environmental and social assessments, monitoring plans, among other key documents – is disclosed to the public. In addition, the projects have an important international dimension. The pulp mills are located on the border with Argentina and involve a multilateral financial institution, the IFC. All of this means the projects receive important public scrutiny in both countries, resulting in large amounts of information on the projects being produced by different stakeholders, including civil society groups, national governments and the financial institutions.
- To date, the use of PF in the pulp sector has been very rare. Indeed, between 1990 and January 2005 only US$1 billion was devoted to PF transactions in the pulp mill sector, which corresponds to only 2.8 per cent of total pulp mill projects.[1] Considering the current shift in pulp sector investments to Southern countries and the need to build larger plants, these projects are likely to be a significant test case for expansion of PF in the sector.

Methodology

The research is based on interviews with key stakeholders conducted in the context of a field visit to Uruguay and Argentina in July 2006. This was complemented by a review of the main literature on the Uruguayan pulp mill projects and its financing process. In particular, this included official documents and grey literature produced by the financial institutions involved, project sponsors, national governments, civil society groups and press documents among others. Special attention was given to information on the regulatory framework governing the investments in the host country and to information regarding the environmental and social due diligence processes conducted by the financial institutions involved in the loan.

---

[1] M. Spek, *Financing Pulp Mills. An Appraisal of Risk Assessment and Safeguard Procedures* (Bogor: CIFOR, 2006) (available at: www.cifor.cgiar.org/publications/pdf_files/Books/BSpek0601.pdf).

Scope of the research

This case study focuses on the process of negotiation of the PF loans and the application of IFC guidelines for conducting environmental and social assessments and the Equator Principles (EP).

The research presented some limitations. A key restraint was the non-availability of the contractual agreements between the lending banks and the borrowers. Commercial banks do not have a disclosure policy and keep information regarding their due diligence processes away from the public domain on the grounds of client confidentiality. Hence, researchers faced a major obstacle in trying to determine if stabilization clauses or other contractual arrangements in the particular projects would have an impact on sustainable development and/or human rights. Information available on the issue mostly came from civil society groups involved in the projects.

Moreover, the analysis of this study was mainly carried out during the first phase of the pulp mill project, when the original plants were about to be constructed near each other in Fray Bentos, in the Río Negro Department of Uruguay, on the border with Argentina. Much of the controversy, at the time, focused on the financial institutions' due diligence process and its lack of consideration of the cumulative impacts of the two mills. However, after so much controversy, ENCE decided to relocate its mill further south in late 2006 and sold it, due to financial difficulties, to other paper mill companies in 2009 before the plant was completed.

A final limitation comes from the nature of the issues to be analysed. These mostly refer to contractual terms, processes and the stakeholders' motivations to enter into the agreements and conduct these processes. These processes and motivations can be explained by many different factors and can also be found in other types of financing structures. They are not exclusive to the use of PF instruments.

Structure of the chapter

This chapter is structured as follows. After this brief introduction, it provides background information on the projects and their financing, before looking at the legal framework governing the investments in the host country and their links with sustainable development and human rights issues. The chapter then focuses on the lenders' approach to sustainable development, and in particular concentrates on the environmental and social due diligence processes conducted by the main multilateral financial institution involved in the loans – the IFC – and then looks to the processes followed by the commercial banks. The final section includes a critical analysis of the main links between the PF arrangement and sustainable development, looking at both opportunities and challenges that need to be addressed.

About the projects and their financing

Project descriptions

The purpose and location of the projects

Orion project   The Orion project is owned by the Uruguayan subsidiary of the Finnish company Botnia SA and involves the construction of a greenfield eucalyptus kraft pulp mill and a related port. The pulp mill has the capacity to produce 1 million metric tonnes a year of air-dried pulp (ADP) for the international market. The Orion project is located in Fray Bentos, the capital of the Río Negro Department of Uruguay, on the border with Argentina. The city is located some 230 km north-west of Montevideo and has an estimated population of 23,000. Fray Bentos is an important trade conduit as it is located on the Uruguay River and next to an international bridge that connects Uruguay to Argentina.

CMB project   The project sponsor of Celulosas de M'Bopicuá (CMB) is the Spanish group ENCE, and the project was to be operated by a wholly owned subsidiary of ENCE. The project originally involved the construction of a greenfield eucalyptus kraft pulp mill with a capacity of 500,000 tonnes a year of ADP also for the international market. The original site of the CMB project was in M'Bopicuá, a district also located in the Río Negro Department, 12 km north of Fray. In 2006, however, ENCE decided, with the consent of the governments of both Argentina and Uruguay, to relocate the pulp mill to Punta Pereira in the Colonia Department, on the Río de la Plata, some 2,000 km from the original location.[2] The new project had a planned capacity of 1 million tonnes a year.[3]

The Orion and CMB projects together constituted the largest private investment ever in Uruguay. Although the CMB project decided to relocate in late 2006, the reason why this chapter analyses both of

---

[2] The Uruguayan NGO Guayubira reported that there were even plans by ENCE to pull out of Uruguay's paper mill business altogether; see: www.guayubira.org.uy/comunicados/traslado.html.

[3] ENCE, Annual Report 2006, Letter from the Chairman, 2006, available at: www.ence.es/pdfs/Memoria_Ence_2006.pdf.

them is that key to the controversy regarding the two projects was their accumulated environmental and social impacts.

Production

Orion project   When operating at full capacity, the mill uses 3.5 million cubic metres of wood raw material a year. About 70 per cent of this wood is supplied from the plantations of Botnia's subsidiary Compañía Forestal Oriental (FOSA), most of which are situated near Fray Bentos. FOSA is a company specializing in eucalyptus cultivation, founded in Uruguay in 1990.[4] It currently owns 100,000 hectares of land, of which around 60 per cent is either planted or suitable for planting.[5] FOSA's plantations, activities and entire procurement chain have received Forest Stewardship Council (FSC) certification. Of this, 10 per cent will come from a long-term wood supply contract already signed with the Otegui Group. The remaining 20 per cent of the wood needed will be procured through long-term contracts with private forest owners, funds, foundations or cooperatives in Uruguay and Argentina. The technology to be used by the project is elemental chlorine-free (ECF). The bleached eucalyptus pulp produced by the mill will be sold largely to the paper mills of Botnia's owners in Europe and Asia.[6]

CMB project   The original CMB project would have produced bleached eucalyptus kraft pulp (BEKP) using an ECF process. The primary raw material would have been eucalyptus wood grown within about a 300 km radius of the mill, almost two-thirds of which would be sourced from EUFORES, an ENCE-owned affiliate while the remaining one-third would have come from independently owned suppliers. The pulp was due to be sold on the world market.

The relocated ENCE project in Punta Pereira was to be ready to operate in 2009 before it was sold to[7] Stora Enso and Arauco[8] in a 50/50 transaction. The purchase agreement was completed in October 2009 and

[4] In December 2006, Botnia's forestry activities in Uruguay were merged into one company, Forestal Oriental, joining FOSA and Tile Forestal. See 'Botnia's forestry operations in Uruguay merged into one company', press release, 12 July 2007, available at: www.botnia.com.
[5] See Metsä-Botnia website: Forestal Oriental, available at: www.metsabotnia.com/es/default.asp?path=284,1530,599.
[6] *Ibid.*   [7] ENCE, Annual Report 2006.
[8] Both companies are pulp and paper manufacturers; Stora Enso is of Finnish–Swedish origin and Arauco Chilean.

included approximately 130,000 hectares of owned land and plantations, and 6,000 hectares of leased lands and other operations owned by Grupo ENCE in the central and western areas of Uruguay. Within a year, the companies will decide how to develop their joint venture investment. As part of this transaction, the companies are also to acquire the Terminal Logística M'Bopicuá (TLM).[9]

Construction and costs

The total cost of the Orion plant was US$1.2 billion. Botnia conducted the civil engineering project (construction) and Andritz Oy, an Austrian company, supplied and assembled all the machinery for the plant.[10] The agreement involved a fibre line extending from wood handling through to pulp drying, as well as a chemicals recovery system. The value of the order was over €200 million. With the exception of the pulp dryers, all the main equipment – representing more than half of the order – was manufactured in Finland.[11] Botnia also contracted the Finnish chemicals group Kemira to supply the required chemicals. To this end Kemira built a chemical plant on site involving a total investment of €60 million.[12] Honeywell and Alstom supplied the entire automation system and the air pollution control systems for the mill, respectively. Regarding the civil engineering project, Botnia had some 17 or 18 contracts with Uruguayan companies involving more than 2,600 workers.[13] By November 2007 the pulp mill started its operations and between May 2008 and April 2009 reached its planned capacity of 1 million tonnes.[14]

---

[9] See ENCE website, at: www.ence.es/noticias.php?Id=210; and also Globenewswire website, at: www.globenewswire.com/newsroom/news.html?d=175684.

[10] Ronald Beare, Managing Director of Botnia SA, personal communication July 2006.

[11] Metsä-Botnia, 'Andritz Oy to supply the main process equipment for Botnia's pulp mill in Uruguay', press release, 18 May 2005, available at: www.metsabotnia.com/en/default.asp?path=204;208;210;211;812;917.

[12] Metsä-Botnia, 'Kemira selected as chemicals supplier for Botnia's pulp mill in Uruguay', press release, 4 October 2005.

[13] Ronald Beare, Managing Director of Botnia SA, personal communication July 2006.

[14] Metsä-Botnia, 'The start-up process of Botnia in Fray Bentos begins today', press release, 9 November 2007, available at: www.metsabotnia.com/en/default.asp?path=204;1490;1491;1541;1546;1927; Metsä-Botnia 'Fray Bentos mill reached its planned production', press release, 5 April 2009, available at: www.metsabotnia.com/en/default.asp?path=204;210;211;2672;2915.

The total planned cost of the original CMB project was US$660 million but after ENCE relocated the plant to Punta Pereira the planned costs escalated to an estimate of US$1,250 million.[15] ENCE started construction works in Punta Pereira in 2008[16] and halted them in 2009.

Project sponsors

Orion project   The Orion project belonged initially to Botnia SA, a company founded in 2003 in Uruguay which was 100 per cent owned by entities controlled by the sponsor (Botnia[17] 82.1 per cent, UPM 12.4 per cent and Metsäliitto 5.5 per cent). However, in 2009 the Orion project ownership changed. UPM-Kymmene signed an agreement to acquire 91 per cent of the Fray Bentos plant[18] while the remaining 9 per cent will remain property of the Uruguayan company Otegui Group.[19] The agreement will be effective and UPM will operate the plant once the project lenders have agreed to the operation.

CMB project   The original CMB project was 100 per cent owned by the Grupo Empresarial ENCE SA of Spain.[20] ENCE specializes in eucalyptus forestry and pulp production and manufactured 1.1 million tonnes of pulp in 2008, making it the second-largest producer of eucalyptus pulp in the world. The main shareholder is Retos Operativos XXI followed by Alcor Holding.

---

[15] EFT, 'Papelera Ence en Colonia. Silencio oficial. El Río de La Plata cambia de nombre', *Equipo Federal del Trabajo*, 21(4) (February 2006), available at: www.news matic.e-pol.com.ar/index.php?pub_id=99&sid=629&aid=17604&eid=21&NombreSeccion =Mercosur&Accion=VerArticulo.

[16] Infobae, 'Avanza la construcción de la segunda papelera en Uruguay', 18 August 2008, available at: www.infobae.com/contenidos/398107-0-0-Avanza-la-construcci%C3% B3n-la-segunda-papelera-Uruguay.

[17] Botnia is owned by the Metsäliitto Group (53 per cent) and UPM-Kymmene Corporation (47 per cent).

[18] UPM, 'UPM signs agreement on restructuring of Botnia ownership', press release, 22 October 2009, available at: http://w3.upm-kymmene.com/upm/internet/cms/upmcms. nsf/prv/UPM_signs_agreement_on_restructuring_of_Botnia_ownership? OpenDocument.

[19] The Otegui group is in the agribusiness sector and owns eucalyptus plantations and sawmills.

[20] ENCE was founded in 1957 and is a partially integrated forestry products company, whose primary assets and activities comprise the ownership and management of forest lands on the Iberian peninsula and in Uruguay (EUFORES) as well as three pulp mills in Spain.

Stakeholders' perceptions of the projects

Key stakeholders include the projects' sponsors, the governments of Uruguay and Argentina, the communities of Fray Bentos (in Uruguay) and Gualeguaychú (in Argentina) and the financial institutions. Stakeholders can be divided into two main groups: those supporting the projects and those opposing them.

Stakeholders supporting the initial projects include: the government of Uruguay, the projects' sponsors (Botnia and ENCE) and the people of Fray Bentos. These stakeholders' key arguments in favour of the projects are based on their contributions to the national economy and employment, including the following points:

- The Orion project involves the largest FDI investment ever in the country, equivalent to some 2 per cent of GDP (based on figures of 2005) and more than 8 per cent of the country's exports annually for an estimated period of thirty years of full production.[21]

- According to Botnia the pulp mill alone will create 8,000 direct and indirect jobs during the construction phase (of which 300 are long-term jobs).[22]

- From a broader perspective, for the Uruguayan government the projects constitute an additional step in the development of the forestry sector in the country. The forestry sector had begun to develop in Uruguay by the late 1980s when the government introduced several economic instruments such as subsidies and soft loans[23] to promote the sector. The cellulose plants therefore constitute a further step in this development pattern. Indeed, in addition to the Orion and CMB projects the Swedish–Finnish company Stora Enso started to purchase land in Uruguay with the intention of establishing fast-growing plantations. The plantations will serve a future Stora Enso pulp mill to be located in the same district of Río Negro.

- The IFC has been supporting the projects since their conception. According to the IFC, as a development institution it is supporting the projects because of the benefits they represent to the national economy and because they fit in with the World Bank Group's long-term strategy for the development of Uruguay, which recommends

---

[21] See IFC website: 'FAQs: Uruguayan pulp mills', at: www.ifc.org/ifcext/lac.nsf/Content/Uruguay_PulpMills_FAQ.

[22] HCG Environment, 'Socio-economic Study of the Impacts of Botnia SA Pulp Mill Project in Uruguay', prepared for Metsä-Botnia, June 2004.

[23] Through the Ley de Promoción Forestal of 1988.

investments in forestry and in the diversification of the country's export base to increase its competitiveness.[24] But according to IFC guidelines, the institution should also aim to increase the projects' local contributions.[25] To this end, the IFC requested further studies and requirements of the projects' sponsors in the context of the due diligence process of the two projects (see below, pp. 439, 443).

On the other hand, those opposed to the projects include the people of Gualeguaychú (in Argentina); and Uruguayan and Argentinian civil society groups supported by international non-governmental organizations (NGOs) and the government of Argentina. The main reasons for opposition are based on the perceived negative sustainable development impacts of the projects and on shortcomings in the due diligence processes conducted by the financial institutions, including the following:

- The positive economic impacts of the projects are overestimated: in the case of Botnia, for example, only a small proportion of the whole investment (less than 20 per cent) would actually be spent in Uruguay.[26] The bulk of the job creation is during the construction phase and would have very little impact on long-term jobs. Also due to the free-zone status[27] granted to the companies there will be almost no revenues paid to the government of Uruguay.
- There are significant concerns associated with potential negative environmental impacts of the projects, such as the effect on water quality due to the use of ECF instead of total chlorine free (TCF). Concerns also relate to the impacts the projects might have on the local population and on other economic sectors such as tourism and agriculture.
- The government of Argentina opposes the project due to potentially negative effects on the Argentinian population of Gualeguaychú and also accuses Uruguay of violation of the 1975 Uruguay River Statute (a bilateral treaty between the two states).
- Several groups from civil society also criticize inadequacies in the environmental and social due diligence proceedings conducted by the IFC.

---

[24] IFC website: 'FAQs', above n. 21.   [25] *Ibid.*
[26] A. Difilippo, 'Uruguay: Advierten que 80% de la inversión de Botnia no llegará al país', Uruguay Ambiental, 2006 available at: www.uruguayambiental.com/noticias/UruguayBotniaInversion.html.
[27] The free-zone status was granted in 2004 for a period of thirty years. See www.presidencia.gub.uy/resoluciones/2004101803.htm.

Project financing

Both projects approached multilateral financing institutions and commercial banks for financial support using the PF mode.

Orion project   Total costs of the Orion project are US$1,200 million, about 60 per cent of which comes from capital invested by Botnia SA and its owners, while the remaining 40 per cent is arranged through external loans. Of these external loans, one part has been applied for from the IFC and the rest from commercial banks.

The final loan arrangement consists of a US$230 million, ten-year export loan covered by Finnvera – the official state-owned export credit agency (ECA) of Finland – and a US$100 million, ten-year IFC B loan. Oy Metsä-Botnia also signed a €300 million, five-year multicurrency revolving credit facility,[28] whose coverage against political risk was provided by the Multilateral Investment Guarantee Agency (MIGA) of the World Bank.[29] The IFC and the Nordic Investment Bank (NIB), on their side, are each committed to a US$70 million loan to Botnia SA. The mandated lead arranger banks for export loan and the IFC B loan are Calyon and Nordea, while Calyon, Danske Bank and Nordea were mandated to arrange the revolving credit facility.[30]

However, it should be noted the financial deal took some time in getting finally arranged. Indeed, ING Bank was initially appointed as the global coordinator together with Nordea as the co-adviser.[31] However, ING decided to pull out in late March 2006 after being targeted by several NGOs opposing the project with the claim that it failed to comply with the EP – an industry standard for conducting environmental and social due diligence.

After ING pulled out, Calyon and the Nordea Group got involved as the main loan arrangers. Nordea is the leading financial services group in the Nordic and Baltic Sea region. Calyon is the corporate and investment banking arm of the French Crédit Agricole Group.

IFC financial support for the project was also delayed by the additional cumulative impact study (CIS) on the environmental and social impact

---

[28] Metsä-Botnia, 'Botnia's Uruguayan pulp mill project's loan agreements signed', press release, 12 March 2007, available at: www.botnia.com/en/default.asp?path=204;1490;1491;1541;1546;1657.

[29] See MIGA website: wwwqa.miga.org/sitelevel2/level2.cfm?id=1072&proj=690&ghol=514.

[30] Metsä-Botnia, 'Botnia's Uruguayan pulp mill', 2007, above n. 28.

[31] Metsä-Botnia, 'Welcome to Botnia's press conference concerning the pulp mill project in Uruguay', presentation by Erkki Varis, Botnia, 7 March 2005.

of the Orion and CMB projects required by the IFC (see below, p. 443).[32]
The final CIS results were published in September 2006, and the respective
boards of directors approved both the IFC loan and the MIGA guarantee on
21 November 2006. When the IFC and the MIGA decided on the loans, they
indicated that '[t]he two organizations, after completing a thorough review
of the facts, are convinced that the mill will generate significant economic
benefits for Uruguay and cause no environmental harm'.[33] Commercial
banks were also awaiting the results of the CIS to decide whether to support
the project. The IFC board of directors decided on the loans in November
2006, while the private banks committed to the project in March 2007.

CMB project   The total cost of the CMB project was US$660 million,
with a US$200 million investment from the IFC. The proposed IFC
investment consisted of an A loan[34] for the IFC itself of about US$50
million and a syndicated B loan from participant financial institutions of
about US$150 million.[35] The Spanish commercial bank Banco Bilbao
Vizcaya Argentaria (BBVA) was the commercial institution leading the
syndicated loan.

Due to delays during 2006 in the IFC proceedings regarding the
financing, CMB approached the Spanish state-owned corporate entity
attached to the Spanish Ministry of Economy and Finance, ICO
(Instituto de Crédito Oficial) for financial support. ICO envisaged the
provision of a US$350 million loan plus interest (7 per cent) to the
company and also asked the Spanish export credit agency CESCE
(Compañía Española de Crédito a la Exportación) to consider providing
risk insurance for ENCE.

[32] Metsä-Botnia, 'President and CEO of Botnia in Nordea Ja Calyon are the main arranging banks for Botnia's pulp mill project in Uruguay', press release, 28 April 2006, available at: www.MetsaBotnia.com/en/default.asp?path=204;208;210;211;1097;1261.
[33] IFC, 'IFC and MIGA board approves Orion pulp mill in Uruguay: 2,500 jobs to be created, no environmental harm', press release, 21 October 2006, available at: www.ifc.org/ifcext/media.nsf/content/SelectedPressRelease?OpenDocument&UNID=F76F15A5FE7735918525722D0058F472.
[34] An A loan is granted directly by the IFC to the borrower and is governed by a single loan agreement. A B loan is a syndicated loan in which the IFC sells shares of the loan to commercial banks but retains the administration of the loan and receives the guarantees. The IFC administers A and B loans by dividing payments proportionately between the A and B loans. See S. Gatti, *Project Finance in Theory and Practice* (London: Elsevier Inc.).
[35] See IFC website: 'Summary of Project Information', at: www.ifc.org/ifcext/lac.nsf/Content/SelectedProject?OpenDocument&UNID=4208C72853E61DF785257045006F993F.

In early October 2006 ENCE announced its decision to relocate the CMB plant (see above, p. 418). As a consequence, the IFC would consider financing the ENCE/CMB plant only once the corporation had the opportunity to assess the project in its new location. However, ENCE did not approach the IFC for a new loan arrangement and instead in 2008 negotiated a syndicated credit with BBVA, Caja Madrid, Sabadell Bank, ICO and Banesto.[36]

The legal framework governing the projects and contentious cases

The legal framework

The legal aspects surrounding the projects are crucial as they shape the framework for the projects' viability and control the allocation of risks between the parties.[37] Contracts must not interfere unduly with the expectation for debt repayment from project revenue. They should be designed to anticipate regulatory problems unique to the project and the environment in which the projects will exist. However, in their aim to reduce or allocate risk between the partners, these contracts may include stabilization clauses or financial arrangements that may interfere with the achievement of sustainable development goals in the host country.[38] According to human rights advocates, stabilization clauses have the potential to insulate the investor from the duty to comply with social and environmental laws that are enacted after the effective date of the investment agreement. Moreover, if the state insists on applying the changed laws it is burdened with paying compensation to the investor for new social and environmental laws. In the case of developing

---

[36] Guayubira, 'Carta de protesta al Presidente José Luis Zapatero por el apoyo del gobierno y de entidades financieras españolas al proyecto de ENCE en Uruguay', press release, 2008, available at: www.guayubira.org.uy/celulosa/creditos.html.

[37] S. L. Hoffman, *The Law and Business of International Project Finance* (2nd edn, The Hague: Kluwer Law International, 2001).

[38] According to a study conducted for the IFC and the United Nations Special Representative to the Secretary-General on Business and Human Rights on stabilization clauses and human rights, lenders consider essential the inclusion of stabilization clauses in financial contracts for the bankability of a project, especially for projects with non-recourse financing. A. Shemberg and A. Motoko, *Stabilization Clauses and Human Rights* (2008), para. 18 (available at: www.iisd.org/pdf/2008/dci_stabalization.pdf). The Botnia project falls into the latter category, as loan payments are solely sourced from the revenue stream of the project.

countries, this is very likely as rapid legislative development is normal as part of bringing the country up to the latest international standards.[39]

Two main legal frameworks govern the relationship between the government of Uruguay and the two projects' sponsors: bilateral investment agreements between the government of Uruguay and the respective governments of the country of origin of the sponsors and the Law NR 15.921 regulating the free-zone status of the projects.

Bilateral investment agreements

The investment agreement between Uruguay and Finland was signed in March 2002 and ratified by the Uruguayan Congress in April 2004. The agreement covers different aspects of inflow investment including: the promotion of investment between the two countries, non-discrimination, expropriation, compensation, revenue repatriation and controversy resolution.[40]

The agreement has been strongly criticized by different civil society groups. Main criticisms are that the agreement has been 'tailored to Botnia's needs'[41] and that the company only guaranteed the investment on the condition this agreement between the two governments was signed.[42]

Criticisms also refer to the potential implications of articles 6 and 9 of the agreement. Article 6 deals with compensation issues establishing compensation for economic losses deriving from a number of causes, including 'demonstrations' (*manifestaciones* in Spanish) that might affect the company.[43] Several stakeholders have interpreted this article to mean that if public demonstrations were to affect the company, the

[39] See R. Suda, 'The Effect of Bilateral Investment Treaties on Human Rights Realization and Enforcement', Global Law Working Paper 01/05, 2005, available at: www.law.nyu.edu/global/workingpapers/2005/ECM_DLV_015787.
[40] Parlamento Uruguay, 'Republica de Finlandia–Uruguay Acuerdo relativo a la promoción y protección de inversiones, España', Republica Oriental del Uruguay Poder Legislativo, 2006, available at: www.parlamento.gub.uy/htmlstat/pl/acuerdos/acue17759.htm.
[41] Teresa Pérez, Grupo Guayubira, personal communication, June 2006.
[42] M. Cabrera, 'Fábrica de celulosa en Fray Bentos – El escándalo de Botnia', Sol y Luna, 84 (April–May 2005), available at: http://letras-uruguay.espaciolatino.com/cabrera_miguel/celulosa_fray_bentos.htm.
[43] R. Gentili, 'Análisis de Coyuntura sobre el ALCA y el MERCOSUR No. XXVII, Enero a Marzo de 2006', Projeto de Analise da Conjuntura Brasileira, 2006, available at: www.lpp-uerj.net/outrobrasil/docs/1842006184740_Analise_Rafael_N%C2%BA27%20-%20Abr06.doc ; Guayubira (NGO), 'Guayubira position on the Investment Agreement between Uruguay and Finland', available from: www.guayubira.org.uy/english.html no date. L. Vales, 'Como Tener la Pelota bien Atada: El Usurero Pacto Binacional que la

Uruguayan government would have to compensate the company for any resulting losses. Article 9 deals with the resolution of controversy and establishes that in case of controversy between the company and the government of Uruguay the former would have the right to decide whether the case be ruled in a domestic or international court.[44]

The bilateral investment agreement between Uruguay and Spain[45] was signed in April 1992, prior to ENCE's arrival in Uruguay through EUFORES in 1990 and well after the development of the CMB pulp mill project.

Free-zone status

Both pulp mills were granted free-zone status. According to article 19, Law NR 15.921:[46] 'Users of the Free Zones shall be exempted from all national tax, created or to be created, including those requiring by law a specific exemption, as regards any activity carried out therein.' This means the companies will be 100 per cent exempt from profit tax, capital tax, VAT and import and export taxes. The free-zone status was granted to the companies in October 2004 for a period of thirty years. In return, the companies will have to pay to the government of Uruguay an annual fee determined by the highest of three different options: (a) 5 per cent of the gross income attributable to direct and indirect area services; (b) US$30,000; or (c) a variable annual sum that is calculated by multiplying U$1,000 by an established number of hectares agreed in the free-zone annex resolution. If either option (b) or (c) is used to calculate the annual fee, from 2006 onwards, the sum has to be adjusted until the expiration

Papelera Botnia le impuso a Uruguay', *Corriente Praxis*, 2006, available at: www.corrientepraxis.org.ar/spip.php/spip.php?page=imprimir_articulo&id_article=261.

[44] Although controversial, the articles in the bilateral investment treaty that have been criticized are part of the full protection and security standard common to this type of agreement. According to Luke Eric Peterson, this protection could be interpreted in a tribunal of arbitration, as it has been in some cases, as a due diligence standard and not a strict liability one that will generate automatically the right to compensation. For more on this issue, see L. E. Peterson, 'Human Rights and Bilateral Investment Treaties: Mapping the Role of Human Rights Law within Investor–State Arbitration', 2009, available at: www.ddrd.ca/site/_PDF/publications/globalization/HIRA-volume3-ENG.pdf.

[45] Parlamento Uruguay, 'España–Uruguay Promoción y Protección Recíproca de las Inversiones entre la República Oriental del Uruguay y el Reino de España', Republica Oriental del Uruguay Poder Legislativo, no date, available at: www.parlamento.gub.uy/htmlstat/pl/acuerdos/acue16444.htm

[46] Ley de Zonas Francas Nº. 15921 del 17 de diciembre de 1987, available at: www.zonafrancacolonia.com/ley.htm.

of the free zone using the Consumer Price Index – All Urban Areas established by the US government.[47]

The free-zone status granted to the companies has been the target of significant criticism by those opposing the projects. They argue that the free-zone status of the companies means there will be very little economic benefit to the country while the potential environmental and social damage will be significant.[48] Moreover, they argue that the projects' profits will be taxed in Finland and Spain, leading to a net transfer of revenue from Uruguay to these countries. Opponents also argue that, in the case of Botnia, the company only decided to proceed with the investment on the condition that the government of Uruguay granted the free-zone status.

On the other hand, Botnia argues that the free-zone status is needed to ensure the stability of Botnia's customs and tax treatment in the long term.[49]

The articles of the free-zone regulation related to tax exemptions and other fiscal benefits that regulate the relationship between the government of Uruguay and Botnia's special purpose vehicle (SPV) arguably constitute a stabilization clause that stops the government of Uruguay from imposing a more onerous taxation or tariff regime in the thirty-year period.

The Uruguay River Statute and the case at the International Court of Justice

At international level, the construction of the two pulp mills initiated a series of disputes between the governments of Argentina and Uruguay, a

---

[47] Annex 1, Resolution that established free trade zone for Botnia Fray Bentos, available at: www.ursea.gub.uy:8080/web/mnormativo.nsf/617834097FAB944E03256F33005458A8/ $file/Res%20URSEA%2027-004.pdf?OpenElement.

[48] See CEDHA *et al.* (2006), Equator Principles Compliance Complaint Regarding Proposed Pulp Paper Mill Investment in Fray Bentos, Uruguay. From Center for Human Rights and Environment (CEDHA) Argentina; Eco La Paz, Argentina; Amigos de la Tierra, Argentina; BankTrack – The Netherlands; Maan Istavaat – Friends of the Earth, Finland; Guayubira, 'Guayubira position', 35; Redes, Movimiento Mundial p/los Bosques, Amigos de la Tierra, Uruguay; Amis de la Terre, France; and Friends of the Earth International to Calyon of Crédit Agricole – France, 18 May 2006, CEDHA, Córdoba, Argentina, available at: www.cedha.org.ar/en/initiatives/paper_pulp_mills/compliance-complaintcalyon.pdf.

[49] Metsä-Botnia, 'Uruguayan government grants free trade zone status to Botnia pulp mill project', press release, 2004, available at: www.metsabotnia.com/en/default.asp?path=204;208;210;211;577;752.

controversy that has been adjudicated at the International Court of Justice (ICJ) in The Hague.[50]

Political background to the ICJ case

In January 2006 Argentina decided to take the Uruguay government before the ICJ after the High Level Technical Group (GTAN is the Spanish acronym) completed its work without reaching an agreement.

GTAN is a group of authorities from both Argentina and Uruguay set up in May 1995 by the presidents of the two countries following Argentinian opposition to the construction of the mills and the complaint that Uruguay was infringing the obligations under a bilateral treaty between both countries for the protection of the River Uruguay. GTAN was entrusted with the task of exchanging information and analysing the impacts of the projects. The group had 180 days, between August 1995 and January 2006, to carry out the study and was to produce its first report at the end of this period. However, during the process the Argentinian delegation complained that Uruguay did not hand over all the relevant available information and finally concluded in its report in January 2006 that due to the technology being used by the projects, the geographical location, the proximity to populated areas and the fragility of the aquatic ecosystem, the environment could not be preserved at the highest international level.

Before Argentina launched the petition before the ICJ, on 11 March 2006 the Uruguayan and Argentinian presidents reached a ninety-day agreement to halt the projects to allow further social, economic and environmental impact studies to be carried out and asked both companies to halt construction during this period and civil society groups to stop protests that were interrupting free transit in border bridges between Argentina and Uruguay.

However, Botnia only halted the plant construction for ten days and this was not due to financial pressure for loan repayment under the PF scheme. The loans were not in place yet and the company was financing the construction stage with its own assets. According to the company, construction works continued due to the lack of any official statement

---

[50] *Case concerning Pulp Mills on the River Uruguay (Argentina v. Uruguay)*, Request for the Indication of Provisional Measures, ICJ Order, 13 July 2006; and ICJ Judgment, 20 April 2010. Uruguay launched its own application for Provisional Measures against Argentina, for which the ICJ also made an Order on 23 January 2007. All ICJ orders and the (final) judgment are accessible at: www.icj-cij.org.

from the government of Uruguay on the issue[51] but those opposing the projects hold the view that Botnia's decision responded to fear of damaging the company's share prices in the Helsinki and NY stock exchanges.[52]

The government of Argentina strongly criticized the Uruguayan government for failing to order Botnia to halt construction activities. The government of Uruguay, on its part, argued that it did not have the legal authority to bring construction of the two plants to a halt.[53] Uruguay's refusal was probably because both companies had legal permits for construction in place and there was also the bilateral investment agreement between Uruguay and Finland to consider. An imposition by the Uruguayan government on Botnia to halt construction had the potential to give rise to a claim by Botnia under article 6 of the bilateral investment agreement.[54] Article 6 regulates compensation for losses under the most favoured nation clause and includes as one of the grounds for compensation demonstrations that create losses to the company. Although *sensu stricto* the order to suspend construction works would have come from the GTAN decision, the company could have argued that the GTAN was in the first place established because of the strength of opposition to the project expressed in several demonstrations that took place near Botnia's future plant.

After the failure of the bilateral negotiations, the two governments filed a series of complaints before different international organizations including Mercosur and the ICJ.

The 2006 ICJ order and 2010 ICJ judgment

On 4 May 2006, Argentina filed a claim against Uruguay at the ICJ and asked for so-called provisional measures. According to court documents, Argentina argues that it wants the construction of the two mills halted because Uruguay violated the 1975 Treaty by improperly and unilaterally authorizing the construction of the plants without prior

---

[51] Helsingin Sanomat, 'Metsä-Botnia continues construction of Uruguay pulp mill despite appeal by two presidents', Helsingin Sanomat international edition, 2006, available at: www.hs.fi/english/print/1135219124992.

[52] CEDHA, 'Botnia Decides to Ignore Argentine and Uruguayan Presidents' Request to Stop Construction, due to Risks to Stock Value on European Markets', 2006, available at: www.cedha.org.ar/en/more_information/botnia-continues-construction.php.

[53] M. Valente, 'Argentina: Uruguay Rejects President's Plea to Halt Pulp Mills', bilaterals. org, 2006, available at: www.bilaterals.org/article.php3?id_article=3977.

[54] Gentili, 'Análisis de Coyuntura', above n. 43; Valente, 'Argentina', above n. 53; Guayubira, 'Guayubira position'.

consultation. Under the 1975 treaty, all issues concerning the River Uruguay must be agreed by both countries. Argentina is concerned that the projects will jeopardize the environment of the River Uruguay and its area of influence affecting more than 300,000 residents in the town of Gualeguaychú, who are concerned about the significant risk of pollution of the river, deterioration of diversity, harmful effects on health and damage to fishery resources. Uruguay, on the other hand, argues that the mills will generate jobs and be under strict environmental control. On 13 July 2006 the ICJ issued its ruling on provisional measures and rejected the request.[55] The Court ruled that the construction of the mills posed no serious threat to the environment and could continue while the judges evaluated the potential risks of the pulp plants once they began operation. The final ruling of the Court was delivered on 20 April 2010 and confirmed that Uruguay had not breached any substantive obligation under international law vis-à-vis Argentina. However, the ICJ ruled in the *Pulp Mills* (*Merits*) decision that: 'it may now be considered a requirement under general international law to undertake an environmental impact assessment [EIA] where there is a risk that the proposed industrial activity may have a significant risk in a transboundary context, in particular, on a shared resource'.[56] The Court concluded that Uruguay had failed to fulfil its procedural obligation to notify and allow Argentina to participate in the transboundary EIA exercise prior to approving the proposed projects. Moreover, due diligence, and the duty of vigilance and prevention which it implies, would not be considered to have been exercised if a (state) party planning works liable to affect the regime of the river or the quality of its waters did not undertake an environmental impact assessment on the potential effects of such works.[57]

On the other hand, the ICJ was unable to confirm that the conduct of such a transboundary EIA exercise would necessarily require states to provide for consultation and public participation of the affected populations within the states potentially affected by the proposed project(s), as required by the 1991 Espoo Convention, which neither Uruguay nor

---

[55] For the ICJ resolution and the history of the proceedings, see ICJ press release 'Pulp Mills on the River Uruguay (*Argentina* v. *Uruguay*). The Court finds that the circumstances, as they now present themselves to it, are not such as to require the exercise of its power to indicate provisional measures', available at: www.icj-cij.org/icjwww/ipresscom/ipress2006/ipresscom_2006-28_au_20060713.htm.

[56] *Case concerning Pulp Mills on the River Uruguay*, ICJ Judgment, para. 204, pp. 60–1, above n. 50.

[57] *Ibid.*

Argentina is party to.[58] The ICJ here appears to be making a distinction between the lack of requirement for public participation in the trans-boundary EIA context, and its requirement during normal EIA procedures. Nevertheless, the Court held that public consultation had in fact taken place in the present case.[59] This appears to confirm the prescient observation by Knox that rather than extending the public participation principle across territorial boundaries, it is the principle of non-discrimination as to the potential extra-territorial effects of significant infrastructure projects that was applied in this case.[60]

As part of the arguments presented by Uruguay against the request for provisional measures, the representative of the government and one of its experts argued that if the Court ordered a halt to the construction of the mills, Uruguay would face irreparable damage. They specified that both companies have expressly stated that they would not wait for a decision by the Court to start with the project but would take their investments to another country.[61] Although the government of Uruguay did not elaborate further on the legal obligations that it had already contracted with both companies as part of its legal arguments in its response to Argentina, it is clear that it was under other pressures to continue with the projects which were the product of former negotiations and contractual arrangements.

In the case of Botnia, the government had already authorized the creation of the private free trade zone in favour of Botnia's SPV, Botnia Fray Bentos SA (part of the PF arrangement). In virtue of that agreement, Uruguay was obliged to allow Botnia Fray Bentos SA to operate in the free zone for a period of thirty years subject to environmental licences that were to be processed in due course and that both the government and company anticipated were going to be granted. According to article 25 of Law 15.921,[62] that regulates all free zones, the resolution authorizing the free zone is a contract and the state is under obligation to guarantee all tax and fiscal exemptions for the duration of the contract. The government had agreed to grant tariff preferences and tax exemptions to Botnia Fray Bentos in return for

---

[58] *Ibid.* para. 216, p. 64.   [59] *Ibid.* para. 219.
[60] John Knox, 'The Myth and Reality of Transboundary Environmental Impact Assessment', *American Journal of International Law*, 96(2) (April 2002), 291–319.
[61] ICJ Public Sitting, 8 June 2006 Verbatim Record, available at: www.icj-cij.org/docket/files/135/13128.pdf.
[62] Law 15.921, 17 December 1987, available at: www.zfrancas.gub.uy/espanol/legislacion/leyes/ley15921.pdf.

a guarantee investment of US$29,000,000 in infrastructure and US$913,000,000 in the actual plant.

The Treaty of Asunción, Mercosur and the 2007 ICJ order

The citizens of Gualeguaychú, an Argentinian town on the border with Uruguay, have been at the centre of the social movements opposing the plants by continuous demonstrations. They have been blocking the transit over border bridges connecting Argentina and Uruguay.[63]

Due to the disruptions caused by the blockades, in April 2006, Uruguay submitted a petition before the dispute settlement mechanism of Mercosur[64] against Argentina, arguing that Argentina was in violation of the Treaty of Asunción in relation to the free movement of goods and services between countries (article 1). Uruguay argued that Argentina did not act to lift or prevent the blockades hindering in that way the rights of Uruguay under the treaty.

The Ad-Hoc Court under the Mercosur treaty regime ruled in favour of Uruguay and decided that Argentina had violated its regional obligations in the framework of the Asunción Treaty. However, the ruling did not have any practical implications as the Ad-Hoc Court decided not to rule against any blockades that could occur in the future within the same framework. Currently, the citizens of Gualeguaychú continue obstructing the traffic across the border bridge that connects Gualeguaychú and Fray Bentos.

In the ruling, the Ad-Hoc Court recognized the right to freedom of expression of the people of Gualeguaychú whilst at the same time established that the exercise of such right is not of an absolute nature

---

[63] It is reported that the blockades of the bridge have continued and will continue at least until the ICJ ruling. 'El Bloqueo de Ruta contra Botnia sigue Dividiendo a Gualeguaychu', *La Voz*, available at: www.lavoz901.com.ar/despachos.asp?cod_des=90000&ID_Seccion=12.

[64] Within Mercosur, the Olivos Protocol for the Settlement of Disputes establishes the use of an ad hoc arbitration court formed by three arbitrators as the mechanism for dispute settlement when a dispute has not been solved by negotiation (articles 9–10). The award granted by the court can be submitted for a review. According to article 26 of the Protocol the decision of the ad hoc court and (if utilized)the review court is binding upon the parties and constitutes *res judicata* (articles 26–27). Laudo del Tribunal arbitral AD HOC de MERCOSUR, *Omisión del Estado Argentino en Adoptar Medidas Apropiadas para Prevenir y/o Hacer Cesar los Impedimentos a la Libre Circulación Derivados de los Cortes en Territorio Argentino de vías de Acceso a los Puentes Internacionales Gral. San Martín y Gral. Artigas que unen la República Argentina con la República Oriental del Uruguay*, Mercosur, available at: www.mercosur.int/t_generic.jsp?contentid=375&version=1&channel=secretaria.

and that the blockades in turn hindered the right to freedom of movement and goods of third parties. It found Argentina responsible for the violation because it allowed its citizens to block the bridges for very long periods of time. However, it also accepted that Argentina acted in good faith, and therefore rejected any claims for monetary compensation in favour of Uruguay.

After the Mercosur decision Uruguay requested provisional measures before the ICJ on 23 January 2007. Uruguay argued before the Court that the blockades violate and constitute a threat of irreparable harm to the rights that are the subject matter of the case before the Court. The ICJ found that the circumstances in the case did not fulfil the requirements for the order of provisional measures. According to the Court, there was no 'imminent risk of irreparable prejudice to the rights of Uruguay'. It also established that since 2006, construction works in the Botnia plant had advanced significantly and therefore Uruguay did not demonstrate before the court that there was an imminent risk.[65] As a consequence, Argentina does not have the obligation under international law to halt the demonstrations against the pulp mill projects.

Lenders' approach to environmental and social due diligence

IFC due diligence

According to IFC environmental and social guidelines, the Orion and CMB plant mill projects were classified as environmental and social review category-A projects.[66] The framework within which the IFC determines due diligence for category-A projects is guided by:

- IFC's procedure for environmental and social review of projects (ESRPs) (1998);
- IFC's OP 4.01 policy on environmental assessment (EA) (1998);
- IFC's policy on disclosure of information;
- sector-specific guidelines within the IFC Pollution Prevention and Abatement Handbook (1999, final version) – in this case, for pulp and paper mills); and

---

[65] *Case concerning Pulp Mills on the River Uruguay*, ICJ Order, para. 50, above n. 50.

[66] According to the IFC, a category-A project is one that is 'expected to have significant adverse, social and/or environmental impacts that are diverse, irreversible or unprecedented'. IFC, 'Definition of project categories', available at: www.ifc.org/ifcext/disclosure.nsf/Content/Project_Categories.

- in addition, IFC has safeguard policies addressing specific issues such as international waterways (OP 7.50), involuntary resettlement, natural habitats, indigenous peoples, cultural property and forestry.

A description of IFC due diligence for each project is provided below.

Orion's EA process

The project sponsor Botnia had approached the IFC by mid-2004. As a result the IFC prepared its Project Data Sheet – Early Review on 10 August 2004, for the Orion project. In February 2005, after discussions between the IFC and the Orion project's sponsor, a mandate letter was signed and the IFC began the project's due diligence process.[67]

At the time the IFC became involved in the project (early 2005) the processes for review and disclosure of the environmental impact assessment by the competent authority in Uruguay, DINAMA (Dirección Nacional de Medio Ambiente)[68] were largely complete. Therefore, when the IFC commenced the due diligence process, Botnia had already received the environmental permit from DINAMA (see Box 13.1 for details). As a result, the IFC conducted the social and environmental due diligence process from the EIA documentation produced by the sponsor to DINAMA and the Back-to-Office Report (BTO) from MIGA's appraisal visit to the project in January 2005.

On the basis of the information provided in these documents, the IFC raised issues concerning the need to assess the cumulative impacts of the Orion and CMB projects, to which Botnia responded that the issue was addressed in an additional analysis provided to DINAMA between September 2004 and January 2005. Concerns about air and water quality were other issues raised by the IFC to which the sponsor replied that air quality indices would not be affected by the project and the proposed treatment of Fray Bentos's wastewater by Orion would improve the water quality.[69] A site visit by IFC's environmental team in late March/early

---

[67] CAO, *CAO Audit of IFC's and MIGA's Due Diligence for two Pulp Mills in Uruguay Final Report*, Office of the Compliance Advisor/Ombudsman International Finance Corporation Multilateral Investment Guarantee Agency, 22 February 2006.

[68] The EIA was submitted to DINAMA on 31 March 2004 and after several requests for supplementary information and analysis covering a range of topics, on 6 December 2004, DINAMA instructed Botnia to commence the process of public participation. The Orion environmental permit was released by DINAMA on 15 February allowing the specified construction works to start within twenty-four months following notification of the order and for operations to start within forty-eight months of the start of construction.

[69] CAO, *CAO Audit*.

BOX 13.1 **Orion EIA process for DINAMA**

The Orion project's EIA was submitted to DINAMA on 31 March 2004. DINAMA's review up to December 2004 involved six requests for supplementary information and analysis covering a range of topics, including assessment of the cumulative impacts of the Botnia and CMB projects in relation to water, air and odour. A seventh request was made on 20 December 2004, and the response to this was dated 17 January 2005.

On 6 December 2004, DINAMA instructed Botnia to announce the beginning of the public disclosure period with a public hearing to be held in Fray Bentos on 21 December 2004. Botnia printed and distributed 3,000 copies of the EA summary and opened a public consultation office in Fray Bentos for the week of 13 December 2004. Botnia announced the consultation in local newspapers and on radio and TV stations in the Fray Bentos area, including adjacent towns and across the river in the city of Gualeguaychú, Argentina.

The permit was released for public disclosure on 14 February 2005. During the fourteen-day notification period, one appeal was lodged by the NGO group Guayubira, which reserved its right to specify the appeal at a later date.

The Orion environmental permit dated 15 February 2005 sets out the EIA submission and review process, lists the main issues raised at the public hearing on the EIA, notes that the issues raised during the public notices and the hearing in connection with the permit were properly taken into account in DINAMA's examination of the application, and sets out thirty-four conditions attached to the permit. These conditions include information and access to be provided to DINAMA, additional plans and studies to be completed at various stages, project-specific emission limits, monitoring and monitoring plan requirements, participation of Botnia in an environmental performance committee to include local government and community representatives, proposals for a revised location of the on-site landfill, acquisition and management of a conservation area, and construction of a cycle way.

April 2005 was also conducted. Issues related to the Ontur Terminal at Nueva Palmira, on the other hand, were not considered as the port was finally considered as a non-associated facility to the Orion project.

Moreover, the IFC did not require a public consultation and disclosure plan as it considered the consultations undertaken by the sponsor under DINAMA's requirements were adequate.

On April 2005 the IFC considered the EIA complete in all respects and also obtained permission for the release of a set of twenty documents from the sponsor.[70] The provisional board date was set for 23 June,

---

[70] *Ibid.*

indicating that the pre-board sixty-day disclosure requirement was initiated. The IFC's due diligence process regarding the Orion project has received a lot of criticism. Several NGOs in Uruguay and Argentina, the population from the locality of Gualeguaychú, the government of Argentina and other international institutions have challenged the adequacy of the EIA study on several technical issues as well as the public participation and the disclosure processes conducted by the IFC.

Regarding technical issues, considerable concern was expressed about the adequacy of the assessment on matters such as the site of choice, area of influence, socio-economic impacts, concerns about the technology of choice and impacts on other sectors. Box 13.2 summarizes three specific examples of where the EIA is said to fall short.

Concern about the impacts of the Orion project was further exacerbated by the fact that at the time the IFC's due diligence process was taking place, the CMB project also commenced its process of approval by the IFC. Therefore, stakeholders opposing the projects expressed their worries about the environmental and social cumulative impacts of the projects and hence the need to conduct a separate study on the cumulative impacts of the Orion and CMB projects together.[71]

As a result of the increasing amount of criticism of the two projects, the IFC decided to undertake additional enquiries in the context of social and environmental due diligence. Later in 2005 the IFC ruled that an additional study on cumulative impacts was needed.

CMB's EA process

The CMB project had also already completed the process for review and disclosure of the EIA by the Uruguayan environmental authority DINAMA and received the environmental permit prior to the IFC's disclosure of the EA and related documents in late July 2005. Indeed, the EA was submitted to DINAMA in January 2003, the public participation process commenced in July 2003 and the environmental permit was issued in October 2003 (see Box 13.3).

The IFC determined that the EIA produced by ENCE for DINAMA needed to be supplemented to fulfil its requirements for a category-A project. The IFC therefore requested additional information on issues such as IFC policies and safeguards, cumulative assessment and social and economic impacts – including impacts on tourism on the Argentinian side

---

[71] The EIA approved by DINAMA contained an annex with an assessment of the cumulative impacts of the Orion and CMB projects but it was based on obsolete technical data.

BOX 13.2 **Examples of shortcomings in Botnia's EIA**

According to the Centre for International Forestry Research (CIFOR), Botnia's EIA report, while apparently comprehensive, lacks clarity on a number of critical issues, and falls far short of what a proper assessment of the mill should have considered. CIFOR highlights three concrete examples of where the EIA report is insufficient: forestry, land use and traffic impact.

Forestry: the pulp mill will have a production capacity of 1 million tonnes per annum and will obtain its wood supply from sustainably managed plantations but the report does not clearly show from where this fibre will be sourced, and how incremental plantation land will need to be planted to meet this demand. The report states that some of this eucalyptus wood will come from FOSA of which Botnia is part-owner, while the balance will be sourced externally. According to the report, the mill will have an annual fibre demand of 3.5 million cubic metres, which CIFOR assumes refers to debarked volume. FOSA's plantation stands totalled 31,754 ha in 2004. In the same year, there were a further two certified plantations with stands of 13,059 ha and 5,040 ha respectively. The report gives no information about the productivity of these plantations; however, it does mention fungal attacks on the eucalyptus, implying less than optimal productivity. Even at optimal pro-duction, these stands are insufficient to meet future wood demand. The total amount of plantations in Uruguay is recorded at 575,000 ha, but this total is nationwide, and not restricted to eucalyptus. Charts of future fibre supply meanwhile show that ample resources will be available, presumably by assuming that wood can be imported from adjacent Argentinian provinces. The report nevertheless concedes that there is a fibre deficit, and in the section on wood harvesting states: 'As of the present wood volume, by the turn of the first decade, the apparent shortage of wood resources will be covered with the wood coming from plantations established from 2003 onwards.' In the section on recommendations, it states that 'Foster invest-ments if present harvesting technologies are considerably limiting the available wood.' This recommendation is found too vague to be of use. There is no dis-cussion about what the impact would be if the necessary investments in plantations were not made, nor what would happen if any of the other mills that are on the drawing board were to be realized. The fibre deficit is not mentioned in the summary and the conclusions do not make any mention of the concerns of the surrounding population.[72]

---

[72] In reaction to the CIFOR report in May 2006 Botnia issued a press release arguing that the raw material has been secured from the beginning of the project and that the CIFOR report was based on old studies. For more information, see Botnia, 'The raw material has been secured from the beginning of the project', press release, 24 May 2006, available at: www.metsabotnia. com/en/default.asp?path=204;208;210;211;1097;1271. In addition to this, according to experts, monocultures, such as the eucalyptus plantations in Uruguay, that have been established and have replaced the grasslands have negative impact on water resources. For more on this issue,

Land use: if the mill is to obtain its fibre from sustainably managed plantations, more of these will have to be established. This is conceded by the report. The report does not provide a meaningful analysis of how the establishment of these plantations would impact land used by the current economic activities of the population, such as agriculture, cattle farming, etc.

Infrastructure: the report discusses traffic loads and infrastructure. The point is made that road maintenance is the responsibility of the Road Directorate regarding national roads, and the municipality regarding other non-forest roads. The analysis for Río Negro shows that the cost for this municipality will be US$1 million p.a. but this is balanced against US$1.4 million in inflows. The report is silent on the cost of road maintenance in the other two departments (as Uruguay's states are referred to) through which wood will be transported, but that derive few taxes from the mill. The traffic volume generated by the wood transport is calculated to be 20 per cent of the magnitude of long-distance trucking traffic to and from Montevideo. But because this traffic will not be going to Montevideo, there will be no overburden. This paints an overly optimistic picture. The daily transport of 10,000 tonnes of wood necessitates 324 trucks to make 1.5 round trips a day. So, on certain stretches of road close to the mill there will be incessant trucking volume. This will have a deteriorating impact on the road condition, and also result in considerable traffic delays to the farmers that rely on these roads to take their cattle and crops to the market. No effort is made to estimate the latter impact. The national/municipal authorities may be responsible for road maintenance, but the critical issue is whether they will have the funding. This is dependent not only on how taxes are shared between the central and municipal government, but also on whether any tax is actually being paid directly. CIFOR argues that many large industrial companies are experts at working the tax code to their full advantage to minimize actual tax payments and illustrates this point with the example of Aracruz in Brazil. In Botnia this point is even more relevant considering the free-zone status granted to the company, though the CIFOR study did not mention this. The free-zone status means that Botnia will only be paying the government a fixed annual fee of US$30,000. Furthermore the CIFOR study argues that given the actual low level of income taxes paid on forestry activities, despite large reported profits, any unwillingness of the relevant department to do proper road maintenance works should not come as a major surprise.

Source: M. Spek, *Financing Pulp Mills: An Appraisal of Risk Assessment and Safeguard Procedures*, CIFOR, Bogor, 2006, available at: www.cifor.cgiar.org/publications/pdf_files/Books/BSpek0601.pdf

see C. Lang, 'Plantations, Poverty and Power', 2008, available at: www.wrm.org.uy/publications/Plantations_Poverty_Power.pdf; and C. Perez Arrarte, 'Plantaciones Forestales e Impacto sobre el Ciclo de Agua', 2007, available at: www.natbrasil.org.br/Docs/monoculturas/cartilha_aguaXeucaliptos_uruguai.pdf.

BOX 13.3 **CMB's EIA process for DINAMA**

In the case of the CMB project, the EA was submitted to DINAMA on 8 January 2003, and following review by DINAMA was publicly disclosed locally on 26 May 2003. The public hearing on the EA was held in Fray Bentos on 21 July 2003. The environmental permit was issued on 9 October 2003, and was valid for twenty-four months in which to begin construction and for forty-eight months from the start of construction to begin operations.

The permit for the CMB project included conditions such as the development of environmental management plans prior to construction and operation, monitoring and monitoring plan requirements, specifications for pollution control and other technical aspects, emission limits, requirements to present a solid waste disposal project for approval by DINAMA prior to construction, and participation in an environmental monitoring commission led by DINAMA. The environmental permit was revised in April 2004, with an amended table of air emission limits.

---

of the Uruguay River.[73] CMB submitted the requested information and a visit by IFC specialists was recommended to take place in July 2005.

These specific additional requirements might be explained by the fact that the IFC started CMB's due diligence process during the sixty-day public disclosure period on the Orion project. By that time, the Orion project had already raised considerable concern on both sides of the Uruguay River.[74]

Given that CMB conducted public consultation prior to the EA presentation to DINAMA in 2003, the IFC requested that ENCE prepare a PCDP (public consultation and disclosure policy) according to IFC guidelines based on the process conducted for DINAMA.

However, civil society groups from both sides of the Uruguay River and the Argentinian government all expressed concerns about the impacts of the CMB project. In particular, they argued that the supplement to the EIA still only superficially addressed the cumulative impacts of the projects and was also insufficient in addressing the indirect impacts and the effects on Argentina (Gualeguaychú). They also challenged the adequacy of the public consultation process and IFC disclosure policy.

As established above, in July 2005 the IFC finally determined the need to conduct a separate CIS for the CMB and Orion projects as an

---

[73] CAO, *CAO Audit.*   [74] *Ibid.*

additional step in the identification of the environmental and social impacts of the projects.

The CMB document package (supplementary EA, ESAP, PCDP and a project disclosure sheet, among others) was finally disclosed on 29 July 2005.

The CIS process

The IFC decided to commission a separate CIS. The decision to request a more comprehensive CIS was needed both to inform the IFC's decision making and to ensure credibility of the due diligence process, particularly in the eyes of external stakeholders.[75] On the other hand, according to the IFC's Compliance Advisor/Ombudsman (CAO), by taking the decision to commission an additional study of the cumulative impacts, the IFC essentially indicated there had been a shortcoming in its earlier due diligence.[76] Indeed civil society organizations, in September 2005, filed a complaint to the CAO based upon perceived violations of the due diligence processes conducted by the IFC (and MIGA) on the CMB and Orion projects (see below, pp. 445–50).

The IFC wrote separate terms of reference for the CIS study by August 2005, to which additional requirements were added by the CAO later in November 2005.[77] The draft addressed more than thirty issues, ranging from social and economic (such as the effects on traffic, labour supply and tourism in the region) to environmental issues such as air quality,

---

[75] IFC, 'IFC response to the CAO audit of IFC's and MIGA's due diligence for two pulp mills in Uruguay', March 2006, available at: www.cao-ombudsman.org/html-english/documents/
IFCCAOAuditofOrionandCMBPulpMillsIFCManagementResponseENGLISH.PDF.

[76] CAO, *CAO Audit.*

[77] With regard to process, these include: transparency; participation; and an agreed protocol and clearly defined timetable for consultation and disclosure. With regard to content, the CAO requests that the IFC ensure it includes an assessment of: BAT; and social and environmental impacts – in particular effects on agriculture, tourism and fisheries. And finally, possible options for mitigation of any impacts. For more information see: CAO, *Compliance Advisor Ombudsman Office (CAO) of the IFC and MIGA Preliminary Assessment of the Complaint on the Celulosas de M'Bopicuá and Orion Projects in Uruguay Preliminary Assessment*, Report, 16 November 2005, available at: www.cao-ombudsman.org/html-english/documents/CAOUpdatedMediaAdvisory.pdf.

water quality and biodiversity.[78] Together with the release of the CIS, the IFC commenced the consultation process for the study for a minimum of sixty days prior to any decisions by the IFC.[79]

However, the draft CIS has been subject to significant criticism by those opposing the construction of the pulp mills.[80] Main concerns include a lack of impartiality on the part of the consultants who conducted the CIS; a lack of adequacy of the technical team to give appropriate treatment to basic environmental issues in Uruguay; and failure to comply with the additional requirements made by the CAO. Criticism has also been made of the fact that the CIS failed to properly address specific technical issues such as: discussion of choice of site; environmental impacts of massive eucalyptus plantations on groundwater; selection of second-rate technology; impacts on drinking water for local communities; and social impacts derived from impacts on other sectors (e.g. tourism); as well as inconsistencies with earlier EIA reports, for example, regarding available wood supply.[81] The participatory process has also been criticized for its failure to involve all the key relevant stakeholders in the consultation process and the lack of rules of engagement, among other things.

As a result of the controversy around the draft CIS, the IFC decided to hire two Canadian experts to audit the whole EIA process including the individual EIA documents provided by the companies, the draft CIS and the comments provided by the other stakeholders. The audit's results – known as the Hatfield report – were released in late March 2006 and acknowledged several of the problems raised by civil society.[82]

In their review, the experts state that 'assertions that the CIS, Botnia and CMB [Celulosas de M'Bopicuá – the ENCE project] have not provided sufficient information on the proposed design, operating procedures and environmental monitoring for the mills are generally

---

[78] For details on the CIS draft, see: www.ifc.org/ifcext/lac.nsf/Content/Uruguay_Pulp_Mills_CIS.
[79] IFC, 'Cumulative impact study on Uruguayan pulp mills released by World Bank Group', press release, 19 December 2005, available at: www.ifc.org/ifcext/pressroom/ifcpressroom.nsf/PressRelease?openform&7EAD4F8DB16D8D1D852570DC006756DA.
[80] For a complete list of comments on the CIS study sent to the IFC, see: www.ifc.org/IFCExt/CumulativeImpact.Nsf/Comments2?OpenView&count=100000000.
[81] See, for example, Spek, *Financing Pulp Mills*.
[82] Hatfield, *Cumulative Impact Study – Uruguayan Paper Mills*, Hatfield Consultants Ltd, 26 March 2006, available at: www.ifc.org/ifcext/lac.nsf/Content/Uruguay_Pulp_Mills_TOR.

valid'.[83] They identified a need for additional information and analysis to substantiate the environmental impacts of the CMB and Orion pulp mill projects and also recommended some technical improvements for consideration that could enhance the environmental performance of both mills.

The experts found that concerns that the mills would cause catastrophic environmental damage were unsupported and they did not question the location of the two plants or the use of ECF technology to bleach the paper pulp. However, they did acknowledge some environmental advantages in the TCF process and criticized the CIS for failing 'to provide a solid justification for the ECF approach versus the TCF option'. Further, the experts highlighted a lack of supporting information that the mills would actually use BAT (best available technology) in all aspects of their design and operations. Indeed, in their comparison of twenty-four aspects of BAT with the available mill design data, they found that the Botnia and ENCE projects only complied with five.

Overall, after reviewing the main weaknesses of the three studies the experts set forth seventy critical recommendations, involving both the construction and operational phases of the plants. The IFC's acceptance of these observations as a condition for approving the credit and insurance sought by the two companies would imply making corrections to the final version of the CIS and Botnia and ENCE would have to adjust their plans for the factories, which could modify the timeframes involved. The Hatfield report was made public by the IFC in April 2006.

On the basis of the Hatfield report, in May 2006 the IFC produced an 'action plan' indicating the remaining steps needed to complete their environmental and social due diligence process for the two pulp mill projects in Uruguay. The plan addresses recommendations included in the Hatfield report and stakeholders' comments in the draft CIS and specifies the need to collate and analyse additional information on the following key issues:

- plant process technology: evaluate possible technological and process improvements, and verify that plant operations will utilize BAT techniques and will, at least, meet Integrated Pollution Prevention and Control (IPPC)/BAT Reference (BREF) environmental performance standards;

---

[83] IFC, 'Action plan to complete environmental studies on pulp mill projects addresses recommendations from independent experts', press release, 9 May 2006, available at: www.ifc.org/ifcext/media.nsf/content/SelectedPressRelease?OpenDocument&UNID= E4E38161D7BB335085257169006B3910.

- plan site selection: provide additional information that substantiates the companies' decision to locate the plants near Fray Bentos;
- Río Uruguay water quality and aquatic resources: provide a more detailed review of data on baseline water quality and fisheries to assess the impact of effluent discharge;
- air quality: revise emissions models;
- tourism: provide additional baseline information and analysis of the tourism industry within the area of influence of the two proposed pulp mills;
- forest plantations: undertake additional review of mill-related plantation forestry operations and their impacts; and
- emergency response and environmental management/monitoring plans: provide additional detail on each company's management plans.

The CIS review took between sixty and ninety days to complete, starting with the appointment of the independent consultants. Once the CIS had been reviewed and updated by the consultants, it was reviewed by the panel of independent Canadian experts to verify consistency and responsiveness to the findings and recommendations in their report. On 21 July 2006 the Canadian environmental consultancy firm EcoMetrix was appointed by the IFC to review the December 2005 draft CIS.

The revised CIS was released in September 2006. Upon completion of the work done by EcoMetrix, the independent panel reviewed once again the final CIS and indicated that it addresses the key findings and recommendations of the Hatfield report in April 2006. In October 2006 the independent panel released its report with its conclusions. It found that the proposed mills are designed in accordance with BAT, as defined by IPPC and other regulatory agencies experienced with pulp industry issues, and the operations emissions and effluents will not pose environmental threat or impacts on the health of people in the area, on either side of the River Uruguay. The expert panel also suggested certain conditions that IFC may wish to consider incorporating into any eventual agreement to finance the projects. The proposed protocol should ensure that future operations of the pulp mills are environmentally sound in practice. The suggested measures for IFC to consider in any loan agreement include:[84]

---

[84] For details, see *Expert's Panel Report on the Final CIS for the Uruguayan Pulp Mills*, 14 October 2006, at: www.ifc.org/ifcext/lac.nsf/Content/Uruguay_PulpMills_ExpertsReport_Oct06.

- Verification that the process DINAMA has defined to develop monitoring programmes (both on effluent discharge and air quality) is implemented. Such monitoring programmes should be compatible with DINAMA's requirements.[85]
- Verification that all mill systems and personnel are ready to start before doing so. This could be based on the mill's commissioning protocols.
- After the mills are commissioned, verification that ambient air and reception-water monitoring is proceeding as planned, and any outstanding issues are being resolved.
- Audit of mills' environmental and social performance every six months for the first two years. This could be based on the various programmes discussed in the CIS.

The expert panel report also highlights some potential positive environmental impacts:

- Reduction on dioxin discharges from existing mills due to the use of a plant to manufacture sodium chlorate.
- A reduction in Biochemical Oxygen Demand (BOD) caused by discharges into the Río Uruguay, as Botnia expressed a willingness to treat the domestic sewage of Fray Bentos in the mill's activated sludge plant.
- The burning of black liquor and wood waste would generate more electricity than needed, contributing approximately 5 per cent of Uruguay's needs to the national grid.[86]

Opponents of the projects state that the EcoMetrix study and Hatfield report fail to consider the impacts on other sectors – notably tourism. The pulp industry is a contaminating industry and thus it is incompatible with

---

[85] Since the Botnia plant started its operation, EcoMetrix has issued performance results every six months. The reports established that the plant has been in compliance with the air and quality standards projected in the CIS and EIA and within the limits approved by DINAMA. See full report at: www.ifc.org/ifcext/lac.nsf/Content/Uruguay_Pulp_Mills. In contradiction to EcoMetrix's assessment, some environmentalists argue that so far the plant is contaminating. See E. J. Matta, 'Letter to the Editor: The Pollution Load Caused by ECF Kraft Mills, Botnia-Uruguay: First Six Months of Operation', *Int. J. Environment and Health*, 3(2) (2009).

[86] Since UPM Kymmene bought all the shares in the Uruguayan operations, it is not clear what will happen with Botnia's initiatives in this regard.

the tourism industry. They also argue the Hatfield report fails to consider impacts on the Guaraní Aquifer.[87]

Finally, on 21 November 2006 the boards of directors of IFC and MIGA approved the Orion project loan (see above, pp. 426ff.).[88] Although the IFC was considering support for both the Orion and CMB projects, it decided to put CMB on hold after the decision of the company in early October 2006 to relocate its plant.[89] From the information available it seems that CMB did not approach the IFC again for its relocated operation.

IFC and MIGA are not taking any position on the eventual outcome of the case brought by Argentina pending with the ICJ.

The complaint filed with the CAO

The alleged shortcomings in the due diligence processes conducted by the IFC (and MIGA) on the CMB and Orion projects also resulted in a complaint lodged in September 2005 by the Argentinian NGO, the Center for Human Rights and Environment (CEDHA) to the IFC's CAO. The CAO is the body that reviews policy compliance of IFC projects.[90] The complaint was based upon violation of IFC (and MIGA) policy including issues such as:

- IFC operational policy OP4.01 on environmental assessments in issues such as area of influence; choice of site, transboundary impacts; and no meaningful consultation process;
- IFC disclosure policy; and
- IFC operational policy OP7.50 on projects on international ways.

In November 2005, the CAO requested an audit of the IFC's (and MIGA's) compliance with internal due diligence procedures up to the point of public disclosure of the environmental assessments of the two projects (July 2005). The audit did not review the IFC's decision to commission a separate cumulative impact assessment released in

---

[87] CEDHA, 'Yet another unbelievable IFC disclosure error on environmental report of Uruguay mills reaction: local communities plan new roadblocks to oppose mills', press release, 10 October 2006, available at: www.cedha.org.ar/en/more_information/ifc-disclosure-error-uruguay.php; S. Godinot, 'Usine Botnia (Uruguay): risques majeurs pour le Crédit Agricole', Les Amis de la Terre, France, 21 December 2006, available at: www.amisdelaterre.org/Usine-Botnia-Uruguay-risques.html.

[88] IFC, 'IFC and MIGA', above n. 33.   [89] ENCE, Annual Report 2006.

[90] CEDHA, 'Letter of complaint re: IFC Orion project no. 23817 and Celulosas de M'Bopicuá, IFC project no. 23681', available at: www.cedha.org.ar.

December 2005. However, on the basis of the audit the CAO issued some specific requirements of the CIS report.

The CAO concluded in its final report of March 2006 that the IFC's decision to commission an additional CIS in July 2005 essentially signalled a shortcoming in its earlier due diligence process. Regarding how the IFC applied its policies and procedures, the CAO found that:

> IFC's due diligence to satisfy itself that the EAs were complete in all material respects prior to disclosure was inadequate and not in compliance with the organization's Disclosure Policy, resulting in disclosure of EAs that were not complete. In addition to the inadequacy of the due diligence pertinent to this specific EA, CAO concludes that IFC's ESRPs more generally are not currently supportive of compliance with IFC's Disclosure Policy requirements. In other words, although the procedures are followed, they are not rigorous or robust enough to sufficiently support an outcome that is in compliance with the Disclosure Policy.[91]

Based on its findings, the CAO provides several recommendations on the IFC's procedure for ESRPs. In particular it recommends:

- that IFC systematically document its appraisal of the adequacy of clients' social and environmental processes and documentation prior to public disclosure of EA documents;
- that the IFC outline the findings of its environmental and social due diligence in detail;
- implementation of procedures that clearly define the process to be followed where shortcomings are identified in clients' social or environmental documentation or processes after disclosure;
- establishment of clear procedures of collaboration when the IFC and MIGA are involved in the same project. It should include the sharing of information and the documentation of the rationale for key decisions; and
- implementation of procedures to verify that the documentation posted on the external websites is accessible, correct and consistent during the entire disclosure period.

In response to the CAO audit, the IFC argued that the CAO's audit was undertaken and completed while IFC due diligence was under way and before the analysis was complete and the final recommendations sent to the board. The IFC also refers to the need to focus on outcomes and the intentions of policies and staff and says that in this sense staff decisions were fully consistent with practice and the broader objectives

---

[91] CAO, *CAO Audit*, 25.

BOX 13.4 IFC's due diligence process on the Orion and CMB projects' timeline

- mid-2004: Botnia approached IFC;
- 10 August 2004: IFC released Orion Project Data Sheet – Early Review;
- February 2005: IFC started Orion's due diligence process;
- late March/early April 2005: IFC site visit on Orion project;
- April 2005: IFC posted Orion's category-A disclosure sheet on the Infoshop and sixty-day disclosure process commenced;
- June 2005: ENCE sent supplementary EA to IFC; IFC removed 'Chinese wall' between the Orion and CMB projects teams;
- July 2005: IFC specialists visited CMB; IFC decided that an additional CIS was necessary; IFC's disclosure of CMB EA and related documents;
- August 2005: IFC started with the CIS; IFC meetings with stakeholders and government officials in Gualeguaychú, Buenos Aires and Montevideo;
- September 2005: CEDHA filed a complaint to the CAO and it was accepted;
- November 2005: CAO placed additional requirements on the CIS;
- 19 December 2005: IFC releases draft CIS and begins a sixty-day consultation period;
- January–February 2006: IFC stakeholder consultations on CIS in Uruguay and Argentina;
- end of February 2006: end of consultation period;
- March 2006: Canadian experts released audit's results; CAO concluded its final report;
- 11 April 2006: expert panel's report is made public by IFC;
- 9 May 2006: IFC makes public the 'action plan' to incorporate experts' recommendations into final CIS;
- 21 July 2006: EcoMetrix appointed to revise the CIS;
- September 2006: final CIS is released;
- early October 2006: ENCE announces its decision to relocate the CMB mill;
- 14 October 2006: expert panel's report with the conclusion is made available;
- 21 November 2006: IFC and MIGA board of directors approve the loan and the guarantee to the Orion project, respectively; and
- March 2007: Orion Project's loan agreement signed.

---

of IFC policy and procedures to improve development outcomes.[92] The IFC states that the recommendations made by the CAO are taken into account in the new ESRP and disclosure policy.[93]

---

[92] IFC, 'IFC response to the CAO audit', above n. 75.

[93] The ESRP and disclosure policy framework was reviewed and accepted by the IFC board of directors on 21 February 2006 to be implemented from 30 April 2006.

A new complaint about the plant operation has been launched by the Environmental Civic Assembly of Gualeguaychú and is in its review process.[94]

Commercial banks' due diligence

During recent years a growing number of commercial banks have been adopting policies to conduct environmental and social risk assessments of the projects they are involved in. Notably, in 2003 several major commercial banks endorsed the EP, a set of guidelines for managing social and environmental risks by the PF industry. The EP are based on the IFC's environmental and social safeguard policies and apply to PF transactions over US$10 million.[95]

Information on the due diligence processes being conducted by the key banks involved in the financing of the projects is provided below. In general, the information is rather scarce as commercial banks do not have any disclosure policy and they are reluctant to provide information on clients due to the need for commercial confidentiality.

The Orion project

The ING Bank was originally appointed as the lead arranger of the B loan. ING is one of the leading advocates of the EP, endorsing them in July 2003. Moreover, ING is one of only eight banks[96] to have adopted publicly a human rights policy on their financing decisions.[97]

However, ING's support for the Orion project was subject to sustained pressure from international civil society groups[98] who argued that the bank's support for the project ran against its commitment to invest responsibly and did not comply with the EP. In December 2005 an NGO filed an EP-compliance complaint against ING regarding the loan to Botnia. The complaint identifies the relevant violations to the EP and also informs ING of other legal and procedural actions that are

---

[94] For latest developments on this complaint, see www.cao-ombudsman.org/cases/case_detail.aspx?id=152.

[95] A revised version of the EP (EP II) was released in July 2006. The EP II sets US$10 million as the new threshold for EP to apply.

[96] The other banks are ABN AMRO, Barclays, HBOS, Rabobank, Société Générale, Standard Chartered and Westpac.

[97] A. Durbin, S. Hertz, D. Hunter and J. Peck, 'Shaping the Future of Sustainable Finance – Moving from Paper Promises to Performance', WWF-UK with BankTrack, January 2006.

[98] For example, BankTrack in Netherlands and CEDHA in Argentina.

under way and/or imminent against the government of Uruguay, against the IFC and against sponsor-company representatives. It also identifies violations of human rights and environmental law.[99] The complaint also highlights the enormous risks for ING involvement in these projects in terms of legal process, public opposition and mounting international advocacy against the types of unsustainable development promoted by the project sponsors and requests ING to cease any and all consideration of financing Botnia.

Responding to the EP complaint in a letter dated 20 December 2005, ING highlights the importance for the bank that the projects they finance are developed in a sound environmental and social manner.[100] Moreover in a letter from ING to the Business Rights Resource Center making reference to the same complaint it further states the bank was considering participating in the financing of the project subject to the results of the CIS being conducted by the IFC and in particular ING would review the project's compliance by reviewing the CIS's results in light of the following regulations and guidelines: ING's business principles; applicable Uruguayan environmental and social laws; applicable regulations issued by the Comisión Administradora del Río Uruguay (CARU) established by Argentina and Uruguay; the EP; and BAT guidelines derived from the European Union's Integrated Pollution Prevention Control (IPPC) Directive.[101]

Two additional letters were sent by the same NGO to the ING Group in February and March 2006 respectively informing on latest developments and mounting pressure on the bank to withdraw. In April 2006, two weeks before the annual shareholders meeting, ING decided to pull out of the financing of Botnia's project.

There has been a lot of speculation about the reasons for ING's decision to pull out of the financing. On the one hand, ING declined to explain the rationale for the decision on the grounds of client confidentiality. In a letter to campaign groups, however, the bank explicitly said

---

[99]   CEDHA, 'Equator Principles Compliance Regarding Proposed Pulp Paper Mill Investment in Fray Bentos Uruguay From the Center for Human Rights and Environment (CEDHA) to ING of the Netherlands', 2005, available at: www.cedha. org.ar/en/initiatives/paper_pulp_mills/complaint-letter-to-ing-eng.pdf.

[100] Letter available at: www.cedha.org.ar/en/initiatives/paper_pulp_mills/letter-ing-equator-principle.pdf.

[101] See CEDHA, 'ING Letter to Business and Human Rights Resource Center – 22 December 2005', available at: www.cedha.org.ar/en/initiatives/paper_pulp_mills/ing-response-cedha-22-dec-2005.pdf.

that the decision was made jointly with the project sponsor and was not related to the project's compliance with the EP. On the other hand, others said ING's withdrawal was related to the project's inconsistencies with IFC safeguards and the EP, but that the banks would never admit this as a reason since they might face lawsuits from the sponsors.[102] Others attribute the bank's decision to the negative publicity generated by the project. After ING pulled out, the Swedish finance group Nordea and the French bank Calyon were appointed by Botnia as the main arranging banks for the financing of Botnia's pulp mill project in Uruguay.[103]

Nordea is the leading financial services group in the Nordic and Baltic Sea region whose major shareholder is the State of Sweden (19 per cent). In 2007, the Uruguayan Congress approved a host government agreement (HGA) with the bank (Law No. 18.117) similar in terms to the bilateral investment agreement signed with Finland. This is the first agreement of its type that Uruguay has signed with a private investor.[104] The HGA provides for better terms than those given individually to the country members of the bank (article 10). As part of its provisions, the HGA prohibits the disclosure to the public of any documentation during a potential arbitration. It also includes a most-favoured nation clause, tax exemptions, immunity for Nordean employees, authorization for the import or acquisition of the foreign currency necessary for the implementation of its activities and free capital repatriation.[105]

Like ING, Nordea has been targeted by civil society groups who criticize its support for the project and the lack of transparency regarding how the bank is performing its due diligence process on the project. There are also accusations about Nordea not being in compliance with international corporate social responsibility and human rights obligations. Nordea's answer to the criticisms is that the bank cannot disclose information on how it is conducting its due diligence due to the fact the

---

[102] Daniel Taillant, Executive Director CEDHA, personal communication, July 2006.
[103] Metsä-Botnia, 'Nordea and Calyon are the main arranging banks for Botnia's pulp mill project in Uruguay', press release, 28 April 2006, available at: www.metsabotnia.com/en/default.asp%3Fpath%3D204%3B208%3B210%3B211%3B1097%3B1261+calyon+botnia&hl=en&gl=uk&ct=clnk&cd=1.
[104] For more on this issue, see C. Faristein *et al.*, *Soberanía de los Pueblos e Intereses Empresariales*, 2008, pp. 66–9. See website of Redes Amigos de la Tierra Uruguay, at: www.redes.org.uy.
[105] Framework Agreement Nordic Investment bank and Uruguay, available at: http://200.40.229.134/htmlstat/pl/acuerdos/acue18117.htm.

company operates under strict banking confidentiality rules.[106] Nordea adopted the EP in February 2007.[107]

Calyon is the corporate and investment banking arm of Crédit Agricole, and is one of the original signatory banks to the EP. Calyon argues it has integrated the EP into the credit process by investing in people through an extensive training scheme involving the IFC.[108] In July 2005 Calyon endorsed the revised version of the EP (EP II).

Calyon involvement in the financing of the project has also been heavily criticized by civil society groups. In May 2006, nine civil society organizations filed a complaint against Calyon for violations of the EP due to Calyon's support for the construction of the Orion project.[109] The complaint was modelled on similar terms to that presented to the ING group in December 2005. There were also criticisms that the bank is using client confidentiality as a barrier to avoid disclosure of its involvement in the project.

Calyon responded to criticism by saying it was awaiting the results of the assessment made by the IFC to determine the environmental and social impacts of the mills.[110] Moreover, it affirmed it would abandon the project if the IFC environmental impact assessment proves to be negative.[111] The bank signed the loan in March 2007.

Finnvera is the Finnish ECA, which has given its largest guarantees, among others, to the wood-processing industry.[112] Regarding environmental standards in its activities, Finnvera complies with Finnish legislation for domestic activities, and orients its further environmental policies at sector-specific practices. The company claims that its 'environmental policy is in line with practices followed by export credit agencies in Finland's principal competitor countries'.[113]

---

[106] See 'Nordea Response to CEDHA, 10 May 2006', available at: www.cedha.org.ar/en/initiatives/paper_pulp_mills/letter-to-cedha-10-may-06.pdf.

[107] See www.equator-principles.com/.

[108] Euromoney, 'Putting Principles into Practice', Principle Finance, October 2004, available at: www.equator-principles.com/ef3.shtml.

[109] See 'Calyon France Compliance Complaint – May 18th 2006', available at: www.cedha.org.ar/en/initiatives/paper_pulp_mills/compliance-complaint-calyon.pdf.

[110] Daniel Taillant, Executive Director CEDHA, personal communication 27 July 2006; Oliver Balch, 'Uruguay: mills act as test case', Financial Times, 9 June 2006.

[111] Mercopress, 'With or without IFC support, Botnia's mill goes ahead', Mercopress South Atlantic's News Agency, 2006, available at: www.mercopress.com/Detalle.asp?NUM=8137.

[112] Finnvera, 'Finnvera, Interim Report June 2006', 2006, available at: www.finnvera.fi/index.cfm?id=5766.

[113] See Finnvera homepage, at: www.finnvera.fi/index.cfm?id=2773.

The CMB project

The BBVA was the lead arranger of the commercial banks loan to ENCE. The BBVA endorsed the EP in 2004 and on 6 July 2006 announced that it had adopted the EP II. However, like other banks supporting the Uruguayan mills, the BBVA has been targeted by civil society institutions that oppose the project. In December 2006, an EP-compliance complaint was lodged against BBVA regarding the loan to ENCE, under similar terms to those lodged against the banks supporting Botnia.

Moreover, the BBVA has also endorsed the UN Global Compact. By endorsing the Global Compact banks commit themselves to applying the core four labour standards/eight labour conventions to their own operations. However there is criticism that to date none of them has developed a specific labour policy applicable to its lending operations.[114]

The BBVA argued it was considering financial support for ENCE but it was waiting for the IFC's environment assessment report to advance with the project.[115] There is no available information about whether the bank would be involved in the financing of the project in its new location.

Critical analysis of the links between PF, sustainable development and human rights

The case studies of the pulp mills Orion and CMB in Uruguay show there are positive and negative impacts on sustainable development associated with the use of PF. The following describes those main links.

Sustainable development opportunities that arise from PF institutions' environmental and social due diligence

- There are some positive links that can be expected when the IFC is involved in a PF arrangement:
  - IFC involvement helps to reduce key environmental risks of the projects it funds: the IFC has a comprehensive set of procedures for conducting environmental and social assessments, which it applies – though not without shortcomings – to all the projects it funds. This allows the internalization of key environmental and social risks of the project from the beginning, thus reducing the

[114] Durbin et al., 'Shaping the Future'.
[115] Paul de Clerk, Friends of the Earth Netherlands, in Balch, 'Uruguay: mills act as test case'.

project's risk. IFC also has a mandate to increase the development contribution of the projects it funds.

- IFC involvement sends a strong signal to other financial institutions regarding the environmental and social 'health' of the projects: due to the IFC role in the political risk mitigation of the projects, the IFC's decision on whether or not to finance a project or to ask for additional requirements on environmental and social grounds sends a strong signal to other financing institutions (i.e. commercial banks).

- IFC involvement provides an EIA process more open to public scrutiny: the IFC has a disclosure policy which means its due diligence processes are more open to public scrutiny than, for example, when only commercial banks are involved. IFC disclosure policy provides an opportunity for other stakeholders to have an influence on the process. This can be realized either by providing insight into unaddressed or poorly addressed areas or by being vigilant as to whether the IFC is sticking to its own policies for conducting environmental and social assessments. In the specific case of the pulp mills, as a result of stakeholders' comments on the process, the IFC has had to include several modifications and additional requirements to the original EIAs and has had to commission a separate CIS study, which has also been reviewed due to criticism from civil society. The IFC acceptance of the recommendations provided in the Hatfield report as a condition for approving the credit (for example, on BAT or including measures to mitigate impacts on other sectors, i.e. tourism, artisan fisheries, agriculture) would imply that Botnia and ENCE would have to make some adjustments to their plans for the factories. This would thus lead to a reduction in the risks of negative impacts of the projects.

- The IFC has established a clear mechanism in case of non-compliance, which provides opportunities to improve environmental and social practice: the CAO is the body that reviews policy compliance of IFC projects. In the case of the pulp mills, NGOs filed a complaint to the CAO accusing the IFC of shortcomings in its due diligence on the projects. The CAO concluded that the IFC was indeed failing to comply with some of its own policies for conducting ESIAs and accordingly filed some recommendations to improve IFC practice. The CAO recommendations were taken into account in its new IFC policies.

- IFC intervention provides an opportunity to improve domestic environmental and social performance: several of the additional requirements included in ESIA studies of the pulp mills produced for the IFC or in the subsequent CIS were not addressed – at least not with the same level of detail – in the EIA studies that the project sponsors produced for the environmental authority (DINAMA). The IFC's additional requirements and the whole debate on the impacts of the projects held between the IFC and civil society have provoked further debate at DINAMA on the impacts of the projects and some of these elements are now being included in later updates of the projects by DINAMA or are being required for new projects. Some examples include a requirement of tertiary treatment for effluents; the requirement of analysis of site viability; and the introduction of an environmental permit for operation that will be granted for only three years after which it has to be renewed. Broadly speaking, IFC participation and the whole debate held with the civil society have also raised standards in Uruguay in terms of the transparency and public participation relating to the EIA processes.[116]

- Commercial banks' commitment to the EP provides an opportunity to improve environmental and social practice: the three loan arrangers in the projects have endorsed the EP. The EP banks are committed to conduct environmental and social assessments according to IFC guidelines. The introduction of the EP provides opportunities therefore to internalize key environmental and social risks of a project from the beginning, reducing the project's risk and improving the sustainable development impacts of the projects funded through PF.
- EP provide a window of opportunity to scrutinize commercial banks' practice: since EP correspond to a public commitment made by the banks endorsing them and the EP are linked to familiar procedures such as the IFC guidelines, they provide a window of opportunity for civil society to intervene in the process and to promote or advocate better practice where non-compliance is suspected. One of the principal motivations of the banks to engage with the EP is to have some assurance that their financing decisions for such commercial activities will not become subject to negative publicity.[117] Therefore, the potential risk to banks' reputation from NGOs for non-compliance with the EP is key to whether or not

[116] Ronald Beare, Managing Director of Botnia SA, personal communication July 2006.
[117] Spek, *Financing Pulp Mills*.

banks back a project. On the other hand, due to the EP being based on IFC guidelines, serious questions will arise regarding commercial banks' social and environmental due diligence if they decide to finance the projects when the IFC decides not to.

Sustainable development opportunities that could potentially arise from PF contracts

- The cash flow waterfall contract used in PF could be extended to include provisions to guarantee environmental performance and human rights. Within these types of contracts, lock-up and cash sweep clauses are included to guarantee that project cash flows are used first for loan repayments when the contract is not performing to expectation. Equally, lock-up clauses could be used by EP banks to stop distributions and demand compliance with human rights and environmental standards otherwise a cash sweep can be applied, impeding the sponsor's access to any project distributions.

Sustainable development challenges that arise from PF institutions' environmental and social due diligence

- EP banks are self-restricted by IFC due diligence process, thereby missing the possibility of ensuring a broader sustainable development approach to financing decisions: as explained below, several factors make commercial banks rely on IFC due diligence process. However comprehensive the IFC process is, it lacks a holistic approach to different types of industries and specific country conditions. In the present case, the effects on the tourism and on deforestation were overlooked.
- Timing: project construction begins before the due diligence processes of the IFC and other commercial banks have been completed. This means there are fewer opportunities for the IFC and other commercial banks to have a real influence on the environmental and social impacts of the projects as there is less flexibility in terms of the scope for amending an action or, for example, to change the choice of site. Though this is consistent with IFC policy it goes against good international ESIA practice. As concluded in the examination of the BTC pipeline in Chapter 12, this points to the need to align IFC policy with good ESIA international practice by commencing construction

activities only once the due diligence activities have been completed. On the other hand, this might result in clashes with national laws when there are government permits already in place for project construction to begin.

- Poor implementation of environmental and social policies by the financial institutions: these can be explained by different factors including:
  - Lack of institutional capacity to assess the environmental and social issues associated with the projects. While the IFC has an explicit commitment to maximize the development impacts of the projects it finances, which allows for the existence of environmental and social experts in the staff, the existence of experts on social and environmental issues within the commercial banks is still poor. According to CIFOR there is a cost element here. However, in the case of Calyon, some progress has been made as the bank, assisted by the IFC, is training its staff in the implementation of EP.
  - Even where there are properly trained in-house staff dealing with environmental and social issues, in general there is poor communication between those responsible for financing the project and those conducting the environmental and social assessment. This means there is no feedback between these groups and the latter are usually relegated to conducting a checklist of environmental and social issues rather than affecting the terms of the loan.[118] This applies both to the IFC and commercial banks.
  - Broadly, there is a lack of sectoral (pulp mill) technical expertise within the commercial banks, which may also be contributing to the lack of understanding of the environmental and social risks associated with the projects. As noted earlier, pulp mill sector companies rarely use PF to fund their projects.
- Lack of transparency: a common criticism made of commercial banks is that they use 'client confidentiality' as a barrier to avoid disclosure of their involvement in PF transactions. Indeed, in contrast to the IFC, commercial banks do not have a disclosure policy and therefore they keep information regarding their due diligence process out of the public domain on the grounds of client confidentiality. This has been found to be the case for all three commercial banks known to be involved in the projects: Calyon, Norea and BBVA. This points to

---

[118] Daniel Taillant, Executive Director of CEDHA, personal communication, July 2006.

the need for commercial banks to endorse some type of disclosure policy.

- Passive attitude of commercial banks: commercial banks prefer to rely on the social and environmental due diligence conducted by the IFC or on the information provided by the sponsors rather than conducting their own assessment. This is suggested by the fact that all the commercial banks known to be involved in the projects – Calyon, Nordea and BBVA – were waiting for the results of the IFC's due diligence to decide on whether to proceed with lending. On the one hand, this might reflect the aforementioned fact that due to the political risk mitigation effect the IFC has on lending, commercial banks often follow any IFC decision. On the other hand, this passive attitude might also reflect the commercial banks' poor in-house capacity to carry out environmental and social assessments, especially on the forestry–pulp mill sector and hence their preference to rely on the participation of the IFC or other multilateral agencies.
- EP lack of mechanisms or procedures when things do not work: the case of the Uruguayan pulp mills also highlights another issue linked to the effectiveness of the EP – the lack of an independent mechanism or set of procedures for addressing complaints. Indeed, EP have a whole set of procedures to follow for assessing environmental and social risk. But when things do not work or there are claims about banks' compliance with EP, as happened with the Uruguayan pulp mills, there is no ombudsman or equivalent mechanism to whom plaintiffs can address their concerns (except the commercial banks themselves). In order to address this weakness, several civil society organizations working on international responsible banking have suggested that the EP banks follow the mode of the CAO set by the IFC.[119] The grievance mechanism established in the EP (principle 6) only allows the complainant to have recourse to the borrower, not the financial institutions.
- Compliance after the loan is repaid: financial institutions should be responsible for the whole life of the projects they fund and not only until repayment of the loan has been completed. In the Orion and CMB projects, financial institutions provided for monitoring activities during the construction phase. However, there are several impacts that might occur during the pulp mills operation, which

---

[119] Johan Frijns, coordinator of BankTrack, in Balch, 'Uruguay: mills act as test case'.

will also require monitoring. Moreover, at present there is no evidence that any of the financial institutions involved are providing for monitoring activities or considering any leverage points to ensure that project sponsors continue to comply with the terms agreed in the ESIAs once the loan is repaid. Environmental groups in Uruguay also claim that ENCE is leaving an 'environmental debt' due to deforestation and consequent biodiversity loss followed by replacement with single specie monocultures to source the plant. Although the CMB plant did not use PF when relocating its operation, the same applies to the Botnia plant.

14

The Newmont and AngloGold mining projects

NII ASHIE KOTEY AND POKU ADUSEI

Introduction

In recent times, corporations operating in the extractive industry sectors of developing countries have increasingly resorted to project finance (PF) in place of more conventional methods of financing their operations, such as equity and conventional commercial corporate borrowing. The obvious advantage of PF is that the project itself and its assets are used as security for loans advanced to the project. This means that the risks that lenders assume as well as the liabilities of the project sponsors are all tied to the project and therefore lenders cannot, except in highly limited circumstances, have recourse to the assets of project sponsors or shareholders of the corporation floating and executing the project in the event of default.

In tandem with the increased recourse to PF by business enterprises engaged in natural resource extraction, there has also been an emerging trend whereby PF institutions require that borrowers incorporate the protection of fundamental human rights and principles of sustainable development into their implementation plans. For these financial institutions, project lending serves as a leveraging device that is used to obtain commitment by extractive industry firms to comply with norms and principles of fundamental human rights and sustainable development as contained in the laws of the host country and international legal instruments. The International Finance Corporation (IFC), the private sector arm of the World Bank, and banks that subscribe to the Equator Principles (EP) have adopted this practice of requiring borrowing companies to incorporate human rights and sustainable development principles and practices into their operations.

But while the linkage between PF and human rights protection and/or sustainable development may seem straightforward in theory, the empirical evidence would seem to tell an entirely different story. The question is whether in practice, corporations that resort to PF as a lending mechanism possess better records on human rights and sustainable development than those that do not. What happens after the 'moment of leverage' (e.g. closing of the PF deal with lenders) has passed? Can regulators, investors and citizens hold the project sponsors (e.g. a multinational mining corporation) accountable for end-running the provisions of the PF agreement dealing with human rights and sustainable development issues?

This chapter critically examines the practical dimensions of the linkage between PF, human rights and sustainable development in Ghana. More specifically, it examines the Newmont Ghana Gold Limited (NGGL) Ahafo Project and AngloGold Ashanti's Obuasi operations as case studies. Whereas the NGGL project is largely, if not wholly, financed through project lending, AngloGold Ashanti's Obuasi mine is financed largely through equity contributions and conventional commercial borrowing. The question posed in this joint case study is whether this makes any difference in terms of their respective records on human rights and sustainable development? If not, why not?

The study is divided into five sections, inclusive of this introduction. The next section provides the analytical framework for the study and an overview of the investment agreement and the stability agreement between the government of Ghana and NGGL and AngloGold respectively. Then, the chapter gives an account of the constitutional and legislative frameworks in respect of Ghana's mining sector. The next section examines empirical data relating to the two case studies and further provides a number of proposals for reform, while the final section concludes with some key recommendations.

Overview of the projects and PF mechanisms

Analytical framework

Relying on the Brundtland Report of 1987, Tilton defines sustainable development as 'behaviour by the present generation that does not prevent future generations from enjoying a standard of living at least comparable to its own'.[1] The significance of this definition is that it takes cognizance of the well-respected inter-generational equity principle that

---

[1] John E. Tilton, 'Exhaustible Resources and Sustainable Development, Two Different Paradigms', *Resources Policy*, 22(1–2) (1996), 91–7.

land (and for that matter the environment) belonged to our forefathers, and that it also belongs to the present generation, who are trustees of the environment for the future generation. Closely related to the issue of sustainability is the concept of human rights which is defined to include all entitlements that inure to the benefit of the human race. It is against this backdrop that proponents of human rights and sustainable development have sought to agitate against all acts and/or omissions in the mining sector that undermine the quality of the environment and make the survival of the human generation unsustainable. Professor Kasim Kasanga, a former minister of Ghana and a renowned land economist, aptly captures the concerns of most traditional farming communities (now mining communities) in Ashanti, Western and Brong Ahafo Regions as follows:

> Surface mining now poses the greatest threat to both commercial and subsistence farming in Ghana. Cocoa is as important as gold, if not more important. Cocoa is a long yielding investment between 40 and 50 years. Cocoa farms are inter-planted with food crops, to feed farmers. Even though there is some slash and burning involved in the initial land clearing, the environmental damage is negligible in comparison with surface mining. Some Cocoa farmers who are victims of surface mining operations in the Dunkwa-On-Offin area are being offered 9,000 Cedis [US$1] per tree. A mature Cocoa tree is capable of yielding half a bag of Cocoa beans and farmers are currently being paid 112,500 Cedis per bag of Cocoa (i.e. 62.5 kg). In effect a farmer, who is offered 9000 Cedis for a lost Cocoa tree, could obtain 55,250 Cedis [US$6] from that tree for just one season and the returns to this Cocoa tree could last for between 40 and 50 years. The gross injustice to these helpless village farmers is clear. If a free society cannot help the majority who are poor, it cannot save the few who are rich.[2]

The strife has brought on board governments, international organizations and civil society organizations to set mining industry standards to ensure that the public interest, human rights and sustainable development are well served. Illustrative of this was the agitation by the communities in the Ahafo South District of Ghana which led to the negative review of NGGL's environmental impact assessment (EIA) Report by the US Environmental Protection Agency (EPA). Despite initial resistance by some of the mining companies, they are reconsidering their policies for fear of litigation or the possible revocation of their operating licences.

---

[2] Kasim Kasanga, 38th Anniversary Lectures of Ghana Academy of Arts and Sciences, 1997. The current price of a bag of cocoa in Ghana is about US$58.

Sometimes financing mechanisms also tend to influence the standards of compliance adopted by these mining companies. A good example is the IFC condition that all potential beneficiaries of project financing adhere to the EP to manage the social and environmental risks of projects in the extractive sector.[3] PF for the purposes of this study encompasses 'a method of funding in which the lender looks primarily to the revenues generated by a single project, both as the source of repayment and as security for the exposure'[4] as against conventional methods of borrowing from banking institutions with other forms of security. It is on the basis of this financing mechanism that standards such as social and environmental assessment standards, land acquisition and involuntary resettlement standards, pollution prevention standards and effective disclosure of project-related information are prescribed. In Ghana, whether these PF mechanisms and the related-prescribed standards have achieved their expected positive results in the protection of human rights and the promotion of sustainable development will be examined in this chapter.

Newmont Ahafo project

NGGL, a company existing under the laws of Ghana, entered into an investment agreement with the government of Ghana on 17 December 2003 to conduct mining operations in the Ahafo area of the Brong Ahafo Region of Ghana. As part of the agreement, NGGL undertook, among other things, to follow generally accepted world mining industry standards and procedures in the exploration, development, production, financing and reclamation.[5] The government of Ghana for its part undertook not to expropriate, confiscate, destroy, disrupt or wrongly take possession of the company.[6] The agreement further states that in the event of such nationalization or expropriation under article 20 of the 1992 Constitution, the government shall pay prompt, adequate and effective compensation in accordance with the principles of international law. In additions, the government of Ghana undertook not to engage in acts or omissions that adversely affect the smooth operations

---

[3] See International Finance Corporation's Performance Standards on Social and Environmental Sustainability (30 April 2006).
[4] *Basel Committee on Banking Supervision*, International Convergence of Capital Measurement and Capital Standards (November 2005).
[5] See article 1.20 of the investment agreement between Newmont and the Government of Ghana.
[6] *Ibid.* article 9.7.

of the company, and to further extend to the company equal treatment accorded to any other person or entity.[7]

The investment agreement also sought to provide a cap on the extent to which the government can impose taxes on the company. Section 41.1a of the agreement states that the aggregate of corporate income tax applicable to NGGL shall not exceed 32.5 per cent. This percentage is expected to come down to 30 per cent as soon as NGGL becomes listed on the Ghana stock exchange. Section 15.5 of the agreement concerns itself with environmental compliance and reclamation. Here, NGGL undertakes to conduct its mining activities in order to limit the adverse impact to the environment and to comply with the existing laws of Ghana. The difficulty is that any subsequent legislation passed by the parliament of Ghana imposing extra compliance burden on the company can be challenged, since that may violate the terms of the investment agreement.[8] Additionally, the agreement provides that NGGL pays compensation to owners of private lands or any person who lawfully occupies a land affected by the grant of the mineral right. Private land is defined in the agreement to include creeks, streams, rivers or bodies of waters located on the land owned by a person other than the government. Despite the presence of this provision, the policy of NGGL is that compensation is not paid to owners of lands that have not been cultivated and this has become a constant source of conflict between the villagers and the mining company.

The Ahafo project currently involves 299 square miles of land covered by mining and prospecting licences (representing 774 square kilometres), and 322 square miles of land covered by reconnaissance licenses (representing 834 square kilometres) together with approximately a 30-mile strike length.[9] The present size of the Ahafo Project represents a significant growth of 125 per cent between 2003 and 2004 alone. The commencement of the mining activities and/or the execution of projects incidental thereto in 2004 have actually affected some communities and have the potential to affect more communities in the future. The affected communities include, but are not limited to, villages/towns such as

[7] *Ibid.* article 9.10.
[8] For an in-depth analysis of the 'regulatory chill' effects of such clauses within investment agreements for the progressive development of environmental laws and standards in Ghana, see Kyla Tienhaara, 'Mineral Investment and the Regulation of the Environment in Developing Countries: Lessons from Ghana', *International Environmental Agreements*, 6(4) (2006), 371–94.
[9] See NGGL official website: www.newmont.com/en/operations/projectpipeline/ahafo.

Kenyasi, Ntotoroso, Gyedu, Tawiakrom, Kodiwohiakrom, Kwakyekrom, Dongokrom, Yamfo, Dokyikrom, Wamahinso and Atuahenekrom, all in the Brong Ahafo Region of Ghana. In May 2006, an independent review team comprising Tasneem Salam and Frederic Giovannetti found that a total number of 1,701 households and 1,568 structures have been affected by the mining project.[10] The report further indicated that 9,575 individuals have been affected as a result of mining-related activities. This figure is contradicted by WACAM (Wassa Communities Affected by Mining), which gives the total number of displaced inhabitants as 28,000. As a result, NGGL has sought, among other things, to adopt measures aimed at reducing the impact of their operations on the local inhabitants via the payment of compensation, resettlement schemes and the provision of basic infrastructures in mining communities. According to the Compliance Monitoring Report of NGGL, the number of affected buildings for which compensation has been paid stands at 100 per cent.[11] Also, the number of resettlement houses built stands at 93 per cent, and the number that the expected owners have taken possession of stands at 87 per cent.[12]

The financing of the NGGL Ahafo project substantially originates from the International Finance Corporation (IFC), the private lending arm of the World Bank. The IFC on January 2006 approved US$75 million to finance NGGL's Ahafo project and thus sought to commit the NGGL to various IFC evaluation processes and international standards of mining practices in order to address the social and environmental concerns of the project. However, an interview with Daniel Owusu-Koranteng, the executive director of WACAM, revealed that the US government abstained from voting to approve the funding granted to Newmont on the basis of the US government's dissatisfaction with the NGGL EIA. According to him, this was the result of the negative review of NGGL's EIA undertaken by the US EPA.

Operations of AngloGold Ashanti

AngloGold Ashanti operates three main mines in Ghana located at Obuasi, Iduapriem and Bibiani. The Obuasi mine, the subject of this

---

[10] See NGGL-Ahafo Project: External Social Compliance Monitoring Report, prepared by Tasneem Salam and Frederic Giovannetti for IFC and Newmont Mining Corporation, at 2–3. A more recent (fifth) independent external compliance review dates from January 2007. See Newmont's website.
[11] Ibid. [12] Ibid.

chapter, comprises both surface mining and underground mining and it covers an area of more than 411 square miles (over 1,070 square kilometres) of land. Some of the communities affected by the mining activities include Ayanfuri, Gyaman, Sansu, Fobinso, Abnabna, Dadieso, Ntwintina and Nkonya. The project is wholly owned by AngloGold Ashanti and is financed through borrowings from banking institutions such that as of 31 December 2005 AngloGold had borrowings of US $1,894 million.[13] The Ashanti project is also financed through floating and selling of shares to the public, and the company is estimated to have paid US$5 million in royalties in 2005 to the government of Ghana and a total corporate social investment expenditure of US$266,206 was spent in Obuasi.[14]

Unlike NGGL which operates under an investment agreement, AngloGold-Ashanti operates under a stability agreement, which was ratified by the parliament of Ghana on 18 February 2004. The said stability agreement is the legal instrument that gives effect to the mining lease entered into between Ashanti and the government of Ghana on 5 March 1994 to permit the former to engage in the exploration, development and production of minerals until 4 March 2054.[15] The agreement among other things requires Ashanti to submit detailed reports of its investment activities and more generally confirm whether AngloGold has materially complied with its obligations to the government by January 2009 and January 2024. In the area of corporate taxation the government of Ghana undertook to maintain the corporate tax payable by Ashanti at the rate of 30 per cent for a period of fifteen years from the date of commencement.[16] The Government further undertook that within a period of fifteen years of the commencement of operations, Ashanti's operational activities shall not be adversely affected by any new enactment, orders, instruments or any action appertaining thereto. Although the stability agreement does not insulate the mining project from existing laws regarding human rights and sustainable development, it could affect the free exercise of governmental authority to impose additional standards aiming at the promotion and respect of human rights.

---

[13] See AngloGold Ashanti: Risk Management Report, at 7. See: www.anglogold.com/.
[14] *Ibid.*
[15] Stability agreement between the government of Ghana and AngloGold Ltd.
[16] *Ibid.* article 2.03.

AngloGold on its part undertook to establish and maintain a community trusts fund to assist the affected mining communities in Ghana. Schedule 4.01(b) of the agreement commits Ashanti to contribute 1 per cent of profit annually into the fund to assist community work. In addition, it undertook to implement programmes pertaining to training, fighting malaria and improving health, safety and working conditions.[17] A fundamental philosophy of the company is that its operations and activities should contribute towards long-term sustainable development and that communities should be better off for AngloGold Ashanti having been there. According to the company, it maintains contact with the chiefs and traditional authorities, including paying homage – particularly to the Asantehene, the king of the Ashanti at significant events.

Legal and regulatory contexts of the projects

The 1992 Constitution

The Constitution contains a chapter on natural resources generally, with specific provisions dealing with minerals. In terms of Article 257 all minerals in their natural state found in Ghana are property of the state. Such minerals are vested in the president in trust for the people of Ghana.[18] The nature of the president's *trusteeship* was the subject matter of a suit before the High Court in *Adjaye & Ors* v. *Attorney General*.[19] The plaintiffs in this case were contesting the government's sale of part of its 55 per cent shares in the then Ashanti Goldfields Company Limited (now AngloGold Ashanti). It was the case of the plaintiffs that because the constitutional provision vested minerals in their natural state to the president in trust for the people of Ghana, it was improper for the government to divest itself of the said shares without the consent of the beneficiaries (i.e. the people of Ghana). This raised a number of issues, namely: (a) was there a trust created when the government acquired its 55 per cent stake in Ashanti?; (b) was there a breach of trust occasioned by the public share offer?; and (c) were the plaintiffs, as ordinary citizens of Ghana, entitled to bring an action to enforce the trust, if any? Relying on the decision of the English courts in *Tito and Ors* v. *Waddell*,[20] Aryeetey J. held that the Constitution did not create

---

[17] *Ibid.* Schedule 4.01(c).   [18] See Article 257, Clause 6.
[19] High Court, Accra (1994) (unreported).
[20] See *Tito and Ors* v. *Waddell* (No. 2) (1977) 1 Ch. 106.

a trust in the ordinary sense of the word and that it merely created a governmental obligation that could not be enforced in court. Following the *Tito* case closely, he held that the trust referred to in Article 257 of the Constitution was a trust in the higher sense of a governmental obligation and not a trust in the lower sense of a fiduciary relationship enforceable in court.

The president's trusteeship in respect of minerals in their natural state does not necessarily give the executive branch of government exclusive control over the management of mineral resources in the country. This is because Article 268 of the Constitution invests parliament with the power to ratify all transactions or contracts granting rights for the exploitation of natural resources in the country. Thus any agreements entered into by the president, acting through the minister for mines or the minerals commission cannot become operational until they have received the requisite legislative approval. Parliament may however exempt any such agreement from the requirement of ratification. Further, such agreements may be scrutinized by the courts for their conformity with the Constitution.

The Minerals and Mining Act 2006 (Act 703)

The substantive legislation on mining is the Minerals and Mining Act. The Act re-enacts the ownership regime relating to minerals contained in the Constitution.[21] In addition, the government has a number of ownership-related rights. In terms of s. 43 of the Act, the government has a 10 per cent free carried interest in the rights and obligations of the holder of a mineral right in Ghana. In other words, the government automatically becomes a shareholder in any mining venture but without the obligation to pay for its shares when they are allotted. Further, the government has a right of pre-emption over all minerals exploited in Ghana, including the exploitation of minerals in the territorial waters, the exclusive economic zone and the continental shelf. Finally, it is provided in s. 60 of the Act that the minister for mines may by notice require any mining company to issue a 'special share' to the state free of any consideration. The rights to be conferred by the issue of such special share are determined by negotiation between the minister and the company concerned. But the Act provides explicitly that the special share does not entitle the government to dividends nor does it confer

---

[21] See Minerals and Mining Act 2006 (Act 703), s. 1.

voting rights on the government. However, the government is entitled to notice of meetings of shareholders and may attend and speak at such meetings.

Under the Act, the power to grant mineral rights is vested in the minister for mines, acting on behalf of the president and on the recommendations of the Minerals Commission. Pursuant to this power, the minister can negotiate, grant, revoke and suspend mineral rights accorded to any person under any agreement for the exploitation and utilization of minerals in the country. Mineral rights are granted subject to the fulfilment of a number of conditions, including:

- the appointment by the mining company of a qualified and experienced manager to take charge of the mineral operations;
- obtaining the necessary permits and approvals from Ghana's Forestry Commission and Environmental Protection Agency (EPA) for the protection of natural resources, public health and the environment;
- agreement to pay the prescribed royalties upon commencement of mining; and
- respect for the surface rights of occupants of the land covered by the mining lease.

The mining lease is the principal legal instrument for the conferment of mineral rights towards the development of a mine or mines. It is an agreement between the mining company and the government for an initial period of about thirty years. The lease term may be shorter than thirty years if the company applying for it agrees that it be shortened.[22] The initial period can however be renewed upon an application to that effect by the mining company.[23] Once granted, the lease entitles its holder to conduct mineral operations within the area or areas covered by it; exploit and market minerals obtained from such exploitation; dump mining and or other waste products in accordance with its environmental impact statement; and carry out activities incidental to its mining operations.

Where the investment relating to a mining lease is in excess of US$500 million, the minister for mines has discretionary power to enter into a development agreement with the grantee company. The development agreement should incorporate terms and conditions for the effective development of the grantee company's operations including stability

---

[22] *Ibid.* s. 41   [23] *Ibid.* s. 44

arrangements, environmental protection and settlement of disputes in accordance with the dispute settlement mechanisms provided for under the Act.[24] With respect to stability arrangements, the minister has authority to enter into a stability agreement with any mining company irrespective of the level of its investment. The essence of the stability agreement would be to ensure that, within a period of fifteen years from the execution of the agreement, the company does not suffer from adverse legislative changes or subsequent modifications to the levels of customs duties, royalties and other taxes or from changes to the laws relating to exchange control, capital transfer and remittance of dividends. Any stability agreement signed with a mining company is subject to ratification by parliament. The study established that whereas NGGL has entered into a development agreement with the government of Ghana in accordance with the Act, AngloGold continues to operate under a stability agreement for unexplained reasons and/or for corporate comfort.

The Environmental Protection Act 1994 (Act 490)

Under the Environmental Protection Act 1994, the Environmental Protection Agency (EPA) is charged with the responsibility of ensuring control and prevention of discharge of waste into the environment. The Act further empowers the EPA to protect and improve the quality of the environment.[25] The EPA is also mandated to issue permits and pollution abatement notices as well as directives, procedures or warnings in relation to pollution prevention and control. Related to this is the power of the EPA to prescribe standards and guidelines on pollution of air, water and land and to conduct investigations into environmental issues. Where any of these statutory obligations is not performed to satisfaction, the EPA could be sued for an order of the prerogative writ of mandamus to compel it to do so. An action in that nature formed the subject of a suit between the Center for Public Interest Law (CEPIL) on the one hand and Bonte Gold Mines (now liquidated), the EPA and the Minerals Commission on the other hand. In *CEPIL* v. *Bonte, EPA and Minerals Commission*,[26] the plaintiff, an NGO dedicated to the protection of the environment, sued among other things to compel the Ghana EPA to perform its statutory obligations to demand US$2 million reclamation bond from Bonte Ltd before the latter commenced its mining operations.

---

[24] *Ibid.* s. 49.   [25] Act 490, s. 2(d).   [26] Suit No. AP6/05.

The plaintiff also seeks an order to compel the EPA to ensure that Bonte Ltd takes remedial steps to 'reverse' the destruction to the environment and water bodies in Bonteso in the Ashanti region.

The Minerals Commission Act 1993 (Act 450)

The Minerals Commission was established for the regulation and management of utilization of mineral resources of Ghana and the coordination of the policies in relation to them. Specifically, the Commission is mandated under the Act to make recommendations of national policy for exploration and exploitation of mineral resources. Besides its crucial role in the granting of all mineral rights in Ghana, the Commission is also responsible for monitoring the implementation of all bodies with responsibility for minerals and to report to the minister. The Commission collaborates with the EPA in the development of general guidelines on how mining activities can be carried out in an environmentally responsible manner. In the pending *CEPIL* v. *Bonte* suit the Minerals Commission has joined as a third defendant, and the plaintiff claims against it relief similar to those being claimed against the EPA because of its statutory obligations under Act 450.

Approaches to human rights and sustainable development

Newmont Ahafo project

Human rights

Since November 2005, NGGL has worked with outside experts to investigate and benchmark human rights issues and management challenges using a variety of tools. The first attempt to develop such human rights standards vis-à-vis the mining sector took place at a mineral resources workshop in Princeton University in which NGGL's Ahafo project served as a case study for a draft 'Human Rights Protocol for Mining Companies'. Generally such instruments developed by mining companies are geared towards tackling issues of compensation for landowners, environmental pollution, and resettlement of displaced communities and the execution of other sustainable projects.

Compensation   Most of the villages affected by the NGGL's mining activities are reputed to be among the major cocoa and food growing areas in Ghana. Because of the negative impact of the mining activities, issues of compensation have become a constant source of conflict between the company and the local farmers. As described in the NGGL's resettlement action plan (RAP), compensation has been paid to project-affected people according to parameters set by the elected Resettlement Negotiation and Compensation Committee and on the basis of non-coerced, prior and informed consent.[27] According to the company, compensation included full replacement cost of structures, assistance with moving personal belongings, efforts to improve former living standards and compensation for crops. Land, housing, infrastructure and other compensation were provided to the adversely affected population at a total cost of over US$13 million.[28] WACAM, an advocacy NGO engaged in championing the cause of deprived communities, has criticized NGGL for paying a meagre US$7 for destroying a cocoa tree which could yield cocoa beans to the value of about US$20 per year for over thirty years. It also noted that there were many people who worked as farm labourers that did not benefit from any compensation package because those persons were not owners of the farms destroyed.

Another contested issue relates to the position taken by NGGL that there is no mechanism currently in Ghanaian law to allow unused land to be compensated.[29] The study established that no payments have been made by NGGL to the owners of fallow land that have been affected by the mining project because, in the view of the company, land unlike crops and structures is not an asset held at household level. This position is clearly undesirable and indeed not supported by law since the obvious negative impact of the loss of unused land is not consistent with accrued rights of landowners in the communities. It also contradicts the importance of access to land for sustainable farming practices and ensuring food security for individuals in the mining community. It is for this reason that NGGL, in collaboration with an NGO called Opportunities

---

[27] See report prepared by Newmont for IFC entitled *Social and Community Development of the Ahafo Region: Collaboration to Promote Project Benefits, Vision and Commitments* (October 2005), p. 2. Available at Newmont's website.

[28] *Ibid.*

[29] *Ibid.* p. 3. Section 74(1) of Act 703 on compensation principles states that '[T]he compensation to which an owner or lawful occupier may be entitled may include compensation for (a) deprivation of the use or particular use of the natural surface of the land or part of the land; (b) loss of or damage to immovable properties; (c) in the case of land under cultivation, loss of earnings or sustenance suffered by the owner or lawful occupier, having due regard to the nature of their interest in the land; and (d) loss of expected income, depending on the nature of crops on the land and their life expectancy.'

Industrialization Centres International (OICI),[30] is adopting measures aimed at facilitating the acquisition of land, through established channels, by farmers who need replacement land.

Resettlement   NGGL in its August 2005 RAP indicated that it has built some 399 houses in two resettlement villages to improve the lot of inhabitants. In addition, the company has sought to develop programmes to assist vulnerable persons in the affected communities during the life of the project.[31] In the course of this study, most of the residents in the resettled communities complained about the size of the rooms constructed for them by the company. The study also established that some of the landlords in Kwakyekrom for instance have refused to move to the new settlement at Ntotoroso because of NGGL's unilateral reduction of the number of rooms built as replacements. Major concerns expressed also included the lack of involvement of the affected persons in the planning and design of the resettlement policies.

Land access   Replacing the affected landowners with alternative land is seen as a critical aspect of livelihood restoration, as the vast majority of affected people predominantly rely on farming. The mine area covers 2,426 hectares of farmland. Out of this, 1,965 hectares were actively cropped and in the view of the company were compensated for.[32] This means that uncultivated lands were not compensated for when they were taken by the company. An independent assessor's report submitted to IFC posits that 'it is not possible for the project to compensate fallow land, and this approach is consistent with legislation'.[33] As already alluded to elsewhere, such an unexamined view of Ghana's law is not correct and it violates Article 20 of Ghana's 1992 Constitution and s. 74 of Act 703, both of which deal primarily with compensation principles. A related issue in the independent assessor's report was that no compensation was paid to persons who were involved in alcohol preparation

---

[30] The Opportunities Industrialization Centers International (OICI) Ghana website is at: www.oicighana.org/.
[31] Newmont-IFC report.
[32] See Salam and Giovannetti, Compliance Monitoring Report, at 3.
[33] See Frederic Giovannetti, *Newmont Ahafo: Independent Assessment of Resettlement Implementation* (December 2005). Moreover, in Giovannetti and Salam, Compliance and Monitoring Report, on pp. 6 and 7, the reviewer recommended that NGGL implement the planned fallow land study in 2007 in order to assess the project impact on fallow land availability and use and design mitigation measures.

since it was difficult to distinguish well-established akpeteshie tappers from fake ones.[34]

The research further established that little progress has been made to ensure and facilitate access of affected people to alternative land. A survey of land access by the OICI indicates that as many as 53 per cent of interviewed settlers in Kenyasi and 37 per cent in Ntotoroso state that they have no land to cultivate.[35] It becomes more crucial since the affected persons can only access NGGL's financial assistance if they are able to secure at least 2 acres of land for themselves. It also came to light that the workings of the grievance logging system were identified to be defective. Streamlining it therefore can help to maintain a good relationship with the community. Recommendations previously made to improve the lot of vulnerable people have been identified by the company as one of the priority areas that are yet to be implemented. The external social compliance report of the company also recommended among other things that gender considerations be factored into the development of the project to address the need of women and youths.

Water and sanitation   Following media reports of the disposal of faecal matters into the River Asuopre by NGGL, water samples from the Asuopre River, River Tano and water supplied to the residents of Kenyasi, Ntotroso and Kwakyekrom were collected for scientific analysis by an expert of the Ghana Centre for Environmental Impact Analysis (CEIA). The results of the testing showed that levels of dissolved oxygen, BOD, turbidity and conductivity were within acceptable limits prescribed by WHO and Ghana EPA. The report however concluded that colonies of total viable bacteria, E. coli, salmonella and shigella were above the acceptable limits and hence posed significant health hazards to residents who drink from all water bodies sampled in the study.[36] This study also revealed that NGGL has constructed a dam on Subiri River, which until then served as the source of drinking water for villages such as Dokyikrom, Yawusukrom, Dongokrom, Tawiakrom, Subiriegya and Kodiwohia. The water schemes to supply water to the affected villages were identified to be non-functional and this finding is corroborated by

---

[34] Salam and Giovannetti, Compliance and Monitoring Report.   [35] *Ibid.*

[36] See Samuel Obiri, *Water Sampling and Analysis of River Asuopre and some Water Bodies within the Concession of NGGL – Ahafo Project in Kenyasi* submitted to WACAM with funding from Rights and Voice Initiative (RAVI) and Oxfam America.

the report of the independent assessor, and the resettlers were being supplied with water by water tankers.[37] Besides the health hazards associated with the drinking water, the construction of the dam has also blocked the access road of the people of Dokyikrom, and has isolated other communities such as Yawusukrom and Oseitutukrom.

Sustainable development and environmental protection

Sustainable livelihoods: the Sustainable Development Foundation Under this Foundation, Newmont has committed to work with the local communities to support specific capacity-building and infrastructure development projects. It is envisioned that the NGGL Ahafo South project will commit 1 per cent of gross operational profit plus US$1 per ounce produced to fund the foundation and related development initiatives beginning in 2006. This level of funding is projected to contribute approximately US$650,000 per year based on current projected cash flows.[38] The company's commitment to full and regular public consultation includes continuous assessment of stakeholders, easy access to relevant information, regular release of information, and appropriate and consistent messages. In the view of NGGL management, communication with stakeholders will provide information on the progress of work and ensure awareness of special programmes throughout the life of the mine. The problems already identified as confronting the communications and grievance response systems continue to hamper some of these initiatives.

Environmental management and closure planning According to the company, post-closure land use and management provide potential opportunities related to land productivity and sustainability, resource management and livelihood enhancement.[39] And therefore NGGL's commitments towards environmental mitigation and enhancement include planning towards closure and these measures are set out in the NGGL's EIA. It is instructive to state that testing standards used in the NGGL EIA have been criticized by the US government as not meeting international standards and the standards prescribed by the US EPA. The US EPA review states among others that 'Newmont did not use any of the conventional Acid Base Accounting (ABA) testing procedures

[37] Salam and Giovannetti, Compliance and Monitoring Report, p. 5.
[38] Newmont report, *Social and Community Development of the Ahafo Region*, p. 6
[39] *Ibid.* p. 11

accepted by [US EPA, US Bureau of Land Management, British Columbia, etc.] but instead used an in-house acid base accounting method'.[40] This according to the US EPA rendered the NGGL EIA deceptive and for that matter failed to address and prevent the generation of acid resulting from the production of acid mine drainage. The US EPA review also pointed out the lack of provisions in the NGGL EIA that require the latter to conduct proper monitoring at the locations where mining wastes are discharged.[41] Dissatisfaction of NGOs such as WACAM and CEPIL with the company's EIA is articulated by Michael Warner saying that: 'NGOs have questioned whether the provisions [of NGGL EIA] assure that local communities will be adequately consulted, and whether environmental impact assessment reports will be open to full public scrutiny.'[42]

Sustainable livelihood enhancement   Newmont's programme goal and commitment is to enhance livelihood capacity of an estimated 2,000 households through income-generating activities and alternative livelihoods.[43] According to the company, it intends to create and strengthen local small-to-medium enterprises (SMEs) to benefit around 1,500 people. And therefore NGGL is developing and implementing a micro-credit scheme for affected people and will provide initial funds to the level of US$200,000 for SME development for 2006. Also, the company has defined a number of livelihood enhancement initiatives to help Project-affected people re-establish their livelihoods or create new ones. An extensive livelihood survey, independently undertaken by OICI in September 2003, examined, among other things, the existing socio-economic levels, including literacy and gender statistics and characteristics of communities in the Ahafo concession area.

Based on the data from the livelihood survey and from intensive consultation and engagement with local stakeholders, a comprehensive and sustainable community development programme – the Livelihood Enhancement and Community Empowerment Program (LEEP) – was developed by OICI on behalf of Newmont Ghana Gold. The programme

---

[40] John Hillenbrand, US Environmental Protection Agency Review: Newmont Ahafo South Project EIA 28/12/05, p. 1.

[41] *Ibid.* p. 3

[42] Michael Warner, 'The New International Benchmark Standard for Environmental and Social Performance of the Private Sector in Developing Countries: Will it Raise or Lower the Bar? Overseas Development Institute, Opinion (February 2006), at 1, at: www.odi.org.uk/publications/opinions.

[43] Newmont report, *Social and Community Development of the Ahafo Region*, p. 4.

is intended to enhance the livelihood of people in the mine take area. The LEEP programme targets households that have been economically displaced by the project and households that are physically displaced and resettled or relocated by the project. The communities have however rejected the claims that the LEEP project would restore their livelihood, alleging that LEEP was in reality a means to drive farmers away from their land and provide access to lands for the company. In their view, the company only directs them to contact OICI, an NGO that the former (Newmont) had contracted under the pretext of assisting them to acquire alternative land. This study can confirm that a major drawback to this somewhat laudable initiative is the lack of trust of the intermediary being used by the company to execute the project. Thus one could argue that the human rights and environmental risks mitigation measure used by the company (the LEEP programme to mitigate effects of displacement and destruction of livelihood) has backfired against its original intent by creating mistrust in the community and possibly creating a conflict risk.

Agriculture and food security   Through a variety of means including agricultural development and training projects, NGGL has promised to work with partners to improve food and cash crop production for 750 households and reduce post-harvest and storage losses by 5 per cent for 750 households. The focus will be to improve the agricultural potential of farmers in the Ahafo area to include both Newmont-managed land and the adjacent farm lands near and around the mine site. These purported policies of the NGGL aimed at promoting agriculture and ensuring food security ran counter to the position taken by NGGL management that the taking away of fallow land is not subject to payment of compensation. It is submitted that the success of the initiative depends on successful execution of programmes to provide the displaced farmers with viable alternative land, and in some cases with seedlings, seeds, etc. to start cultivating new farms since most of the farmers have lost virtually everything as a result of the mining activities.

Education and capacity building   Newmont has indicated its commitment to increase the level of education in the project-affected area via both infrastructure and capacity building. NGGL has therefore promised to establish a Newmont community scholarship to support selected students to undertake further education. The company also intends to construct or rehabilitate schools to increase access to quality education, skills training and recreation. A new school has been completed at the Kenyase 2 resettlement village. Additional classrooms and staff facilities have also been added to the new school built at Ntotoroso resettlement site. In addition, NGGL has sought to enhance the technical and vocational skills for 600 youths for direct employment in the construction phase of the project through a partnership with the Ghana National Vocational and Training Institute and at the Newmont training centre at Yamfo. The timeline for executing the training project has been criticized by WACAM as inadequate since, in its view, it was impossible to train persons to acquire sufficient knowledge in metalwork, masonry and administration as required under the EIA within three weeks. According to the company, financial management seminars for locals are being held and partnerships with local universities and technical facilities are being set up.[44]

Objective assessment and performance evaluation   Reports published by NGGL indicate that assessments and evaluations have been undertaken with the aim of meeting the standards set by the IFC. For instance, Newmont's Ghana project was assessed in early September 2005 under the corporation's internal five star management system. There is also a programme which requires sites to be assessed by external assessors on their systems and performance against sets of standards in the three disciplinary areas of environment, health and safety and social responsibility. The results of these assessments are used as the basis of continuous improvement for the sites and used for Newmont's public reports. Inasmuch as NGGL can be credited as having a better disclosure system than AngloGold, there are some important public interest data, according to the US EPA, that have been excluded from its EIA. This includes the lack of information on acid produced by Newmont in its acid rock drainage mining.

Leveraging knowledge, expertise and collaborative association   The company seeks broad collaboration between the private sector, civil society and the government to leverage knowledge, opportunity, resources and expertise to multiply benefits beyond those directly associated with the company. Existing major partnerships for the Ahafo project include collaborations with OICI; Conservation International (biodiversity and forests); University of Colorado Medical School (health baseline

[44] *Ibid.* p. 8.

assessments); Planning Alliance (resettlement programme); Ghana Wildlife Society (endangered species and conservation education), USAID Ghana and the International Finance Corporation (environmental and social responsibility in general for the project).[45] It is however interesting to note that NGGL has not established a healthy partnership with local NGOs such as WACAM, CEPIL and the Third World Network (TWN) which have been very critical of the activities of Newmont. The study established that isolating these community organizations and public interest-oriented organizations makes nonsense of the purported collaborative initiative of NGGL.

Employment   The company has estimated that the expected workforce for operations is approximately 570, comprising 40 expatriates, 180 skilled Ghanaians and 350 unskilled Ghanaians. In addition to these direct employees, the company has also promised to hire around 350 contract service providers on a regular basis. Also the company, with its training programmes, has implemented a wholly local hiring policy for its unskilled workforce – achieving 98 per cent for the construction phase – which it intends to continue through into operation. In its view, the local workforce has deliberately been selected according to a geographically representative, community-based residence assessment, and comes from the breadth and length of the mine lease area.[46] To minimize the potentially negative social impacts of having a large group of workers residing near a community not their own, NGGL uses a fleet of more than thirty buses to take the workers to and from their homes every day. The difficulty is that there are some displaced farmers who cannot take part in the employment initiative due its manual nature.

Community health   In the course of the study we also learned about mine-related diseases via community interviews. The commonest diseases include skin rashes, malaria and acute headaches. NGGL is collaborating with the Kintampo Health Research Centre in the Brong Ahafo region on a project to undertake a detailed baseline health survey to assess the well-being and health status of the people of the Asutifi and Tano districts. It is likely that the recommendations of these studies will lead the company to look at strengthening of the Community-Based Health Planning and Services (CHPS) programme, the upgrading of some local health facilities, the expansion of malaria interventions and

---

[45] *Ibid.* p. 7.   [46] *Ibid.* p. 8.

a continuation of its programmes to improve accessibility to clean water and adequate sanitation infrastructure.[47]

Another serious health risk in the area is HIV/AIDS. NGGL has a comprehensive policy which creates an HIV/AIDS programme for employees including awareness raising, prevention and treatment. The company has employed a full-time AIDS specialist and an HIV/AIDS steering committee has been formed. Employees have been surveyed for baseline medical information and the company will train peer counsellors and community educators. A major criticism of the company's disease control policies is that they are mainly targeted at its workers.

Grievance process and disclosure   The company has sought to provide avenues for hearing the concerns of the villagers and to provide answers to those concerns. However, most of the villagers interviewed expressed lack of trust for OICI, the intermediary organization contracted by NGGL to liaise with the communities. It is therefore not surprising that the grievances response system was adjudged ineffective by an independent assessor because of the difficulties in channelling community grievances to the management or having access to the management to ventilate concerns. It would be interesting to examine how the present grievance procedure works and compare the reality with the recommendations of the *IFC Stakeholder Engagement Handbook* chapter on grievance mechanisms where the IFC recommends that in grievance processes, 'as with the broader process of stakeholder engagement, it is important that management stays informed and involved so that decisive action can be taken when needed to avoid escalation of disputes'. A major challenge for companies engaging with communities seems to be trust building. It would be interesting to see where, in the case of Newmont, the problems for trust building lie.

AngloGold Ashanti

According to AngloGold, efforts to maintain good community relations and to contribute towards long-term sustainable development of the communities hinge on the following business principles:

---

[47] *Ibid.* p. 9.

- forging and enhancing strong partnerships between the company and its stakeholders, including employees, their families and dependants, the communities and society in general;
- regular consultation and engagement to achieve peaceful and harmonious coexistence with the communities, governmental agencies and civil society in general;
- undertaking social investment initiatives in the communities and other areas where the company can make short- and long-term meaningful contributions in the socio-economic sphere;
- promoting capacity building and alternative livelihood programmes; and
- the provision of assistance in the areas of education, agriculture, health and sanitation.[48]

A major obstacle to this research in respect of the operations of AngloGold relates to Ashanti's relative lack of sufficiently disclosed data on its official website. Even though the company has set out in detail the processes that must be followed to obtain records, it has failed to differentiate between public interest records and private confidential records, thereby subjecting almost every significant piece of data to an equally stringent requirement for disclosure.

Human rights

Security and human rights   Quite recently, the issue of unlawful artisanal mining on the AngloGold concession area has become a major cause of conflict between the company and some of the persons displaced by the mining activities. Thus, while the company is making ongoing attempts to engage with the artisanal miners or 'galamsey' operators to stay out of the lease area and to protect its property, clashes have occurred between the artisanal miners and the company, resulting in injuries to both groups. On 21 May 2005 tensions between the mine and galamseyers again increased when a group of twenty-one military personnel and police assisted Obuasi management in destroying fifteen to twenty illegal pits, constructed by galamseyers around the Ellis and West shafts.[49]

A further incident occurred on 21 June 2005 when one Awudu Mohammed, a galamsey suspect, was shot by AngloGold Ashanti security staff. A comprehensive internal investigation was undertaken and the company has maintained its original contention that Awudu

---

[48] See AngloGold website at: www.anglogold.com for details.   [49] *Ibid.*

Mohammed was injured by falling on the spikes of a security gate when he tried to avoid arrest. The position of the company was however contradicted by the Medical Officer who examined the victim. These incidents, among others, have led to the company being on the receiving end of allegations of human rights abuses by two NGOs, the TWN and WACAM. Even though AngloGold Ashanti recognizes that these NGOs have a significant role to play in the communities, this chapter can conclude that they have often been sidelined.

Sustainable development and the environment

Discussions around sustainable enterprises   AngloGold in collaboration with the Centre for Biodiversity Utilization and Development (CBUD) has sought to develop a range of sustainable livelihood projects which it could assist in establishing. Funded by the Royal Netherlands Embassy in Accra, the CBUD aims to stimulate and promote sustainable development through the use of natural resources, paying equal attention to conservation. Some of the projects it has proposed for future development include duck, rabbit and pig farming; honey production; aquaculture; and seedling nurseries. In accordance with AngloGold Ashanti's request, however, the initial ventures were limited to training in snail and indigenous leafy vegetable farming; and grasscutter rearing. The total CBUD budget for capacity building and start-up costs in these ventures was estimated at US$84,660.

The study established that out of about 5,000 people who applied to take part in the projects, 1,000 were selected to take part in concurrent training in snail and vegetable farming and 100 for grasscutter rearing which has high start-up costs. Criteria for acceptance were that participants originated from the Ayanfuri enclave and, to ensure the security of ventures, that they owned a piece of land next to their home. This additional requirement that the applicant needs to own land unfortunately barred most of the displaced villagers from benefiting from the project even though some participants who did not own land were asked by the community chief to make land available for individual projects. Although the neighbouring Obuasi mine has a projected life of over thirty years, AngloGold Ashanti has given assurances that a programme of skills transfer will be extended to the eight communities in and around the mine, to ensure that sustainable livelihood programmes are firmly in place long before mine closure.

While the programme has been fairly successful to date, the company admits it has not been without its challenges. The identifiable challenges according to the company include but are not limited to the following:

- meeting the 2010 closure plan deadline, which the EPA has indicated is too ambitious;
- aligning community support with the mine's objectives;
- creating organized markets for products (currently produce reverts to the CBUD when markets cannot be found); and
- preparing for business expansion well ahead of the CBUD's scope of one year.

Environmental protection   AngloGold Ashanti's environmental philosophy and practice are guided by the company's business principles and environmental policy.[50] AngloGold's operations are subject to the environmental laws, rules and regulations of the countries in which they are situated. AngloGold Ashanti has formally adopted ISO 14001 as the standard for the company's environmental management system during 2005 and has successfully achieved certification of all its operating mines, including Obuasi. A dark spot in Ashanti's environmental record occurred in 2005 when large amounts of tailings material escaped into the external environment. The surrounding downstream communities of Kokoteasua, Abompekrom and Nkamprom were affected by the spillage and the company deployed the necessary staff and resources to clean up the spillage and assess damage, with the intention of paying compensation to affected communities. One of the authors however found out that most of the affected communities never received any compensation.

Use of cyanide   The use of cyanide in the recovery of gold is seen by the company as critical to the viability of its operations and AngloGold used an estimated 5,954,000 kilograms of cyanide in 2005. However, the use of cyanide and its accidental spillage has in the past polluted the water bodies of the communities in and around the mining areas of AngloGold. Media reports had it that oranges produced from Obuasi and its surrounding villages have become 'poisonous' due to their high acidic content, and the cause, according to the reports, was the use of the

---

[50]   www.ashantigold.com/Values/Environmenta.htm.

cyanide in the mining in the area. It is however noted that these claims have not yet been validated by scientific analysis.

Procurement   According to AngloGold Ashanti and as part of its contribution to sustainable development, the company tries to procure goods and services locally. At Obuasi it is estimated that about 12 per cent of the company's material requirements are sourced from local businessmen. The transport of employees and of materials to and from the mine is handled by local private companies. Foodstuff and drinks for the employees' club houses and the canteen are sourced from businesses in the area. The director of WACAM downplayed this initiative and stated that most of the displaced inhabitants may not even dream of owning viable businesses in order to benefit from AngloGold's so-called procurement benefits.

Managing health threats   One of AngloGold Ashanti's objectives is to implement an integrated campaign at the mine, targeting a 50 per cent decrease in the incidence of absenteeism within two years. The integrated malaria control campaign is planned to start in Obuasi and all outlying villages within the Obuasi municipal assembly area. In addition, a malaria control centre has been established at Sansu to coordinate the programme. According to AngloGold, the programme aims to develop, implement and sustain a campaign that:

- reduces the severe burden of malaria at Obuasi; major capital project to come on stream;
- promotes community development and all means of preventive measures; and
- assists health practitioners in early detection and treatment of malaria, in partnership with relevant stakeholders and in line with the government's malaria policy.

HIV response programmes are also in place at all the operation centres to deal with the impact on both employees and their communities. According to the company, the HIV prevention programmes were developed under the auspices of the Ghana Employers' Association and the Ghana AIDS Commission. The communities interviewed however criticized the company for failing to attend to the very health-related problems including increased cases of malaria that its mining activities had created in the communities. According to the villagers, the company's health policies focus primarily on its staff in an attempt to maintain higher productivity.

Communication and consultation   From the perspective of the company, interactions with communities within the Obuasi Mine Concession are managed through monthly consultative meetings with the chief and some opinion leaders. The research however established that the substance of this consultative process in most of the communities is doubtful since the supposedly consultative committee members have never been summoned for any meeting. Some of the villagers also blamed their chief for having compromised their independence in order to get contracts from the company.

Capacity building at Ayanfuri mine   Ayanfuri, part of the greater Obuasi mine in Ghana, is the subject of the country's first decommissioning plan following the pit's closure in September 2001. AngloGold maintains that prior to this, there was no national legislation in Ghana governing mine closure, which in certain instances resulted in foreign-owned miners leaving the country and abrogating their environmental and social responsibilities. The research however confirmed that the above position of AngloGold does not represent the true state of Ghanaian law since the Minerals Commission Act, the Environmental Protection Act and its enabling Environmental Assessment Regulations have been in force since 1993, 1994 and 1999 respectively. And this is further evidenced by the request from Ghana's EPA to Ashanti to submit a formal decommissioning plan. While much preparatory work was done to address issues like public safety, site stability, revegetation, provision of social infrastructure and sustainable livelihood support, it was not until AngloGold Ashanti was formed that the decommissioning plan finally got under way in July 2004. This, in the view of the company, was an important exercise in rebuilding community trust since much of the mine's rehabilitated land was found to be suitable for sustainable livelihood support projects, including mined-out pits containing water which could be used for aquaculture.

Key conclusions and recommendations

This chapter has sought to analyse two mining concessions in Ghana and to assess their human rights and sustainable development credentials in the light of their divergent funding bases. While NGGL primarily receives its project funding from the IFC, a private sector arm of the World Bank, AngloGold essentially receives its finding through borrowings from banking institutions and the sale of shares. For instance, before a company becomes eligible for financing from the IFC, the IFC applies its performance standards to manage social and environmental risks and impacts, and to enhance development opportunities. The object of this chapter as indicated earlier is to establish whether there is a nexus between any of the two mechanisms for project financing vis-à-vis the safe execution of the mining project without causing excessive damage to the environments and the lives of the inhabitants in the communities.

It is important to note that examination of the publicly disclosed data reveals that AngloGold has been very reluctant to disclose any independent assessment reports respecting its operations, even if such assessments have been done. With respect to the NGGL, perhaps the IFC as the core financier has become an important check on its activities since even if the NGGL fails to disclose such project-related documents that same information may be found on the IFC website. In addition, the standards of prescription imposed as conditions for the granting of the IFC loan appear to have thrust the activities of the NGGL more into the international spotlight and further put it under the microscope of the international financier. The US EPA's negative review of the NGGL's EIA illustrates this point.

A common thread that runs through the Newmont and AngloGold projects is that some attempts have been made by both companies to adopt policies aimed at alleviating the negative impact of the activities of mining on the communities. Notwithstanding this, the study shows that those policies have not been entirely successful in protecting the fundamental human rights of the inhabitants and ensuring sustainable livelihoods for the affected communities. Thus, the reality of the situation in most of the mining communities contradicts the somewhat glamorous ideals being propagated by the mining companies on their websites in respect of sustainable development and the protection of human rights.

The study also established that long years of operations of AngloGold in Ghana appear to have safeguarded the interest of the company from most of the contentious issues such as compensation for land, farms and resettlements. Put differently, the communities seemed to accept AngloGold as having come to stay, and therefore most of the initial agitations against the company have become history. The case of NGGL is different since it is now attempting to entrench its establishment and has not yet been embraced by the communities. Moreover, most of the inhabitants displaced by the operations of NGGL are still alive and the 'pain' is still fresh in their minds.

Notwithstanding the shortcomings identified in the operations of both AngloGold and NGGL, the mining-related information available in respect of the operations of the two companies suggests on the face of it that NGGL operations are subject to higher, and probably preferable, standards of compliance than those of AngloGold. This leads to the conclusion that the use of PF mechanisms supported by the IFC whereby human rights protection and sustainable development standards are clearly set down for compliance is preferable to the conventional form of financing such as equity being used by AngloGold. Thus, the participation of a (public) international institutional lender can arguably lead to improved transparency, international scrutiny and as a consequence to better compliance with standards. Whether this particular form of PF generates *better* compliance in comparison to other types of PF methods is still questionable.

15

Overview and recommendations

SHELDON LEADER AND RASMIYA KAZIMOVA

Overview

These chapters have investigated ways in which PF can potentially affect, both positively and negatively, key social and environmental concerns. Before we move to summarize the findings and conclude with a list of recommendations, it is useful to place the earlier arguments in the context of the recent financial crisis; a crisis which throws into relief several of the major concerns raised in the book.

A recent report by UNCTAD on the impact of the crisis on investment strategies indicates that most transnational corporations surveyed 'are still grappling with the short-term impacts of the crisis, [though] a sizable majority expect the business environment to improve substantially by 2012.'[1] One of the direct effects of the crisis is that many companies have shifted their geographical priorities towards developing and transition countries.[2]

The financial crisis therefore continues to cast its shadow, with an effect both on those who demand and those who supply investment. On the demand side, the fact that less money is flowing into national treasuries creates extra pressures on governments to try to continue to meet social demands for infrastructure development and certain other key public spending needs through the utilization of private financing techniques, including that of PF. In a risky environment, both politically and economically, PF continues to be a logical choice within the envelope of investment strategies. On the supply side, PF lenders are concentrating on fewer projects, and commercial banks and investors are less willing to go ahead with a project unless the prospective rate of

---

[1] UNCTAD, *World Investment Prospects 2010–12*, p. 4; at: www.unctad.org/en/docs/dia-eia20104_en.pdf
[2] *Ibid.* p. 5.

economic return is fairly watertight. Guarantees of the completion of the project sought from sponsors have become more comprehensive and the period of their liability to the lender, prior to the non-recourse phase, has typically been extended.[3]

PF is not, in quantitative terms, the dominant mode of finance. As a recent BankTrack report points out, PF provides well under 5 per cent of capital raised through commercial lending and investment banking. The report goes on to point out that 'its use is decreasing, due to the high financial risks for the banks associated with that form of financing'.[4] However, that observation must not obscure the fact that PF is likely to continue to play a major role in some of the world's largest investment projects: projects with profound potential impacts on the surrounding societies. In the current climate private lenders look more intensely than usual for support from public ECAs and bodies such as the IFC, the latter being 'flooded with applications' according to the journal *Project Finance International*.[5]

The financial crisis creates both a threat and an opportunity for social and environmental standards. Economic actors and governments are naturally tempted to lower the constraints on PF in order to accelerate economic recovery. At the same time, for policy makers who see the problem of social unrest in various parts of the world that can result from poor adherence to such standards, this is an opportunity to require of borrowers that they subscribe yet more firmly to the norms set by international human rights standards, the EP and IFC standards. It is a pivotal moment.

Several of the foregoing chapters have recommended steps that might help to strengthen the links between PF and social concerns. It is useful to recall some of the main themes on which they have focused. The initial note is a positive one: the social and environmental norms surrounding the international use of PF have at least started a process of focusing and heightening attention on this mode of finance. They have turned the EP into, as was argued in Chapter 4, the pre-eminent self-regulation instrument in their respective fields, with their principles and standards both

---

[3] Communication from M. Roland Kahale, Banque BNP Paribas 27 November 2009; see also 'Not too bad – PF in 2009', *Project Finance International*, January 2010, at www.pfie.com.

[4] *Banking it Right*, October 2009, at: www.banktrack.org/show/pages/about_banktrack, p. 6

[5] *Project Finance International*, December 2009, p. 46.

accepted and applied by a significant number of the private PF lending banks around the world.

At the same time, it is important for the future to strengthen the grip of those principles, as well as other norms governing PF. The positive social and environmental impacts of PF should not be undermined by the negative. Some major areas of concern, highlighted in several chapters, are considered below.

The withdrawal option

When projects reach a stage at which they enter into a 'pure' non-recourse phase, some project sponsors are attracted to the possibility that they will be able to withdraw from their involvement and be insulated from liability arising from the fact that they are not obligated on the loan; and that they are protected from liabilities for the other obligations of the SPV to third parties since the company will usually have separate legal personality and its shareholders, including the sponsor, enjoy standard limited liability – unless there are special grounds for the corporate veil separating the SPV from the project sponsor to be pierced. While this possibility is not likely to appeal to companies with concerns about repeat business from lenders, generating overall concern for their reputations, there are sponsors who are not unduly concerned about either. In the event that something goes awry with the project and there is an urgent need for additional equity to be injected, the sponsor might reject supporting the project further and instead walk away. This could potentially result in unmet claims by accident victims, employees made redundant, etc.

Information flows and project decision-making

As seen in several of the case studies, there are points at which crucial information about a project is either too little or too late in its availability. There is insufficient access to information about the way in which the social and environmental risks are evaluated by lenders or by those borrowers implementing the project, especially to those potentially affected by the decisions taken. Equally, information relevant to the concerned parties is not always made available early enough in the decision-making process – information which should reach into the earliest considerations regarding the design and location of projects. Here, there are legal principles that can be borrowed from other fields of law in which commercial decisions and social impacts of those decisions are linked. Many such norms require the provision of sufficient information, and within adequate time to allow meaningful participation and reaction by the stakeholders concerned to take place.[6]

Interviews with project contractors referred to in earlier chapters identified a certain level of frustration arising from their perception that they are often brought into the process of decision making about the essential characteristics of a project when it is too late for their participation to be meaningful, and where their expertise would have made a difference. The result, they argue, is that project deadlines and other completion requirements are sometimes set at unrealistic levels – optimal perhaps in financial terms, but carrying greater hazards than they need to. Similar arguments in favour of participation in the series of decisions can be made on behalf of those stakeholders who stand to be affected by project design and location.

Completion deadlines and operational schedules

At various points in the foregoing chapters it has been argued that concerns about the reliability of income streams in PF projects can create pressures for meeting targets that can jeopardize environmental and health and safety concerns. This is not to say that PF is solely responsible for such pressures on project performance. As was pointed out in Chapter 5, often there are other factors as well: the need for a facility to fit in with a larger web of projects being completed; the need to respond to a fluctuating market, etc. However, insofar as the terms of finance risk add to such pressures, it is important to see how these potential effects can be curbed.

Criteria for project evaluation

Balancing commercial and non-commercial interests

PF commitments raise more acutely than do many other investment decisions both the tensions and the complementarities between commercial and social concerns. That mix is, of course, present in many quarters. However, because of the close calculations about operating

[6] See, for example, the European Framework Directive on Information and Consultation 2002/14/EC, concerning employee rights when e.g. corporate restructuring is being planned.

conditions and returns on loans that this form of finance imposes, the need for an appropriate protocol for striking balances is strong. The discussion of human rights impact assessment tools in Chapter 7 implies that it is often a mistake to think in all-or-nothing terms here. That is, the choice is often at the margins, calling for a partial compromise on optimal commercial returns and a greater provision for basic rights concerns, or vice versa. It may be in any given situation that the 'business case' for respecting basic rights runs out of the incentives it can provide, while social and environmental risks remain. At that point, the protection of basic social rights and environmental protection carry independent weight: they continue to make demands even though it might not be in the optimal interest of the investor to acknowledge these demands. Nowhere is this requirement more salient than in the analysis of risk. All sides agree that it is important to deal with risk of social and environmental damage by investment in a given project, but they differ strongly about the way to go about it.

Risk

As was seen in several chapters, the dominant concerns about risk to a project and to investment will in turn inform the way different underlying risks are allocated between the parties, as well as the choice of mitigation techniques. Once all the risks are cushioned 'financially', PF lenders are not that concerned about the way in which underlying problems are being taken care of, unless this could seriously damage their reputation and thus their activities in the long run. Environmental and social risks matter a great deal, but as means to another end: that of minimizing obstacles to a steady return on the loan made. Any further form of social protection that could trouble that stable return will face an uphill battle to be accepted. This may be one explanation for the higher costs charged for loans where there are higher levels of democratic accountability of host governments, as established in Chapter 8. It may also explain the fact that, as indicated in interviews reported in Chapter 9, project-rating agencies are not inclined to downgrade a project if environmental or social risks are present but pose no threat to the reliability of a project as a debtor.[7]

These views can affect a project company's enthusiasm for two possible strategies towards risk that were canvassed in the chapters: one is to give priority to avoidance by proactive measures, including slowing

---

[7] Chapter 9, n. 21.

down or stopping a project so that the damage does not arise. The other is to build in compensation provisions out of company resources, standing ready to pay for any accidents, environmental pollution, and other damage that arises for which the project is legally accountable. As a general proposition it is clear, and all sides would agree, that avoidance of damage is superior to compensation for damage done. However, the difficult decision arises when the line dividing the one from the other has been drawn. The approach taken by the IFC, as discussed in Chapter 5, is to press for the avoidance of damage unless it is not 'financially feasible' to do so. Everything then turns on what counts as 'feasible'. The avoidance strategy will often be more expensive than the compensation approach, given that the latter can be paid for out of the revenues generated from the project income (prior to royalties and other taxation payments to the host government), while slowing or stopping the project will reduce or even end this income stream. Human rights principles, however, require greater commercial sacrifice – as they do whenever such rights are at risk. If slowing or stopping a project by government demand in order to put right a social or environmental problem threatens in a particular situation to make the investment no longer viable per se, thus engaging the indirect expropriation principles discussed in Chapter 9, then a difficult policy choice emerges: how can the very viability of a project be balanced against the need to avoid certain damage to local populations. Whatever the legitimate choice is in a situation such as this, it is not clear that it is a choice that can be safely left solely in the hands of project lenders, project sponsors and the management of SPVs.

Methods of regulation

The details of PF arrangements are largely under the control of the parties to the contracts structuring the project: from the lenders through to those owning, constructing and operating it. There is, however, a regulatory role for host governments as well as home governments. The host government is in a position to set the terms on which it may be granting a concession to a company wanting to develop, for example, a mineral resource; or more generally the terms on which it will allow, through an investment treaty, business to be done within its borders. The home government is in a position to regulate by the conditions it might attach to the financial and other guarantees it is willing to provide to its enterprises investing abroad. Finally, there is potential regulation arising through the terms on which project insurance is provided. It is useful to divide these modes of regulation in the way set out below.

Direct regulation

While a PF structure is worked out between lenders and borrowers, this arrangement often sits alongside the investment contract that the SPV will have made with the host government, together with other regulations that the government might impose. Apart from the commercial aspects of the project, these contracts may contain further undertakings on the part of the SPV not to damage certain rights of local populations, such as the supply of adequate water to surrounding farmers in a mining operation. Whatever might be the agreement reached about the loan repayment, these terms will have to take account of the requirements of such contracts and other domestic regulatory measures. A host government has the potential ability to sue under the contract, often before an international arbitrator, for a breach of an undertaking such as this. In addition, the investment contract can, by special terms, leave space for direct suit before domestic courts for violation of, for example, local environmental or health and safety legislation by individuals, as discussed in those chapters that consider the BTC Human Rights Undertaking. Within such space for domestic litigation, a proactive approach to the avoidance of damage can find itself backed by an injunction.

Indirect regulation

In addition to these direct modes of regulation there are other, less direct forms which nevertheless carry a strong potential to induce the lenders and users of PF to take social and environmental standards seriously. One of these, as investigated in Chapter 9, is to be found in project insurance. There the discussion turned, *inter alia*, on the need to avoid insuring against damage in a way that causes that damage to fall within the umbrella of risks to third parties provoked by a moral hazard. This would require clearer apprehension of those risks by insurers, as well as willingness and readiness to reject providing a policy in cases when availability of a particular cover could heighten the risk of damage to human rights and environmental protection. For example, express carve-outs when providing a political risk insurance (PRI) cover for stabilization clauses, for regulatory changes to strengthen the level of environmental protection, would be an example of a good practice for an ECA aiming to respect the EP. Indeed, the very spirit of the EP may require this. Beyond the reach of the EP, an effort to orient project insurance in this way would call for a requirement imposed by host or home governments. Since these governments often declare support for basic rights and environmental protection as a priority when allowing FDI to take place, this would be a point of entry for such a requirement.[8] For similar reasons, it should be possible for home governments to condition the project insurance provided under schemes such as the US Overseas Private Investment Corporation (OPIC) on the meeting of such standards.

Proposed reforms

Several changes to the norms and practices framing PF could strengthen an investor's ability to deliver on a project's social and environmental objectives. A two-part agenda, consisting of regulations and a code of practice, should cover the following areas.

Regulation by host/home states and lenders should:

(1) Strengthen project sponsor accountability in the event of an SPV's failure to meet the EP and/or IFC standards. This would include qualifications to the non-recourse feature of lending in situations in which the SPV is not able to continue payments under the loan while also meeting the costs of avoiding or compensating for social and/or environmental damage.

(2) Provide greater openings under PF arrangements for avoidance of damage to third parties as opposed to reliance on compensation once damage has happened.

(3) Narrow the range of stabilization clauses in investor/state contracts in order to open the way for application to projects of changes in domestic law and regulation by host states, in order to allow the latter to meet their international human rights, social and environmental obligations.

Codes of practice should provide for:

(4) Guidance to lenders and sponsors for the maintenance of reserve funds in the SPV adequate to cope with the effects of stopping or slowing the speed of project construction or operation in order to

---

[8] See the arguments in Chapter 9. Valuable insights on these points have also been provided by Ms Beata B. Wlodarczak, LL.M., senior lawyer at TMF Group, Amsterdam.

prevent reasonably foreseeable damage from occurring as opposed to compensating it once it has taken place.

(5) Earlier consultation with lenders and contractors about project standards and schedules for completion of work.

(6) Consideration of human rights and environmental protection as separately identifiable concerns from the very inception of the project.

(7) The creation of a link between a project's compliance with the EP/IFC standards and its eligibility for insurance against certain commercial losses.

(8) Greater attention paid to possible moral hazards arising from project insurance.

(9) Social and environmental impacts of projects to be taken into greater account by rating agencies specialising in PF. Assignment by these agencies of independent weight to core values advanced in the EP/IFC project standards even when observing these standards does not enhance the economic viability of the project, or reduce commercial risk to the investing parties.

(10) Introducing temporary tax exemptions or other incentives in return for companies using social, environmental and human rights impact assessment tools and internalizing international norms and principles.

These proposals can be fed into the design and implementation of project impact assessment tools. The EPs and IFC project standards should reflect these requirements.

INDEX